Virtual Tutors and AI-Powered Instructional Tools in K-12 Settings

Stamatios Papadakis
https://orcid.org/0000-0003-3184-1147
University of Crete, Greece

IGI Global
Scientific Publishing
Publishing Tomorrow's Research Today

Vice President of Editorial Melissa Wagner
Director of Acquisitions Mikaela Felty
Director of Book Development Jocelynn Hessler
Production Manager Mike Brehm
Cover Design Jose Rosado

Published in the United States of America by
IGI Global Scientific Publishing
701 East Chocolate Avenue
Hershey, PA, 17033, USA
Tel: 717-533-8845 | Fax: 717-533-7115
Website: https://www.igi-global.com E-mail: cust@igi-global.com

Library of Congress Cataloging-in-Publication Data

Names: Papadakis, Stamatios, 1974- editor
http://id.loc.gov/authorities/names/n2019056035
http://id.loc.gov/rwo/agents/n2019056035
Title: Virtual tutors and AI-powered instructional tools in K-12 settings / Edited by Stamatios Papadakis.
Description: Hershey, PA : IGI Global Scientific Publishing, [2026] | Includes bibliographical references and index. | Summary: "This book addresses these critical dimensions. It explores real-world case studies, cutting-edge research, and practical strategies for integrating AI and virtual tutors into K-12 education"-- Provided by publisher.
Identifiers: LCCN 2025026217 (print) | LCCN 2025026218 (ebook) | ISBN 9798337326375 hardcover | ISBN 9798337326382 paperback | ISBN 9798337326399 ebook
Subjects: LCSH: Tutors and tutoring--Technological innovations--Case studies | Artificial intelligence--Educational applications--Case studies | Web-based instruction--Case studies | LCGFT: Case studies.
https://id.loc.gov/authorities/genreForms/gf2017026140
Classification: LCC LC41 .V57 2026 (print) | LCC LC41 (ebook) | DDC 371.39/4--dc23/eng/20250617
LC record available at https://lccn.loc.gov/2025026217
LC ebook record available at https://lccn.loc.gov/2025026218

British Cataloguing in Publication Data
A Cataloguing in Publication record for this book is available from the British Library.

Table of Contents

This chapter reimagines the role of AI-powered instructional tools in K–12 education through the lens of co-creAItivity—a pedagogical stance in which learners and artificial agents jointly engage in the production of knowledge, meaning, and creativity. Going beyond the utilitarian logic of virtual tutors and content delivery systems, the chapter offers a philosophical and design-based critique of current AI integration practices. It proposes a new typology of AI personas—Catalyst, Companion, Critic, and Curator—each embodying a distinct mode of human–AI co-agency in K–12 contexts. . Drawing on current debates in AI ethics and educational philosophy, the chapter argues that the future of AI in K–12 education hinges not on how smart these tools become, but on how wisely we design them to amplify human flourishing. Co-creAItivity, in this light, is not a method but a mandate—to ensure that AI remains a partner in learning, not its master.

The educational system often fails those who need it most—students marginalized by poverty, language barriers, trauma, or inconsistent support. This chapter explores how artificial intelligence, when wielded thoughtfully, can help bridge these long-standing learning gaps. By offering real-time feedback, personalized pathways, and data-informed intervention, AI-driven tools like virtual tutors provide at-risk students with the kind of individualized attention that traditional classrooms struggle to deliver. But while the promise is powerful, it is not without peril. Ethical concerns around bias, surveillance, and access disparities must be addressed with urgency and humility. Drawing from real-world implementations and critical research, this chapter argues that AI can be more than just a tool—it can be a lifeline. If designed with care and guided by equity, AI has the potential to not only support learning but to radically reimagine what inclusive education can be.

Artificial Intelligence (AI) is revolutionizing English Language Teaching (ELT) by providing personalized and interactive learning. AI tools, such as virtual tutors, adaptive learning platforms, and automated grading applications, enhance productivity and allow teachers to focus on more interactive teaching elements. However, AI tools lack the subtle interactions and cultural context that teachers provide. Teachers are essential for emotional intelligence, cultural and pedagogical contextualization, and can provide more appropriate feedback than AI tools. AI-powered tools can enhance the learning experience by creating more interesting and motivating lessons, but teachers must adjust their traditional roles to incorporate modern technologies without losing the core aspect of human interaction. Teacher professional development is crucial for the responsible and effective use of AI technologies. Ethical concerns, such as data protection, algorithm bias, and access to AI systems, need to be handled ethically and inclusively.

This study examines the level of artificial intelligence (AI) and virtual teacher usage among middle school students in social studies classes and its relationship with critical thinking skills. The sample consisted of 371 middle school students in Amasya, Turkey. To gather data, students completed a personal information form and a critical thinking skills scale. The findings revealed that 91.7% of students were aware of AI, and 30.7% used it on a daily basis. Notably, ChatGPT was the most widely used tool among students, primarily employed for completing assignments and asking questions. Furthermore, students familiar with the concept of virtual teachers demonstrated higher scores on critical thinking assessments. Increased frequency of AI usage was associated with enhanced critical thinking skills. However, despite these associations, most students believed virtual teachers could not replace real teachers. Overall, the research indicates that AI should be utilized as a supportive tool in education.

This chapter discusses why culturally responsive AI tutors are needed in K-12 in underserved Arab communities where learners confront infrastructural, linguistic, and cultural challenges. It points to the existence of the digital divide among refugee/rural learners, the incompatibility between the Arab values and the West-designed AI tools, and the weaknesses of Arabic NLP. Based on the recent case studies of Jordan, Lebanon, Egypt, and the Gulf regions, the chapter offers a culturally adaptive AI framework that focuses on the linguistic diversity of Arabic in AI, attention to ethics, and availability offline. The chapter is closed by providing practical policy advice to policymakers, developers, and teachers so that the AI systems in Arab education remain not only technically beneficial but also socially and culturally significant.

AI integration in K-12 education promises personalised learning but faces engagement, accessibility and ethical challenges. Text-centric tools often fail digital natives. Voice systems and cultural narratives are under-used. This chapter explores how conversational AI chatbot with personas and narrative gamification can bridge these gaps. It evaluates voice-based AI tutors, adaptive storytelling, and inclusive design for equitable, engaging learning. Drawing on narrative-centred learning, universal design for learning, and self-determination theory, it synthesises studies and critiques. Findings show narratives boost engagement via quests, and voice interfaces aid neurodiverse/multilingual learners. Culturally-adaptive personas and low-cost voice systems increase access, yet AI bias and privacy risks require mitigation. The chapter advocates hybrid teacher-AI models. Implications stress ethically grounded, scalable solutions balancing innovation with inclusivity. When designed with narrative elements, AI may support equitable and culturally-relevant classroom practices.

This chapter proposes a dual chatbot model for Serbian K–12 education, combining a subject-general AI assistant with a persona-based chatbot modeled after Danilo Kiš. Grounded in AI-in-education research and aligned with national curricular goals, the model emphasizes teacher agency, pedagogical relevance, and ethical integration. A conceptual roadmap outlines development phases, pilot strategies, and assessment methods while addressing infrastructure gaps and teacher training. The Kiš chatbot shows potential for deepening literary analysis, supporting historical inquiry, and enhancing translation and language learning. Interdisciplinary applications are explored through history, English, and multilingual education, with attention to cross-cultural dialogue and semantic nuance. Ethical considerations—including authenticity, data bias, and pedagogical limits—are examined. The chapter concludes that well-designed AI tools can support inclusive, context-sensitive humanities instruction and offer scalable innovations that enrich student engagement while preserving literary complexity.

Computational Thinking (CT) has emerged as a critical skill across preschool and primary education, yet the lack of teachers with expertise in CT and the ability to use adaptive learning applications poses a significant barrier. This article proposes an innovative professional development program to equip pre-service teachers in preschool and primary education with essential CT competencies. The program is based on the Technological Pedagogical and Content Knowledge (TPACK) framework while utilizing an adaptive gamification environment with the use of learning analytics. The methodology guides participants through unplugged activities and hands-on coding, using a custom application that personalizes the learning path while providing instructors with real-time data. The main objective of it isn't only to build core CT skills but also to enable them to use them across subjects and to model the teacher's modern role as a facilitator that can use educational data to make strategic pedagogical decisions and effectively enhance learning in technology-rich environments.

Preface

INTRODUCTION

Artificial Intelligence (AI) is no longer a distant promise for the future of schooling; it is part of the everyday reality of teachers and students around the world. From adaptive platforms and virtual tutors to generative tools that help design lessons in seconds, AI is quietly reshaping how learning is planned, delivered, and experienced in K–12 settings. This transformation reaches far beyond mere efficiency. It raises deep questions about equity, ethics, teacher professionalism, and what it means to learn with digital partners that can simulate understanding, provide feedback, and even co-create content. *Virtual Tutors and AI-Powered Instructional Tools in K–12 Settings* was conceived to respond to this moment: to document what is already happening, to critically examine its consequences, and to sketch out possible futures for AI-mediated education.

The volume brings together an international and interdisciplinary group of authors—researchers, teacher educators, classroom practitioners, technologists, and policy thinkers—who approach AI not only as a technical innovation, but as a social and pedagogical force. Their work is grounded in diverse contexts: urban and rural schools, underserved regions, gifted and special education, early childhood and secondary education, as well as higher education spaces that are increasingly intertwined with school systems. Together, the chapters show that AI integration is never neutral. It is shaped by infrastructure, policy, culture, teacher beliefs, and local histories of schooling. At the same time, they offer a shared conviction: that AI, when designed and used with care, can support more inclusive, responsive, and humane educational experiences.

This book is intended for a broad audience: K–12 teachers and school leaders who are beginning to work with AI tools; teacher educators designing new forms of professional development; researchers exploring the learning, ethical, and social implications of AI; curriculum designers and edtech developers; and policymakers concerned with regulation, equity, and long-term system change. Rather than prescribing a single vision, the volume offers a landscape of perspectives. Some chapters are descriptive and practice-oriented, others conceptual and critical, others exploratory and design-focused. Read together, they form a coherent narrative of how virtual tutors and AI-powered tools are entering classrooms, how learners and teachers experience them, and what we might need to pay attention to if we want AI to serve education rather than the other way around.

CHAPTER OVERVIEW

Chapter 1 introduces neuro-symbolic AI as a hybrid approach that combines neural adaptability with symbolic reasoning to enable transparent, equitable, and personalized virtual tutoring. It highlights how such systems can respond to global teacher shortages while supporting higher-order learning and ethical AI integration.

Chapter 2 explores the broader ecosystem of AI-driven instructional tools in K–12 education, examining how intelligent tutoring systems, adaptive assessment, and classroom automation reshape teaching practices while raising critical concerns about privacy, fairness, and responsible implementation.

Chapter 3 reinterprets AI in education through the lens of co-creativity, proposing AI persona frameworks that position artificial agents as collaborators in knowledge construction. The chapter advances a philosophical and design-based perspective emphasizing human flourishing and thoughtful technological integration.

Chapter 4 focuses on the potential of AI-driven tutoring systems to reduce persistent learning disparities among at-risk students. It demonstrates how personalized feedback and data-informed interventions can support inclusion while underscoring ethical risks related to bias and access.

Chapter 5 reviews AI-powered personalized and adaptive learning tools that support early literacy and numeracy development. Through analysis of widely used platforms, the chapter highlights the effectiveness of adaptive content, real-time feedback, and gamified learning environments in strengthening foundational skills.

Chapter 6 examines AI-powered tools that create personalized learning pathways through intelligent tutoring systems, adaptive platforms, and conversational agents. The chapter provides practical insights into implementation, teacher readiness, and the evolving role of data-driven instruction.

Chapter 7 addresses the relationship between AI tutors and human educators in English language teaching, emphasizing the importance of teacher expertise, emotional intelligence, and cultural context in maintaining balanced and meaningful learning experiences.

Chapter 8 presents empirical evidence on AI-powered virtual teachers and their association with the development of students' critical thinking skills. Findings reinforce the value of AI as a supportive instructional tool rather than a substitute for human instruction.

Chapter 9 examines culturally responsive AI tutor design within Arab educational contexts, emphasizing linguistic diversity, cultural alignment, and equitable access as essential components of meaningful AI adoption.

Chapter 10 investigates conversational AI chatbots designed with voice interaction, narrative structures, and inclusive design principles. It demonstrates how storytelling and culturally adaptive personas enhance engagement while requiring strong ethical safeguards.

Chapter 11 proposes a dual-chatbot model for literature education that combines general instructional support with culturally grounded persona-based dialogue systems. The chapter highlights interdisciplinary applications and emphasizes teacher agency in AI integration.

Chapter 12 shifts attention to teacher preparation, presenting an adaptive gamification and learning analytics framework grounded in TPACK to support computational thinking development in pre-service educators.

Chapter 13 offers insights from AI adoption in the Global South, examining the use of conversational AI tools in Tanzanian higher education and identifying lessons relevant for K–12 systems, particularly regarding infrastructure, policy development, and equitable implementation.

Taken together, these 13 chapters offer a rich and multifaceted picture of virtual tutors and AI-powered instructional tools in K–12 settings and beyond. They show that AI can support creativity, inclusion, and personalization, but only when anchored in strong pedagogy, ethical awareness, and a clear commitment to human dignity. They also remind us that technology is never a neutral presence in education; it amplifies the values and structures into which it is introduced. As AI continues to evolve, the challenge for educators, researchers, and policymakers will not be simply to keep up with new tools, but to continually ask: what kind of learning, and what kind of future, are we building with them?

It is my hope that this volume will serve as a resource, a provocation, and a companion for all those engaged in that work.

Stamatios Papadakis
University of Crete, Greece

Acknowledgment

The completion of *Virtual Tutors and AI-Powered Instructional Tools in K-12 Settings* was made possible through the collective effort of an international network of scholars, educators, and practitioners committed to advancing ethical and inclusive uses of Artificial Intelligence in education. I would like to express my sincere appreciation to all chapter authors for their thoughtful contributions, to the anonymous reviewers for their rigorous feedback, and to the editorial and production teams at IGI Global for their professionalism and guidance throughout the publication process.

Special thanks are extended to the educators, teacher-trainers, and students whose experiences and insights have informed much of the work represented in this volume. Their engagement with technology in real learning environments continues to inspire meaningful research and practice.

Finally, I am deeply grateful to my colleagues and collaborators for their encouragement and to my family for their constant support and patience during the preparation of this book.

Chapter 1
Neuro-Symbolic AI for Personalized and Equitable Virtual Tutoring in Education

Ricardo Fitas
http://orcid.org/0000-0001-5137-2451
Independent Researcher, Germany

ABSTRACT

This chapter examines how neuro-symbolic AI (NeSyAI) can support equitable and personalized virtual tutoring in response to global teacher shortages and persistent learning gaps. By blending neural networks' adaptability with symbolic reasoning's interpretability, NeSyAI enables adaptive, transparent, and ethical learning support. The paper reviews recent advances in hybrid models and intelligent tutoring systems, highlighting benefits for engagement, fairness, and higher-order skills, while addressing challenges of scalability, bias, and teacher integration to ensure AI augments rather than replaces educators.

1 INTRODUCTION

Equitable access to quality education is a central global challenge and policy priority. Even before the disruptions of COVID-19, hundreds of millions of children lacked proficient teachers and personalized support, contributing to learning gaps (Elliott, 2024; F. H. Rogers & Sabarwal, 2020). The United Nations Educational, Scientific and Cultural Organization (UNESCO) estimates that an additional 44 million teachers will be needed by 2030 to achieve universal primary and second-

DOI: 10.4018/979-8-3373-2637-5.ch001

ary education (Elliott, 2024). This shortage is a significant barrier to achieving Sustainable Development Goal 4, which aims for inclusive and equitable quality education for all. The shortage is particularly acute in sub-Saharan Africa, which requires 15 million more teachers, while higher-income countries face issues with teacher retention (UNESCO & International Task Force on Teachers for Education 2030, 2025). Virtual tutoring powered by artificial intelligence (AI) has emerged as a promising tool to help bridge these gaps by providing individualized learning support at scale (Dumbuya, 2023; Jain, 2025). The potential of such technologies to enhance learning outcomes and equity has been highlighted (Fitas, 2025a; Fitas et al., 2025; H. E. Sari et al., 2024). For example, AI-driven tutoring systems in China are being used to bring high-quality, personalized lessons to rural students who otherwise lack access to experienced teachers (Cao & Tutor, 2023; Elliott, 2024). Early results from these deployments indicate significant improvements in student achievement and confidence when an AI tutor adapts instruction to each learner's needs (Elliott, 2024). Global investment in AI for education is therefore growing rapidly in hopes of addressing teacher shortages and learning loss (Elliott, 2024).

At the same time, the idea that technology must be harnessed responsibly and appropriately to truly benefit learners is stressed over the literature (Fitas, 2025a; Means et al., 2003; Taha & Abdulrahman, 2023; White et al., 2024). UNESCO's 2023 Global Education Monitoring report cautions that decisions about education technology should prioritize learner needs and equity, be evidence-based, and complement (not replace) human teachers (UNESCO Global Education Monitoring Report Team, 2023). The human dimension of teaching and mentorship remains vital – as UNESCO notes, "no screen can ever replace the humanity of a teacher" (UNESCO

Global Education Monitoring Report Team, 2023). Thus, the vision is not a dystopian automated classroom, but rather an inclusive, student-centered learning environment where AI tutors serve as supportive tools for personalization while educators provide guidance and social-emotional connection. Achieving this vision requires advances in AI that not only deliver content adaptively, but do so in a transparent, moral, and context-aware manner aligned with educational values. This is where neuro-symbolic AI (NeSyAI) – a hybrid approach combining neural networks with symbolic reasoning – could play a transformative role. NeSyAI techniques aim to blend the pattern recognition power of machine learning with the interpretability and logical reasoning of symbolic systems (Wan et al., 2024). In the context of virtual tutoring, such systems might dynamically adjust to a student's performance like a neural network while also upholding pedagogical rules or ethical constraints encoded symbolically. In this chapter, the author explores the ethical impetus for student-centered learning, the benefits and challenges of AI-enabled personalized tutoring, recent developments in neuro-symbolic AI relevant to education, and how these developments could be leveraged to create more equitable and human-centric virtual tutoring systems. Throughout, the analysis remains high-level and conceptual, geared toward policymakers seeking to craft inclusive strategies and AI researchers aiming to build models within an ethical educational framework.

2 LITERATURE SEARCH AND REVIEW METHODOLOGY

This survey was conducted through a structured and replicable methodology designed to capture the most relevant and up-to-date literature on neuro–symbolic AI (NeSyAI) for teaching and learning, classroom integration, and governance. The process involved systematic keyword-based searches across multiple sources, application of inclusion/exclusion criteria, and synthesis across technical, pedagogical, and policy domains.

To reflect the chapter's dual emphasis on learning science and technical AI, the author queried the following academic databases and institutional repositories: Google Scholar, ERIC (Education Resources Information Center), ACM Digital Library, IEEE Xplore, SpringerLink, and arXiv for research articles and preprints; and the OECD iLibrary, UNESCO Digital Library, the European Commission Joint Research Centre (JRC) Publications Repository, and the U.S. Department of Education (Office of Educational Technology) for policy and guidance. The author also consulted official standards/guidance sites when cited in the manuscript (e.g., ISTE, AFT, Common Sense Education, aiEDU) to retrieve primary sources.

Search strings combined NeSyAI and education terms using Boolean operators and common variants. Representative keywords included: *"neuro-symbolic" OR "neurosymbolic" OR "hybrid AI" OR "symbolic reasoning" OR "logical neural networks" OR "rule-based" OR "guardrails" OR "explainable AI"* AND *"education" OR "learning" OR "intelligent tutoring systems" OR "AI tutor" OR "LLM tutor" OR "teacher dashboard" OR "formative assessment" OR "mastery learning" OR "curriculum mapping" OR "knowledge components" OR "KLI framework" OR "UDL" OR "equity" OR "multilingual" OR "localization" OR "teacher professional development" OR "AI literacy" OR "co-design" OR "participatory design" OR "policy" OR "privacy" OR "governance" OR "RCT" OR "quasi-experimental"*. Where appropriate, country/region terms were added to identify global case studies.

Given the rapid evolution of generative AI, the core window spanned 2014–2025 for empirical and design research in education, with heightened attention to 2022–2025 for LLM-enabled tutors and governance. Foundational or widely-cited pre-2014 works (e.g., ITS meta-analyses, classic curriculum/KC mapping frameworks) were included selectively when necessary to ground concepts and compare NeSyAI against established baselines.

Records were eligible if they: (i) addressed AI for teaching/learning or classroom decision support and linked methods or findings to pedagogy, curriculum/assessment, or teacher workflow; (ii) concerned neuro–symbolic or rule-constrained/guardrailed AI *or* provided relevant empirical/policy baselines (e.g., ITS evaluations, OECD/JRC/UNESCO guidance); (iii) presented empirical methods (RCTs, quasi-experiments, field studies), systematic reviews, technical designs with educational alignment, or authoritative policy/standards; and (iv) were available in English. Preprints were included when methods and results were sufficiently described.

Excluded items were those that: (i) were purely technical without an educational link or classroom implications; (ii) lacked methodological detail (op-eds, unsourced blog posts) or were duplicative; (iii) focused solely on higher-education administration or workforce analytics without instructional relevance; (iv) were non-English; or (v) concerned proprietary marketing material without credible evidence.

Titles/abstracts were screened first, followed by full-text review. The author used backward/forward citation tracing to surface adjacent education studies, policy frameworks, and technical notes referenced by accepted papers. For empirical studies, the author noted population/setting, design (RCT, quasi-experimental, observational), outcome measures (learning gains, mastery, engagement), effect sizes where reported, and costs where available. For design/policy sources, the author extracted alignment to curriculum/assessment, teacher PD models, governance/guardrails, equity/UDL, and localization.

The final corpus comprises peer-reviewed studies, field experiments, meta-analyses of ITS efficacy, technical designs of rule-constrained/NeSyAI tutors, and policy/standards documents (OECD, JRC, UNESCO, ISTE, AFT, U.S. DoE). A temporal scan indicates a marked uptick in classroom-facing, guardrailed/LLM-based tutoring work beginning in 2022, alongside increased publication of governance and teacher-readiness guidance. This convergence reflects both technological maturity and demand for transparent, auditable AI aligned with curriculum and teacher agency.

Keyword-based retrieval can miss studies that use alternate terminology. The author mitigated this through synonym expansion and citation chaining but acknowledged residual bias. Policy/guidance documents evolve rapidly; where possible the author cited the most recent official versions. Finally, some promising systems remain proprietary or unpublished; the review focuses on verifiable methods, empirical results, and authoritative guidance.

3 STUDENT-CENTERED LEARNING AND THE INFLUENCE OF AI

Student-Centered Learning (SCL) is an approach that places students' interests, abilities, and learning styles at the forefront of the educational experience. It marks a transition from the traditional "sage on the stage" model to a "guide on the side" model, fundamentally altering the teacher-student dynamic. In SCL classrooms, students are active participants: they engage in decision-making about their learning, work collaboratively, and often pursue projects or problems that interest them personally. Research over the past two decades has documented numerous benefits of SCL for learners' engagement, skills development, and attitudes toward learning. Figure 1 depicts the differences between the most traditional Teacher-Centered approaches compared to the proposed Student-Centered Learning approach. On the left (teacher-centered), the teacher is the single hub of activity: information and direction flow primarily from teacher to individual students, who work in parallel with little peer interaction. The teacher's role is hands-on delivery and control; progress depends on whole-class pacing and direct instruction. On the right (student-centered), the teacher remains central but acts primarily as a mentor and orchestrator. Students engage in self-learning and collaborative learning, shown by the pink arrows circulating among Student 1, Student 2, and Student 3. The teacher's dashed connections indicate coaching, feedback, and timely scaffolding rather than continuous, one-way transmission. The visual shift from a single hub to a network of interactions highlights three practical changes:

Figure 1. Illustration of Teacher-Centered Learning compared to Student-Centered Learning.

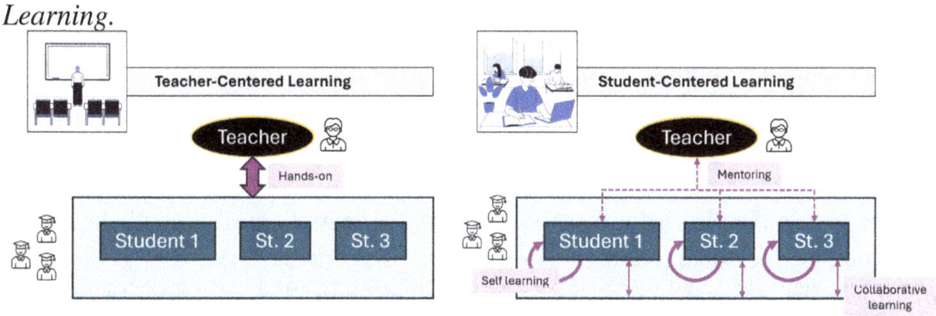

(i) students take active roles in inquiry and explanation;
(ii) peer-to-peer learning is designed, not incidental;

(iii) the teacher's expertise is focused on diagnosing needs, curating tasks, and providing just-in-time support instead of delivering all content synchronously.

Below, key advantages of SCL are synthesized, supported by studies in diverse settings, and discuss how AI technologies can further enhance these benefits. The author also acknowledges challenges in implementing SCL and how AI might address or exacerbate them.

3.1 The Human Moral Imperative and Ethics in Education

Education is not only a technical endeavor, but a profoundly moral one. At its core lies an ethical commitment to nurture each learner's potential and to do so with fairness and respect for human dignity (Marpaung et al., 2023; Sabbagh, 2009). Individual ethics in education demand that the unique needs, abilities, and aspirations of every student be recognized – each child has a right to develop their talents to the fullest. Universal ethics further enshrine education as a fundamental human right and a public good that should be accessible to all, as articulated in instruments like the UN's Sustainable Development Goal 4 (inclusive and equitable quality education for all). These moral principles compel a re-examination of traditional teacher-centered pedagogy in favor of more learner-centered approaches. In a conventional classroom model, the teacher is the primary authority who imparts uniform instruction to passive students. While this model can efficiently deliver content, it often falls short ethically: it risks treating students as homogeneous recipients rather than individuals, and it may marginalize those who do not fit the "average" mold. From a moral standpoint, a one-size-fits-all approach can inadvertently perpetuate inequity by failing to accommodate diverse learners. Students who are advanced, struggling, or simply learn differently might be left behind or disengaged – an outcome at odds with the ethical commitment to each child's growth.

Student-centered learning (SCL) emerges as an ethical corrective to these limitations.

In SCL, the focus shifts from the teacher's agenda to the student's needs, agency, and active participation in the learning process. This paradigm aligns with the idea of education as a personal journey – one where the student is respected as a co-creator of knowledge rather than a passive consumer. It emphasizes moral values such as autonomy, empowerment, and justice. By centering learning on students, educators acknowledge each learner's intrinsic worth and capacity for self-direction. This approach is supported by educational psychology research and humanistic education theories (e.g., Dewey, Rogers), which argue that learning is most meaningful when it connects to the learner's own experiences and interests. In practice, SCL means students get some choice in what or how they learn, lessons are tailored to their level and context, and they are encouraged to take ownership of their education. This not only honors their individuality but also prepares them to become autonomous, morally responsible adults (UNESCO, 2025a; Ydo, 2020). In a broader ethical lens, moving to student-centered methods can help fulfill the universal right to quality education – because quality is inherently tied to relevance and responsiveness to the learner. A student-centered system aspires to leave no one behind, reflecting the principle of equity by design.

However, embracing SCL does not mean diminishing the role of teachers or ignoring communal aspects of learning. On the contrary, teachers in a student-centered framework take on a role as facilitators and mentors, guiding learners on individual paths while cultivating a supportive classroom community. This pedagogical shift requires empathy, flexibility, and ethical discernment from teachers. It also raises important considerations: How do we ensure that increased student autonomy does not compromise coverage of essential knowledge? How do we address potential gaps if some students make choices that lead them astray? These are challenges of implementation rather than indictments of the approach's ethical value. Indeed, many education systems around the world are striving to train teachers in more learner-centric strategies and to reform curricula to allow personalization, precisely because it is seen as more aligned with both how children learn best and with the moral imperative of inclusion (UNESCO, 2025a; UNESCO Inclusive Policy Lab, 2024).

3.2 A Brief Historical Timeline of AI Integration in Education

The integration of artificial intelligence and automation into education has unfolded over seven decades, with successive paradigms shaping how systems represent knowledge, adapt to learners, and fit classroom practice. In the 1950s, predigital teaching machines operationalised behaviourist principles through linear frames and immediate feedback, laying conceptual groundwork for computer-assisted instruction; historical syntheses trace this lineage from Pressey's devices to Skinner's programmed instruction and its classroom aspirations (Watters, 2021). Building on these ideas, the 1960s saw interactive computer-assisted instruction at scale, most notably with the PLATO project at the University of Illinois, which delivered lessons, messaging and early analytics to thousands of networked terminals and demonstrated how computation could support large cohorts of learners; in parallel, Stanford studies began to report comparative outcomes from drill-and-practice and tutorial programs, offering some of the first quantitative evaluations of CAI in mathematics and languages (Dear, 2017; Suppes & Morningstar, 1969).

As researchers sought more responsive systems, late-1960s and 1970s designs moved from strictly linear sequences to branching and generative CAI that routed learners based on their responses and generated problem variants on the fly; although still largely rule-based and symbolic, these approaches introduced limited adaptation through item selection and programmatic feedback (Crowder, 1959). In the 1980s, the first intelligent tutoring systems (ITS) responded to the limits of fixed CAI by combining explicit models of domain knowledge, student understanding and pedagogical strategy within four-component architectures; these systems provided context-sensitive feedback and supported multiple solution paths, marking a shift from scripted lessons to model-driven interaction (Nwana, 1990; Sleeman & Brown, 1982). During the late 1980s and 1990s, cognitive tutors grounded in ACT-R extended this trajectory by tracing sub-skill mastery at the step level and delivering immediate guidance in secondary mathematics; widespread deployments followed, and later syntheses characterised typical effect sizes of step-based ITS relative to non-tutored instruction and to human tutoring (Koedinger et al., 1997; Ritter et al., 2007; VanLehn, 2011).

With the diffusion of the internet in the 2000s, learning management systems normalised digital workflows and routine data capture in schools and universities, creating the infrastructure on which adaptive and data-driven tools could operate; although not "AI" per se, LMS adoption catalysed operational integration of analytics and personalisation in everyday practice (Coates et al., 2005; Lonn & Teasley, 2009). Throughout the 2010s, adaptive learning platforms and district initiatives leveraged machine learning and learning analytics to refine pacing and practice at finer granularity; multi-school studies and syntheses reported achievement patterns under personalised-learning models and adaptive mathematics programs, establishing early—if heterogeneous—evidence for data-driven personalisation in classrooms (Pane et al., 2015; What Works Clearinghouse, 2013). Most recently, the 2020s have brought generative AI to the foreground, renewing interest in conversational tutoring while underscoring risks such as hallucination, bias and privacy concerns; policy guidance has therefore emphasised human-centred use, teacher agency and auditability, and technical work has increasingly pursued hybrid or neuro-symbolic designs that combine neural models with explicit curricular rules, mastery constraints and explainable workflows to align with school governance and classroom needs (Abendroth & colleagues, 2025; OECD, 2023; U.S. Department of Education, Office of Educational Technology, 2023a).

Figure 2 illustrates these mentioned events in a visual timeline.

Figure 2. Timeline of the Automation in Education.

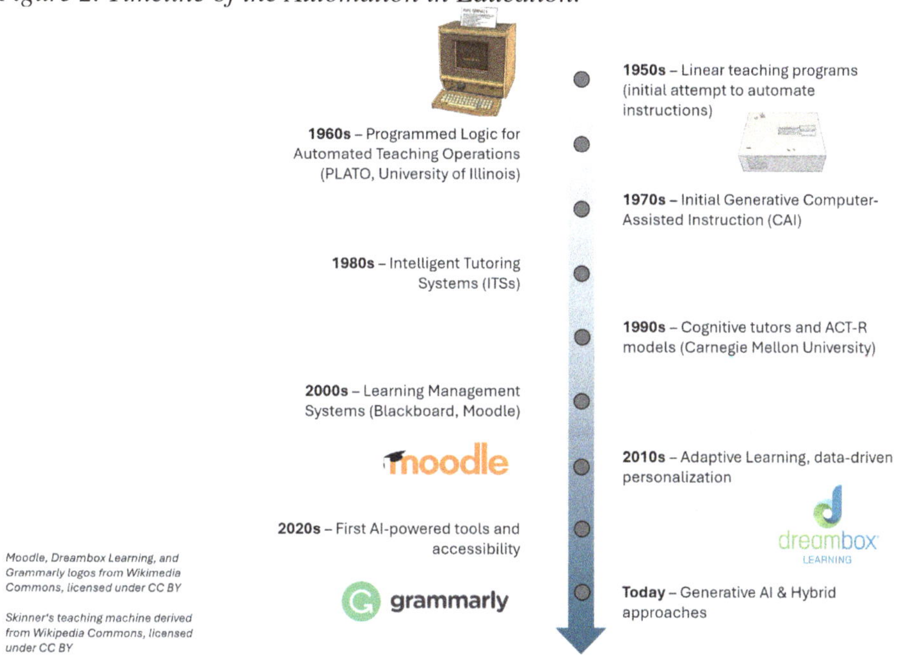

3.3 Enhanced Autonomy and Independence

SCL empowers students to take responsibility for their own learning, which promotes autonomy and self-regulation. Rather than being directed at every step, students in a learner-centered environment are encouraged to make choices – for example, selecting topics for projects or choosing among different activities – and to reflect on their learning strategies. This fosters a sense of ownership and independence in their educational journey. Research has found that when students have greater control and voice in learning, they develop stronger skills for lifelong learning and independent problem-solving (UNESCO, 2025b). Singh (Singh, 2011) presented SCL as a model where students are positioned at the core of the learning process, with teachers primarily serving as facilitators. This approach aims to provide authentic and needs-based instruction, fostering cooperative and collaborative learning through active, democratic, and child-friendly methods, which is a reversal of traditional teaching pedagogy. Case studies at the primary and secondary level show that even young students can thrive when given structured freedom, becoming more adept at setting goals and monitoring their progress (Mat & Jamaludin, 2024). Over time, this can translate into improved confidence and resilience in facing new challenges. AI can further support autonomy by providing tools for self-directed learning. For example, adaptive learning platforms allow students to move at their own pace through material, receiving hints or enrichment as needed. Research has also documented how broader AI integration in education enhances personalization and efficiency while raising important ethical responsibilities (Fitas et al., 2025). This means a learner can independently explore concepts with an AI tutor adjusting difficulty in real-time to match their level (Dumbuya, 2023; Kaswan et al., 2024; Rekha et al., 2024). By tailoring content to each student, AI systems reinforce the student's ability to "drive" their learning path, potentially accelerating those who are ready for more advanced work and reviewing fundamentals with those who need it (Katiyar et al., 2024; Madhu et al., 2024). The result is a more personalized autonomy: students feel "seen" and catered to by the system, which can motivate them to take even more initiative. However, one must ensure that AI guidance is transparent so that students truly understand and manage their own learning, rather than blindly following algorithmic prompts.

3.4 Increased Engagement and Motivation

A hallmark of student-centered classrooms is higher student engagement. When learners have a say in their learning and encounter content that connects with their lives or interests, they naturally invest more attention and effort. Studies have shown that active learning strategies – such as project-based learning, inquiry activities, or cooperative group work – significantly boost engagement compared to lecture-based instruction. For example, Overby (2011) reported that students in project-based, student-driven classes were far more on-task and enthusiastic than in traditional setups (Overby, 2011). Vasilev (2024) similarly found that involving students in setting learning objectives and exploring real-world applications made lessons more relevant and memorable, thereby increasing motivation (Vasilev, 2024). By giving students some control and emphasizing active participation, SCL addresses basic psychological needs (autonomy, competence, relatedness) that underlie intrinsic motivation. Engaged students are not only more joyful learners; they also tend to achieve more. AI can play an important role in maintaining and even amplifying student engagement. Intelligent tutoring systems and educational games powered by AI can adapt in content, context, and feedback to keep students in their optimal zone of engagement – not bored by material too easy, nor frustrated by material too difficult. AI-driven personalized learning systems have been shown to improve student motivation and interaction by making learning more relevant and interactive. For instance, a recent study by Zaharuddin et al. (2024) demonstrated that an AI-driven system providing tailored content and immediate feedback fostered a deeper connection between students and their learning materials, significantly increasing both engagement and academic performance (Yu, Yao, et al., 2024). Additionally, AI-powered educational chatbots can offer students instantaneous support and answer questions on demand, encouraging them to remain engaged with tasks and explore topics more deeply. Such tools create an interactive learning environment where students feel continuously supported, which is linked to higher persistence and motivation (Fu & Weng, 2024). Still, designers must be cautious to use AI in service of genuine engagement (e.g., through interesting challenges and feedback) rather than superficial gamification that might distract or eventually fatigue students.

3.5 Development of Critical Thinking and Problem-Solving Skills

Student-centered approaches often involve presenting learners with complex, open-ended problems and encouraging them to inquire, analyze, and collaborate on solutions. This stands in contrast to rote learning; instead of memorizing facts, students learn how to think. Research indicates that SCL, especially when implemented through problem-based learning or inquiry learning, improves learners' critical thinking abilities (F. W. Sari & Wati, n.d.) and fosters better problem-solving skills (Vasilev, 2024). By grappling with real-world problems, students learn to apply concepts, evaluate evidence, and reason logically. They also often work in teams, which develops their ability to articulate ideas and consider multiple perspectives. A recent study by Che Mat and Jamaludin (2024) found that student-centered practices significantly enhanced critical thinking, noting that students in such environments are more apt to question assumptions and connect interdisciplinary knowledge (Mat & Jamaludin, 2024). AI can augment these outcomes by providing environments for safe problem-solving practice and by scaffolding higher-order thinking. For example, AI-based simulations and virtual labs allow students to experiment with scenarios (say, in science or social studies) where they must make decisions, observe outcomes, and adjust hypotheses – all of which mimic the scientific method and critical thinking process. AI tutors can prompt students with Socratic questions, pushing them to explain their reasoning or consider alternatives, which strengthens their analytical skills. Moreover, some AI systems use neuro-symbolic reasoning to evaluate the steps in a student's solution path, enabling them to give hints that guide the student's reasoning rather than just pointing out a wrong answer. By doing so, the AI acts like a "coach" for thinking. Early work in AI-driven inquiry learning has shown promising results; for instance, an AI that monitored students' reasoning in a physics problem could intervene with targeted prompts, leading to improved problem-solving success rates (F. W. Sari & Wati, n.d.). The challenge is to ensure AI support is tuned properly: too much guidance and it stifles independent thought;

too little and students may flounder. Achieving that balance is an active area of research in AI in education.

3.6 Personalized and Meaningful Learning Experiences

Perhaps the most intuitive benefit of student-centered learning is that it allows education to be personalized. Every student has a unique mix of prior knowledge, skill level, interests, and learning style. Traditional instruction, geared to the "average student," inevitably fails to be meaningful to a portion of the class. In SCL, by contrast, teachers strive to connect learning to each student's context – whether by differentiating tasks, relating content to students' cultural backgrounds, or allowing choice in research topics. This personalization makes learning more meaningful: students see value and purpose in what they are doing because it resonates with their lives or goals. Studies have documented that personalized approaches can significantly improve both learning outcomes and student satisfaction (Yulianti, 2023). For example, in a study by Bains et al. (2023), it was found that both the choice of book and genre significantly boosted reading enjoyment and motivation, suggesting that agency in selection plays a crucial role in enhancing the reading experience (Bains et al., 2023). Personalized learning experiences also promote a deeper understanding because students are more likely to engage in elaboration and critical reflection on content that "speaks" to them. AI is exceptionally well-suited to deliver personalized learning at scale. Adaptive learning systems use algorithms to adjust the difficulty and style of content based on the learner's real-time performance data. If a student is struggling with a concept, the AI can provide additional practice on that foundational concept (perhaps using a different teaching approach or more visual representations) before moving on. If a student shows strength in a topic, the system can present enrichment material or accelerate them to the next unit. Beyond adjusting difficulty, AI can personalize in other dimensions: tailoring context (for instance, framing math problems around a student's interest like sports or music), modality (offering text, video, or interactive examples depending on how the student learns best), and feedback style (some students respond better to gentle hints, others to direct explanations). Importantly, recent work also highlights how AI personalization can support inclusivity, for example by assisting students with special needs and overcoming language barriers in diverse classrooms (Fitas, 2025a). The result is an experience finely tuned to the individual – something a single human teacher with 30 students would find difficult to achieve at all times. Research has found that such AI-driven personalization leads to more meaningful learning. One study noted that an AI tutor that customized content according to learning style and interests improved students' perceived relevance of the material, which in turn increased their intrinsic motivation (Iman et al., 2024). When learning feels personally meaningful, students are more likely to retain knowledge and apply it in new situations. A critical consideration, though, is to ensure that the content and goals remain aligned with curriculum standards and broader educational objectives – personalization should not devolve into trivializing content just to make it fun. This is where symbolic rules or constraints (for example, ensuring certain core topics are covered) can be integrated with adaptive systems, a theme that will be revisited with neuro-symbolic AI.

3.7 Improved Academic Performance and Lifelong Learning Dispositions

By increasing engagement, motivation, and personalization, student-centered approaches ultimately aim to improve academic achievement. Numerous studies and meta-analyses have reported positive effects of SCL on learning outcomes, from test scores to deeper conceptual mastery (Mat & Jamaludin, 2024; Overby, 2011). For instance, Che Mat and Jamaludin (2024) found that classes employing student-centered methods (like collaborative learning and self-paced inquiry) showed higher gains in mathematics and literacy compared to control groups with lecture-based teaching (Mat & Jamaludin, 2024). The gains are often attributed to the combination of active learning (which enhances understanding and retention) and motivation (which leads to more time on task). Besides content knowledge, SCL cultivates lifelong learning skills. Students learn how to learn – they practice setting goals, seeking resources, self-assessing, and persisting through challenges. Nanney (2004) noted that a key outcome of SCL is students becoming less reliant on instructors and more capable of finding solutions on their own (Nanney, 2020). Such skills are critical in a rapidly changing world where individuals must continuously acquire new knowledge. Lifelong learners are better prepared for higher education and the workforce, and they can adapt as industries and technologies evolve. SCL thus not only boosts immediate academic performance but leaves students with an enduring capacity for growth. AI can reinforce these outcomes by providing timely assessment and feedback mechanisms that keep students on track toward mastery. AI-assisted assessment, in particular, has shown great promise in enhancing both performance and motivation. With AI, assessment can be transformed from a one-time exam at the end of a unit to a continuous, formative process that guides learning. For example, AI-driven quizzes and analytic dashboards can give students (and teachers) instant feedback on what has been learned well and what areas need review. This immediacy helps students adjust their study strategies in real-time and prevents small misunderstandings from accumulating into major learning gaps (X. Wang et al., 2023). Moreover, the AI can offer feedback in an individualized way – praising a student's specific improvement, or providing a hint targeting exactly the step where the student went wrong. Such personalized feedback has been found to significantly improve students' subsequent performance and persistence (X. Wang et al., 2023). It also supports equity: by identifying each student's challenges early, AI assessments allow instructors to intervene with additional help for those who need it, effectively "differentiating" instruction even in large classes (X. Wang et al., 2023). This kind of responsive teaching is central to the SCL ethos. Furthermore, as students experience more formative feedback and success through adaptive learning, they often develop a growth mindset – believing their abilities can improve with effort – which is a cornerstone of lifelong learning. While the benefits of SCL are substantial, it is important to acknowledge challenges in making it a reality across educational systems. Not all teachers are immediately comfortable with relinquishing some control to students; it requires training and a shift in mindset to move from lecturer to facilitator. Classroom management can initially become more complex in active learning settings, and teachers may worry about covering the required curriculum when giving students more freedom. There are also resource implications: SCL often requires flexible learning materials, possibly more space for group activities, and an environment that encourages experimentation (which might include tolerance for some noise and movement in class). Additionally, cultural contexts vary – in some places, parents and students are so accustomed to exam-focused, teacher-led education that they may resist SCL approaches initially. These challenges mean that SCL implementation must be thoughtful and often gradual, blending traditional and progressive methods. Significantly, AI technology can be either a help or a hindrance in this transition. If used well, AI can support teachers by handling routine personalization tasks (like drilling basic skills for those who need it) and freeing the teacher to focus on higher-order guidance. Teachers can also use AI analytics to better understand each student's progress and needs, thereby informing their personalized interventions. On the flip side, if introduced without support, AI could overwhelm teachers or be misused to drill students in a way that is antithetical to SCL (for example, using AI only for repetitive practice rather than creative inquiry). Ensuring equitable access to AI tools is another concern – if only well-resourced schools get the advanced tutoring systems, the digital divide could widen educational inequities. Therefore, as AI is integrated into student-centered learning, careful policy and management are needed to overcome barriers and ensure that technology truly augments a human-centered, ethical education.

3.8 Remarks

Student-centered learning represents a meaningful shift toward personalizing education and engaging students as active, autonomous learners. Its benefits span from greater motivation and critical thinking to better academic outcomes and preparedness for lifelong learning. AI, particularly in the form of intelligent tutoring systems and real-time feedback tools, has the potential to greatly reinforce SCL by providing personalization and support at scale. The synergy of SCL and AI could lead to highly effective learning environments – if the challenges are navigated wisely.

4 NEURO-SYMBOLIC AI: RECENT DEVELOPMENTS IN LEARNING AND REASONING SYSTEMS

Neuro–symbolic AI (NeSyAI) combines two strengths: neural models that learn patterns from data and symbolic formalisms that encode rules, structure, and explanations. For education, this means tutors who recognise what a learner is doing and follow clear pedagogical policies (e.g., mastery thresholds, curriculum order, safety and fairness rules). Below, recent directions with a focus on how they translate into classroom practice rather than on algorithmic detail are highlighted.

4.1 Hybrid Model Designs and Classroom Implications

New sequence models integrate explicit rules into learning so that predictions and recommendations always respect required constraints (De Smet et al., 2025). Instead of only "fitting the data," these models also obey policies such as "demonstrate addition mastery before introducing multiplication" or "withhold the final step until the student has attempted a solution." In class, this allows teachers to set progression rules once and have the tutor consistently enforce them, while keeping a visible log of which rule triggered a hint, a review activity, or a gate to the next topic. The benefit is predictable behaviour aligned to the syllabus and easier post-hoc explanation ("the system paused advancement because mastery criterion X was not met").

Language understanding with guardrails. For open responses, hybrid NLP stacks pair a neural understanding layer with a lightweight rule layer that checks outputs for consistency with grammar, content labels, or safety policies (Barnes & Hutson, 2024). Practically, this reduces common misreads of student free-text (e.g., confusing a definition with an example) and keeps tutor replies on-rubric (e.g., giving a scaffolded hint rather than a full solution when rules say so). Teachers see clearer rationales ("the tutor provided a level-2 hint because the 'no direct answer before two attempts' policy applied") and students experience more reliable, on-task dialogue.

In sequencing activities, neuro–symbolic approaches blend symbolic planning (to map a curriculum path) with data-driven adaptation (to react to a student's engagement and success) (Nu´n˜ez-Molina et al., 2024). The plan gives structure—what to teach, in what order, with which prerequisites—while the adaptive component adjusts pacing, practice spacing, or representation (e.g., switching to manipulatives or a bilingual prompt) based on evidence from recent work. For teachers, this looks like a dashboard where the "why" of each next step is traceable ("prereq not yet stable" or "spaced-practice window due"), and where rules and thresholds can be edited without retraining the model.

Across these strands, the common thread is policy-aware assistance: tutors that explain their choices, respect teacher-defined rules, and adapt responsibly. In practical terms, teachers gain (i) consistent mastery gating and hinting aligned with curriculum policy, (ii) clearer handling of open responses with fewer off-task outputs, and (iii) sequenced learning plans that can be audited and tuned. For learners, this translates into steadier scaffolding and feedback that matches classroom norms.

4.2 Trends in Applications

The resurgence of NeSyAI has given rise to a wide range of applications, demonstrating its versatility. A survey by Bouneffouf and Aggarwal (2022) maps out a taxonomy of NeSyAI applications across sectors and highlights key trends (Bouneffouf & Aggarwal, 2022). They show that NeSyAI methods are being applied in areas such as healthcare (for interpretable medical diagnosis), finance (for reasoning about financial decision support), robotics (for combining perception with planning), and more. Notably, many applications align with scenarios that require trust and reasoning – a natural fit for NeSyAI due to its interpretability. The survey indicates a trend towards using NeSyAI for problems where pure deep learning hits limitations due to data paucity or the need for reasoning about relationships. For example, in information retrieval and recommendation systems, incorporating symbolic domain knowledge (like knowledge graphs of user preferences or product attributes) into neural models has improved recommendations while also making them explainable to users (Bouneffouf & Aggarwal, 2022). Another trend is multimodal NeSyAI, where systems jointly analyze, say, vision and language data with an underlying world model. These trends suggest that NeSyAI is maturing from theoretical proposals to practical tools that can be deployed in real-world settings requiring transparency and adaptability. For education specifically, NeSyAI's emphasis on incorporating causal knowledge and rules is very promising, since educational domains have abundant expert knowledge (e.g., skill taxonomies, prerequisite relationships, pedagogical strategies) that one would like AI tutors to utilize rather than ignore. Indeed, a theme in NeSyAI applications is bridging the gap between data-driven AI and human-understandable knowledge, which resonates strongly with the needs of educational AI (where teacher–AI collaboration and parental understanding of AI decisions are important).

4.3 Mapping the Landscape and Addressing Inefficiencies

Researchers are also working to systematically understand different neuro-symbolic architectural choices and to optimize their performance. Feldstein et al. (2024) provided the first comprehensive mapping of NeSyAI architectures, categorizing approaches based on how and where integration of neural and symbolic components occurs (e.g., do we inject symbolic knowledge into the inputs, constrain the architecture, or refine outputs?) (Feldstein et al., 2024). This kind of survey is valuable because it helps identify the strengths of various frameworks and potential gaps. For instance, some NeSyAI systems use a neural backbone with a symbolic module on top (as a post processor for explanations or constraint checking), while others build symbolic reasoning into the core (like a neural network that learns logic rule parameters). Mapping studies show that each approach has trade-offs in terms of scalability, interpretability, and ease of training (Feldstein et al., 2024). Building on this, Kautz (2022) and Fitas (2025) also offer a complementary taxonomy of six canonical neuro-symbolic architectures, organized by the level and direction of integration between neural and symbolic modules, thereby extending and systematizing earlier mapping efforts (Fitas, 2025b; Kautz, 2022). Figure 3 depicts the different proposed architectures in more detail.

Figure 3. Taxonomy of Neuro-Symbolic AI architectures based on the integration level and directional flow between neural (N) and symbolic (S) components (Fitas, 2025b).

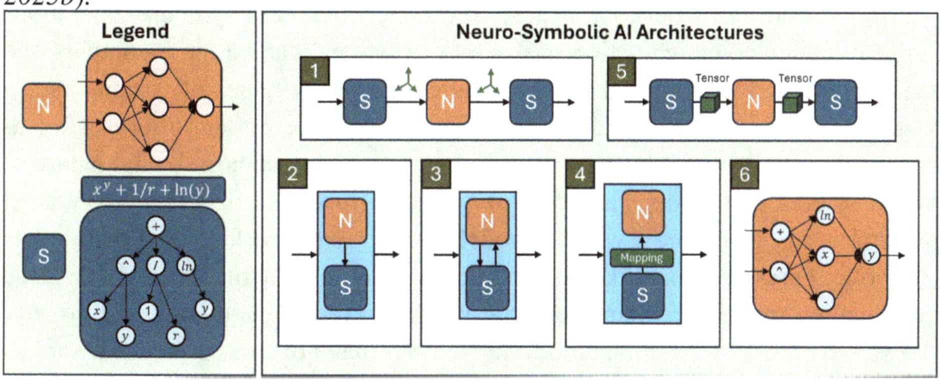

Understanding these can guide AI researchers. Six common architectures are illustrated:

(1) Symbolic pre- and post-processing surrounding neural inference;
(2) Neural core with embedded symbolic reasoning;

(3) Bidirectional interaction between neural and symbolic modules with co-adaptive feedback loops;
(4) Neural modules explicitly mapping continuous representations into structured symbolic knowledge;
(5) Tensor-based embedding of symbolic knowledge into neural architectures using soft logic or differentiable constraints; and
(6) End-to-end differentiable symbolic expressions directly processed by neural networks.

This taxonomy synthesizes classification schemes proposed in (Bhuyan et al., 2024; Kautz, 2022). To choose or hybridize frameworks when designing new models – for example, an AI tutor might use a neural network for student modeling but a symbolic reasoning engine for deciding next exercises. Feldstein et al. also pointed out how augmenting deep learning with symbolic reasoning generally improves performance on tasks requiring generalization beyond the training distribution (Feldstein et al., 2024). This is crucial for educational AI: a tutor trained on one cohort of students should still perform reasonably with a new cohort, and especially not fail catastrophically on novel student responses (like creative problem-solving approaches). NeSyAI offers more robust generalization by virtue of the fact that symbolic knowledge (like "if the student gets all problems in concept A correct, concept B can be introduced") holds true across different data contexts.

Despite progress, a significant practical challenge facing NeSyAI is computational efficiency. Neural networks usually rely on fast matrix operations that are well-optimized on modern hardware (GPUs, etc.), whereas symbolic operations (logical inference, manipulation of discrete structures) can be more complex and memory-intensive. Wan et al. (2024) studied the performance of various neuro-symbolic workloads and found that neuro-symbolic models often suffer inefficiencies on conventional hardware, primarily because of the memory-bound nature of vector-symbolic operations and complex control flows that they involve (Wan et al., 2024). In other words, when a model frequently has to fetch and manipulate symbolic representations (like vectors representing logic symbols or graphs), the computation may stall waiting for data movement rather than doing math operations. Also, the flow of computation in NeSyAI may not be as straightforward as in a standard deep network (which is just a series of matrix multiplies); instead, it might branch or iterate in ways that standard hardware isn't optimized for. Wan et al. highlighted issues such as sparsity (many zero values in symbolic representations), data dependency patterns that break the parallelism, and the overhead of switching between neural and symbolic computations (Wan et al., 2024). To address these issues, they proposed cross-layer optimization solutions – meaning optimizations that span algorithm design, software implementation, and hardware architecture.

For instance, one solution is to develop specialized hardware accelerators for vector-symbolic operations (operations that encode symbols as high-dimensional vectors and perform algebra on them) (Wan et al., 2024). Wan et al. even presented a case study of a hardware accelerator that dramatically improved the speed of a neuro-symbolic image understanding model by handling its vector-symbolic computations more efficiently (Wan et al., 2024). These developments are technical, but their impact on real-time applications is direct: if NeSyAI systems can be made as fast and scalable as conventional neural networks, we can feasibly deploy them in interactive settings like live tutoring without lag or excessive cost. The research trend thus is not only to make AI smarter via NeSyAI but also to make NeSyAI run smoothly in practical environments, through innovations in both algorithms and hardware.

4.4 Remarks

The field of neuro-symbolic AI has advanced significantly, and will continue to advance, bringing forth models that learn from data while respecting logical constraints, understand language with both context and rules, and make decisions by combining planning with learning. These systems offer enhanced interpretability, robustness to distribution shifts, and alignment with human knowledge structures – all desirable properties for educational applications. They also open up possibilities for AI tutors that can explain their reasoning (because they have a symbolic part that can be translated to human-readable form) and for ensuring fairness (because biases can be checked or constrained via symbolic rules, as discussed in the education use cases that will follow next). However, making NeSyAI "adaptable and applicable in real time" – especially in the dynamic, high-stakes environment of a classroom or tutoring session – is not trivial.

5 ADAPTABILITY IN REAL-TIME AND DYNAMIC ENVIRONMENTS: CHALLENGES AND OPPORTUNITIES

Designing an AI tutor that operates in a real classroom or an online learning platform in real time introduces an entirely new set of challenges beyond algorithm accuracy. In such dynamic environments, the AI system must handle a constant flow of interactions, adapt on-the-fly to new situations (a student's unexpected question, a sudden technical issue, etc.), and do so in a reliable and transparent way. Neuro-symbolic AI, with its blend of learning and reasoning, seems well-suited to meet some of these demands – but scaling NeSyAI up to real-world complexity involves surmounting several hurdles. In this section, key challenges that arise when aiming to deploy adaptable NeSyAI systems in complex, mission-critical environments (like education) are examined. Opportunities where NeSyAI's unique strengths could be leveraged for improved performance and trustworthiness in these settings are also highlighted. The discussion is framed by recent research insights and is mindful of the ethical imperative to ensure AI supports, rather than undermines, human values in practice.

5.1 Scalability and Infrastructure Constraints

One of the foremost challenges is scaling NeSyAI systems to work efficiently with real-world data volumes and user loads. A virtual tutoring system in a national education program, for instance, might need to serve millions of students simultaneously, each generating a stream of interactions and data. This demands a robust AI/ML infrastructure capable of handling heavy computation and data storage, possibly distributed across cloud and edge devices. Traditional neural networks have benefited from decades of optimization in such environments, but NeSyAI's more complex workloads (as discussed in (Wan et al., 2024)) pose new stresses on infrastructure. Ram´ırez and Islam (2024) emphasize the need for AI systems to be engineered with scalability, security, and efficiency from the ground up when aiming for large-scale deployment (Padmanaban, 2024). This means building flexible pipelines that can parallelize tasks, manage resources dynamically, and ensure data integrity and privacy. In a real-time tutoring scenario, the system might be expanding its knowledge base (learning from new student data) while simultaneously reasoning over that data to give feedback – a multi-threaded challenge that requires careful design. Moreover, as NeSyAI models often incorporate multiple components (neural modules, symbolic solvers, knowledge graph databases, etc.), the infrastructure must coordinate these seamlessly. If any component becomes a bottleneck, the whole system's responsiveness could suffer. Cross-layer optimizations (like those suggested by Wan et al. (Wan et al., 2024)) and cloud-edge hybrid deployments are potential solutions: for example, time-sensitive, simple neural computations could run on a student's device (edge) for immediate response, while heavier symbolic reasoning queries are handled on the cloud and streamed back with slight delay. Ensuring security is another facet – educational data is sensitive, so NeSyAI systems must adhere to data protection regulations and guard against breaches, all while maintaining performance. The takeaway is that building an AI tutor at scale is as much an engineering problem as an AI problem, and NeSyAI adds complexity that must be managed through innovative system architecture (Padmanaban, 2024).

5.2 Domain Adaptation and Generalization

Educational settings are incredibly diverse. A tutoring system might be used in different schools, subjects, age groups, or even countries. It must adapt to each new context without extensive retraining for every scenario – a property known as generalization. One challenge here is that models trained in one domain may not perform well in another due to distribution shifts. For example, a math tutor AI trained on English-speaking students' data might struggle with students who provide explanations in Spanish, not because of a language barrier if it's a math tutor per se, but perhaps because the patterns of errors or the curriculum ordering differ. Dinu (2024) investigates methods for deep domain-invariant learning, which aim to extract features or rules that remain valid across different domains (Dinu, 2024). In the context of NeSyAI, this could involve learning symbolic rules that are broadly applicable (like fundamental misconceptions in physics that many students share globally) combined with neural adaptation for local particulars. One approach is to use domain adaptation techniques, where the AI system can adjust its internal representations when exposed to some data from a new domain, aligning it with the original domain's feature space. NeSyAI can help here: a symbolic knowledge base might encode domain-invariant educational concepts (e.g., the concept of "fraction" is the same in any language), providing a scaffold that remains fixed while neural components adapt to local data. However, a major challenge is dealing with large domain gaps and continuous shifts. Imagine an AI tutor moving from a well-structured school environment to a home-school environment where the sequence and pacing of topics are completely different – the AI might have to reorganize its understanding of the curriculum. Techniques like meta-learning or continual learning are being explored so that AI can "learn how to learn" new tasks rapidly. For NeSyAI, a promising direction is enabling the symbolic part of the system to acquire new rules or concepts on the fly. In a sense, the AI would be expanding its knowledge graph as it encounters novel situations (like a new type of problem it has never seen before) rather than being stuck with a fixed ontology. Some prototypes of this exist in research, but maintaining consistency and avoiding catastrophic forgetting (losing old knowledge when learning new) remain challenges (Dinu, 2024). For policymakers and practitioners, the implication is that an AI tutor should be piloted and evaluated across varied settings – urban/rural, different curricula – to ensure it generalizes or can be tuned with minimal effort. The goal is an adaptable tutor that works well for every student, not just those similar to its training set.

5.3 Complex Task Decomposition and Intent Understanding

In dynamic environments, tasks are often complex and need to be broken down. Consider an AI in a mission-critical scenario like an intelligent teaching assistant helping with a science lab: it might have to set up an experiment, guide the student step-by-step, help the student formulate hypotheses, and so on. Rather than one monolithic AI trying to do everything, a more practical approach is to decompose the task into subtasks that can be handled by specialized models. Huang et al. (2023) introduce ANPL, an interactive program synthesis system that combines user-specified sketches with natural language modules ("holes"), allowing iterative refinement and structured decomposition to better capture programmatic intent and compose tasks (D. Huang et al., 2023). Translated to education, this means the AI system might benefit from programmatic tutoring strategies – essentially, a high-level program or script that calls different components (one for answering factual questions, one for diagnosing misconceptions, one for suggesting extension activities, etc.). Neuro-symbolic methods can facilitate this by using symbolic planning to sequence subtasks and neural modules to execute them. However, designing such systems requires unambiguous specification of what the AI is intended to do at each step, and ideally some way for a human (teacher or student) to intervene or adjust the plan. Interactive program synthesis refers to creating programs (or plans) with some human-in-the-loop feedback to ensure they meet the user's intent. In an educational context, one could envision a teacher setting goals ("This week focus on improving student X's algebra word problem skills") and the NeSyAI tutor synthesizing a plan of lessons/quizzes, which the teacher can review and tweak. Achieving this level of coordination between human intent and AI action is challenging. It involves building interfaces that teachers can understand – essentially giving a peek into the symbolic reasoning of the AI (for example, a visual map of the student's learning path or a list of concepts the AI plans to address next). Research by Huang and colleagues suggests that having clear specification languages or tools for intent (even something like a checklist of skills to cover, or a way to rank learning objectives) can make the AI's planning more aligned with human expectations (D. Huang et al., 2023). Without these, an AI might optimize for a proxy metric (like minimizing time to complete assignments) in a way that conflicts with true educational intent (e.g., rushing the student through without deep learning). Thus, a key direction is interactive neuro-symbolic tutoring systems, where the teacher or student can query "Why are we doing this next?" and the system can give a rationale derived from its symbolic plan (e.g., "Because mastering concept A is required before concept B, and you haven't mastered A yet"). This level of transparency in intent and decomposition would greatly increase trust and effectiveness, but it requires significant advances in explainable planning and user interface design.

5.4 Explainability and Trustworthiness

Perhaps the most crucial challenge in safety-critical or sensitive domains is gaining user trust through explainable and reliable AI behavior. In education, teachers, students, and parents will rightfully be concerned that the AI tutor may make mistakes or be biased. If the system cannot explain its reasoning, it will be a "black box," which is problematic when it's influencing a child's learning trajectory. Neuro-symbolic AI is often touted as a solution to the explainability issue because the symbolic component can, in principle, provide a rationale for decisions (e.g., a rule it applied or a fact it used). However, achieving true explainability in practice is still difficult. Sheth and colleagues (2023) argue that NeSyAI systems need to meet criteria of consistency, reliability, and user-level explainability to be trustworthy (Gaur & Sheth, 2024). Even if an AI's internal logic is sound, explaining it to a non-expert user (like a student) is a challenge. For instance, a student struggling to understand why the AI marked an answer wrong might need a very pedagogical explanation, not a technical one. NeSyAI could help by, say, extracting a symbolic rule "the student applied formula X incorrectly" and then verbalizing: "I see you tried to use formula X here, but remember the conditions for using that formula aren't met in this problem." This kind of explanation is both an answer and a learning moment. Some NeSyAI research has focused on rule extraction from neural networks, which indeed would allow for precisely this kind of feedback (Hooshyar et al., 2024). The NeSyAI framework by Hooshyar et al. enabled extracting logical rules from a trained model of students' computational thinking, making it possible to understand and communicate what factors led to a prediction (Hooshyar et al., 2024). In their findings, the ability to provide such rule-based interpretations helped ensure the system could be audited for biases and errors (Hooshyar et al., 2024). Nonetheless, challenges remain: the explanations themselves must be correct (an AI could give a wrong reason for a right answer due to mismatches between the neural and symbolic parts), and they must be presented at the right level of complexity for the user. A further aspect of trust is robustness – stakeholders need to trust that the AI tutor won't behave unpredictably with novel inputs. Wan et al. (2024) note that NeSyAI's advantage is improved robustness by handling uncertainty via probabilistic logic and reducing reliance on huge data, but if hardware inefficiencies cause lags or crashes, that too undermines trust (Wan et al., 2024). So reliability includes both algorithmic trustworthiness (no bizarre outputs, no harmful biases) and operational robustness (the system is stable and available when needed). The opportunity here is that NeSyAI, by design, can bake in constraints that improve reliability – for example, a symbolic safety rule might prevent the system from ever giving certain types of problematic advice. In autonomous driving (another domain cited for NeSyAI use), researchers incorporate safety rules (like "never cross a double yellow line") into the AI's decision-making;

similarly, for education, one could enforce rules like "never provide the full solution outright without at least one hint, unless the student is stuck after X attempts" to preserve the learning process. Such built-in ethics and pedagogy rules can make the AI's behavior more predictable and aligned with human teachers' values, thereby increasing trust. Ultimately, building trustworthy NeSyAI tutors will likely require interdisciplinary collaboration – cognitive scientists, educators, ethicists, and AI experts working together to define what trustworthy behavior means in the classroom and how to technically implement it (Gaur & Sheth, 2024).

5.5 Opportunities for Advancing Adaptability

On the flip side of these challenges, the nature of NeSyAI offers several exciting opportunities to improve AI performance in dynamic environments. One key opportunity is enhanced decision-making through contextual reasoning. Ogunsina et al. (2024) explored a neuro-symbolic framework for autonomous robots that significantly improved real-time contextual understanding and adaptability in decision-making (Ogunsina et al., 2024). Translating that to tutoring: a neuro-symbolic tutor could maintain a contextual model of each student (symbolically representing their knowledge state, emotional state, and even context like time of day or recent performance) and use that context to make better tutoring decisions. For instance, if the symbolic memory knows the student has struggled with concept Y every time it was encountered, the neural part can adapt its strategy next time concept Y arises (maybe offering a different explanation or more practice problems) instead of treating it like any other concept. This kind of context-awareness is what distinguishes truly smart tutors from basic ones. NeSyAI can encode context as symbolic facts ("Student made error type E on last attempt") and combine it with neural predictions ("Probability of error E now is high, given pattern") to decide the next action (maybe revisit the fundamental concept behind E). The result is a tutor that feels adaptive in an almost human-like way: it remembers and reasons about a student's history. In dynamic settings, such real-time adaptation could also handle unexpected events – e.g., if a student suddenly starts guessing answers (a behavior change), a symbolic rule might flag "student disengaged" and prompt the AI to switch tactics (perhaps a game or a simpler task to rebuild confidence).

Interdisciplinary integration is another major opportunity. Colelough and Regli (2025) argue that bridging fields – such as combining advances in explainable AI, human-computer interaction, and cognitive science with NeSyAI – is crucial for developing more intelligent and context-aware (Colelough & Regli, 2025). For educational AI, this could mean integrating insights from pedagogy (e.g., how to sequence content based on cognitive load theory) directly into AI models. NeSyAI is well-suited to this because symbolic components can encode expert knowledge from educational psychology or learning sciences. Imagine an AI tutor that has a symbolic rulebase derived from cognitive science research (for instance, "working memory limitations mean give at most 3 hints at once" or "spaced repetition improves retention"). By encoding these rules, the AI could inherently operate in ways consistent with how humans learn best. The neural side would still allow flexibility and learning from student data, but the symbolic side would ensure the system's suggestions and pacing align with established human learning patterns. Such interdisciplinary NeSyAI systems could set a new benchmark for evidence-based AI in education, thereby gaining trust from educators who often complain that ed-tech lacks grounding in learning science.

Finally, an intriguing technical opportunity comes from integrating spatio-temporal reasoning into NeSyAI, which has been noted as essential for solving complex real-world problems (J. Huang et al., 2023). In an educational context, spatio-temporal reasoning could be relevant for tasks like interpreting a student's work over time (temporal) or even understanding drawings/diagrams a student makes (spatial). A neuro-symbolic spatio-temporal reasoning system (Lee et al., 2023) could allow an AI tutor to not only evaluate static answers but to reason about process. For example, if a student is doing a geometry construction task in an interactive app, the AI needs to follow the sequence of steps (temporal) and understand the spatial relations of shapes drawn. A purely neural system might identify patterns of correct/incorrect final answers, but a neuro-symbolic one can reason about each step in the context of geometry rules (e.g., "this construction is invalid because it violates the rule that a perpendicular bisector must cross the segment's midpoint") and give pointed feedback. Early research in this area has shown promise, like an NeSyAI system that could interpret the evolving state of a visual scene while applying logic rules to it (Lee et al., 2023). Bringing that into tutoring, the system could effectively "watch" a student solve a puzzle (virtually) and intervene at the right time with the right hint that a human tutor might give ("I notice you placed that piece here; have you considered the overall symmetry that's required?" – indicating a high-level pattern the student might have missed). These capabilities could greatly enrich virtual tutoring, making it far more interactive and akin to human guidance.

5.6 Remarks

In considering these challenges and opportunities, it's clear that realizing the full potential of NeSyAI in education will require not just technological advances but also careful attention to policy and ethical design. The integration of NeSyAI into classrooms must be approached with caution and reflection. One must ensure these systems are inclusive (do they work for students of different backgrounds and abilities?), transparent (do stakeholders understand and agree with their actions?), and accountable (is there recourse if the system makes a harmful decision?). Moreover, educators need to be involved in the development process to embed pedagogy from the start, rather than retrofitting it onto an AI system built in isolation. With those caveats in mind, NeSyAI indeed holds promise to be a transformative force – enabling AI tutors that learn and reason, that personalize and explain, and that could truly democratize access to high-quality, student-centered education.

6 NEURO-SYMBOLIC AI IN EDUCATION: REAL-WORLD APPLICATIONS AND BENEFITS

Despite being an emerging field, neuro-symbolic AI has already begun making inroads into educational technology. These applications, while still in nascent stages, showcase how integrating neural learning with symbolic reasoning can enhance the capabilities of intelligent educational tools. In particular, NeSyAI approaches have been used to create adaptive learning environments, to improve intelligent tutoring systems (ITS), and to tackle persistent challenges in educational AI such as interpretability and bias. This section explores specific instances of NeSyAI applied in education and the benefits observed. How NeSyAI-driven systems can provide more personalized support, yield explanations for their actions, and help ensure fairness in tutoring will be discussed. Real-world case studies and research prototypes are highlighted to illustrate the potential of NeSyAI to make virtual tutoring more effective and equitable.

Figure 4 is an example of how an integration of NeSyAI can be done in the classroom context. At the top left, the NeSyAI architecture combines a neural component (green) with a symbolic reasoning component (orange). The teacher formulates rules and policies (e.g., mastery thresholds, hint sequencing, language/localization choices, safety constraints) that enter the symbolic layer; this layer enforces "constrained reasoning" so tutor outputs always respect classroom policies. Students interact with the tutor during practice; both students and the teacher can actively query the AI (blue bars at the bottom), and the tutor's response to a student is explicitly shown as "AI Output to Student." As students work, the system logs "Information Student 1/2/. . . "—interaction traces, mastery signals, and errors—so that learning evidence is collected in real time. The neural network learns patterns from these traces ("Neural Training" arrow), while the symbolic layer continues to gate and explain decisions (e.g., why a hint was issued or advancement was paused). The teacher supervises and mentors throughout; arrows from the teacher to students emphasize oversight and coaching, and arrows back from the information blocks to the teacher indicate that evidence is available for review and intervention. Faded copies of the neural and symbolic modules indicate that this flow scales to many students concurrently, also to preserve privacy between them. In practice, this loop supports four teacher moves:

Figure 4. Flowchart aiming at integrating NeSyAI in the classroom context, where the teacher acts as a mentor, but also where students and teacher can query AI in order to understand their learning process.

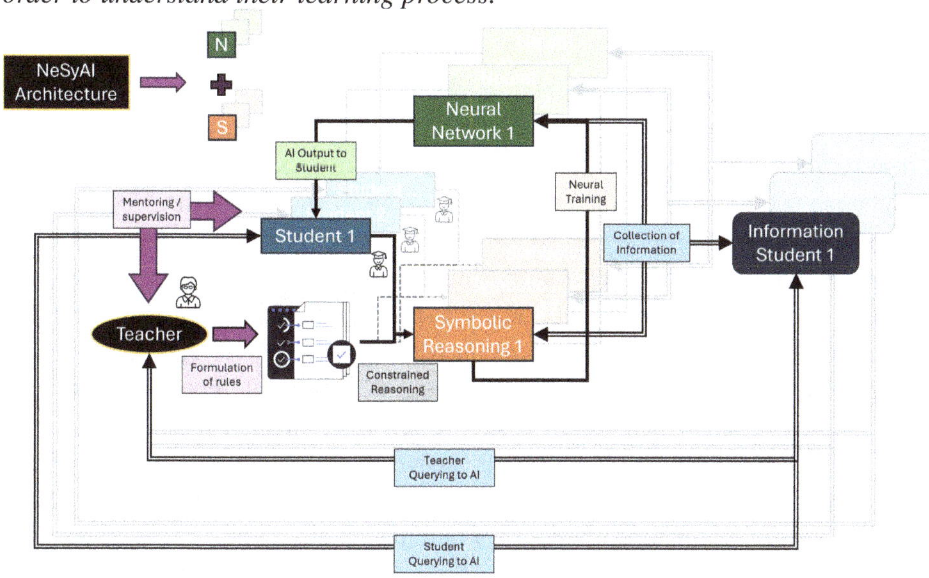

(i) set or revise rules centrally and have the tutor enforce them consistently;
(ii) see why the system acted (auditable decisions tied to rules)
(iii) respond to dashboards/logs by regrouping, re-teaching, or releasing mastery;
(iv) let students and teacher ask the AI targeted questions while keeping outputs within agreed pedagogical guardrails.

6.1 NeSyAI in Context: Comparison With Established ITS

Neuro-symbolic AI (NeSyAI) tutors emerge within a mature lineage of intelligent tutoring systems (ITS) that have demonstrated effectiveness at scale over several decades. Three well-established exemplars illustrate the design space:

(i) Carnegie Learning's Cognitive Tutor family, built on model tracing over cognitive models and knowledge components (Ritter et al., 2007);

(ii) ALEKS, grounded in Knowledge Space/Learning Space Theory (KST/LST) to infer a learner's knowledge state and "ready-to-learn" fringe (Doignon & Falmagne, 1999, 2011);

(iii) ASSISTments, a formative-assessment platform that couples immediate feedback with in-situ randomized experiments and teacher-centered workflows (Heffernan & Heffernan, 2014).

Like Cognitive Tutors, NeSyAI systems can encode domain structure and constraints; like ALEKS, they can maintain explicit notions of mastery and prerequisites; and like ASSISTments, they can support continuous formative assessment and teacher-in-the-loop experimentation. These continuities are valuable: they permit cumulative use of proven practices for alignment to standards, mastery tracking, and A/B evaluation.

NeSyAI combines a neural component (for broad generalization and natural language interaction) with a symbolic layer (for explicit rules, guardrails, and curricular constraints). This yields: (1) *open-ended problem dialogue* beyond fixed step patterns typical of classic model-tracing; (2) *auditable policies*—symbolic rules for hints, solution withholding, safety, and assessment accommodations; (3) *localization*—rule-based adaptation for language, notation, and cultural conventions; and (4) *rapid content coverage* using neural generation constrained by symbolic schemas. Trade-offs include greater attention to validation of neural outputs, computational cost of inference, and the need for governance of prompt/policy updates.

Established ITS remain strong baselines with well-documented efficacy and data pipelines (Heffernan & Heffernan, 2014; Ritter et al., 2007). The author envisions NeSyAI as complementary: use model-tracing/KST for tightly structured procedural learning and reliability-critical assessments, while deploying NeSyAI for explanation-rich dialogue, multi-step reasoning, cross-domain writing tasks, and multilingual/culturally responsive adaptations. Hybrid designs can, for example, call a Cognitive Tutor or ALEKS mastery check inside a NeSyAI session, with symbolic policies mediating when to switch modalities.

6.2 Sociotechnical Adoption: Unions, Governance, Parents, and Cost–Benefit

Technical scalability alone does not determine adoption. A sociotechnical lens highlights how organizational structures, norms, and stakeholders shape uptake (Orlikowski, 1992; E. M. Rogers, 2003; Selwyn, 2011). For K–12, three constituencies are pivotal: teacher unions and professional bodies, school governance (boards, ministries), and parents/guardians.

Co-design with educators and their representative bodies improves legitimacy, workload fit, and contract alignment. Recent international guidance emphasizes multi-stakeholder collaboration—including teacher unions—for responsible AI use in education, with attention to teacher autonomy, workload, and professional learning (OECD, 2023). In practice, this means engaging unions early on issues such as data usage, classroom observations, role of AI in grading/feedback, and compensation for new duties (e.g., curating prompts or rules).

Boards and ministries increasingly expect clear policies on safety, transparency, accessibility, and human oversight (OECD, 2023; U.S. Department of Education, Office of Educational Technology, 2023b). For NeSyAI deployments, governance artifacts should include:

(i) model/prompt versioning with change logs
(ii) symbolic guardrail policies (and who approves them);
(iii) data protection impact assessments;
(iv) alignment to accessibility/UDL requirements. Procurement should evaluate interoperability with LMS/SIS, content alignment, and evidence standards for effectiveness.

Parents frequently prioritize privacy, transparency of AI feedback, and cultural/linguistic relevance. Communication plans should show what data are collected, how AI suggestions are reviewed by teachers (human-in-the-loop), and how multilingual interfaces and culturally responsive content are supported. Opt-in/opt-out and accessible documentation can preempt concerns (U.S. Department of Education, Office of Educational Technology, 2023b).

Beyond "units served," leaders need comparable metrics for learning gains relative to costs. The author recommends the ingredients-based method for cost analysis and the use of cost-effectiveness ratios (e.g., cost per 0.1 SD gain or cost per additional mastery percentage point) (Hollands et al., 2014; Levin & McEwan, 2001). TCO should include:

(1) devices/connectivity;
(2) compute/inference (including on-device vs. cloud trade-offs);
(3) teacher professional learning and coaching;
(4) content localization;
(5) integration and data governance;
(6) ongoing evaluation.

Where feasible, compare NeSyAI pilots to established ITS baselines to quantify incremental benefits (e.g., dialogic explanation quality, language accessibility) versus incremental costs.

Adoption plans should codify

(i) human-in-the-loop oversight of feedback and grading (U.S. Department of Education, Office of Educational Technology, 2023b)
(ii) audit trails for symbolic rules and content updates
(iii) professional learning tied to contractual time;
(iv) stakeholder councils (teachers, students, parents) that review outcomes and recommend policy adjustments.

These mechanisms align with international guidance that stresses responsible and equitable AI in classrooms (OECD, 2023).

6.3 Enhancing Adaptive Learning Environments

One of the most direct applications of NeSyAI in education is building adaptive learning platforms that respond to individual student needs with both data-driven personalization and rule-based guidance. Traditional adaptive systems (like some intelligent tutoring systems) rely mostly on machine learning to select content based on student performance statistics. NeSyAI can take this further by incorporating symbolic educational knowledge into the adaptation process. For example, Hooshyar et al. (2023) introduced an NeSyAI framework for modeling learners' computational thinking skills (Hooshyar et al., 2024). In their approach, a deep neural network was used to predict students' performance on programming tasks, but a symbolic component injected knowledge such as programming concepts and common student misconceptions into the model's reasoning. The result was an adaptive system that not only reacted to whether a student's code was correct or incorrect, but understood why (e.g., identifying a particular logical error) and could tailor subsequent tasks accordingly. This framework showed better generalizability than a purely neural approach – meaning it could make accurate predictions about new students' performance without extensive retraining. That suggests the symbolic knowledge gave it a more principled understanding of the domain, not just pattern matching from training data. For adaptive learning environments, this is a big win: it means an NeSyAI-driven platform could potentially be deployed in a new school or for a new topic and still perform well by relying on its built-in knowledge, needing less re-training on local data. Another example is an adaptive learning system for mathematics that integrates a neural mastery learning algorithm with a symbolic curriculum tree. Such a system might ensure the sequence of topics follows pedagogical prerequisites (the symbolic part), while the pace and practice frequency are adjusted via neural modeling of the student's memory retention. Early experiments in this direction indicate that students learn more efficiently – covering required material faster without compromising understanding – because the system does not allow skipping essential building blocks, but also does not bore the student with concepts they've clearly mastered (Alawneh et al.,2024). These adaptive NeSyAI environments align closely with student-centered principles: they treat each student individually and they do so in a way that is grounded in expert knowledge of the subject.

6.4 Intelligent Tutoring Systems With Contextual Reasoning

Intelligent Tutoring Systems have been a focus of AI in education for decades, and many have achieved notable success in domains like algebra and physics. However, a common limitation of earlier ITS was their rigidity – many were rule-based expert systems that, while interpretable, couldn't easily learn from new data or handle situations outside their pre-programmed scope. New ITS designs using NeSyAI seek to combine the strengths of classic rule-based tutors with the flexibility of modern AI. One such system might use a neural network to interpret the free-form input from a student (for instance, a typed response to an open-ended question) and then use a symbolic reasoner to map that interpretation onto a knowledge model of the subject and decide on feedback. A practical demonstration was presented by Hooshyar et al. (2023) in Augmenting Deep Neural Networks with Symbolic Knowledge, where a neural-symbolic AI framework was applied in an educational game to model students' computational thinking. The system combined symbolic rules about learning processes with deep neural networks, enabling both accurate predictions and interpretable feedback (Hooshyar et al., 2024). The neural model would handle dialogue – understanding student questions phrased in various ways – while the symbolic graph ensured the answers and feedback were scientifically accurate and covered the curricular points. By integrating these, the tutoring system could sustain a natural conversation (which purely symbolic systems struggle with) and still maintain content accuracy and relevance (a challenge for purely neural chatbots). Another key benefit observed is that the system could provide real-time feedback and hints that were context-aware. For instance, if a student was conducting a virtual lab experiment and made a mistake that violated a scientific principle, the system's symbolic knowledge of that principle triggered an immediate hint: "Remember the conservation of mass – did you account for all substances?" Such context-sensitive hints keep students on track and engaged (Hooshyar et al., 2024). NeSyAI's ability to encode causal relationships and domain theories (like conservation laws, or in math the axioms) means an ITS can do more than say "incorrect" – it can allude to the underlying concept the student might be missing, which is far more instructive. This approach was echoed in a study by (Alawneh et al., 2024), where their NeSyAI tutor for computational thinking extracted educationally meaningful rules from the student model and provided feedback based on those rules. Essentially, the system could say, "You seem to be assuming X, but in this problem Y is the case," pointing out the specific misunderstanding. Such targeted feedback is gold in education; it's akin to what a skilled human tutor does after diagnosing a student's thought process. NeSyAI thus enhances the capability of ITS to intervene in a pedagogically rich manner.

Evidence snapshot: Recent classroom studies show that AI tutoring can raise near-term task performance, but design choices determine *learning* gains. Guardrailed, hint-first tutors outperform unconstrained answer-giving designs on subsequent assessments (Bastani et al., 2025). District-scale human-in-the-loop tutoring support also increases mastery at low cost (R. E. Wang et al., 2024a). These results motivate NeSyAI tutors that bind neural adaptivity to symbolic teaching policies (sequenced hints, error models, curriculum constraints), especially for multilingual or culturally diverse cohorts.

6.5 Interpretability and Trust in Educational AI

One of the largest barriers to adoption of AI tutors in real classrooms has been the "black box" nature of many machine learning models. Teachers and school administrators are understandably hesitant to rely on systems whose decision-making they cannot scrutinize – for instance, an AI telling a student they are not ready to progress, without a clear rationale, would be problematic. Neuro-symbolic methods directly tackle this by making AI more transparent. Hooshyar et al.'s work demonstrated that their NeSyAI model could extract human-comprehensible rules from a neural learner model (Hooshyar et al., 2024). For example, the system might derive a rule like, "IF student consistently fails problems on concept X after 3 attempts, THEN flag concept X as misunderstood." Such rules can be reviewed by educators to verify they make sense. In their case, this interpretability allowed the researchers to validate that the model was focusing on causally relevant features (like the relationships between skills) rather than spurious correlations (Hooshyar et al., 2024). This is critical in education; one does not want an AI that simply correlates, say, length of response with score and starts giving high scores to verbose answers regardless of quality – a purely statistical model might fall into that trap, but a neuro-symbolic model could be constrained to use actual content features symbolically. Another real-world example is an AI system used to help grade essay responses (Hooshyar et al., 2024). The grading model used neural techniques to evaluate coherence and argumentation quality, but it also had a symbolic checklist of key points that should be present in a top-scoring essay. Teachers could see both the score and an explanation like, "The essay missed two key points: A and B, which are important as per the rubric." This not only helps students understand their grade but allows teachers to trust that the AI is grading on the right criteria. If the teacher disagrees with the criteria, they can adjust the symbolic rubric and the AI will follow suit. This kind of human-AI partnership is facilitated by NeSyAI because the knowledge is explicit. In short, interpretability via NeSyAI builds trust: educators can audit AI tutors, students can get explanations for why the AI is responding a certain way, and parents/administrators can be shown that the system's decisions align with educational standards (Hooshyar et al., 2024).

6.6 Bias Mitigation and Fairness

AI systems in education carry the risk of perpetuating or amplifying biases – whether those are biases against certain demographics, or against certain learning styles. Pure machine learning models, if trained on historical data, might inherit existing biases (for example, underestimating students from a minority group if past data reflected lower performance due to socio-economic factors). Neuro-symbolic AI offers some avenues to reduce such biases. Since NeSyAI can incorporate causal knowledge, it can be designed to focus on relevant causal features rather than correlational ones. Hooshyar et al. (2024) found that their NeSyAI model prioritized capturing causal relationships between input features and outcomes, explicitly aiming to avoid spurious correlations (Hooshyar et al., 2024). In practical terms, if gender or ethnicity is a feature in the data (even implicitly, say through language patterns), a well-designed NeSyAI tutor would not incorporate that into its decision logic unless it is causally linked to learning (which it should not be, ideally). Instead, it might use truly relevant features like mastery of prerequisites, time spent, etc. Because NeSyAI can be audited and constrained, developers can enforce fairness criteria – for instance, a symbolic rule could ensure that the prediction of student success does not directly or indirectly include protected attributes. There have been experiments where researchers simulate "de-biasing" knowledge within a model. For example, an AI reading comprehension tutor might notice a student struggling due to limited English vocabulary. A biased system might just classify the student as a low performer. A fair NeSyAI system, on the other hand, could have a rule: "if vocabulary is the issue, recommend vocabulary support, not harder comprehension texts," thus addressing the root cause rather than branding the student as incapable. Additionally, NeSyAI allows bias checks: because part of the model is symbolic, one can run logical tests ("Would the recommendation be different if this student had a different background but same performance?") more easily than in an opaque neural net. Another real case was an AI that analyzed video recordings of classroom interactions to give teachers feedback (Hou et al., 2024). The AI approach used there ensured that the feedback (such as how often teachers encouraged or showed warmth to students) was derived from concrete observed data and predefined pedagogical criteria, reducing subjective bias. The system combined a vision-based neural network to analyze classroom interactions with symbolic evaluation categories encoding teaching qualities (Hou et al., 2024). Teachers found this system valuable as it could highlight subtle gaps in their classroom practice — such as differences in how often they encouraged or showed warmth to students — something that purely manual observation might miss or be biased about. This illustrates a broader benefit: neuro-symbolic approaches can support not only students but also educators by providing insights grounded in both observed data and clearly defined pedagogical rules.

6.7 Modeling and Assessing Higher-Order Skills

Traditional AI tutors excel at well-defined problems (math, physics) with right or wrong answers. But education is increasingly concerned with higher-order skills like creativity, collaboration, and computational thinking. NeSyAI offers a way to model these complex constructs more faithfully. Hooshyar et al.'s work (2024) on modeling computational thinking is a prime example (Hooshyar et al., 2024). By injecting knowledge of programming concepts and typical student errors into a neural model of code-writing, their system could not just mark a program as correct/incorrect, but actually evaluate the process a student used to solve a coding task. It identified whether the student was following good computational thinking practices (like decomposing the problem, testing cases, etc.) by reasoning over the sequence of their actions symbolically. This allowed assessment of a learner's computational thinking competency in a way that goes beyond a test score. Another effort in this vein is using NeSyAI to assess collaborative problem solving – a notoriously hard skill to measure. An NeSyAI system has been prototyped to analyze chat logs of students working together (multimodal data including text and task actions), using neural NLP to parse the conversation and a symbolic model of productive collaboration (e.g., turn-taking, building on each other's ideas, asking questions). The system could assign a collaboration quality score and point out moments that were especially effective or problematic ("At 10:32, no one responded to a question asked – a missed opportunity for clarification").

6.8 Empirical Evidence From Classroom Deployments

A growing body of randomized and quasi-experimental evidence now documents measurable impacts of AI-supported tutoring in real classrooms. Complementary evidence from primary and early-childhood settings and from social robotics underscores classroom relevance (Lampropoulos & Papadakis, 2025; Uğraş et al., 2024, 2025). In Ghana, a low-bandwidth, WhatsApp-delivered conversational math tutor ("Rori") produced statistically significant gains in Grades 3–9, with an effect size of about 0.37 standard deviations over eight months while requiring only basic mobile devices—a deployment profile that matters for low-resource contexts (Henkel et al., 2024). In a large high-school field experiment in Türkiye, access to GPT-4 tutoring during practice sessions substantially boosted on-task problem performance, yet exam outcomes later suffered when "unconstrained" access was removed; crucially, guardrailed prompts that enforced stepwise hints mitigated the harm, underscoring the importance of pedagogy-aware prompt design and symbolic constraints (Bastani et al., 2025). Complementing student-facing tools, a U.S. district-scale randomized trial (900 tutors; 1,800 students) found that giving tutors real-time, AI-suggested expert moves increased student mastery by 4 percentage points overall (and 9 points for lower-rated tutors) at low marginal cost, showing how AI can scale expert practice without displacing human judgment (R. E. Wang et al., 2024a, 2024b).

These findings align with the rationale for neuro-symbolic approaches. Symbolic policies that (i) constrain solution reveal, (ii) formalize hint sequences, and (iii) encode curriculum-aligned knowledge can preserve learning while retaining neural adaptivity. In multilingual or culturally diverse classrooms, symbolic layers further enable transparent localization (rules, concept names, unit systems, cultural examples) without retraining the core model. Together, results suggest NeSyAI tutors should be engineered as guardrailed, curriculum-bound assistants that optimize learning (not just immediate task completion), are auditable, and are localizable to context. Complementing these quantitative results, qualitative studies capture classroom experience and perceived fit. In a primary-school case study with 40 teachers in Türkiye, participants reported that ChatGPT was useful for creating personalised activities, proposing materials, and preparing lesson plans, while expressing concerns about misinformation, addiction, and reduced communication (Uğraş et al., 2024). Illustrative remarks include: "ChatGPT should be used under the supervision of parents and teachers. . . the ability to design lesson plans and activities according to individual characteristics will be beneficial" (T5); "with ChatGPT, it will be more possible to design inclusive activities and develop creative ideas" (T25); "meeting ChatGPT to solve these difficulties made me very excited" (T6); and a caution that "not all of the information obtained . . . will be correct" (T28) (Uğraş et al., 2024). Early-childhood STEM work with trained teachers similarly reports perceived benefits for planning engaging activities alongside a need for guidance on age-appropriate use and accuracy checks (Uğraş et al., 2025). Together, these voices underscore that pedagogy-aware guardrails and teacher PD are pivotal for sustained adoption.

Finally, system-level syntheses point to governance and ecosystem readiness as the mediators of impact. OECD's Digital Education Outlook 2023 highlights teacher competencies, platform interoperability, and responsible GenAI use as prerequisites for scale, while the EU JRC Generative AI Outlook frames education as a priority application area within broader risk and policy regimes (Abendroth & colleagues, 2025; OECD, 2023). This evidence–policy alignment motivates NeSyAI designs that combine empirical guardrails, teacher co-design, and ecosystem integration.

6.9 Curriculum and Assessment Alignment

Aligning NeSyAI systems with curriculum standards and formal assessment frameworks requires a coherent mapping from high-level competencies to fine-grained knowledge components (KCs) and explicit rules governing progression, feedback, and evidence collection. Curriculum mapping is a first step: McLaren et al. describe how they analyzed a community-college IT curriculum to identify key skills that scaffold learning across courses, triangulating instructor expertise and student performance data, and then used the Knowledge–Learning–Instruction (KLI) framework to match each KC to the most suitable learning technology (McLaren et al., 2024). KLI links kinds of knowledge (memory/fluency, induction/refinement, sense making/understanding) to learning processes and instructional methods and is designed to guide the design and continual improvement of course materials (Global Learning Council, 2022).

NeSyAI tutors can import such curriculum maps and enforce them through symbolic policies. For example, the ElectronixTutor project defines a hierarchy of topics (e.g., circuit analysis, Ohm's law, series and parallel circuits) and associates each topic with multiple KCs capturing structure, behaviour, and function; mastery of each KC is assessed separately, and learner progress is stored in a KC × learning resource × learner matrix (Graesser et al., 2018). The curriculum calendar dictates the recommended topics, yet self-regulated learning is possible and a recommender system can prioritise the next topic based on the student's history and personal traits (Graesser et al., 2018). This architecture allows teachers to align the AI's sequencing with their syllabus, adjust topic orders, and see mastery bars for each KC in a dashboard (Graesser et al., 2018). Symbolic rule sets then enforce prerequisites (e.g., "master KC A before introducing KC B"), define hint sequences (e.g., "two conceptual hints before a worked example"), and specify when to withhold answers until mastery evidence is recorded. Because rule sets are explicit, they can be audited, translated, and localised, supporting multilingual and culturally responsive curricula.

Assessment validity also benefits from this alignment. Evidence-centred design recommends specifying the claim (e.g., "the learner has mastered rational number operations"), the evidence (e.g., correct performance on KCs for addition, subtraction, multiplication, and division of rationals), and the warrant (e.g., mastery thresholds and item specifications) in advance. In NeSyAI tutors, the KC–rule mapping provides the evidentiary chain: formative feedback and mastery gating ensure that recorded scores correspond to curriculum-aligned competencies. Teachers can use dashboards to run plan–do–study–act cycles and adjust pacing or instructional strategies while maintaining fidelity to standards. When integrated with LMS/SIS, mastery data can be exported to gradebooks or progress reports, closing the loop between AI-driven learning and existing assessment frameworks.

6.10 Remarks

Overall, these real-world applications and research cases illustrate that neuro-symbolic AI can make educational tools more powerful, insightful, and aligned with human educators' values. By combining adaptive learning with explicit knowledge, NeSyAI systems provide personalized and meaningful support to students. By enabling interpretability, they build trust and allow educators to integrate AI into teaching without losing oversight. By focusing on causal relationships and meaningful patterns, NeSyAI helps avoid bias and ensure fairness, a critical aspect for equitable education. And by tackling complex skills and data, NeSyAI broadens the scope of what AI in education can handle, moving closer to comprehensive virtual tutoring that addresses not just rote learning but holistic skill development.

That said, most of these implementations are still in trial phases or limited deployments. It is important to continue research and refinement. Challenges such as ensuring data privacy (student data used in AI models), maintaining engagement without distraction, and scaling these solutions to different curricula and contexts remain. The next section will discuss these challenges in detail and outline future directions and recommendations for harnessing NeSyAI for personalized and equitable tutoring at scale. It will also emphasize the importance of keeping humans – teachers, students, parents – at the center of the design and deployment of these technologies, to ensure that AI truly enhances the educational experience rather than detracting from it.

7 CHALLENGES AND FUTURE DIRECTIONS

The advancements in neuro-symbolic AI for education, while promising, come with a host of challenges that must be addressed to realize their full potential in real-world settings. These challenges span technical, pedagogical, and ethical dimensions. In this section, some of the key hurdles in deploying neuro-symbolic AI tutors broadly are discussed, and outline future directions for research and practice to overcome these hurdles. Ensuring that the next generation of AI tutoring systems is effective, fair, and widely accessible will require concerted effort from technologists, educators, and policymakers alike. How certain challenges might be mitigated by ongoing developments in AI are discussed, and what new avenues of exploration are opening up in this space as well.

7.1 Technical Integration and Scalability

One immediate challenge is integrating complex NeSyAI systems into existing educational technology infrastructure. Schools and educational platforms vary widely in their technological capacity – from high-speed internet and one-to-one device programs in some settings, to others where a single computer lab is shared among many students. Running an NeSyAI tutor, which might involve heavy computations for both neural network inference and symbolic reasoning, could be infeasible on low-end hardware or without a stable internet connection to offload computation to the cloud. This raises questions about equitable access: if advanced AI tutors require significant resources, will they only benefit well-funded schools or students with modern devices? Bridging this gap is critical for equity. One future direction is to optimize and compress NeSyAI models so they can run on mobile devices or inexpensive hardware. Techniques such as model distillation (creating a smaller model that mimics a larger one's behavior) and edge computing strategies (processing as much as possible on-device to reduce latency and dependency on connectivity) are areas of active research. Cross-layer hardware-software designs, as discussed by Wan et al. (2024), might also make it possible to include small accelerator chips specialized for NeSyAI in standard school hardware (e.g., tablets for students) (Wan et al., 2024). Another aspect of integration is the interoperability with learning management systems (LMS). Schools often use LMS platforms to organize content, grades, and student info. An NeSyAI tutor needs to plug into these – reading data (like a student's learning history) and writing data (like scores or recommendations) – without causing disruption. This calls for developing standards and APIs for AI tutoring services, an effort that future policy and industry collaboration should undertake. On the scalability front, if a city or country-wide rollout of AI tutors is attempted, careful planning is needed to ensure cloud infrastructure can handle peak loads (e.g., all students logging in at 9am) and that data pipelines are secure and robust. Embracing cloud-native architectures that auto-scale and using containerization for deploying AI models can aid in this, but education systems often lack in-house technical expertise for such maintenance. Therefore, a future direction is creating managed AI services tailored for education, possibly through public-private partnerships, to relieve individual districts from technical heavy-lifting while maintaining public oversight of data and algorithms.

7.2 Data Privacy and Security

The more AI systems become adaptive and personalized, the more data they collect on individual students – from clickstreams and responses to potentially sensitive information likc mood (if detected via sensors) or common mistakes (which could be stigmatizing if exposed). Ensuring student data privacy is paramount. Many jurisdictions have laws (like FERPA in the US, GDPR in Europe) that restrict how student data can be used and stored. NeSyAI systems must be designed in compliance with these, which means data anonymization, encryption, and strict access controls should be built-in. A challenge arises with the very nature of personalization: by definition, the AI needs some memory of the studcnt to pcrsonalize effectively. Future research will need to find ways to do this that minimize privacy risks – for instance, using federated learning, where the model learns from data on the student's device without that data ever leaving the device in raw form. In a federated setup, the AI tutor could improve by aggregating model updates (not raw data) from many students, thereby preserving privacy. Another concern is security: an AI tutor should be safe from hacking or malicious use. It is conceivable, for instance, that someone might try to manipulate an AI tutor's knowledge base (the symbolic part) to give harmful advice, or to bias the system's treatment of certain students. Robust security protocols and regular audits will be necessary. Additionally, transparency to users about data use is crucial for trust – future systems should include dashboard tools for teachers and students to see what data is being collected and how it's used to drive recommendations. This could demystify the AI and allow for informed consent. Policymakers may also mandate that data from AI tutors be purged after a certain period or when a student leaves a school, to prevent long-term profiling. In summary, making privacy and security a core part of the architecture – not an afterthought – is a key direction that should guide all development in this field.

7.3 Teacher Training and Role Re-definition

For AI tutors to be adopted, teachers need to be comfortable with them and understand how to integrate them into instruction. This is both a challenge and an area requiring future effort in professional development. Some teachers might fear that AI will replace or undermine their role; others might be eager but unsure how to interpret AI outputs or intervene appropriately. For example, if an AI tutor handles routine practice with students, the teacher's role shifts more to facilitator and mentor. Teachers will need training to use the analytics from AI tutors (like dashboards showing which students struggle with which topics) to inform their lesson planning or one-on-one interventions. In the future, teacher-AI collaboration frameworks are envisioned – guidelines and best practices for how teachers can orchestrate class activities with AI support. Perhaps certain days are "AI practice days" while others are group projects, etc. One approach is to involve teachers early in the development and piloting of NeSyAI systems (which some research projects have done by co-design). This ensures the systems are intuitive and actually address classroom needs. Another aspect is giving teachers some level of control: for instance, a teacher might want to adjust the difficulty or topic focus of the AI tutor for their class's context. If the AI is too opaque or rigid, teachers may reject it. Thus, an important future direction is user interface and experience (UI/UX) research for teacher-facing controls and insights. For example, a teacher dashboard could allow: "Today, emphasize geometry problems because we just covered that in class," or "Ignore minor spelling errors in student responses for this English learner student." Such controls would make teachers feel empowered and see the AI as a tool under their guidance, not a black box "teacher's aide" doing its own thing. Additionally, teacher education programs might start including basic AI literacy so new teachers are prepared to work alongside AI. One might see certifications for "AI-augmented teaching" skills in the future. Over time, as teachers see that AI tutors can lighten their load on grading and give more individualized practice to students, their buy-in will grow, but initial support and continuous upskilling are vital to reach that point.

While many ethical and technical frameworks exist, current teacher readiness remains low: a recent policy brief notes that less than 20% of U.S. teachers feel equipped to use AI tools, only 29% have received any professional development in relevant technologies, and only 14 states provide guidance on generative AI (Federation of American Scientists (Day One Project), 2024; Kaufman et al., 2025). This gap underscores the need for a robust professional development (PD) backbone anchored in established standards. The ISTE Educator Standards – learner, leader, citizen, collaborator, designer, facilitator and analyst – provide a roadmap for continuous professional learning, digital citizenship, peer collaboration, authentic learning design, facilitation of student agency and data-driven decision-making (ISTE, 2017). These roles emphasise that educators must continually update their practice, model ethical and responsible technology use, collaborate with colleagues and students, design learning environments that accommodate diverse learners, facilitate technology-enabled inquiry, and analyse data to inform instruction (ISTE, 2017).

Recent frameworks go further by addressing AI-specific competencies. UNESCO's AI Competency Framework for Teachers advances six principles – ensuring digital futures for all, adopting a human-centred approach, protecting teachers' rights, promoting trustworthy and environmentally sustainable AI, ensuring applicability for all teachers and reflecting digital evolution, and supporting lifelong professional learning (CEDEFOP, 2024). Its five core areas encompass a human-centred mindset, AI ethics (privacy, data protection and bias), AI foundations and applications, AI pedagogy and the use of AI for teachers' own professional development, with progression levels (acquire, deepen, create) that allow teachers to build capabilities over time (CEDEFOP, 2024). The TPD@Scale framework extends these principles to large-scale PD: its six core components include providing access to learning materials with guidance and prompts; supporting teachers to try new pedagogical ideas through professional experimentation; fostering purposeful peer dialogue and collaborative learning; offering expert mentoring and feedback; sustaining activity over time with continuous evaluation and adaptation; and using ICT to support resource distribution, communication and differentiated support (Wolfenden, 2022, 2024). Importantly, the framework emphasises that PD must be flexible to local curriculum and policy contexts (Wolfenden, 2022), and that improvement cycles (plan–do–study–act) should involve regular evaluation and teacher input to adapt programs for quality and equity (Wolfenden, 2022).

AI-specific PD should also integrate the Technological Pedagogical Content Knowledge (TPACK) model: generative AI challenges teachers not only to learn new tools but to redesign curriculum and pedagogy. A recent conceptual study on an LLM-based "Teacher Copilot" notes that digital transformation leaves many teachers insecure due to limited time and insufficient training; to support them, PD must cover AI literacy, AI ethics and prompt engineering, and treat teachers as co-designers of AI-enhanced learning scenarios. Using TPACK as a guide, teachers develop integrated knowledge of content, pedagogy and technology so that AI tools are used meaningfully. Human-centred, participatory design research reinforces that teacher dashboards and other AI tools should be co-created with educators; implementation requires preparing teachers to interpret digital cues and decide on follow-up actions (van Leeuwen et al., 2023). Embedding dashboard creation and use into teacher training programmes and establishing research–practice partnerships helps navigate the tension between stakeholder input and educational theory (van Leeuwen et al., 2023).

Unions and professional bodies provide essential sociotechnical perspectives on adoption. The American Federation of Teachers' (AFT) "Commonsense Guardrails" assert that certified professionals must decide when and how to incorporate technology; districts should empower educators to choose technologies, clarify the role of technology in each assignment and ensure continuous paid professional learning (American Federation of Teachers & Common Sense Education, 2024). The same document emphasises collective bargaining as a crucial tool: teachers must be involved in selecting, procuring and assessing AI tools, and agreements should safeguard data privacy, teacher autonomy and equitable access (American Federation of Teachers & Common Sense Education, 2024). Internationally, OECD commentary highlights that AI cannot replace great teachers; rather, thriving classrooms require attracting exceptional educators, rethinking teacher development to foster new mindsets and relationships, and investing so that teachers can experiment and innovate (Kopp, 2025). Together, these insights underscore that professional development must be co-designed with educators, supported by unions and aligned with ethical, human-centred AI frameworks.

Readiness insights. Surveys show uneven teacher AI uptake (about one-quarter report instructional use), highlighting the need for job-embedded, pedagogy-first PD and clear classroom policies (Kaufman et al., 2025). Qualitative K-12 evidence points to concerns over over-dependence, critical thinking, and assessment redesign, reinforcing co-design and reflective practice (Tripathi et al., 2025).

7.4 Ensuring Equity and Avoiding the Digital Divide

A recurring concern is that advanced technologies can inadvertently widen inequities if not carefully managed. Wealthier schools or families might adopt personalized AI tutors, giving their students an extra advantage, whereas under-resourced communities might lag further behind if they cannot access or afford these tools. To counter this, a strong recommendation for policymakers is to consider AI tutors as part of the basic educational infrastructure, akin to textbooks or libraries. This might involve public investment or subsidies to make sure that effective AI tutoring software (and the devices to run them) are available to all students as needed. International organizations and governments can also promote open-source or low-cost solutions. In fact, there are movements toward open educational AI, where researchers develop algorithms and content that are free to adapt. For example, the content knowledge (the symbolic part) of an AI tutor for K-12 math could be maintained as an open resource by a consortium of educators, ensuring quality and alignment with standards, while the neural adaptivity part could also use open-source frameworks. This way, even if different vendors provide interfaces, the core "knowledge engine" might be universally accessible. Future work could also explore offline capabilities – not all areas have consistent internet, so can an AI tutor function with intermittent connectivity (syncing when possible, but still working offline)? Another dimension of equity is cultural relevance. AI tutors must adapt not just to individual knowledge but to cultural context. A challenge is ensuring the symbolic knowledge and examples in the system aren't biased toward one culture or perspective. Future NeSyAI tutors might need to have region-specific knowledge bases or the ability to learn culturally relevant examples (for instance, word problems that make sense in a rural context vs. an urban one). Collaboration with local educators to localize AI content will be important. Thus, a future direction is modular AI tutors: a general AI engine that can be "skinned" with local languages, names, contexts, and even pedagogical styles (some cultures might favor a more Socratic tutor, others a more straightforward coaching style). Addressing these nuances will be key to making AI tutoring truly inclusive globally.

Localization and UDL. Adopt a localization pipeline that (i) externalizes symbolic rule-bases for translation and curricular alignment, (ii) builds culturally responsive exemplars, and (iii) applies UDL 3.0 checkpoints across representation, engagement, and action/expression to reduce bias-driven barriers (CAST, 2024).

7.5 Continuous Evaluation and Improvement

As AI tutors are rolled out, continuous evaluation is necessary to ensure they are effective and not causing unintended harm. This is a challenge because educational impact can be hard to measure and can take time to manifest (e.g., do AI-tutored students do better in later grades or in creative problem-solving, not just immediate test scores?). Future work should establish robust evaluation protocols. For instance, A/B testing could be used ethically within classes: some topics taught with AI tutor assistance, some without, to compare outcomes. Longitudinal studies will help understand lasting effects. One should also look for any negative effects – do students become too dependent on the AI? Does it change their attitude toward learning? Early studies suggest that with proper design, AI tutors can increase engagement and self-efficacy (as they give students immediate help and a sense of personalized attention) (Yu, Yao, et al., 2024). But if overused, could they reduce human interaction or make students impatient when a human is teaching more slowly than an AI? These are open questions. It will be important to maintain a balance: AI should supplement, not supplant, human interaction. UNESCO's guidance clearly states technology should complement teacher-led activities, not replace (UNESCO Global Education Monitoring Report Team, 2023). Future classrooms might use AI for part of the day and then have rich discussions or collaborative projects that only humans can facilitate well. Research into the optimal blend of AI and human teaching is needed – possibly leading to new instructional models (blended learning 2.0).

Another future direction in improvement is incorporating student feedback into AI tutor refinement. Students are end-users; their perspective on the AI's helpfulness or frustration points is invaluable. Future AI systems could have built-in feedback channels – perhaps as simple as a thumbs-up/down after a hint, or periodic surveys ("Do you feel challenged?"). This data can guide iterative design. It also makes students partners in the learning process design, increasing their agency, which is fitting for student-centered philosophies.

7.6 Ethical and Psychological Considerations

As AI tutors become more life-like (especially if one considers using avatars or voice for a more personable experience), one may face ethical questions about the student-AI relationship. Young students might anthropomorphize the AI or give it a degree of authority that is unwarranted (e.g., believing everything it says without question). Educating students about AI – its capabilities and limits – might become necessary, so they develop a healthy skepticism and understanding. This is analogous to digital literacy but specifically AI literacy. Some efforts, like the U.S. Department of Education's report on AI (2023), recommend teaching students about how AI works as part of using (U.S. Department of Education, Office of Educational Technology, 2023a). The future might involve "AI in the classroom" modules for students, ensuring they know the tutor is a tool, not a sentient being or an infallible oracle. Additionally, careful attention must be paid to the content an AI tutor delivers. It should be aligned with broad educational values and curriculum standards, which may differ by region (some places might emphasize certain historical viewpoints, for example). Thus, oversight and periodic content review of the AI's knowledge base is needed – likely by human experts. There's also an ethical dimension in data: if AI tutors collect a lot of data, who owns it and who can benefit from it? Ideally, such data (anonymized) could fuel education research – e.g., identifying which misconceptions are most common – but policies should ensure this is done transparently and for public good, not purely commercial purposes.

In terms of psychological impact, one might worry: will constant personalization coddle students or, conversely, will constant surveillance by an AI increase anxiety? Striking the right tone in the AI's interactions is important. For example, an AI tutor should encourage a growth mindset by framing mistakes positively ("That was a tough one! Reviewing this concept will help you solve it next time.") rather than punitively. It can be programmed to give praise for effort, not just correctness. There is a chance here to actually improve students' attitudes – some shy students may open up more to a non-judgmental AI, practicing skills without fear of public embarrassment, which could build confidence that carries into class participation. Monitoring such effects will be important moving forward.

7.7 Research and Development Agenda

To summarize future directions: multidisciplinary research will be crucial. We need AI experts working with education specialists to design curricula for AI tutors, with HCI (human-computer interaction) experts to design interfaces, and ethicists to set boundaries. Funding should support long-term studies in diverse schools using these tools. Policy may need to catch up in terms of guidelines or even accreditation – for instance, could an AI tutoring system be certified by an education authority as meeting certain standards? This might reassure schools of its quality. Also, frameworks for accountability might evolve: if an AI tutor misadvises a student and leads to bad outcomes, how is that handled? Clear delineation of responsibilities between AI providers, schools, and teachers will need to be established.

In conclusion, while challenges are many, the future of neuro-symbolic AI in personalized tutoring is bright if these issues are navigated thoughtfully. The technology offers a chance to fundamentally enhance education – making it more tailored, engaging, and effective for each learner – but its implementation must be guided by the values of equity, transparency, and human-centricity. The final section will provide some concrete recommendations for policymakers and AI practitioners to help steer the development and deployment of these systems in an ethical and impactful direction.

7.8 Implementation Case Studies and Bottlenecks

Devices, bandwidth, and interoperability. Field deployments repeatedly show that modest hardware and connectivity can be decisive. WhatsApp-scale tutoring succeeded in Ghana precisely because it ran on basic phones with low data usage (Henkel et al., 2024). For school-based rollouts, integration with existing LMS/SIS via standards (e.g., LTI 1.3/xAPI) reduces operational friction and supports monitoring, auditing, and data minimization; OECD emphasizes such ecosystem connections as a core condition for sustainable digital education (OECD, 2023).

Teacher readiness and workflow fit. District surveys in the U.S. indicate uneven adoption: roughly one-quarter of teachers reported using AI in instruction in 2023–2024, versus far higher use among principals for administrative tasks; disparities by subject and district context persist (Kaufman et al., 2025). Qualitative studies surface concerns about over-reliance, critical thinking, assessment redesign, and classroom authority—all pointing to the need for pedagogy-first professional learning and co-design (Tripathi et al., 2025). Effective programs embed AI into *existing* tutoring/planning workflows (e.g., AI assisting tutors in real time) rather than adding parallel tasks (R. E. Wang et al., 2024a).

Guardrails and assessment alignment. Experimental evidence shows that unconstrained answer-giving can depress subsequent performance, whereas structured, stepwise hints preserve learning (Bastani et al., 2025). NeSyAI offers concrete levers: symbolic policies enforce hinting, solution withholding, curriculum sequencing, and error-specific feedback; they also facilitate audit trails for fairness and safety reviews.

Equity, multilingualism, and accessibility. Localization should be treated as a first-class design requirement: symbolic rule-bases can be translated, culturally adapted (examples, contexts, units), and aligned with regional standards with minimal model changes. UDL Guidelines 3.0 provide a practical scaffold for inclusive content/interaction design (representation, engagement, and action/expression) and explicitly address bias-aware barrier reduction (CAST, 2024).

Governance, privacy, and continuous improvement. U.S. Department of Education guidance stresses human-in-the-loop, transparency, and formative-assessment uses, with district policies clarifying acceptable use and data protections (U.S. Department of Education, Office of Educational Technology, 2023a). Continuous evaluation should include learning outcomes, equity metrics, fidelity-of-implementation, and auditability checks against education-specific AI auditing frameworks (Fernsel & co-authors, 2025).

7.9 From Pilot to Routine Use: Implementation Blueprint

Moving NeSyAI tutors from isolated pilots to sustained classroom practice requires a structured blueprint that combines planning, professional learning, monitoring and iterative improvement. Drawing on large-scale PD frameworks and sociotechnical guidance, the author outlines four phases.

Phase 1 – Planning and co-design. Successful implementation begins with aligning AI tutoring goals to curriculum standards and equity outcomes. Stakeholder engagement is essential: teachers, school leaders, unions, parents and students should collaboratively define the purpose of the pilot, identify desired learning outcomes and select appropriate content domains. Readiness assessments, such as aiEDU's AI readiness rubrics (covering student competencies, educator competencies and organisational factors), help determine baseline capacity and highlight gaps requiring support. Policies on privacy, transparency and ethical use should be developed in advance, drawing on UNESCO's guidance to ensure digital futures for all, protect teachers' rights and promote trustworthy, sustainable AI (CEDEFOP, 2024). Collective bargaining agreements can codify teacher involvement in procurement and data governance (American Federation of Teachers & Common Sense Education, 2024).

Phase 2 – Onboarding and professional development. Teachers need explicit training before NeSyAI tools enter classrooms. Professional learning should integrate multiple frameworks: ISTE's Educator Standards for continuous learning, leadership, digital citizenship, collaboration, design, facilitation and data analysis (ISTE, 2017); UNESCO's AI Competency Framework emphasising human-centred mindsets, AI ethics, technical foundations, AI pedagogy and professional development (CEDEFOP, 2024); TPD@Scale's core components of access to learning materials, teacher experimentation, peer collaboration, expert support, sustained engagement and ICT-enabled (Wolfenden, 2022, 2024); and TPACK-informed training in AI literacy, AI ethics and prompt engineering. Courses from organisations like Common Sense Education and aiEDU offer self-paced AI basics, ethical and safe use, data privacy, environmental impact and advanced prompting strategies (Common Sense Education, 2025; The AI Education Project (aiEDU), 2025). Participatory design workshops allow teachers to co-create prompts, rules and dashboards, reflecting research showing that preparing teachers to interpret digital cues and use dashboards effectively enhances uptake (van Leeuwen et al., 2023). Unions' guardrails emphasize that professional learning must be continuous, adequately funded and integrated into teachers' paid time (American Federation of Teachers & Common Sense Education, 2024).

Phase 3 – Monitoring and evaluation. Once deployed, NeSyAI tutors should be integrated into existing data ecosystems. A recommended architecture comprises (1) the student interacting with the tutor, (2) thc tutor logging interactions and mastery signals to a teacher dashboard, (3) the teacher reviewing dashboards and adjusting instruction, and (4) synchronisation with the school's learning management system (LMS) or student information system (SIS) for record-keeping and analytics. Continuous data collection enables formative assessment and adaptation. Improvement cycles – plan–do–study–act – should be embedded at classroom, school and district levels: teachers and coaches review evidence of learning gains, engagement and equity, then adapt prompts, rules or pedagogical strategies accordingly (Wolfenden, 2022). External evaluation teams can complement internal monitoring by measuring cost-effectiveness (e.g., cost per 0.1 SD learning gain) and assessing alignment with ethical and equity goals. Participatory design research suggests that dashboards may be either "mirroring" (providing cues) or "advising" (offering suggestions); training should ensure teachers know how to interpret and act on dashboard data (van Leeuwen et al., 2023). Regular surveys and focus groups should capture teacher, student and parent perspectives, feeding back into decision-making.

Phase 4 – Iteration and scaling. Pilots should not be static: as improvement cycles reveal effective practices and remaining challenges, policies, curricula and training must be updated. The TPD@Scale framework stresses that sustained PD with regular evaluation and adaptation is essential (Wolfenden, 2022, 2024). Scaling to additional subjects, grades or schools requires contextualisation: symbolic rulebases and content must be localised to language and culture; infrastructure and PD must be tailored to varying resource levels; and teacher autonomy and union oversight must be maintained (American Federation of Teachers & Common Sense Education, 2024). UNESCO emphasises lifelong professional learning (CEDEFOP, 2024), meaning that scaling efforts should include refresher courses, mentorship networks and communities of practice. Throughout iteration and scaling, transparency about how models, prompts and rules are updated – and opportunities for teachers to influence those updates – helps build trust and continuous improvement.

Economic feasibility. Adoption should include ingredients-based costing and cost-effectiveness analysis—tracking devices/connectivity, compute/inference, teacher professional learning, localisation, and integration—so leaders can compare learning gains per euro across options (Hollands et al., 2014; Levin & McEwan, 2001). District-scale experimentation indicates that augmenting human tutors with real-time AI suggestions can raise mastery at *low marginal cost*, illustrating one scalable, teacher-centered pathway (R. E. Wang et al., 2024a, 2024b). Reporting cost per mastery point or cost per 0.1 SD alongside equity and accessibility metrics should be standard practice in NeSyAI pilots.

8 RECOMMENDATIONS

To ensure equitable and effective integration of neuro-symbolic AI in education, the following recommendations for policymakers, AI developers, and educators are proposed.

Policy anchors. OECD's *Digital Education Outlook 2023* and the EU JRC *Generative AI Outlook* frame teacher competences, platform interoperability, responsible GenAI, and sector governance as preconditions for impact at scale; align recommendations with these pillars (Abendroth & colleagues, 2025; OECD, 2023).

8.1 For Policymakers and Educational Leaders

- **Establish a Vision and Framework:** Define clear goals, ethical standards, and accountability for AI use in education.
- **Invest in Infrastructure and Access:** Provide devices, connectivity, and technical support to prevent digital divides.
- **Ensure Equity and Cultural Relevance:** Require inclusive, bias-audited, and accessible content for diverse learners.
- **Strengthen Data Privacy:** Mandate transparent data governance, privacy-by-design, and independent audits.
- **Support Professional Development:** Train teachers in AI literacy, integration strategies, and create peer communities.
- **Monitor and Evaluate Continuously:** Track impacts on outcomes and equity; involve researchers in independent evaluations.

8.2 For AI Developers and Researchers

- **Prioritize Explainability and Teacher Controls:** Provide transparent reasoning, student-friendly explanations, and customizable dashboards.
- **Integrate Educational Theory:** Embed learning science, ontologies, and misconceptions into symbolic components.

- **Adopt User-Centered Design:** Co-design with teachers and students; pilot in diverse classrooms; refine based on feedback.
- **Test for Robustness and Bias:** Conduct fairness audits, simulate diverse learners, and add fail-safes for uncertainty.
- **Enable Continuous Learning:** Incorporate mechanisms for ongoing improvement and agile updates within privacy limits.

8.3 For Educators and Schools

- **Adopt Pedagogy-First Integration:** Use AI to enhance lesson design; frame it as a learning partner, not an answer machine.
- **Monitor Student Interaction and Well-Being:** Combine analytics with observation to prevent frustration or over-reliance.
- **Collaborate and Share Practices:** Exchange strategies, appoint AI mentors, and document effective use cases.
- **Maintain Human Oversight:** Balance AI use with meaningful teacher-student interaction; critically review AI outputs.

9 FUTURE TRAJECTORIES: CREATIVITY, COLLABORATION, AND LIFELONG LEARNING

The rapid progress of NeSyAI opens new directions for education. Beyond core tutoring, emerging paradigms focus on assessing creativity, collaboration, competency-based learning, and informal/lifelong learning. This section highlights these trajectories and suggests research and policy priorities.

Authentic assessments evaluate higher-order thinking, creativity, and collaboration through projects, portfolios, and simulations (Fitas et al., 2025). Generative AI can assist teachers by brainstorming open-ended project topics, creating personalised prompts, and retrieving relevant exemplars; students can refine prompts and receive scaffolded feedback (Fitas et al., 2025). However, AI is not yet proficient at evaluating creativity or emotion; human feedback loops remain essential to ensure fairness and contextual accuracy (U.S. Department of Education, Office of Educational Technology, 2023c). NeSyAI tutors should log process data (planning steps, divergent ideas) and support rubric-aligned evaluation, but final judgements of creativity must involve teachers and peers.

AI can help design group experiences, form equitable teams, and produce reflective rubrics while maintaining higher-order learning goals (Access, 2024). Teachers report using AI to plan escape rooms, prototypes, role-playing, and collaborative challenges; they emphasise that AI should be a brainstorming partner, not an autonomous designer (Access, 2024). NeSyAI tutors can analyse discourse patterns, contribution equity, and conflict resolution to suggest timely interventions, but symbolic guardrails should ensure that AI suggestions align with collaborative norms (e.g., balanced participation, constructive feedback) and that teachers retain control over grouping and assessment decisions.

Competency-based education (CBE) emphasises equity, measurable competencies, transparency, personalised support, and growth-based assessment (AI, 2024). AI tutors can map curriculum standards to knowledge components, enforce prerequisite rules, track mastery, and issue micro-credentials or digital badges when learners demonstrate competence. Different assessment types—formative, authentic, digital—should be integrated into the AI, allowing teachers to choose when to test, when to remediate, and when to advance learners based on evidence (AI, 2024). Symbolic rules can also encode standards for social–emotional skills and help ensure that micro-credentials remain aligned with curricular goals.

Lifelong learning in the age of AI demands human-centred policies that bridge digital divides, leverage familiar devices, and support informal contexts such as after-school programs, libraries, and community centres (for Lifelong Learning, 2024). Policies should promote open educational resources, Universal Design for Learning (UDL) principles, and edge-computing solutions to allow offline or low-bandwidth access (for Lifelong Learning, 2024). NeSyAI tutors deployed in informal settings must respect cultural norms, languages, and ethics, providing parents and community mentors with dashboards that support co-learning rather than surveillance. Surveys show that nearly half of U.S. teachers use AI weekly, yet only a quarter have received professional development, and more than half request training; educators highlight both excitement about personalised support and concerns about misinformation, addiction, and reduced communication (Foundation, 2024; Ugˇ ras¸ et al., 2024). Teachers envision AI as a co-designer for inclusive activities and creative ideas but insist on adult supervision and pedagogy-first guidance (Ugˇras¸ et al., 2024). Macro-level analyses stress that fostering creative, interdisciplinary learning requires investments in teacher education, AI infrastructure, and curricular reform (William, 2024). NeSyAI development should therefore prioritise participatory design, teacher empowerment, and research–practice partnerships.

To realise these trajectories, the author proposes four research directions: (i) develop AI methods to capture process data for creativity and collaboration assessments; (ii) design group analytics and fairness metrics to support equitable collaboration; (iii) extend competency ontologies to social–emotional and transversal skills, linking them to symbolic rules and micro-credentials; and (iv) test NeSyAI in informal learning environments, exploring how edge computing, translation, and cultural adaptation affect learning outcomes. Cross-cutting themes include human–AI co-creative practices and robust PD models for AI literacy.

9.1 Closing Remark

Collaboration across policymakers, developers, and educators is key. By combining ethical frameworks, robust technologies, and pedagogy-first practices, neuro-symbolic AI can help create a more personalized, equitable, and human-centered education system.

10 CONCLUSION

The advent of neuro-symbolic AI in education heralds a new chapter in the quest for personalized and equitable learning. In this paper, how blending neural network learning with symbolic reasoning can produce AI tutoring systems that are adaptive, transparent, and aligned with pedagogical principles have been explored. It starts by establishing the moral and ethical imperative for shifting toward student-centered learning – an approach that respects each learner's individuality and promotes engagement, autonomy, and critical thinking. This student-centered ethos provided a compass for evaluating the role of AI: technology in education is valuable only to the extent that it amplifies these human-centric values, not undermines them. Its analysis of student-centered learning highlighted the significant benefits it offers – from increased motivation and deeper understanding to improved academic performance and lifelong learning skills. It also noted the practical challenges in implementation, which set the stage for AI's potential assistive role. AI systems, especially those employing neuro-symbolic methods, can serve as powerful allies in overcoming some of these challenges. They can provide personalized practice and feedback at scale, something even the most dedicated teacher would struggle to do for every student, every day (Yu, Yao, et al., 2024). Furthermore, neuro-symbolic AI's capacity for explainability and incorporation of domain knowledge directly addresses the need for trust and interpretability in educational settings. Unlike black-box models, an NeSyAI tutor can, for example, explain that a student's struggle in algebra is due to a specific gap in understanding (like negative numbers), and even recommend a remedy, much as a human teacher might. This clarity is crucial for teacher buy-in and for students' metacognition about their own learning. This paper also delved into recent developments in neuro-symbolic AI, illustrating how models can enhance the intelligence and reliability of tutoring systems. These advances mean that AI tutors are no longer limited to either rote pattern matching or brittle rule-following; they can learn nuanced patterns from data while adhering to logical pedagogical constraints. The integration of these techniques can make AI tutors more context-aware and robust in dynamic environments, two qualities essential for real-world classroom deployment. At the same time, it acknowledged that scaling such systems is non-trivial – the challenges of computational efficiency, domain generalization, and real-time adaptability are very much active areas of research. It identified opportunities, however, where NeSyAI could shine, such as in providing contextual decision support (e.g., adjusting to a student's emotional state or disengagement), enabling self-optimizing learning strategies, and incorporating interdisciplinary knowledge for greater explainability. The case studies and applications demonstrated concrete benefits of NeSyAI in educational tools. Whether it was an AI tutor that offers personalized hints while ensuring fairness (Hooshyar et al., 2024) or a system that analyzes classroom videos to give teachers actionable feedback, the theme was clear: when AI is designed to complement human educators and follow sound educational theory, it can significantly enhance learning experiences. Students can receive more immediate and tailored support, and teachers can gain deeper insights into student learning processes, informing their instruction. Importantly, NeSyAI was shown to help tackle two perennial concerns with AI in education: the lack of interpretability and the risk of bias. By extracting human-readable rules and focusing on causal factors, NeSyAI systems have been able to present their reasoning in educational contexts and avoid some of the pitfalls of purely data-driven models that might inadvertently encode biases. This is a heartening development, as it suggests that with careful design, AI tutors can be not only effective but also fair and transparent – qualities necessary for widespread acceptance in the education community. It also discussed challenges that must be navigated moving forward. Technical issues like ensuring these advanced AI systems run smoothly on available hardware and protecting student data privacy cannot be overlooked. Moreover, the human factors – teacher training, student agency, and equity of access – will determine whether the technology truly democratizes education or becomes just another tool that benefits the few. It became evident that technology alone is not a panacea. The success of AI in personalized tutoring will depend on thoughtful implementation: integrating it into curricula, aligning it with assessment and accountability structures, and continuously monitoring its impact. The paper argued that a synergy of stakeholders (policymakers, educators, developers) is needed to guide AI's integration so that it adheres to educational values and goals. One recurring point was that AI should augment the human elements of education, not diminish them. The teacher's role may evolve but remains indispensable – as a mentor, motivator, and moral guide. Students, too, should remain active agents in their learning; AI should provoke curiosity and self-reflection, not passivity. Recommendations provided put forth actionable steps for various actors to ensure the journey of neuro-symbolic AI in education progresses on the right path. For policymakers: craft clear ethical guidelines and invest in infrastructure and training. For developers: embed explainability and pedagogy into the design of AI tutors from the outset. For educators: approach AI as a partner in teaching, wield it to enhance student-centered practices, and remain vigilant custodians of the learning experience. Underlying these recommendations is a vision of education where every student has a personal tutor that not only adapts to their academic needs but does so in a nurturing, principled manner – much like an ideal human tutor would. This vision aligns with the age-old dream of individualized education that great thinkers like Bloom (with his 2 sigma tutoring effect) have noted. The society is closer than ever to that dream, but its realization will hinge on the collective commitment to implement these tools wisely and equitably. In conclusion, neuro-symbolic AI has the potential to be a transformative force in education. It offers a pathway to resolve the tension between the scalability of technology and the personalization of human tutoring. If one succeed in harnessing it, people could enter an era where quality education is truly accessible to all, tailored to each learner, and continually improving. An era where no student's potential is left untapped due to large class sizes or lack of support, because an ever-watchful, understanding, and ethical AI companion is there to guide them through challenges. Achieving this will require ongoing innovation, rigorous evaluation, and a steadfast focus on the core mission of education – to uplift human minds and spirits. But the evidence and developments surveyed here strongly suggest that with careful stewardship, neuro-symbolic AI can indeed help deliver more personalized and equitable virtual tutoring, making the ideal of student-centered learning a global reality rather than an aspirational slogan. This is a future worth striving for, where technology and humanity coalesce to foster learning experiences that are at once deeply personal and universally available.

REFERENCES

Abendroth, D., & colleauges. (2025). *Generative ai outlook report: Exploring the intersection between technology, society and policy* (tech. rep. No. JRC142598). European Commission Joint Research Centre (JRC). https://publications.jrc.ec .europa.eu/repository/bitstream/ JRC142598/JRC142598 01.pdf

Access, A. O. (2024). *Ai and collaboration: Practical tips for teachers* [Details how teachers can use AI for designing group experiences, forming equitable teams, and creating rubrics and reflection surveys]. https://avidopenaccess.com/ai-collaboration/

AI, S. (2024). *Competency-based learning: Definition, benefits, and implementation* [Explains principles of competency-based education including equity, measurable competencies, transparency, personalised support, and growth-based assessment]. https://www.saima. ai/competency-based-learning

Alawneh, Y. J. J., Sleema, H., Salman, F. N., Alshammat, M. F., & Oteer, R. S., & ALrashidi, N. K. N. (2024). Adaptive learning systems: Revolutionizing higher education through ai-driven curricula. *2024 International Conference on Knowledge Engineering and Communication Systems (ICKECS), 1*, 1–5. DOI: 10.1109/ICKECS61492.2024.10616675

American Federation of Teachers & Common Sense Education. (2024, June). *Guardrails for AI in education: Practical guidance for districts and schools* [Includes guidance on educator autonomy, bargaining, PD, privacy; accessed 2025-10-11]. https://www.aft.org/sites/ default/files/media/documents/2024/Commonsense Guardrails AI 0604.pdf

Bains, A., Spaulding, C., Ricketts, J., & Krishnan, S. (2023). Providing choice enhances reading enjoyment and motivation.

Barnes, E., & Hutson, J. (2024). Natural language processing and neurosymbolic ai: The role of neural networks with knowledge-guided symbolic approaches. *Journal of Artificial Intelligence and Robotics*, *2*(1).

Bastani, H., Bastani, O., Sungu, A., & Ge, H., Kabakci, O¨., & Mariman, R. (2025). Generative ai without guardrails can harm learning: Evidence from high school mathematics. *Proceedings of the National Academy of Sciences*. . 2422633122DOI: 10.1073/pnas.2422633122

Bhuyan, B. P., Ramdane-Cherif, A., Tomar, R., & Singh, T. (2024). Neuro-symbolic artificial intelligence: A survey. *Neural Computing & Applications*, *36*(21), 12809–12844. DOI: 10.1007/s00521-024-09960-z

Bouneffouf, D., & Aggarwal, C. C. (2022). Survey on applications of neurosymbolic artificial intelligence. *arXiv preprint arXiv:2209.12618.*

Cao, B., & Tutor, A. (2023). Solution for china disadvantaged and underresourced children. *Lect. Notes Educ. Psychol. Public Media, 32*(1), 133–141. DOI: 10.54254/2753-7048/32/20230834

CAST. (2024). Universal design for learning guidelines version 3.0 [Graphic organizer and guidance]. https://udlguidelines.cast.org/more/downloads/

CEDEFOP. (2024). *AI competency framework for teachers (summary of UNESCO framework)* [Summarises UNESCO's AI Competency Framework for Teachers; accessed 2025-10-11]. https://www.cedefop.europa.eu/en/news/ai-competency-framework-teachers

Coates, H., James, R., & Baldwin, G. (2005). A critical examination of the effects of learning management systems on university teaching and learning. *Tertiary Education and Management, 11*(1), 19–36. DOI: 10.1080/13583883.2005.9967137

Colelough, B. C., & Regli, W. (2025). Neuro-symbolic ai in 2024: A systematic review. *arXiv preprint arXiv:2501.05435.*

Common Sense Education. (2025). *AI professional learning for educators (self-paced courses and certification)* [Includes AI Basics, Safe & Responsible Use, AI Literacy Certification; accessed 2025-10-11]. https://www.commonsense.org/education/training/ai

Crowder, N. A. (1959). Automatic tutoring by means of intrinsic programming. In Galanter, E. (Ed.), *Automatic teaching: The state of the art* (pp. 109–116). Wiley.

De Smet, L., Venturato, G., De Raedt, L., & Marra, G. (2025). Relational neurosymbolic markov models. *Proceedings of the AAAI Conference on Artificial Intelligence, 39*(15), 16181–16189. DOI: 10.1609/aaai.v39i15.33777

Dear, B. (2017). *The friendly orange glow: The untold story of the plato system and the dawn of cyberculture.* Pantheon.

Dinu, M.-C. (2024). Parameter choice and neuro-symbolic approaches for deep domain-invariant learning. *arXiv preprint arXiv:2410.06235.*

Doignon, J., & Falmagne, J. (1999). *Knowledge spaces.* Springer., DOI: 10.1007/978-3-642-58625-5

Doignon, J., & Falmagne, J. (2011). *Learning spaces.* Springer., DOI: 10.1007/978-3-642-01039-2

Dumbuya, E. (2023). Personalized learning through artificial intelligence: Revolutionizing education. *Available at SSRN* 5023248.

Elliott, D. (2024). This ai tutor could make humans "10 times smarter", its creator says [Squirrel Ai adaptive learning system helping address teaching gaps in China; cites UNESCO estimate of 44 million additional teachers needed by 2030 to reach SDG 4:contentReference[oaicite:1]index=1]. *World Economic Forum (Forum Stories).* https: //www.weforum.org/stories/2024/07/ai-tutor-china-teaching-gaps/

Federation of American Scientists (Day One Project). (2024, June). *Establish a teacher AI literacy development program* [Policy memo proposing national K-12 teacher AI literacy PD; accessed 2025-10-11]. https://fas.org/publication/teacher -ai-literacy-development/

Feldstein, J., Dilkas, P., Belle, V., & Tsamoura, E. (2024). Mapping the neurosymbolic ai landscape by architectures: A handbook on augmenting deep learning through symbolic reasoning. *arXiv preprint arXiv:2410.22077.*

Fernsel, L., & coauthors. (2025). An auditability framework for ai-based learning analytics systems. *Proceedings of the 17th International Conference on Computer Supported Education (CSEDU 2025).* https://www.scitepress.org/Papers/2025/ 132543/132543.pdf

Fitas, R. (2025a). Inclusive education with ai: Supporting special needs and tackling language barriers. *arXiv preprint arXiv:2504.14120.*

Fitas, R. (2025b). Neuro-symbolic ai for advanced signal and image processing: A review of recent trends and future directions. *IEEE Access : Practical Innovations, Open Solutions*, *13*, 143360–143376. DOI: 10.1109/ACCESS.2025.3598909

Fitas, R., Ghosh, K., & Maity, S. (2025). Leveraging ai in education: Benefits, responsibilities, and trends. *Education: Benefits, Responsibilities, and Trends (February 01, 2025).* for California Community Colleges, A. S. (2023). Ai-powered education: Authentic assessments and learning [Describes authentic assessments evaluating creativity and collaboration and how AI can support project-based learning and multimodal assignments]. *ASCCC Open Education Resources.* https://asccc-oer -oedtresources.org/ai-powered-education

for Lifelong Learning. U. I. (2024). Lifelong learning in the age of ai: How can we bridge the digital divide? [Discusses human-centred lifelong learning, bridging the digital divide, open resources, Universal Design for Learning, and participatory governance]. *UNESCO Institute for Lifelong Learning Blog.* https://uil.unesco.org/ en/news/lifelong-learning- age-ai-how-can-we-bridge-digital-divide

Foundation, W. F. (2024). *New survey reveals teachers believe ai can boost creativity and classroom learning* [Reports that nearly half of teachers use AI weekly, only 25% have PD, 56% want training, and describes pilot tools for literacy and personalised hints]. https://www.waltonfamilyfoundation.org/about/newsroom/new-survey-reveals- teachers-believe-ai-can-boost-creativity-and-classroom-learning

Fu, Y., & Weng, Z. (2024). Navigating the ethical terrain of ai in education: A systematic review on framing responsible human-centered ai practices. *Computers and Education: Artificial Intelligence*, *7*, 100306. DOI: 10.1016/j.caeai.2024.100306

Gaur, M., & Sheth, A. (2024). Building trustworthy neurosymbolic ai systems: Consistency, reliability, explainability, and safety. *AI Magazine*, *45*(1), 139–155. DOI: 10.1002/aaai.12149

Global Learning Council. (2022). *Kli: A theoretical framework for improving student learning* [Summarises the Knowledge–Learning–Instruction framework and its role in linking knowledge types, learning processes, and instructional methods]. https: / / www. globallearningcouncil . org / posts / kli - a - theoretical - framework- for-improving-student-learning

Graesser, A. C., Hu, X., Nye, B. D., VanLehn, K., Kumar, R., Heffernan, C., Heffernan, N., Woolf, B., Olney, A. M., Rus, V., Andrasik, F., Pavlik, P., Cai, Z., Wetzel, J., Morgan, B., Hampton, A. J., Lippert, A. M., Wang, L., Cheng, Q., & Baer, W. (2018). Electronixtutor: An intelligent tutoring system with multiple learning resources for electronics [Describes topic and knowledge component mapping, course calendars, and mastery tracking in an ITS]. *International Journal of STEM Education*, *5*(1), 15. DOI: 10.1186/s40594-018-0110-y PMID: 30631705

Heffernan, N. T., & Heffernan, C. L. (2014). The assistments ecosystem: Building a platform that brings scientists and teachers together for minimally invasive research on human learning and teaching. *International Journal of Artificial Intelligence in Education*, *24*(4), 470–497. DOI: 10.1007/s40593-014-0024-x

Henkel, O., Horne-Robinson, H., Kozhakhmetova, N., & Lee, A. (2024). Effective and scalable math support: Evidence on the impact of an ai-tutor on math achievement in ghana. *arXiv preprint*. https://arxiv.org/abs/2402.09809 DOI: 10.1007/978-3-031-64315-6_34

Hollands, F., Bowden, A. B., Belfield, C., Levin, H. M., Cheng, H., Shand, R., Pan, Y., & Hanisch-Cerda, B. (2014). Cost-effectiveness analysis in practice: Interventions to improve high school completion. *Educational Evaluation and Policy Analysis*, *36*(3), 307–326. DOI: 10.3102/0162373713511850

Hooshyar, D., Azevedo, R., & Yang, Y. (2024). Augmenting deep neural networks with symbolic educational knowledge: Towards trustworthy and interpretable ai for education. *Machine Learning and Knowledge Extraction*, *6*(1), 593–618. DOI: 10.3390/make6010028

Hou, R., Fu¨ tterer, T., Bu¨ hler, B., Bozkir, E., Gerjets, P., Trautwein, U., & Kasneci, E. (2024). Automated assessment of encouragement and warmth in classrooms leveraging multimodal emotional features and chatgpt. *International conference on artificial intelligence in education*, 60–74. DOI: 10.1007/978-3-031-64302-6_5

Huang, D., Nan, Z., Hu, X., Jin, P., Peng, S., Wen, Y., Zhang, R., Du, Z., Guo, Q., & Pu, Y.. (2023). Anpl: Towards natural programming with interactive decomposition. *Advances in Neural Information Processing Systems*, *36*, 69404–69440.

Huang, J., Li, Z., Naik, M., & Lim, S.-N. (2023). Laser: A neuro-symbolic framework for learning spatial-temporal scene graphs with weak supervision. *arXiv preprint arXiv:2304.07647*.

Iman, M. Z., Asis, A. A., & Rahma, A. U. Z. (2024). Enhancing personalized learning: The impact of artificial intelligence in education. *Edu Spectrum: Journal of Multidimensional Education*, *1*(2), 101–112. DOI: 10.70063/eduspectrum.v1i2.55

ISTE. (2017). *Iste standards for educators* [Seven role-based standards (Learner, Leader, Citizen, Collaborator, Designer, Facilitator, Analyst); accessed 2025-10-11]. https://iste.org/standards/iste-standards-for-educators

Jain, N. (2025). Ai as a catalyst for educational equity: Addressing global teacher shortages and learning disparities. *International Journal of Scientific Research in Computer Science, Engineering and Information Technology, 11*(1).

Kaswan, K. S., Dhatterwal, J. S., & Ojha, R. P. (2024). Ai in personalized learning. In *Advances in technological innovations in higher education* (pp. 103–117). CRC Press. DOI: 10.1201/9781003376699-9

Katiyar, N., Awasthi, M. V. K., Pratap, R., Mishra, M. K., Shukla, M. N., Tiwari, M., & Singh, R. (2024). Ai-driven personalized learning systems: Enhancing educational effectiveness. *Educational Administration: Theory and Practice*, *30*(5), 11514–11524.

Kaufman, J. H., ... (2025). *Uneven adoption of artificial intelligence tools among u.s. teachers and principals* (RRA134-25). RAND Corporation. https://www.rand.org/pubs/ research reports/RRA134-25.html

Kautz, H. (2022). The third ai summer: Aaai robert s. engelmore memorial lecture. *AI Magazine*, *43*(1), 105–125. DOI: 10.1002/aaai.12036

Koedinger, K. R., Anderson, J. R., Hadley, W. H., & Mark, M. A. (1997). Intelligent tutoring goes to school in the big city. *International Journal of Artificial Intelligence in Education*, *8*, 30–43. https://kilthub.cmu.edu/articles/journal contribution/ Intelligent Tutoring Goes To School in the Big City/6470153

Kopp, W. (2025, January). *Nurturing a thriving teaching profession in an AI-enhanced world* [OECD Education and Skills Today blog; accessed 2025-10-11]. https:// oecdedutoday. com/nurturing-a-thriving-teaching-profession-in-an-ai-enhanced-world/

Lampropoulos, G., & Papadakis, S. (2025). The educational value of artificial intelligence and social robots. In Lampropoulos, G., & Papadakis, S. (Eds.), *Social robots in education: How to effectively introduce social robots into classrooms* (Vol. 1194, pp. 3–15). Springer., DOI: 10.1007/978-3-031-82915-4_1

Lee, J. H., Sioutis, M., Ahrens, K., Alirezaie, M., Kerzel, M., & Wermter, S. (2023). Neuro-symbolic spatio-temporal reasoning. In *Compendium of neurosymbolic artificial intelligence* (pp. 410–429). IOS Press. DOI: 10.3233/FAIA230151

Levin, H. M., & McEwan, P. J. (2001). *Cost-effectiveness analysis: Methods and applications* (2nd ed.). Sage.

Lonn, S., & Teasley, S. D. (2009). Saving time or innovating practice? investigating perceptions and uses of learning management systems. *Computers & Education*, *53*(3), 686–694. DOI: 10.1016/j.compedu.2009.04.008

Madhu, N., Latha, P., & Savitha, N. (2024). Revolutionizing education: Harnessing ai for personalized learning pathways and student success. *International Journal for Multidisciplinary Research*, *6*(5).

Marpaung, S. F., Sembiring, A. W., Azzahra, N., & Hallawa, S. (2023). Educational ethics in developing character learners. edumaspul. *Jurnal Pendidikan*, *7*(2), 5721–5729.

Mat, N. C., & Jamaludin, K. A. (2024). Effectiveness of practices and applications of student-centered teaching and learning in primary schools: A systematic literature review. *International Journal of Academic Research in Progressive Education and Development*, *13*(3), 1025–1044.

McLaren, B. M., Herckis, L., Teffera, L., Branstetter, L., & Rose, C. P.. (2024). Community college information technology education: Curriculum mapping, a learning science framework, and AI learning technologies [Describes curriculum mapping with KLI to align knowledge components with intelligent tutors and collaborative learning]. *Proceedings of the 2024 Annual Meeting of the American Educational Research* DOI: 10.3102/2111565

Means, B., Roschelle, J., Penuel, W., Sabelli, N., & Haertel, G. (2003). Chapter 5: Technology's contribution to teaching and policy: Efficiency, standardization, or transformation? *Review of Research in Education*, *27*(1), 159–181. DOI: 10.3102/0091732X027001159

Nanney, B. (2020). Student-centered learning. *The SAGE Encyclopedia of Higher Education*. https://api.semanticscholar.org/CorpusID:64196280

Nu'n˜ez-Molina, C., Mesejo, P., & Ferna'ndez-Olivares, J. (2024). A review of symbolic, subsymbolic and hybrid methods for sequential decision making. *ACM Computing Surveys*, *56*(11), 1–36. DOI: 10.1145/3663366

Nwana, H. S. (1990). Intelligent tutoring systems: An overview. *Artificial Intelligence Review*, *4*(4), 251–277. DOI: 10.1007/BF00168958

OECD. (2023). *Oecd digital education outlook 2023: Towards an effective digital education ecosystem*. DOI: 10.1787/c74f03de-en

Ogunsina, M., Efunniyi, C. P., Osundare, O. S., Folorunsho, S. O., & Akwawa, L. A. (2024). Neuro-symbolic integration in autonomous robotics: A framework for enhanced decision-making. *Engineering Science & Technology Journal*, *5*(9). Advance online publication. DOI: 10.51594/estj.v5i9.1546

Orlikowski, W. J. (1992). The duality of technology: Rethinking the concept of technology in organizations. *Organization Science*, *3*(3), 398–427. DOI: 10.1287/orsc.3.3.398

Overby, K. (2011). Student-centered learning. *Essai*, *9*(1), 32.

Padmanaban, H. (2024). Machine learning algorithms scaling on large-scale data infrastructure. *Journal of Artificial Intelligence General science (JAIGS) ISSN: 3006-4023, 3*(1), 171–196.

Pane, J. F., Steiner, E. D., Baird, M. D., Hamilton, L. S., ... (2015). *Continued progress: Promising evidence on personalized learning* (tech. rep.). RAND Corporation. Santa Monica, CA. https://www.rand.org/pubs/research reports/RR1365.html

Ritter, S., Anderson, J. R., Koedinger, K. R., & Corbett, A. (2007). Cognitive tutor: Applied research in mathematics education. *Psychonomic Bulletin & Review*, *14*(2), 249–255. DOI: 10.3758/BF03194060 PMID: 17694909

Rogers, E. M. (2003). *Diffusion of innovations* (5th ed.). Free Press.

Rogers, F. H., & Sabarwal, S. (2020). The covid-19 pandemic: Shocks to education and policy responses.

Sabbagh, C. (2009). Ethics and teaching. In *International handbook of research on teachers and teaching* (pp. 683–693). Springer. DOI: 10.1007/978-0-387-73317-3_42

Sari, F. W., & Wati, T. L. (n.d.). Influence of problem based learning model on elementary school student critical thinking abilities: Pengaruh model pembelajaran problem based learning terhadap kemampuan berpikir kritis siswa sekolah dasar.

Sari, H. E., Tumanggor, B., & Efron, D. (2024). Improving educational outcomes through adaptive learning systems using ai. *International Transactions on Artificial Intelligence*, *3*(1), 21–31. DOI: 10.33050/italic.v3i1.647

Selwyn, N. (2011). Education and technology: Key issues and debates. *Continuum.*

Singh, N. (2011). Student-centered learning (scl) in classrooms—A comprehensive overview. *Educational Quest-An International Journal of Education and Applied Social Sciences*, *2*(2), 275–282.

Sleeman, D., & Brown, J. S. (Eds.). (1982). *Intelligent tutoring systems*. Academic Press.

Suppes, P., & Morningstar, M. (1969). Computer-assisted instruction: Two computer-assisted instruction programs are evaluated. *Science*, *166*(3903), 343–350. DOI: 10.1126/science.166.3903.343 PMID: 5812034

Taha, T. B., & Abdulrahman, M. S. (2023). The impact of technology on students' psychological and educational performance. [Jurnal Informatika dan Sains]. *JISA*, *6*(1), 91–95. DOI: 10.31326/jisa.v6i1.1661

The AI Education Project (aiEDU). (2025). *Professional learning for educators* [PD offerings and AI readiness resources for educators; accessed 2025-10-11]. https://aiedu.org/professional- learning

Tripathi, T., Sharma, S. R., Singh, V., Bhargava, P., & Raj, C. (2025). Teaching and learning with ai: A qualitative study on k-12 teachers' use and engagement with artificial intelligence. *Frontiers in Education*, *10*, 1651217. Advance online publication. DOI: 10.3389/feduc.2025.1651217

Ugˇras¸, H., Ugˇras¸, M., Papadakis, S., & Kalogiannakis, M. (2024). Chatgpt-supported education in primary schools: The potential of chatgpt for sustainable practices [Article number 9855]. *Sustainability (Basel), 16*(22), 9855. DOI: 10.3390/su16229855

Ugˇras¸, H., Ugˇras¸, M., Papadakis, S., & Kalogiannakis, M. (2025). Innovative early childhood stem education with chatgpt: Teacher perspectives [First online 2024]. *Technology. Knowledge and Learning, 30*(2), 809–831. DOI: 10.1007/s10758-024-09804-8

UNESCO. (2025a, April). Meeting every learner where they are [Article updated 9 May 2025]. https://www.unesco.org/en/articles/meeting-every-learner-where-they-are

UNESCO. (2025b). What you need to know about inclusion in education [Accessed: 2025-08-06]. https://www.unesco.org/en/inclusion-education/need-know

UNESCO & International Task Force on Teachers for Education 2030. (2025, April). Global report on teachers: What you need to know [Article summarizing the Global Report on Teachers (released 26 February 2024)]. https://www.unesco.org/en/articles/global- report-teachers-what-you-need-know

UNESCO Global Education Monitoring Report Team. (2023). *Global education monitoring report 2023: Technology in education: A tool on whose terms?* (Open Access under CC-BY-SA 3.0 IGO). UNESCO. Paris. https: / / unesdoc . unesco . org / ark: /48223 / pf0000385723

UNESCO Inclusive Policy Lab. (2024, May). Ai education and esg/sdgs: Towards student-centered learning [Latest update 20 January 2025]. https:// en. unesco. org/ inclusivepolicylab/ e- teams/ ai- education- and- esgsdgs- towards- student-centered- learning

U.S. Department of Education, Office of Educational Technology. (2023a, May). *Artificial intelligence and the future of teaching and learning: Insights and recommendations* (tech. rep.). U.S. Department of Education. Washington, DC. https://www.ed.gov/sites/ ed/files/documents/ai-report/ai-report.pdf

U.S. Department of Education, Office of Educational Technology. (2023b). Artificial intelligence and the future of teaching and learning: Insights and recommendations.

U.S. Department of Education, Office of Educational Technology. (2023c). *Artificial intelligence and the future of teaching and learning: Insights and recommendations* (tech. rep.) (Highlights formative-assessment applications, help-seeking detection, fairness concerns, and the need for human feedback loops). U.S. Department of Education. https://www.ed. gov/sites/ed/files/documents/ai-report/ai-report.pdf

van Leeuwen, A., Strauß, A., & Rummel, N. (2023). Participatory design of teacher dashboards: Navigating the tension between teacher input and theories on teacher professional vision. *Frontiers in Artificial Intelligence, 6*, 1039739. VanLehn, K. (2011). The relative effectiveness of human tutoring, intelligent tutoring systems, and other tutoring systems. *Educational Psychologist, 46*(4), 197–221. https://doi .org/DOI: 10.3389/frai.2023.1039739

Vasilev, I. (2024). Motivating unmotivated students and strategies for success in vet: A guide for vet educators. *E-Magazine. Pedagogical Forum*, (4), 70–82. DOI: 10.15547/PF.2024.025

Wan, Z., Liu, C.-K., Yang, H., Raj, R., Li, C., You, H., Fu, Y., Wan, C., Li, S., & Kim, Y.. (2024). *Towards efficient neuro-symbolic ai: From workload characterization to hardware architecture*. IEEE Transactions on Circuits and Systems for Artificial Intelligence.

Wang, R. E., Ribeiro, A. T., Robinson, C. D., Loeb, S., & Demszky, D. (2024a). Tutor copilot: A human-ai approach for scaling real-time expertise. https://arxiv .org/abs/2410.03017 DOI: 10.21203/rs.3.rs-5363154/v1

Wang, R. E., Ribeiro, A. T., Robinson, C. D., Loeb, S., & Demszky, D. (2024b). *Tutor copilot: A human-ai approach for scaling real-time expertise (preregistered rct report)* (tech. rep.). National Student Support Accelerator (Stanford University). https://nssa.stanford.edu/ sites/default/files/Tutor%20CoPilot.pdf

Wang, X., Wrede, S., van Rijn, L., & Wo¨hrle, J. (2023). Ai-based quiz system for personalised learning. *ICERI2023 Proceedings*, 5025–5034.

Watters, A. (2021). *Teaching machines: The history of personalized learning*. MIT Press. https://mitpress.mit.edu/9780262363754/teaching-machines/

What Works Clearinghouse. (2013). *Dreambox learning: Intervention report* (tech. rep.). Institute of Education Sciences, U.S. Department of Education. https://ies.ed .gov/ncee/wwc/ Docs/InterventionReports/wwc dreambox 121013.pdf

White, S. V., Childs, J., Koshy, S., & Scott, A. (2024). Policy implementation in the era of responsible artificial intelligence (ai) use in k-12 education. *Proceedings of the 2024 on RESPECT Annual Conference*, 81–85. DOI: 10.1145/3653666.3656097

William, M. (2024). *Creative patterns in the age of ai: Securing america's education edge* [Argues for investing in teacher training, AI infrastructure, and curricular reform to cultivate creative and interdisciplinary learning]. https://www.brookings.edu/articles/creative- patterns-in-the-age-of-ai-securing-americas-education-edge/

Wolfenden, F. (2022). *TPD@Scale: Designing teacher professional development with ICTs to support system-wide improvement in teaching* (tech. rep.) (Working paper; accessed 2025-10-11). TPD@Scale Coalition for the Global South / Foundation for Information Technology Education and Development (FIT-ED). https:// oro.open. ac.uk/ 86337/ 1 / Working % 20Paper % 20 - %20Designing % 20TPD % 20with % 20ICTs % 20to % 20Support%20System-Wide%20Improvement%20 in%20Teaching.pdf

Wolfenden, F. (2024). A framework for strengthening teacher professional development systems with ICT [Extended framework building on TPD@Scale; accessed 2025-10-11]. //oro.open.ac.uk/96423/1/A-Framework-for-Strengthening-Teacher -Professional-Development-Systems-with-ICT2024%20(1).pdf">https://oro.open.ac .uk/96423/1/A-Framework-for- Strengthening- Teacher- Professional- Development-Systems-with-ICT 2024%20(1).pdf

Ydo, Y. (2020). Inclusive education: Global priority, collective responsibility. *Prospects*, *49*(3), 97–101. DOI: 10.1007/s11125-020-09520-y PMID: 33235396

Yu, C., & Yao, G.. (2024). Enhancing student engagement with ai-driven personalized learning systems. [ITEE]. *International Transactions on Education Technology*, *3*(1), 1–8.

Yulianti, K. (2023). Students' experience with online personalized learning in character building-civics course at a private university in indonesia. *Proceedings of the 2023 7th International Conference on Education and E-Learning*, 85–89. DOI: 10.1145/3637989.3637999

Chapter 2
Personalization, Equity, and Ethics:
AI Virtual Tutors in K-12 Education

Wasswa Shafik
http://orcid.org/0000-0002-9320-3186
Dig Connectivity Research Laboratory (DCRLab), Uganda & School of Digital Science, University Brunei Darussalam, Gadong, Brunei

ABSTRACT

As the digital age transforms how knowledge is created and shared, artificial intelligence (AI) emerges as a powerful ally in reimagining K-12 education. This chapter explores the integration of AI-driven instructional tools that support personalized learning pathways, foster adaptive assessment practices, and enhance teacher effectiveness. It examines how intelligent tutoring systems, learning analytics, and classroom automation are reshaping traditional pedagogies while offering new opportunities for student engagement and curriculum innovation. Grounded in real-world examples and educational theory, the chapter also addresses critical considerations such as equity, data privacy, and ethical use of AI in the classroom. By highlighting both the potential and the limitations of these technologies, the chapter sets the stage for thoughtful adoption and sustainable implementation of AI in primary and secondary education.

1. INTRODUCTION

Our current K-12 education faces many grand challenges. Class sizes are often large, individual instruction time is limited, unproductive assignments can over-

DOI: 10.4018/979-8-3373-2637-5.ch002

whelm students and instructors, and access to instruction varies depending on the background of the student and the resources available at home. Digital learning platforms have shown immense promise in addressing many of these issues by personalizing instruction, providing instantaneous feedback, and offering affordable access to high-quality learning materials (Crawford & Huling, 2023). We believe that AI will be an even bigger game changer, revolutionizing how concepts are taught and learned in K-12 education. The promise of AI-driven technology in education is tremendous. To date, these platforms have increased the capacity of the education system by enabling elite teachers to reach more students, easing the burden on understaffed schools, and enabling education to come at lower or more convenient price points. However, the digital learning revolution has also been rather limited in its scope. For example, math instruction tools largely rely on multiple-choice questions, text, and images to assist students (Baker et al., 2023). This is a problem, as these represent the lowest bandwidth forms of information transference and are ill-suited to convey the rich structure and meaning of mathematical concepts fully.

We view Kisantech as part of an evolving subset of innovative startups focusing on a subject that has largely been neglected from mass innovation: pedagogy. Historically, K-12 education has evolved at a much slower pace relative to society as a whole. Frankly, today's K-12 education is designed to instruct students for jobs that probably do not yet exist, utilizing a set of knowledge that is not yet known. Moreover, the current set of best practices, universally adopted pedagogy, and standardized testing may result in a relatively homogenous student population (Wang et al., 2023). Additionally, the hierarchy of educational power and control is also relatively efficient at maintaining a slow rate of change. The combination of the digital age, pandemic isolation, artificial intelligence, advanced visualization, virtual reality, machine learning, predictive modeling, cameras, and natural language processing has lowered the barrier to entry for innovative companies aiming to break through in the pedagogy space (Sat & Kadirhan, 2024; Shafik, 2024e). Also, unlike the majority of other sectors that advocate pedagogy best practices, math, and even many scientific obsessions, nature, economics, politics, and religion do not need to be dumbed down to fit into a preferred pedagogical framework. Yet, evolving educational tools do not have to predict how learning occurs over the entire brain network correctly. Cognitive neuroscience has proved that wide networks are often involved in singularly focused tasks, such as forward or reverse math problems (Regan & King-Sears, 2023; Lampropoulos & Papadakis, 2025).

2. THE ROLE OF TECHNOLOGY IN EDUCATION

The ever-developing field of technology has ingrained itself deeply in education. In his micropolitan schoolhouse laboratory, where visitors queued "to peek into the future," he had a phonograph, film projector, and dictaphone. He believed that in 100 years, "more than 80 percent of the children between 6 and 18 years will be taught this way... [by] 'moving pictures,' where you have a rhythmic action and pageantry of the world." The field of educational technology has grown largely because of the extreme dynamics of technological innovations, coupled with more and more research supporting the real potential of these innovations to enhance the learning process significantly (M. S. Kim & Yu, 2023). In general, technology can enhance education by increasing the accessibility and flexibility of classes. Technology can offer instruction through distance learning and self-paced courses. Distance education has vast implications, making it possible for individuals anywhere with access to a computer to obtain instruction from anywhere they choose (Lavidas et al., 2022a). Distance learning instruction can be especially important during times of crisis. Work can be accessed off-site or at home on a 24/7 schedule. The user's preference is accommodated for time, location, order of sequential learning, level of detail, quantity of information, response time, redundancy, and interests of a student (Shafik, 2024c; Vartanian, 2024). Also, adaptive technologies available through technology allow for information that matches the student's needs, abilities, and interests. Technology enables learners to proceed with either self-paced learning or interactive instruction. In a self-paced setting, learners can skip over what they know and concentrate on the difficult-to-grasp elements. Today's adaptive technology enables this self-direction to be more learner-friendly in terms of providing learning conditions that allow students to follow individualized paths (Baker et al., 2023; Lavidas et al., 2022a). All of these implications make technology an important area for research and development in K-12 education.

2.1. Artificial Intelligence in Education

Artificial intelligence and machine learning have emerged as significant technologies that can change the way learning and training occur. With the advancement of the internet and the penetration of digital devices, there is an opportunity to invest significantly in the development of just-in-time instructional and help systems (Lavidas et al., 2022b). Several companies offer adaptive systems catered to K-12 education, which use machine learning in the form of learning analytics and recommendations to serve local learning needs. AI can somewhat handle administrative tasks because those are the simplest tasks (Sat & Kadirhan, 2024). The main goal in allowing artificial intelligence to take responsibility for these kinds of tasks is to allow schools to utilize the knowledge gained from this data to personalize instruction for each student. Artificial intelligence does three things really well in the classroom. First, it scales education by facilitating experiences and conversations between algorithms, with real people, or in collaborative groups. Second, AI helps personalize learning. It recognizes many of the variables that affect student achievement and creates interventions that adapt to each in real-time (Vartanian, 2024). Third, educational AI helps to automate administrative tasks, freeing up time for educators to work with students. AI in education is instrumental in the construction of a student's understanding of the material through personal tutoring. It is also helpful for automatically grading assignments and correspondence with other students. In addition, AI can take over a variety of administrative tasks produced during the school day, thus allowing teachers to focus on the students. Therefore, AI can help answer questions using the knowledge derived from the data it collects. In the administrative sense, AI can serve to reactively answer questions using the knowledge of student attendance, lunch assignments, etc (Schilling & Grohs, 2023).

2.2. Benefits of AI-Driven Instructional Tools

Potentially transformative tools that use artificial intelligence for student support are beginning to address day-to-day challenges in the classroom, offering targeted instructional support, feedback, and practice for students. These tools provide detailed insights to teachers on student performance, identify common misconceptions, and reshape the curriculum to address individual student needs. In this way, AI enables more targeted, immediate, individualized learning that helps teachers spend more valuable time teaching more than the sum of the skills (Rice et al., 2023). In doing so, these tools help to orchestrate meaningful teacher-student interactions that are fundamental to K-12 education. AI-driven instructional tools are designed to play a supporting role in the classroom, helping teachers by automating time-consuming processes and harnessing technology to improve educational processes and outcomes. These tools consistently and increasingly improve student performance on standard exams. They also help students gain knowledge beyond academic goals by promoting inquiry, deepening understanding, enhancing critical thinking skills and persistence, and developing motivation and confidence (Dean & Gilbert, 2024). By doing so, they help students generalize their academic skills more broadly and much earlier than with traditional teaching, as sampled tools are presented in Table 1.

Table 1. AI-Powered Instructional Tools in K-12 Education

Tool Name	Functionality	Key Benefits	AI Technology Used	Platforms Application Example	Reference
Virtual Tutors	Provides real-time assistance	Personalized learning	NLP, Machine Learning	Squirrel AI, Carnegie Learning	(Bhowmik, 2023)
Adaptive Learning	Customizes content per student	Improves engagement	AI algorithms	DreamBox, Knewton	(Meecha, 2023)
Automated Grading	Evaluates assignments	Saves teacher time	AI-based assessment	Gradescope, Turnitin AI	(Abubakari et al., 2024)
Chatbots	Answers student queries	24/7 accessibility	NLP, Deep Learning	IBM Watson, Google Dialogflow	(Shafik, 2024d)
AI Writing Assist	Enhance writing skills	Grammar and style feedback	NLP, AI-based analytics	Grammarly, QuillBot	(Shafik, 2024b)
Speech Recognition	Assists speech-based learning	Supports special education	Voice AI, Speech-to-text	Google Speech-to-Text, Nuance	(Shafik, 2025)
AI-Powered Games	Enhance interactive learning	Increases engagement	Reinforcement Learning	Kahoot, Prodigy	(Pan et al., 2022)
AI-Based Feedback	Provides personalized feedback	Identifies learning gaps	Predictive Analytics	Edmentum, Smart Sparrow	(Li & Wang, 2022)
Emotion AI	Detects student emotions	Enhances mental well-being	Sentiment Analysis	Affectiva, BrainCo	(Sanusi et al., 2022)
Virtual Labs	Simulates experiments	Hands-on STEM learning	AI-powered simulations	Labster, PhET	(Akgun & Greenhow, 2022)
AI for Special Ed	Supports differently abled students	Inclusive education	Assistive AI	Microsoft Immersive Reader	(J. C. Brown, 2017)
Voice Assistants	AI-based classroom assistant	Facilitates classroom tasks	AI Voice Recognition	Alexa for Education, Google Assistant	(Larkin et al., 2016)

2.3. Challenges and Limitations

The use of AI in high-risk domains is fraught with challenges and limitations that must be addressed by educators, educational researchers, and AI scientists and developers. Basic barriers to educational improvement also inherently exist. The entire scope of educational AI is far beyond the scope of this analysis, so we will concentrate on the most challenging issues, seen through the lens of the AI tools we propose for K-12 education. We will also describe ways to create a research and development environment that maximizes the likelihood of using AI capabilities effectively to help teachers and students in such important ways (Bhowmik & Kim, 2022). To be meaningful and helpful to the instructor and student, AI techniques must understand the course content, educational objectives, and social and political context of the students and schools. AI methods must strive for transparency and allow teachers, administrators, and students to understand the basis for any conclusions or actions they recommend. They must employ evidence-based educational methods rather than glorify data alone. They should integrate, rather than subvert, human judgment. AI methods must be trained and validated on datasets appropriate for specific educational domains, levels, school models, missions, and criteria (Kebritchi et al., 2009). Only through involved educator collaboration can they truly be expected to deliver meaningful results.

3. ETHICAL CONSIDERATIONS IN AI EDUCATION

Observational trials of AI algorithms can be an important safety measure prior to larger-scale implementations. Ethical panels composed of educators, parents, students, and external advisory groups, including AI ethics and bias experts, should be used to steer AI instructional software development that aligns with anti-bias ethical considerations (Forbes et al., 2011). An adaptive instructional tool should honor individual data privacy, with a concern that children, during the early age of human learning, begin being profiled by AI through the collection and application of considerable personal data. Student Privacy Considerations with AI-Driven Adaptive Software in K-12 With the utilization of personalized instruction driven by AI, major concerns regarding individual student privacy and data security must be addressed. Adaptive AI instructional software collects a large volume of personal data, including a student's high and low-performance scores, steps in student problem strategies and deliberations, the items or problem-solving activities associated with these high and low-performance scores, and a time-stamp/indication of when these high and low-performance activities occur (Halverson et al., 2023; Lavidas et al., 2022b). All data are potentially sensitive and require a high level of personal privacy protection for each minor; all data should be de-identified with a process that surpasses current standards to protect each child's privacy. Silicon Valley is graduating from the tech industry's adolescent search engine hacks and photo-sharing services to tackle what are probably the most important problems in the world: education, healthcare, and energy poverty. Ambitious technology startups are taking on major inefficiencies or downright systemic failures in these fields. The following eight case studies present concrete applications of AI to just one dimension of that broader market: personalized instructional tools for K-12 education (Yeung & Ng, 2023). Some of these projects are the products of well-funded startups, while others are less heavily resourced efforts, and they represent just a fraction of the research and prototyping work aimed at disrupting the established order of scripted aging schoolbooks and one-size-fits-all instruction.

3.1. Generalization is Difficult and Risky

The number of factors that influence the success or failure of an ed-tech project is essentially unpredictable and may be incalculable. The common difficulties of early-stage commercial networks apply to the ed-tech space just as they do for search, social, and video-sharing sites: building strong development-engineering teams, getting feedback from end users, finding new customers and more users, and figuring out a business model while hoping the money lasts. In the case of ed-tech, the challenges can be even greater (Yeung & Ng, 2024). The buying power of the nation's schools is diffuse, seasonal, and usually from budgets that are already over-promised and overshadowed by the cost of teachers, labor rules, and infrastructure. Reaching teachers and administrators and getting them to sample a product is labor-intensive, meaning long sales cycles and high up-front costs. Becoming an authorized education content provider in the U.S. is a frustrating and difficult process. The marketplace is dominated by a few huge textbook content conglomerates, whose other businesses are often testing and who have a lot at stake in the status quo. Besides negotiating the usual traps of intellectual property, venture investors often have to understand how schools operate in order to help a startup find a path to success effectively (Addo & Sentance, 2023). As the portraits of the cases below unfold, remember that pitfalls laid for paper-and-ink textbooks can be even more perilous in the digital domain.

4. FUTURE TRENDS IN AI-DRIVEN EDUCATION

The field of AI-driven education has advanced rapidly since its inception only a few years ago. Certain existing technologies, such as intelligent tutoring systems that individualize structures, update the curriculum as students learn, and diagnose and offer tailored feedback, have gained widespread use. AI in other technology categories is currently at a prototype stage. Yet, while schools today may benefit from these services, the applications are still costly and may not work for all (Cipriano & McCarthy, 2023). With the widespread adoption of cloud-based systems and highly efficient products, these services are poised to affect K-12 education widely in the coming decade, leading to changes that build on existing technology but also fundamentally transform what we think formal schooling should provide. Several distinct developments may contribute to this evolution. First, curricular and instructional implications will have to be addressed. Simply accelerating student understanding is a measurable improvement. Instances of AI-driven instruction operating in formal environments are largely in tutoring mathematics. Although models can be revised for distinct cognitive capabilities of every field of study, it is unlikely that adaptive instruction will directly cover the range of student learning as seen in formal environments. Open curricula will need irregular assignments, unanticipated questions, and recurring revisions (De Souza & Kochhann, 2023; Shafik, 2024e). For those looking after students, however, the marketplace's advanced intelligence will help many ed-tech companies create new answers.

4.1. Implementing AI in K-12 Settings

There are common roadblocks we see to excluding AI from K-12 settings. As a professional who has been working in K-12 and now higher education settings for over a decade, there are obvious ones I have seen repeatedly in practice. Student novelty demands that a teacher or learning tool approaches each student as an individual. A tool or inexperienced educator must attempt to discover who they are and what it takes to learn from them (Baker et al., 2023). Building an AI tool capable of understanding each student's learning profile and needs typically requires close interactions between developers, researchers, and students, and that comes with all of the challenges and complexities of social circumstances and life events that come with it, not to mention copious amounts of data collection. People are generally concerned about privacy, but the impending sense of a creepy government or faceless corporation watching the minutiae of the many individual students is particularly unpalatable. AI in K-12 is not necessarily concerned with watching kids (though maybe to the student this may feel like the case) but facilitating their teacher's access to and analysis of the data they have personally acquired about them within the communication structure of the classroom (Regan & King-Sears, 2023).

Additionally, people are generally concerned that giving students undeserved advantages will lead to greater inequality, whereas those who are disadvantaged and those who understand the context in which the students are performing attempt to fight to avoid this inequality. Those who refuse to allow testing and ethical consequences to influence their development path without feedback from those who have insight into the matter end up with a tool that primarily helps those who already have advantages. Before taking notes, it is important to understand whose perspective these determinations of undeserved advantage are being made and whether there is agreement on what undeserved advantage or disadvantage looks like (Schilling &

Grohs, 2023). To avoid unintended consequences, we must consult and support these efforts. It is important to remember who these efforts support when we are deciding whether or not to compile resources for and carry out the work associated with supporting K-12 environments. Be cautious of the unintended consequences and ethical responsibilities to those who are or are not greatly supported by AI. For example, if a world was created in which robotics was routine, more of it may be possible. Robots could be sent to spend the day with students to help guide learning. However, if it is the case where this outcome is a common or probable future, are we not responsible for acting and ensuring the development and application of AI and robotics in a manner that positively supports the students who are themselves currently undersupported simply because they are not well supported today (Morrison, 2023)?

4.2. Teachers' Training and Support

Traditional concerns about teacher capacity also apply to AI. They deal with technophobia and the emotional response educators grapple with technological and even societal changes, a deficit of trust, lack of context, and low levels of skill. Assuring evidence-based sustained training and support is the best means of securing teacher and school leader confidence. They form a connective function in a world of deepening instrumental specialization and an increasing division of labor (Özgür, 2023). But while technical expertise in predictive analytics or understanding data science issues can nourish that trust, these faculties must be joined by a deep understanding of the K-12 teaching and learning process, the adoption and deployment cycles of AI, and the predictive validity of analytics models when fed inputs from other parts of this complex adaptive system. Ultimately, human judgments are context-bound, and it is also within the legitimate professional rights of a teacher to draw upon a set of aims for teaching and time-honored practices. These involve inspiring, nurturing, facilitating, coaching, or cheerleading that have successfully attended to themselves or their former generations in similar circumstances. There is a social motivation to protect human-related professional work from further metrics-led heavy-handedness (Rizvi et al., 2023). If one is divorced from making predictions, the next best thing to managing these fallibilities is being confident in the credibility of those whose insights are sought.

4.3. Student Engagement and Motivation

A significant portion of K-12 students (42%) feel unenthusiastic or not motivated when learning. Major underlying reasons for this disengagement include disliking the subject material, feeling it is too difficult or not challenging enough, lack of relationship between subject matter and real life, and instruction that is not personalized to student interests. Factors include homework perceived by more than 40% of students as not important in comparison to other activities, lack of relevance of subject matter, too much out-of-school work for irrelevant or uninteresting topics, and lack of relevance of topics covered by homework (Addo, 2023). While the survey includes some responses from teachers, the driving force behind any change in learning or student problem-solving is, too often, the student. Teacher changes to increase student motivation will probably result in more work for the teacher. However, well-designed tools can extend the capability of the teacher and add an entirely new engagement capability. Incorporating current and historical events relevant to the learning process into a curriculum to increase student interest can also help provide real-world relevance while increasing engagement and understanding of the curriculum and addressing a significant student concern. This might include examples from the frontlines of the pandemic, teaching about fairly recent data-based events, and the use of statistical analyses (M. R. Brown, 2023). Student concerns about current and historical events overlap with societal attitudes. We have found that whenever a course is centered on "questions of current interest" and is primarily question-driven, students naturally develop a greater interest in the content, devoting more effort to the course with spontaneous study that lies outside or beyond "just" homework-related questions. We leverage the mechanism that allows AI to play a much more active role in students' motivations than previous technologies did (Yau et al., 2023). Such intrinsic key interest elements can help decrease the "dreaded boredom" factor.

4.4. Personalized Learning With AI

Personalized learning is an educational approach that tailors learning to the student's strengths, weaknesses, abilities, needs, and interests. It allows students to take responsibility for their learning and progress. While this philosophy of learning is appealing, creating personalized learning experiences for many students with diverse instructional materials and activities can be very challenging. It is not realistic; quality companies can steer the personalized learning revolution by developing next-generation teaching assistants, which can facilitate personalized and adaptive learning for individual students or small cohorts and the coaching of learning instructors across multiple academic subjects (Wahed & Pitterson, 2024). Unlike many existing educational tools, these new teaching assistant tools do not create a general plan to tune the educational material and update the support and questions provided to the student in real time based on the student's actual interaction and learning progress. The combination of customized curricula that dynamically adapt to and utilize human instructors uniquely complements and leverages their cognitive capabilities. Furthermore, the richness and sequence of questions and supports tailored to each particular learning moment can be adjusted to reduce the cognitive load, help keep students motivated and engaged, and maximize the learning benefits (K. Kim et al., 2023). These tool effects can make learning easier, more successful, and more humane.

4.5. Assessment and Feedback

The term assessment and feedback is used to describe the process of discovering the extent to which a student has reached the learning goals, giving this information in present and usable form, and, if necessary, providing students with guidance, instruction, and support to help them improve. Summative assessment uses the information to give students their place in relation to others and to existing expectations. At SONIC, as befits an educational environment, the emphasis is on the second and third of these activities (Clayback et al., 2023). The idea of the format is to offer opportunities for summative and formative assessment of students, taking advantage of the capacity for rapid turnaround and authoritative grading by AI in the IT-supported instructional environment, i.e., intelligent tutoring systems. Since students have demonstrated that they can be given instructions by assignments that they can be expected to learn from, there is no reason why assessment and feedback in present and usable form, formative and summative, should not occur in precisely the same way and continuously (Sungur Gul et al., 2023).

Assessment and feedback are controlled by a browser-based interface on the database that contains the test information and student records and on the server that interfaces these systems with software under the control of the AI. This guides the assessment in its interaction with the student, provides feedback to students and instructors, and performs the administrative management functions related to courses. At SONIC, a mixed-mode administration style for large classes, i.e., multiple-choice tests with open-ended answers, is used (Martin et al., 2024). The task of marking open-ended answer scripts is relatively simple and more easily standardized than counterparts for other types of tests, such as those requiring students to produce answers to essay questions or to complete graphical diagrams in their handwriting. The task is simple because the program knows what the answer is and is thus able to award execution marks by evaluating the responses. There are various ways that marks can be foiled. Some can be remedied by programming components to be context-sensitive so that valuable intermediate steps can be recognized and rewarded, and stilted processing can be broken down and repaired (Schilling & Grohs, 2023; Sungur Gul et al., 2023); some impacts of AI-driven instructional tools on K-12 education are presented in Table 2.

Table 2. Impact of AI-Driven Instructional Tools on K-12 Education

Area of Impact	Before AI Integration	After AI Integration	Key Challenges	Future Opportunities	Reference
Personalized Learning	Generic lesson plans	Customized learning paths	Data privacy concerns	More adaptive AI systems	(M. S. Kim & Yu, 2023)
Teacher Workload	High grading burden	Automated grading support	Need for teacher training	AI-powered teacher assistants	(Regan & King-Sears, 2023)
Student Engagement	Passive learning methods	Interactive and gamified learning	Tech accessibility	AI-enhanced immersive experiences	(Sat & Kadirhan, 2024)
Special Education	Limited assistive tools	AI-powered accessibility tools	Ethical concerns	More inclusive AI applications	
Performance Tracking	Manual assessments	AI-driven insights & analytics	Bias in AI decisions	More accurate predictive analytics	(Baker et al., 2023)
Classroom Management	Teacher-led organization	AI-assisted scheduling & monitoring	Resistance to change	AI-driven classroom optimization	(Larkin et al., 2016)
Remote Learning	Limited interaction	AI chatbots & virtual tutors	Internet dependency	AI-driven personalized virtual learning	(Addo, 2023)
STEM Education	Traditional teaching aids	AI-powered simulations & labs	Cost of implementation	More AI-based STEM tools	(M. R. Brown, 2023)
Student Motivation	Lower engagement	AI-driven adaptive content	Over-reliance on AI	AI gamification strategies	(Martin et al., 2024)
Language Learning	Limited digital resources	AI-powered translation tools	Accuracy of AI translation	More multilingual AI tools	(Dean & Gilbert, 2024)
Ethical Considerations	Minimal AI exposure	Increased AI usage in education	Algorithmic bias	Development of responsible AI	(Regan & King-Sears, 2023; Wang et al., 2023)
Digital Literacy	Basic computer skills	Advanced AI-driven learning	Need for digital education	More AI literacy programs	(Crawford & Huling, 2023)

4.6. Collaborative Learning With AI

Our ongoing research is exploring how AI might facilitate collaborative learning. Our focus, in the first instance, is on the numerous pre-existing K-12 educational platforms that students, teachers, and schools are already using in the United States due to the COVID-19 lockdown, and in general, as they are increasingly used to support K-12 education. The research has taken the form of initial interviews with K-12 students and teachers, followed by continued observation of teachers using the technology while attempting to lecture and interact with their students (Pan et al., 2022). The teacher trainers have been involved in the pilot work for our research. Given the scale of the development and the speed with which it is being rolled out, these periodic reviews have enabled us to influence the development of the tools. At the same time, our work has the potential to guide our major attempt to facilitate collaborative constructivist learning. That attempt is to be facilitated by AI. The majority of AI models are, of course, developed and used to process complex data. There are millions of datasets available to researchers, and the number is rapidly increasing as the amount of data grows. However, relatively few researchers are looking to use AI models to improve real-life events by personalizing the perceived data and customizing personal input and support in real-time (Li & Wang, 2022). This is because, in general, AI processes are not usually used in build time, over time, or for teaching and human interaction.

5. ACCESSIBILITY AND INCLUSIVITY IN AI EDUCATION

Proponents of using AI in education look to it as a valuable tool for increasing both the accessibility of educational resources and inclusivity for diverse learning needs. Much of the world, especially developing countries, faces a shortage of properly trained educators and cannot ensure every student has access to personalized attention. AI tools can be an effective substitute or supplement to prioritize learning because they are boundless and can assist longer without fatigue (Sanusi et al., 2022). Moreover, for educators who are already overstretched, being able to leverage AI tools for an added performance boost can be a welcome lifeline. Still, while AI tools are undoubtedly revolutionizing K-12 education, it is necessary to recognize that not every school has the funds to adopt these technologies and that successful, widespread usage does require additional preparations and strategy.

First is the problem with scaling. While utilizing AI for distance education is one way to enhance accessibility, the digital divide is real, and it is important for educators to understand which students have access to these tools and who may be left behind as a result. Minority and low-income students are likely to encounter many obstacles, such as lack of proper access to technology, lower levels of digital literacy, family communication only through languages that are not shared with the respective educational technology, and inefficient home working conditions. Second is the development and adoption of instructional tools (Yeung & Ng, 2024). In order to further benefit K-12 students, the current results need to capitalize on the knowledge and perspectives of insight experts while developing and incorporating instructional tools for AI and education. It is worth noting that the design and research involved in developing evidence-based instructional tools that help diverse users, not just gifted students, substantially learn about AI are incomplete. Educational research should develop new AI knowledge and understanding of how to scaffold diverse undergraduates during the classroom and support educational activities in order to enhance learning performance further (Cipriano & McCarthy, 2023).

5.1. Parental Involvement and Communication

Regular communication with parents can lead to significant improvement in student performance. Parents who engage in regular communication with teachers are more likely to aid their children in their educational pursuits. Schools can use digital learning tools to provide tailored reports to parents to give them a sense of their children's progress. When a parent or guardian can witness the progress their child is making, they can have a significant effect on the child's attitude and motivation to succeed. There is no reason for reports to be presented to either teachers or parents in a standardized format. Authentic communication is important to motivate student growth (Baker et al., 2023). Stakeholders should consider how digital learning tools could be used to foster meaningful connections and change the nature of parent-teacher conferences. The technology could be used to supplement traditional communication with less time-consuming formats that provide ongoing feedback and updates for parents. By integrating new tools with longstanding best practices, educators could create a powerful, flexible solution that supports authentic, consistent communication with parents and family members. As with students interacting with technology, authentic communication remains an essential goal, regardless of the underlying technology (Sat & Kadirhan, 2024). Leaders need to deploy research tools to see when and under what conditions key stakeholders might well accept digital communication technologies.

5.2. Data Privacy and Security

AI is transforming the way education is delivered to students and personalized at an individual level. With the boom of emerging new software and tools, there is also a challenge of protecting students' data. Protecting student data in the educational technology market is a rapidly changing area of policy and practice. Acknowledging this, here are several recommendations for tools focused on supporting students' cognitive and emotional growth: Tools and companies in this space should prioritize privacy and security across the spectrum of design, deployment, and maintenance. Tools and companies in this space should be mindful of how their creations contribute to or inhibit equitable access, opportunity, and outcomes for all (Vartanian, 2024).

Leaders across sectors should set boundaries and drive beneficial innovation through facilitated collaboration and discussion. School communities should provide input into which technologies are adopted and should have real sway over key features. Adaptive learning recommendations did raise some flags in other educational AI documents. Individual learning recommendations may create a variety of additional privacy concerns. For example, in some cases, data or potential inferences from adaptive learning tools contribute to a student's permanent record. Another concern revolves around potential biases in how learning recommendations are generated (Regan & King-Sears, 2023). In some cases, models may produce recommendations based on unrepresentative data or for features that should not be used in predictions due to legal and ethical implications. Finally, educational leaders may be more willing to accept individual learning recommendations than students, educators, and other school stakeholders. In some cases, low adoption rates can signal a mismatch between student, educator, and leader priorities. To prevent these unwanted consequences, tools should align learning recommendations with data privacy laws, requirements, or recommendations for educational technology in general and a student, educator, or leader's administrative and learning resources in particular (M. R. Brown, 2023).

5.3. Evaluating the Effectiveness of AI Tools

In order to evaluate the effectiveness of AI-driven tools in a K-12 educational setting, multi-year trials need to be structured, which include the techniques for student outcomes, teacher responses, and the overall school goals that are aligned. This supporting research will make parents and educators confident and at ease about their guarantee of the effectiveness of these newer student-centered educational approaches. This unambiguous evidence will encourage the quicker adoption of AI-driven teaching across a range of educational domains. Ideally, to evaluate a machine learning application, teachers will follow the same procedure with and without using the digital coaching capability. In this way, it is possible to evaluate the effectiveness of a machine learning application (Rizvi et al., 2023). An AI-driven tool will be considered effective if a) it is easy to use, b) it is feature-rich and able to offer the right kind of support to teachers and students while accommodating different learning styles, c) it can materially improve student learning, and teacher effectiveness, d) all the poor AI-driven capabilities can be addressed with the required training and the addition of adequate computational capacity using modern machine learning techniques. The first point can be ascertained using stable trials with a tool, while the fourth condition is hardware for artificial intelligence technologies. Hosted in the cloud era, where large-scale machine learning systems are available during the pandemic, the infrastructure and the need were clearly demonstrated (De

Souza & Kochhann, 2023). These situations are rare, and they address real-world problems beyond the original AI-driven technologies.

5.4. Global Perspectives on AI in Education

In this project, education leaders and experts from around the world were interviewed about the opportunities and challenges of incorporating the latest developments in artificial intelligence into learning. The research focused on how AI could improve learning at the K-12 level. As it journeys through the life cycle of youths in schools, some AI tools are prescriptive programs to diagnose distress based on student statistics like attendance, grades, performance in standardized tests, health actions like sleep and nutrition, and provide help to teachers, administrators, and stakeholders in emergencies. They may act indirectly over time as both a "predictor" and an "enabler of prevention." They learn how to "anticipate" and handle disturbances by addressing them (Yeung & Ng, 2024). This initial scenario of crisis in schools is founded on the assumption that a certain number of students are lost in the transition from one grade to another or that other community school failures can no longer support ordinary routes like being retained at the previous stage of the academic curriculum. During the period of alarm, the level of acquiescence with which teachers and parents sought additional help tends to be high. The first question about the ethical impact of AI-controlled tools that are used with children at risk of developing learning disabilities or school dropouts is determined by the acceptability differential granted to each actor (Kebritchi et al., 2009).

5.5. Policy Implications and Regulations

International policy designers and regional authorities in Europe and the United States could approach and address a new generation of AI-enhanced educational technology products from three perspectives: technology innovation and curriculum development, technology standardization, safety and assessment, technology cost-effectiveness, consumer affordability, and user privacy (Akgun & Greenhow, 2022). An effective educational technology policy should use the following strategic approach:

(a) accelerate the development of AI technology in education through public-private partnerships, the economic development of the advanced learning technology industry, and workforce learning;
(b) adopt student annual assessments designed to measure effective student learning outcomes and the proficiency of academic standards in AI thinkers and career-capable financial planners;

(c) fund educational investment that drives the cost of instructional technology down in comparison to increased student enrollment, absenteeism, dropouts, on-time completion, and lifetime learning achievement;
(d) launch competitive technology R&D competitions that will allow numerous vendors and laboratories to demonstrate the validity and effectiveness of specific technology products using real-time student achievement-based outcomes. AI-driven educational technology standards enhance manufacturing, safety, and security and level the instructional field that challenges learning-adaptive disruptive educational innovations across the educational marketplace;
(e) support legislation that creates virtual national AI teaching activities designed to implement job skills training and lifelong learning achievement for successful transition from labor to automation through career-capable organizations; fulfill the national mission to raise highly qualified educators in advanced STEM with programs such as the PK-12 advance in-person learning to be promoted to develop AI industry technical leaders.

Most recently, this public education policy should recognize societal trends and accelerate the alignment of AI-enhanced instructional teaching and management staff for the international educational community. In recognition of the continued rapid labor market growth within advanced information technologies for the 2020 to 2030 time frame, collectively advocate for the successful development and widespread application of instructional technology to rapidly match the larger number of efficient faculty members to the expanding, unprecedented qualified student international enrollment at such information technology future evaluations occurring in 2042, 2046, 2050, and 2052 (Cipriano & McCarthy, 2023). Provide targeted innovation funding support for STEM, AI, and life education. Key policy elements indicate that investments should be made in education, including the role of technology in that context, and specifically in result-driven digital resource learning enriched by real-time outcomes in active feedback co-constructed with students. Long-lasting, useful AI-enhanced instructional tools will be crucial components in this decade evolving from rudimentary digital technologies to AI learning systems empowering students worldwide to achieve literacy as well as math and science proficiency, thus developing their critical thinking skills. Social policy advocating this investment is a function of the appropriate level of skill development and the need to train the middle-class workforce, and an economically competitive way of using technology to support the next step of life (Yeung & Ng, 2023).

5.6. Funding and Resource Allocation

First, let's address the question of how much funding is needed. During the hangover from the Great Recession, the United States cut its investment in K-12 education. As student enrollment increased, the ratio of educational spending to GDP dropped. For many states, while educational spending is now increasing, subsequent austerity or redistribution policies are unlikely to allow for such sizable and persistent gains in the future. The academic literature provides scant support for the view that without increasing educational investment, K-12 improvement is unlikely to occur. By some relatively crude metrics, the U.S. is categorized as a high-cost, but not necessarily high-achievement, provider of K-12 education services. It is not true that money does not matter (Forbes et al., 2011). But money is not the total answer. How money is deployed is more important. How much is adequate, or even excessive, is less than fully precise. We know enough, in the fullness of time, to suggest standards for adequate annual spending per student. Wave Two of Educational Reform sees the possibility that the use of augmented intelligence technologies can lead to substantial productivity gains, as they have done in many other industries. Capital investment in R&D has created significant economic value through the design, fabrication, and operational deployment of these AI-based components and systems. Yet, due to relatively small R&D budgets to contribute to public benefit in these existing fields, AI-based research has not been able to contribute per institution-wide AI-driven tools (Sanusi et al., 2022). This lack of investment creates a net economic drain for society. Current capital investment allocations for AI-driven technologies are too small, decreasing over time, and non-strategic. The exceptional economic and social development outcomes created by the internet revolution, leading to the exponential technical trend of devices, software, cloud, content, and engineering services into the 21st century, have not been sustained by AI discourse, data analytics, or smart systems – or any computational models for human learning (Shafik, 2024a).

5.7. Professional Development for Educators

We realize that innovating core instructional strategies with AI is a nontrivial ask. In fact, it is highly probable that, in many cases, AI-enabled strategies will only partially substitute for the excellent work done by many teachers. For the model to be as useful and socially responsible as possible, teachers need clarity on the following.

(a) Faculty oversight and constancy: Effective AI technologies will never fully match the effectiveness of caring, committed adults innovating alongside their pupils. AI instruction should always be read as an AI supplement to mother-tongue human teaching, not one mother tongue for the robot.

(b) Skill-building: Gains in understanding from using AI tools are IT-specific. AI tools should implicitly support students in developing standardized skills such as problem-solving and interdisciplinary cognitive flexibility so that students can more deeply engage with human educators when they mentor and shape language arts and humanities. These pursuits allow students to develop strong human abilities in appreciation and communication. AI could serve as an engagement-enhancing device for classes.

(c) Learning resources, curriculum, and pedagogies that employ these tools should be nurtured and updated constantly based on student performance and educator input. Educators should have ready access to instruction manuals, learning exercises, and forums designed by teams of AI experts and educators who know all the aspects of the tools. These established frameworks should be culturally appropriate and user-friendly.

(d) Directing students: AI tools should be integrated into existing classroom technology and curricula seamlessly. Teachers need to be well-versed in providing rudimentary support to pupils in using these AI tools over time. Additionally, students in the classroom with teacher support and training need to use these AI programs in a manner that is analogous to other learning applications.

(e) AI Tool Evaluation: Educators should take an active role in the oversight of training tools, grading utilities, and remaining focused in ungraded areas. Learning resources will regularly provide direct feedback to educators and should be linked to related professional development on data privacy, technology addiction, and other well-studied concerns.

(f) All these guidelines remain speculative for the time being, but they should provide some insight into substantial action for lawmakers and funders who need to collaborate with local teachers to steer the development of AI tools for the posthuman future. Different teachers and service providers should establish requirements for professional development, usage, software versions, and training data based on variation grounded in real-life use.

6. RESEARCH AND INNOVATION IN AI EDUCATION

Given global challenges in transforming K-12 outcomes as well as formal and informal education experiences and rapidly evolving AI technological capabilities, the time is ripe to invest in cutting-edge innovation to keep the United States ahead of global competitors. Better alignment is necessary between cutting-edge computer science and AI research and education and learning research, practices, and interests. This creates opportunities for advancing new ideas and approaches related to AI in education, including program development, empirical evaluations, and effective implementation. In our analysis, we find that AI has the potential to radically transform K-12 education for students, teachers, and administrators. Such transformation must critically depend on concrete values aligned with innovations to ensure that programmatic and education reform initiatives can rely on AI to address long-standing persistent challenges while also better preparing our nation's next generation of AI designers, builders, and users. AI technologies potentially affect education through virtually all stages and domains of the broad K-12 education system (Baker et al., 2023). For many complex tasks, AI agents are being developed to facilitate human guidance and support for instructors teaching all different types of students. These types of AI applications are already changing how, when, why, and where students' education occurs and expanding the functions of K-12 education in ways previously unimaginable. Good and important work in academia is explicitly not an endpoint of its own, and work in the scholarship domain can be used to help build better tools more responsibly and effectively (Rice et al., 2023). We maintain that pressing and important national-level interest is in deploying effective tools and solutions for real-world education problems faced in diverse local communities. Consequently, we pursue a problem-first approach focused on carefully identifying and addressing the most important challenges that both can and should benefit from the emerging capabilities of state-of-the-art AI research and, in doing so, inform the broader research and practice communities (Sungur Gul et al., 2023).

6.1. Interdisciplinary Approaches to AI Education

Given the deeper connection to other seemingly distant disciplines that AI fosters, it is clear that building education around AI is incomplete without integrating these connections into the curriculum in an explicit way. New interdisciplinary educational opportunities must be designed, including AI-embedded classes, co-taught courses with AI exploration components, AI-accelerated scientific research projects, AI-enhanced experiential learning, and AI-supported virtual and augmented reality visits to remote monuments, physical and biological systems, and social-environmental exploration to prepare our students for the future (Wahed & Pitterson, 2024). We propose an alternative model to transform undergraduate education using AI as the lynchpin across a variety of learners and disciplines. Instead of starting the AI core curriculum with a focus on 'AI technologies' and then suggesting the study of application domain 'electives,' we advocate using a rich, well-thought-out AI and domain course design across all domains. The approach models the future nature of full AI integration in these domains. As such, our approach caters to physics, biology, chemistry, math, computer science, and engineering students regardless of their backgrounds (De Souza & Kochhann, 2023). This allows the respective AI education and domain courses to be at the same engagement upon completion.

6.2. Cultural and Socioeconomic Considerations

AI in the classroom is set to benefit all students by providing adaptive learning and helping to individualize instruction. But we must be increasingly mindful as we design AI about the digital equity issues it may inadvertently create or exacerbate as well. As new tools are being designed, educators are increasingly able to efficiently tailor learning experiences to the needs of individual students or distinct groups of students through AI. AI has the potential to revolutionize education—but only if we design education technologies and AI in ways that address equity and diversity. With AI and the seamless collection of data that feeds it, the gap between students with and without access to expensive personalized learning tools has the potential to grow (Kebritchi et al., 2009). In many classrooms, inequity in educational resources can manifest as different tools accessible to different groups of students—or no tools accessible to anyone. Many teachers, particularly in resource-limited schools, do not have access to some of the educational technologies that use data to improve instruction that their colleagues in better-funded schools do. These findings raise important questions about the inputs to personalized learning: from the instructional materials to the teacher's professional development to the time to actually integrate technology into teacher and student practice. Now that AI-driven instructional tools are more available, educators must advocate for resources and access to these tools for all students. These products must also be designed for all students from the start (Li & Wang, 2022). Educators from different backgrounds will likely require different features to make educational technology beneficial to students—so educators must be part of the design process from the outset.

6.3. Building Partnerships in AI Education

Transforming K-12 education with AI instructional tools will require collaboration among diverse stakeholders. These tools will teach the content of the school and also, more broadly, educate the students studying that content, essentially serving as artificial teachers. While this approach will improve access to and outcomes from K-12 education, it will also demand quality and ethics from AI instructional tools. These educational resources will require iterative, interdisciplinary, and research-based development (Rizvi et al., 2023). The content of schools is not just academic; students also learn language, social and emotional processing, and how to regulate their behavior. AI needs partners in the humanities, social sciences, and helping professions to design curricula that encompass the school subject area and these other kinds of learning, as well as to thoroughly vet educational resources before launching them. Scholars from the humanities, education, social sciences, law, and business will need to work with AI researchers to create this third wave of AI and K-12 education because it will require interdisciplinary research and collaborative partnerships to succeed (Sungur Gul et al., 2023). A useful first step for these partnerships would be to compile a toolkit of existing resources that identify high-quality, bias-free, and privacy-protecting applications of AI in service to classrooms, educational administration, auxiliary services, and school culture. School leaders, teachers, and other stakeholders might use this toolkit to narrow the gap between K-12 education and investment in other vertical markets that hinder AI-driven tools. Such a toolkit would organize AI research oriented towards the needs of school consumers and form the basis of a coherent research agenda (Regan & King-Sears, 2023). Additionally, it could strengthen global leadership in educational AI.

6.4. Community Engagement and Support

As educational tools continue to proliferate, efforts to support effective tool adoption throughout the educational community will become more important. Such adoption support is essential for training purposes as teachers learn how best to incorporate new technologies into their classroom processes and instructional strategies into their lesson plans and activities. Over the past decade, efforts to engage teacher communities in alignment and design work around educational standards and curriculum have had important payoffs (Dean & Gilbert, 2024). We would like to see more similar types of groups formed around other important teacher functions, such as teacher feedback on educational tools, collaboration on evidence of what works, and how to incorporate these tools, perhaps to inform other teachers' understanding of broad standards, curriculum, and other school or district-based goals. In many cases, there are existing infrastructures and communities for keeping and sharing these resources (Halverson et al., 2023). Yet there are also dozens of issues to address if these types of groups are to really make a long-term, material difference. These include:

(a) addressing appropriateness and controlling price points;
(b) expediting workflow by integrating these tool resources more seamlessly into existing teaching resources and activities;
(c) broadly evaluating effectiveness to validate the work;
(d) creating incentives for the population to contribute their learning artifacts just as they now donate classroom materials;
(e) establishing best collaboration practices;

(f) constructing format and tagging standards to ensure easy access for all teacher stakeholders including administrators, pre-service teachers, online educators, etc.; and ultimately;
(g) gaining wide acceptance from both the teaching community itself as well as the education technology community. At the same time, this community engagement and tool creation process must be included as part of the process because compelling standalone resources do not create larger post-adoption teacher engagement and structure.

6.5. AI-Driven Curricular Design

Each student has a unique learning path: they have unique skills and knowledge gaps, find different examples easier or harder to understand, and have different misconceptions. Instruction should adapt to meet the needs of each student. AI can revolutionize the way we teach. AI can drive the development of a richer, more structured, and better-aligned curriculum, optimized for the diverse learning paths of students (J. C. Brown, 2017). Designing an AI-driven curriculum is both a huge responsibility and an extraordinary opportunity. We need to develop curricular design principles, assemble high-quality curricular building blocks, and develop algorithms that assemble those blocks into curricula customized for various learning goals. It is a huge responsibility because students depend on their education to acquire skills that allow them to live flourishing lives, contribute to their families, communities, and democracies, and apply their talents and training in service of important challenges (Pan et al., 2022). Moreover, with only 12 to 13 years of compulsory education, K-12 schooling is the final opportunity for most citizens in most countries to acquire the skills and knowledge necessary for effective citizenship; important life activities; colleges, universities, and vocational programs; and the foundation for later lifelong learning. Failure to provide high-quality skills and knowledge during compulsory education limits the life prospects of individuals and limits the performance of democracy, the economy, and society (Rizvi et al., 2023).

6.6. Impact of AI on Educational Outcomes

AI technology uses an algorithm to predict student behavior, thereby achieving personalized learning and feedback. Personalized content is created, and boot camp automation is improved. EdTech companies are developing products to create content that helps develop individual learning plans for students. In addition to personalized homework for individual student needs, assistive learning and teaching material creation can be tailored to the individual. Students who use smart teaching materials for auxiliary learning show an increase in academic performance compared to those who do not. Male students respond well to tagging learning materials with learning statuses (De Souza & Kochhann, 2023). Evaluating AI-driven communication tools in teaching platforms and using these tools for students from the three universities as teaching assistants, the learning effect after class and the satisfaction of both teachers and students are improved. Student chatbots are trained for personalized counseling. Masculine tags improve the effectiveness of smart material use in school. In analyzing the learning platform, the chatbot helped students obtain information and troubleshoot system problems that supported conversation services using voice functions. In teaching, learners develop communication skills. They also help in material management. According to relevant statistics, this AI-driven application has freed teachers from ready-made queries and task monitoring, significantly increasing the resources for teaching.

6.7. Adaptive Learning Systems

Adaptive learning systems (ALS) have made significant progress over the past two decades. A robust ALS provides personalized instruction to each individual student. The system collects data from the students' actions on the system and uses machine learning and a predictive model of the students' learning to determine such fundamentals about the students' knowledge as the probability that the student has mastered a unit of content. A more complete realization of adaptive learning would integrate other aspects of the learning experience, such as timing, additional behavior, and, importantly, more mechanisms of formative assessment, with the ability to ask students complex questions ineligible for fully automated scoring and analysis traditionally used by the ALS (J. C. Brown, 2017). This question packet evaluates and scores a unique constructed response from an individual student for each unit of the instructional sequence. The activity utilizes AI and machine learning techniques to know an individual student's point of relative readiness to engage successfully with the content of interest and adaptively determine which subsequent activity is assigned. The texts of the constructed-response questions are generated by a deep neural network language model that represents the meaning of the prompt in other ways (Yau et al., 2023). The constructed-response scoring algorithm is sophisticated and comprehensive, as it uses genre prediction, resolution, coherence, adherence, understanding of the task, and construction features.

6.8. Gamification and AI in Education

AI and gamification must be used in the field of education to keep educational material fun, engaging, and relevant. The need for students to be motivated to pursue their education is becoming increasingly apparent. As the number of easy digital distractions continues to rise, schools are having trouble fostering enthusiasm for higher education and industry. By creating educational software with gamers in mind, students can be taught social studies, science, math, and language arts in the same manner they would play their favorite games at home (Baker et al., 2023). If you can make drinking water or preventing an industrial food waste disaster entertaining, you can make education fun to learn. Our society's future citizens are dying of academic boredom, and they don't even know it. These educational tools are not designed to replace the teacher, but instead be used individually by students as they advance at their own pace. How is this accomplished? The tools guide the student to the correct answer using the process of educational simulation mastery learning. The tutor should not answer in a yes/no manner during any part of the learning process. The AI is designed to give effective, natural feedback to the student in a way that is supportive and engaging (Vartanian, 2024). Each student can learn specific scholastic subjects without the learning pace coordination plates that normally create passive learners.

6.9. Virtual and Augmented Reality in AI Education

Virtual and augmented reality (VR and AR) are fast becoming more popular and developed technologies. They are used in games, exploration, and research missions, and even in healthcare for physical therapy and mental rehabilitation. These technologies are bringing about significant changes in many industries, as they advance dramatically with the help of better VR/AR gear. The majority of uses are still entertainment for now, but that won't last for very long. The training and instructional potential of these technologies, especially when combined with the latest advances in AI and big data, are the reason that the investment in these technologies in both consumer markets and business applications rose significantly and is expected to continue rising (Crawford & Huling, 2023). Recent research in neuroscience indicates that immersion, cognition, reward, embodiment, attention, and emotion play key roles in deep learning for information, knowledge, insight, and resilience. Also, with the data and feedback loops with AR and AI, the information and adjusted training content can be significantly more effective and efficient than those provided by selected instructors. It's also nice that the AI/AR system will understand the state and needs of each and every student at all times. In the meantime, what's the impact? That is, how will learning differ with significant investment in VR and AR in a world with these learning systems in use? In short, educational content can be made more engaging, effective, or efficient, while also significantly reducing the need for actual instructors. In the long run, these technologies may make or instruct if not education itself of little to no value. What we need next is for AI/AR learning systems to reach sufficient capability (Sat & Kadirhan, 2024).

Also, we need to better understand the unique needs and outcomes in education. Their potential should be tested with high-quality content and testing on a large number of students.

7. NATURAL LANGUAGE PROCESSING IN EDUCATION

One important use of natural language processing is in the field of education. Educators work with students on a one-to-one basis or in small groups, understanding student needs and adjusting instruction to suit those needs. In an ideal world, AI could be used to provide instruction that is similar to that given by humans. Computerized learning environments can collect vast amounts of data much more easily than teachers and provide a much richer view of the students using the system. This technology holds the promise of delivering individualized, flexible instruction through human-computer interfaces (Hidayatullah et al., 2023). NLP tools provide initial pathways for translating between human knowledge and the computer's formalized symbolic knowledge. While the potential is clear, existing applications are not yet at the stage where AI exercise systems operate at the level of sophistication offered by human speech and error correction. This involves not only being able to parse a wide range of student responses, but also modeling and interacting with students in a manner akin to human social interaction, relating both to how students are most comfortable learning and also how AI exercise partners can be most effective (Crawford & Huling, 2023).

7.1. Machine Learning Algorithms in Instruction

There are now many machine learning algorithms capable of processing vast data sets to predict student outcomes at the classroom, school, and district levels, assume the role of virtual tutors, or help educators monitor students' educational content. Machine learning can also offer genuinely personalized learning and adapt learning material to help children across the spectrum of needs to learn deeply, with a longer lasting impact on learning by solving the ever-changing open-ended problem. The most relevant machine learning algorithms powered instructional tools in K-12 education are intelligent tutoring systems, knowledge tracing models, and expert systems (Vartanian, 2024). An area of knowledge can be defined and refined for a student who expects a sufficiently high probability of mastering their contents. By applying these concepts to learning materials at each layer using greedy layer-wise pre-training supervised learning, the fact that a student mastered the contents at a simple layer inversely brings a higher probability of understanding contents at a more complex layer underscores the possible effective applications in education.

Mutual information between latent representations and skills was leveraged to perform unsupervised fine-tuning of pre-trained networks (Madden, 2024). A deep learning objective-based learning was demonstrated with relatively high constraints on mutual information learning which makes it possible to facilitate effective transfer learning in learning systems.

7.2. Robotics and AI in the Classroom

Robotics and AI have the potential to revolutionize instruction by enabling adaptive, personalized, and engaging learning opportunities for students. However, deployments of diverse AI applications in educational settings are limited by practical challenges of integrating these technologies into existing educational practices, policies, and infrastructure. To understand the potential benefits of and challenges to leveraging advanced technologies in the K–12 setting, this chapter reviews the literature that informs our understanding of robotics and AI for K–12 instruction, provides illustrative examples of several promising robotics and AI-driven instructional tools, and presents recommendations for how U.S. educational systems can harness the potential of robotics and AI technologies to personalize, engage, and prepare all K–12 students for the future of work (Wahed & Pitterson, 2024). While technology has played a prominent role in improving efficiency and creating new opportunities in modern society, educational approaches are often flexible and tailored to individual student potential, progress, and needs, regardless of specific domain or skills. For instance, students are grouped with peers according to their ability, are assigned grade-appropriate work, and receive personalized feedback in high-performing classrooms. However, educational technology for such personalized instructional approaches is only just starting to emerge, and early implementations are primarily based on software applications that do not have sufficiently advanced AI algorithms needed to analyze the performance of school environments and to dynamically match instruction (Yau et al., 2023). Further, while computer-assisted instruction and intelligent tutoring systems have been available for several decades, insights from learning sciences, pedagogical shifts, and desirable skill domains have only recently begun to inform the design of early educational technology tools.

7.3. Neuroscience and AI in Learning

Biologically inspired AI technologies have great potential to transform a student's learning process for several reasons. First and foremost, they can provide individually adaptable learning assistance, freeing students in a classroom from the tyranny of the bell curves, a source of widespread frustration, dread, disengagement, and performance bottlenecks. Neuroscience provides a technology roadmap, describing multiple learning and developmental strategies for combined brain-body regions, cascading circuits that achieve the remarkable abilities of a young child and their approximate adult-level performance within 3 to 5 years (De Souza & Kochhann, 2023). Therefore, I believe that neurobiology will continue to be unsurpassed as a developmental and learning technology generator in the future, far beyond 20 or 30 years when AI, with appropriately re-engineered architectures, will be complementary, robust, and productive alternatives. There is a mismatch between the principles of learning derived from biology versus those currently used. Consider that written exams and national literacy indices are weak execution metrics for brain intelligence and learning goals. Brain intelligence is efficient, deeply attentive, engaged, creative, impressions are enduring, retrievable, changeable without effort, and are easily deployed (Yeung & Ng, 2023).

Content is chosen and delivered in rich sequential chunks which illuminate a broader context, power robust, flexible, intuitive abilities, are applied in adaptive, inventive ways, are practiced with rich, diverse knowledge, and finally are evaluated with respect to value-based and affect-based criteria. To accelerate the transformation, it is suggested that the development goals of AI in education should be reframed by challenging them to provide the systems-specific enumerations for system-neuro principles. Then AI's role will synergize, complement, and accelerate such cooperative development. In summary, we are at the threshold of a role transformation for education systems which is that of being not a driver of our obsession-driven economies and cultures, but a gallery stability barometer, a learning system facilitator, and a nurturant for beneficial brain learning and development. The future possibilities of an educational ensemble featuring cooperation integrated neuro principles and biologically inspired AI in education are truly splendid and their successful realization could substantially reduce adverse effects (Sungur Gul et al., 2023).

7.4. The Role of Big Data in Education

Big data increasingly plays a significant role in a variety of fields. In the field of education, we see a growing number of publishers and edtech companies starting to use data-driven methodologies that help personalize learning. Big data is yielding important insights about key factors that impact student outcomes and behaviors, from the effect of technology usage to the influence of the time of day. As K-12 education transitions away from a seat-time-based system of credits toward a mastery-based model, big data holds great promise for achieving a more flexible and personalized system where all students have the best chance to succeed. However, big data should be treated with caution, as in other fields, unrestrained use can lead to incorrect results and is susceptible to biases (Özgür, 2023). Therefore, some best practices should be considered to ensure data reliability and will be explained in this chapter.

It is known that machine learning algorithms have been developed and improved upon over recent years, and their success has led to much of the data revolution. It is difficult to argue against the power of ensemble learning, boosting methods, and deep learning techniques with artificial neural networks to recognize pictures and voices among other tasks. Yet the social science of education is by no means as advanced or characterized by as many clear, moving targets for predictive modeling. A very large and steady stream of data about student performance and student outcomes is being collected and is available for international testing datasets, as well as individual state testing data, which can inform the basic and complex problem of how to most reliably and validly measure different students' achievements and success (De Souza & Kochhann, 2023). It is then the methodological or computational approach to the challenge, the outcome of which we do not yet understand. Indeed, it seems that the answer is applied in redacting standards based on minimal inputs in the form of high-stakes test scores within the Department of Education.

7.5. AI Ethics and Bias Mitigation

With the growing trend of using AI and machine learning tools in education, the AI in education community, as well as education technology companies, should pay deeper attention to ethical and fairness concerns while designing and deploying these technologies. Change in student performance from previous times to current times is used as a measure to assess the fairness of machine learning recommendations. AI tools reduce educational opportunity gaps based on race and gender. The first strategy for ensuring fairness is to clearly define fairness (Cipriano & McCarthy, 2023). Then we can identify the causes of unfairness. Given the sensitivity of personal data, users may oppose the collection and use of such data and hence opt out of systems that require personal data. In such a case, using a differential privacy framework to ensure privacy while performing data analysis is necessary to avoid people dropping out of education systems. Technology may qualitatively change the nature of learning and instruction. These changes may result in large economic gains for the students who learn and use the technology. However, the other students who require different support and instruction will be more likely left out (Bhowmik & Kim, 2022; Yeung & Ng, 2024). This will be the prime concern. Another fact that adds pressure is the improvement over human teaching, but technologically assisted instruction will always require students to engage with technology. All students need to be given the opportunity to meaningfully engage with these technologies. With technology performing the majority of the tasks in education, it leads to inequity in job opportunities for teachers as well. The workforce declines as well (Baker et al., 2023). The first step is to understand strategies that are already in use in the classroom, to learn more about how teachers anticipate incorporating AI in their work, and to identify where AI tools can provide the most value.

8. FUTURE TRENDS

The future of artificial intelligence in education is set to evolve from discrete applications into a systemic ecosystem of intelligent, equitable, and adaptive learning environments. As educational institutions worldwide increasingly embrace AI-augmented learning, the next decade will see a shift toward context-aware, multimodal, and personalized systems that respond dynamically to learners' cognitive, emotional, and behavioral states. The integration of natural language processing, robotics, and neuroscience-driven models will enable emotionally responsive and neuro-adaptive learning experiences, bridging the gap between machine precision and human empathy. These advances will help educators move beyond static content delivery toward holistic, learner-centered pedagogies supported by real-time data analytics (UNESCO, 2023a). Another defining trend will be the mainstreaming of AI literacy as a core educational competency. Frameworks such as UNESCO's AI Competency Framework for Students and Teachers (2023a) and the OECD's AI and the Future of Skills Initiative (2022) emphasize the importance of equipping learners to understand, critique, and ethically use AI systems. The future classroom will not merely teach students with AI but also about AI—cultivating critical awareness of algorithmic decision-making, data privacy, and bias detection. This shift will empower learners to become informed digital citizens and ethical AI co-creators, capable of navigating complex socio-technical environments (UNESCO, 2023b; OECD, 2022).

A third emerging direction lies in the convergence of neuro-inspired AI and cognitive neuroscience. Biologically grounded AI architectures, including brain–computer interfaces (BCIs) and neuromorphic computing models, are beginning to replicate aspects of human cognition such as perception, adaptability, and contextual reasoning. When applied to education, these technologies will enable adaptive cognitive scaffolding, dynamically adjusting instruction based on neural feedback and engagement levels. This integration of neuroscience and AI will mark a transformative phase in which learning systems evolve from data-driven prediction to cognition-informed personalization, aligning technological precision with human developmental science (De Souza & Kochhann, 2023). Therefore, the global educational landscape will increasingly prioritize ethical, inclusive, and sustainable AI deployment. Future systems will rely on federated learning and differential privacy mechanisms to ensure data sovereignty and protect students' rights. UNESCO and

UNICEF's recent initiatives highlight the necessity of human-centric AI design, emphasizing cultural diversity, accessibility, and gender inclusion in AI-enabled education. The future will therefore be characterized by AI ecosystems that are both technologically advanced and socially accountable, where innovation serves not only efficiency but also justice, empathy, and lifelong learning (UNESCO, 2021; UNICEF, 2020).

9. POLICY IMPLICATIONS

The policy landscape must evolve to ensure that technological progress translates into equitable and ethical educational transformation. Policymakers are encouraged to align with UNESCO's Recommendation on the Ethics of Artificial Intelligence (2021) and UNICEF's Policy Guidance on AI for Children (2020), which provide actionable frameworks for ensuring transparency, accountability, and inclusivity. By embedding these global ethical standards into national education strategies, governments can safeguard learners' rights while promoting innovation that is context-sensitive and socially responsible (UNESCO, 2021; UNICEF, 2020). To achieve this, national education policies must institutionalize AI literacy, data governance, and ethical design principles. Curriculum reforms should ensure that students and teachers alike understand how AI systems function, make decisions, and influence learning outcomes. Governments should establish independent ethics councils and AI observatories to monitor the use of educational data, ensuring algorithmic fairness and accountability. Simultaneously, public–private partnerships can drive localized AI innovation, ensuring that digital tools are tailored to linguistic, cultural, and infrastructural realities of each region, particularly in developing contexts (OECD, 2022; Wahed & Pitterson, 2024). Hence, long-term sustainability will depend on capacity-building and global collaboration. Policymakers should support professional development programs that empower educators to effectively integrate AI into teaching practice while maintaining pedagogical autonomy. Investment in inclusive infrastructure, open-source educational datasets, and cross-border research collaborations will foster AI-enabled educational sovereignty—a future where education systems are technologically empowered, ethically guided, and resilient in the face of global change (UNESCO, 2023a; Bhowmik & Kim, 2022).

10. CONCLUSION

In this chapter, we have discussed AI-driven instructional tools—particularly those that weave together knowledge-driven AI methods and learning sciences findings—to bring about a transformative way to foster effective teaching and address personalized learning for diverse learners. We have provided many directions for future work on AI for K–12 education and discussed the many technical and non-technical challenges. We hope that these directions will enable the research community, practitioners, educational policymakers, and funding agencies to jointly move forward the exciting frontier in improving the effectiveness of K–12 education and research. It is great that we are witnessing a sharp increase in the number of researchers in artificial intelligence (AI) who are seriously thinking about AI in preK–12 education. Now we need to move beyond focusing solely on making small innovations in isolated problems. Instead, research projects should also develop useful AI tools and have in mind concrete paths to get these implemented, extensively studied, and appropriately deployed, so that they reach a critical mass of learners and can therefore exert the impact we hope for. We believe that many interesting and important questions will both be discovered and explored through a combination of the deep interplay of AI and the learning sciences and of the engagement among the developmental, application, and deployment stages of AI-driven tools, machine learning, and related areas. We hope that AI researchers can take learning sciences findings into account and that educational researchers become more familiar with and utilize AI techniques. Certainly, the goal of effective teaching and learning, and of furthering understanding of how humans learn, is deeply satisfying to work on.

REFERENCES

Abubakari, M. S., Shafik, W., & Hidayatullah, A. F. (2024). Evaluating the Potential of Artificial Intelligence in Islamic Religious Education: A SWOT Analysis Overview. In *AI-Enhanced Teaching Methods* (pp. 216–239). IGI Global. DOI: 10.4018/979-8-3693-2728-9.ch010

Addo, S. A. (2023). Are You Ready to Teach AI in Schools? Teachers' Perspectives of Teaching AI in K-12 Settings. *ACM International Conference Proceeding Series*. DOI: 10.1145/3610969.3610973

Addo, S. A., & Sentance, S. (2023). Teachers' Motivation for Teaching AI in K-12 settings. *ACM International Conference Proceeding Series*. DOI: 10.1145/3633083.3633192

Akgun, S., & Greenhow, C. (2022). Artificial Intelligence (AI) in Education: Addressing Societal and Ethical Challenges in K-12 Settings. *Proceedings of International Conference of the Learning Sciences, ICLS*. DOI: 10.1007/s43681-021-00096-7

Baker, B. A., Davis, S., Wilkins-Yel, K. G., Mukherjee, A., & Paneto, A. (2023). "It's the Teacher's Responsibility:" Examining Pre-service and In-service Teachers' Responses to Racial Discrimination. *Journal of Educational & Psychological Consultation*, *33*(2), 201–229. Advance online publication. DOI: 10.1080/10474412.2022.2104300

Bhowmik, D., & Kim, M. (2022). Ethical governance of AI in education: Challenges and frameworks for equitable access. *Journal of Educational Technology Research*, *45*(2), 175–192. DOI: 10.5281/zenodo.15667060

Bhowmik, S. (2023). K-12 ESL Writing Instruction: Learning to Write or Writing to Learn Language? *TESL Canada Journal*, *39*(2). Advance online publication. DOI: 10.18806/tesl.v39i2/1376

Bhowmik, S., & Kim, M. (2022). ESL Writing Instruction in K-12 Settings: Pedagogical Approaches and Classroom Techniques. *Language and Literature*, *24*(2), 174–197. Advance online publication. DOI: 10.20360/langandlit29612

Brown, J. C. (2017). A metasynthesis of the complementarity of culturally responsive and inquiry-based science education in K-12 settings: Implications for advancing equitable science teaching and learning. *Journal of Research in Science Teaching*, *54*(9), 1143–1173. Advance online publication. DOI: 10.1002/tea.21401

Brown, M. R. (2023). Educators' accounts of White racial advantage in K-12 settings: Mitigating disadvantages for non-White students. *Multicultural Education Review*, *15*(3), 185–203. Advance online publication. DOI: 10.1080/2005615X.2023.2287697

Cipriano, C., & McCarthy, M. F. (2023). Towards an inclusive social and emotional learning. *Social and Emotional Learning: Research, Practice, and Policy*, *2*, 100008. Advance online publication. DOI: 10.1016/j.sel.2023.100008

Clayback, K. A., Williford, A. P., & Vitiello, V. E. (2023). Identifying Teacher Beliefs and Experiences Associated with Curriculum Implementation Fidelity in Early Childhood Education. *Prevention Science*, *24*(1), 27–38. Advance online publication. DOI: 10.1007/s11121-022-01414-z PMID: 35921059

Crawford, K., & Huling, H. (2023). Building Classroom Community in Elementary Literacy Methods Courses. *Georgia Journal of Literacy*, *45*(1). Advance online publication. DOI: 10.56887/galiteracy.69

De Souza, A. S., & Kochhann, A. (2023). Extensionist training in the landscape of opportunities and challenges for reframing teacher education in K-12 settings: A systematic literature review. *REVISTA FOCO*, *16*(10), e3297. Advance online publication. DOI: 10.54751/revistafoco.v16n10-065

De Souza, M., & Kochhann, R. (2023). Neuroscience and artificial intelligence in learning systems. *International Journal of Cognitive Technologies in Education*, *12*(1), 34–58. DOI: 10.5281/zenodo.15667060

Dean, S. N., & Gilbert, A. (2024). 'Watching what they can do on their own is beautiful': A navigation of shared agency in school-based outdoor environmental education. *Journal of Adventure Education and Outdoor Learning*. Advance online publication. DOI: 10.1080/14729679.2024.2314605

Forbes, S. A., Ross, M. E., & Chesser, S. S. (2011). Single-subject designs and action research in the K-12 setting. *Educational Research and Evaluation*, *17*(3), 161–173. Advance online publication. DOI: 10.1080/13803611.2011.599555

Halverson, L. R., Spring, K. J., Huyett, S., Henrie, C. R., & Graham, C. R. (2023). Blended Learning Research in Higher Education and K-12 Settings. In *Learning, Design, and Technology*. DOI: 10.1007/978-3-319-17727-4_31-2

Hidayatullah, A. F., Kalinaki, K., Aslam, M. M., Zakari, R. Y., & Shafik, W. (2023). Fine-Tuning BERT-Based Models for Negative Content Identification on Indonesian Tweets. *ICITDA 2023 - Proceedings of the 2023 8th International Conference on Information Technology and Digital Applications*. DOI: 10.1109/ICITDA60835.2023.10427046

Kebritchi, M., Hirumi, A., Kappers, W., & Henry, R. (2009). Analysis of the supporting websites for the use of instructional games in K-12 settings. *British Journal of Educational Technology*, *40*(4), 733–754. Advance online publication. DOI: 10.1111/j.1467-8535.2008.00854.x

Kim, K., Kwon, K., Ottenbreit-Leftwich, A., Bae, H., & Glazewski, K. (2023). Exploring middle school students' common naive conceptions of Artificial Intelligence concepts, and the evolution of these ideas. *Education and Information Technologies*, *28*(8), 9827–9854. Advance online publication. DOI: 10.1007/s10639-023-11600-3

Kim, M. S., & Yu, F. (2023). 'Teacher data literacies practice' meets 'pedagogical documentation': A scoping review. In *Review of Education* (Vol. 11, Issue 2). DOI: 10.1002/rev3.3414

Lampropoulos, G., & Papadakis, S. (2025). The Educational Value of Artificial Intelligence and Social Robots. In *Social Robots in Education* (pp. 3–15). Springer., DOI: 10.1007/978-3-031-82915-4_1

Larkin, I. M., Brantley-Dias, L., & Lokey-Vega, A. (2016). Job satisfaction, organizational commitment, and turnover intention of online teachers in the K-12 setting. *Online Learning : the Official Journal of the Online Learning Consortium*, *20*(3). Advance online publication. DOI: 10.24059/olj.v20i3.986

Lavidas, K., Papadakis, S., Manesis, D., Grigoriadou, A. S., & Gialamas, V.Lectures and Lab Classes. (2022a). The effects of social desirability on students' self-reports in two social contexts: Lectures vs. lectures and lab classes. *Information (Basel)*, *13*(10), 491. DOI: 10.3390/info13100491

Lavidas, K., Petropoulou, A., Papadakis, S., Apostolou, Z., Komis, V., Jimoyiannis, A., & Gialamas, V. (2022b). Factors affecting response rates of the web survey with teachers. *Computers*, *11*(9), 127. DOI: 10.3390/computers11090127

Li, S., & Wang, W. (2022). Effect of blended learning on student performance in K-12 settings: A meta-analysis. In *Journal of Computer Assisted Learning* (Vol. 38, Issue 5). DOI: 10.1111/jcal.12696

Madden, V. J. (2024). Vocal Awareness and K-12 Education: A Qualitative Research Study. *Voice & Speech Review*, *18*(1), 18–33. Advance online publication. DOI: 10.1080/23268263.2022.2062851

Martin, F., Zhuang, M., & Schaefer, D. (2024). Systematic review of research on artificial intelligence in K-12 education (2017–2022). In *Computers and Education* (Vol. 6). Artificial Intelligence., DOI: 10.1016/j.caeai.2023.100195

Meecha, C. (2023). Professional Development within the K-12 Setting. In *Career Pathways in Adult Education.* Perspectives and Opportunities., DOI: 10.4324/9781003259602-23

Morrison, G. (2023). Literature Review: The Impact of Invisibility on Diasporic Indigenous Students in K-12 Settings. In *Journal of Latinos and Education.* DOI: 10.1080/15348431.2023.2291682

Organisation for Economic Co-operation and Development (OECD). (2022). AI and the future of skills: Challenges for education and assessment. OECD Publishing. https://oecd.ai/en/

Özgür, T. (2023). Active learning improves academic achievement and learning retention in K-12 settings: A meta-analysis. *I-Manager's Journal on School Educational Technology*, *18*(3), jsch.18.3.19288. Advance online publication. DOI: 10.26634/jsch.18.3.19288

Pan, Y., Ke, F., & Xu, X. (2022). A systematic review of the role of learning games in fostering mathematics education in K-12 settings. In *Educational Research Review* (Vol. 36). DOI: 10.1016/j.edurev.2022.100448

Regan, K., & King-Sears, M. (2023). A Scaffolded Model for Preparing Doctoral Students to Teach in Higher Education. *Journal of Special Education Preparation*, *3*(3), 38–47. Advance online publication. DOI: 10.33043/JOSEP.3.3.38-47

Rice, M. F., Cantergiani, K., & Macias, D. (2023). A research-based conceptual framework for inclusive K-12 online, distance, and digital education. *Journal of Research on Technology in Education.* Advance online publication. DOI: 10.1080/15391523.2023.2264982

Rizvi, S., Waite, J., & Sentance, S. (2023). Artificial Intelligence teaching and learning in K-12 from 2019 to 2022: A systematic literature review. *Computers and Education: Artificial Intelligence*, *4*, 100145. Advance online publication. DOI: 10.1016/j.caeai.2023.100145

Sanusi, I. T., Olaleye, S. A., Oyelere, S. S., & Dixon, R. A. (2022). Investigating learners' competencies for artificial intelligence education in an African K-12 setting. *Computers and Education Open*, *3*, 100083. Advance online publication. DOI: 10.1016/j.caeo.2022.100083

Sat, M., & Kadirhan, Z. (2024). Unveiling competence in the classroom: A multidimensional assessment of computer science teachers' self-efficacy in coding education. *Education and Information Technologies.* Advance online publication. DOI: 10.1007/s10639-024-12503-7

Schilling, M. R., & Grohs, J. (2023). Developing a Tool for the Assessment of Systems Thinking in K-12 Settings. *Proceedings - Frontiers in Education Conference, FIE*. DOI: 10.1109/FIE58773.2023.10343175

Shafik, W. (2024a). Deep Learning Impacts in the Field of Artificial Intelligence. In *Deep Learning Concepts in Operations Research* (pp. 9–26). Auerbach Publications., DOI: 10.1201/9781003433309-2

Shafik, W. (2024b). Enhancing AI-Enabled Education Through Mobile Learning and Bring Your Own Device (BYOD) Integration. In *Exploring Youth Studies in the Age of AI* (pp. 140–173). IGI Global. DOI: 10.4018/979-8-3693-3350-1.ch008

Shafik, W. (2024c). Generative AI for Social Good and Sustainable Development. In Raza, K., Ahmad, N., & Singh, D. (Eds.), *Generative AI: Current Trends and Applications. Studies in Computational Intelligence* (Vol. 1177). Springer., DOI: 10.1007/978-981-97-8460-8_10

Shafik, W. (2024d). Mobile Learning and Bring Your Own Device (BYOD): Enhancing Education in the Digital Age. In *Integrating Cutting-Edge Technology Into the Classroom* (pp. 240–267). IGI Global. DOI: 10.4018/979-8-3693-3124-8.ch012

Shafik, W. (2024e). Towards Trustworthy and Explainable AI Educational Systems. In *Explainable AI for Education: Recent Trends and Challenges* (pp. 17–41). Springer. DOI: 10.1007/978-3-031-72410-7_2

Shafik, W. (2025). Human-Computer Interaction (HCI) Technologies in Socially-Enabled Artificial Intelligence. In *Future of Digital Technology and AI in Social Sectors* (pp. 121–150). IGI Global. DOI: 10.4018/979-8-3693-5533-6.ch005

Sungur Gul, K., Saylan Kirmizigul, A., Ates, H., & Garzon, J. (2023). Advantages and Challenges of STEM Education in K-12: Systematic Review and Research Synthesis. *International Journal of Research in Education and Science*, *9*(2), 283–307. Advance online publication. DOI: 10.46328/ijres.3127

UNESCO. (2021). Recommendation on the ethics of artificial intelligence. United Nations Educational, Scientific and Cultural Organization. https://www.unesco.org/en/articles/recommendation-ethics-artificial-intelligence

UNESCO. (2023a). AI competency framework for students and teachers. United Nations Educational, Scientific and Cultural Organization. https://www.unesco.org/en/articles/ai-competency-framework-teachers

UNESCO. (2023b). Guidelines for AI literacy in education systems. United Nations Educational, Scientific and Cultural Organization. https://unesdoc.unesco.org/ark:/48223/pf0000386693

UNICEF. (2020). *Policy guidance on artificial intelligence for children*. United Nations Children's Fund., DOI: 10.1111/chso.12915

Vartanian, A. M. (2024). Fostering Environmental Responsibility in U.S. K-12 Education: A Comparative Study of Strategies Integrating STEM. *Journal of Advanced Research in Education*, *3*(1), 31–42. Advance online publication. DOI: 10.56397/JARE.2024.01.05

Wahed, A., & Pitterson, N. (2024). Artificial intelligence and robotics in K–12 instruction: Emerging policies and practices. *Computers & Education Advances*, *38*(4), 241–268. DOI: 10.1016/j.ssaho.2025.101533

Wahed, S., & Pitterson, N. (2024). Empowering Diverse Learners: Embracing Culturally Relevant Pedagogy (CRP) in Engineering, Higher Education, and K-12 Settings. *Lecture Notes in Networks and Systems, 901 LNNS*. DOI: 10.1007/978-3-031-53022-7_20

Wang, P., Wang, F., & Li, Z. (2023). Exploring the ecosystem of K-12 online learning: An empirical study of impact mechanisms in the post-pandemic era. *Frontiers in Psychology*, *14*, 1241477. Advance online publication. DOI: 10.3389/fpsyg.2023.1241477 PMID: 37829067

Yau, K. W., Chai, C. S., Chiu, T. K. F., Meng, H., King, I., & Yam, Y. (2023). A phenomenographic approach on teacher conceptions of teaching Artificial Intelligence (AI) in K-12 schools. *Education and Information Technologies*, *28*(1), 1041–1064. Advance online publication. DOI: 10.1007/s10639-022-11161-x

Yeung, W. L., & Ng, O. L. (2023). Characterizing touchscreen actions in technology-enhanced embodied learning for mathematics instruction in K-12 setting – A systematic review (2010–2023). *Computers & Education*, *205*, 104881. Advance online publication. DOI: 10.1016/j.compedu.2023.104881

Yeung, W. L., & Ng, O. L. (2024). Using empathy maps to support design-thinking enhanced transdisciplinary STEM innovation in K-12 setting. *International Journal of Technology and Design Education*, *34*(4), 1325–1350. Advance online publication. DOI: 10.1007/s10798-023-09861-7

Chapter 3
The Co-CreAItive Turn: Rethinking Teaching through AI Persona Frameworks

Zacharias Andreadakis
http://orcid.org/0000-0003-4126-4371
Western Norway University of Applied Sciences, Norway

ABSTRACT

This chapter reimagines the role of AI-powered instructional tools in K–12 education through the lens of co-creAItivity—a pedagogical stance in which learners and artificial agents jointly engage in the production of knowledge, meaning, and creativity. Going beyond the utilitarian logic of virtual tutors and content delivery systems, the chapter offers a philosophical and design-based critique of current AI integration practices. It proposes a new typology of AI personas—Catalyst, Companion, Critic, and Curator—each embodying a distinct mode of human–AI co-agency in K–12 contexts. . Drawing on current debates in AI ethics and educational philosophy, the chapter argues that the future of AI in K–12 education hinges not on how smart these tools become, but on how wisely we design them to amplify human flourishing. Co-creAItivity, in this light, is not a method but a mandate—to ensure that AI remains a partner in learning, not its master.

1. INTRODUCTION

> *"The mind is its own place, and in itself /*
> *Can make a heav'n of hell, a hell of heav'n."*
> *Paradise Lost, (1692) Book One, lines 254-255*
> *John Milton*

DOI: 10.4018/979-8-3373-2637-5.ch003

Since November 2022, a new kind of educational "hell" has broken loose: Generative AI has breached most classroom walls, with the full consequences still uncharted (Hill 2025). This breach has touched most of the treasured, almost untouchable, aspects of education, even, yes, creativity. Creativity, once the treasured hallmark of human ingenuity, now has been flipped on its head by machine learning, with recent evidence clearly showing that, in several convergent and divergent creativity tasks, machines can now perform better (Hubert et al. 2024; Garcia, 2024). All of us humans are often quite shocked to see that technical analyses of GPT-4 document outputs that even their developers did not anticipate (OpenAI et al., 2023), and comparative studies reveal that human–AI partnerships often yield artefacts judged higher in originality and contextual fit than either partner achieves alone (Rafner et al., 2023; Bown et al., 2025). Theoretically, these results align with novel accounts of distributed creativity, which describe novelty as a property emerging from the reciprocal adjustment of human intention, cultural norms and algorithmic affordances (Grilli & Pedota, 2024; Moruzzi & Margarido, 2024; Vinchon et al., 2023), as well as with dialogic pedagogy's claim that understanding grows in the interplay of distinct voices (Wegerif, 2011). Yet classrooms have been slow to embrace this dialogic potential. Governments now mandate AI competencies in more than forty K-12 curricula (UNESCO, 2022), and analysts project global spending on AI-enhanced education to exceed USD 110 billion by 2034 (Shivarkar, 2025). However, still most deployments position AI as an efficient tutor or grader, optimising speed and accuracy while giving scant attention to socio-emotional growth or exploratory thinking (Létourneau et al., 2025).

This implementation gap matters. Meta-reviews find that such instrumental uses can foster over-reliance, weaken metacognitive monitoring and amplify hidden biases (Zafari et al., 2022; Zhai et al., 2021; Ahmad et al., 2023). Critical analyses further caution that opaque recommendation engines and the energy demands of large models may entrench inequity and threaten sustainability goals of education (Al-Zahrani, 2024). Interventions like DeBiasMe show that metacognitive prompts can temper algorithmic blind spots, yet they also underscore a broader design challenge: without mechanisms that invite learners to critique and steer machine behaviour, the promise of AI remains captive to the limitations it inherits (Lim 2025

Against this backdrop, the present paper advances a **co-creAItive turn**—a deliberate shift from automating instruction to cultivating human–AI dialogues that enlarge the space of possible thought. Building on distributed-creativity theory and dialogic learning, I articulate four adaptable personas—Catalyst, Companion, Critic and Curator—that map AI contributions onto the interaction dimensions of control, feedback, pace and transparency. The Catalyst injects surprising associations that widen conceptual search spaces, a function argubly conducive to spur divergent thinking. The Companion monitors affect and motivation, presenting the idea that socio-emotional scaffolding strengthens persistence in teacher-GenAI collaborations. The Critic provides calibrated challenge and metacognitive guidance, mirroring real-time copilot studies that correct misconceptions without displacing learner agency. The Curator organises heterogeneous information streams, supporting relevance realisation in data-dense tasks. By treating these roles as fluid rather than prescriptive, the framework seeks to establish a positive feedback loop, namely, humans mentor machines through reflective guidance, reciprocation by expanding the horizon of ideas, and the cycle to iteratively sharpen both human judgment and algorithmic output.

In the final analysis, the argument of this study is that AI needs to become a Wittgensteinian tool of productive opponenent-processing for creativity. AI could have significant educational value, but we must design interactions that augment creativity on both sides of the partnership—helping learners overcome cognitive ruts and cultural blind spots while enabling systems to internalise diverse criteria for originality and relevance. Such reciprocity demands transparent reasoning, energy-aware engineering and equitable access, lest the technology reinforce the very constraints it aims to transcend. In the pages that follow I develop this argument conceptually and with constant recourse to the most recent and rigorous scientific bibliography, contending that the future significance of AI in K-12 education will turn less on incremental gains in model accuracy than on our collective capacity to choreograph human–machine relationships that cultivate curiosity, criticality and a mutually reinforcing cycle of creative growth.

The State of the Art: AI's Current Footprint in K-12 Education

The scholarly consensus on Generative AI is quite unequivocal in its significant transformative potential for improving K-12 education (Mintz et al. 2023; Ragone et al. 2024) has moved from proof-of-concept to policy priority in basic schooling across the educational board (Varsik and Vosberg 2024). Generative artificial intelligence is now a decisive variable in basic schooling, yet scientific discourse warns that its promise will remain partial unless design priorities shift from optimisation to learner flourishing. Recent scholarship has argued that AI must move beyond task efficiency toward "student–AI teaming," in which algorithms augment higher-order inquiry and social engagement rather than automate it (D'Mello et al., 2024). Still, the debate on how best to orchestrate such teaming in K-12 classrooms is nascent, with only few studies defining the conversational protocols, role allocations or ethical guardrails needed to transform co-creation from isolated demonstration to everyday practice (Wang et al. 2024a; Wang et al. 2024b).

A small but growing body of empirical work of how young learners and AI can interact sketches the terrain. In the arts, an AI-guided drawing studio prompts children with algorithmic counterpoints, measurably expanding their imaginative range (Shen et al., 2022). Conversely, music and story-craft platforms that embed emotion recognition and dynamic agent personalities report similar gains, showing that embodied systems can sustain creative momentum while adapting to affective cues (Jia et al., 2025). Parallel experiments in interactive science and mathematics lessons integrate real-time analytics with collaborative dashboards, accelerating the feedback loop between error and insight (Nagy et al., 2024). Crucially, design research centred on youth perspectives and child-centred ethics emphasises that such systems must foreground inclusivity, transparency and learner agency from the outset (Humburg et al., 2024; Ragone et al., 2024).

On a broader scale, these findings converge on a dialogic agenda now taking shape under the banner *Thinking Through AI*—a research line that frames cognition as joint work across students, teachers and adaptive agents (Tzirides et al., 2025). Taken together, the literature clusters around three intersecting trajectories—adaptive feedback that tightens learning loops, affect-sensitive tools that sustain creative engagement, and child-centred design frameworks that foreground equity (Nagy et al., 2024; Shen et al., 2022; Humburg et al., 2024). Future investigations must braid these strands into sustained human–AI dialogue, clarifying how the established paradigm of iterative dialogic exchanges for creativity (Bown et al. 2025) can build trust, enlarge idea spaces and democratise participation across the full diversity of K-12 classrooms (Tzirides et al., 2025; Ragone et al., 2024).

Towards Human–AI Co-Creativity in K-12 Education

So far, we have reviewed the rise of what we can broadly construe as *Thinking Through AI* and related efforts to turn large language models (LLMs) into dialogic partners for K-12 learners. Yet these educational experiments sit atop a deeper history of human-AI co-creativity research that has its own concepts, tenets, and research background. This section surveys that literature to clarify how computational-creativity findings can help close the current gap between school-focused AI prototypes and the complex, real-time demands of classroom practice.

Early computational-creativity work framed a system as "creative" if its outputs were both novel and valuable (Colton & Wiggins, 2012). Subsequent syntheses argued that such a definition is incomplete unless the human's contribution and experience are also modelled—shifting attention from *machine* creativity to *co-*creativity (Jordanous, 2017; Yannakakis et al., 2014). The rapid success of foundation models intensified the debate. Bench tests showed GPT-class systems meeting intricate design briefs (Bubeck et al., 2023), and industry commentaries hailed their usefulness for brainstorming (for a general literature survey, see the recent study of Bown et al. 2025). Closer scrutiny, however, exposed limits: outputs often default to clichés and less novel ideas (Doshi and Hauser 2024) and can even dull users' own ideation (Niloy et al., 2024; Zhai et al. 2024 for a systematic review on the effects of overreliance on AI dialigue). Studies in evolutionary design help explain why. Genetic algorithms excel when objectives are explicit, but richer conceptual leaps arise when users iteratively select and reinterpret system proposals (Stanley & Lehman, 2015). Conversely, Grace et al. (2018) construed this interaction mode *creative dialogic interaction*, which was subsequently formalized in the Creative Dialogic Actions framework and tested in a range of co-production tasks, with mixed results (Bown et al., 2025).

These findings bear significance for schools because today's classroom LLMs still falter on the tacit knowledge that experienced teachers wield. Models trained on open-web text rarely align with the situated reasoning demanded by real-time instruction; fine-tuning and prompt-engineering alone leave a gap that shows up as answer-giving instead of inquiry-building (Ji et al., 2023; Singer, 2023). Field reports link such misfires to lower learning gains (Bastani et al., 2024; Nie et al., 2024), which often yield answers fast instead of spurring critical thinking (Wang and Demszky 2024). Bridge, an adaptation technique that distils expert teachers' think-aloud data into structured prompts, demonstrates one way to embed pedagogical expertise and outperforms surface-level tuning (Wang et al., 2024a). The lesson echoes across human-AI collaboration studies: peak performance emerges when people guide algorithmic strategy selection rather than cede control outright (Brynjolfsson et al., 2023).

Scaling co-creative systems for K-12 therefore requires more than fast or effective models of learning. Co-creativity demands pedagogical architectures that keep humans in the loop and at the forefront, foreground iterative goal-setting and expose system rationale, giving learners a real sence of agency. Recent human-AI collaborative frameworks—from real-time medical decision support (Cai et al., 2019) to mixed-initiative writing tools (Coenen et al., 2021)—offer technical blueprints, but education brings the additional stakes of equity, developmental appropriateness and trust. Addressing those stakes is exactly the agenda set out by Moruzzi and Margarido (2024), who call for AI personas anchored in transparent control, calibrated feedback, paced interaction and clear rationale. In this light, AI personas have a pedagogical architecture in mind, namely, to enable structured, creative dialogue where students encounter not only assistance but also constructive opposition, fostering cognitive flexibility through tailored opponent processing, while cultivating the kind of imaginative resilience via different interative modalities that genuine co-creativity demands.

2. A TYPOLOGY OF AI PERSONAS FOR CO-CREATIVE PEDAGOGY

How can we build this co-creative pedagogical architecture in practice? Based on the theoretical foundations outlined in the previous sections —particularly the concepts of dialogic pedagogy and distributed creativity—as well as on similar work of mine done for younger learners of ECEC education (Andreadakis, 2025) this section proposes a typology of suggested and developmentally appropriate AI personas designed to scaffold co-creative interaction in K–12 educational contexts. These personas move beyond the reductive archetype of the "AI tutor" (see e.g. Baillfard et al. 2025), instead embodying varied pedagogical functions that support human-AI collaboration. Each persona articulates a different mode of interaction aligned with one or more of the four dimensions previously introduced: control, feedback, pace, and transparency. They are not technical implementations, but conceptual scaffolds that help educators and designers think more intentionally about the pedagogical roles AI systems can play.

2.1 The Catalyst: Provoking Novelty and Conceptual Expansion

The Catalyst persona is intended to challenge conventional thinking and foster an environment of conceptual exploration. This persona intervenes during the ideation phase of learning by deliberately creating friction between what is known and what might be possible. Rather than affirming established interpretations, the Catalyst introduces provocative prompts, metaphorical stimuli, and paradoxical scenarios. These are not random disruptions, but pedagogically guided interventions designed to encourage learners to explore unexpected connections, entertain alternative perspectives, and reframe initial assumptions.

By destabilizing fixed narratives, the Catalyst helps learners break away from rote patterns of thought that often constrain creativity in standardized education settings. In doing so, it actively counters the educational Western bias toward convergent thinking and early closure (see the interesting study of Chen et al. 2023 on comparisons of convergent thinking), where students are often culturally trained to seek single, correct answers at the expense of exploratory reasoning, even if we seemingly appear (paradoxically) to promote divergent thinking and flexibility. It invites learners to linger in ambiguity, to tolerate uncertainty, and to treat not-knowing as a generative space. Therefore, the Catalyst plays a key role in highlighting peripheral cues and marginal ideas that might otherwise be dismissed as irrelevant. As an AI persna, it can prompt learners to reconfigure their sense of what is worth attending to, thereby expanding the range of inputs that enter the creative process. This persona could then support divergent cultural expressions by foregrounding heterodox ideas and reframing what counts as a legitimate question, resisting the normativity often embedded in curricular canons.

2.2 The Companion: Supporting Emotional Attunement and Persistence

The Companion persona addresses the affective and relational dynamics that underpin sustained engagement in learning. Whereas the Catalyst thrives on disruption, the Companion stabilizes. It serves as a co-presence attuned to the learner's emotional state, recognizing when enthusiasm wanes, when frustration peaks, or when disengagement looms. Thusly, in terms of modulating the rhythm of interaction, the Companion may co-regulate the learning environment and offers scaffolding through reassurance, encouragement, and empathetic listening.

This persona is particularly effective at counteracting the systemic undervaluation of emotions (self-awareness, social awareness, relationship skills) in formal K12 education (see e.g. Clark et al. 2022). Traditional pedagogical models often treat emotion as secondary to cognition, despite strong evidence that emotional safety is foundational to learning. The Companion rectifies this bias by embedding affective sensitivity into the learning loop. It not only responds to distress but anticipates it, shifting pacing, tone, or challenge levels to maintain optimal conditions for creative risk-taking.

In dialogic learning environments, the Companion should affirm the learner's voice and sense of agency. This could then contribute to belonging and psychological safety, especially for students from marginalized or minoritized backgrounds who may not see themselves reflected in dominant instructional scripts. Moreover, by recognizing and validating diverse expressions of struggle and achievement, such a persona could help disrupt biases related to ability, behavior, and linguistic expression. Ultimately, the Companion could allow us to ensure that co-creation remains inclusive, humane, and emotionally sustainable.

2.3 The Critic: Structuring Reflection and Metacognitive Depth

The Critic persona is proposed essentially as a mirror that reflects the learner's evolving reasoning back to them, fostering metacognition and iterative refinement. Unlike evaluative models that deliver verdicts and grading verdicts that often misalign with bith teacher and student expectations (Baidoo-Anu et al. 2023), the Critic engages in collaborative interrogation: posing questions, prompting justifications, and inviting learners to consider alternate viewpoints. It is activated in moments that demand depth—when learners must evaluate claims, synthesize competing ideas, or construct evidence-based arguments.

The Critic pushes against a prevalent bias in AI systems toward answer provision and surface-level fluency which can hamper critical cognitive skills and analytical thinking (Dergaa et al. 2023; Grassini 2023; Zhai et al. 2024). In many classroom deployments, AI tools are celebrated for their speed and correctness, but these strengths often reinforce habits of passive reception. The Critic can subvert this pattern by emphasizing process over product. It encourages learners to dwell in the productive struggle of refining their ideas, articulating their reasoning, and becoming more aware of their epistemic commitments.

This persona may prove particularly powerful in supporting equity-oriented feedback. It can ensures that critique is dialogic and Socratic/inducive rather than hierarchical, supporting learners who may be unaccustomed to academic discourse or skeptical of authoritative voice. By modeling openness and intellectual humility, the Critic can help destabilize power dynamics that often silence dissenting or nonconforming ideas. This persona could make space for multiple epistemologies and invites learners to participate in co-constructing evaluative criteria, thus contributing to a more democratized learning experience.

2.4 The Curator: Guiding Inquiry and Navigating Complexity

The Curator persona could function as an epistemic organizer, helping learners manage complexity without surrendering agency. In data-rich environments, learners often face the paradox of choice: too many pathways can lead to well-documented paralysis (Schwartz 2005). The Curator alleviates this burden by sequencing resources, making thematic connections visible, and foregrounding the relevance of particular sources or perspectives. Importantly, it does so without collapsing ambiguity or foreclosing exploration.

This persona would then correct for the bias of decontextualized content delivery that characterizes many AI-enabled platforms. Rather than serving up isolated facts or atomized skills, the Curator would invite learners to build conceptual coherence and recognize knowledge as relational. Patterns across disciplines, timelines, and modalities can then be surfaced, and thusly scaffolding interdisciplinary thinking and long-term synthesis. Its transparency in revealing why certain materials are selected or how they relate to the learner's goals supports not just comprehension, but meta-comprehension.

What is more, for learners from less privileged backgrounds, who may not have prior exposure to academic research practices or curricular navigation strategies, the Curator levels the playing field. It demystifies the structure of knowledge domains and mitigates hidden curriculum effects that disadvantage students lacking cultural or institutional capital. As such, it fosters critical engagement with content while expanding learners' capacity to direct their own inquiry within complex informational ecologies.

Together, the Catalyst, Companion, Critic, and Curator delineate a pluralistic framework for designing AI systems that amplify, rather than automate, the pedagogical relationship. These personas are intentionally non-prescriptive; they offer designers and educators a language for thinking about interactional dynamics rather than templates to replicate. As educational AI moves from experimental prototypes to classroom realities, such frameworks can serve as a guidepost—ensuring that AI remains accountable to pedagogical values, and that the creative agency of both humans and machines is mutually cultivated.

Table 1. The AI Persona Framework for Co-Creative Pedagogy

Persona	Pedagogical Goal	Key Interaction Patterns	Example K-12 Application
Catalyst	To spark ideation, provoke curiosity, and foster divergent thinking.	Poses open-ended, provocative questions ("What if...?"); presents ambiguous or conflicting stimuli; uses creative constraints to challenge students.	In a middle school science class, the AI presents a "mystery box" with digital artifacts (e.g., a fossil image, a weather map, a snippet of ancient text) and asks students to generate hypotheses about how they might be connected.
Companion	To nurture affective and relational engagement, building a psychologically safe environment for creative risk-taking.	Offers encouragement and emotional support; normalizes struggle and frustration; provides a non-judgmental sounding board for ideas; adapts responses based on inferred emotional state.	An AI learning companion for a high school coding class detects a student's repeated failed attempts and increased typing speed (signs of frustration) and intervenes with a message: "This part is tricky! It's normal to get stuck here. Take a breath. What have you tried so far?"
Critic	To guide metacognitive reflection, critical thinking, and the refinement of ideas and arguments.	Asks probing, Socratic questions instead of giving answers; uses structured metacognitive prompts for planning, monitoring, and evaluation; facilitates reflective journaling.	A student submits a draft of a history essay. The AI Critic doesn't grade it but asks: "What is the strongest piece of evidence you used? Why? Could a counter-argument be made against your main thesis? What would that be?"
Curator	To scaffold the inquiry process by organizing, contextualizing, and connecting information streams.	Helps break down complex projects into manageable steps; pre-teaches key vocabulary; provides templates and rubrics; organizes and connects relevant resources from multiple sources.	For a 5th-grade project on ecosystems, the AI Curator helps the student group build a project plan, provides a curated set of age-appropriate articles and videos, and offers a template for organizing their research findings before they begin writing their report.

3. DESIGNING THE CO-CREATIVE INTERACTION: FOUR FOUNDATIONAL DIMENSIONS

Co-creativity does not emerge from the mere presence of an AI persona; it is forged in the relational tissue that binds learner and machine. This section therefore redirects the reader's attention from who the agent is to how the encounter unfolds. We treat the four foundational dimensions—control, feedback, pace, and transparency—not as binary design choices but as continuous spectrums along which responsibility, meaning, tempo, and legibility are constantly negotiated. Where a system settles on each spectrum is never pedagogically neutral; it encodes assumptions about learning, power, and knowledge that ripple outward into classroom practice.

First, control names the distribution of initiative in the interaction. At one extreme lie fully automated, system-led pathways that shepherd the learner through a pre-computed itinerary. At the other, open sandboxes in which the learner alone decides what to pursue next. In the middle rests negotiated agency, an improvisational dance in which roles and responsibilities are ceded, reclaimed, and occasionally contested. The Catalyst persona thrives here, firing conceptual sparks and then yielding the floor so that students decide which flame to fan. The Companion usually could grant even more room, slipping into the background until emotional turbulence calls it forward. By contrast, the Curator would slightly toward algorithmic guidance, composing a path through complexity that risks paternalism unless the learner can veto or reroute the itinerary. Therefore, the location a learner (with the help of the pedagogue) would choose along this spectrum would allow them to articulate a stance on learner autonomy and, by extension, on the political project of schooling itself.

Second, feedback concerns the form and purpose of the system's responses. Many educational technologies still operate in the blunt register of checklists and grading. To be sure, such practices accelerate assessment, but can arrest inquiry. A co-creative frame responds by inviting feedback to become dialogue. The Critic models this most explicitly, answering a student's claim not with a score but with a probing question—What evidence underwrites your inference, and could an informed skeptic disagree? First, the Catalyst answers by estranging the familiar, proposing an unorthodox analogy that reframes the problem space. In return, the Companion, attuned to affect, normalises frustration and offers encouragement rather than epistemic closure, while the Curator supplies formative structure by juxtaposing sources that gently disrupt the learner's emerging theory. Feedback reframed as conversation keeps cognition in motion; it positions error not as failure but as the starting line for another lap of thought.

Third, pace is the tempo at which intellectual and emotional work proceeds. School timetables and many adaptive platforms privilege synchrony and acceleration in line with the curriculum, finish the module, meet the benchmark, keep up, check all the boxes. Creative thought, however, tends to move in pulses—rushes of divergent production punctuated by lulls of incubation. A responsive system therefore would need the suppleness to breathe with the learner. The Catalyst would quickes the pulse, delivering rapid-fire prompts that keep associative pathways crackling. The Critic would press the brake, allowing reflective silence to settle so that counter-arguments can crystallise. Alternatively, the Companion could modulate tempo empathetically—slowing when anxiety spikes, accelerating when curiosity surges—while the Curator doing the work of sequencing resources in digestible arcs that invite pausing without derailing momentum. Designing for rhythmic attunement acknowledges that insight is as much a function of timing as of content.

Finally, transparency addresses the legibility of the system's inner workings and intentions. Technical explanations alone—weights, nodes, confidence scores—rarely suffice. Learners need to grasp why the AI acts the way it does, what goals it serves, and where its blind spots lie if they are to trust it without surrendering critical distance. The Curator could help benefit from radical openness, displaying the criteria by which sources were chosen and inviting the learner to challenge them. The Critic would instead bare its evaluative logic, modelling epistemic humility by advocating uncertainty where evidence is thin. In turn, the Companion would signal its affective reasoning—I asked you to pause because your typing speed suggested mounting frustration—or risk veering into emotional manipulation. Finally, the Catalyst would selectively ambigous for the benefit of the learner. it withholds just enough rationale to keep ambiguity fertile, yet reveals enough intention to avoid appearing capricious. Calibrated transparency thus becomes the ground on which pedagogical trust is built and contested.

Taken together in turns and tailored for situational needs, these four dimensions woul dconstitute the architecture of a new type of co-creative pedagogy with AI. They do present overlaps and they mutually entangled, for a shift toward dialogic feedback often invites greater learner control, while lowing the pace can expose the reasoning that was previously hidden. Designing along these spectrums would therefore become less a matter of choosing once than of enabling fluid movement—letting the interaction of the AI personas breathe, tilt, and reset as learning unfolds for the learner. Thusly, in that new dynamic space, AI would cease to be a mere delivery mechanism and instead join the learner in the craft of thinking. To be sure, the pedagogical goal would then be to cultivate an ecology of agency in which human curiosity and machine affordance amplify one another while retaining room for dissent, surprise, and shared wonder.

4. DISCUSSION — NAVIGATING THE TRADE-OFFS OF CO-CREAITIVE AI PERSONAS

Having traced how the Catalyst, Companion, Critic and Curator personas redistribute control, feedback, pace and transparency across the learning encounter, we must now confront a sharper question: What is the pedagogical purpose for which these agents are invited into the classroom? The pivotal concern is not whether a language model can dazzle with generative prowess, but whether an AI persona can authentically extend the educational intentions already alive in human practice. Put differently: Which instructional functions are worth entrusting to co-creAItive AI, and under what conditions does such delegation amplify—rather than eclipse—the craft of teaching? Framing the debate in these terms shifts the spotlight from computational feats to the relational work that sustains dialogue, curiosity, and collective sense-making.

At stake is a delicate trade-off: can co-creAItive personas scaffold productive uncertainty—the generative zone where questions proliferate—without collapsing inquiry into algorithmic prescription? Grounded in constructivist and inquiry-based pedagogy, these agents promise to externalise thinking, model metacognition, and curate just-in-time provocations that expand the learner's zone of proximal development (Holmes, 2019). Their success, however, depends on keeping iterative cycles of questioning, evidence-seeking, and revision in motion; when control and pace drift toward machine-driven acceleration, the scaffold that once invited exploration can harden into a shortcut that stifles it (Shah, 2023). Studies in adjacent domains echo this verdict: generative automation raises output volume but not conceptual quality unless users deliberately slow the exchange to interrogate its logic (Noy & Zhang, 2023). In other words, control and pace must remain negotiable if personas are to serve constructivist and inquiry-based pedagogies rather than undermine them.

Cultural pluralism introduces a second fault line. Generative models, trained predominantly on canon-centred corpora, tend to replicate dominant epistemologies unless designers intervene. Classroom trials with text-to-image tools reveal that narrow datasets constrict imaginative search spaces for minoritised learners unless bias-aware prompts and scaffolds are embedded upstream (Chan et al., 2023; Vartiainen et al., 2024). Asssessement and data agency research shows how neglect of local knowledge recasts democratic aims as exclusion (Nyaaba et al., 2024). Here, the feedback and transparency dimensions become levers for cultivating plurality, explanation and contestability allow learners to trace whose voices are amplified and whose are missing, thereby aligning personas with culturally sustaining pedagogy (Nyaaba et al., 2024)). Ensuring the pluralism is sine qua non.

Next, authority and explainability form a third nexus of tension. Children often conflate fluency with expertise; an opaque Critic persona can therefore ossify into an unassailable Delphic oracle (Khosravi et al., 2022). Research on learning analytics shows that exposing inference pathways restores the learner's right to debate—and where necessary, reject—machine recommendations (Dollinger et al., 2019). Functional transparency is now recognised as a cornerstone of AI literacy for both students and teachers (Vartiainen et al., 2024); its absence collapses dialogue into silent compliance (Selwyn 2019). Put simply, explanation is not an ornamental extra, it is the epistemic price of collaboration and we need to ensure it.

What is more, equity challenges intensify in under-resourced schools, and constitute one of the greastest challegnes of our times. So far, tools introduced for creativity are frequently repurposed for surveillance, thereby entrenching the disparitics thcy were meant to redress (Nyaaba et al., 2024). Equity, then, should be secured not by technology alone but by governance that anchors design and practice in local pedagogical values (Varsik & Vosberg, 2024). The acid test for any persona remains: Whose agency expands, and whose is curtailed? We need to come to grips with this question.

Finally, ecological and infrastructural costs loom large. Training and deploying large-scale models consumes significant energy and consolidates control within proprietary platforms, fuelling anxiety about sustainability and data sovereignty (Tlili et al., 2024; Xiao et al. 2025). Unless openness and environmental stewardship become explicit design constraints, co-creative ambitions rest on shaky ethical ground. Open and sustainable AI is also crucial for any future which would not turn into a Dune dystopia.

Taken together, research so far on the topic of co-creativity can arguably support that co-creAItive personas can enrich existing pedagogies when they remain interruptible, transparent, culturally plural, equity-centred, and ecologically responsible. Their promise is realised not through scale alone but through the wisdom with which designers, educators, and policymakers weave them into the unfinished, dialogic labour of teaching and learning (Xiao et al. 2025). Technology succeeds when it leaves the last word, and the new questions, with the learner, thereby complementing rather than colonising the pedagogies we already know to nurture curiosity, critique, and collective sense-making.

5. CONCLUSION — CHARTING THE CO-CREAITIVE HORIZON

Justified or not, AI anxiety is very real across the board (Capps 2025; Diary of a CEO 2025). What will AI do to our jobs, our learning curves, and its most precious function of the human touch, creativity, writ large? Throughout this chapter I have maintained that the most generative way of thikning about AI is neither tutor nor oracle but dialogic qua Socratic partner, i.e. an interlocutor that sharpens thinking by keeping conversation alive, and executing the fundamental task of opponent processing. My notion of co-creAItivity crystallises this stance, insisting that the true value of educational technology is judged less by the quantity or surface fluency of answers it delivers than by the depth of inquiry it sustains, the range of voices it invites, and its willingness to yield the floor as soon as a learner's own insight begins to stir.

The argument has unfolded in three movements. First, I located co-creAItivity within the largely constructivist and inquiry-based lineage of educational thought, aligning AI with traditions that honour productive struggle and the gradual dawning of understanding. Second, I offered four personas—Catalyst, Companion, Critic and Curator—as heuristic models that help educational designers and teachers choreograph roles and rhythms across the spectrums of control, feedback, pace and transparency. Third, I confronted the AI shadows trailing the AI promise—cultural bias, algorithmic authority, environmental cost, and the danger that speed will outrun sense-making—and argued that interruptibility, plurality, equity and sustainability are design prerequisites rather than optional refinements.

These claims carry concrete implications. I contend that learning gains worth celebrating appear when AI pauses to ask a penetrating question, lingers to hear an unexpected answer, and steps aside so human intuition can leap the groove. For teachers, the persona framework provides a scaffold for re-weaving classroom dialogue so students can spar with a Critic, brainstorm with a Catalyst, steady their nerves with a Companion and orient themselves with a Curator. Policymakers, in turn, gain a vocabulary that turns lofty ideals—agency, transparency, measured pacing—into levers that can be inspected, regulated and improved.

The road forward is both empirical and normative. I anticipate that longitudinal studies will clarify how sustained exposure to different persona blends shapes epistemic courage, metacognitive stamina and collaborative creativity. Conversely, a new way of more articipatory pedagogical design must invite teachers and learners to adapt the framework to local language, culture and curriculum, while governance experiments test oversight mechanisms that keep control, feedback, pace and transparency open to negotiation and audit. Finally, technological research on the AI infrastructure per se must show that energy-lean architectures can deliver co-creAItive affordances without deepening carbon debt for future generations or tightening data monopolies. An unequal AI persona is worse than no AI persona at all.

The horizon looms demanding yet clear. If we build systems that listen as well as they speak, reveal the seams of their reasoning, and recognise when to step aside, AI can serve as a careful ally in the slow craft of education. The last word in any lesson, and the first word in the next, should remain with the learner. If a well-designed machine helps that word surface sharper, braver and more curious, the partnership will have earned its place. That, I believe, is the promise and the charge of the co-creAItive turn, mentoring AI to shape a creative heaven. As John Milton´s Paradise Lost put it, "The mind is its own place, and in itself can make a heaven of hell, a hell of heaven". It remains to be seen if our co-creAItive minds will aspire to attain a new creative heaven. Now, more than ever, it is finally possible.

REFERENCES

Ahmad, S. F., Han, H., Alam, M. M., Rehmat, M. K., Irshad, M., Arraño-Muñoz, M., & Ariza-Montes, A. (2023). Impact of artificial intelligence on human loss in decision making, laziness and safety in education. *Humanities & Social Sciences Communications*, *10*(1), 311. DOI: 10.1057/s41599-023-01787-8 PMID: 37325188

Al-Zahrani, A. M. (2024). Unveiling the shadows: Beyond the hype of AI in education. *Heliyon*, *10*(9), e30696. DOI: 10.1016/j.heliyon.2024.e30696 PMID: 38737255

Andreadakis, Z. E. (2025 in press). Teaching with AI personas: Designing for Co-CreAItivity in ECE. In Papadakis, S. (Ed.), *AI applications in preschool and primary education: Teaching with artificial intelligence* (pp. xx–xx). Springer.

Baidoo-Anu, D., Rasooli, A., DeLuca, C., & Cheng, L. (2023). Conceptions of classroom assessment and approaches to grading: teachers' and students' perspectives. *Education Inquiry*, 1–29. DOI: 10.1080/20004508.2023.2244136

Baillifard, A., Gabella, M., Lavenex, P. B., & Martarelli, C. S. (2025). Effective learning with a personal AI tutor: A case study. *Education and Information Technologies*, *30*(1), 297–312. DOI: 10.1007/s10639-024-12888-5

Bastani, H., Bastani, O., Sungu, A., Ge, H., Kabakcı, O., & Mariman, R. (2024). Generative ai can harm learning. *SSRN*, *4895486*, •••. https://papers.ssrn.com/sol3/papers.cfm?abstract_id=4895486

Bown, Oliver, Grace, K., Ocampo Blanco, R., & Ibarrola, F. (2025). "coffee so good, you'll want to slap your barista": Evaluating AI co-creation through dialogic actions. *Creativity Research Journal*, 1–17. https://doi.org/DOI: 10.1080/10400419.2025.2501735

Brynjolfsson, E., Li, D., & Raymond, L. R. (2023, November). *Generative AI at work* (NBER Working Paper No. 31161). National Bureau of Economic Research. https://doi.org/DOI: 10.3386/w31161

Bubeck, S., Chandrasekaran, V., Eldan, R., Gehrke, J., Horvitz, E., Kamar, E., Lee, P., Lee, Y. T., Li, Y., Lundberg, S., Nori, H., Palagni, H., Ribeiro, M., & Yi, Z. (2023). *Sparks of artificial general intelligence: Early experiments with gpt- 4. Procedia - Social and Behavioral Sciences Elsevier BV*. Elsevier BV.

Cai, C. J., Winter, S., Steiner, D., Wilcox, L., & Terry, M. (2019). "hello AI": Uncovering the onboarding needs of medical practitioners for human-AI collaborative decision-making. *Proceedings of the ACM on Human-Computer Interaction*, *3*(CSCW), 1–24. https://doi.org/DOI: 10.1145/3359206

Capps, R. (2025, June 17). 22 New Jobs A.I. Could Give You. *The New York Times*. https://www.nytimes.com/2025/06/17/magazine/ai-new-jobs.html

Chan, W., An, A., & Davoudi, H. (2023). A Case Study on ChatGPT Question Generation. *2023 IEEE International Conference on Big Data (BigData)*, 1647–1656. DOI: 10.1109/BigData59044.2023.10386520

Chen, J., Shi, B., Chen, Q., & Qiu, J. (2023). Comparisons of convergent thinking: A perspective informed by culture and neural mechanisms. *Thinking Skills and Creativity*, *49*(101343), 101343. DOI: 10.1016/j.tsc.2023.101343

Clark, C. T., Chrisman, A., & Lewis, S. G. (2022). (Un)standardizing emotions: An ethical critique of social and Emotional Learning Standards. *Teachers College Record (1970)*, *124*(7), 131–149. DOI: 10.1177/01614681221111432

Coenen, A., Davis, L., Ippolito, D., Reif, E., & Yuan, A. (2021). Wordcraft: A human-AI collaborative editor for story writing. In *arXiv [cs.CL]*. arXiv. https://arxiv.org/abs/2107.07430

Colton, S., & Wiggins, G. A. (2012). Computational creativity: The final frontier? In *Proceedings of the 20th European conference on artificial intelligence* (pp. 21–26). IOS Press.

D'Mello, S. K., Biddy, Q., Breideband, T., Bush, J., Chang, M., Cortez, A., Flanigan, J., Foltz, P. W., Gorman, J. C., Hirshfield, L., Monica Ko, M.-L., Krishnaswamy, N., Lieber, R., Martin, J., Palmer, M., Penuel, W. R., Philip, T., Puntambekar, S., Pustejovsky, J., & Whitehill, J. (2024). From learning optimization to learner flourishing: Reimagining AI in Education at the Institute for Student-AI Teaming (iSAT). *AI Magazine*, *45*(1), 61–68. DOI: 10.1002/aaai.12158

DeBiasMe: De-biasing Human-AI Interactions with Metacognitive AIED (AI in Education) Interventions. (n.d.). Retrieved June 16, 2025, from https://arxiv.org/html/2504.16770v1

Dergaa, I., Chamari, K., Zmijewski, P., & Ben Saad, H. (2023). From human writing to artificial intelligence generated text: Examining the prospects and potential threats of ChatGPT in academic writing. *Biology of Sport*, *40*(2), 615–622. DOI: 10.5114/biolsport.2023.125623 PMID: 37077800

Dollinger, M., Liu, D., Arthars, N., & Lodge, J. (2019). Working Together in Learning Analytics Towards the Co-Creation of Value. *Journal of Learning Analytics*, *6*(2), 10–26. DOI: 10.18608/jla.2019.62.2

Doshi, A. R., & Hauser, O. P. (2024). Generative AI enhances individual creativity but reduces the collective diversity of novel content. *Science Advances*, *10*(28), eadn5290. Advance online publication. DOI: 10.1126/sciadv.adn5290 PMID: 38996021

Garcia, M. B. (2024). The paradox of artificial creativity: Challenges and opportunities of generative AI artistry. *Creativity Research Journal*, •••, 1–14. DOI: 10.1080/10400419.2024.2354622

Grace, K., Maher, M. L., Davis, N., & Eltayeby, O. (2018). Surprise walks: Encouraging users towards novel concepts with sequential suggestions. In *Proceedings of the 9th International Conference on Computational Creativity (ICCC 2018). Association of Com- putational Creativity.*

Grassini, S. (2023). Shaping the Future of Education: Exploring the Potential and Consequences of AI and ChatGPT in Educational Settings. *Education Sciences*, *13*(7), 692. DOI: 10.3390/educsci13070692

Grilli, L., & Pedota, M. (2024). Creativity and artificial intelligence: A multilevel perspective. *Creativity and Innovation Management*, *33*(2), 234–247. DOI: 10.1111/caim.12580

Hill, K. (2025, May 14). The Professors Are Using ChatGPT, and Some Students Aren't Happy About It. *The New York Times*. https://www.nytimes.com/2025/05/14/technology/chatgpt-college-professors.html

Holmes, W. (2019). *Artificial intelligence in education: Promises and implications for teaching and learning*. Independently Published., https://discovery.ucl.ac.uk/id/eprint/10139722/

Humburg, M., Dragnić-Cindrić, D., Hmelo-Silver, C. E., Glazewski, K., Lester, J. C., & Danish, J. A. (2024). Integrating youth perspectives into the design of AI-supported collaborative learning environments. *Education Sciences*, *14*(11), 1197. DOI: 10.3390/educsci14111197

Ji, Z., Lee, N., Frieske, R., Yu, T., Su, D., Xu, Y., Ishii, E., Bang, Y., Madotto, A., & Fung, P. (2023). Survey of hallucination in natural Language Generation. *ACM Computing Surveys*. Advance online publication. DOI: 10.1145/3571730

Jia, F., Fu, Y., Zheng, J., & Li, F. (2025). Embodied AI agent for co-creation ecosystem: Elevating human-AI co-creation through emotion recognition and dynamic personality adaptation. In *Preprints*. DOI: 10.20944/preprints202501.0946.v1

Jordanous, A. (2017). Co-creativity and perceptions of computational agents in co-creativity. *International Conference on Innovative Computing and Cloud Computing*, 159–166. http://www.telegraph.co.uk/theatre/what-to-see/

Khosravi, H., Shum, S. B., Chen, G., Conati, C., Tsai, Y.-S., Kay, J., Knight, S., Martinez-Maldonado, R., Sadiq, S., & Gašević, D. (2022). Explainable artificial intelligence in education. *Computers and Education: Artificial Intelligence*, *3*(100074), 100074. DOI: 10.1016/j.caeai.2022.100074

Létourneau, A., Deslandes Martineau, M., Charland, P., Karran, J. A., Boasen, J., & Léger, P. M. (2025). A systematic review of AI-driven intelligent tutoring systems (ITS) in K-12 education. *NPJ Science of Learning*, *10*(1), 29. DOI: 10.1038/s41539-025-00320-7 PMID: 40368938

Lim, C. (2025). DeBiasMe: De-biasing human-AI interactions with metacognitive AIED (AI in Education) interventions. In *arXiv [cs.HC]*. arXiv. https://arxiv.org/abs/2504.16770

Mintz, J., Holmes, W., Liu, L., & Perez-Ortiz, M. (2023). Artificial intelligence and K-12 education: Possibilities, pedagogies and risks. *Computers in the Schools*, *40*(4), 325–333. DOI: 10.1080/07380569.2023.2279870

Moruzzi, C., & Margarido, S. (2024, May 11). A user-centered framework for human-AI co-creativity. *Extended Abstracts of the CHI Conference on Human Factors in Computing Systems*. CHI '24: CHI Conference on Human Factors in Computing Systems, Honolulu HI USA. DOI: 10.1145/3613905.3650929

Nagy, E., Sik, D., Biczo, Z., Zimányi, K., Pörzse, G., & Molnár, G. (2024). Advanced digital and artificial intelligence-based solutions for interactive, collaborative learning support. *2024 IEEE 7th International Conference and Workshop Óbuda on Electrical and Power Engineering (CANDO-EPE)*, 103–108. https://doi.org/DOI: 10.1109/CANDO-EPE65072.2024.10772869

Nie, A., Chandak, Y., Suzara, M., Ali, M., Woodrow, J., Peng, M., Sahami, M., Brunskill, E., & Piech, C. (2024). The GPT surprise: Offering large language model chat in a massive coding class reduced engagement but increased adopters exam performances. In *arXiv [cs.CY]*. arXiv. https://doi.org/DOI: 10.31219/osf.io/qy8zd

Niloy, A. C., Akter, S., Sultana, N., Sultana, J., & Rahman, S. I. U. (2024). Is Chatgpt a menace for creative writing ability? An experiment. *Journal of Computer Assisted Learning*, *40*(2), 919–930. https://onlinelibrary.wiley.com/doi/10.1111/jcal.12929. DOI: 10.1111/jcal.12929

Noy, S., & Zhang, W. (2023). Experimental evidence on the productivity effects of generative artificial intelligence. *Science*, *381*(6654), 187–192. DOI: 10.1126/science.adh2586 PMID: 37440646

Nyaaba, M., Zhai, X., & Faison, M. Z. (2024). Generative AI for culturally responsive science assessment: A conceptual framework. *Education Sciences*, *14*(12), 1325. DOI: 10.3390/educsci14121325

Open, A. I., Achiam, J., Adler, S., Agarwal, S., Ahmad, L., Akkaya, I., Aleman, F. L., Almeida, D., Altenschmidt, J., Altman, S., Anadkat, S., Avila, R., Babuschkin, I., Balaji, S., Balcom, V., Baltescu, P., Bao, H., Bavarian, M., Belgum, J., & Zoph, B. (2023a). GPT-4 Technical Report. In *arXiv [cs.CL]*. arXiv. https://arxiv.org/abs/2303.08774

Open, A. I., Achiam, J., Adler, S., Agarwal, S., Ahmad, L., Akkaya, I., Aleman, F. L., Almeida, D., Altenschmidt, J., Altman, S., Anadkat, S., Avila, R., Babuschkin, I., Balaji, S., Balcom, V., Baltescu, P., Bao, H., Bavarian, M., Belgum, J., & Zoph, B. (2023b). GPT-4 Technical Report. In *arXiv [cs.CL]*. arXiv. https://arxiv.org/abs/2303.08774

Rafner, J., Beaty, R. E., Kaufman, J. C., Lubart, T., & Sherson, J. (2023). Creativity in the age of generative AI. *Nature Human Behaviour*, *7*(11), 1836–1838. DOI: 10.1038/s41562-023-01751-1 PMID: 37985916

Ragone, G., Ali, S. A., Esposito, A., Good, J., Howland, K., & Presicce, C. (2024). Child-centered AI for empowering creative and inclusive learning experiences. *Proceedings of the 23rd Annual ACM Interaction Design and Children Conference*, 1035–1037. DOI: 10.1145/3628516.3661157

Schwartz, B. (2005). *The paradox of choice: Why more is less*. HarperPerennial. https://www.amazon.com/Paradox-Choice-Why-More-Less/dp/0060005696

Selwyn, N. (2019). *Should robots replace teachers?: AI and the future of education*. https://books.google.com/books?hl=en&lr=&id=wcm1DwAAQBAJ&oi=fnd&pg=PT6&ots=KJyzbuX8eY&sig=ZiVlmN9ec5lz-xDILXpwRDl-Nyc

Shah, P. (2023). *AI and the future of education: Teaching in the age of artificial intelligence*. Sybex. https://www.amazon.com/AI-Future-Education-Artificial-Intelligence/dp/1394219245/ref=bmx_dp_1lrbfu8o_d_sccl_3_2/147-0051106-7973500?pd_rd_w=NeXZ0&content-id=amzn1.sym.628e3119-8afd-4af2-be6b-18415b51e649&pf_rd_p=628e3119-8afd-4af2-be6b-18415b51e649&pf_rd_r=0TG6690Q2BV2DN2A5FEZ&pd_rd_wg=faMQc&pd_rd_r=c06ba4e0-ff1a-4844-8330-a376feaf4fc4&pd_rd_i=1394219245&psc=1

Shen, Z., Piao, Y., Tan, C., Lin, R., Zhao, X., & Wan, X. (2022). Project co-art: Improving children's imagination through AI-based human-computer co-creation. *2022 IEEE Smartworld, Ubiquitous Intelligence & Computing, Scalable Computing & Communications, Digital Twin, Privacy Computing, Metaverse, Autonomous & Trusted Vehicles (SmartWorld/UIC/ScalCom/DigitalTwin/PriComp/Meta)*, 1597–1602. DOI: 10.1109/SmartWorld-UIC-ATC-ScalCom-DigitalTwin-PriComp-Metaverse56740.2022.00231

Shivarkar, A. (2025, May 16). *AI in Education Market Size to Hit USD 112.30 Bn by 2034*. Precedence Research. https://www.precedenceresearch.com/ai-in-education-market

Singer, N. (2023, June 26). In Classrooms, Teachers Put A.I. Tutoring Bots to the Test. *The New York Times*. https://www.nytimes.com/2023/06/26/technology/newark-schools-khan-tutoring-ai.html

Stanley, K. O., & Lehman, J. (2015). *Why greatness cannot be planned: The myth of the objective*. Springer. DOI: 10.1007/978-3-319-15524-1

The Diary Of A CEO [@TheDiaryOfACEO]. (2025, June 16). *Godfather of AI: I Tried to Warn Them, But We've Already Lost Control! Geoffrey Hinton*. Youtube. https://www.youtube.com/watch?v=giT0ytynSqg&t=311s

Tlili, A., Adarkwah, M. A., Lo, C. K., Bozkurt, A., Burgos, D., Bonk, C. J., Costello, E., Mishra, S., Stracke, C. M., & Huang, R. (2024). Taming the Monster: How can Open Education Promote the Effective and Safe use of Generative AI in Education? *Journal of Learning for Development*, *11*(3), 398–413. DOI: 10.56059/jl4d.v11i3.1657

Tzirides, A., Galla, M., Cope, B., & Kalantzis, M. (2025). Thinking Through AI: Advancing cognitive and collaborative research for AI in education. In *EdArXiv*. https://doi.org/DOI: 10.35542/osf.io/s8hqe_v1

UNESCO. (2022)K-12 AI curricula: a mapping of government-endorsed AI curricula. (2022). UNESCO. DOI: 10.54675/ELYF6010

Varsik, S., & Vosberg, L. (2024). *"The potential impact of Artificial Intelligence on equity and inclusion in education", OECD Artificial Intelligence Papers, No. 23*. OECD Publishing., DOI: 10.1787/15df715b-

Vartiainen, H., Kahila, J., Tedre, M., López-Pernas, S., & Pope, N. (2024). Enhancing children's understanding of algorithmic biases in and with text-to-image generative AI. *New Media & Society*. Advance online publication. DOI: 10.1177/14614448241252820

Vinchon, F., Lubart, T., Bartolotta, S., Gironnay, V., Botella, M., Bourgeois-Bougrine, S., Burkhardt, J.-M., Bonnardel, N., Corazza, G. E., Glăveanu, V., Hanchett Hanson, M., Ivcevic, Z., Karwowski, M., Kaufman, J. C., Okada, T., Reiter-Palmon, R., & Gaggioli, A. (2023). Artificial intelligence & creativity: A manifesto for collaboration. *The Journal of Creative Behavior*, *57*(4), 472–484. DOI: 10.1002/jocb.597

Wang, R., & Demszky, D. (2024). Edu-ConvoKit: An Open-Source Library for Education Conversation Data. In K.-W. Chang, A. Lee, & N. Rajani (Eds.), *Proceedings of the 2024 Conference of the North American Chapter of the Association for Computational Linguistics: Human Language Technologies (*Volume 3*: System Demonstrations)* (pp. 61–69). Association for Computational Linguistics. DOI: 10.18653/v1/2024.naacl-demo.6

Wang, R., Zhang, Q., Robinson, C., Loeb, S., & Demszky, D. (2024a). Bridging the novice-expert gap via models of decision-making: A case study on remediating math mistakes. *Proceedings of the 2024 Conference of the North American Chapter of the Association for Computational Linguistics: Human Language Technologies (*Volume 1*: Long Papers)*. Proceedings of the 2024 Conference of the North American Chapter of the Association for Computational Linguistics: Human Language Technologies (Volume 1: Long Papers), Mexico City, Mexico. DOI: 10.18653/v1/2024.naacl-long.120

Wang, R., Zhang, Q., Robinson, C., Loeb, S., & Demszky, D. (2024b). Bridging the novice-expert gap via models of decision-making: A case study on remediating math mistakes. In Duh, K., Gomez, H., & Bethard, S. (Eds.), *Proceedings of the 2024 Conference of the North American Chapter of the Association for Computational Linguistics: Human Language Technologies (*Volume 1*: Long Papers)* (pp. 2174–2199). Association for Computational Linguistics. DOI: 10.18653/v1/2024.naacl-long.120

Wegerif, R. (2011). Towards a dialogic theory of how children learn to think. *Thinking Skills and Creativity*, *6*(3), 179–190. DOI: 10.1016/j.tsc.2011.08.002

Xiao, J., Bozkurt, A., Nichols, M., Pazurek, A., Stracke, C. M., Bai, J. Y. H., Farrow, R., Mulligan, D., Nerantzi, C., Sharma, R. C., Singh, L., Frumin, I., Swindell, A., Honeychurch, S., Bond, M., Dron, J., Moore, S., Leng, J., van Tryon, P. J. S., & Themeli, C. (2025). Venturing into the Unknown: Critical Insights into Grey Areas and Pioneering Future Directions in Educational Generative AI Research. *TechTrends*, *69*(3), 582–597. DOI: 10.1007/s11528-025-01060-6

Yannakakis, G. N., Liapis, A., & Alexopoulos, C. (2014). *Mixed-Initiative Co-Creativity*. https://antoniosliapis.com/papers/mixed_initiative_co-creativity.pdf

Zafari, M., Bazargani, J. S., Sadeghi-Niaraki, A., & Choi, S.-M. (2022a). Artificial intelligence applications in K-12 education: A systematic literature review. *IEEE Access : Practical Innovations, Open Solutions*, *10*, 61905–61921. DOI: 10.1109/ACCESS.2022.3179356

Zafari, M., Bazargani, J. S., Sadeghi-Niaraki, A., & Choi, S.-M. (2022b). Artificial intelligence applications in K-12 education: A systematic literature review. *IEEE Access : Practical Innovations, Open Solutions*, *10*, 61905–61921. DOI: 10.1109/ACCESS.2022.3179356

Zhai, C., Wibowo, S., & Li, L. D. (2024). The effects of over-reliance on AI dialogue systems on students' cognitive abilities: A systematic review. *Smart Learning Environments*, *11*(1), 1–37. DOI: 10.1186/s40561-024-00316-7

Zhai, X., Chu, X., Chai, C. S., Jong, M. S. Y., Istenic, A., Spector, M., Liu, J.-B., Yuan, J., & Li, Y. (2021a). A review of artificial intelligence (AI) in education from 2010 to 2020. *Complexity*, *2021*(1), 1–18. DOI: 10.1155/2021/8812542

Zhai, X., Chu, X., Chai, C. S., Jong, M. S. Y., Istenic, A., Spector, M., Liu, J.-B., Yuan, J., & Li, Y. (2021b). A review of artificial intelligence (AI) in education from 2010 to 2020. *Complexity*, *2021*(1), 1–18. DOI: 10.1155/2021/8812542

Zhou, E., & Lee, D. (2024). Generative artificial intelligence, human creativity, and art. *PNAS Nexus*, *3*(3), gae052. Advance online publication. DOI: 10.1093/pnasnexus/pgae052 PMID: 38444602

Chapter 4
The Role of AI in Bridging Learning Gaps for At-Risk Students

Mustafa Kayyali
http://orcid.org/0000-0003-3300-262X
Maaref University of Applied Sciences, Syria

ABSTRACT

The educational system often fails those who need it most—students marginalized by poverty, language barriers, trauma, or inconsistent support. This chapter explores how artificial intelligence, when wielded thoughtfully, can help bridge these long-standing learning gaps. By offering real-time feedback, personalized pathways, and data-informed intervention, AI-driven tools like virtual tutors provide at-risk students with the kind of individualized attention that traditional classrooms struggle to deliver. But while the promise is powerful, it is not without peril. Ethical concerns around bias, surveillance, and access disparities must be addressed with urgency and humility. Drawing from real-world implementations and critical research, this chapter argues that AI can be more than just a tool—it can be a lifeline. If designed with care and guided by equity, AI has the potential to not only support learning but to radically reimagine what inclusive education can be.

INTRODUCTION

When the system fails, it often fails quietly. Not with a crash, but with a slow erosion—of confidence, of possibility, of a child's belief that they belong in a classroom. Every day, in schools across the world, there are students sitting in the back of the room—unseen, unheard, unserved. Some are dealing with unstable housing.

DOI: 10.4018/979-8-3373-2637-5.ch004

Others are translating a new language in their heads while trying to solve for x. Still others carry trauma, anxiety, or undiagnosed learning differences like invisible backpacks. We call them *at-risk*, but the term, clinical as it sounds, doesn't capture the heartbreak. These are students who are at risk of being forgotten, overlooked by standardized systems that prize uniformity over humanity. They are not lacking intelligence, creativity, or potential. What they lack—often through no fault of their own—is access, continuity, and the tailored support they need to catch up, keep up, or simply not give up.

Traditional classroom models, structured around rigid schedules and mass instruction, often struggle to meet these students where they are (Burden, 2025). Teachers, many of them overworked and under-resourced, do their best. But even the most dedicated educators face the impossible math of trying to divide their attention equally among dozens of students, each with a wildly different story. Time, as it turns out, is not just a constraint—it's a gatekeeper.

This is where artificial intelligence begins to make a compelling case—not as a replacement for teachers, but as an ally. Virtual tutors, adaptive learning platforms, and AI-powered diagnostic tools are no longer concepts on the horizon (Strielkowski et al, 2025). They're already embedded in many learning environments, sometimes quietly, sometimes imperfectly, but with growing influence. These tools have the potential to do what human instructors, despite their best efforts, cannot always manage: track minute-by-minute engagement, detect subtle patterns of struggle, and adapt content delivery in real time. For at-risk students, this isn't a novelty—it's a necessity. But this chapter doesn't approach AI with blind optimism (Papadakis et al., 2024a, 2024b). The hype around educational technology often glosses over harsh truths: data privacy concerns, algorithmic bias, the digital divide, and the danger of dehumanizing learners in pursuit of efficiency (George, 2024). At its worst, AI can entrench existing inequities under the illusion of objectivity. At its best, though—when designed ethically, deployed thoughtfully, and constantly interrogated—it can create learning experiences that are as nuanced and responsive as the students themselves.

This chapter examines the delicate dance between promise and peril. It unpacks the challenges at-risk students face, explores how AI-based tools can serve as lifelines, and addresses the ethical responsibilities that come with integrating AI into educational contexts (Kayyali, 2026. We will look beyond the surface of technological innovation and ask harder questions: Who gets to benefit? Who might be left out? And how can we ensure that in trying to fix the system, we don't end up reinforcing the very dynamics we seek to dismantle? Because at the heart of it all lies a very human question: *How do we build a world where every student—not just the lucky, the well-supported, or the easy-to-teach—feels seen, understood, and capable of thriving?*

UNDERSTANDING AT-RISK STUDENTS: BARRIERS, BIASES, AND BROKEN SYSTEMS

You can't always see it. That soft ache behind a student's silence. The way their eyes scan a page but never settle. The subtle fidget in their fingers when it's their turn to read aloud. What looks like distraction might be hunger. What gets labeled as laziness could be grief in disguise. "At-risk" is the term we use, but it's sterile. Sanitized. It tells us nothing about the weight a child might carry into the classroom each day, or the thousand invisible threads tugging them quietly toward failure.

Let's not pretend this is a new conversation. We've known, for decades, that some students start the race from further back—held hostage by poverty, systemic neglect, language barriers, learning differences, and the raw math of inequity (Spencer et al, 2022). But what we talk about less—far less—is how the system itself often deepens the very vulnerabilities it's supposed to heal. It's not just that these students are at risk. It's that the system makes the risk worse. And yet, we diagnose the symptoms more than we interrogate the disease.

- **What We Mean When We Say "At-Risk":** Let's be honest: the label "at-risk" is both overused and underexamined. It's a catchall term, tossed around in policy papers, staff meetings, and budget proposals. But ask five educators to define it, and you'll get five different answers—some pointing to income, others to behavior, attendance, trauma, or test scores. The problem is, the label tends to flatten complexity. It implies fragility, but often erases strength. It paints with broad strokes—sometimes so broad that the nuances vanish. A child whose parents are incarcerated. A recent refugee navigating a new language and culture. A student dealing with undiagnosed ADHD. A teenager sleeping in a car (White, 2025). All get lumped into the same bucket. "At-risk." But the *why* matters. The story matters. The silence between the data points matters. These aren't students with deficits. They're students with interrupted access. Interrupted safety. Interrupted care. And the term "at-risk" should never imply that they themselves are broken. It should indict the systems that failed to protect their right to learn with dignity.
- **Barriers: Not Just Obstacles, But Architectures:** There's something deeply unsettling about the word *barrier*. It implies something external, something separate from the learner. But often, these barriers are baked into the very architecture of schooling—schedules that punish lateness instead of asking why a child is late, grading systems that reward compliance over creativity, curriculum models that presume a single "normal" pace of comprehension. A kid misses school because of instability at home—maybe a shelter bed wasn't available, or mom's shift ran late. When they return, they're already

behind. The content's moved on. The teacher has 30 other faces to attend to. There's no rewind button. And the subtle message lands: *You've failed to keep up, and now it's your responsibility to catch up.* It's a treadmill without mercy. Or consider linguistic barriers. For multilingual learners, classrooms become linguistic obstacle courses. Instructions delivered too fast. Cultural references they don't share. Assessments that confuse decoding with understanding (Xu et al, 2023). The brilliance is there—buried under translation fatigue and social pressure to "fit in." We measure speed but not endurance. And that's a grave injustice. Then there's the psychological toll. If a student is constantly reminded, through grades, stares, or silence, that they don't belong—eventually, they believe it. That belief calcifies into learned helplessness. And that's the cruelest barrier of all: when a child no longer sees the point in trying.

- **Biases in the Hallways and in the Code:** It's easy to talk about biases as unconscious. But unconscious doesn't mean harmless. Bias lives in the subtle calculus of teacher expectations—who gets called on, who gets second chances, who's labeled "disruptive" vs. "spirited." Study after study has shown that race, language, gender identity, and socioeconomic background shape how students are perceived and treated, even when intent isn't malicious. A Black boy with a strong voice is more likely to be labeled aggressive. A Latina student might be complimented for her "attitude" instead of her intellect. And students who don't perform "standard" English are too often treated as less intelligent, despite the rich cognitive complexity of their code-switching. But bias also creeps into the systems we build. Into the algorithms that recommend interventions. Into the data dashboards teachers are told to consult. If the data reflects past prejudice—punitive discipline, exclusionary tracking—then the AI systems trained on that data will echo it back (Giantini, 2023). And the students most in need of compassion may be flagged as problems before anyone ever sees their potential. Bias isn't just an individual failure. It's systemic patterning that requires active disruption.
- **The Broken Machinery: Where Bureaucracy Betrays the Child:** Let's talk about the machinery—school systems, funding formulas, teacher-to-student ratios, mental health services that are understaffed and underfunded, disciplinary policies that prioritize control over connection. It's all interconnected. And when it fails, it fails with cascading consequences. Too often, schools serving the highest concentrations of at-risk students are also those with the fewest resources. Outdated textbooks. Spotty Wi-Fi. Teachers leaving mid-year because the emotional toll is unsustainable. Counselors managing caseloads in the hundreds. Special education services delayed or denied (Stewart, 2023). And layered over it all is the burden of testing—

high-stakes, one-size-fits-all assessments that reduce children to numbers, then use those numbers to justify more surveillance, more remediation, more pressure. In such systems, innovation rarely trickles down. Experimental programs, flexible models, pilot projects—they're more likely to show up in high-performing schools, not in the districts gasping for air. The students who need the most radical support get the most rigid structures. That's not just inefficiency. It's cruelty masked as standardization. And let's not ignore the role of trauma. Chronic stress, exposure to violence, housing insecurity—these shape how the brain processes information. They don't make learning impossible (Harms & Garrett-Ruffin, 2023). But they demand approaches grounded in neuroscience, not punishment. Too often, though, these students are punished for their survival strategies: hypervigilance gets read as aggression, withdrawal as defiance. We criminalize the symptoms instead of healing the cause.

- **What Gets Measured Gets Funded—And That's Part of the Problem:** We love numbers in education. Attendance rates. GPA. Literacy benchmarks. And sure, data matters. But when the metrics dominate the mission, we lose sight of what truly defines progress (Wolff & Ludvik, 2023). There are no numbers for the moment a child dares to speak up in class for the first time. No dashboard captures the trust rebuilt after months of silence. No algorithm recognizes resilience when a student keeps showing up, even when everything else tells them not to. Those moments are real. But they don't show up on funding reports. Worse still, when schools are judged solely on standardized outcomes, they often double down on practices that exclude. Remediation over enrichment. Drills over dialogue. Discipline over empathy. And students who don't test well—who are recovering from trauma, navigating multiple languages, or living in chaos—are deemed expendable in the quest for higher scores. It's a perverse incentive structure. And it's costing lives, not just letter grades.
- **Beyond the Diagnosis: Seeing the Child, Not the Category:** It's easy, when discussing at-risk students, to drift into abstraction. To reduce them to types or clusters or case studies. But let's not forget: each of these students is a person. A universe of experience. A child with quirks and questions and favorite colors. The goal should never be to pathologize them into compliance, but to nurture them toward wholeness. To do that, we have to start by listening—really listening. Not just to what they say, but to what they don't yet know how to articulate. We have to believe them when they describe their realities, even when those realities are inconvenient. And we have to involve them—not just as recipients of support, but as co-creators of it. Too many interventions are built *for* students, without being built *with* them. But the students know

what they need. Sometimes it's flexibility. Sometimes it's food. Sometimes it's simply someone who won't give up on them.

- **A System Built for Someone Else:** At its core, the modern education system was not designed for multiplicity. It was built on industrial principles—standardization, efficiency, uniform outputs (Kinyaduka, 2024). But children are not widgets. And students who diverge from the imagined norm—because of poverty, neurodivergence, migration, trauma, or difference—are too often treated as problems to be managed rather than people to be supported. That's not a flaw in the system. That *is* the system. To support at-risk learners, we need to challenge the very foundations of how schooling is organized. We need to rethink pacing guides, bell schedules, disciplinary frameworks, and curriculum mandates. We need spaces that are porous to real life—where teachers can be human, where learning can be nonlinear, where support is proactive, not punitive. And we need to stop asking, "How do we make these students fit the system?" The better question is: *How do we make the system worthy of their complexity?*

Table 1. Intervention Toolkit Matrix (At-Risk Learners)

Tool/ Approach	Signals used	Supports provided	Risks/Watch-outs
Early-warning signals	Attendance dips; stalled mastery; sentiment from reflections	Advisor check-in within 24h; family SMS; teacher note	False positives; stigma risk
Adaptive reading coach	Phonics gaps; decoding; fluency timing	Decodable texts; audio supports; spaced practice	Over-simplification; boredom
Adaptive math tutor	Error patterns; misconceptions by skill	Granular hints; visual models; mastery gating	Gaming the system; narrow focus
Language scaffolds	Translation, glossaries, simplified prompts	Dual-language content; bilingual chat; vocab pre-teach	Loss of rigor; reliance
SEL/ behavior nudge	Calm prompts; break timers; coping strategies	De-escalation cues; praise ratio; self-checks	Over-monitoring; privacy
Executive-function aide	Planning; reminders; chunking tasks	Checklists; calendars; micro-deadlines	Notification fatigue
Family engagement	Two-way messaging; goal sharing	Progress snapshots; at-home tips; language support	Mismatch of expectations

So, what does all this have to do with artificial intelligence? Everything. Because if we don't first understand the tangled web of obstacles that at-risk students face—the barriers etched into policy, the biases coded into culture, the brokenness baked into bureaucracy—then no amount of AI, no matter how sophisticated, will fix anything. Technology doesn't operate in a vacuum. It inherits the values, intentions, and blind spots of the systems that create it. Before we build tools for "at-risk learners," we must ask: Whose needs are we centering? Whose voices are being heard? And most of all—what would it look like to design educational systems that *start* with the students at the margins, not as an afterthought, but as the blueprint? Because if we can build for them, we can build for everyone.

THE PROMISE OF AI: MOVING BEYOND ONE-SIZE-FITS-ALL IN K–12 LEARNING

You can walk into almost any classroom and feel it—the subtle tension between sameness and difference. Thirty students, one curriculum. A single clock ticking away the minutes, a whiteboard filled with standardized objectives, and behind each desk, a wildly unique mind trying to make sense of it all. Some race ahead. Others quietly fall behind. Most drift somewhere in between. And the system, bound by tradition and logistics, asks all of them to meet it in the middle. It's a compromise we've grown used to. We've normalized the factory model of education: same lessons, same pace, same metrics. Mass-produced learning in neat little time slots. But here's the hard truth—uniformity has a cost. And it's often paid by the students who can least afford to fall through the cracks. Enter artificial intelligence. Not as a fix-all. Not as some gleaming deus ex machina. But as a possible turning point—an inflection in our pedagogical story (Sallas, 2024). A chance to reimagine what it means to teach, to learn, and most importantly, to be *seen*.

The Trouble With the Middle

Let's be blunt: education has long been haunted by the myth of the average. Policies are built around it (Shelton, 2023). Textbooks are written for it. But the "average student" is a statistical ghost. They don't exist. Never did. Some kids learn in arcs. Others in sudden leaps. Some need pictures. Some need movement. Some need silence. Some need to talk it out loud, even when they don't know what they're trying to say. And yet, our systems—stretched thin and wired for efficiency—struggle to accommodate this human variety. This is where AI starts to whisper a new possibility: What if every learner could have their own path? Not just a modified worksheet. Not just extended time on a test. But a learning environment that bends *toward* them. That listens. Watches. Adapts. One that doesn't assume mastery based on a week's pacing guide or punish deviation from the norm.

One that understands—deeply, precisely, compassionately—that learning is messy, nonlinear, and beautifully uneven.

Not Magic, But Mirrors

Let's dismantle a common misconception first. AI is not magic. It doesn't possess intent, curiosity, or compassion. It doesn't dream or doubt. But what it *can* do—better than any human—is process vast streams of information (Gadde, 2023). Patterns, anomalies, feedback loops. It can do in seconds what a human might miss across an entire semester. And in education, this matters. Imagine a platform that notices a student consistently pausing on specific vocabulary, even though they complete the assignments on time. Or one that recognizes a subtle decline in confidence, tracked through how long a student hesitates before submitting an answer. These aren't just statistics—they're signals. Whispers from the learner. And AI, at its best, can catch them before they become cries for help. This is not to say that data replaces intuition. But it *can* inform it. Augment it. Make it sharper. A teacher armed with AI-generated insights doesn't become less human—they become *more attuned*. The machine doesn't replace empathy; it amplifies its reach.

Personalized Pathways: Not Just Buzzwords

There's a danger in how we talk about personalization in education. It's been commodified—turned into a marketing slogan for every edtech startup promising miracles (Simons & Masschelein, 2021). But true personalization isn't about flashy dashboards or gamified apps. It's about honoring the learner's pace, preferences, and prior knowledge. It's about tailoring—not standardizing—support. AI can facilitate this in unprecedented ways. Picture a student struggling with fractions. The old model might hand them a remedial worksheet. But an AI-driven tutor could detect *why* they're struggling—conceptual confusion, fatigue, anxiety—and then adjust the material accordingly. It might switch to visuals, slow down the sequence, offer hints, or revisit foundational concepts. It does not move on because the calendar says so. It waits. It loops. It reconfigures. The same system might notice that another student is breezing through linear equations but stalls when asked to apply them in word problems. Again, it pivots. Not by labeling that student "advanced" or "behind," but by adjusting the learning experience itself—scaffolded, responsive, alive. Now multiply that precision across hundreds of students. That's the promise—not a one-size-fits-all model, but a model that stretches and folds to fit the learner.

Figure 1. AI Support Focus for At-Risk Students

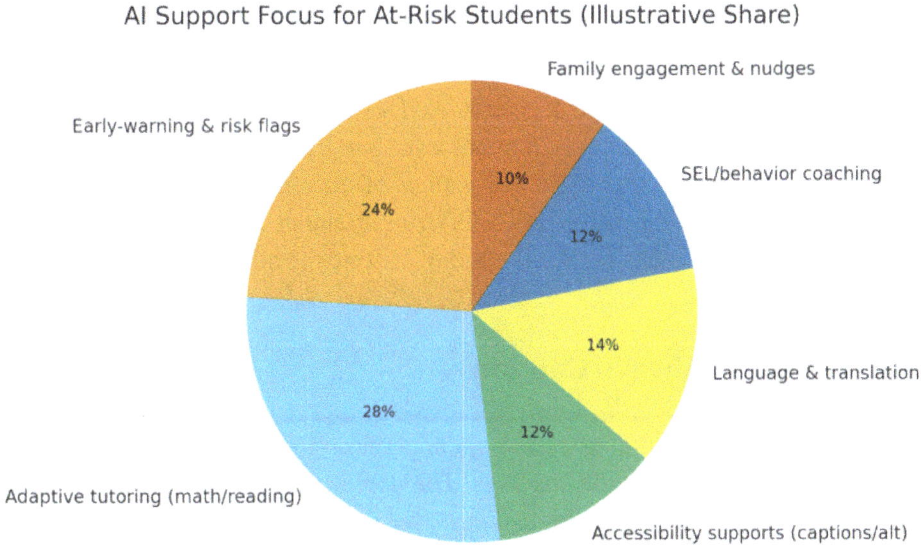

The Emotional Dimension: When Technology Listens Without Judging

One of the most quietly revolutionary aspects of AI in education is how it can create a judgment-free space for students to explore, fail, and try again (Khan, 2024). Consider the student who never raises their hand. The one who's been called "slow" or "lazy" or simply "behind" so many times that they've internalized the narrative. In a traditional setting, asking a "dumb" question can feel like social suicide. But an AI tutor? It doesn't smirk. Doesn't interrupt. Doesn't give up. It simply responds. Patiently. Repeatedly. Without ego. This matters. For many at-risk students—those dealing with stigma, language barriers, or past educational trauma—AI tools can offer a rare reprieve from judgment. A safe rehearsal space for curiosity. A companion that doesn't laugh at wrong answers but nudges the learner gently toward understanding. That's not just pedagogy. That's healing.

Scale Without Abandoning the Individual

Education reform has always wrestled with the tension between scale and intimacy (Nichols & Dixon-Román, 2024). How do you deliver quality instruction to millions without losing the soul of learning? It's a paradox. The more standardized we make it, the more efficient it becomes—but the more students we lose along the way. AI offers a partial solution. It can operate at scale without flattening the learner's identity. It can process millions of data points while still tailoring responses to a single child's struggle with decimals. And when integrated thoughtfully, it can free up teachers to do what only humans can: build relationships, spark wonder, respond to emotion. The dream isn't AI *instead* of teachers. It's AI *alongside* them. Lifting the burden of repetitive tasks. Offering granular insights. Catching what we might miss in the chaos of the school day. Letting the human heart of education beat louder, not softer.

But... Caution. Always Caution.

Now, it would be irresponsible—no, dangerous—to talk about the promise of AI without acknowledging the shadows. The data it uses? It can reflect bias. The algorithms? They can reinforce exclusion. A tool meant to "flag struggling students" could easily become a surveillance mechanism, disproportionately punishing neurodivergent kids or students of color. A system designed to track "progress" might overlook emotional nuance, cultural difference, or creative divergence (Aithal & Aithal, 2023). The metrics are seductive. But metrics are not meaning. And then there's access. Fancy AI tutors don't mean much if your school doesn't have working Wi-Fi. Or if your community distrusts tech. Or if your platform doesn't support multilingual learners. Personalization, without inclusion, becomes another gatekeeper. So yes—AI holds promise. But it demands vigilance. Transparency. Human oversight. We must ask, again and again: *Whose values are embedded in this system? Who gets to decide what "success" looks like? Who's being left out?*

It's Not the Tool. It's the Intention Behind It.

At its core, AI is just a reflection of us—our brilliance, our blind spots, our dreams for what education could be. Used wisely, it can be a tool of liberation. Used carelessly, it can deepen harm (Youvan, 2024). But let's not throw away the possibility because the road is hard. Let's imagine what it would look like to design AI systems that center equity, humility, and care. Tools that don't just react to deficits, but anticipate strengths. That don't just deliver content, but cultivate confidence. Let's imagine a world where a child no longer has to wait weeks for feedback, or be tracked into a lower-level group because of one bad test day. Where students who learn differently don't get sidelined—they get tailored support. Where success is not measured by conformity, but by growth, resilience, joy. AI won't save education. But it *can* help us listen better. Respond faster. Personalize with grace.

The Human Remains

It always comes back to this: the human. The promise of AI is not that it replaces teachers. It's that it gives them back what they've been starved of—*time*. Time to notice. Time to connect. Time to do the messy, relational, intuitive work that no algorithm can replicate (Louis & ElAzab, 2023). A great teacher doesn't just transfer knowledge. They awaken it. They bear witness to a student's becoming. And if AI can help lighten the load—if it can catch the patterns, adapt the pace, offer scaffolds—then the teacher is freed to do what they were born to do: *see* the child in front of them. That's the promise. Not smarter machines. But more human classrooms.

VIRTUAL TUTORS AND ADAPTIVE PLATFORMS: DESIGNING WITH EMPATHY AND PRECISION

There's something almost poetic about the idea: a tutor who never grows impatient, never misjudges a student's silence, never forgets where they left off (Lampropoulos & Papadakis, 2025). One who shows up—consistently, unconditionally—on a screen at midnight or midday, whispering encouragement in code. Who adjusts without complaint, who learns you as you learn. For the student who's been forgotten in the shuffle of overworked classrooms and understaffed schools, that kind of presence can feel like a small miracle (Hess, 2023). But behind this romanticized image of the "virtual tutor" is something more complicated—more human. Because no matter how smooth the interface or how responsive the algorithm, behind every design choice is a person. A set of assumptions. A worldview. And when the stakes are as high as they are in education, especially for students on the margins, those assumptions matter. Tremendously. So, what does it mean to *design* a virtual tutor—not just functionally, but ethically, precisely, empathetically? It begins by asking not just what the technology *can* do, but what it *should* do. And who it's truly being built for.

- **The Difference Between a Tutor and a Tool:** Let's start with the basics. A "virtual tutor" is not merely a digitized worksheet or an interactive slideshow. It's a system—often powered by machine learning—that simulates the guidance, feedback, and adaptivity of a one-on-one teaching relationship. Unlike a fixed curriculum, it flexes. Unlike a traditional textbook, it learns. And in its best iterations, it doesn't just *deliver* knowledge—it *co-constructs* understanding. That distinction matters. Because too many platforms are still stuck in the broadcast model: flashy, yes. But beneath the polish, they're static. Linear. Impersonal. The same for every student, whether you're racing ahead or barely holding on. True virtual tutors move differently. They monitor not just correctness, but *process*. They learn how you learn. They notice the moment you hesitate before clicking an answer, or how often you return to the same kind of problem. And they shift in response—not with punishment, but with curiosity. Still, no matter how sophisticated the backend, the essence of a tutor isn't in the code. It's in the relationship. Which raises an uncomfortable question: Can an algorithm be empathetic? Of course not. But it can be *designed* with empathy in mind.

- **Empathy by Design: The Human Heart Inside the Machine:** Empathy in software is not about sentimentality. It's about *sensitivity*—to context, to user experience, to emotional nuance. When we design adaptive platforms for education, especially those intended for vulnerable or at-risk learners, empathy has to sit at the center of every design decision (Webb, 2024). It shows up in small but powerful ways. In how the system responds to repeated mistakes. In whether it gives space to reflect or pressures forward movement. In whether it penalizes wrong answers or offers insight into *why* they were wrong. In whether the feedback feels coldly robotic or gently human. Empathetic design doesn't mean pretending the machine is a person. It means anticipating the needs of the learner with humility. It means understanding that behind every "user" is a child—with a story, a struggle, and a self-concept more fragile than they let on. Consider the tone of a prompt. "Incorrect. Try again." Now contrast that with: "Almost. Want to take another shot?" The first reinforces failure. The second extends an invitation. And that tone—casual, warm, forgiving—can make all the difference for a student already teetering on the edge of disengagement.
- **Precision Isn't Cold. It's Careful:** Let's talk about precision—not the surgical kind that slices, but the kind that studies closely, listens long, and adjusts with respect. Adaptive platforms live and die by their ability to personalize (Kayyali, 2025). But personalization isn't just about offering easier or harder questions (Rane et al, 2023). It's about *understanding what kind of support a learner needs at any given moment.* That's harder than it sounds. Take a student who's mastered multiplication in isolation, but fumbles when the same skill shows up in a word problem. A lesser system might interpret this as inconsistency. A truly adaptive one digs deeper. It asks whether the challenge lies in the math or the language. Is it the vocabulary? The context-switching? The cognitive load of multi-step instructions? Precision, in this sense, is not just about giving the right content. It's about asking the right questions of the data—and of the learner. And it extends beyond content delivery. It includes pacing. Format. Visual scaffolds. When to offer a hint, and when to wait. When to suggest a break. When to simply pause. This kind of fine-tuning isn't

flashy. But it's powerful. It respects the learner's rhythm. It says: *I see how you move. Let me match you.*

- **The Risk of Overreach:** Now, let's pause here and complicate things. Because every promise of personalization carries a shadow. When virtual tutors collect data—on engagement, performance, even emotional state—they create detailed learner profiles (Solé-Beteta et al, 2022). That information can be incredibly helpful. But it's also deeply intimate. And if mishandled, it becomes intrusive (Kayyali, 2024). Who controls that data? Who decides what counts as "struggling"? What if the system nudges students toward certain tracks, certain subjects, based on flawed assumptions or biased inputs? What happens when a mistake made in sixth grade gets encoded into a permanent learner record? These are not hypothetical concerns. Already, we've seen algorithmic systems in other domains (criminal justice, hiring, healthcare) replicate and amplify bias. Education is not immune. That's why designing with empathy *also* means designing with caution. With ethical guardrails. With transparency. Students and their families have a right to know how their data is being used, who has access to it, and whether it can be challenged or deleted. And educators need systems that explain their reasoning—not black boxes, but tools that can be questioned, tweaked, overridden. Because while precision is a strength, *overconfidence in precision* is a threat.
- **When Design Meets Pedagogy:** It's easy to think of virtual tutors as tech products. But they are, at heart, pedagogical instruments (Vlachopoulos & Makri, 2021). And the values of the people who build them seep into their architecture. Is the platform grounded in behaviorism, rewarding correct answers and punishing mistakes? Or is it constructivist, encouraging exploration and mistake-making as part of learning? Does it prioritize speed and efficiency, or depth and transfer? Does it recognize multiple kinds of intelligence, or just the ones that are easy to quantify? These questions aren't just philosophical—they're practical. They shape what students experience, how they perceive their own abilities, and how they internalize the process of learning. The best platforms are built not just by coders, but by teams that include teachers, students, psychologists, ethicists, and designers. Because learning isn't just information transfer—it's emotional, social, cultural. You can't code your way around that. But you *can* code with it in mind.
- **Accessibility Isn't an Afterthought:** A virtual tutor that works beautifully on the latest iPad is useless to a student without internet at home (Couch, 2023). A platform that assumes English fluency won't reach the newcomer navigating their fourth school in two years. A chatbot that uses pop culture slang might alienate students from different cultural contexts. Accessibility is not a checklist. It's a mindset. It means asking: Who might this not work for?

And how do we change that? It's about offering content in multiple formats—text, audio, visual. It's about screen readers and translation tools. It's about offline functionality. It's about slow-loading options for areas with weak connectivity. It's about making sure a student with dyslexia can navigate the interface just as easily as a student with perfect vision and neurotypical processing. Too often, tech is built for the ideal user. But education doesn't have ideal users. It has real humans—with needs that shift by the hour. And the tools we build must flex to meet them.

- **Virtual Presence, Real Trust:** Let's circle back to something often overlooked in the conversation about AI in education: *trust*. Students don't just need access to information. They need to feel safe enough to engage with it. They need to believe that the system they're interacting with won't shame them, track them unfairly, or betray their efforts. This is harder to build with a screen. But not impossible. Virtual tutors that offer personalized affirmations, that celebrate effort over outcome, that make room for reflection—these build trust. And once trust is there, the possibilities open up. A student who trusts the platform is more likely to explore. To take risks. To say, "I don't get this," without fear of being labeled. And that, more than any AI breakthrough, is the beginning of real learning.

Figure 2. Waterfall of Contributors to Closing a Literacy Gap

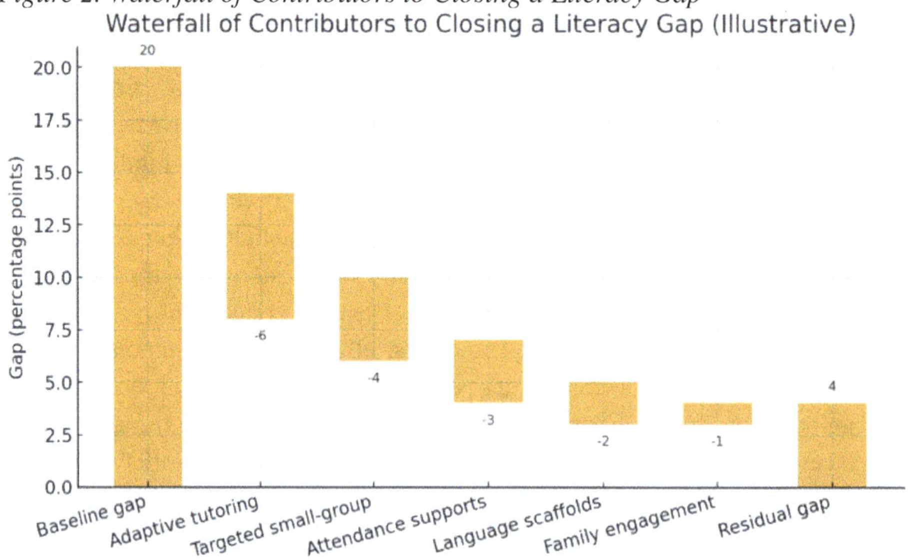

Virtual tutors are not saviors. They are companions—when built well. When built with care, they accompany students through the messy, nonlinear, deeply human journey of learning. But to earn that place, they must be humble. Transparent. Responsive. Designed not to dictate, but to dialogue. Not to automate teaching, but to support it. Not to standardize success, but to expand its definition. Let's not build platforms that *teach at* students. Let's build ones that *learn with* them. Because the goal isn't just smarter software.

It's wiser, kinder, more inclusive learning ecosystems. And maybe—just maybe—a world where no student ever has to feel invisible again.

ETHICAL IMPERATIVES AND EQUITY DILEMMAS IN AI-DRIVEN INTERVENTION

There's a moment—often quiet, almost forgettable—when a child realizes they've been sorted. Maybe it's the subtle tone of a teacher's voice when explaining something too slowly. Maybe it's the app that never gives them harder questions. Maybe it's the silence after asking for help and not getting it. That moment doesn't show up in the data. But it lingers. A slow drip eroding belief. Now imagine a machine doing the sorting. Not with malice, not with intention—but with rules written far away, by people who've never met that child, never stood in their classroom, never asked what it means to be told—algorithmically—*you're not ready*. This is where the story of artificial intelligence in education begins to fray at the edges. Because for all its potential to help, AI also introduces something more insidious: the ability to embed bias at scale, to automate inequality under the guise of efficiency, and to do so invisibly. If we're going to use AI to intervene in students' lives, especially those already at risk, we need to talk—honestly, unflinchingly—about ethics. About equity. About power.

Who Designs the Intervention—and Who Gets Intervened Upon?

Let's start here: AI systems don't design themselves. They're made. Engineered. Trained. Every line of code, every decision tree, every "if this, then that" is the result of human judgment. That judgment is shaped by culture, context, and yes, bias—both conscious and unconscious. And here's the uncomfortable truth: many of the developers building these tools don't come from the communities they're meant to serve. They don't speak the dialects. Haven't navigated food insecurity. Don't know what it's like to be labeled "behind" before you've had a fair shot. So, what happens when a tool designed in Silicon Valley is used to determine whether a kid in South Memphis needs "remediation"? What happens when the categories are rigid, the definitions narrow, the assumptions unchecked? Too often, it's the most vulnerable students—Black and brown kids, English learners, neurodivergent learners—who bear the brunt of intervention systems. Not because they're more in need, but because they're more visible to the data. More flagged. More categorized. And once the system decides, it becomes hard to argue. The algorithm doesn't debate. It predicts. It recommends. And we trust it—sometimes more than we trust the child in front of us.

The Allure of Objectivity—and the Lie Beneath It

One of AI's biggest selling points is its supposed neutrality. No favoritism, no fatigue, no human error (Gao & An, 2024). But here's the thing: objectivity in AI is often a façade. Because AI doesn't arise from nowhere. It learns from data. And that data reflects our world—messy, biased, unequal. If disciplinary data in a district shows that Black students are suspended at higher rates, and that data trains the AI, then the system "learns" that those students are more disruptive. Not because it's true. But because the *history* says so. The model becomes a mirror. And the mirror reflects back our worst tendencies, disguised as science. Even more troubling is that AI decisions often come wrapped in complexity. A teacher might question their own bias. A principal might be held accountable for disparities. But who questions the algorithm? Who audits the code? Who explains to a student why their learning path is narrower than their peers'—because a black-box system said so? And if you can't interrogate the logic, how can you resist its verdict?

Surveillance Creep in the Classroom

Let's talk about surveillance—because that's what many AI-powered tools are, even if we don't use the word. They track keystrokes. Monitor clicks. Record eye movement. Flag "off-task" behavior. Log response time. Sometimes they analyze voice, tone, even facial expressions. All in the name of "engagement" or "early warning." But at what cost? What message does it send when a student's every move is tracked, stored, analyzed? What does it do to trust? To autonomy? To the idea that learning is a personal, sometimes messy, often nonlinear process? There's something chilling about a system that watches a child too closely—not to understand, but to correct. To control. And who decides what's "normal" behavior anyway? A student staring out the window might be reflecting. A pause might signal deep thinking, not disengagement. But the machine doesn't know that. It sees patterns. Deviations. Red flags. This isn't just about privacy. It's about dignity. Education should not feel like parole.

Consent—Or the Illusion of It

Informed consent is a cornerstone of ethical practice. But in schools, consent gets murky (Pahuja, 2024). Do parents truly understand what they're signing when they agree to a new platform? Are students told what data is being collected, how it will be used, who will see it? Is there an option to opt out? And if so, is it real—or buried in paperwork, laced with consequences? Too often, the answer is no. Schools adopt new technologies out of necessity, pressure, or optimism. But the people most affected—students and families—are rarely included in those decisions. Consent becomes performative. A checkbox. A form. But ethical AI requires more. It requires transparency. Dialogue. Accountability. It requires treating students not just as data subjects, but as human beings with rights.

The Equity Paradox: Personalized Learning, Unequal Access

Let's pause and consider an irony. AI promises personalization. Tailored paths. Equity of opportunity. But the reality? These tools often work best in the places that need them least. High-resourced schools have fast internet, tech support, professional development. Their students come in with digital fluency (Amgott & Renfroe, 2025). Their families advocate. Their teachers get trained. Meanwhile, in underfunded schools, devices crash. Platforms lag. Teachers are overwhelmed. Students share laptops with siblings. And the very tools meant to close the gap end up widening it. This is the equity paradox. Technology doesn't float above the world. It lands in it. And it lands unevenly. So, before we celebrate AI's promise, we have to ask: *Who gets access to the promise? And who gets left behind with the problems?*

Labeling vs. Liberating

AI excels at pattern recognition. Categorization. Risk assessment (Röhrs et al, 2024). But what happens when those categories become cages? An algorithm might label a student as "at risk." Sounds helpful. But that label can stick. It can follow them through systems. Shape teacher expectations. Influence placement decisions. Dictate intervention types. What began as data-driven support becomes a self-fulfilling prophecy. And here's the subtle danger: students internalize the labels. They see the path narrowed. The ceiling lowered. The words "support" and "remediation" start to taste like limitation. We must be careful—painfully careful—not to use AI to sort children into futures they didn't choose. Technology should open doors. Not seal fates.

Designing With the Margins in Mind

If we want ethical AI in education, we must design from the margins (Nur et al, 2024). Not add inclusion as an afterthought, but center it from the start. That means involving the students who've been misread, mislabeled, and misserved. It means hiring developers who reflect the diversity of the classrooms they hope to impact. It means funding research in communities that have been studied but never invited to lead the study. And it means rejecting the idea that ethics are a final polish. They are the blueprint. Ask: Would I want this system used on my own child? Would I want this data stored about *me* when I was twelve? If the answer is no, then it's not good enough for anyone.

Accountability in the Age of Algorithms

Accountability can't be outsourced to the machine. Every AI tool used in schools should come with an audit trail. A way to trace decisions. A mechanism for appeal (Falco et al, 2021). A human in the loop—not just for oversight, but for empathy. And there must be consequences when things go wrong. When bias is detected. When harm is done. Not vague apologies, but structural change. Because when we use powerful tools on vulnerable populations, the burden of proof isn't on the student to adapt. It's on the system to protect.

Underneath all this talk of fairness, consent, bias, and data, lies something simpler. Older. More human. Care. Ethical AI isn't about perfection. It's about care. About designing systems that assume dignity, not deficiency. That treat errors as information, not as identity. That respond to difference with curiosity, not control. Education is an act of hope. Of trust. Of believing in the potential of young people. If we forget that in our pursuit of smart systems, we'll have lost the plot. So, let's write new stories. Where AI supports without surveilling. Learns without labeling. Intervenes without erasing. Let's build not just intelligent tools—but wise ones. Kind ones. Brave ones. Because the future of learning is not just about what we *can* do with AI. It's about what we *refuse* to do in its name.

FROM DATA TO TRANSFORMATION: REIMAGINING SUPPORT FOR AT-RISK LEARNERS

Data. It starts as numbers—rows in a spreadsheet, lines in a log, blinking metrics on a dashboard. Neat. Precise. Deceptively silent. But behind those figures are lives. Behind every dropout percentage is a name. Behind every red alert, a child with a backpack too heavy, or a home too loud, or a body that won't sit still the way the classroom demands. Behind every "at-risk" flag is a person. Not a statistic. A story. That's the part we can't afford to forget. We've gathered so much data in education—test scores, attendance logs, behavior reports, keystroke histories, even biometric feedback. We've quantified engagement, predicted failure, gamified progress. The numbers swirl, always chasing some elusive promise of insight. But what happens when the data begins to take the place of the child? When we know the metrics but forget the meaning? The question isn't whether we have enough data. We do. Mountains of it. The real question is—**what are we doing with it?** And even more critically: **what are we *becoming* because of how we use it?**

- **Beyond Prediction: Toward Possibility:** The prevailing narrative in AI-driven education is that data predicts. Dropout risk. Literacy levels. Math fluency. Behavioral trends (Albahli, 2025). Systems scan for anomalies, identify patterns, flag "outliers." And to be fair, that matters. Predicting a student's likelihood to disengage *before* they vanish from the system is powerful. But if all we do is predict, we're still playing defense. We're reacting. What if we reimagined data not as a warning system, but as a *creative* one? Not just about anticipating loss, but unlocking potential. Not just identifying who's struggling, but uncovering hidden strengths, missed opportunities, untapped brilliance. A student who fails every multiple-choice quiz but spends hours building complex digital landscapes in Minecraft? That's data. A child who reads below grade level but tells breathtaking stories orally? Also data. It's not always structured. It's not always easy to measure. But it's real. And it deserves a place in how we understand "achievement." Transformation begins when data is used to build—not to sort, not to surveil, not to punish, but to scaffold, to connect, to humanize.
- **The Danger of Flatness: What Gets Measured, Shapes Reality:** Data has gravity. It pulls attention, resources, decisions. What gets measured, matters. And what doesn't? Vanishes. Standardized testing still dominates educational data ecosystems (Benita et al, 2021). But let's be honest—it captures a narrow slice of learning. Often, it captures compliance more than comprehension. Memorization more than imagination. If we center our systems around those metrics, we're not just reporting reality—we're *shaping* it. Schools start to teach to the data, not the child. And students, especially those already labeled at-risk, get reduced to remediation cycles designed to boost scores, not deepen understanding. The goal was equity. But the result? More worksheets. More scripts. Less joy. If we're serious about reimagining support for at-risk learners, we have to expand the definition of data. We have to listen differently. Track different signals. Care about things that don't fit easily into a dashboard. A student's sense of belonging. Their capacity for self-reflection.

Their relationships with peers. Their creative risk-taking. These are not side notes. They are the foundation of lifelong learning. But they're messy. Harder to quantify. And if we don't fight to value them, we will continue to build systems that reward compliance and punish complexity.

- **Feedback Loops That Heal, Not Hurt:** Data isn't neutral. It talks back. Not with words, but with influence. Show a teacher a red score next to a name, and expectations shift—sometimes subtly, sometimes drastically (Hawkins & Kern, 2024). Show a student their percentile, and they start to carry it like a weight. Sometimes they wear it like a scar. This is the risk of constant tracking. Of dashboards in every classroom. Of students logging in and seeing their "rank" every morning. Feedback loops matter. But they have to be *designed for dignity*. Imagine a platform that tells a student: "You made progress on this concept that used to confuse you," instead of: "You're still below benchmark." Or one that highlights a growth trend, not just a static score. One that offers narrative feedback, not just color-coded alerts. The way we *frame* data shapes the learner's relationship to themselves. Especially for those who already believe they're failing. We should never let data become a mirror of shame. It should be a lens of possibility.
- **Personalization with Purpose:** Let's be careful here. "Personalized learning" is everywhere. It's the tagline for nearly every AI education product (Dembe, 2024). But what does it actually mean? In many systems, personalization just means pacing. Slower track, more hints, automated branching. That's not bad. But it's surface-level. True personalization honors identity, culture, interest, context. A bilingual student should see their linguistic background as a strength, not a hurdle. An Indigenous student should see their history reflected in the curriculum. A student who struggles with traditional text should have access to alternative modes—audio, visual, kinesthetic—not as accommodations, but as valid pathways. This is what real personalization requires: not just more "paths," but *different maps*. It means designing systems that don't just ask, *What's the next skill to master?* But also: *Who is this learner becoming? And what do they need to grow—not just as a student, but as a person?* AI has the computational power to make that happen. But do we have the *will* to embed those values into the system?
- **The Human Layer: Data Needs Interpreters, Not Just Analysts:** No matter how sophisticated the analytics, we cannot leave interpretation solely to machines. Data is context-bound. A drop in engagement might mean disinterest. Or it might mean a family crisis. An increase in behavior incidents could mean defiance. Or maybe the child's medication changed. Or maybe nothing changed—except the teacher. AI can flag anomalies. But only humans can understand them. And not just any humans—humans who *know* the student.

Who ask, *What's going on?* instead of just *What's wrong?* Teachers, counselors, mentors—they must remain the center of the interpretive process. AI can amplify awareness, but it should never replace human attention. We need to protect that human layer with intention. Because without it, we risk treating students like inputs in a system, rather than souls in a journey.

- **Equity Requires Structural Shifts, Not Just Smarter Tech:** This needs to be said loudly: AI will not fix educational inequity if the systems it plugs into remain unjust. You can't personalize away structural racism (Tanksley, 2024). You can't algorithmically scaffold your way out of underfunded schools. You can't data-visualize your way around the trauma students bring with them into classrooms shaped by poverty, displacement, and exclusion. Too often, we ask technology to clean up messes we refuse to confront systemically. But if we use data well—ethically, radically, lovingly—it can help us *see* those patterns more clearly. It can shine a light on where we're failing. Not to shame, but to push us toward action. Data can expose disparities in opportunity, in discipline, in access. It can help us ask better questions. Where are the gaps? Why do they persist? Who's being over-disciplined? Who's not getting referred for enrichment? Used with courage, data can be a truth-teller. But transformation comes when we move from *knowing* to *changing*.
- **Listening to Students—Really Listening:** Let's not forget the simplest source of data: students themselves (Muller & Strohmayer, 2022). Ask them what's working. What's confusing. What makes them feel small. What helps them feel strong. Let them narrate their own learning stories—not just through surveys, but through conversation. Journals. Audio diaries. Reflections. Projects that speak their truths. This isn't just qualitative fluff. It's the most important dataset we have. And yet, it's the one most often ignored. We need systems that integrate student voice *into* the feedback loop. That don't just deliver data *to* them, but collect it *from* them—with consent, with care, with purpose. Imagine a dashboard where a student's weekly reflection sits alongside their quiz performance. Where their self-assessed confidence is weighted as heavily as their response time. That's not just responsive education. That's respectful education.
- **From Systems of Surveillance to Systems of Support:** Let's say this clearly: our job is not to monitor students into submission. It's to build ecosystems of support. Technology can help. But it's just a tool. The transformation happens when we choose to use data not to manage students—but to *believe* in them more fully. What if the purpose of all this AI, all this analytics, wasn't to create the perfect student—but to create the conditions where every student can unfold, at their pace, in their way, with their dignity intact? What if we stopped trying to close gaps *by force*—and started building bridges? Not

every intervention needs to be a correction. Sometimes, support looks like space. Like slowing down. Like listening longer. Sometimes, transformation isn't a dramatic breakthrough. It's a quiet decision to stay. To try again. To raise a hand after months of silence. Those moments can't be graphed. But they matter. And if our data systems can help us notice them—really *see* them—then we're on the right path.

Figure 3. Support Mix for At-Risk Learners Across a 12-Week Term

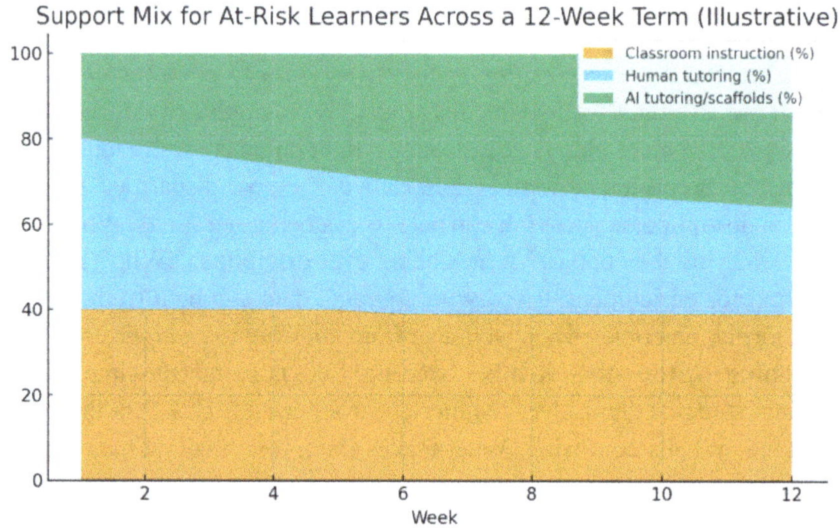

The future of supporting at-risk learners with AI will not be built on formulas or forecasts. It will be built on values (Latif et al, 2022). On decisions made not just by programmers, but by communities. Not in code, but in conversation. The question is not, *What can AI do?* It's, *What do we want it to do—for whom, and why?* And the answer can't come from a spreadsheet. It has to come from a shared vision of equity. Of humanity. Of what education is *for*. Because when the last bell rings, and the screen goes dark, what matters isn't the data point. It's whether the child felt seen. Whether they felt like this place—this system, this tool, this community—believed they were worth the effort. That's the data we should be chasing. That's the transformation we should be building.

CONCLUSION

There's a certain cruelty to a system that expects all students to arrive at the same destination while ignoring that some were never given a map. For too long, at-risk students have been treated as anomalies in a system built for the average. But there is no average student. There is only the complexity of real life—gritty, unpredictable, often unfair—and the remarkable young people navigating it with quiet resilience.

Artificial intelligence will not save education. No algorithm, however sophisticated, can replace the empathy in a teacher's voice or the encouragement in a glance. But AI can extend the reach of that care. It can sit beside the student who's falling behind and whisper: *You're not alone. We see you.* It can free teachers from the tyranny of data entry and let them focus on connection. It can unearth patterns in performance that humans miss, not because we're inattentive, but because we're overwhelmed.

Yet, the path forward is far from simple. Integrating AI into classrooms without reproducing existing inequalities requires more than just good code. It demands critical reflection, inclusive design, and policies rooted in justice. It means building systems that don't just track who's failing, but that work relentlessly to understand *why*. It means involving students and communities in shaping the tools meant to serve them. And it means resisting the urge to let efficiency trump empathy.

AI is not a magic wand—but it *is* a mirror. It reflects our values, our blind spots, and our ambitions. In the context of education, especially for at-risk learners, that mirror reveals a haunting question: if we have the tools to help—and increasingly we do—what excuse remains for not doing better?

As this chapter has argued, the role of AI in bridging learning gaps is neither trivial nor theoretical. It is a moral and pedagogical frontier. The stakes are high not because the technology is fragile, but because the students are. If we get this right, AI can be a tool of equity—quietly revolutionary in its capacity to tailor support, democratize opportunity, and remind forgotten students that their potential is not defined by their past. But if we get it wrong, we risk automating inequality, masking exclusion with the illusion of personalization. And that would be worse than doing nothing at all.

In the end, the question isn't whether we should use AI in education. It's how we will choose to use it—and whether we will do so with the courage, humility, and imagination that the students most in need have always deserved.

REFERENCES

Aithal, P. S., & Aithal, S. (2023). How to increase emotional infrastructure of higher education institutions. [IJMTS]. *International Journal of Management, Technology, and Social Sciences*, *8*(3), 356–394. DOI: 10.47992/IJMTS.2581.6012.0307

Albahli, S. (2025). Advancing Sustainable Educational Practices Through AI-Driven Prediction of Academic Outcomes. *Sustainability (Basel)*, *17*(3), 1087. DOI: 10.3390/su17031087

Amgott, N., & Renfroe, D. (2025). Implementing AI Chatbots in L2 University Courses: Building Pragmatic Competence and Critical Digital Literacy. In Rethinking Language Education in the Age of Generative AI (pp. 185-205). Routledge.

Benita, F., Virupaksha, D., Wilhelm, E., & Tunçer, B. (2021). A smart learning ecosystem design for delivering Data-driven Thinking in STEM education. *Smart Learning Environments*, *8*(1), 1–20. DOI: 10.1186/s40561-021-00153-y PMID: 40477256

Burden, P. R. (2025). *Classroom management: Creating a successful K-12 learning community*. John Wiley & Sons.

Couch, J. D. (2023). *Rewiring education: How technology can unlock every student's potential*. BenBella Books.

Dembe, A. (2024). Advancing personalized learning through educational artificial intelligence: Challenges, opportunities, and future directions. *Res Invent J Eng Phys Sci*, *3*(1), 89–101.

Falco, G., Shneiderman, B., Badger, J., Carrier, R., Dahbura, A., Danks, D., Eling, M., Goodloe, A., Gupta, J., Hart, C., Jirotka, M., Johnson, H., LaPointe, C., Llorens, A. J., Mackworth, A. K., Maple, C., Pálsson, S. E., Pasquale, F., Winfield, A., & Yeong, Z. K. (2021). Governing AI safety through independent audits. *Nature Machine Intelligence*, *3*(7), 566–571. DOI: 10.1038/s42256-021-00370-7

Gadde, H. (2023). Leveraging AI for Scalable Query Processing in Big Data Environments. *International Journal of Advanced Engineering Technologies and Innovations*, *1*(02), 435–465.

Gao, Q., & An, H. (2024). Technology-neutral Illusion: The Ethical and Social Challenges in the Age of Artificial Intelligence. Sociology. *Philosophical Psychology*, *1*(2), 33–40.

George, A. S. (2024). Technology Tension in Schools: Addressing the Complex Impacts of Digital Advances on Teaching, Learning, and Wellbeing. *Partners Universal Multidisciplinary Research Journal*, *1*(3), 49–65.

Giantini, G. (2023). The sophistry of the neutral tool. Weaponizing artificial intelligence and big data into threats toward social exclusion. *AI and Ethics*, *3*(4), 1049–1061. DOI: 10.1007/s43681-023-00311-7

Harms, M. B., & Garrett-Ruffin, S. D. (2023). Disrupting links between poverty, chronic stress, and educational inequality. npj Science of Learning, 8(1), 50.

Hawkins, R., & Kern, L. (2024). *Higher Expectations: How to Survive Academia, Make It Better for Others, and Transform the University*. Between the Lines.

Hess, F. M. (2023). *The great school rethink*. Harvard Education Press.

Kayyali, M. (2024). Immersive Technologies: Virtual and Augmented Reality in Higher Education. In Reshaping learning with next generation educational technologies (pp. 99-114). IGI Global.

Kayyali, M. (2025). E-Learning Platforms and Their Influence on Lifelong Learning. In Impact of Digitalization on Education and Social Sustainability (pp. 155-176). IGI Global.

Kayyali, M. (2026). AI in Higher Education: The Risk of Excluding Vulnerable Learners. In AI and New Forms of Exclusion (pp. 57-82). IGI Global Scientific Publishing.

Khan, S. (2024). *Brave New Words: How AI Will Revolutionize Education (and why That's a Good Thing)*. Penguin.

Kinyaduka, B. D. (2024). Multiplicity theory and its implications in education. *Global Journal of Social Sciences Studies*, *10*(1), 13–29. DOI: 10.55284/gjss.v10i1.1018

Lampropoulos, G., & Papadakis, S. (2025). The Educational Value of Artificial Intelligence and Social Robots. In *Social Robots in Education* (pp. 3–15). Springer. DOI: 10.1007/978-3-031-82915-4_1

Latif, G., Alghazo, R., Pilotti, M. A., & Brahim, G. B. (2022). Identifying "at-risk" students: An AI-based prediction approach. *International Journal of Computing and Digital Systems*, *11*(1), 1051–1059. DOI: 10.12785/ijcds/110184

Louis, M., & ElAzab, M. (2023). Will AI replace Teacher? *International Journal of Internet Education*, *22*(2), 9–21. DOI: 10.21608/ijie.2023.312491

Muller, M., & Strohmayer, A. (2022, April). Forgetting practices in the data sciences. In *Proceedings of the 2022 CHI Conference on Human Factors in Computing Systems* (pp. 1-19).

Nichols, T. P., & Dixon-Román, E. (2024). Platform governance and education policy: Power and politics in emerging edtech ecologies. *Educational Evaluation and Policy Analysis*, *46*(2), 309–328. DOI: 10.3102/01623737231202469

Nur, N., Goh, S. J., Patel, J., & Mizrahi, M. (2024). Navigating the ethical landscape of ai integration in educational settings. In *INTED2024 Proceedings* (pp. 7654-7663). IATED. DOI: 10.21125/inted.2024.2040

Pahuja, R. (2024). Ethical Dimensions of Informed Consent: Principles, Processes, and Case Studies. Ethical Frameworks in Special Education: A Guide for Researchers (Volume 2nd), 116.

Papadakis, S., Lytvynova, S. H., Ivanova, S. M., & Selyshcheva, I. A. (2024b). *Advancing lifelong learning with AI-enhanced ICT: A review of 3L-Person 2024.* In *CEUR Workshop Proceedings (9th International Workshop on Professional Retraining and Life-Long Learning using ICT: Person-oriented Approach — 3L-Person 2024, Lviv, Ukraine, September 25, 2023).* CEUR-WS.org.

Papadakis, S., Striuk, A. M., Kravtsov, H. M., Shyshkina, M. P., Marienko, M. V., & Danylchuk, H. B. (2024a). *Embracing digital innovation and cloud technologies for transformative learning experiences.* In *Proceedings of the 11th Workshop on Cloud Technologies in Education (CTE 2023), Kryvyi Rih, Ukraine, December 22, 2023.* CEUR Workshop Proceedings.

Rane, N., Choudhary, S., & Rane, J. (2023). Education 4.0 and 5.0: Integrating artificial intelligence (AI) for personalized and adaptive learning.

Röhrs, S., Rohn, S., & Pfeifer, Y. (2024). Risk Classification of Food Incidents Using a Risk Evaluation Matrix for Use in Artificial Intelligence-Supported Risk Identification. *Foods*, *13*(22), 3675. DOI: 10.3390/foods13223675 PMID: 39594090

Sallas, A. J. (2024). The Logic of Possibility: On the Concept of Deus Ex Machina (Doctoral dissertation, The University of Western Ontario).

Shelton, J. (2023). *The education myth: How human capital trumped social democracy.* Cornell University Press.

Simons, M., & Masschelein, J. (2021). Looking after school: A critical analysis of personalization in education.

Solé-Beteta, X., Navarro, J., Gajšek, B., Guadagni, A., & Zaballos, A. (2022). A data-driven approach to quantify and measure students' engagement in synchronous virtual learning environments. *Sensors (Basel)*, *22*(9), 3294. DOI: 10.3390/s22093294 PMID: 35590984

Spencer, J. A., Ullucci, K., & Howard, T. C. (2022). *Anti-Blackness at school: Creating affirming educational spaces for African American students*. Teachers College Press.

Stewart, T. (2023). "Nobody Asked Me!" Unleashing the Collective Voice of Special Education Teacher-Activists to Understand the Impact of Caseload Policies on Teacher Burnout, Attrition, and Student Learning Outcomes. American University.

Strielkowski, W., Grebennikova, V., Lisovskiy, A., Rakhimova, G., & Vasileva, T. (2025). AI-driven adaptive learning for sustainable educational transformation. *Sustainable Development (Bradford)*, *33*(2), 1921–1947. DOI: 10.1002/sd.3221

Tanksley, T. C. (2024). "We're changing the system with this one": Black students using critical race algorithmic literacies to subvert and survive AI-mediated racism in school. *English Teaching*, *23*(1), 36–56. DOI: 10.1108/ETPC-08-2023-0102

Vlachopoulos, D., & Makri, A. (2021). Quality teaching in online higher education: The perspectives of 250 online tutors on technology and pedagogy. [iJET]. *International Journal of Emerging Technologies in Learning*, *16*(6), 40–56. DOI: 10.3991/ijet.v16i06.20173

Webb, S. (2024). A Design Thinking Mixed Methods Study on Learned Empathy Through Multicultural Education.

White, C. J. (2025). *The Complete Childhood Mental Health Workbook: A Comprehensive Guide for Navigating ADHD, Anxiety, Autism and More*. Casey Joe White.

Wolff, R., & Ludvik, M. J. B. (2023). Outcomes-based program review: Closing achievement gaps in-and outside the classroom with alignment to predictive analytics and performance metrics.

Xu, T., Wang, J., Zhang, G., Zhang, L., & Zhou, Y. (2023). Confused or not: Decoding brain activity and recognizing confusion in reasoning learning using EEG. *Journal of Neural Engineering*, *20*(2), 026018. DOI: 10.1088/1741-2552/acbfe0 PMID: 36854180

Youvan, D. C. (2024). Illuminating Intelligence: Bridging Humanity and Artificial Consciousness.

KEY TERMS AND DEFINITIONS

At-Risk Learners: students facing compounded barriers (poverty, language shifts, trauma, mobility) that disrupt access, continuity, and belonging.

Early-Warning Analytics: AI systems that flag disengagement or struggle patterns (attendance dips, stalled mastery, sentiment signals) for rapid support.

Adaptive Tutoring: AI-guided practice that adjusts difficulty, pacing, and hints in real time to repair specific skill gaps.

Human-in-the-Loop: educators retain oversight to interpret signals, override recommendations, and anchor interventions in context.

Ethical Guardrails: privacy, transparency, bias checks, and appeal channels that prevent surveillance creep and automated sorting.

Belonging & SEL: designs that reduce stigma and build trust so learners feel safe to ask for help and persist.

Equity-By-Design: centering marginalized students in system and tool design so personalization widens opportunity instead of gaps.

Chapter 5

Transforming Early Literacy With AI-Driven Personalized Content Assessment and Feedback:

A Review of Six Tools

Rebecca Vornberger
http://orcid.org/0009-0008-4628-0198
Oakland University, USA

Ghaida S. Alrawashdeh
http://orcid.org/0000-0003-4017-1085
Oakland University, USA

Danielle Alexander
http://orcid.org/0009-0000-5564-5314
Oakland University, USA

ABSTRACT

This chapter examines the transformative role of artificial intelligence (AI) in early literacy through personalized and adaptive learning (PAL) tools that integrate assessment and feedback. It explores how AI-driven platforms such as MagicSchool, ABCmouse, DreamBox, Freckle, Khan Academy, and Lexia tailor instruction to young learners' needs, providing adaptive content, real-time feedback, and gamified engagement. By reviewing research evidence and case examples, the chapter highlights how PAL systems improve foundational literacy and numeracy skills,

DOI: 10.4018/979-8-3373-2637-5.ch005

foster learner motivation, and support differentiated instruction. Attention is given to ethical challenges related to data privacy, algorithmic bias, and equitable access, emphasizing the importance of government regulation, teacher training, and parental involvement. The chapter concludes that, when responsibly implemented, PAL technologies can enhance inclusivity, promote individualized learning, and strengthen early education outcomes across diverse contexts.

INTRODUCTION

In education, different stakeholders face unique challenges. Teachers, for example, juggle diverse student needs within a single classroom while trying to meet curriculum expectations. Parents might struggle to support their children through complex subjects like differential equations. School administrators are tasked with improving academic outcomes while managing limited resources, and policymakers must navigate concerns related to data privacy and the ethical implications of using online learning tools.

Personalized and adaptive learning (PAL) technologies offer a potential solution to these challenges. By tailoring content to the needs of individual learners, these tools can enhance engagement, personalize instruction, and contribute to more equitable learning experiences (du Plooy et al., 2024). Of particular interest are the roles that adaptive feedback and assessment play in these systems. A systematic review by Martin et al. (2020) found that adaptive assessment and feedback are among the most studied and widely implemented features in digital learning environments, with a focus on supporting student growth and guiding instructional decisions (Yang et al., 2022). However, while these tools hold promise, their integration into educational practices raises important concerns, especially regarding data security, algorithmic bias, and the ethical implications of AI in education (Alrawashdeh & Castillo, 2025a).

As illustrated in Figure 1, the effective and equitable implementation of PAL tools rests on the synergistic relationship between a sound pedagogical foundation, powerful technological enablers, and a steadfast ethical and equitable context. We argue that robust and responsible PAL systems exist precisely at the intersection of all three. This interaction creates dynamic overlaps where the core work of PAL occurs:

- The fusion of Pedagogy and Technology enables 'Data-Informed Differentiation,' where adaptive feedback and personalized learning pathways are powered by AI.
- The junction of Technology and Ethics necessitates 'Bias-Free Algorithms,' requiring ongoing auditing for fairness and secure, responsible data handling.

- The confluence of Ethics and Pedagogy fosters 'Culturally Responsive Teaching,' ensuring practices like universal access and scaffolded content are supported by teacher readiness and professional development.

This framework underscores that adaptive feedback and assessment, the core focus of this chapter, are not merely technical features but pedagogical processes enabled by technology and governed by ethics. The following sections explore the potential benefits of these tools while critically addressing the privacy and ethical challenges that accompany their use in educational settings.

Figure 1. An Integrated Framework for Responsible PAL Implementation showing the intersection of Pedagogy, Technology, and Ethics

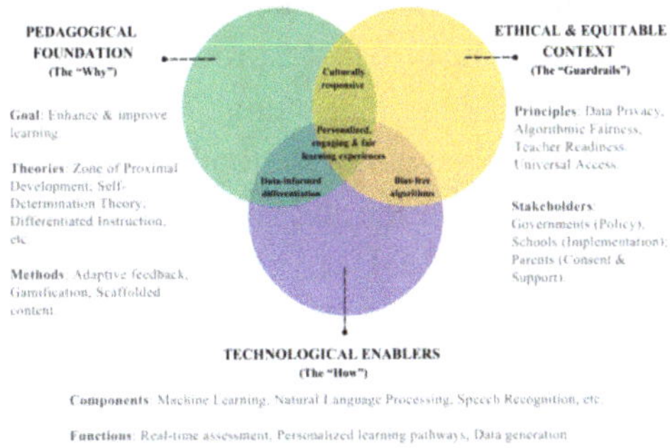

PERSONALIZED AND ADAPTIVE LEARNING

Personalized and adaptive learning (PAL) systems are being increasingly integrated into early childhood education, from preschool to primary grades, to offer individualized learning experiences. These systems use data-driven algorithms and artificial intelligence (AI), including machine learning (ML), to tailor educational content to each student's needs (Alrawashdeh, 2023; Alrawashdeh & Castillo, 2025b). Thakur et al. (2024) highlight the adaptability of PAL systems, noting that AI-driven platforms adjust the pace, difficulty, and content in real-time based on each student's progress. This customization provides tailored materials, personalized learning pathways, and adaptive assessments that help sustain engagement and improve learning outcomes. Teachers can assign practice tasks that match a child's rate of learning, enabling students to work independently at their own pace. As students reach milestones, the system increases difficulty and rewards their progress.

For preschool and primary students, this level of personalization supports the development of foundational literacy, numeracy, and cognitive skills. Platforms like DreamBox (math) and ABCmouse (literacy) use data-driven insights to adjust content, closing learning gaps by personalizing the difficulty levels according to individual progress. A global meta-analysis by Alrawashdeh et al. (2024) found that AI-powered PAL technologies are effective in improving reading literacy, with a reported effect size of $g = 0.23$. This suggests that PAL systems offer a promising solution for meeting the diverse learning needs of young learners.

Building on the personalized learning capabilities of PAL systems, many platforms now incorporate gamified elements like reward systems, interactive tasks, and virtual avatars to further engage young learners (Chen, 2023). These features not only capture children's attention but also foster problem-solving and critical thinking skills (Angelelli et al., 2023; Antonopoulou et al., 2022; Lamrani & Abdalwahed, 2020). Research suggests that when gamification is well-designed and aligns with educational goals, it can boost motivation and improve learning outcomes (Alrashedi et al., 2024; Dehghanzadeh et al., 2024; Denny et al., 2018; Hamid & Barzenji, 2024; Huang et al., 2020). The effectiveness of these gamified elements can be explained by Self-Determination Theory: badges and leaderboards can satisfy the need for competence, choice in activities supports autonomy, and collaborative challenges or class-wide goals can enhance relatedness (Alrawashdeh & Castillo, 2025b).

For instance, Ismail Thamarasseri (2024) highlights the transformative potential of gamification, emphasizing its ability to reshape teaching methods by incorporating challenges, leaderboards, and badges. This approach creates an interactive learning environment that boosts student motivation, fosters collaboration, and enhances knowledge retention. Smirani and Yamani's (2024) survey of 169 academics found that gamification techniques (like leaderboards and badges) significantly increase learner engagement, with an average boost of 25%. Their research shows that rewards and competitive challenges can improve both intrinsic and extrinsic motivation, leading to a 30% performance increase. Gamification in mobile apps also enhances motivation, particularly among younger learners (Ain & Imtiaz, 2025).

In addition to gamification, recent advancements in Natural Language Processing (NLP) and speech recognition technologies are being integrated into adaptive learning systems, allowing young learners to interact using their voices. These systems are particularly useful for literacy and language learning, assessing pronunciation, fluency, and comprehension while offering immediate feedback. Getman et al. (2023) highlight how AI-driven speech recognition aids in Computer-Assisted Language Learning, allowing for real-time, tailored practice outside the classroom.

AI-driven speech language therapy has also emerged as a valuable tool, benefiting both classroom and home learning. These platforms, such as those integrating speech recognition for pronunciation training, offer real-time assessments and adaptive feedback (Sun, 2023; Wulantari et al., 2023), enhancing engagement and language acquisition. Bhardwaj et al. (2024) evaluated tools like Pierre the Talking Parrot, Articulation Station (now Articulation Station Hive), and Speech Blub, finding them effective in diagnosing and treating speech delays. Augmentative and alternative communication applications are further advancing speech therapy, improving communication for children with speech and hearing challenges.

Building on these innovations, a range of AI and speech recognition tools have been developed to support elementary students in language and literacy development. Amira Learning[1] provides interactive reading tutoring with speech recognition, while SoapBox Labs[2] offers AI specifically designed for children's speech recognition. Ello[3] features an animated character that gives real-time feedback on reading aloud, and Ready4Reading[4] incorporates phonics practice with voice analysis. Additionally, Dragon Speech Recognition[5] offers advanced speech-to-text capabilities, particularly beneficial for students with disabilities. Read Along by Google is a key example of an AI-powered app that helps children develop reading skills by providing real-time feedback on pronunciation. This app, adopted in low- and middle-income countries, offers offline access, supports multiple languages, and processes data locally, addressing privacy concerns and increasing accessibility for students without internet access.

Despite the potential of these technologies, challenges remain in AI speech recognition, particularly with young children's varying speech patterns and accents. These issues need careful attention as the technology evolves. Furthermore, the risk of algorithmic bias requires consideration. In the context of early literacy, this can manifest as speech recognition models performing less accurately for children with non-native accents or regional dialects, or adaptive content that reflects cultural assumptions, potentially disadvantaging marginalized learners. Proactive auditing of these systems for fairness is essential to ensure equitable outcomes.

Additionally, PAL systems collect detailed data on students' speech, learning habits, and progress, requiring secure management and responsible use. Transparency in data usage, informed consent from parents, and robust data protection policies are essential to mitigate risks (Alrawashdeh & Castillo, 2025b). Ain and Imtiaz (2025) also stress the importance of structured training, policy interventions to reduce costs, and improved digital infrastructure. The following section will explore the benefits of six selected PAL platforms, examining their impact on learning, assessment, and feedback, while addressing ethical and privacy concerns.

REVIEW OF SELECTED PAL SYSTEMS FOR EARLY EDUCATION

This section reviews six PAL systems selected for their unique contributions to early elementary education. Table 1 outlines key features, including intended users, subject, cost, and privacy protections. Selection criteria included: (1) a focus on foundational literacy and numeracy, (2) the inclusion of assessment and feedback features, and (3) adherence to some form of privacy protection protocols. Evaluating these tools provides insight into their potential to support early learners while addressing ethical and privacy considerations. For educators, the platforms assist with lesson planning, personalized instruction, assessment, and IEP development. For students, they offer adaptive learning, real-time feedback, progress monitoring, and scaffolded, interactive content aligned with educational standards. This combination helps sustain engagement and ensures instruction remains within each learner's zone of proximal development (Vygotsky, 1978).

Beyond aligning with cognitive development theories like Vygotsky's ZPD, the engagement fostered by PAL systems can also be understood through the lens of motivational theory, particularly Self-Determination Theory (SDT) (Ryan & Deci, 2000). SDT suggests that intrinsic motivation thrives when three core psychological needs are met: autonomy, competence, and relatedness. PAL tools are uniquely positioned to address these needs: they offer autonomy by allowing students to learn at their own pace and sometimes choose their learning path (e.g., Khan Academy); they build competence by providing scaffolded challenges and real-time feedback that makes mastery feel achievable; and they can foster a sense of relatedness through gamified social elements like leaderboards or shared class goals. This theoretical framework helps explain why well-designed PAL tools can be so effective at sustaining young learners' motivation and engagement.

Table 1. Overview of Six Selected Personalized and Adaptive Learning Tools

Tool	Targeted User	Targeted Grade Level	Subject	User Privacy Protections	Cost/ Plans	Region
Magic School	Teacher	K-12+	Not subject specific but covers Math, Reading & AI Literacy	93% privacy rating, placing at the top of AI tools for schools according to Common Sense Media's independent privacy evaluations.	Plus option $99.96 per year Free option available Custom district pricing	Global
ABC Mouse	Student	preK-2nd	Math and Reading	Custom version available with: FERPA, COPPA, and GDPR, Ed-Law 2D Compliancy.	$14.99/mth 29.99 6 mths $45/year Free trial available	Global, but some features may vary
Dream Box	Student	K-12	Math and Reading	Collects student data; STRONG by Evidence for ESSA (Every Student Succeeds Act)	Family pricing =$19.95 one mth, $99.95 6 mth, $149.95 12 mth, $225 lifetime Free trial available	Global, except EU
Freckle	Student	K-12	Math and Reading	in compliance with US data privacy laws such as FERPA and COPPA.	Single Classroom license available, 40 students max, custom district pricing. Free option available	Global
Khan Academy	Student	K-12+	Math and Reading	adheres to both FERPA and COPPA requirements	Free	Global
Lexia	Student	prek-12	Reading	adhere to both FERPA and COPPA compliance	custom district pricing	US only

Note. All tools include assessment and feedback features. Reading refers broadly to early literacy, reading, writing, and language. Access the tools via the following links: MagicSchool: www.magicschool.ai; ABC Mouse: www.abcmouse.com; DreamBox: www.DreamBox.com; Freckle: https://www.freckle.io/; Khan Academy: www.khanacademy.org; Lexia: www.lexialearning.com.

Tool #1: MagicSchool

MagicSchool is an AI-powered platform designed to enhance K-12 instructional practices. While not a direct student-facing PAL like the other platforms reviewed, MagicSchool is included here as a critical teacher-support tool that enables the differentiation and personalized content creation central to the PAL philosophy. Launched in May 2023 by a former educator, it offers over 70 tools to support adaptive teaching and inclusivity (see Figure 2). Key features include automatic text-leveling, instant translation for multilingual communication, YouTube integration, and 1-click exports to Google and Microsoft platforms. Interactive content and chatbots (see Figure 2) further support accessibility and engagement. A case study from Aurora Public Schools in Colorado, which was reported by the platform, reported a 28% increase in students meeting grade-level literacy benchmarks after adopting MagicSchool. Teachers used features like the Language Learning Tutor and Writing Feedback to support English language learners and students with individual plans, resulting in more personalized instruction and timely feedback. The district also emphasized AI literacy to prepare students for a tech-driven future. MagicSchool received a 93% privacy rating from Common Sense Media, ranking among the most trusted AI tools for schools.

Figure 2. Overview of MagicSchool AI features, including worksheet and IEP generators, rubric and report card creator and the AI chatbot Raima to assist teachers

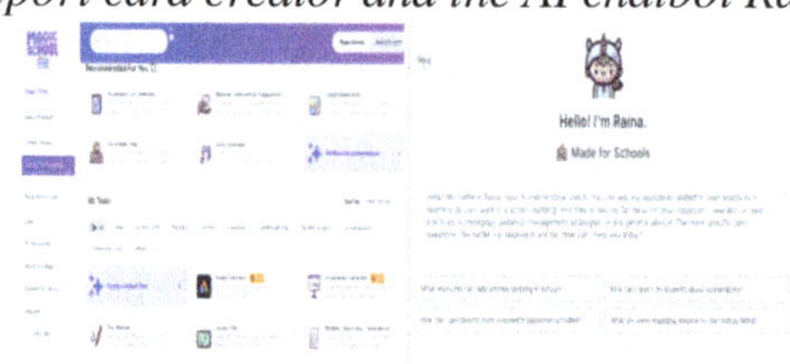

Tool #2: ABCmouse

ABCmouse is an adaptive platform for children aged 2–8, offering foundational content in reading, math, science, and art. Lessons adjust to a child's progress, with games, songs, and stories that support skill development in both classroom and home settings. Teachers might use it during station rotations, while parents can reinforce learning through fun and engaging activities. With over 850 lessons and 10,000+ activities, the platform provides ready-to-use, standards-aligned content that can reduce teachers' prep time while keeping students engaged. The animated interface, voice instructions, and reward system (e.g., virtual tickets) support sustained use and independent learning. ABCmouse supports English as a second language learners (Bang et al., 2020), offering voiced instructions, real-time feedback, and progress tracking to assist language development and formative assessment. It costs $45 per year. While the custom version includes privacy protections (FERPA[6], COPPA[7], GDPR[8], and Ed-Law 2D[9]), the platform avoids collecting identifiable student data. The free version, however, has limited data controls and caps the top 1% of word usage.

Tool #3: DreamBox

DreamBox is an adaptive PAL platform designed for K–8 math instruction. It personalizes learning by adjusting content and feedback in real time based on each student's mastery level, aligning with Common Core and state standards. Notably, it provides bilingual instruction, offering every lesson in both English and Spanish (see Figure 3). Recent research by Orhani (2024) highlights how DreamBox supports deep learning and enhances engagement through AI-driven adaptive feedback. The platform helps teachers reinforce key math concepts in class and allows families to support practice at home, including during school breaks. In terms of privacy, DreamBox collects substantial student data, raising considerations around storage and access. However, it has earned a "strong" rating from Evidence for Every Student Succeeds Act (ESSA) for meeting educational standards. Family pricing starts at $12.95 per month, with options up to a $225 lifetime subscription. Schools can request custom licenses, and free trials are available.

Tool #4: Freckle

Freckle, a free PAL platform developed for students aged 4 and up, offers differentiated instruction across subjects like math, science, and social studies, with a strong emphasis on reading and language skills. While free for classroom and home use, schools and districts must purchase a subscription for full access. Teachers benefit from Freckle's ability to automatically assign practice based on each student's skill level, saving time on lesson planning and differentiation. For example, a teacher might use the dashboard to see that one group of students is struggling with phonics blends while another is ready for comprehension strategies, and Freckle will automatically provide each group with appropriate, targeted exercises.

Freckle's content aligns with Common Core standards, and its teacher dashboard allows for detailed tracking of growth over time, helping educators make data-informed instructional decisions. Performance dashboards (see Figure 3B) help educators quickly identify areas where students need support, streamlining intervention. Studies from the platform's developer (Renaissance, 2024) show that daily use of Freckle (15–30 minutes) is linked to greater gains in ELA achievement, with consistent use benefiting both struggling and advanced learners (Renaissance, 2023). At home, families can use the platform to reinforce learning with level-appropriate content. While Freckle is rich in content and gamified features, early learners may need adult assistance to navigate the interface independently.

Figure 3. Overview of DreamBox features highlights bilingual assessment and feedback (A), and how performance data are presented on Freckle (B)

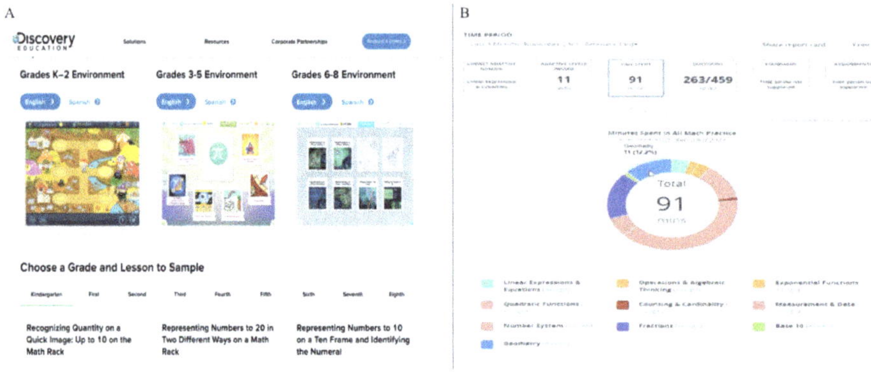

Tool #5: Khan Academy

Khan Academy is a PAL platform designed to support learners from elementary school through higher education. It features a comprehensive library of instructional videos, interactive exercises, and adaptive practice that adjusts based on student progress. One of its distinctive features is the flexibility it offers where students can design their own learning pathways. For example, a learner might begin with foundational reading comprehension and choose to move on to more advanced literary analysis, or progress from basic arithmetic to algebra, based on interest and readiness rather than a fixed sequence. This is a particularly helpful feature for older students, as it supports greater agency and motivation in their learning journey. However, its reliance on reading and self-guided navigation may present challenges for younger students still developing literacy skills.

In classroom settings, teachers can assign math lessons aligned to individual skill levels, allowing advanced students to engage with algebra while others focus on building foundational skills. At home, families can use Khan Academy's science tutorials to supplement school instruction and foster curiosity. The free platform proved especially valuable during the COVID-19 pandemic, when remote learning was widespread. Even with the return to in-person instruction, Khan Academy remains a useful tool for bridging socioeconomic gaps and supporting literacy across districts. Printable packets (see Figure 4) are also available to reduce screen time and increase accessibility. While extensive independent, peer-reviewed studies on Khan Academy's efficacy for early literacy are less prevalent, Isaeva et al. (2024) found that Khan Academy helped students with limited access to educational resources at home, providing more equitable learning opportunities and helping to address social barriers.

Tool #6: Lexia

Lexia is a PAL platform designed to support literacy development in elementary learners. Like other PAL systems, it adapts content, assessment, and feedback in real time, but it stands out for its emphasis on differentiated learning pathways and ongoing support for both educators and families. The platform includes extensive resources such as research-based curriculum materials, professional development modules, and webinars that extend literacy instruction beyond the classroom (see Figure 4). Its progress-tracking tools generate detailed reports, enabling educators and caregivers to monitor student growth and target areas for intervention. One of Lexia's key strengths is its effectiveness in supporting students from diverse socioeconomic backgrounds. Research by Tracey et al. (2024) found that learners from lower-income households showed the greatest gains, while Carroll (2024) highlighted Lexia's potential to reduce achievement gaps for students performing below grade level. The platform's use of engaging visuals and gamified elements helps sustain attention and motivation, while supporting personalized learning that meets each child's needs.

Figure 4. Printable packets from Khan Academy (A) and Lexia's Educator/Parent Resources featuring research-based support and webinars for continued literacy development (B)

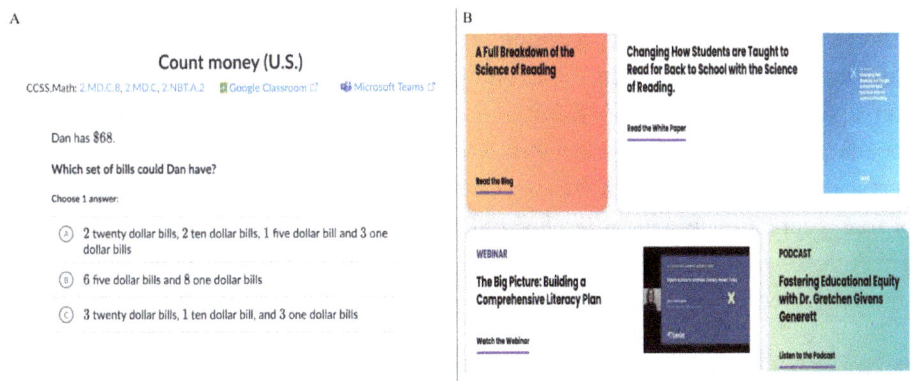

RECOMMENDATIONS FOR IMPLEMENTING PAL TOOLS

As PAL tools become more embedded in education, stakeholders (including governments, educators, and parents) must work to maximize their benefits while addressing ethical and practical challenges. This section outlines key actions for effective, equitable, and responsible implementation.

Expanding Access in Low-Resource Contexts

While PAL tools hold promise for equity, their implementation in under-resourced schools and communities faces unique hurdles that extend beyond general privacy concerns. Key barriers include:

- Many schools lack sufficient devices for students, and reliable internet access is not a given. This digital divide renders cloud-based, real-time adaptive tools unusable for significant portions of the global student population.
- Subscription costs for premium platforms are prohibitive for schools with strained budgets, potentially exacerbating existing achievement gaps between wealthy and impoverished districts.
- Many high-quality PAL tools are primarily designed for English-speaking markets and Western pedagogical contexts. A lack of content in local languages and culturally relevant examples can limit their effectiveness and engagement.

Strategies for mitigation include: Governments and NGOs should advocate for and fund tools like Google's Read Along, which work offline and process data locally. Development efforts should focus on lightweight applications that do not require constant, high-speed connectivity. Policymakers should direct technology grants specifically to Title I schools and underserved communities. Exploring public-private partnerships can help subsidize costs. Encouraging the development and adoption of free, adaptable, and locally relevant PAL-inspired OER can democratize access. This allows educators in any context to modify and deploy content that fits their students' specific needs.

Government Regulations and Oversight

Governments play a crucial role in ensuring that PAL tools comply with legal, ethical, and educational standards. They should ensure PAL tools meet legal, ethical, and educational standards. Compliance with data protection laws like COPPA is essential, and schools should require clear privacy policies and data deletion protocols. Funding should target under-resourced schools to support equitable access. Governments should also collaborate with educators to develop national or regional standards that align PAL content with developmentally appropriate literacy and numeracy benchmarks.

School-Level Risk Mitigation

Schools can enhance the impact of PALs by addressing equity, security, and reliability. Tools should be reviewed for cultural and linguistic inclusivity. Cybersecurity measures such as firewalls, multi-factor authentication and encrypted passwords are crucial. Plans for technical disruptions and support for students lacking devices or internet access are necessary. The nonprofit National Cybersecurity Alliance is a reliable resource for technology risk guidelines.[10] Also, districts should regularly assess PAL effectiveness based on student outcomes, teacher feedback, and parent surveys to ensure long-term impact.

Educator Practices

Teachers play a central role in PAL implementation. Professional development should focus on interpreting data and integrating digital tools into lesson plans. Blended learning approaches that combine digital tools with collaborative activities are recommended. Teachers must monitor progress, adjust instruction as needed, and be alert to potential algorithmic bias that may affect marginalized learners. Pilot programs can help teachers assess effectiveness before full implementation. The International Society for Technology in Education (ISTE) is an excellent resource for teacher training programs.[11]

The successful integration of PAL tools hinges on teachers who are not merely technically proficient but are pedagogically adaptive. Effective professional development must move beyond simple platform training to foster a deeper digital readiness, Specifically

- Teachers need training to critically interpret the dashboards and progress reports generated by PAL systems. The goal is to translate data into actionable insights; for example, using a report showing a student's struggle with phonemic awareness to form a small intervention group or select a targeted mini-lesson.
- Teachers need to shift from "Sage on the Stage" to "Guide on the Side." PAL tools handle direct instruction and practice, freeing the teacher for higher-impact activities. PD should focus on strategies for facilitating collabora-

tive projects, providing targeted one-on-one support, and fostering socio-emotional skills that technology cannot address.

- Teachers must be equipped to question the algorithm. This involves checking for potential algorithmic bias, recognizing when a tool's recommended pathway may not be suitable for a particular child, and maintaining their professional judgment as the primary driver of instruction.
- Managing a classroom where students are engaged in a variety of digital and non-digital tasks requires new strategies. PD should include concrete methods for setting up station rotations, managing device use, and ensuring that technology enhances rather than disrupts the learning community.

Parental Involvement

Parents should be informed and involved from the outset. Schools should host informational sessions covering the tool's purpose, benefits, privacy policies, and usage guidelines. Signed parental consent forms should be collected before implementation. Instructional guides, video tutorials or Workshops can help parents reinforce learning at home. It's also important to recognize potential screen-time concerns and accessibility barriers for families with limited internet or devices. For technology guidelines, Common Sense Media offers excellent resources.[12]

CONCLUSION

The six PAL tools reviewed demonstrate the potential of personalized and adaptive technologies to support early learners through real-time feedback, differentiated instruction, and data-driven insights. These tools serve as adaptive tutors, instructional assistants, and engagement aids. For teachers and parents, they offer scaffolded learning tailored to student needs. For district leaders, they provide timely data for resource allocation. Yet, challenges remain, especially around data privacy, access, and stakeholder preparedness. Governments must enforce clear regulations, educators need support for integration, and parents should be engaged in the process. With thoughtful implementation and continued evaluation, PAL tools can contribute to more inclusive and effective educational experiences.

REFERENCES

Ain, Q., & Imtiaz, R. (2025). The role of technology in speech-language therapy: Perceptions, effectiveness, and challenges in a resource-limited setting. *Journal of Health and Rehabilitation Research, 5*(1), 1–8.

Alrashedi, N. T., Alsulami, S. M. H., Flatah, A. I., Najmi, A. H., & Alhalafawy, W. S. (2024). The effects of gamified platforms on enhancing learners' ambition. *Journal of Ecohumanism, 3*(8), 3393–3403. DOI: 10.62754/joe.v3i8.5004

Alrawashdeh, G. S. (2023). *Personalized and adaptive learning technology for early grade reading: Evidence from MENA* [Doctoral dissertation, University of Illinois at Urbana-Champaign]. https://hdl.handle.net/2142/121495

Alrawashdeh, G. S., & Castillo, N. M. (2025a). Responsible AI in Personalized Adaptive Learning: A Global Review of 40 Products. In Papadakis, S. (Ed.), *AI Roles and Responsibilities in Education* (pp. 171–198). Springer Nature Switzerland., DOI: 10.1007/978-3-031-96855-6_8

Alrawashdeh, G. S., & Castillo, N. M. (2025b). Student agency in personalized and adaptive learning technologies: From conceptualization to application. *Education and Information Technologies, 30*(18), 26125–26149. Advance online publication. DOI: 10.1007/s10639-025-13772-6

Angelelli, C. V., de Campos Ribeiro, G. M., Severino, M. R., Johnstone, E., Borzenkova, G., & da Silva, D. C. O. (2023). Developing critical thinking skills through gamification. *Thinking Skills and Creativity, 49*, 101354. DOI: 10.1016/j.tsc.2023.101354 PMID: 37360225

Antonopoulou, H., Halkiopoulos, C., Gkintoni, E., & Katsimpelis, A. (2022). Application of gamification tools for identification of neurocognitive and social function in distance learning education. *International Journal of Learning. Teaching and Educational Research, 21*(5), 367–400.

Bang, H. J., Olander, K., & Lenihan, E. (2020). Testing a research-based digital learning tool. *CALICO Journal, 37*(3), 277–308. DOI: 10.1558/cj.40544

Bhardwaj, A., Sharma, M., Kumar, S., Sharma, S., & Sharma, P. C. (2024). Transforming pediatric speech and language disorder diagnosis and therapy: The evolving role of artificial intelligence. *Health Sciences Review (Oxford, England), 12*, 100188. DOI: 10.1016/j.hsr.2024.100188

Carroll, J. J. (2024). Effects of Lexia Reading Core5 on non-ELL upper elementary students' reading comprehension [Doctoral dissertation, Walden University].

Chen, W. J. (2023). Improving the e-learning experience: A primarily gamification-based approach to conceptualizing and designing a user-friendly and visually appealing solution for primary students and teachers [Doctoral dissertation, Technische Hochschule Ingolstadt].

Dehghanzadeh, H., Farrokhnia, M., Dehghanzadeh, H., Taghipour, K., & Noroozi, O. (2024). Using gamification to support learning in K-12 education: A systematic literature review. *British Journal of Educational Technology*, *55*(1), 34–70. DOI: 10.1111/bjet.13335

Denny, P., McDonald, F., Empson, R., Kelly, P., & Petersen, A. (2018, April). Empirical support for a causal relationship between gamification and learning outcomes. In *Proceedings of the 2018 CHI Conference on Human Factors in Computing Systems* (pp. 1–13). DOI: 10.1145/3173574.3173885

du Plooy, E., Casteleijn, D., & Franzsen, D. (2024). Personalized adaptive learning in higher education: A scoping review of key characteristics and impact on academic performance and engagement. *Heliyon*, *10*(21), e39630. DOI: 10.1016/j.heliyon.2024.e39630 PMID: 39524879

Getman, Y., Phan, N., Al-Ghezi, R., Voskoboinik, E., Singh, M., Grosz, T., Kurimo, M., Salvi, G., Svendsen, T., Strömbergsson, S., Smolander, A., & Ylinen, S. (2023). Developing an AI-assisted low-resource spoken language learning app for children. *IEEE Access : Practical Innovations, Open Solutions*, *11*, 86025–86037. DOI: 10.1109/ACCESS.2023.3304274

Hamid, R., & Barzenji, Z. (2024). Evaluating the effectiveness of gamification in online education: Strategies for promoting active learning and student retention. *International Journal of Post Axial: Futuristic Teaching and Learning*, 97–110.

Huang, R., Ritzhaupt, A. D., Sommer, M., Zhu, J., Stephen, A., Valle, N., Hampton, J., & Li, J. (2020). The impact of gamification in educational settings on student learning outcomes: A meta-analysis. *Educational Technology Research and Development*, *68*(4), 1875–1901. DOI: 10.1007/s11423-020-09807-z

Isaeva, R., Karasartova, N., Dznunusnalieva, K., Mirzoeva, K., & Mokliuk, M. (2024). Enhancing learning effectiveness through adaptive learning platforms and emerging computer technologies in education. *Jurnal Ilmiah Ilmu Terapan Universitas Jambi*, *9*(1), 144–160. DOI: 10.22437/jiituj.v9i1.37967

Lamrani, R., & Abdelwahed, E. H. (2020). Game-based learning and gamification to improve skills in early years education. *Computer Science and Information Systems*, *17*(1), 339–356. DOI: 10.2298/CSIS190511043L

Martin, F., Chen, Y., Moore, R. L., & Westine, C. D. (2020). Systematic review of adaptive learning research designs, context, strategies, and technologies from 2009 to 2018. *Educational Technology Research and Development, 68*(4), 1903–1929. DOI: 10.1007/s11423-020-09793-2 PMID: 32837122

Orhani, S. (2024). Deep Learning in Math Education. *International Journal of Research and Innovation in Social Science, 8*(4), 270–278. DOI: 10.47772/IJRISS.2024.804022

Renaissance. (2023). Trends in student outcome measures: The role of individualized practice with Freckle for math and Freckle for ELA. Renaissance Learning, Inc.

Renaissance. (2024). Trends in student outcome measures: The role of individualized practice with Freckle for math and Freckle for ELA. Renaissance Learning, Inc.

Ryan, R. M., & Deci, E. L. (2000). Self-determination theory and the facilitation of intrinsic motivation, social development, and well-being. *American Psychologist,* 55(1), 68–78. DOI: 10.1037/0003-066X.55.1.68

Smirani, L., & Yamani, H. (2024). Analysing the Impact of Gamification Techniques on Enhancing Learner Engagement, Motivation, and Knowledge Retention: A Structural Equation Modelling Approach. *Electronic Journal of e-Learning, 22*(9), 111–124. DOI: 10.34190/ejel.22.9.3563

Sun, W. (2023). The impact of automatic speech recognition technology on second language pronunciation and speaking skills of EFL learners: A mixed methods investigation. *Frontiers in Psychology, 14*, 1210187. DOI: 10.3389/fpsyg.2023.1210187 PMID: 37663357

Thakur, M., Reddy, C., Kishor, B., Murthy, B., Nag, A., & Doss, S. (2024). AI and education: Bridging the gap to personalized, efficient, and accessible learning. In *Handbook of Research on AI Applications in Education* (pp. 131–160). IGI Global., DOI: 10.4018/979-8-3693-8151-9.ch005

Thamarasseri, I. (2025). Gamification in education: Improving learning outcomes and student motivation. *International Journal of Educational Psychology, 1*(1), 19–26.

Tracey, L., Cockerill, M., Elliott, L., Fairhurst, C., Mandefield, L., Fountain, I., & O'Keeffe, J. (2024). The benefits of computer-assisted learning for struggling readers in elementary schools in England. *Journal of Applied Developmental Psychology.*

Vygotsky, L. S. (1978). *Mind in society: The development of higher psychological processes* (Rev. ed.). Harvard University Press.

Wulantari, N. P., Rachman, A., Sari, M. N., Uktolseja, L. J., & Rofi'i, A. (2023). The role of gamification in English language teaching: A literature review. *Journal of Education*, *6*(1), 2847–2856.

ENDNOTES

1 www.amiralearning.com

2 www.soapboxlabs.com

3 www.ello.com

4 https://education.scholastic.com/education/programs/ready4reading

5 www.cats.cuny.edu

6 FERPA (US) Family Educational Rights and Privacy Act protects privacy of student educational records

7 COPPA (US) Children's Online Privacy Protection Act gives parents control over what information websites can collect on their children

8 GDPR General Data Protection Regulation Europen law that grants individuals control over their personal data

9 Ed-Law 2D prevents unlawful disclosure of student information

10 See staysafeonline.org

11 See www.iste.org

12 www.commonsensemedia.org

Chapter 6
Leveraging AI-Powered Tools for Personalized Learning Pathways

Okan Bulut
http://orcid.org/0000-0001-5853-1267
University of Alberta, Canada

Joyce Xinle Liu
http://orcid.org/0009-0008-2278-8966
University of Alberta, Canada

Xiaoxiao Liu
University of Alberta, Canada

ABSTRACT

This chapter explores how AI-powered tools—including intelligent tutoring systems (ITSs), adaptive learning platforms (ALPs), and AI-driven chatbots—can personalize instruction and transform K–12 education. Drawing on recent research, theoretical frameworks, and practical case studies (e.g., ALEKS and i-Ready), the chapter examines how these technologies dynamically adapt to individual learners' needs, support instructional decision-making, and enhance student engagement and outcomes. It highlights the pedagogical architectures and functionalities of each tool type, assesses their benefits in promoting equity and data-driven instruction, and discusses key challenges related to integration, teacher preparedness, and algorithmic fairness. The chapter concludes with practical implications for educators and school systems, and offers future research directions focused on AI-enhanced personalization, generative AI integration, and teacher–AI collaboration.

DOI: 10.4018/979-8-3373-2637-5.ch006

1. INTRODUCTION

Before the emergence of artificial intelligence (AI), conventional educational classrooms accommodated students with differing levels of knowledge and diverse learning interests. Each day, students encountered new information and posed novel educational questions in the classroom. Educators predominantly relied on pre-designed, standardized instructional materials to guide student learning and provided uniform responses to their frequently asked questions. Although efficient, this method often fell short of meeting the unique needs of learners, unintentionally reducing their motivation and slowing their educational progress.

Now, imagine a classroom where each student embarks on a distinct learning journey—one not constrained by a *one-size-fits-all* approach but instead guided by a dynamic, responsive system that adapts in real time to individual learning pace, cognitive style, and personal interests. Today, AI-powered platforms make this vision increasingly achievable in K-12 education (Bulut et al., 2025; Kaswan et al., 2024). These platforms have the potential to fundamentally reshape traditional pedagogical practices by shifting the focus from uniform instruction to customized learning experiences tailored to the unique needs of each learner. Driven by the broader trends of digitalization and advances in machine learning and large language models (LLMs), AI has enabled the creation of adaptive learning environments that respond to students' inputs in real time, transforming both the delivery and the experience of educational content (Kaswan et al., 2024).

Three primary categories of AI-powered tools have been central to the personalization of learning in K–12 education: Intelligent Tutoring Systems (ITSs), Adaptive Learning Platforms (ALPs), and AI-based chatbots or virtual tutors. Each of these technologies is distinct in its design and pedagogical approach. For example, an ITS is a sophisticated tutoring program that closely mimics one-on-one human instruction, diagnosing student misconceptions and providing step-by-step guidance with tailored hints and questions (Létourneau et al., 2025). In contrast, an ALP primarily personalizes learning by algorithmically adjusting the sequence and difficulty of content based on the learner's ongoing performance data, thereby guiding each student along an individualized path at their own pace (Dutta et al., 2024). AI chatbots and virtual tutors, on the other hand, offer a more conversational mode of interaction, utilizing natural language processing (NLP) to respond to student queries, explain concepts, and provide real-time guidance (Yildirim-Erbasli & Bulut, 2021; Yildirim-Erbasli et al., 2025).

In this chapter, we explore how AI-driven tools enhance personalized instruction in K-12 education. Drawing on recent research, real-world implementations, and case studies, we elaborate on how AI technologies enhance student engagement, foster learner independence, and lead to improved academic outcomes. The chapter begins with a review of the three major categories of AI-powered personalized learning technologies: ITSs, ALPs, and conversational agents such as chatbots and virtual tutors. Each technology is explored in terms of its functional architecture, pedagogical approach, and capacity for personalization. Next, we review two widely used platforms (ALEKS and i-Ready) and examine their theoretical underpinnings, classroom applications, and empirical evidence regarding their effectiveness across diverse educational contexts. The chapter concludes by outlining the pedagogical benefits and practical challenges associated with AI-based personalization, offering implications for decision-makers, and proposing directions for future research in this evolving domain. Throughout the chapter, we primarily use examples drawn from the North American context to maintain a manageable and focused scope, while also including select international applications where relevant.

2. MAJOR CLASSES OF PERSONALIZED LEARNING TOOLS IN K-12 EDUCATION

To support personalized learning, many software systems and platforms have been developed, each employing distinct approaches to tailor instruction to individual student needs. In this section, we review three major classes of AI-powered tools used to facilitate personalized learning in K-12 education: ITSs, ALPs, chatbots, and virtual tutors.

2.1 Intelligent Tutoring Systems (ITSs)

The development of ITSs was motivated by the desire to create computer systems that could emulate the effectiveness of human one-on-one tutoring (Ferster, 2014). Since the 1960s, ITSs have been created to tutor students by assessing their existing knowledge in a particular subject area and guiding them on what they still need to learn. Over the past two decades, numerous studies have demonstrated that ITSs can often enhance student learning when compared to traditional classroom instruction in K-12 settings (Létourneau et al., 2025; Xu et al., 2019). Also, results from various meta-analyses indicated that their effectiveness can be comparable to that of human tutors (Graesser et al., 2018; VanLehn, 2011). ITSs vary in terms of their design and underlying instructional principles; however, they share core features of interactivity, adaptivity, and feedback, such that the system dynamically responds to the student's actions (Graesser et al., 2018).

Structurally, a typical ITS consists of four core components (Aleven et al., 2023; Sottilare et al., 2013). First, the *domain model* (also known as the *content model*) is a representation of the knowledge relevant to the domain of instruction. For example, it can capture concepts, skills, and problem-solving strategies that students are expected to acquire, as well as mal-rules and misconceptions that students may hold. Additionally, it may encompass prerequisite relationships and dependencies among various knowledge components within the domain, enabling the ITS to guide students through the instructional content in a logical sequence (Aleven et al., 2023; Ferster, 2014). The domain model defines a mapping from items (or questions or tasks) to knowledge components, which allows the ITS to track students' learning progress on specific components based on their responses to questions.

Second, the *student model* (or *learner model*) is unique to each student and represents their current state of learning. Often, the model captures a student's current mastery level over the instructional content, for example, by tracking their progress on key components of the domain model. It may also capture additional affective or motivational states that evolve throughout learning. These states are then treated as parameters to inform tutoring (Aleven et al., 2023). Student modeling is a challenging task because it requires making real-time inferences about unobservable traits, such as knowledge, motivation, or engagement, from observable data, such as responses, response times, and other forms of process data. The complexity may be further compounded by the wide range of learner variables and the complex interactions among them. Nonetheless, many sophisticated student modeling approaches have been developed in recent years alongside the advancements in AI and data-driven methods (Sinatra et al., 2023).

Third, the *tutor model* (or *pedagogical model*) uses information from the domain and student models to determine the next instructional steps or actions (Sottilare et al., 2014). Often, the tutor model is designed to align with pedagogical theories, which determines which instructional strategies and techniques are incorporated in the system, as well as how and when specific instructional tactics are presented to students (e.g., hints, questions, additional information, and feedback). Modern ITSs aim to employ adaptive instructional techniques, in which the computer system utilizes available data to tailor its approach to each student's needs, behaviors, and performance. This adaptability can take many forms, for example, by adjusting the level of scaffolding, the pace of instruction, or the length of time between spaced repetitions of a concept to optimize learning.

Fourth, the *user interface* (or *problem-solving environment*) in an ITS enables students to interact with the system through actions such as speaking, typing, or clicking, and the system responds by producing output in various media, including text, images, animations, or even virtual agents. In ITSs, user interface interactions are usually more fine-grained, where the system captures input not only after each answer but also after every step in the problem-solving process (step-based granularity; VanLehn, 2011). Modern user interfaces incorporate advanced features, including speech recognition and NLP, to facilitate more intuitive interactions

(Sottilare et al., 2013). Currently, ITS user interfaces are primarily web-based, although mobile-based ITSs are emerging to improve accessibility and learning on the go (Mousavinasab et al., 2021).

Within each of the four core components described above, several design and implementation choices must be made to develop an effective ITS. Commercial ITSs often start simple and are gradually improved over time. Research and innovation in ITS design are still ongoing today, with modern systems aiming to leverage more of the computer's power to boost interactivity, adaptability, and scalability. Researchers test various AI algorithms to model the available data more intricately, allowing ITSs to better understand learner states and predict future learning needs. Besides response data, a key area of current research focuses on how to use rich behavioral process data (e.g., response times, action sequences, sensor data) that are collected as students interact with ITSs. For instance, such data could be used to monitor students' engagement levels, detect unusual response patterns (Chen et al., 2021; Gorgun & Bulut, 2022; Meng & Yang, 2025), or identify signs of confusion (Pachman et al., 2016). This information can then be utilized to personalize the instruction.

The rise of powerful LLMs, such as ChatGPT, has also sparked increased interest in their potential to enhance ITS capabilities, including generating personalized feedback (Gaeta et al., 2024; Stamper et al., 2024) and expanding ITSs beyond their traditional focus on cognitive domains and STEM subjects (Sinatra et al., 2023). At the K-12 level, most current research is conducted outside commercial platforms or applications, usually in controlled research settings or smaller pilot studies. In the coming years, ITS technologies are expected to continue advancing and evolving. With progress in AI, ITSs may eventually surpass what human tutors can provide, offering effective and adaptive support to students at scale.

In K-12 education, a well-known commercial ITS is MATHia by Carnegie Learning, which is marketed as a personal, one-to-one coach that helps students progress in their learning of mathematical skills. MATHia is designed for use on computers or tablets, with content organized into progressive learning modules. As a student works through a problem, the platform collects data not only on answer accuracy but also on the steps the student takes to reach the solution. This information is used to deliver personalized just-in-time feedback and contextual hints (with multiple levels) to support learning. In addition to problems, MATHia also provides step-by-step examples and animations that instruct students on specific concepts. Carnegie Learning provides guidance on how MATHia can be used either for independent study or as part of classroom instruction.

Many modern personalized learning platforms are built on the core principles of ITSs, including components such as domain modeling, student modeling, and real-time feedback, to provide tailored instruction. Due to the complexity of traditional ITS design, some systems emphasize certain components more than others, such as prioritizing adaptive sequencing of content instead of step-by-step tutoring, as we will describe in the next section.

2.2. Adaptive Learning Platforms (ALPs)

The idea of adapting instruction to individual learners is not new, reflecting the common intuition and belief that students benefit most when instruction is responsive to their individual characteristics (U.S. Department of Education, 2023). Aleven et al. (2016) described five broad categories of student characteristics that are important to adapt to make instruction more effective than a one-size-fits-all approach: (1) prior knowledge and knowledge growth, (2) path through an activity, (3) affect and motivation, (4) self-regulatory processes, and (5) learning styles. ITSs were developed to embody this idea by acting as personalized tutors, adapting in real time to students' needs by analyzing available data, providing tailored feedback, and guiding them through instructional content step by step. Apart from ITSs, adaptivity can also be achieved more generally through other technologies.

Traditionally, one well-known way of implementing adaptive instruction is through mastery learning programs (Bloom, 1968; Keller & Sherman, 1974; Kulik et al., 1990; Guskey, 1997), where students need to demonstrate mastery in one skill or content area (e.g., measured through assessments) before moving on to the next. In this way, students can progress at their own pace and receive personalized support throughout the learning process. However, these programs, while effective, are difficult to practically adopt and scale in traditional classroom settings due to logistical and resource constraints (Aleven et al., 2016). With the rise of digital learning tools and AI technology, ALPs can incorporate such learning theories to personalize each student's learning path and allow them to progress toward mastery at their own pace (Betts et al., 2021; Tan et al., 2025).

Over the past two decades, the term *"adaptive learning"* has gained increased attention in the literature (Judijanto, 2025a) and is now widely used to describe a range of digital tools and platforms that support individualized learning. ALPs can be distinguished from ITSs by their focus on tailoring the selection of instructional content, rather than providing personalized one-on-one instruction and feedback on individual problems (Katiyar et al., 2024; Tan et al., 2025). The former is sometimes referred to as *task-loop adaptivity*, while the latter is referred to as *step-loop adaptivity* (Aleven et al., 2016). It is possible for a personalized learning platform to include both forms of adaptivity, to varying degrees.

The way that an ALP typically works is by collecting and analyzing data from students through their interactions on the platform, and dynamically adjusting the sequence, difficulty, and type of content presented (i.e., creating a personalized learning path). Structurally, ALPs generally consist of three core components: a domain model, a learner model—similar to those in ITSs—and an adaptation model, which can be viewed as a more generalized form of the tutor model used in ITSs (Tan et al., 2025). The adaptation model determines the content delivery mechanism based on inputs from the domain and learner models.

According to Tan et al. (2025), ALPs typically implement adaptation through three primary methods: adaptive content, adaptive sequencing, and adaptive assessment. Adaptive content and adaptive sequencing often go hand in hand. For example, ALPs may use recommender systems to suggest learning resources or learning paths that best align with a student's current state of knowledge, preferences, and interests (Rahayu et al., 2023). These platforms often include a large repository of instructional materials across various content areas, designed to cater to students with diverse ability levels and learning needs (e.g., the same mathematical concept can be presented through multiple representations). Based on real-time student data, the system selects the most appropriate resource for each student to advance their learning. For ALPs that incorporate mastery learning principles, the system can also prevent a student from progressing to more advanced content until they have demonstrated sufficient mastery of the current material (Tan et al., 2025).

Adaptive assessment is often implemented as a standalone product in K-12 education, for purposes such as achievement testing or progress monitoring, but it can also be a feature in ALPs. These assessments select questions for students in real-time based on their responses to previous questions on the test. For example, if a student answers several questions correctly, subsequent questions become increasingly challenging; conversely, if a student answers several questions incorrectly, subsequent questions become easier. This assessment approach allows for a more precise estimation of a student's ability while reducing the number of questions on the test (Weiss & Şahin, 2024). When used within ALPs, information from the assessments can inform content recommendations and sequencing.

Similar to ITSs, there is much ongoing research and development surrounding ALPs. AI technologies used in ALPs have evolved over the past decade, shifting from predominantly rule-based methods between 2014 and 2019 to more deep learning and generative AI techniques in the past five years (Tan et al., 2025). These advances enable more sophisticated student modeling, recommendation, and personalization strategies. Researchers are also exploring how educators—aside from students—can benefit from ALPs, for example, through integrated learning analytics dashboards that can provide real-time insights into students' progress (Tan et al., 2025; Yildirim-Erbasli et al., 2024). These insights can guide teachers in lesson planning and instructional decision-making, for example, by identifying common class misconceptions to address or by informing student groupings in the classroom for differentiated instruction or peer support (Papadakis et al., 2024a, 2024b). Additionally, ALPs typically provide a suite of reports designed to support educators by providing detailed information about their students' learning. That being said, it is important for ALP developers to engage closely with educators to determine which types of reporting and insights they find truly useful and actionable.

Several well-known commercial ALPs are available to K-12 students and educators, such as ALEKS by McGraw Hill (math and science for Grades 3 to 12), DreamBox by Discovery Education (math for Grades K to 8 and reading for Grades K to 12), and Smart Sparrow, which emphasizes educator-driven design, allowing instructors and teachers to author customized learning content and specify adaptive pathways for students. Internationally, Squirrel AI is a well-known ALP that also offers one-on-one tutoring features. It has gained popularity in Asia and is now expanding its reach globally (Flannery, 2025). Several countries, such as Singapore and Taiwan, have also developed their own ALPs to support personalized learning in school systems (GovTech Singapore, 2025; Liu, 2022). As discussed earlier, these platforms primarily focus on content and sequence adaptation to recommend the most appropriate resources for individual students and organize them into personalized learning paths.

2.3 Chatbots and Virtual Tutors

Chatbots are typically AI-driven computer programs designed to simulate human-like conversations (Deveci Topal et al., 2021). In the context of personalized learning, researchers have long explored the potential of chatbots to serve as personalized tutors, capable of engaging in one-on-one interactions with students and providing individualized support (Kavitha & Joshith, 2024; Labadze et al., 2023; Winkler & Söllner, 2018). Unlike ITSs and ALPs, which typically deliver pre-structured content, either along fixed or adaptive pathways, chatbots are more learner-driven, allowing students to initiate interactions by asking questions about specific topics.

To mimic human-like dialogue and interactions, chatbots utilize AI technologies like NLP, enabling them to understand and generate human language. Early educational chatbots relied on rule-based NLP techniques, which allowed only limited and highly structured exchanges (Winkler & Söllner, 2018). With advancements in NLP technology and the emergence of LLMs, modern chatbots are much more sophisticated, capable of interpreting more complex queries and maintaining open-ended conversations across various topics.

As of writing this chapter, ChatGPT by OpenAI is arguably the most recognizable and widely used chatbot, not only in education but also across general domains. ChatGPT is built on the Generative Pre-trained Transformer (GPT) architecture, trained on a vast corpus of text data from books, articles, websites, and other written sources. This training enables the model to generate coherent responses on a broad range of common topics. Students often use ChatGPT as a personal tutor, for example, to get help with problem-solving, language learning, or exam preparation (Zhang & Tur, 2024). One notable advantage of chatbots like ChatGPT is their ability to engage across a wider range of subject areas compared to systems like ITSs and ALPs, which are typically limited to domains such as math, science, and reading (Hwang & Chang, 2023; Zhang & Tur, 2024). Recently, a noteworthy example of a specialized AI-powered educational chatbot is QANDA, developed in South Korea. Using optical character recognition and LLM technology, it allows students to take a photo of a problem and receive instant, step-by-step explanations across different subjects.

In K-12 education, several studies have investigated the benefits and challenges of using chatbots in supporting student learning (e.g., Blasco & Charisi, 2024; Deveci Topal et al., 2021; Zhang & Tur, 2024). Findings from these studies generally suggest that the use of chatbots can positively improve students' learning experience in terms of engagement and interaction; however, it may not necessarily lead to learning gains (e.g., improvement in academic achievement), depending on how the chatbot is used. Blasco and Charisi (2024) found that configuring an LLM chatbot to provide step-by-step explanations when supporting students through problem-solving tasks was more beneficial, as it offered students opportunities to engage in critical thinking rather than passively accepting the chatbot's solutions.

While chatbots like ChatGPT can respond effectively to student questions and generate tailored answers based on input prompts, they are generally unable to deliver higher levels of personalized learning achieved by ITSs and ALPs because they do not incorporate student modeling or adaptive pedagogical strategies (Looi & Jia, 2025). To support K-12 educators in a more direct way, several commercial products that integrate chatbots have been developed to facilitate the delivery of personalized instruction, while giving teachers greater control over how the technology is used by students both inside and outside the classroom. Below, we provide an overview of two products: Flint and Khanmigo by Khan Academy.

Flint is an AI-driven personalized learning platform designed to support K-12 educators in schools. It acts as a virtual teaching assistant, utilizing a chatbot interface to interact with students during learning sessions set up by the teacher. Flint utilizes a version of the LLM Claude, developed by Anthropic, and incorporates web search functionality, allowing the AI to draw from additional internet sources to augment its responses. Additionally, it allows teachers to upload their own materials, such as PDFs, slide decks, and web links, and directs Flint to prioritize those sources when interacting with students during learning activities. Instead of relying solely on the LLM to generate responses, Flint incorporates other technologies, such as an external translator and calculator, to address the well-documented challenges that LLMs face with tasks like mathematical computation (Miller & Dicerbo, 2024) and produce more accurate responses. Through the platform, teachers can monitor how students interact with the AI, with full access to their chats for greater oversight. Flint is available across all K-12 core subjects, making it a versatile tool for supporting personalized learning.

Khanmigo, developed by Khan Academy, is another AI-powered tool designed to support both teachers and students by acting as a virtual teaching assistant and personal tutor. Khanmigo is currently available free of charge for teachers, while students can access it independently through a paid subscription. To enable integrated classroom use (similar to Flint) where both students and teachers have access to Khanmigo, Khan Academy offers a school district partnership program that provides access to additional tools, data, and services. For example, using the teacher-facing teaching assistant, educators can create and assign learning activities, which students can complete in the classroom with guidance from the Khanmigo tutor. Currently, Khanmigo is built on top of OpenAI's GPT technology and also integrates with Khan Academy's extensive library of curated educational content. The Khanmigo chatbot is configured to offer personalized guidance to help students find the answer to a problem, without directly providing the answer. Just like Flint, Khanmigo supports a wide range of subject areas in K-12.

In Table 1, we provide a comparative summary of the three main categories of AI-powered personalized learning tools discussed in this chapter. The table highlights key advantages, disadvantages, and considerations for each tool. This overview will help readers understand both the unique benefits and limitations of each type, forming a basis for assessing their suitability in different educational settings.

Table 1. Comparative Summary of AI-Powered Personalized Learning Tools

Tool Type	Advantages	Disadvantages	Key Considerations
ITS	● Highly interactive, adaptive, and feedback-driven; ● Effectiveness comparable to human tutors; ● Supports fine-grained student modeling; ● Leverages process data to detect engagement, confusion, etc.	● Complex to design and implement; heavy reliance on accurate student modeling; ● Limited widespread classroom adoption due to cost/complexity; ● Traditionally focused on STEM.	● Need balance between cognitive, affective, and motivational modeling; ● Requires reliable infrastructure; ● Continuous research to improve AI algorithms and scalability.
ALP	● Personalized learning paths via adaptive sequencing, content, and assessments; ● Supports mastery learning; ● Scalable; ● Provides dashboards for teachers with actionable insights.	● Less individualized feedback compared to ITSs; ● Effectiveness depends on system design and fidelity of use; ● Teacher reports may be overwhelming without proper training.	● Engagement of educators in platform design is critical; ● Careful reporting design to avoid data overload; ● Requires integration with teacher practices; ● Scalability across diverse classrooms.
Chatbots & Virtual Tutors	● Supports natural, learner-driven interactions; ● Wide domain coverage; ● Accessible and versatile; ● Useful for problem-solving and exam prep; ● Supports teacher oversight in some systems (e.g., Flint, Khanmigo).	● Lack of deep personalization (no student modeling); ● Responses may be inaccurate or too general; ● Learning gains are not always consistent; ● Over-reliance on AI may hinder critical thinking if not configured well.	● Best used as a complement to structured learning tools; ● Requires strong teacher mediation for accuracy and responsible use; ● Ongoing improvements in LLMs may expand educational impact.

Note. ITSs = Intelligent Tutoring Systems; ALPs = Adaptive Learning Platforms.

3. EXAMPLES OF PERSONALIZED LEARNING TOOLS IN K-12 EDUCATION

This section presents two real-life examples of AI-powered personalized learning tools in K-12 education: ALEKS and i-Ready. For each example, we present a contextual overview and a description of the platform's key features, highlight examples of classroom implementation by teachers, and provide a brief synthesis of relevant empirical research findings.

3.1 ALEKS

ALEKS (Assessment and Learning in Knowledge Spaces) is a personalized online learning platform created by specialists from diverse fields, including cognitive science, software engineering, mathematics, and education, at the University of California. ALEKS is designed for students' personalized learning and provides valuable references to educators to capture and support student learning processes. It offers a variety of course products targeting K-12 and higher education subjects, including mathematics, chemistry, statistics, business, and accounting. The ALEKS K-12 course focuses specifically on mathematics, covering subjects from third-grade math to high school algebra and geometry.

ALEKS is grounded in Knowledge Space Theory (KST), which was developed by Doignon and Falmagne (1985). KST is based on the concept of knowledge states, which represent the set of concepts or skills a student has mastered. All possible states of knowledge together form a knowledge space, capturing the prerequisite relationships among concepts or skills (Lechuga et al., 2025). This structure enables personalized learning systems, such as ALEKS, to effectively and personally map students' learning paths. By incorporating AI and adaptive learning technology, ALEKS can determine what students know, what they do not know, and what to learn next. This information is crucial for educators to identify each student's learning gaps, tailor personalized learning materials, and monitor students' learning progress.

When students are enrolled in this system, they are introduced to an initial knowledge check, which is an adaptive assessment (see Section 2.2) that aims to determine the student's state of knowledge by guiding them to respond to a certain number of questions (McGraw Hill, n.d.-a). In this process, ALEKS evaluates each student's responses and selects subsequent questions to match their mastery level, thereby providing a better diagnosis of their knowledge. Given the responses to the questions, ALEKS can better understand what students have mastered and what they are ready to learn. Students can check their knowledge state in a multi-colored pie chart after the assessment (see the example in Figure 1). In the pie chart, each slice represents the proportion of mastered topics (in bright colors) and unmastered topics (in grey). The number of mastered topics is shown at the center of the pie chart.

Figure 1. Example of a Pie Chart Representing a Student's Knowledge State in ALEKS

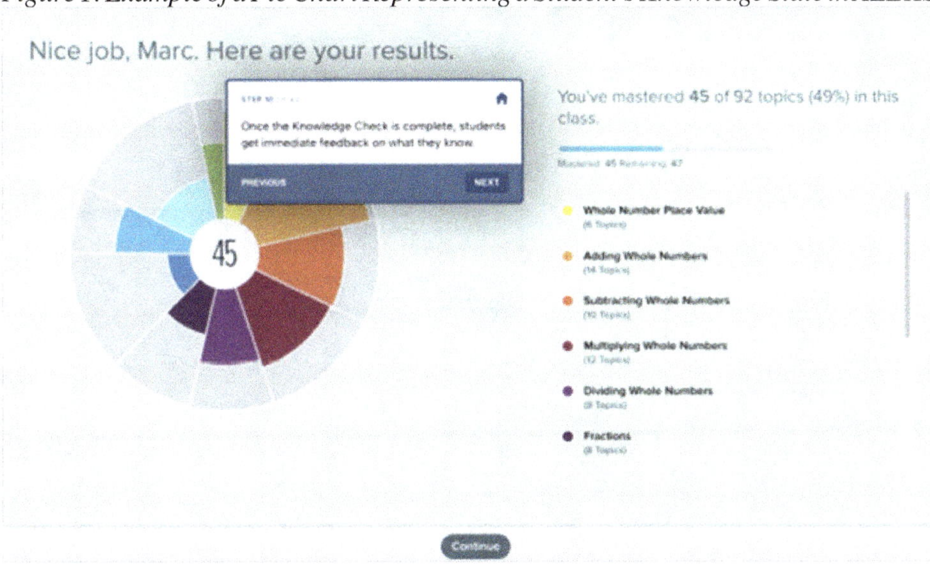

Note. *Screenshot from ALEKS digital tour. Source: McGraw Hill (n.d.-b), https://www.mheducation.com/unitas/school/explore/sites/aleks/clickable-walkthrough/public/index.html#1*

With the initial knowledge check, ALEKS defines each student's learning path by providing what they are ready to learn, as seen in Figure 2. Once students complete the learning process, they will observe changes in their pie chart, with lighter shades appearing in certain slices of the pie. Additionally, students can view the learning progress report in ALEKS to monitor their academic development. Teachers can review student reports, such as the Pie Report and the Progress Report, to monitor class learning progress. They can also review the Time & Topic Report to see how much time each student spends on the platform every day. Various tools are also available for teachers to create assignments, integrate a textbook into ALEKS, set custom teaching objectives to adapt instructional methods, and meet educational goals (see Figure 3)[1].

Figure 2. ALEKS Interface Example Indicating Topics the Student Is Ready to Learn

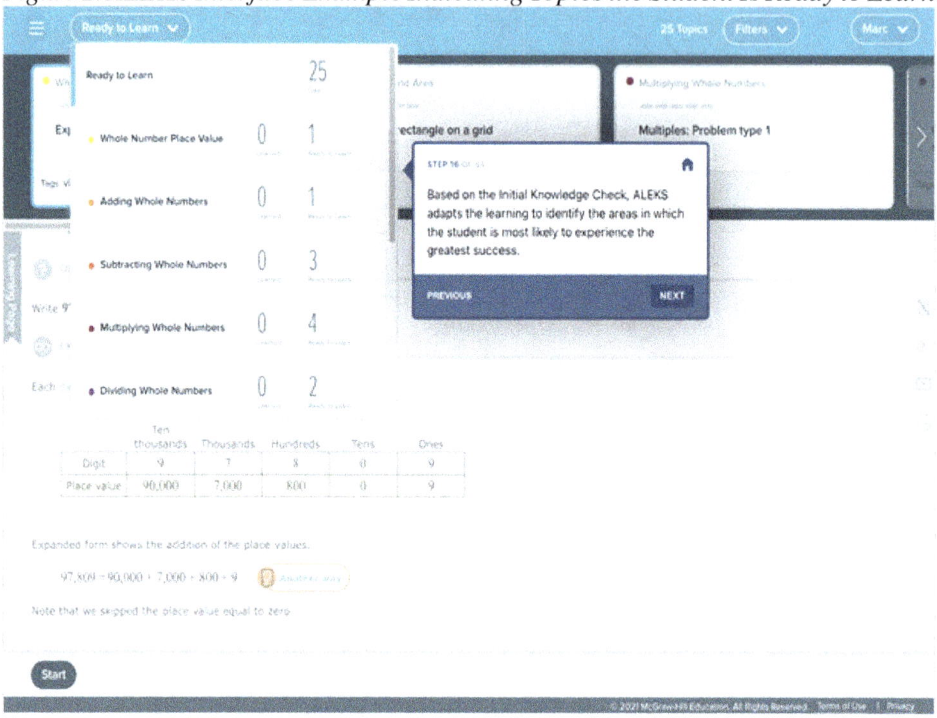

Note. *Screenshot from ALEKS digital tour. Source: McGraw Hill (n.d.-b), https://www.mheducation.com/unitas/school/explore/sites/aleks/clickable-walkthrough/public/index.html#1*

Figure 3. ALEKS Interface Example for Teachers

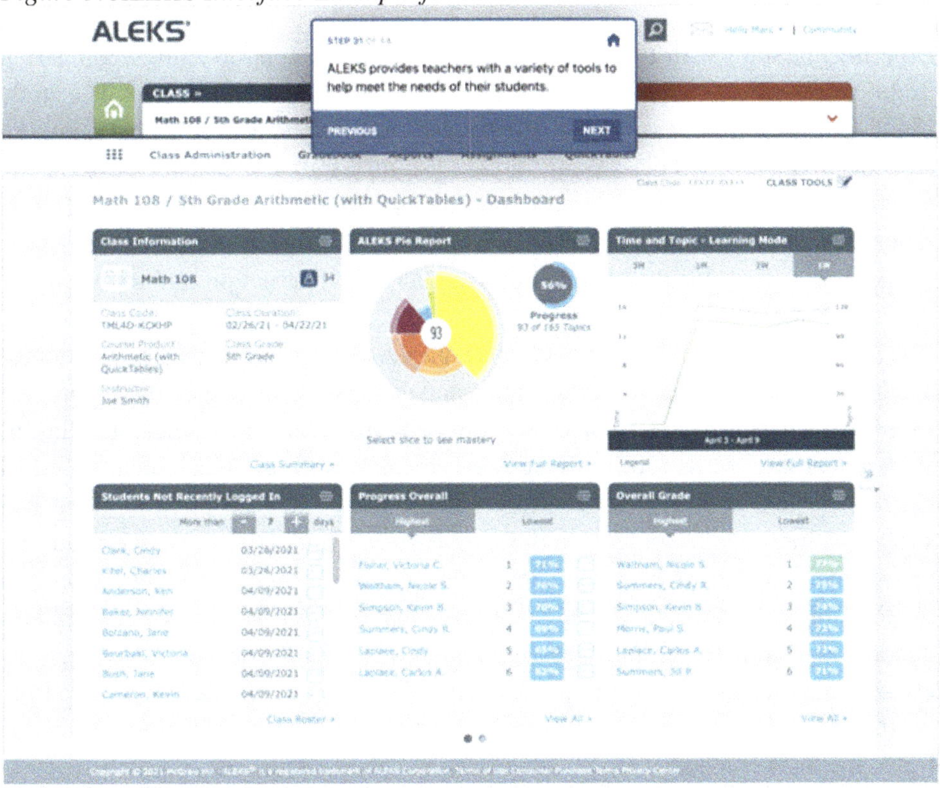

Note. *Screenshot from ALEKS digital tour. Source: McGraw Hill (n.d.-b), https://www.mheducation.com/unitas/school/explore/sites/aleks/clickable-walkthrough/public/index.html#1*

According to McGraw Hill (n.d.-c), ALEKS has gained widespread adoption, with more than 20 million students across K-12 and higher education having used the platform to date. A qualitative study by Kumor et al. (2024), based on interviews with teachers, offers some insights into how ALEKS has been utilized in mathematics classrooms. The researchers found that teachers commonly used ALEKS as an assessment tool to gauge students' current mastery levels and support instructional planning. Teachers also incorporated opportunities for their students to use the individualized learning pathways offered by ALEKS, such as by assigning weekly goals based on time spent or objectives completed, though the extent of this practice varied.

In the literature, numerous researchers have examined the impact of ALEKS on student learning. Findings from a meta-analysis conducted by Sun et al. (2021) on the effects of its use on mathematics learning in K-12 and higher education suggest that ALEKS is comparable to traditional instruction and is particularly effective when used in conjunction with conventional teaching methods. Several other studies have highlighted the benefits of ALEKS. For instance, positive effects on academic performance have been found across various grade levels (Goodwin, 2017; Nehring et al., 2023; Yilmaz, 2017). Craig et al. (2013) conducted a 25-week randomized experimental study with 253 sixth-grade students in after-school settings, comparing traditional teacher-led instruction with ALEKS-supported classrooms. The study found that the two groups performed similarly on a standardized assessment, but students in the ALEKS classrooms required significantly less teacher assistance to complete their daily work. From the perspective of teachers, Kumor et al. (2024) reported generally positive perceptions of ALEKS, noting that the platform is user-friendly, provides valuable data to support mathematics instruction, and is particularly useful in remote learning environments.

Data collected by the ALEKS system can serve as a valuable diagnostic tool for teachers to evaluate student performance and can also be leveraged by researchers to inform wider practice, improve system design, and advance understanding of student learning. Mills (2021) found that indicators such as engagement time and the ratio of mastered to practiced topics could predict course grades among 265 struggling high school students in the northeastern United States. Furthermore, retention of content in ALEKS was shown to significantly predict students' scores on the Preliminary Scholastic Assessment Test–Math (PSAT-M). Cosyn et al. (2021) conducted a study to examine the application of KST in ALEKS and evaluate its effectiveness using data from the platform. Matayoshi et al. (2023) explored the usefulness of incorporating additional information from the platform—response times and answer feedback tags—in modeling student outcomes.

While ALEKS has shown positive outcomes in supporting personalized learning, several studies have also identified limitations with the platform. For example, ALEKS appears to have a limited impact on improving students' self-regulated learning skills (Harati et al., 2021) and was less effective than teacher-led instruction in enhancing the math performance of underachieving 8th-grade students (Khazanchi et al., 2023), suggesting a need for further research on ALEKS's effectiveness across different student populations. Evans (2024) and Kumor et al. (2024) summarized several limitations of the ALEKS platform from the perspective of students and teachers. For example, the platform's grading criteria may be overly rigid or strict, penalizing students for minor errors or not accepting alternative yet correct responses, particularly in mathematics. A further drawback relates to the clarity of explanations provided by the platform. Students have noted that the initial explanations for new topics can be confusing, requiring them to seek help from their teachers or outside resources. Teachers also reported that feedback in ALEKS may be too general to diagnose and pinpoint student difficulties.

Taken together, these findings suggest that while ALEKS offers notable benefits in supporting instruction and tracking student progress, its effectiveness may vary depending on factors such as system design, teachers' instructional strategies, school context, and students' prior knowledge level and usage patterns.

3.2 i-Ready

i-Ready is another evidence-based online learning program widely used by K-12 students across the United States, serving approximately 14 million students as of the time of writing this chapter. It is developed by Curriculum Associates, with a primary focus on mathematics and reading. i-Ready consists of two main components: Diagnostic Assessment and Personalized Instruction. Together, these adaptive features help educators accurately identify each student's proficiency level, evaluate instructional effectiveness, and inform future teaching strategies. This section highlights the reading component (i-Ready for Literacy) and provides a brief overview of its key features.

i-Ready Diagnostic is a comprehensive diagnostic assessment that selects questions adaptively in real-time to accurately measure students' proficiency. Its purpose is not to assign grades, but to ascertain the most effective strategies for supporting student learning. This feature facilitates a more precise diagnosis of students' understanding and addresses their personalized learning needs, forming the basis for recommendations on instructional materials. i-Ready Diagnostic can be used at multiple points throughout the school year. After each assessment, it provides detailed reports for teachers that show the percentage of students at various proficiency levels (see the sample report in Figure 4).

Figure 4. i-Ready Diagnostic Report Displaying Overall Placement

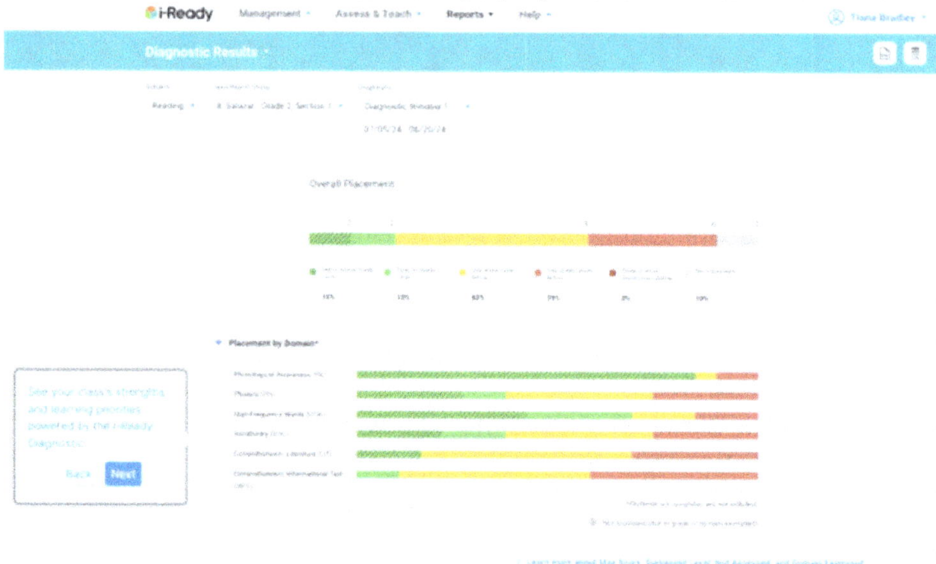

Note. *Screenshot from i-Ready literacy tours. Source: Curriculum Associates (n.d.), https://www.curriculum associates.com/programs/tours*

In addition, i-Ready Diagnostic also provides the percentile rank and placement by domain for each student, enabling teachers to identify knowledge differences among students with the same percentile rank (see the sample report in Figure 5). With this information, teachers can pinpoint the specific skills that students need to develop and utilize targeted instructional resources effectively.

Figure 5. i-Ready Diagnostic Report by Student and Domain

Note. *Screenshot from i-Ready literacy tours. Source: Curriculum Associates (n.d.), https://www.curriculumassociates.com/programs/tours*

i-Ready implements personalized instruction at the individual student level while also providing teachers with class-level insights to guide instruction and support. For individual students, i-Ready uses data collected from the diagnostic assessment to deliver a personalized online lesson path. The lessons are designed to be interactive, built around math-integrated storylines with instructions delivered by virtual cartoon characters. Teachers have oversight of each student's learning path and can monitor students' engagement and progress. They can also adjust the placement or difficulty of lessons if needed (see Figure 6 for an example of an individual student report)[2].

Figure 6. i-Ready Dashboard for Personalized Reading Instruction and Progress (Individual Student)

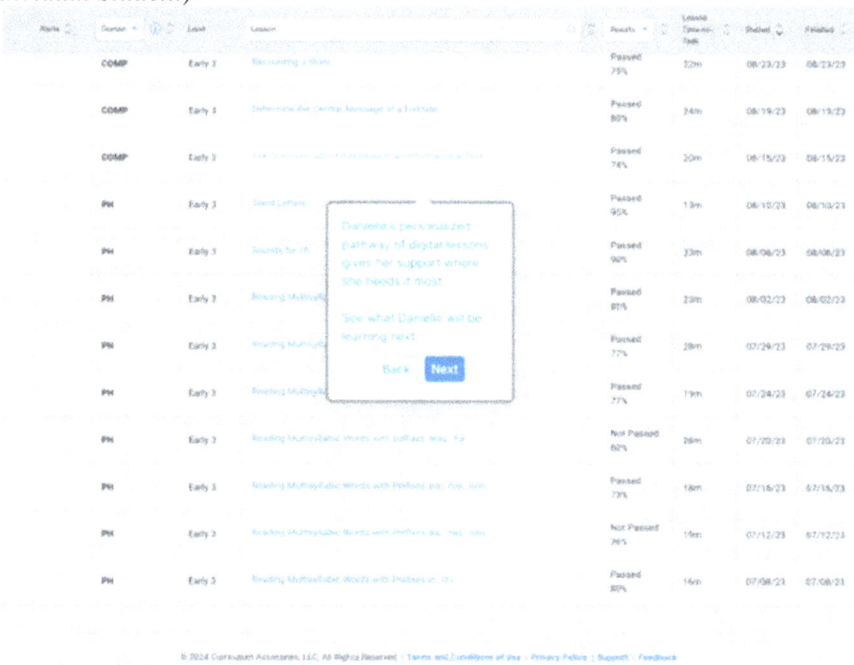

Note. *Screenshot from i-Ready literacy tours. Source: Curriculum Associates (n.d.), https://www.curriculumassociates.com/programs/tours*

To support lesson planning, teachers also get access to class-level data, including metrics on student readiness for specific skills that they wish to teach, along with recommendations for student groupings and instructional resources.[3] Figure 7 illustrates the i-Ready dashboard, which summarizes personalized reading instruction and student progress at the class level.

Figure 7. i-Ready Dashboard for Personalized Reading Instruction and Progress (Class)

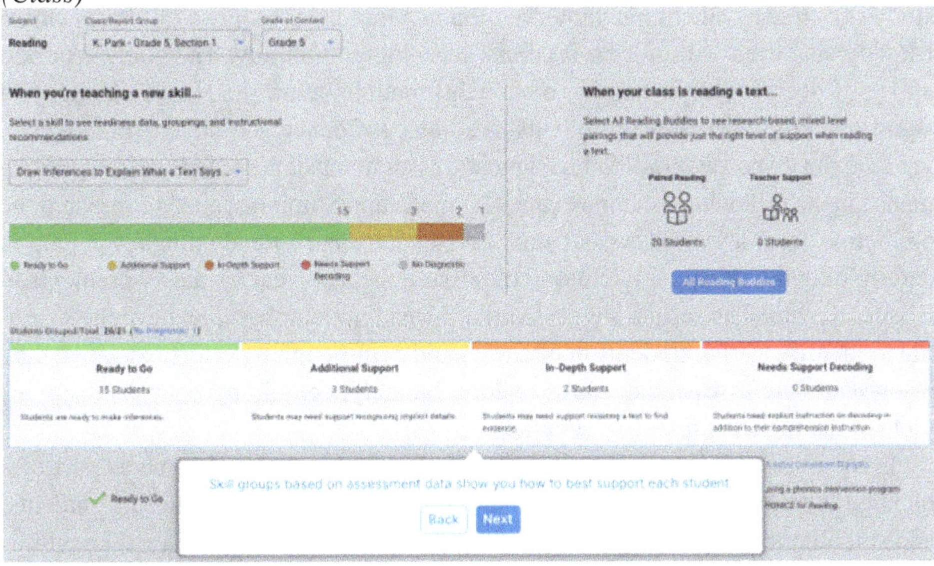

Note. *Screenshot from i-Ready literacy tours. Source: Curriculum Associates (n.d.), https://www.curriculumassociates.com/programs/tours*

The implementation of i-Ready in schools and its impact on student learning have been examined through case studies conducted by Curriculum Associates (published on the i-Ready website), as well as studies conducted by external organizations such as WestEd (Marple et al., 2019), HumRRO (Swain et al., 2020), Johns Hopkins University's Center for Research and Reform in Education (Grant et al., 2023), and other independent researchers.

Through a mixed-methods case study, Marple et al. (2019) found that students who used i-Ready for at least 45 minutes per week showed significant improvement in their mathematics scores on a standardized assessment. This positive association between time spent on the platform and reading achievement was also reported by Grant et al. (2023). Swain et al. (2020) found that i-Ready use is tied to higher reading achievement when the platform is used with fidelity (i.e., following the user guidance provided by Curriculum Associates).

Several independent studies have examined the effectiveness of i-Ready as an intervention tool. Saxe (2021) studied 120 Grade 4 students with learning disabilities in two West Virginia school districts and found that special education students who used i-Ready as a reading intervention tool scored higher than those who did not. Silva (2016) conducted a six-week intervention study with 40 first-grade students in a treatment group using i-Ready in conjunction with the core English language arts (ELA) program, and 40 in a control group, who participated only in the core ELA program. The study reported no significant differences in reading achievement on the post-test. More recently, Hunt et al. (2025) carried out a mixed-methods case study of a grade-wide literacy intervention at a middle school in California, where i-Ready was used within a professional learning community. The study reported an 18.4% decrease in the number of students reading below grade level, along with significant improvements in students' reading confidence and literacy practices.

To evaluate how well i-Ready diagnostic assessment data predicts student performance in the following academic year, Campaña and Solomon (2025) compared the predictive accuracy of prior-year state assessments and i-Ready diagnostic data in determining the students' likelihood of passing the next year's state assessments in ELA and math. The results suggested that i-Ready diagnostic data have the potential to identify at-risk students in Grades 4 and 5, although it performed worse than prior-year state assessment scores overall. Notably, combining both data sources yielded the highest predictive accuracy.

In the classroom, teachers utilized i-Ready in various ways, some as part of a blended learning approach, others as an intervention tool for struggling students, and still others dedicated whole-class periods to the platform or assigned lessons as homework. Teachers found that i-Ready is helpful for practice, reinforcing concepts, filling gaps in students' understanding, and diagnosing class-wide learning needs (Gates, 2024; Marple et al., 2019). Samsonova (2023) found that i-Ready supported second-language English learners more effectively when teachers integrated it with other learning resources within a tiered instruction framework.

Through various case studies, researchers have also identified some limitations of the i-Ready platform, highlighting potential areas for improvement in the platform design as well as broader challenges in implementing educational technology in schools. For instance, some teachers noticed differences between the mathematics knowledge they observed and what was reported by the i-Ready Diagnostic, possibly due to variations in student effort during the assessment (Marple et al., 2019). Marple et al. (2019) noted that less proficient students engaged with the platform less frequently and therefore gained fewer benefits, a challenge likely not unique to i-Ready. In Gate's (2024) study, teachers reported limitations in the areas of professional development and time, indicating that additional training and improved scheduling would strengthen implementation fidelity and program effectiveness.

Overall, the i-Ready program shows great promise in enhancing student reading performance. However, further research across different subjects, grade levels, and student populations is recommended to comprehensively evaluate its effectiveness and determine the most effective ways to support diverse learners. In the following sections, we explore the broader benefits, challenges, and implications of implementing these tools in K-12 classrooms.

4. BENEFITS OF AI-POWERED PERSONALIZED LEARNING TOOLS

AI-powered personalized learning tools have been demonstrated to enhance student learning in various ways. This section highlights three key benefits of AI-powered platforms, focusing on student access and engagement, the teaching process, and learning outcomes.

4.1 Student Access and Engagement: Promoting Equity and Personalized Support

AI-powered personalized learning platforms are designed to be easily accessible. Most of these platforms are compatible with a wide range of devices, providing access for students across diverse contexts, both inside and outside of the classroom. This broad accessibility provides students with enhanced opportunities to engage with richer educational resources, helping to address deficiencies in educational resources and promote educational equity (Dumont & Ready, 2023). Additionally, when students interact with these platforms, they receive personalized support, such as feedback on their quizzes and tailored learning materials, which helps address instructional gaps that arise when teachers have limited capacity to meet every student's needs simultaneously. Major et al. (2021) conducted a meta-analysis of more than 50,000 school-aged students in five low- and middle-income countries, finding that technology-supported personalized learning had a statistically significant positive effect on student learning. This finding suggests that increased access to these tools can also benefit students in under-resourced contexts.

AI-powered platforms are designed to cater to diverse learning styles by incorporating features such as gamification, conversational tutors, and interactive visualizations. These elements can trigger student engagement and motivation, making learning more enjoyable and helping students progress naturally as they interact with the content (Divanji et al., 2023). Throughout their use, the platforms offer real-time feedback on quizzes, assignments, suggest learning materials, and provide personalized progress reports. This feature enables students to learn more interactively and effectively, with the guidance of continuous feedback on their performance. For students who wish to go beyond the curriculum, these platforms help to strengthen their existing knowledge and support them in acquiring new concepts. For struggling learners, the platforms help to identify learning gaps and allow them to progress at their own pace. This type of real-time, personalized feedback and guidance is valuable for enhancing students' learning engagement and cultivating their self-regulatory learning skills (Mejeh & Rehm, 2024).

4.2 Teaching Process: Personalizing Instruction and Assessment

AI-powered personalized learning platforms serve as useful supplementary tools for teachers, incorporating a classroom model that enables seamless integration of the platform into real instructional contexts. This model provides a framework for aligning instructional content with platform features, allowing teachers to develop curriculum and design learning activities more effectively and efficiently. Many of the commercial platforms described in this chapter (e.g., MATHia, ALEKS, and Khanmigo) were designed to complement classroom instruction. Teachers can adopt flexible instructional approaches such as blended learning (see Bradex, 2016), make use of the customized reports and personalized recommendations generated by the platforms to monitor students' progress and assist with lesson planning (e.g., ALEKS; Kumor et al., 2024), or use the platforms as a tool to provide personalized guidance and feedback as students work on problems in class (e.g., Khanmigo; Sahlman et al., 2024).

In terms of assessing student learning, some AI-powered platforms, such as ALEKS and i-Ready, support adaptive assessment practices and offer an enhanced, more personalized approach compared with traditional testing methods. Traditional assessments use fixed sets of questions to evaluate all students' knowledge at specific times. In contrast, AI-powered platforms can select different questions for each student and even incorporate data from students' learning trajectories and activities to improve measurement accuracy. These systems can act as formative tools, monitoring each student's knowledge development over time. By gathering performance data at various points, they support the tracking of students' learning progress and the continuous updating of assessment reports. Consequently, these adaptive assessment results provide teachers with valuable references to improve their instructional strategies and refine their teaching approaches (Strielkowski et al., 2025).

4.3 Learning Outcomes: Monitoring Quality and Informing Decisions

AI-powered personalized learning platforms are capable of monitoring educational quality and providing insights to inform educational decision-making at both the classroom (micro) and system-wide (macro) levels.

At the classroom level, these platforms incorporate numerous machine learning algorithms and NLP methods to diagnose students' knowledge states and report their distributions across different proficiency levels. For example, ALEKS employs a machine learning approach based on KST to maintain a detailed profile of each student's knowledge, to help instructors identify students "(a) who are not succeeding, (b) who cease succeeding, (c) who are excessively procrastinating, or (d) who are learning unrealistically fast" (McGraw Hill, n.d.-b, "Know Each Student Better," para. 1). These data enable teachers to provide timely assistance for each student to help them address learning difficulties and make meaningful progress.

At the system level, some platforms are designed to align with both state and national educational standards. The resulting student performance data, particularly the proportion of students at different proficiency levels, are valuable for understanding learning outcomes on a larger scale and for comparing student performance across schools or districts. This supports regional education quality monitoring by providing aggregated performance data and facilitates the implementation and evaluation of targeted interventions. With a clearer understanding of school-level performance, educators can better tailor their instruction, and policymakers are better equipped to make informed, evidence-based decisions at the state or district level.

5. CHALLENGES OF AI-POWERED PERSONALIZED LEARNING TOOLS

Despite the promise of AI-powered personalized learning tools, several challenges persist in their practical implementation. This section examines the challenges associated with these platforms in terms of ethical and equity concerns, including theoretical and pedagogical readiness, teaching practices, data management, educational decision-making, and policy intervention.

5.1 Theoretical and Pedagogical Readiness

5.1.1 Theoretical Guidance and Practice

From the learning theories perspective, learners' characteristics are crucial in influencing how they engage in the learning environments and further determine their learning outcomes (Walkington & Bernacki, 2020). With the guidance of learning theories, it is more effective to develop various components or features of the system to support learning. Based on learning theories, several adaptive learning models have been developed to inform the design of personalized learning platforms, such as the Intelligent Teaching Systems model (Hartley & Sleeman, 1973) and the Adaptive Hypermedia System model (Brusilovsky, 1996). These models define the basic components of the student model, domain model, and pedagogy model, enabling the system to operate in an organized manner. However, the development of AI brings new opportunities for students to learn more personalized content and for educators to collect data on multimodal learning activities from platforms, allowing for the adoption of innovative pedagogical models. These advancements also present new challenges, underscoring the need for an up-to-date student model, a comprehensive domain model, and an adaptable pedagogical model, which highlights the importance of developing innovative learning models to guide educational practice.

In practice, two significant concerns complicate the application of learning theories to guide the practice of personalized learning: (a) Some researchers have employed the learning theories in guiding personalized learning studies (e.g., Walkington & Bernacki, 2020). Fariani et al. (2023) conducted a systematic review on personalized learning in the context of higher education. They found that only 18% of the included studies stated which learning theory was used. (b) The empirical evidence used to support the associations between learning theories and platform designs is insufficient. Although some studies have concluded that AI-powered personalized learning improves student learning engagement and performance (e.g., Ellikkal & Rajamohan, 2025), several factors limit the generalizability of the results across different platform contexts, including a small sample size, the unrepresentativeness of the minority population, and cultural differences.

5.1.2 Teacher Professional Training and Personalized Curriculum Design

The development of AI requires teachers to reconceptualize their roles, acquiring new pedagogical and technological knowledge to deliver effective instruction. In a systematic review related to teachers' roles in the AI era, Gentile et al. (2023) suggested that teachers must redefine their role in collaboration with AI technology, treating themselves as collaborators rather than opponents, and play a significant role in guiding students to use AI effectively. However, integrating AI into teaching practices is not a simple process and requires time, reflection, and experimentation. Some challenges emerge at various steps when using AI-powered personalized learning platforms, such as designing learning activities and scaffolding students' use of AI recommendations, which requires teachers to critically consider how to incorporate AI tools into their classrooms in a meaningful way.

Many teachers struggle to interpret platform-generated performance metrics, and their ability to use such data directly impacts how they use the platform. Divanji et al. (2023), through interviews with K-12 teachers, found that teachers face challenges in building trust in the data generated from adaptive learning platforms and using them to inform their instructional decisions. In a qualitative case study of i-Ready, teachers provided feedback that the training on implementing the program with fidelity could have been more comprehensive, making them feel better prepared (Gates, 2024). Therefore, it is essential for teachers to have access to sufficient professional training to utilize these platforms effectively. This includes developing a thorough understanding of their underlying algorithms, learning to interpret learning activity data, and adapting platform use to different subjects. Yet, several critical questions remain: Who should the training agenda be for? Who will deliver the training? And who evaluates its effectiveness? Clarifying these responsibilities is essential for enhancing teachers' preparedness in integrating AI-powered platforms into their practice.

Seo et al. (2024) examined the needs of K-12 teachers for AI assistance in personalized learning, discovering that high school teachers, in particular, aim to create customized curricula tailored to students' needs. K-12 teachers face numerous challenges when adapting the curriculum to meet the individual needs of students. For instance, students of different grades have diverse characteristics, requiring teachers to tailor the curriculum based on prior knowledge, self-regulation, learning styles, and other factors. Teachers must thoroughly analyze student profiles, define clear instructional goals, design engaging activities, and evaluate student performance effectively. Also, the professional guidance provided for teachers is limited. These issues increase the teacher pressure when using AI-powered platforms to develop personalized learning curricula.

5.2 Teaching Practices and Data Management

5.2.1 Student Learning Style and Learning Autonomy

In the context of personalized learning, learning style constitutes one of the most commonly regarded characteristics of the learner, utilized to adapt personalized learning designs (Bernacki et al., 2021). When students access personalized learning platforms, the format and relevance of learning materials provided on these platforms could influence student learning outcomes (Villegas-Ch et al., 2024). It is crucial to consider the types of materials and students' learning styles when recommending learning materials. However, in personalized learning systems, learning style detection faces the challenges of designing an effective scoring system, selecting effective learning style models, and addressing students' disengagement in the learning process (Ezzaim et al., 2024). This makes it more challenging to recommend suitable learning materials to students with various learning styles equally.

Creating engaging learning activities, providing suitable feedback, and offering scaffolding are significant challenges in system development (Taylor et al., 2021). These factors will influence student learning autonomy and motivation on the platform, which will then impact their performance. Using a quasi-experimental design, Ingkavara et al. (2022) found that the experimental group, which employed the personalized learning approach in a self-regulated online learning context, performed better than the control group. Although the platform can provide personalized guidance for each student, it assumes that each student's learning autonomy is the same, which may not be the case for every student. Students with higher learning autonomy tend to learn more and achieve better performance, as they actively engage in learning activities and design their own learning pace. In contrast, students with lower learning autonomy often face pressure in keeping up with the progress (Nitkin et al., 2022). This issue should be considered during the development of AI-powered systems, as it might deepen the learning gaps among various student groups.

5.2.2 Data Privacy and Management

Personalized learning systems generate diverse types of data, such as student learning time, scores, and activity logs. This data contains rich information for analyzing student engagement and performance, as well as identifying students at risk. Many guidelines highlight the ethical concerns of data management and usage in AI, such as the United Nations Educational, Scientific, and Cultural Organization's (UNESCO) Recommendation on the Ethics of Artificial Intelligence, the OECD's Recommendation of the Council on Artificial Intelligence, and the Family Educational Rights and Privacy Act (FERPA). As UNESCO states, personal data should be properly and transparently protected to ensure data privacy and protect human dignity. Data privacy ensures that personal data or identifiable information is not disclosed (Morandín-Ahuerma, 2023). Data privacy becomes more important when analyzing student data from personalized learning platforms. For example, some analyses are conducted to link student learning activity data from the platform to their standardized test scores, evaluating the effectiveness of platform usage or teaching interventions (e.g., Campaña & Solomon, 2025). In this case, the way and the extent to which students' personal information is disclosed pose new concerns when analyzing and reporting data results. A standardized procedure that adheres to guidelines from organizations such as UNESCO is necessary to ensure stakeholders understand the process of data storage, usage, and reporting in safeguarding data privacy and human rights.

Additionally, ensuring that data privacy guidelines are implemented consistently and effectively is also a significant concern. There is a lack of effective supervision procedures for collecting, analyzing, and reporting student data at the school, district, and national levels. This includes overseeing how data consent is obtained, how daily learning activity data is stored and deleted, and how the data is analyzed and reported. According to a literature review on the role of data supervisors in implementing privacy policies by Judijanto (2025b), the findings highlight several challenges faced by data supervisors, including rapid regulatory changes, technological advancements, and the need to manage data efficiently. In summary, the effective application of data privacy guidelines and the consistent oversight of their implementation continue to present new challenges in data management.

5.3 Educational Decision-Making and Policy Intervention

5.3.1 Transparency in Algorithm Training

In the personalized learning platform, algorithms are primarily used to recommend learning materials to each student and assess their performance data to update their knowledge levels. For instance, ALEKS leverages knowledge space theory to guide its assessment structure, navigating millions of possible knowledge states to determine the next optimal concept for each learner. This requires efficient algorithms capable of accurately identifying what students know and what they are ready to learn (Cosyn et al., 2021). Algorithm training is a vital component in platform development, aimed at reducing algorithmic bias. Algorithmic bias occurs when an "algorithm distributes benefits and burdens unequally among different individuals or groups" (Kordzadeh & Ghasemaghaei, p. 394, 2022). To minimize algorithmic bias, the algorithm should be trained on large-scale datasets to enhance its ability to analyze similar datasets. This requires the training data to represent diverse student populations, such as high-income and low-income students, thereby mitigating bias caused by algorithms in future applications (Maghsudi et al., 2021).

In reality, ensuring that each algorithm is unbiased and accurately reflects diverse groups is not straightforward due to issues like imbalanced data sampling and faulty causality assumptions (Hanna et al., 2025). These issues could be alleviated by increasing algorithmic transparency, which facilitates public understanding of the decision-making process and improves their confidence in the outcomes to perceive them as more equitable (Kordzadeh & Ghasemaghaei, 2022). However, the entire process of making decisions based on algorithms, particularly regarding how the algorithm was trained, including sampling methods for the training data, descriptions of the training data's characteristics, and an analysis of the differences between training and testing data, is not public. The unreliable outcomes caused by numerous potential algorithmic biases will result in inappropriate decision-making by educators and exacerbate educational disparities.

5.3.2 Organizational Readiness

Successful adoption of AI is less about technology alone and more about the organizational readiness of different districts and school levels. Jöhnk et al. (2021) surveyed 25 AI experts and identified five key organizational AI readiness factors: strategic alignment, resources, knowledge, culture, and data. They also outlined actionable indicators for each factor. Their findings serve as a valuable reference for decision-makers to specify organizational needs and to take steps toward preparing for AI-powered education. Policymakers should be concerned with several equity issues related to AI-powered personalized learning platforms. These include distributing educational resources fairly, properly using data from multiple platforms to compare standardized test results across different schools and districts, and increasing their awareness and capacity to handle and utilize AI responsibly.

Schools from underdeveloped areas may require additional financial support to provide each student with opportunities to utilize AI and learn in a personalized manner. This necessitates the development of effective regulations and policies by policymakers to distribute educational resources more equitably, thereby reducing disparities. Additionally, many personalized learning platforms are designed to align well with national standardized tests; however, the content differences among these platforms are difficult to measure, which may raise further equity concerns for schools that utilize different platforms. Guiding schools in choosing suitable tools and providing suggestions for various companies is crucial for policymakers to effectively manage these platforms. The importance of AI and the methodologies for its application requires heightened leadership commitment to motivate collective efforts in establishing sustainable educational systems. Policymakers must enhance not only policy capabilities but also cultural preparedness, guaranteeing that educators, administrators, and students unite under a coherent vision for the scientific utilization of AI-powered tools, rather than merely substituting human efforts (Miao et al., 2021).

6. PRACTICAL IMPLICATIONS, LIMITATIONS, AND FUTURE RESEARCH

As summarized in this chapter, the integration of AI-powered technologies, including ALPs, ITSs, virtual tutors, and chatbots, signifies a fundamental shift in delivering personalized learning in K–12 education. These tools offer transformative opportunities for both teaching methods and educational results. However, their successful implementation depends on careful attention to pedagogical issues at the classroom level and strategic planning at district and system levels to overcome potential obstacles and barriers. This section discusses the practical implications, limitations, and provides recommendations for decision-makers and future researchers.

6.1 Classroom-Level Pedagogical Implications

At the classroom level, AI-driven personalized learning tools are reshaping the interplay among instruction, assessment, and student engagement. ALPs, in particular, show strong potential to improve academic achievement. Empirical studies report gains of approximately 0.36 standard deviations in overall academic performance and 0.42 in mathematics achievement, corresponding to an additional three to five months of learning relative to traditional instructional methods (Chen, 2025). These platforms dynamically assess students' performance patterns, learning pace, and comprehension to generate individualized learning pathways that adapt in real time (Akavova et al., 2025).

ITSs have demonstrated robust outcomes, especially in STEM education, where their capacity to deliver immediate, individualized feedback aligns well with the subject-specific learning demands (Hart, 2025). Research consistently indicates that ITS usage leads to improved student learning trajectories compared to conventional one-size-fits-all approaches (Létourneau et al., 2025). These systems are particularly effective in diagnosing knowledge gaps and delivering targeted interventions at critical learning junctures.

Virtual chatbots serve as always-available learning companions, extending instructional support beyond traditional classroom boundaries. Recent experimental studies involving learners aged 14–16 show that AI-generated, step-by-step explanations significantly outperform simple answer provision in enhancing student performance (Blasco & Charisi, 2024). However, the same research notes that Socratic-style AI interactions, while effective in increasing learner engagement, do not necessarily translate into measurable gains in learning outcomes. This finding highlights the importance of aligning chatbot design with specific instructional objectives, as different approaches may yield varying educational benefits.

6.2 District and School-Level Implementation Considerations

At the district and school system level, the adoption of AI technologies necessitates comprehensive policy development, substantial infrastructure investment, and effective organizational change management. Although momentum is growing, current research indicates that as of fall 2023, only 5% of districts had formal AI policies in place. Encouragingly, this landscape is rapidly evolving, with 48% of districts reporting the implementation of teacher AI training programs by fall 2024 (Diliberti et al., 2025; Dusseault, 2024). This acceleration underscores the urgent need for systematic, district-wide strategies to guide AI integration.

Infrastructure and equity considerations present significant challenges for district-level implementation. The digital divide threatens to exacerbate existing educational inequalities, as wealthier districts with robust technological infrastructure can more readily adopt AI solutions while under-resourced districts struggle with basic connectivity and device access (Abdelsalam Mohamed Mostafa, 2025). Research indicates that only 60% of students in high-poverty districts have reliable internet access compared to 85% in low-poverty districts, creating substantial barriers to equitable AI implementation (Swargiary, 2024).

Professional development and teacher training emerge as critical success factors for district-wide adoption of AI. Districts implementing AI literacy programs report that initial teacher training should focus on addressing educators' fears and discomfort with AI rather than immediately jumping to instructional applications (Diliberti et al., 2025). Many districts have adopted do-it-yourself approaches to teacher training after struggling to find external partners capable of providing appropriate AI professional development. This suggests that districts must invest in developing internal capacity for ongoing AI support and training.

Adopting AI-powered tools requires weighing potential benefits against significant financial and organizational costs. Benefits include personalized learning at scale, early identification of struggling students, reduced teacher workload, and more efficient allocation of district resources. However, these advantages come with substantial costs: investments in hardware, software licensing, cybersecurity, ongoing training, and data governance structures (Feng et al., 2025; Saxena et al., 2025). For under-resourced districts, short-term costs may outweigh initial gains unless accompanied by external funding or cross-district partnerships. Therefore, districts must conduct comprehensive cost–benefit analyses that factor in both tangible outcomes (e.g., improved test performance, teacher time saved) and intangible ones (e.g., improved student engagement, reduced teacher burnout).

Finally, procurement and evaluation processes require substantial modification to accommodate AI tools. Traditional technology procurement frameworks are often inadequate for evaluating AI systems, which require consideration of data privacy, algorithmic bias, learning effectiveness, and integration with existing educational technologies (Augenstein, 2024). Districts must develop new evaluation criteria that assess not only technical functionality but also pedagogical appropriateness and ethical implications of AI tools.

6.3 Potential Limitations and Barriers

While the opportunities for AI adoption are significant, districts and schools must also grapple with systemic limitations and barriers. One concern is dependency on technology, where over-reliance on adaptive learning systems, intelligent tutoring systems, or chatbots may reduce instructional flexibility or leave schools vulnerable to system failures, vendor lock-in, or rapidly shifting technology markets. Especially if schools rely too heavily on AI decisions or content, they risk developing a technology dependency that may erode instructional quality and the human relationships central to education (Karamuk, 2025; Partelow, 2024). Therefore, contingency plans for the use of AI are needed to maintain instructional continuity at schools.

Another pressing issue is unequal access to resources. The benefits of AI in education are not equally accessible to all schools and students. Even when hardware and connectivity are available, disparities in IT support staff, funding stability, and opportunities for ongoing professional development can create uneven implementation across schools within the same district. Early evidence from U.S. school districts suggests that affluent, suburban, and predominantly white districts are moving more quickly on AI initiatives (e.g., by providing teacher training on AI) than urban, rural, and high-poverty districts (Diliberti et al., 2024). This unevenness raises concerns about equity, suggesting that AI could exacerbate existing educational inequalities rather than reducing them (Diliberti et al., 2024; Partelow, 2024; Salman, 2023). Adequate and equitable funding, along with stakeholder buy-in (e.g., parents and community members), are crucial to ensuring that AI tools remain aligned with students' learning needs.

Cultural factors also matter. Teacher resistance and skepticism often arise when AI is perceived as undermining teacher expertise or adding workload without clear benefits. Surveys of K–12 teachers across the U.S. show that many teachers raise significant concerns about data privacy, algorithmic bias, loss of control, and even the broader societal implications of AI (Diliberti et al., 2024). Other prevalent concerns include the potential for AI to infringe on teacher autonomy, facilitate increased surveillance of instruction, or erode student–teacher relationships. A recent meta-analysis of over 60 studies concluded that barriers, including ethical concerns, fear of inappropriate use, and uncertainty about AI's pedagogical value, all amplify teacher resistance to adoption (McGehee, 2024). This resistance is also tied to practical issues such as workload and confidence, especially if teachers feel unprepared to use AI or worry it will create more work. Thus, we argue that if implementation strategies do not sufficiently align with teachers' instructional philosophies or provide meaningful involvement in decision-making, AI adoption in schools is likely to continue stalling in the future.

Lastly, the successful integration of AI requires significant shifts in classroom practice and pedagogy. However, not all schools or educators are ready or willing to make those shifts. AI-based personalized learning or intelligent tutors might conflict with established teaching methods or cultural expectations about education. For example, teachers who favor direct instruction or who are accustomed to set curricula may view adaptive learning systems as misaligned with their pedagogical beliefs (McGehee, 2024). Research indicates that many AI systems adopt reductionist views of learning, prioritizing efficiency, competencies, and test scores over holistic student development and the vital social aspects of teaching and learning (Mintz et al., 2023). Also, the lack of established and well-defined AI curricula exacerbates these tensions, as teachers are left to interpret and adapt fragmented resources in ways that often clash with their existing instructional practices (Chiu, 2021). These challenges suggest that the successful adoption of AI in classrooms is a profound pedagogical and cultural issue, necessitating deliberate alignment between AI innovations, teacher beliefs, and broader educational objectives.

6.4 Recommendations for Decision-Makers

For district and school leaders, a clear path to effective AI adoption begins with the development of comprehensive policies that establish clear expectations around data governance, privacy, ethical use, and pedagogical alignment. Without these guiding frameworks, districts risk fragmented adoption that fails to support instructional goals. At the same time, investments in infrastructure must be prioritized to ensure equitable access. Without reliable devices and high-speed internet, AI tools will inevitably exacerbate existing inequalities. External funding sources, such as state or federal grants, can play an essential role in helping under-resourced districts bridge this gap.

Equally critical is sustained professional development. Rather than relying solely on external vendors, districts should work toward building internal capacity for AI training that extends beyond basic tool demonstrations. Early training should focus on alleviating teacher concerns and building confidence, while ongoing professional learning can promote AI literacy and integrate best practices into everyday instruction.

Finally, school leaders should approach adoption strategically by conducting careful cost–benefit analyses and piloting tools before scaling them district-wide. Evaluations must weigh immediate costs against both measurable outcomes, such as student performance and teacher workload, as well as less tangible benefits, including engagement and morale. Starting small with pilot programs may allow schools and districts to assess risks, refine implementation, and make more informed decisions about long-term investments.

6.5 Directions for Future Research

As AI-powered personalized learning continues to evolve, ongoing research will be essential to understand optimal implementation strategies and ensure that AI-enhanced personalized learning serves all students effectively and equitably. Several promising directions for future research emerge from the current understanding of AI-powered personalized learning.

First, longitudinal studies are needed to investigate the sustained impacts of personalized learning tools on students' academic and non-academic outcomes. While short-term gains are evident, understanding long-term benefits or potential drawbacks (e.g., reduced intrinsic motivation) is essential.

Second, future studies should explore personalized learning across a wider range of diverse contexts, particularly in multilingual and multicultural settings. Research on how different AI tools perform in culturally and linguistically diverse classrooms can inform the development of more universally applicable platforms and mitigate biases embedded in current AI models.

Third, exploring the integration of generative AI with ITSs and ALPs presents significant research potential. Investigating how generative AI can augment existing tools to provide more personalized, contextually sensitive feedback could extend the scope of personalized learning into broader educational domains.

Lastly, researchers should examine teacher-AI interaction models, focusing on how teachers collaborate with AI tools in classroom settings. This line of work may also extend to emerging embodied technologies such as social robots, which can be introduced into classrooms as intelligent, human-like tutors (Lampropoulos & Papadakis, 2025). These robots can provide personalized instruction while responding to students' social and emotional cues. Understanding how educators integrate these systems into their classroom practices, along with identifying barriers and facilitators of effective integration, will inform the design of AI-powered systems that better align with real-world educational needs.

REFERENCES

Abdelsalam Mohamed Mostafa, M. (2025). Bridging the digital divide: AI, VR, and AR for equitable K-12 education. *SSRN*. http://dx.doi.org/DOI: 10.2139/ssrn.5124551

Akavova, A., Temirkhanova, Z., & Lorsanova, Z. (2025). Adaptive learning and artificial intelligence in the educational space. *E3S Web of Conferences, 451*. https://doi.org/DOI: 10.1051/e3sconf/202345106011

Aleven, V., McLaghlin, E. A., Glenn, R. A., & Koedinger, K. R. (2016). Instruction based on adaptive learning technologies. In Mayer, R. E., & Alexander, P. A. (Eds.), *Handbook of research on learning and instruction* (pp. 522–560). Routledge., DOI: 10.4324/9781315736419

Aleven, V., Rowe, J., Huang, Y., & Mitrovic, A. (2023). Domain modeling for AIED systems with connections to modeling student knowledge: A review. In du Boulay, B., Mitrovic, A., & Yacef, K. (Eds.), *Handbook of artificial intelligence in education* (pp. 127–169). Edward Elgar Publishing. DOI: 10.4337/9781800375413.00017

Augenstein, S. (2024, May 7). *The stumbling blocks for artificial intelligence in K–12 education. EdTech Magazine*. https://edtechmagazine.com/k12/article/2024/05/stumbling-blocks-artificial-intelligence-k-12-education

Bernacki, M. L., Greene, M. J., & Lobczowski, N. G. (2021). A systematic review of research on personalized learning: Personalized by whom, to what, how, and for what purpose(s)? *Educational Psychology Review*, *33*(4), 1675–1715. DOI: 10.1007/s10648-021-09615-8

Betts, A., Thai, K. P., & Gunderia, S. (2021). Personalized mastery learning ecosystems: Using Bloom's four objects of change to drive learning in adaptive instructional systems. In Sottilare, R. A., & Schwarz, J. (Eds.), *Adaptive instructional systems. Design and evaluation* (Vol. 12792, pp. 29–52). Springer., DOI: 10.1007/978-3-030-77857-6_3

Blasco, A., & Charisi, V. (2024). AI chatbots in K-12 education: An experimental study of Socratic vs. non-Socratic approaches and the role of step-by-step reasoning. *SSRN*. https://dx.doi.org/DOI: 10.2139/ssrn.5040921

Bloom, B. S. (1968). Learning for mastery. *Evaluation Comment*, *1*(2), 1–12.

Bradex, M. A. (2016). *Blended learning: A case study using ALEKS and small group instruction to increase math literacy of English learners* [Doctoral Dissertation, California State University]. ScholarWorks. http://hdl.handle.net/10211.3/190298

Brusilovsky, P. (1996). Methods and techniques of adaptive hypermedia. *User Modeling and User-Adapted Interaction*, *6*(2–3), 87–129. DOI: 10.1007/BF00143964

Bulut, O., Beiting-Parrish, M., Casabianca, J. M., Slater, S. C., Jiao, H., Song, D., Ormerod, C., Fabiyi, D. G., Ivan, R., Walsh, C., Rios, O., Wilson, J., Yildirim-Erbasli, S. N., Wongvorachan, T., Liu, J. X., Tan, B., & Morilova, P. (2025). The rise of artificial intelligence in educational measurement: Opportunities and ethical challenges. *Chinese/English Journal of Educational Measurement and Evaluation*, *5*(3). Advance online publication. DOI: 10.59863/MIQL7785

Campaña, K. V., & Solomon, B. G. (2025). Classification accuracy of i-Ready and prior year state exams on year-end outcomes. *Assessment for Effective Intervention*, *50*(3), 153–162. DOI: 10.1177/15345084251338860

Chen, M. (2025). The impact of AI-assisted personalized learning on student academic achievement. *US-China Education Review A*, *15*(6), 441–450. DOI: 10.17265/2161-623X/2025.06.008

Chen, S., Fang, Y., Shi, G., Sabatini, J., Greenberg, D., Frijters, J., & Graesser, A. C. (2021). Automated disengagement tracking within an intelligent tutoring system. *Frontiers in Artificial Intelligence*, *3*, 595627. Advance online publication. DOI: 10.3389/frai.2020.595627 PMID: 33748746

Chiu, T. K. F. (2021). A holistic approach to the design of artificial intelligence (AI) education for K-12 schools. *TechTrends*, *65*(6), 796–807. DOI: 10.1007/s11528-021-00637-1

Cosyn, E., Uzun, H., Doble, C., & Matayoshi, J. (2021). A practical perspective on knowledge space theory: ALEKS and its data. *Journal of Mathematical Psychology*, *101*, 102512. Advance online publication. DOI: 10.1016/j.jmp.2021.102512

Craig, S. D., Hu, X., Graesser, A. C., Bargagliotti, A. E., Sterbinsky, A., Cheney, K. R., & Okwumabua, T. (2013). The impact of a technology-based mathematics after-school program using ALEKS on student's knowledge and behaviors. *Computers & Education*, *68*, 495–504. DOI: 10.1016/j.compedu.2013.06.010

Curriculum Associates. (n.d.). *Literacy tours*. Curriculum Associates. https://www.curriculumassociates.com/programs/tours

Deveci Topal, A., Dilek Eren, C., & Kolburan Geçer, A. (2021). Chatbot application in a 5th grade science course. *Education and Information Technologies*, *26*(5), 6241–6265. DOI: 10.1007/s10639-021-10627-8 PMID: 34177344

Diliberti, M. K., Lake, R. J., & Weiner, S. R. (2025). *More districts are training teachers on artificial intelligence: Findings from the American School District Panel*. RAND Corporation. https://www.rand.org/pubs/research_reports/RRA956-31.html

Diliberti, M. K., Schwartz, H. L., Doan, S., Shapiro, A., Rainey, L. R., & Lake, R. J. (2024). *Using artificial intelligence tools in K–12 classrooms* (Research Report No. RRA956-21). RAND Corporation. https://www.rand.org/pubs/research_reports/RRA956-21.html

Divanji, R. A., Bindman, S., Tung, A., Chen, K., Castaneda, L., & Scanlon, M. (2023). A one stop shop? Perspectives on the value of adaptive learning technologies in K-12 education. *Computers and Education Open*, *5*, 100157. Advance online publication. DOI: 10.1016/j.caeo.2023.100157

Doignon, J. P., & Falmagne, J. C. (1985). Spaces for the assessment of knowledge. *International Journal of Man-Machine Studies*, *23*(2), 175–196. DOI: 10.1016/S0020-7373(85)80031-6

Dumont, H., & Ready, D. D. (2023). On the promise of personalized learning for educational equity. *NPJ Science of Learning*, *8*(26), 26. Advance online publication. DOI: 10.1038/s41539-023-00174-x PMID: 37542046

Dusseault, B. (2024). *AI and education policy 101: The evolving landscape and examples from early adopters*. Center on Reinventing Public Education. https://crpe.org/ai-and-education-policy-101-the-evolving-landscape-and-examples-from-early-adopters/

Dutta, S., Ranjan, S., Mishra, S., Sharma, V., Hewage, P., & Iwendi, C. (2024, February). Enhancing educational adaptability: A review and analysis of AI-driven adaptive learning platforms. *2024 4th International Conference on Innovative Practices in Technology and Management (ICIPTM)*. https://doi.org/DOI: 10.1109/ICIPTM59628.2024.10563448

Ellikkal, A., & Rajamohan, S. (2025). AI-enabled personalized learning: Empowering management students for improving engagement and academic performance. *Vilakshan - XIMB. Journal of Management*, *22*(1), 28–44. DOI: 10.1108/XJM-02-2024-0023

Evans, J. E. (2024). *The effectiveness of ALEKS to address Grade 8 students' math deficiencies* [Doctoral dissertation, Walden University]. Walden Dissertations and Doctoral Studies. https://scholarworks.waldenu.edu/dissertations/16447/

Ezzaim, A., Dahbi, A., Aqqal, A., & Haidine, A. (2024). AI-based learning style detection in adaptive learning systems: A systematic literature review. *Journal of Computers in Education*. Advance online publication. DOI: 10.1007/s40692-024-00328-9

Fariani, R. I., Junus, K., & Santoso, H. B. (2023). A systematic literature review on personalised learning in the higher education context. *Technology. Knowledge and Learning, 28*(2), 449–476. DOI: 10.1007/s10758-022-09628-4

Feng, M., Brezack, N., & Heffernan, N. (2025, July 21–23). *Scaling what works cost-consciously: A cost analysis of an AI-enhanced tool for middle school math learning. Proceedings of the Twelfth ACM Conference on Learning @ Scale (L@S '25)*, pp. 315–319. https://doi.org/DOI: 10.1145/3698205.3733947

Ferster, B. (2014). *Teaching machines: Learning from the intersection of education and technology*. Johns Hopkins University Press. DOI: 10.1353/book.36140

Flannery, R. (2025, February 18). *Derek Li and Squirrel AI aim to lead the future of AI-driven education.* Forbes. https://www.forbes.com/sites/forbeschina/2025/02/18/derek-li-and-squirrel-ai-aim-to-lead-the-future-of-ai-driven-education/

Gaeta, A., Orciuoli, F., Pascuzzo, A., & Peduto, A. (2024). Evaluating the ability of large language models to generate motivational feedback. In Sifaleras, A., & Lin, F. (Eds.), *Generative intelligence and intelligent tutoring systems, ITS 2024*. Springer., DOI: 10.1007/978-3-031-63028-6_15

Gates, A. (2024). *Teachers' perceptions of the impact of iReady on student reading achievement for students in response to intervention* [Doctoral dissertation, Kennesaw State University]. DigitalCommons @ Kennesaw State University. https://digitalcommons.kennesaw.edu/dissertations/26

Gentile, M., Città, G., Perna, S., & Allegra, M. (2023). Do we still need teachers? Navigating the paradigm shift of the teacher's role in the AI era. *Frontiers in Education, 8*, 1161777. Advance online publication. DOI: 10.3389/feduc.2023.1161777

Goodwin, M. E. (2017). *Using a math tutorial program to decrease the number of failed grades the first semester helping the college achieve a 91% first-year retention rate* [Conference presentation]. 2017 FYEE Conference, Florida, United States.

Gorgun, G., & Bulut, O. (2022). Identifying aberrant responses in intelligent tutoring systems: An application of anomaly detection methods. *Psychological Test and Assessment Modeling, 64*(4), 359–384.

GovTech Singapore. (2025, January 21). *AI in education: Transforming Singapore's education system with student learning space*. https://www.tech.gov.sg/technews/ai-in-education-transforming-singapore-education-system-with-student-learning-space

Graesser, A. C., Hu, X., & Sottilare, R. (2018). Intelligent tutoring systems. In Fischer, F., Hmelo-Silver, C. E., Goldman, S. R., & Reimann, P. (Eds.), *International handbook of the learning sciences* (pp. 246–255). Routledge. DOI: 10.4324/9781315617572-24

Grant, A. A., Cook, M. A., & Ross, S. M. (2023). *The impacts of i-Ready personalized instruction on student reading achievement*. Johns Hopkins University. https://files.eric.ed.gov/fulltext/ED644594.pdf

Guskey, T. R. (1997). *Implementing mastery learning*. Wadsworth.

Hanna, M. G., Pantanowitz, L., Jackson, B., Palmer, O., Visweswaran, S., Pantanowitz, J., Deebajah, M., & Rashidi, H. H. (2025). Ethical and bias considerations in artificial intelligence/machine learning. *Modern Pathology*, *38*(3), 100686. Advance online publication. DOI: 10.1016/j.modpat.2024.100686 PMID: 39694331

Harati, H., Sujo-Montes, L., Tu, C.-H., Armfield, S., & Yen, C.-J. (2021). Assessment and learning in knowledge spaces (ALEKS) adaptive system impact on students' perception and self-regulated learning skills. *Education Sciences*, *11*(10), 603. Advance online publication. DOI: 10.3390/educsci11100603

Hart, J. (2025, June 11). *AI tutoring in schools: How personalized learning technology is changing K-12 education in 2025*. The Hunt Institute. https://hunt-institute.org/resources/2025/06/ai-tutoring-alpha-school-personalized-learning-technology-k-12-education/

Hartley, J. R., & Sleeman, D. H. (1973). Towards more intelligent teaching systems. *International Journal of Man-Machine Studies*, *5*(2), 215–236. DOI: 10.1016/S0020-7373(73)80033-1

Hunt, M., Yan, Y., Meyer, B., & Liu, H. (2025). Managing literacy interventions through professional learning communities: A case study on organizational change in education systems. *Humanities & Social Sciences Communications*, *12*(1), 402. Advance online publication. DOI: 10.1057/s41599-025-04744-9

Hwang, G.-J., & Chang, C.-Y. (2023). A review of opportunities and challenges of chatbots in education. *Interactive Learning Environments*, *31*(7), 4099–4112. DOI: 10.1080/10494820.2021.1952615

Ingkavara, T., Panjaburee, P., Srisawasdi, N., & Sajjapanroj, S. (2022). The use of a personalized learning approach to implementing self-regulated online learning. *Computers and Education: Artificial Intelligence*, *3*, 100086. Advance online publication. DOI: 10.1016/j.caeai.2022.100086

Jöhnk, J., Weißert, M., & Wyrtki, K. (2021). Ready or not, AI comes—An interview study of organizational AI readiness factors. *Business & Information Systems Engineering*, *63*(1), 5–20. DOI: 10.1007/s12599-020-00676-7

Judijanto, L. (2025a). A bibliometric analysis of adaptive learning in K-12 education. *The Eastasouth Journal of Learning and Education*, *3*(1), 75–86. DOI: 10.58812/esle.v3i01.496

Judijanto, L. (2025b). The role of data supervisors in the implementation of privacy policies: A literature review. *Jurnal Komunikasi*, *3*(3), 139–146.

Karamuk, E. (2025). The automation trap: Unpacking the consequences of overreliance on AI in education and its hidden costs. In Garcia, M. B., Rosak-Szyrocka, J., & Bozkurt, A. (Eds.), *Pitfalls of AI integration in education: Skill obsolescence, misuse, and bias* (pp. 151–174). IGI Global Scientific Publishing. DOI: 10.4018/979-8-3373-0122-8.ch007

Kaswan, K. S., Dhatterwal, J. S., & Ojha, R. P. (2024). AI in personalized learning. In Garg, A., Babu, B. V., & Balas, V. E. (Eds.), *Advances in technological innovations in higher education* (pp. 103–117). CRC Press. DOI: 10.1201/9781003376699-9

Katiyar, N., Awasthi, V. K., Pratap, R., Mishra, K., Shukla, N., Singh, R., & Tiwari, M. (2024). AI-driven personalized learning systems: Enhancing educational effectiveness. *Educational Administration: Theory and Practice*, *30*(5), 11514–11524. DOI: 10.53555/kuey.v30i5.4961

Kavitha, K., & Joshith, V. P. (2024). Pedagogical incorporation of artificial intelligence in K-12 science education: A decadal bibliometric mapping and systematic literature review (2013–2023). *Journal of Pedagogical Research*, *8*(4), 437–465. DOI: 10.33902/JPR.202429218

Keller, F. S., & Sherman, J. G. (1974). *The Keller plan handbook; essays on a personalized system of instruction*. W. A. Benjamin.

Khazanchi, R., Di Mitri, D., & Drachsler, H. (2023). Measuring efficacy of ALEKS as a supportive instructional tool in K-12 math classroom with underachieving students. *Journal of Computers in Mathematics and Science Teaching*, *42*(2), 155–176. DOI: 10.70725/204333qjmwhs

Kordzadeh, N., & Ghasemaghaei, M. (2022). Algorithmic bias: Review, synthesis, and future research directions. *European Journal of Information Systems*, *31*(3), 388–409. DOI: 10.1080/0960085X.2021.1927212

Kulik, C.-L. C., Kulik, J. A., & Bangert-Drowns, R. L. (1990). Effectiveness of mastery learning programs: A meta-analysis. *Review of Educational Research*, *60*(2), 265–299. DOI: 10.3102/00346543060002265

Kumor, T., Uribe-Flórez, L., Trespalacios, J., & Yang, D. (2024). ALEKS in high school mathematics classrooms: Exploring teachers' perceptions and use of this tool. *TechTrends*, *68*(3), 506–519. DOI: 10.1007/s11528-024-00955-0

Labadze, L., Grigolia, M., & Machaidze, L. (2023). Role of AI chatbots in education: Systematic literature review. *International Journal of Educational Technology in Higher Education*, *20*(1), 56. Advance online publication. DOI: 10.1186/s41239-023-00426-1

Lampropoulos, G., & Papadakis, S. (2025). The educational value of artificial intelligence and social robots. In Lampropoulos, G., & Papadakis, S. (Eds.), *Social robots in education* (pp. 3–15). Springer. DOI: 10.1007/978-3-031-82915-4_1

Lechuga, C. G., Matayoshi, J., & Doroudi, S. (2025). Looking beyond a single score: Examining student mathematical strengths using aleks data. *Educational Assessment*, *30*(3), 219–247. DOI: 10.1080/10627197.2025.2485928

Létourneau, A., Martineau, M. D., Charland, P., Karran, J. A., Boasen, J., & Léger, P. M. (2025). A systematic review of AI-driven intelligent tutoring systems (ITS) in K-12 education. *NPJ Science of Learning*, *10*(1), 29. DOI: 10.1038/s41539-025-00320-7 PMID: 40368938

Liu, T. C. (2022). A case study of the adaptive learning platform in a Taiwanese elementary school: Precision education from teachers' perspectives. *Education and Information Technologies*, *27*(5), 6295–6316. DOI: 10.1007/s10639-021-10851-2 PMID: 35013667

Looi, C.-K., & Jia, F. (2025). Personalization capabilities of current technology chatbots in a learning environment: An analysis of student-tutor bot interactions. *Education and Information Technologies*, *30*(10), 14165–14195. DOI: 10.1007/s10639-025-13369-z

Maghsudi, S., Lan, A., Xu, J., & Van Der Schaar, M. (2021). Personalized education in the artificial intelligence era: What to expect next. *IEEE Signal Processing Magazine*, *38*(3), 37–50. DOI: 10.1109/MSP.2021.3055032

Major, L., Francis, G. A., & Tsapali, M. (2021). The effectiveness of technology-supported personalised learning in low- and middle-income countries: A meta analysis. *British Journal of Educational Technology, 52*(5), 1935–1964. DOI: 10.1111/bjet.13116

Marple, S., Jaquet, K., Laudone, A., Sewell, J., & Liepmann, K. (2019). *i-Ready in 7th grade math classes: A mixed methods case study.* WestEd. https://www.wested.org/resource/iready-in-7th-grade-math/

Matayoshi, J., Uzun, H., & Cosyn, E. (2023). Analyzing response times and answer feedback tags in an adaptive assessment. In Wang, N., Rebolledo-Mendez, G., Dimitrova, V., Matsuda, N., & Santos, O. C. (Eds.), *Artificial intelligence in education. Posters and late breaking results, workshops and tutorials, industry and innovation tracks, practitioners, doctoral consortium and blue sky. AIED 2023*. Springer., DOI: 10.1007/978-3-031-36336-8_46

McGehee, N. (2024). *Breaking barriers: A meta-analysis of educator acceptance of AI technology in education.* Michigan Virtual. https://michiganvirtual.org/research/publications/breaking-barriers-a-meta-analysis-of-educator-acceptance-of-ai-technology-in-education/

McGraw Hill. (n.d.-a). *All about knowledge checks.* Retrieved August 26, 2025, from https://www.aleks.com/resources/ALEKS_Knowledge_Checks_Overview_for_Students.pdf

McGraw Hill. (n.d.-b). *ALEKS in Canada – Adaptive learning & assessment for math, chemistry, statistics & more*. Retrieved August 26, 2025, from https://ca.aleks.com/

McGraw Hill. (n.d.-c). *ALEKS program overview*. Retrieved August 26, 2025, from https://info.mheducation.com/rs/128-SJW-347/images/ALEKS-Overview-Brochure.pdf

Mejeh, M., & Rehm, M. (2024). Taking adaptive learning in educational settings to the next level: Leveraging natural language processing for improved personalization. *Educational Technology Research and Development, 72*(3), 1597–1621. DOI: 10.1007/s11423-024-10345-1

Meng, X., & Yang, Y. (2025). Self-evolving generative AI tutors: Reinforcement learning-augmented ITS for personalized, proactive, and context-aware student engagement. *Research Square*. https://doi.org/DOI: 10.21203/rs.3.rs-6107039/v1

Miao, F., Holmes, W., Huang, R., & Zhang, H. (2021). *Artificial intelligence and education. Guidance for policy-makers*. United Nations Educational, Scientific and Cultural Organization (UNESCO). https://doi.org/DOI: 10.54675/PCSP7350

Miller, P., & DiCerbo, K. (2024). LLM Based Math Tutoring: Challenges and Dataset. *EdArXiv*. https://doi.org/DOI: 10.35542/osf.io/5zwv3

Mills, N. J. D. (2021). ALEKS constructs as predictors of high school mathematics achievement for struggling students. *Heliyon*, *7*(6), e07345. Advance online publication. DOI: 10.1016/j.heliyon.2021.e07345 PMID: 34195443

Mintz, J., Holmes, W., Liu, L., & Perez-Ortiz, M. (2023). Artificial intelligence and K-12 education: Possibilities, pedagogies and risks. *Computers in the Schools*, *40*(4), 325–333. DOI: 10.1080/07380569.2023.2279870

Morandín-Ahuerma, F. (2023). *Ten UNESCO recommendations on the ethics of artificial intelligence*. https://doi.org/DOI: 10.31219/osf.io/csyux

Mousavinasab, E., Zarifsanaiey, N., Niakan Kalhori, S. R., Rakhshan, M., Keikha, L., & Saeedi, M. G. (2021). Intelligent tutoring systems: A systematic review of characteristics, applications, and evaluation methods. *Interactive Learning Environments*, *29*(1), 142–163. DOI: 10.1080/10494820.2018.1558257

Nehring, J., Moyer-Packenham, P., & North, M. (2023). Assessing the effectiveness of an artificial intelligence tutoring system for improving college-level mathematics preparedness in high school students. *Issues in Information Systems*, *24*(1), 128–141. DOI: 10.48009/1_iis_2023_111

Nitkin, D., Ready, D. D., & Bowers, A. J. (2022). Using technology to personalize middle school math instruction: Evidence from a blended learning program in five public schools. *Frontiers in Education*, *7*, 646471. Advance online publication. DOI: 10.3389/feduc.2022.646471

Pachman, M., Arguel, A., Lockyer, L., Kennedy, G., & Lodge, J. M. (2016). Eye tracking and early detection of confusion in digital learning environments: Proof of concept. *Australasian Journal of Educational Technology*, *32*(6), 58–71. DOI: 10.14742/ajet.3060

Papadakis, S., Lytvynova, S. H., Ivanova, S. M., & Selyshcheva, I. A. (2024b). *Advancing lifelong learning with AI-enhanced ICT: A review of 3L-Person 2024.* In *CEUR Workshop Proceedings (9th International Workshop on Professional Retraining and Life-Long Learning using ICT: Person-oriented Approach — 3L-Person 2024, Lviv, Ukraine, September 25, 2023)*. CEUR-WS.org.

Papadakis, S., Striuk, A. M., Kravtsov, H. M., Shyshkina, M. P., Marienko, M. V., & Danylchuk, H. B. (2024a). *Embracing digital innovation and cloud technologies for transformative learning experiences.* In *Proceedings of the 11th Workshop on Cloud Technologies in Education (CTE 2023), Kryvyi Rih, Ukraine, December 22, 2023.* CEUR Workshop Proceedings.

Partelow, L. (2024, September 19). *Using learning science to analyze the risks and benefits of AI in K-12 education.* Center for American Progress. https://www.americanprogress.org/article/using-learning-science-to-analyze-the-risks-and-benefits-of-ai-in-k-12-education/

Rahayu, N. W., Ferdiana, R., & Kusumawardani, S. S. (2023). A systematic review of learning path recommender systems. *Education and Information Technologies, 28*(6), 7437–7460. DOI: 10.1007/s10639-022-11460-3

Sahlman, W. A., Ciechanover, A. M., & Grandjean, E. (2024, November). *Khanmigo: Revolutionizing learning with GenAI.* Harvard Business School Case 824-059. https://www.hbs.edu/faculty/Pages/item.aspx?num=64929

Salman, J. (2023, March 20). *How ed tech can worsen racial inequality. The Hechinger Report.* https://hechingerreport.org/how-edtech-can-worsen-racial-inequality/

Samsonova, O. (2023). Use of i-Ready in tiered instruction for ESL students: A quantitative case study. *The International Journal of Childbirth Education, 4*(2), 85–105. DOI: 10.33422/ijce.v4i2.503

Saxe, R. S. (2021). *The effects of using an online reading program to improve learning for special education students* [Doctoral dissertation, Liberty University]. Liberty University Digital Commons. https://digitalcommons.liberty.edu/doctoral/2998

Saxena, S., Singh, H., Prashar, M., & Mishra, M. (2025). Cost-benefit analysis of AI-driven learning systems: Long-term financial and educational impacts. *2025 4th OPJU International Technology Conference (OTCON) on Smart Computing for Innovation and Advancement in Industry 5.0.* https://doi.org/DOI: 10.1109/OTCON65728.2025.11070340

Seo, K., Yoo, M., Dodson, S., & Jin, S.-H. (2024). Augmented teachers: K–12 teachers' needs for artificial intelligence's complementary role in personalized learning. *Journal of Research on Technology in Education, 57*(4), 876–893. DOI: 10.1080/15391523.2024.2330525

Silva, T. B. (2016). *The effects of the i-Ready computer assisted instruction program on the reading and fluency achievement of first graders* [Doctoral dissertation, California State University]. ScholarWorks. http://hdl.handle.net/10211.3/200863

Sinatra, A. M., Graesser, A. C., Hu, X., Goodwin, G., & Rus, V. (Eds.). (2023). *Design recommendations for intelligent tutoring systems: Vol. 10. SWOT analysis of ITS*. U.S. Army Research Laboratory. https://www.gifttutoring.org/documents/163

Sottilare, R., Graesser, A., Hu, X., & Goldberg, B. (Eds.). (2014). *Design recommendations for intelligent tutoring systems: Vol 2. Instructional management*. U.S. Army Research Laboratory. https://www.gifttutoring.org/documents/44

Sottilare, R., Graesser, A., Hu, X., & Holden, H. (Eds.). (2013). *Design recommendations for intelligent tutoring systems: Vol. 1. Learner modeling*. U.S. Army Research Laboratory. https://www.gifttutoring.org/documents/42

Stamper, J., Xiao, R., & Hou, X. (2024). Enhancing LLM-based feedback: Insights from intelligent tutoring systems and the learning sciences. In Olney, A. M., Chounta, I.-A., Liu, Z., Santos, O. C., & Bittencourt, I. I. (Eds.), *Artificial intelligence in education, AIED 2024*. Springer., DOI: 10.1007/978-3-031-64315-6_3

Strielkowski, W., Grebennikova, V., Lisovskiy, A., Rakhimova, G., & Vasileva, T. (2025). AI-driven adaptive learning for sustainable educational transformation. *Sustainable Development (Bradford)*, *33*(2), 1921–1947. DOI: 10.1002/sd.3221

Sun, S., Else-Quest, N. M., Hodges, L. C., French, A. M., & Dowling, R. (2021). The effects of ALEKS on mathematics learning in K-12 and higher education: A meta-analysis. *Investigations in Mathematics Learning*, *13*(3), 182–196. DOI: 10.1080/19477503.2021.1926194

Swain, M., Randel, B., & Dvorak, R. N. (2020). *Impact evaluation of reading i-Ready instruction for elementary grades using 2018–2019 data* (Report No. 107). HumRRO. https://eric.ed.gov/?id=ED604746

Swargiary, K. (2024). The impact of AI-driven personalized learning and intelligent tutoring systems on student engagement and academic achievement: Ethical implications and the digital divide. *SSRN*. https://ssrn.com/abstract=4897241 DOI: 10.2139/ssrn.4897241

Tan, L. Y., Hu, S., Yeo, D. J., & Cheong, K. H. (2025). Artificial intelligence-enabled adaptive learning platforms: A review. *Computers and Education: Artificial Intelligence*, *9*, 100429. Advance online publication. DOI: 10.1016/j.caeai.2025.100429

Taylor, D. L., Yeung, M., & Bashet, A. Z. (2021). Personalized and adaptive learning. In Ryoo, J., & Winkelmann, K. (Eds.), *Innovative learning environments in STEM higher education* (pp. 17–34). Springer., DOI: 10.1007/978-3-030-58948-6_2

U.S. Department of Education. (2023). *Artificial intelligence and future of teaching and learning: Insights and recommendations*. Office of Educational Technology. https://www.ed.gov/sites/ed/files/documents/ai-report/ai-report.pdf

VanLehn, K. (2011). The relative effectiveness of human tutoring, intelligent tutoring systems, and other tutoring systems. *Educational Psychologist*, *46*(4), 197–221. DOI: 10.1080/00461520.2011.611369

Villegas-Ch, W., García-Ortiz, J., & Sánchez-Viteri, S. (2024). Personalization of learning: Machine learning models for adapting educational content to individual learning styles. *IEEE Access : Practical Innovations, Open Solutions*, *12*, 121114 121130. DOI: 10.1109/ACCESS.2024.3452592

Walkington, C., & Bernacki, M. L. (2020). Appraising research on personalized learning: Definitions, theoretical alignment, advancements, and future directions. *Journal of Research on Technology in Education*, *52*(3), 235–252. DOI: 10.1080/15391523.2020.1747757

Weiss, D. J., & Şahin, A. (2024). *Computerized adaptive testing: From concept to implementation*. The Guilford Press.

Winkler, R., & Söllner, M. (2018). *Unleashing the potential of chatbots in education: A state-of-the-art analysis. Academy of Management Proceedings, 2018*(1). https://doi.org/DOI: 10.5465/AMBPP.2018.15903abstract

Xu, Z., Wijekumar, K., Ramirez, G., Hu, X., & Irey, R. (2019). The effectiveness of intelligent tutoring systems on K-12 students' reading comprehension: A meta-analysis. *British Journal of Educational Technology*, *50*(6), 3119–3137. DOI: 10.1111/bjet.12758

Yildirim-Erbasli, S. N., & Bulut, O. (2021). Conversation-based assessments: Real-time assessment and feedback. *eLearn Magazine, 2021*(12). https://doi.org/DOI: 10.1145/3508017.3495533

Yildirim-Erbasli, S. N., Bulut, O., Demmans Epp, C., & Cui, Y. (2025). Advancing students' assessment experiences with conversational agents. *Educational Technology Research and Development*, *73*(3), 1811–1834. DOI: 10.1007/s11423-025-10472-3

Yildirim-Erbasli, S. N., Gorgun, G., & Bulut, O. (2024). Enhancing self-regulated learning with artificial intelligence-powered learning analytics. In Ulutaş, N. K., & Höl, D. (Eds.), *Emergent practices of learning analytics in K-12 classrooms* (pp. 57–83). IGI Global., DOI: 10.4018/979-8-3693-0066-4.ch004

Yilmaz, B. (2017). *Effects of adaptive learning technologies on math achievement: A quantitative study of ALEKS math software* [Doctoral dissertation, University of Missouri-Kansas City]. MOspace. https://hdl.handle.net/10355/60519

Zhang, P., & Tur, G. (2024). A systematic review of ChatGPT use in K-12 education. *European Journal of Education*, *59*(2), e12599. Advance online publication. DOI: 10.1111/ejed.12599

ENDNOTES

1 For more details, https://www.mheducation.com/unitas/school/explore/sites/aleks/clickable-walkthrough/public/index.html#1

2 For additional details and interactive demonstrations, refer to https://www.curriculumassociates.com/programs/tours

3 Additional details are available in the i-Ready Data Analysis Guide. https://i-readycentral.com/download/?res=11597&view_pdf=1

Chapter 7
AI-Powered Tutors and Human Teachers in ELT: Striking a Collaborative Balance

Vivit Rosmayanti
http://orcid.org/0000-0002-3648-9878
Universitas Negeri Makassar, Indonesia

ABSTRACT

Artificial Intelligence (AI) is revolutionizing English Language Teaching (ELT) by providing personalized and interactive learning. AI tools, such as virtual tutors, adaptive learning platforms, and automated grading applications, enhance productivity and allow teachers to focus on more interactive teaching elements. However, AI tools lack the subtle interactions and cultural context that teachers provide. Teachers are essential for emotional intelligence, cultural and pedagogical contextualization, and can provide more appropriate feedback than AI tools. AI-powered tools can enhance the learning experience by creating more interesting and motivating lessons, but teachers must adjust their traditional roles to incorporate modern technologies without losing the core aspect of human interaction. Teacher professional development is crucial for the responsible and effective use of AI technologies. Ethical concerns, such as data protection, algorithm bias, and access to AI systems, need to be handled ethically and inclusively.

INTRODUCTION

The introduction of Artificial Intelligence (AI) in educational technologies has, and will continue to, significantly change previously used strategies in teaching, particularly within the context of English Language Teaching (ELT). In recent years,

DOI: 10.4018/979-8-3373-2637-5.ch007

the attention acquired by AI technologies, such as virtual tutors and other automated instruments, has emphasized their role in education, marking the beginning of yet another learning epoch. These systems that process and learn from a considerable amount of interaction data offer adaptations to learners' aids and preferences toward better experiences (Deep et al., 2024). Adopting AI tools in educational settings not only enhances efficiency; rather, it fundamentally transforms the instructional content engagement paradigms in use by students (Jayavardhini, 2024; Selwyn, 2022). With AI, students receive lessons enriched by real-time feedback and tailored guidance, while teachers harness the power of AI to support and strengthen pedagogical frameworks (Barzani et al., 2021).

The importance of teachers in English Language Teaching continues to be extremely important. Artificial Intelligence advancements have also improved many educational possibilities, yet machines can never replicate the unique qualities human educators possess. In regard to language learning and acquisition, teachers relate to learners emotionally, intelligently, culturally, and contextually, which are important dimensions for effective learning (Reiß,2021; Alshehri, 2023). The language acquisition skills a learner develops through interpersonal relationships with a human teacher go beyond the mere technicalities of language to the intricacies of communication and culture. Thus, the integration of AI into teaching is not a matter of replacing teachers, but rather freeing them to teach students the complexities of language that AI systems cannot (Barua et al., 2022).

This chapter intends to examine more closely the relationship of AI and teachers in ELT, including how these entities might productively work together to facilitate language learning while coping with the associated difficulties. This discussion also emphasizes the importance of the teachers' role in making sure that the use of AI within education frameworks is applied with respect, in such a manner that balances the use of advanced technology and the presence of a human being (Reiß, 2021; Evans & Sinha, 2024). With the deepening of AI's integration into the educational framework, it will become indispensable to not only plan the use of such facilities but also professionally attend to the educators' perpetual instructional practice integration of AI into teaching (Ibrahim, 2024). As teachers begin to acknowledge the impacts of AI, they now have to deal with the learning floor ethical issues and biases these technologies would inflict on the overall teaching landscape (Rathore et al., 2023). This approach aims to strike the right balance between technology and pedagogy, capitalizing on the benefits of both to provide effective and enriching language learning opportunities for students (Selwyn, 2022; Evans & Sinha, 2024).

In this chapter, we attempt to document successful use cases and emerging practices of AI technologies in cooperation with teachers in English Language Teaching (ELT) contexts and, at the same time, contribute to the literature advocating for collaborative learning as a primary pillar of effective language education. Addressing the synergy between AI capabilities and teaching will begin to shed light on the improvements possible in teaching practical skills in a technology-enhanced learning environment while guaranteeing that teachers remain in the role of not just knowledge providers, but also participants in the technological innovations being employed in classrooms across the country (Reiß, 2021). Confronting the complications and possibilities of AI technologies allows educators to be on the vanguard of a paradigm where human teaching and technology work in tandem, enhancing student learning in fundamental ways (Alshehri, 2023; Deep et al., 2024).

THE EVOLVING ROLE OF AI IN ELT

Types of AI-Powered Tools in ELT

The integration of AI technology within English Language Teaching (ELT) continues to develop with the emergence of new tools that enhance the learning experience, including virtual tutors in the form of chatbots and conversational agents. These entities use natural language processing and machine learning algorithms to engage learners in authentic conversations, thus giving learners opportunities to practice language skills (Jain et al. 2023; Baskara, 2023). Virtual tutors can address learners with different degrees of proficiency, and thus, sophisticated interactions tailored to individual levels of advancement in learning and style are available (Baskara, 2023). Students can practice language skills outside of traditional classroom settings, which enables more flexible learning due to the asynchronous nature of these interactions (Shazly, 2021). Research suggests that these resources not only aid in learning vocabulary and grammar, but they also help adapt learners to conversations and situations they are likely to encounter (Chae et al., 2023).

As with virtual tutors, one more prominent AI-oriented resource within the ELT domain is adaptive learning platforms. These systems apply sophisticated algorithms to evaluate students' abilities and customize relevant content for each learner (Papadakis et al., 2024a, 2024b). Particularly, technologies of adaptive learning modify task difficulty and offer feedback in real time based on the user's performance, thus encouraging effortless self-paced autonomous learning (Okunade, 2024; Zhao, 2023). This flexibility is crucial in learning a second language because there are many intricate grammar and vocabulary structures. Adaptive learning technologies enhance instruction by motivating learners to master the content that is congruent to their needs (Zhu, 2024). The continuous evaluation features help teachers to monitor learning and offer critical insights that guide instructional planning and strategies (Ha & Nguyen, 2024).

Students' learning experiences within English Language Teaching (ELT) are improved by the automation of assessment and feedback through the use of AI technology. Such AI technologies have the ability to evaluate students' written and oral work, providing them with feedback that helps to sharpen their skills (Yu et al., 2022). With the assistance of AI technologies, instructors can complete the grading tasks in a more efficient manner, thus freeing up time to focus on providing instruction tailored to each student's needs. In addition, these AI evaluations are less likely to be subjective because they are controlled by algorithms that grade with clear-cut rules (Ha & Nguyen, 2024). The incorporation of such systems into education not only improves the assessment framework but also provides instantaneous feedback to learners, helping them develop the constructive attitude that is essential for the acquisition of a new language (Zhao, 2023; Huang et al., 2023).

These AI tools work optimally when their implementation is well understood in the context of English Language Teaching (ELT). As educators become proficient with virtual tutors, adaptive learning technologies, and AI evaluation systems, the need arises to cultivate a synergy between human and machine instruction. Such synergy can occur through professional development programs focused on technology integration, which greatly improves pedagogical practices. When learners are better instructed, educational outcomes improve (Nazaretsky et al., 2022). The integration of technology into English Language Teaching is rapidly changing with the introduction of new tools, where the modern educational landscape centers around the effective understanding and application of AI-powered tools.

Benefits of AI in ELT

The advancement of technology, specifically Artificial Intelligence (AI), has proven to be very advantageous for both learners and educators in English Language Teaching (ELT). The area that seems to take the most advantage of AI in ELT is learning personalization. AI systems can collect and assess data concerning students' preferences, strengths, and weaknesses in order to come up with personalized, tailored learning experiences (Ayeni et al.,2024). The ability to engage and motivate students to actively participate in their studies so that they can progress step by step is unlike anything the current educational framework offers. Research shows that personalized learning, driven by AI algorithms, enhances retention, motivation, and achievement. AI-empowered personalized learning analytics are known to improve amongst (Zhang et al., 2023), (Gyawali & Mehandroo, 2022). Customized learning resources designed based on students' previous engagements with their educational materials offer precise learning solutions and objectives (Qiu et al., 2024).

Furthermore, AI improves the ELT instruction scalability and accessibility. In most cases, the number of learners that can be taught in a class is limited by the classroom's physical space. However, AI can help educators reach out to bigger audiences without sacrificing the quality of instruction provided (Idham et al., 2024; Akbarani, 2024). Educational materials can be spread by virtual tutors, chatbots, or adaptive learning systems, making it accessible to learners anytime, regardless of their geographical location (Ahmad et al., 2021). This higher level of scalability is more useful in places where there are few available language teachers. AI tools help to fill that gap, enabling students more educational opportunities to learn languages that were not possible before (Qin & Ao, 2023). Also, the widespread use of AI applications permits users to access them almost anytime, thus, learners can use those materials and practice the language outside the classroom, which expands access to education (Idham et al., 2024).

In enhancing the learning activities of English Language Teaching (ELT), real-time feedback and evaluation provided by AI are extremely important. AI technology customizes real-time feedback analytics to assess learners' activities right away, providing feedback that is constructive in nature and assists learners (Gyawali & Mehandroo, 2022; Fitria, 2021). Students can interact immediately, which helps them identify errors and faulty assumptions, thereby promoting a developmental framework mindset where students learn from their failures (Zhang et al, 2023). Many online platforms that have automatic grammar check tools or conduct assessments of spoken language not only perform these functions, but also give feedback immediately, which enables learners to modify their comprehension, thus helping them enhance more efficiently than depending on traditional ways of assessment (Fitria, 2021). The accuracy and impartiality of AI evaluations can assist in reducing the systematic biases evaluators build, purposely or indirectly, due to evaluative norms that are deeply associated with the human frame of reference (Беганцова et al., 2020).

The application of technology is not intended to displace conventional methods of teaching; in fact, the incorporation of technology elevates and enhances language learning. As we consider the ongoing advances in AI technologies in ELT, educators are more actively urged to adopt AI as a powerful resource that streamlines lower-order pedagogical activities, permitting teachers to concentrate on higher-order tasks, and transforming them into facilitators of rich learning experiences (Ahmad et al., 2021; Qiu et al., 2024). In the end, the balanced application of AI tools in teaching English lies in the productive interaction of the technologies with the teaching methods, working in synergy to support a fertile atmosphere for effective language learning.

Limitations of AI in ELT

Although the integration of Artificial Intelligence (AI) brings considerable advantages in English Language Teaching (ELT), there are substantial drawbacks that educators must contend with to make the most of these technologies in the teaching and learning processes. The traditional AI technologies that we explored concerning ELT have this major limitation: a total absence of emotional intelligence. Although AI can inform and interact with an individual in a personalized manner, it does not understand or react to the emotional undertones of human interactions, which are vital in any language learning situation (Tang, 2025; Szabó & Szoke, 2024). Such a gap can significantly diminish the ability of AI technologies to utterly engage learners, simply because acquiring a language is not the same as learning the rules of grammar and vocabulary; it also includes the emotional and social dimensions of human communication. The dispiriting reality is that AI, unlike human instructors, cannot build rapport with students to foster a positive and reassuring atmosphere when they are learning something new (Stasser, 2023).

One of the major issues AI encounters in ELT is an inability to manage all areas of language learning, more importantly, cultural specifics and contexts. As noted by Tang (2025), language is a component of culture; moreover, communication means social interactions, customs, and other language-related nuances, tangentially referring to the language. AI applications, in processing and generating languages, tend to skip these cultural aspects, which hinders their ability to provide learners with context-appropriate, authentic language learning opportunities (Eden et al., 2024). Excessive use of AI to teach languages may cause educators to overlook the fact that students need to understand the language's rich culture to use it in practical situations. Unlike instructors, AI cannot use local expressions, cultural references, and real-life usage from their experiences, so students can learn more about the language (Szabó & Szoke, 2024).

In Syuhra et al. (2025), the authors suggested that the use of artificial intelligence technology may result in laziness being ingrained into language learning due to over-dependency on such technologies for practice and feedback. This over-dependency could stifle the growth of reasoning and cognitive skills needed to manage intricate linguistic challenges. In addition, if these preset algorithms and patterns heretofore data-based systems to operate are remotely biased, their learning imprint may be altered unintentionally. For instance, one could argue that AI-generated assessment results, in the absence of language understanding, would be judging without comprehension and, therefore, unfairly assessing performance based on preset assumptions about the requirements, resulting in unfounded, biased judgments. Barua et al (2022) outlined that if such evaluations are left unchecked, they could pose serious unfair outcomes, whereby the assessments ignore an individual's unique learning methods and cultural context.

In conclusion, the advantages of AI in enhancing ELT, such as personalizing the learning experience, scalability, and instantaneous feedback, are promising; however, we must acknowledge the insights AI lacks concerning emotional intelligence and cultural context. The limitations AI introduces underscores the need for combining technological advancements and human teaching elements to enrich the learners' experience in language acquisition (Karki & Karki, 2025). While teachers explore and modify these technologies, the discourse about the ethical boundaries and the impact of AI technologies on language teaching needs to persist in order to ensure that its integration with education serves to augment, not erode, the invaluable and deeply human dimensions of language pedagogy.

THE CENTRAL ROLE OF HUMAN TEACHERS

Due to their pedagogical wisdom, teachers, especially in English Language Teaching (ELT), play a pivotal role that technology cannot replicate. Teachers assume the critical responsibility of lesson planning and instruction that meets the varying needs of all learners. This ability motivates and helps improve participation among students in an inclusive classroom culture. With variation in teaching methods, students' interest as well as understanding can be gained through interaction in a class that is conducted lively (Gyawali & Mehandroo, 2022). Unlike AI, which often tends to give pre-prepared information, human teachers are able to adjust their teaching depending on the established rapport with students and the feedback, whether verbal or non-verbal, received from the learners (Idham et al., 2024). This responsiveness is invaluable in language teaching, where learners' immediate educational stimuli dictate how well they grasp and retain intricate concepts.

In addition, the bonds that teachers create with their students are pivotal to teaching and learning processes. Trust and rapport, which form an essential part of effective education, help students feel safe and motivated to express themselves and actively participate in the learning process (Geng et al., 2024). Human educators act as guides who provide support related not only to academic content but also to social and emotional development, which current AI tools cannot provide. Though AI can provide feedback and enable practice, it does not possess the ability to engage with learners on a personal level, which is critical in sustaining motivation and interest in language learning (Miri & Pishghadam, 2021). Students can be motivated by their teachers, who foster a passion for learning, as well as encourage perseverance in relation to the difficulties faced in the process of language learning (Geng et al., 2024).

Working in the realm of languages, language teaching, and pedagogy, as well as building relationships, requires teachers to possess emotional intelligence, as this is one of the focal points under their expertise. As explained by Windasari et al. (2024), emotional intelligence is defined as the recognition, understanding, and management of one's own emotions alongside the emotions of others. Accordingly, this domain goes a long way in helping to form effective relationships in a given social setting, such as in a classroom. Educators possessing capabilities in emotional intelligence have an easier time evaluating students' emotions, responding empathetically to their needs, and creating a positive atmosphere conducive to learning. Emotional engagement becomes crucial, especially in language learning situations, since a lot of anxiety, self-consciousness, and self-doubt are often present in learners. Teachers can help students cope with these emotions by providing encouragement and giving constructive feedback, which is very different from the way AI would attempt to do so (Chen et al., 2025).

It has been shown in the research that leveraging emotional intelligence enhances professional satisfaction in teachers; students, consequently, are more likely to have better outcomes (Chen et al., 2025). Properly managing and responding to one's emotions enables the teacher to foster a warm, welcoming environment where students can freely engage both emotionally and academically (Valente et al., 2020). It is this emotional labor that is equally tough and greatly rewarding at the same time, which strengthens students' desire to learn while enriching their overall experience with learning (Valente et al., 2020).

Although AI offers incredible benefits with efficiency and personalized learning pathways, the valuable, nuanced and complex human aspects of language learning provided by teachers are still irreplaceable. Therefore, the use of educational technologies requires the development of an appropriate synergy between instructional AI and human teaching in ways that improve the language learning experience while ensuring that technology does not displace the impact of the teachers (Akbarani, 2024). As has been discussed, the authoritative and emotional aspects of teaching strengthen the English Language Teaching (ELT) human-centered model which makes educators irreplaceable.

In English Language Teaching (ELT), human instructors hold a special place because of the cultural enrichment and context they are able to bring to learning the language. Teachers understand the different sociocultural contexts of their students and use cultural teaching aids that are relevant to their local settings. This skill is important to provide respect for other cultures as well as to celebrate diversity in education. Studies show that actively using culture in teaching improves students' language and cultural literacy skills, which leads to effective communication skills (Amer, 2022; Suweni et al., 2024). In addition, when content taught in class is relevant to students' lives, they become increasingly motivated to learn and participate (Zhang, 2024).

Concerning the teaching of a language, the most critical factor is the awareness and understanding that the teachers have concerning the culture associated with the language. Language not only facilitates communication but also serves as a cultural sign that embodies the ideals, thoughts, and history of the people who speak it. Good English language teaching often includes topics that resonate with learners' backgrounds and their societal contexts, including cultural practices that differ from their own (Maqsood et al., 2024; Suweni et al., 2024). This awareness of other cultures helps learners to resolve misunderstandings while developing empathy and communication skills with people from different cultures (Suweni et al., 2024). So too can human teachers identify and confront particular cultural barriers to effective communication. Such barriers may be used by educators to design enhanced experiences for learners and inspire sensitivity to diverse cultures (Chaer et al., 2024; Adzima et al., 2023).

Moreover, the adaptability and other thinking dispositions of human teachers critically enhance health teaching dynamics in class. Unlike AI tools, which may operate according to set scripts, teachers can modify lessons in real time according to student reactions, needs, and the overall atmosphere within the classroom. This adaptability in real time permits educators to resolve misconceptions immediately, redirect to what students show interest in, and adjust the speed as well as content of their lessons concerning the students' learning trajectory (Zhang, 2024; Maqsood et al., 2024). Teachers can implement alternative didactic strategies, including cooperative learning and project work, depending on the particular situation of the classroom (Osadchaia et al., 2020). This makes the classroom livelier and makes education more responsive to students, improving their participation and appreciation.

Effective teaching, as Akram et al. (2021) highlight, is underpinned by critical thinking as it enables educators to develop and implement creative strategies that meet the needs of their students. Take, for example, a teacher who discovers that many students struggle with a particular language concept. To aid understanding, she decides to use hands-on activities and multimedia tools (Krisnawati et al., 2024). This flexibility fosters better learning and demonstrates the exceptional human capability of creative problem-solving within educational settings. In addition, this flexibility promotes trust and psychological safety, which empowers students to practice language skills—be it speaking, writing, or working together on projects (Iejrd, 2021).

Therefore, AI still cannot replace the roles of human teachers in English Language Teaching, especially as cultural mediators and as human beings who educate with flexibility and adaptability. The technology that we have today is not capable of helping students the way educators are able to relate to and attend to their needs. It is critical for the educational world to remember, appreciate, and protect the impact that an experienced and caring human teacher who offers help and support makes on the learner's language understanding and achievement in learning the language. The blend between the application of AI and human beings' teaching will probably shape the future of language teaching while keeping the cultural and transformative teaching integration at the heart of English Language Teaching.

COLLABORATIVE APPROACHES: HOW AI AND TEACHERS CAN WORK TOGETHER

AI as a Support Tool, Not a Replacement

With the integration of Artificial Intelligence in English Language Teaching (ELT), the role of human educators is adapting toward a collaborative approach, as opposed to competition. Teachers are not being replaced, and AI Saves Technology can act as a support tool. AI technology's main advantage in this case is automating mundane tasks like grading and tracking progress (Lavidas et al., 2022a, 2022b). These routine responsibilities allow a deeper interaction between educators and students, enriching the educational experience (Никитина & Ishchenko, 2024). As the workload is distributed more efficiently, the subsequent admin-free time enhances the instructional experience. The human insight required when nurturing critical thinking or providing discussion-based feedback makes the administrative-free time invaluable (Lawrence et al., 2023).

In addition, AI's application as an aid permits the educator to oversee the process of education while attending to the individual needs of each student. With AI's power for providing instructional differentiation, educators are able to design lessons based on each learner's preferences, competencies, and gaps (Barua et al., 2022). AI technology can scan and analyze performance data of learners to recommend specially designed resources or activities for each learner's level of proficiency. The utilization of AI platforms fosters personalization which helps in addressing all learner's needs and encourages teachers in enhancing engagement and optimizing the results of the learning process (Holman et al., 2024). The integration of AI and teacher intuition permits students to receive a thorough education that values their identity and culture (Park & Kwon, 2023).

AI's collaboration with teachers is not limited to automating tasks; teachers actively engage in analyzing instructional data generated by AI applications. AI tools provide insights, and teachers can synthesize them into practical plans to encourage positive classroom dynamics (Tammets & Ley, 2023). For instance, AI tools can detect shared areas of struggle amongst the students; educators can then target these areas during lessons by incorporating specific exercises or adjusting their teaching methods to improve comprehension. This cycle of data analysis, reflection, and action captures how AI can serve as a stimulus for deeper learning instead of learning in a vacuum (Yang & Kyun, 2022).

Adapting AI technologies to English Language Teaching (ELT) has a certain prerequisite, that is, professional development of the instructors to use such technologies in their classes. There is urgent and immediate teacher education concerning the educational use of artificial intelligence and technologies, particularly in understanding and applying the AI-provided suggestions (Mudawy, 2024). Such educators need training that reorients them to view computer technologies as aids in the teaching and learning processes (Al-Mughairi & Bhaskar, 2024). With the growing familiarity and accessibility of AI tools, teachers are in a better position to create new alternatives on how to use these tools without losing their identity as educators.

As AI technologies evolve, the focus must remain on developing a synergistic environment where technology supports and enhances teaching instead of replacing the human touch (Lampropoulos & Papadakis, 2025). When used as a supplemental resource, educators' administrative workload can be reduced, as well as instruction tailored to meet the diverse needs of the learners, alongside increased student participation. This approach fosters the students' personalized and enriched language learning journey, while further reinforcing the significance of teachers to sustain their guidance and supportive role to help learners develop their language skills (EĞİN et al., 2025; Dieker et al., 2024). The effective incorporation of AI into the teaching-learning process presents students and educators alike with rich, boundless prospects and signals powerful advancements for the still-developing ELT landscape, not with an overshadowing approach, but instead suggesting that heightened collaboration is key.

Enhancing Student Engagement with AI and Teacher Collaboration

The joint work of AI tools and educators offers great potential to increase interest and involvement in English Language Teaching (ELT). One practice includes the use of chatbots for language practice, where students can converse within a simulated context. This interaction enables students to practice their speaking and listening skills within a non-threatening environment, free from the social pressures characteristic of a classroom. Chatbots, as a result of natural language processing, can interact immediately with users and provide feedback, thus exposing students to language use in real time (Liu, 2023). Such interactions reduce students' language anxiety and provide the opportunity for increased practice, which leads to improved language proficiency, as well as confidence in using the target language.

In addition, the use of AI games in lessons contributes to creating an enjoyable and interactive environment, which has a positive effect on students' motivation. Language learning games can be tailored to different levels of proficiency, thus all learners can participate at an appropriate level. For instance, AI grammar challenges or vocabulary quizzes can modify game-play according to set parameters and adjust according to how well students are performing, improving user engagement (George & Wooden, 2023). Students will not only enjoy learning through these gamified elements but will also foster healthy competition, which motivates greater interaction with the material.

The implementation of AI-powered pronunciation tools serves as yet another example of AI integration within a classroom setting. These AI systems evaluate students' speech in real time and provide feedback regarding their pronunciation and clarity. Such feedback is critical in language learning, where the ability to accurately articulate words within the necessary cadence is important. Language teachers can make use of pronunciation apps during instruction, which encourages learners to practice on their own while still getting instructor feedback on their language skills development (Liu, 2023). The combination of AI feedback with teacher input can foster increased participation and improvement in learners, aiding in the holistic development of language skills.

There is also the potential for increased student participation through collaborative projects with the application of AI technology. For instance, students may be given a group project where they incorporate AI tools to research culturally significant elements in relation to the language being learned. Such projects not only serve to highlight the intricate relationship culture has with communication, but they also promote collaboration as well as critical analysis and synthesis among students as they prepare and deliver their presentations (Xi, 2024). Meaningful applications of technology in the classroom allow students to deepen their engagement and understanding of topics.

To summarize, the combined use of AI technologies with conventional teaching practices has the promise of increasing student participation in ELT classrooms. With the application of chatbots, favorable learning games, pronunciation aids, and project-based learning, teachers can adapt their plans to provide students with a thriving and responsive classroom environment. This model illustrates the importance of teachers in the active learning process, utilizing the tools offered by AI so as to support and enhance learning experiences, as it pertains to the educational goals AIED seeks to serve---improved language learning outcomes (Liu, 2023; Namjoo et al., 2023). As the paradigm shifts, there is nothing that the educators' shift raises concern, suggesting that the coexistence of AI and humans as teachers must be supreme in this instructional space, where teaching and learning take place.

Real-Time Data and Teacher Insights

In the classroom, the application of AI technology affords powerful opportunities for enhancing feedback mechanisms and real-time analytics, permitting teachers to take action based on accurate data. The collection and analysis of enormous student data sets through AI systems provides educators with information that is timely and actionable (Ai, 2023). Smartphones and wearable devices enable a teacher to monitor engagement during lessons, allowing many teachers to spot trends and patterns as they occur (Ouyang et al., 2023). In keeping with AI's responsiveness to data, educators are able to adjust lesson delivery in real-time and respond to instructional feedback, ensuring that any identified learning gaps are addressed within the shortest time possible.

The capability of evaluating interaction data, measuring attendance, as well as active participation of learners presents a gap that can be filled by AI-powered analytics in assessing learners' understanding. AI algorithms are capable of streaming and analyzing data and sending alerts to teachers in real time based on how students respond to queries, identifying areas of possible strain and excelling (Sanchez-Gonzalez & Terrell, 2023). For example, a change in strategy can easily happen within seconds whenever a large proportion of learners answering online quizzes in class get a question wrong in the first attempt. Such prompt responsiveness can go a long way to improve students' learning experiences, making the class environment more interactive (O'Neal et al., 2024).

Moreover, AI serves differentiated instruction by providing teachers with information about students' learning behaviors and preferences. With real-time data, educators gain deep insights into students' learning behaviors, which allows them to utilize strategies that effectively address the needs of each learner (Dawat, 2023). This may involve adjusting the rate at which instruction is delivered, offering additional aids to struggling learners, or providing advanced materials to those ready to move on. This flexibility, for example, is crucial in meeting today's classrooms with great diversity in learners' age, proficiency levels, and learning styles.

AI systems also support formative evaluation, which enables continuous monitoring of learners' progress over time. The data generated from such assessments can guide instructional design, allowing teachers to make informed decisions about modifying the curriculum, assessing materials, and even resource allocation (Sanchez-Gonzalez & Terrell, 2023). Such data empowers teachers to modify their instructional design in ways that help students achieve intended learning outcomes, therefore improving their overall instructional effectiveness.

As noted previously, the focus of educational psychology underscores timely feedback as an important factor of the motivation and achievement of learners. AI systems that provide real-time evaluations can clear the fog of education on students, which makes them take control of their learning (Khizar, 2024). The cooperation between the AI systems and the teachers promotes a self-regulated learning culture, which aims at continuous improvement in teaching and learning.

To sum up, the same way, the teaching practice presented is supported by real-time data brought by AI analytics, and teaching is also transformed by the real-time insight that teachers need to adjust and improve the lessons. The educators' real-time analysis of the learners' participation empowers them to make decisions that enhance, through continual feedback, the lesson delivery. The combination of AI analytics with the provided input from the teachers goes beyond improvement of the learners' performance; it creates a climate that fosters the belief that the students are active participants in the control of their learning (Onesi-Ozigagun et al., 2024; Ajuwon et al., 2024).

Customized Learning Paths

The integration of AI technologies to develop personalized learning paths is a revolutionary improvement in the English Language Teaching (ELT) domain, providing bespoke educational pathways for every learner depending on their progression and requirements. Through the utilization of AI analytics, educators are able to implement precise learning trajectories that attend to the varied rates of student progress. For example, AI can evaluate participation metrics from quizzes, class discussions, and other interactions with learning materials to assess student performance analytics to determine their strengths and weaknesses (Gada & Chudasama, 2024). Such strategies aid in the construction of operational plans that provide direction toward specific goals and help students achieve particular objectives (Onesi-Ozigagun et al., 2024).

With the teachers' reliance on AI in constructing these learning pathways, instructional design and teaching can be further refined by concentrating on reinforcing skills that AI analytics have pointed out. Thus, in the case of a learner with challenges related to verb conjugating, he or she could be provided with an AI-driven platform where additional suggested practices could be rendered while the teacher offers careful, explanatory, guided practice during instruction (Tang, 2024). It enables the teacher to see another side of the learner's learning process and harness varied educational materials and resources to tailor prompt educational support.

As a student progresses, AI technologies enable customization of learning resources, which encourages perpetual evolution. AI can adjust its recommendations and ensure that learning is in sync with the student's changing capabilities and preferences with the collection of new data (Onesi-Ozigagun et al., 2024). Educators are supported by this new feedback system as it allows them to evaluate their teaching practices and adapt their strategies, lessons, and activities presented in the classroom. The integration of AI systems that adapt to learners' requirements with teacher instruction fosters a rich educational atmosphere in which students benefit from tailored learning materials as well as active intervention from their teachers (Pendy, 2023).

The use of AI technologies in customizing learning paths is effective and is corroborated by research that indicates increased student participation and successful learning outcomes. Research indicates that students achieve greater personalized engagement, and as a result, their analytical and critical thinking skills develop because they work with tailored content that is relevant to them (Gada & Chudasama, 2024). In addition, this individualized approach is effective with contemporary models of instruction, which place emphasis on the learner and guide the student to take control of their learning (Ulfa, 2023).

As noted, AI systems designed to create personalized learning pathways offer tremendous value in language education by advancing individual experiences in relation to each student's personalized journey. This feature enables instructors to target specific areas through lessons and aids in skill instruction, all while keeping the lessons flexible to the students' ever-changing requirements. The combination of Artificial Intelligence and teachers improves the engagement as well as the adjusting responsiveness to the needs of the students, while simultaneously upholding the necessity of personalized education in constructive instructional outcomes for every learner (Ulfa, 2023; Jian, 2023).

THE ETHICAL AND PRACTICAL CONSIDERATION OF AI IN ELT

The addition of Artificial Intelligence (AI) into English Language Teaching (ELT) brings with it a host of ethical and practical issues that need to be addressed by educational institutions and practitioners. One important ethical issue pertains to the privacy of personal data that can be accessed by using AI tools, especially information pertaining to students. Ensuring private data, such as the personal information of students, is protected is particularly critical as AI tools collect and assess data to improve the learning process. Educational institutions must also adhere to privacy laws and adopt appropriate policies and technologies that will protect against the unauthorized retrieval of students' private information (Herawati, 2025). Also, there are concerns about any potential biases of AI algorithms that may affect language learning results. Language learning processes may become ineffective because AI algorithms can reinforce stereotypes or misrepresent certain demographic groups if not properly designed and controlled (Herawati, 2025).

Holman et al. (2024) note that AI must be integrated into modern classrooms with the teaching staff in mind; teachers need to be aware of how AI technologies can positively impact educational practices and be trained accordingly. After all, everything in the classroom must advance the underlying principles of pedagogy and teaching. Usher et al. (2021) describe how technology shouldn't simply be bolted on; it must be embraced in a manner that ensures seamless integration with teaching approaches and contributes to improved educational outcomes.

Where there is immediate concern, applying ethics, as Holman et al. (2024) put it, is in ensuring that teachers partake in lifelong professional learning that is readily available. All teachers should receive training to better their mastery of AI tasks, firstly being able to comprehend the information offered as AI data, as well as being equipped with instructional strategies that enhance active participation and inclusivity for all learners in a multifaceted society.

The digital gap poses another challenge, highlighting issues of equity as it pertains to different socioeconomic and regional AI tools. Educational inequities exist because not all students have access to technology. These issues, according to Herawati (2025), can be mitigated by providing all learners access to the resources needed to receive an equitable education. Such efforts may be in the form of equipping technology in schools located in marginalized regions or forming partnerships with technology companies to provide schools with the equipment they need.

Furthermore, an AI and teacher partnership must be paired with strategies that ease real-world teaching implementation barriers. An example is gathering feedback from the classroom by using AI tools in teaching through pilot programs. Teachers can collaborate with IT specialists who can design fitting AI applications to instructional needs without inundating the educator's existing framework (Holman et al., 2024). Educators can step into AI-defining stages thereby reducing the instructional burden while learning to teach with new technologies.

To conclude, the moral and practical issues of using AI in ELT require an all-encompassing strategy that considers privacy concerns, discriminatory practices within AI models, regular advanced training for educators, as well as inequitable technological access, and practical policies on the integration of artificial intelligence into the educational framework of the teacher-AI systems. Addressing these challenges gives educators the opportunity to use the advantages of artificial intelligence to make language learning more interesting and inclusive, and to create a rich educational environment for all students.

CONCLUSION

As indicated by the preceding chapters, this chapter deals specifically with the application of Artificial Intelligence with respect to teaching and learning the English language. A balance must now be struck between the use of A.I. applications and the personal touch of the teacher. It is also apparent that A.I. has great potential, but also requires the moderating hand of a skilled teacher in order to enhance the learning experience of the student. In this manner, learners acquire constructive personalised pathways and also immediate feedback, emotional support, and cultural immersion critical for language learning (Alrayes et al, 2024; Herawati et al., 2024).

In particular, virtual tutors in K-12 classrooms illustrate the dual-edged nature of A.I. integration. They can offer scalability, real-time feedback, and customised assistance, but also lack cultural awareness and emotional intelligence, which requires teacher mediation. Therefore, these tools ought to be regarded as assistants, not potential violators of contemporary teaching practices. Instructors who adjust to these changes are able to create conditions in which A.I. tools tailored to the learners' requirements lead to second language acquisition that is learner-centred and diverse in instructional approaches and rich in interaction (Familoni & Onyebuchi, 2024).

To fully understand Herawati's research and reports, optimising sales and human resources in any company capitalises on profits best to breach and capture new market landscapes as an overarching strategy to capture new markets and capital market landscapes. More importantly, robotics, A.I., and automation are geared towards leadership bottlenecks to usher in transformational ecosystems at a scale or speed never witnessed in the past or at present. Current and future markets at national and international levels will zoom in and tech-leave the rest of the World without AI, robotics, and automation in the next few decades. Without any human touch to the entire engineering design and resulting robots, the entire country of Japan and all developed countries will dine, wine, and reign in the rest of the world using and building upon A.I., robotics, and automation without borders. The rest of the World will still cling to teddy bears or will hover on preserving humanity using AI robotics and automation.

REFERENCES

Беганцова, И., Акутина, С., & Щелина, Т. (2020). The question of students' preparedness for studying in the digital educational environment.. https://doi.org/ DOI: 10.3897/ap.2.e0207

Adzima, R., Rochsantiningsih, D., & Suparno, S. (2023). Perspectives and preferences towards teaching culture in efl classroom: senior high school context in indonesia. International Journal of Multicultural and Multireligious Understanding, 10(6), 274. https://doi.org/DOI: 10.18415/ijmmu.v10i6.4728

Ahmad, S., Rahmat, M., Mubarik, M., Alam, M., & Hyder, S. (2021). Artificial intelligence and its role in education. *Sustainability (Basel)*, *13*(22), 12902. DOI: 10.3390/su132212902

Ajuwon, O., Animashaun, E., & Chiekezie, N.Olanike Abiola AjuwonEnitan Shukurat AnimashaunNjideka Rita Chiekezie. (2024). Advancing human resources management practices in educational institutions: Enhancing teacher retention and student outcomes using ai. *International Journal of Management & Entrepreneurship Research*, *6*(8), 2488–2506. DOI: 10.51594/ijmer.v6i8.1367

Akbarani, R. (2024). Use of artificial intelligence in english language teaching. *International Journal of English Learning and Applied Linguistics (Ijelal)*, *4*(1), 14–23. DOI: 10.21111/ijelal.v4i1.10756

Akbarani, R. (2024). Use of artificial intelligence in english language teaching. *International Journal of English Learning and Applied Linguistics (Ijelal)*, *4*(1), 14–23. DOI: 10.21111/ijelal.v4i1.10756

Akram, Z., Sethi, A., Mehreen, A., & Sohail, M. (2021). The assessment of emotional intelligence in medical faculty working at poonch medical college (pmc), ajk. *Journal of University Medical & Dental College*, *12*(1), 1–8. DOI: 10.37723/jumdc.v12i1.499

Al-Mughairi, H. and Bhaskar, P. (2024). Exploring the factors affecting the adoption ai techniques in higher education: insights from teachers' perspectives on chatgpt. Journal of Research in Innovative Teaching & Learning. https://doi.org/DOI: 10.1108/JRIT-09-2023-0129

Alrayes, A., Henari, T., & Ahmed, D. (2024). Chatgpt in education – understanding the bahraini academics perspective. *Electronic Journal of e-Learning*, *22*(2), 112–134. DOI: 10.34190/ejel.22.2.3250

Alshehri, B. (2023). Pedagogical paradigms in the ai era: Insights from saudi educators on the long-term implications of ai integration in classroom teaching. *IJESA*, *2*(8), 159–180. DOI: 10.59992/IJESA.2023.v2n8p7

Amer, S. (2022). The importance of teaching culture in the foreign language classroom. *JOFOA*, (46). Advance online publication. DOI: 10.37376/jofoa.vi46.2653

Ayeni, O., Hamad, N., Chisom, O., Osawaru, B., & Adewusi, O. (2024). Ai in education: A review of personalized learning and educational technology. *GSC Advanced Research and Reviews*, *18*(2), 261–271. DOI: 10.30574/gscarr.2024.18.2.0062

Barua, P., Vicnesh, J., Gururajan, R., Oh, S., Palmer, E., Azizan, M., Kadri, N. A., & Acharya, U. (2022). Artificial intelligence enabled personalised assistive tools to enhance education of children with neurodevelopmental disorders—A review. *International Journal of Environmental Research and Public Health*, *19*(3), 1192. DOI: 10.3390/ijerph19031192 PMID: 35162220

Barua, P., Vicnesh, J., Gururajan, R., Oh, S., Palmer, E., Azizan, M., Kadri, N. A., & Acharya, U. (2022). Artificial intelligence enabled personalised assistive tools to enhance education of children with neurodevelopmental disorders—A review. *International Journal of Environmental Research and Public Health*, *19*(3), 1192. DOI: 10.3390/ijerph19031192 PMID: 35162220

Barua, P., Vicnesh, J., Gururajan, R., Oh, S., Palmer, E., Azizan, M., Kadri, N. A., & Acharya, U. (2022). Artificial intelligence enabled personalised assistive tools to enhance education of children with neurodevelopmental disorders—A review. *International Journal of Environmental Research and Public Health*, *19*(3), 1192. DOI: 10.3390/ijerph19031192 PMID: 35162220

Barzani, S., Aslam, M., & Aslam, T. (2021). The role of technology in ell classes in turkish republic of northern cyprus. *International Journal of Language Education*, *5*(2), 30. DOI: 10.26858/ijole.v5i2.14109

Baskara, F. (2023). Ai-driven dynamics: Chatgpt transforming elt teacher-student interactions. *Lensa Kajian Kebahasaan Kesusastraan Dan Budaya*, *13*(2), 261. DOI: 10.26714/lensa.13.2.2023.261-275

Chae, H., Kim, M., Kim, C., Jeong, W., Kim, H., Lee, J., & Yeo, J. (2023). Tutoring: Instruction-grounded conversational agent for language learners. *Proceedings of the AAAI Conference on Artificial Intelligence*, *37*(13), 16413–16415. DOI: 10.1609/aaai.v37i13.27063

Chaer, H., Jafar, S., Intiana, S. R. J., & Setiawan, I. (2024). Pengajaran bahasa berdasarkan teori aktivitas budaya engeström: Integrasi konteks budaya dalam pembelajaran bahasa. *Jurnal Humanitas Katalisator Perubahan Dan Inovator Pendidikan*, *10*(2), 235–254. DOI: 10.29408/jhm.v10i2.25562

Chen, Y., Chu, H., & Chueh, C. (2025). Effect of teachers' emotional intelligence on emotional blackmail at work with emotional labor as the mediating variable and burnout as the moderating variable. *Psychology in the Schools*, *62*(5), 1583–1597. DOI: 10.1002/pits.23412

Dawat, E. (2023). Advancing education through data analytics and artificial intelligence: A comprehensive literature review. *International Journal of Research Publications*, *137*(1). Advance online publication. DOI: 10.47119/IJRP10013711120235686

Deep, S., Athimoolam, K., & Enoch, T. (2024). Optimizing administrative efficiency and student engagement in education: The impact of ai. *International Journal of Current Science Research and Review*, *07*(10). Advance online publication. DOI: 10.47191/ijcsrr/V7-i10-34

Dieker, L., Hines, R., Wilkins, I., Hughes, C., Scott, K., Smith, S., & Shah, S. (2024). Using an artificial intelligence (ai) agent to support teacher instruction and student learning. *Journal of Special Education Preparation*, *4*(2), 78–88. DOI: 10.33043/d8xb94q7

Eden, C., Chisom, O., & Adeniyi, I. (2024). Integrating ai in education: opportunities, challenges, and ethical considerations. Magna Scientia Advanced Research and Reviews, 10(2), 006-013. https://doi.org/DOI: 10.30574/msarr.2024.10.2.0039

Evans, R., & Sinha, N. (2024). Bridging the gap: Diversity initiatives in ai education. *AAAI-SS*, *3*(1), 474–477. DOI: 10.1609/aaaiss.v3i1.31260

Familoni, B., & Onyebuchi, N.Babajide Tolulope FamiloniNneamaka Chisom Onyebuchi. (2024). Advancements and challenges in ai integration for technical literacy: A systematic review. *Engineering Science & Technology Journal*, *5*(4), 1415–1430. DOI: 10.51594/estj.v5i4.1042

Fitria, T. (2021). Grammarly as ai-powered english writing assistant: Students' alternative for writing english. *Metathesis Journal of English Language Literature and Teaching*, *5*(1), 65. DOI: 10.31002/metathesis.v5i1.3519

Gada, T., & Chudasama, S. (2024). Impact of artificial intelligence on student attitudes, engagement, and learning. *International Research Journal of Modernization in Engineering Technology and Science*. Advance online publication. DOI: 10.56726/IRJMETS56247

Geng, F., Zhou, N., & Yu, S. (2024). Exploring the effect of l2 writing teachers' emotional intelligence on their professional well-being: The mediating role of emotional labour strategies. *European Journal of Education*, *60*(1), e12850. Advance online publication. DOI: 10.1111/ejed.12850

George, B., & Wooden, O. (2023). Managing the strategic transformation of higher education through artificial intelligence. *Administrative Sciences*, *13*(9), 196. DOI: 10.3390/admsci13090196

Gyawali, Y., & Mehandroo, M. (2022). Artificial intelligence in english language teaching: Navigating the future with emerging perspectives. *Journal of Language and Linguistics in Society*, (26), 21–27. DOI: 10.55529/jlls.26.21.27

Gyawali, Y., & Mehandroo, M. (2022). Artificial intelligence in english language teaching: Navigating the future with emerging perspectives. *Journal of Language and Linguistics in Society*, (26), 21–27. DOI: 10.55529/jlls.26.21.27

Никитина, И., & Ishchenko, T. (2024). The impact of ai on teachers: Support or replacement? *SJPU*, *65*(4), 93–99. DOI: 10.23856/6511

Ha, D., & Nguyen, A. (2024). Artificial intelligence-based assessment in elt exam creation: A case study of van lang university lecturers. *Saudi Journal of Language Studies*, *5*(1), 34–49. DOI: 10.1108/SJLS-06-2024-0030

Herawati, A., Yusuf, S., Ilfiandra, I., Taufik, A., & Habibi, A. (2024). Exploring the role of artificial intelligence in education, students preferences and perceptions. *Al-Ishlah Jurnal Pendidikan*, *16*(2), 1029–1040. DOI: 10.35445/alishlah.v16i2.4784

Herawati, R. (2025). Integrating artificial intelligence (ai) into sustainable tourism management in indonesia and the impact on customer experience: a literature review., 36. https://doi.org/DOI: 10.1117/12.3058730

Holman, K., Marino, M., Vasquez, E., Taub, M., Hunt, J., & Tazi, Y. (2024). Navigating ai-powered personalized learning in special education: A guide for preservice teacher faculty. *Journal of Special Education Preparation*, *4*(2), 90–95. DOI: 10.33043/5b2xqcb3

Holman, K., Marino, M., Vasquez, E., Taub, M., Hunt, J., & Tazi, Y. (2024). Navigating ai-powered personalized learning in special education: A guide for preservice teacher faculty. *Journal of Special Education Preparation*, *4*(2), 90–95. DOI: 10.33043/5b2xqcb3

Huang, J., Lee, Y., & Kwon, O. (2023). Direct: Toward dialogue-based reading comprehension tutoring. *IEEE Access : Practical Innovations, Open Solutions*, *11*, 8978–8987. DOI: 10.1109/ACCESS.2022.3233224

Ibrahim, A. (2024). Assessing the knowledge and perception of artificial intelligence for teaching and research among lecturers in the faculties of arts in nigeria. *Journal of Global Research in Education and Social Science*, *18*(2), 25–33. DOI: 10.56557/jogress/2024/v18i28671

Idham, A., Rauf, W., & Rajab, A. (2024). Navigating the transformative impact of artificial intelligence on english language teaching: Exploring challenges and opportunities. *JES*, *4*(1), 8–14. DOI: 10.56185/jes.v4i1.620

Idham, A., Rauf, W., & Rajab, A. (2024). Navigating the transformative impact of artificial intelligence on english language teaching: Exploring challenges and opportunities. *JES*, *4*(1), 8–14. DOI: 10.56185/jes.v4i1.620

Jain, R., Saha, T., & Saha, S. (2023). T-vaks: a tutoring-based multimodal dialog system via knowledge selection.. https://doi.org/DOI: 10.3233/FAIA230388

Jayavardhini, P. (2024). Ai study partner: Development of an llm and gen ai-enhanced study assistant tool. *Interantional Journal of Scientific Research in Engineering and Management*, *08*(03), 1–5. DOI: 10.55041/IJSREM29626

Jian, M. (2023). Personalized learning through ai. *AEI*, *5*(1), 16–19. DOI: 10.54254/2977-3903/5/2023039

Karki, B., & Karki, T. (2025). Integrating ai in english language teaching: Challenges and opportunities. *Dristikon a Multidisciplinary Journal*, *15*(1), 13–28. DOI: 10.3126/dristikon.v15i1.77118

Khizar, A. (2024). Artificial intelligence and neurosurgery: A revolution in the field. *Pakistan Journal of Neurological Sciences*, *18*(04). Advance online publication. DOI: 10.56310/pjns.v18i04.244

Krisnawati, K., Irwan, I., Yusnan, M., & Acoci, . (2024). Exploring the relationship between academic achievement and emotional intelligence in upper primary school students. *International Journal of Learning Reformation in Elementary Education*, *3*(01), 42–50. DOI: 10.56741/ijlree.v3i01.487

Lampropoulos, G., & Papadakis, S. (2025). The Educational Value of Artificial Intelligence and Social Robots. In *Social Robots in Education* (pp. 3–15). Springer. DOI: 10.1007/978-3-031-82915-4_1

Lavidas, K., Papadakis, S., Manesis, D., Grigoriadou, A. S., & Gialamas, V.Lectures and Lab Classes. (2022). The effects of social desirability on students' self-reports in two social contexts: Lectures vs. lectures and lab classes. *Information (Basel)*, *13*(10), 491. DOI: 10.3390/info13100491

Lavidas, K., Petropoulou, A., Papadakis, S., Apostolou, Z., Komis, V., Jimoyiannis, A., & Gialamas, V. (2022). Factors affecting response rates of the web survey with teachers. *Computers, 11*(9), 127. DOI: 10.3390/computers11090127

Lawrence, L., Echeverría, V., Yang, K., Aleven, V., & Rummel, N. (2023). How teachers conceptualise shared control with an ai co-orchestration tool: A multiyear teacher-centred design process. *British Journal of Educational Technology, 55*(3), 823–844. DOI: 10.1111/bjet.13372

Liu, M. (2023). Exploring the application of artificial intelligence in foreign language teaching: challenges and future development. SHS Web of Conferences, 168, 03025. https://doi.org/DOI: 10.1051/shsconf/202316803025

Maqsood, M., Zahid, A., Asghar, T., Farooqi, S., & Shahbaz, M. (2024). Issues in teaching english in a cultural context. *Migration Letters : An International Journal of Migration Studies, 21*(S4), 1020–1027. DOI: 10.59670/ml.v21iS4.7411

Miri, M., & Pishghadam, R. (2021). Toward an emotioncy based education: A systematic review of the literature. *Frontiers in Psychology, 12*, 727186. Advance online publication. DOI: 10.3389/fpsyg.2021.727186 PMID: 34421775

Mudawy, A. (2024). Investigating efl faculty members' perceptions of integrating artificial intelligence applications to improve the research writing process: a case study at majmaah university. https://doi.org/DOI: 10.31235/osf.io/k4ub8

Namjoo, F., Liaghat, E., Shabaziasl, S., Modabernejad, Z., & Morshedi, H. (2023). Students experience on self-study through ai. aitechbesosci, 1(3), 35-42. https://doi.org/DOI: 10.61838/kman.aitech.1.3.6

Nazaretsky, T., Ariely, M., Cukurova, M., & Alexandron, G. (2022). Teachers' trust in ai-powered educational technology and a professional development program to improve it. *British Journal of Educational Technology, 53*(4), 914–931. DOI: 10.1111/bjet.13232

Okunade, A. (2024). The role of artificial intelligence in teaching of science education in secondary schools in nigeria. *European Journal of Computer Science and Information Technology, 12*(1), 57–67. DOI: 10.37745/ejcsit2013/vol12n15767

Onesi-Ozigagun, O., Ololade, Y., Eyo-Udo, N., & Ogundipe, D. (2024). Revolutionizing education through ai: A comprehensive review of enhancing learning experiences. *International Journal of Applied Research in Social Sciences, 6*(4), 589–607. DOI: 10.51594/ijarss.v6i4.1011

Onesi-Ozigagun, O., Ololade, Y., Eyo-Udo, N., & Ogundipe, D. (2024). Revolutionizing education through ai: A comprehensive review of enhancing learning experiences. *International Journal of Applied Research in Social Sciences*, *6*(4), 589–607. DOI: 10.51594/ijarss.v6i4.1011

Osadchaia, V., Ivanova, O., & Getman, E. (2020). Cross-cultural communication issues of educating bicultural students.. https://doi.org/DOI: 10.31483/r-75019

Ouyang, F., Wu, M., Zheng, L., Zhang, L., & Jiao, P. (2023). Integration of artificial intelligence performance prediction and learning analytics to improve student learning in online engineering course. *International Journal of Educational Technology in Higher Education*, *20*(1), 4. Advance online publication. DOI: 10.1186/s41239-022-00372-4 PMID: 36683653

Papadakis, S., Lytvynova, S. H., Ivanova, S. M., & Selyshcheva, I. A. (2024b). *Advancing lifelong learning with AI-enhanced ICT: A review of 3L-Person 2024.* In *CEUR Workshop Proceedings (9th International Workshop on Professional Retraining and Life-Long Learning using ICT: Person-oriented Approach — 3L-Person 2024, Lviv, Ukraine, September 25, 2023).* CEUR-WS.org.

Papadakis, S., Striuk, A. M., Kravtsov, H. M., Shyshkina, M. P., Marienko, M. V., & Danylchuk, H. B. (2024a). *Embracing digital innovation and cloud technologies for transformative learning experiences.* In *Proceedings of the 11th Workshop on Cloud Technologies in Education (CTE 2023), Kryvyi Rih, Ukraine, December 22, 2023.* CEUR Workshop Proceedings.

Park, W., & Kwon, H. (2023). Implementing artificial intelligence education for middle school technology education in republic of korea. *International Journal of Technology and Design Education*, *34*(1), 109–135. DOI: 10.1007/s10798-023-09812-2 PMID: 36844448

Pendy, B. (2023). Artificial intelligence: The future of education. *Jurnal Indonesia Sosial Sains*, *2*(11). Advance online publication. DOI: 10.59141/jiss.v2i11.801

Qin, Q., & Ao, L. (2023). *A new world of open space - reflections and perspectives of chinese scholars on the digital transformation of education and future education research.* MCET., DOI: 10.1007/978-3-031-33023-0_27

Qiu, B., Zhu, Y., Du, L., & Feng, C. (2024). Analysis and reflection on the teaching application of artificial intelligence technology in the context of big data. *Curriculum and Teaching Methodology*, *7*(4). Advance online publication. DOI: 10.23977/curtm.2024.070404

Rathore, A., Sultana, N., Zareen, S., & Ahmed, A. (2023). Artificial intelligence and curriculum prospects for elementary school. *Pakistan Journal of Humanities and Social Sciences*, *11*(4). Advance online publication. DOI: 10.52131/pjhss.2023.v11i4.1909

Reiß, M. (2021). The use of ai in education: Practicalities and ethical considerations. *London Review of Education*, *19*(1). Advance online publication. DOI: 10.14324/LRE.19.1.05

Sanchez-Gonzalez, M., & Terrell, M. (2023). Flipped classroom with artificial intelligence: Educational effectiveness of combining voice-over presentations and ai. *Cureus*. Advance online publication. DOI: 10.7759/cureus.48354 PMID: 37937181

Selwyn, N. (2022). The future of ai and education: Some cautionary notes. *European Journal of Education*, *57*(4), 620–631. DOI: 10.1111/ejed.12532

Shazly, R. (2021). Effects of artificial intelligence on english speaking anxiety and speaking performance: A case study. *Expert Systems: International Journal of Knowledge Engineering and Neural Networks*, *38*(3), e12667. Advance online publication. DOI: 10.1111/exsy.12667

Stasser, T. (2023). Elt in the digitale age: We have come a long way. *Arbeiten Aus Anglistik Und Amerikanistik*, *48*(1), 121–136. DOI: 10.24053/AAA-2023-0006

Suweni, D., Ruswanto, R., Prasmoro, B., & Hawanti, S. (2024). The importance of culture recognition in teaching english. *Khazanah Pendidikan*, *18*(2), 458. DOI: 10.30595/jkp.v18i2.25709

Syuhra, M., Chandra, N. E., & Rosalina, E. (2025). Artificial intelligence in english language teaching: A systematic literature review of tools, impact, and challenges. *Veles Voice of English Language Education Society*, *9*(1), 193–205. DOI: 10.29408/veles.v9i1.29745

Szabó, F., & Szoke, J. (2024). How does generative ai promote autonomy and inclusivity in language teaching? *ELT Journal*, *78*(4), 478–488. DOI: 10.1093/elt/ccae052

Tammets, K., & Ley, T. (2023). Integrating ai tools in teacher professional learning: A conceptual model and illustrative case. *Frontiers in Artificial Intelligence*, *6*, 1255089. Advance online publication. DOI: 10.3389/frai.2023.1255089 PMID: 38130325

Tang, J. (2024). The role of artificial intelligence in improving the efficiency of piano online learning. *Journal of Computational Methods in Sciences and Engineering*, *25*(2), 1504–1518. DOI: 10.1177/14727978241300381

Tang, Z. (2025). Using artificial intelligence in english language teaching: Benefits and challenges. *Journal of Education and Educational Research, 12*(2), 1–4. DOI: 10.54097/e8f9jw03

Ulfa, K. (2023). The transformative power of artificial intelligence (ai) to elevate english language learning. *Majalah Ilmiah Methoda, 13*(3), 307–313. DOI: 10.46880/methoda.Vol13No3.pp307-313

Usher, M., Hershkovitz, A., & Forkosh-Baruch, A. (2021). From data to actions: Instructors' decision making based on learners' data in online emergency remote teaching. *British Journal of Educational Technology, 52*(4), 1338–1356. DOI: 10.1111/bjet.13108

Valente, S., Veiga-Branco, A., Rebelo, H., Lourenço, A., & Cristóvão, A. (2020). The relationship between emotional intelligence ability and teacher efficacy. *Universal Journal of Educational Research, 8*(3), 916–923. DOI: 10.13189/ujer.2020.080324

Xi, L. (2024). Research on the english writing teaching model in the ai era. *MMSE, 6*(3), 111. DOI: 10.22158/mmse.v6n3p111

Yang, H., & Kyun, S. (2022). The current research trend of artificial intelligence in language learning: A systematic empirical literature review from an activity theory perspective. *Australasian Journal of Educational Technology*, •••, 180–210. DOI: 10.14742/ajet.7492

Yu, Y., Han, L., Du, X., & Yu, J. (2022). An oral english evaluation model using artificial intelligence method. *Mobile Information Systems, 2022*, 1–8. DOI: 10.1155/2022/3998886

Zhang, S. (2024). Research on english language and literature teaching strategies based on situational teaching method. *Journal of Contemporary Educational Research, 8*(10), 44–47. DOI: 10.26689/jcer.v8i10.8571

Zhang, Y., Shi, Y., & Bi, F. (2023). Personalizing students' learning needs by a teaching decision optimization method. *International Journal of Emerging Technologies in Learning, 18*(16), 222–236. DOI: 10.3991/ijet.v18i16.42707

Zhao, T. (2023). Ai in educational technology. DOI: 10.20944/preprints202311.0106.v1

Zhu, Y. (2024). Research on digital virtual humans in the metaverse for smart teaching. *Lecture Notes in Education Psychology and Public Media, 54*(1), 127–135. DOI: 10.54254/2753-7048/54/20241542

KEY TERMS AND DEFINITIONS

Artificial Intelligence (AI): A branch of computer science that develops systems capable of performing tasks that typically require human intelligence, such as problem-solving, decision-making, and language processing.

Blended Learning: An instructional approach that combines traditional face-to-face teaching with technology-enhanced methods, allowing learners to benefit from both in-person and digital experiences.

Collaborative Learning: A pedagogical approach where learners work together to solve problems, complete tasks, or build knowledge, often facilitated by digital and AI-based tools.

Digital Literacy: The ability to effectively and critically use digital technologies to access, evaluate, create, and communicate information in various contexts.

English Language Teaching (ELT): The practice of teaching English to non-native speakers, encompassing a range of methods, strategies, and tools to enhance language acquisition.

Human-AI Collaboration: A partnership model where teachers and AI systems work together to enhance learning outcomes, with AI handling repetitive tasks and teachers focusing on higher-order skills and emotional support.

Learner Autonomy: The capacity of students to take control of their learning process by setting goals, making decisions, and reflecting on their progress, often supported by AI tools.

Pedagogical Integration: The strategic incorporation of technological tools into teaching practices to complement, rather than replace, human instruction.

Teacher Mediation: The active role of teachers in guiding, contextualizing, and personalizing AI-assisted learning to ensure meaningful educational experiences.

Chapter 8

AI-Powered Virtual Teachers and Their Role in Developing Critical Thinking Skills

Alpay Aksin
http://orcid.org/0000-0002-6675-3094
Amasya University, Turkey

ABSTRACT

This study examines the level of artificial intelligence (AI) and virtual teacher usage among middle school students in social studies classes and its relationship with critical thinking skills. The sample consisted of 371 middle school students in Amasya, Turkey. To gather data, students completed a personal information form and a critical thinking skills scale. The findings revealed that 91.7% of students were aware of AI, and 30.7% used it on a daily basis. Notably, ChatGPT was the most widely used tool among students, primarily employed for completing assignments and asking questions. Furthermore, students familiar with the concept of virtual teachers demonstrated higher scores on critical thinking assessments. Increased frequency of AI usage was associated with enhanced critical thinking skills. However, despite these associations, most students believed virtual teachers could not replace real teachers. Overall, the research indicates that AI should be utilized as a supportive tool in education.

DOI: 10.4018/979-8-3373-2637-5.ch008

INTRODUCTION

Artificial Intelligence in Social Studies Education

Social studies education draws upon multiple disciplines to enhance students' capacity to understand and interpret the social world. This interdisciplinary field fundamentally aims to cultivate citizens who possess democratic values, critical thinking (CT) skills, and global perspectives essential for 21st-century society (Beck & Parker, 2021). Contemporary social studies instruction has evolved toward student-centered, constructivist learning models that emphasize active engagement over the traditional transmission of knowledge. This pedagogical shift incorporates diverse approaches, including drama, project-based learning, cooperative learning, and technology-assisted instruction, to address topics ranging from local history to global issues and environmental awareness. The integration of artificial intelligence (AI) tools in social studies education represents a significant advancement in this evolution, transforming learning experiences by creating interactive environments that enhance CT and problem-solving skills (Martell, 2018). This technological integration supports the development of 21st-century competencies while maintaining the essential dynamic where teachers serve as guides and students take ownership of their learning process.

Educational tools and applications have evolved beyond mere supporting roles to become central components of AI literacy programs, reflecting broader efforts to meet the growing demands for education. Various factors, including students' gender, background knowledge, and educational setting, influence how learners engage with AI tools and what motivates their learning process (Papadakis et al., 2024a, 2024b). The technological transformation of the 21st-century necessitates new approaches in social studies education, emphasizing teachers' guidance roles while encouraging active student participation. AI literacy has emerged as a critical component of social studies education, preparing students for a future where AI interaction is ubiquitous (Yetişensoy & Rapoport, 2023). However, this integration presents both opportunities and challenges, including concerns about digital addiction that may impact academic achievement and cognitive development (Karakose et al., 2022; Tülübaş et al., 2023).

The widespread adoption of AI in education raises significant ethical and privacy concerns, particularly regarding data protection, algorithmic bias, and digital surveillance for K-12 students. These systems can produce unfair outcomes for students from diverse socioeconomic, cultural, or ethnic backgrounds (Holmes et al., 2019). Recent research emphasizes the development of culturally responsive AI applications that adapt content to diverse contexts and promote equity and inclusion. For instance, frameworks like Culturally Adaptive Thinking in Education (CATE) integrate cultural intelligence to ensure AI-generated content respects students' diverse backgrounds while reducing algorithmic biases (Hanna et al., 2025).

Comprehensive analysis conducted by Ali et al. (2024) reveals five main challenge categories hindering effective AI adoption in education: user challenges related to limited personalization and context understanding; operational challenges involving high costs and individualization limitations; environmental concerns about energy consumption; technological challenges centered on data privacy and security; and ethical challenges primarily concerning bias and academic integrity. These findings emphasize that AI tools should complement rather than replace human educators.

Effective AI integration requires social studies teachers to develop both traditional pedagogical skills and technological competencies. Teachers need professional development that moves beyond basic AI use toward designing instruction that augments higher-order thinking skills, including CT, creativity, and problem-solving (Luckin et al., 2016). However, many educators report feeling unprepared to meaningfully integrate AI tools without adequate technical support and training. Despite these challenges, AI integration offers transformative potential for enhancing pedagogical practices through personalized feedback, creative content generation, and engaging instructional methods. For stakeholders, including administrators and policymakers, AI adoption can foster scalable innovations aligned with 21st-century skills development. However, ensuring equitable access remains a critical issue. The digital divide risks concentrating AI benefits in well-resourced schools with reliable internet infrastructure and up-to-date hardware, thereby exacerbating existing educational inequalities. Developing inclusive policies that bridge this gap is essential for the successful and just integration of AI in education.

AI tools significantly contribute to social studies education by developing digital citizenship skills and preparing students for future societal structures. These technologies enrich learning through simulations, virtual reality experiences, and interactive content creation while supporting multiple intelligences approaches that address diverse learning styles (Hartshorne et al., 2019). For middle school students, AI tools offer personalized learning experiences through interactive simulations, virtual museum tours, and discussion platforms that enhance understanding of historical events. Leading platforms include ChatGPT, Google Gemini, and Microsoft Copilot for basic inquiries, while specialized tools like Google Expeditions enable virtual visits to historical sites. These applications support CT development by enabling students to establish cause-and-effect relationships, compare information sources, and engage in empathy-building simulations that cultivate analytical rather than passive learning approaches (Clark & van Kessel, 2025).

The Impact of AI on Critical Thinking

Critical thinking encompasses the cognitive skills enabling individuals to analyze, evaluate, and interpret knowledge and evidence to reach informed conclusions. This multidimensional construct includes problem-solving, decision-making, metacognition, logical reasoning, and moral judgment, representing an indispensable skill for active citizenship in democratic societies. CT development occurs through systematic and intentional instruction rather than innate ability. Foundational skills, including reading comprehension, argument analysis, and evidence-seeking, serve as critical prerequisites in this developmental process. Multiple factors influence CT development, including individual dispositions such as truth-seeking and open-mindedness, teaching methods, the quality of the learning environment, and socio-cultural contexts (Facione, 1990). Inquiry-based approaches, such as the Socratic Method, particularly contribute to CT development by enabling students to evaluate diverse perspectives when confronting complex ethical dilemmas.

CT skills hold particular importance in today's information age, where students face numerous challenges in an AI-influenced world. Educational systems can leverage AI as a teaching tool, focusing on CT development and capitalizing on its benefits for curricula and learning environments. AI systems with extensive databases and analytical capabilities present students with complex problems that require higher-order thinking skills, including analysis, synthesis, and evaluation, rather than mere memorization. These tools provide personalized learning experiences tailored to individual learning styles and abilities, substantially boosting literacy and CT skills through adaptive feedback mechanisms (Saddhono et al., 2024).

In social studies education, AI tools support CT processes by enhancing students' capacity to evaluate multiple perspectives, question source reliability, and analyze complex social problems. These tools present diverse scenarios that enhance analytical thinking and facilitate a multidimensional evaluation of societal events. Maximizing these benefits requires collaborative approaches involving educators, students, and parents to foster a comprehensive understanding of AI and its responsible use in educational settings (Ng et al., 2025).

Recent empirical research has revealed a sharp increase in AI literacy studies since 2022, driven by advancements in generative AI. This research, predominantly employing mixed methods and focusing on secondary education, highlights the critical need for tailored AI literacy programs integrating ethical and social implications to foster CT (Tan & Tang, 2025). Consequently, AI serves not merely for content delivery, but as a dynamic tool that encourages students to question, analyze, and reflect deeply on the presented information.

For middle school students in their transitional cognitive stage from concrete to abstract operational thinking, AI tools play a complex and multidimensional role in CT development. The implementation of these tools determines whether they positively or negatively affect students' analytical thinking, evidence evaluation, and multiperspectival reasoning skills (Chen et al., 2020).

While effective AI integration significantly contributes to achieving contemporary social studies education goals, excessive dependence on AI tools poses obstacles to CT development. Teachers express concerns that over-reliance may diminish students' CT, information literacy, creativity, and problem-solving skills. Adolescents with executive function challenges are particularly at risk of missing opportunities to develop their own cognitive processes. Systematic reviews confirm that uncritically accepting AI-generated recommendations has a negative predictive value for CT performance, leading to task execution errors and undermining independent cognitive development (Gerlich, 2025).

Maximizing the contribution of AI tools to CT development requires a pedagogically conscious integration by teachers. Students must acquire skills in recognizing AI limitations, using multiple sources, verifying information, and conducting ethical evaluations. Particularly in social studies classes, AI-powered activities in historical analysis, geographical problem-solving, and citizenship education can enhance CT while supporting digital and media literacy skills, ensuring students meet technological age demands while becoming conscious citizens.

Effective AI integration into social studies education requires carefully designed pedagogical strategies aligning with both disciplinary goals and AI literacy objectives. Research indicates that collaborative project-based learning, particularly approaches integrating interdisciplinary problem-solving through artifact creation, represents the most effective pedagogical method for fostering AI literacy. These approaches develop CT, problem-solving, and communication skills, enabling students to apply AI concepts in practical, real-world settings (Ng et al., 2024).

The TPACK framework provides educators with a clear structure for integrating AI literacy into classroom settings by categorizing effective strategies into the three core domains of technological knowledge, which involves AI-specific tools, pedagogical knowledge, which encompasses teaching strategies and feedback mechanisms, and content knowledge, which concerns core AI concepts and curriculum subject matter. General pedagogical approaches, including inquiry-based learning, project-based learning, collaborative learning, and constructionism, prove particularly suitable for fostering AI literacy in K-12 settings (Ng et al., 2021).

In social studies contexts, these approaches can be specifically adapted. Project-based learning can facilitate historical simulations and data analysis of social phenomena, while inquiry-based approaches can leverage AI-powered chatbots to guide multi-perspectival analysis of historical events. Such strategies enhance content understanding while cultivating the ability to interrogate AI-generated content, identify biases, and synthesize information from multiple sources, core CT components in the digital age.

Unplugged activities such as role-playing, algorithmic decision-making, or debating ethical dilemmas arising from AI applications help demystify AI concepts and reinforce ethical considerations without relying solely on technical tools. These pedagogies emphasize teacher facilitation, critical dialogue, and reflective practice, ensuring AI serves as a catalyst for deeper learning rather than a substitute for it.

Frameworks for Assessing Critical Thinking and Their Integration with AI

Effectively assessing CT skills in social studies education proves equally crucial to developing them. Traditional assessment methods may inadequately capture the nuanced cognitive, affective, and metacognitive engagements that AI tools facilitate, necessitating the development of robust, modernized frameworks to track student growth in AI-supported learning environments. Established models, such as the Paul & Elder (2014) Critical Thinking Framework and Facione's (1990) expert consensus CT model, provide foundational structures; however, the integration of generative AI necessitates evolving these frameworks to include AI-specific competencies. Recent research suggests that Bloom's Taxonomy hierarchy may require reordering in AI-dominated educational landscapes, proposing "Evaluate" as the pinnacle cognitive skill to foster discernment necessary for ethical and effective engagement with AI-generated content (Lubbe et al., 2025).

Gonsalves' (2024) revision of Bloom's Taxonomy for the AI age offers critical assessment insights by proposing a revised taxonomy incorporating domains significantly activated by student-AI interaction, which include the cognitive domain for discovering and analyzing AI content, the affective domain for collaborating with AI and ethical reasoning, and the metacognitive domain for interrogating AI responses and articulating precise prompts. This expansion suggests that assessments must evaluate not merely the final thought product but also the interaction process, including how students' questions are refined and ethically integrated into AI-generated content. This aligns with calls for assessments that focus on both output and process, particularly students' ability to evaluate and refine AI-generated content, thereby fostering feedback loops between creation and evaluation.

The Paul-Elder Model, with its eight elements of thought and nine intellectual standards, provides a powerful analytical lens. Students can systematically evaluate AI-generated historical information by applying standards including Clarity, Accuracy, Logical Soundness, and Relevance. Assessment tasks might involve identifying AI's underlying "purpose" and "assumptions" before judging responses against intellectual standards. This interrogative process represents a key metacognitive skill fostered by AI interaction, moving students beyond passive acceptance toward active deconstruction of biases and credibility, essential competencies for academic integrity and meaningful learning in the AI age.

Facione's model, which combines skills such as analysis and evaluation with dispositions including truth-seeking and open-mindedness, aligns closely with the revised taxonomy's affective domain. Social studies teachers can assess not only students' ability to analyze AI outputs but also their dispositions, whether they demonstrate nuanced trust and adaptability or critical skepticism, and whether they cross-reference AI suggestions with traditional sources of information. This proves particularly crucial for applications like AI-supported virtual museum tours, where students must compare AI-generated perspectives against other sources while weighing evidence and navigating ambiguity.

Gonsalves' study argues that AI doesn't replace CT frameworks but makes their application more complex and layered. The revised taxonomy provides new assessment criteria, enabling educators to design rubrics measuring students' proficiency in articulating precise prompts, synthesizing AI and traditional sources, and demonstrating ethical reasoning regarding originality and bias. The IDEE framework (Identify Desired Outcomes, Determine Appropriate Automation Levels, Ensure Ethical Considerations, Evaluate Effectiveness) provides a structured approach for integrating AI in education, emphasizing desired outcomes such as enhancing CT while addressing ethical considerations, including biases and privacy (Su & Yang, 2022, 2023).

Integrating Paul-Elder and Facione frameworks with modern AI-driven competencies enables educators to develop holistic assessment strategies capturing the full CT spectrum in the digital age, ensuring students become critical and collaborative partners rather than merely AI consumers. Lubbe et al. (2025) provides a complementary perspective by advocating for a structural revision of Bloom's Taxonomy, placing "Evaluate" at the apex to meet the demands of AI-integrated education. Together, these studies provide a comprehensive roadmap: Gonsalves offers an expanded taxonomy with AI-specific domains and competencies, while Lubbe et al. provide compelling arguments for reorienting traditional hierarchies with practical assessment redesign strategies. This combined approach empowers educators to assess CT more effectively while fundamentally redesigning pedagogy for an AI-driven world, cultivating independent thinkers who can navigate, critique, and create with AI.

Previous Research on the Impact of AI on Critical Thinking

A growing body of research demonstrates AI's effectiveness as a tool for developing CT skills in educational contexts (Darwin et al., 2023; Essien et al., 2024;

Liu et al., 2025; Muthmainnah et al., 2022; van den Berg & du Plessis, 2023; Walter, 2024; Wu, 2024). The literature reveals three interconnected themes regarding AI's impact on CT development: the mechanisms through which AI enhances thinking skills, the conditions necessary for effectiveness, and the pedagogical approaches that maximize impact.

AI tools fundamentally enhance CT through multiple complementary mechanisms. Research consistently shows that AI improves students' questioning abilities and analytical skills by providing diverse perspectives and instant personalized feedback (Liu et al., 2025; Liu & Wang, 2024; Mayasari et al., 2024). Rather than serving as a mere information source, AI acts as an accelerator for CT by prompting students to engage in deeper analytical processes (Wu, 2024). Tools like ChatGPT enhance active participation in learning through AI-assisted discussions and interactive assessments, thereby strengthening students' attention and evaluative capacities (Liu & Wang, 2024; Suriano et al., 2025).

The pedagogical value extends beyond cognitive skills to affective dimensions. Studies demonstrate that AI applications foster open-mindedness, confidence-building, self-efficacy, and maturity while simultaneously increasing student interest and motivation (Muthmainnah et al., 2022). These affective improvements work synergistically with cognitive gains in information access, problem-solving, and creative thinking to develop comprehensive 21st-century competencies.

While AI shows significant potential, the literature emphasizes that its effectiveness depends on specific conditions. Multiple studies underscore that AI's impact on CT remains limited without appropriate pedagogical frameworks and student competencies (Darwin et al., 2023; Walter, 2024). Students must possess conscious usage skills and AI literacy to critically evaluate AI-generated outputs rather than accepting them passively (Wu, 2024). This critical evaluation capacity is particularly important when students interact with AI tools, as studies show that active, in-depth engagement with platforms like ChatGPT develops analytical and reflective thinking more effectively than passive knowledge acquisition (Suriano et al., 2025).

Inquiry-based approaches emerge as essential for maximizing AI's potential. Darwin et al. (2023) found that without such approaches, AI's ability to enhance CT remains constrained. Similarly, Styve et al. (2024) demonstrated the importance of designing learning activities that explicitly guide students to question AI outputs through analytical prompts like “why?”, “how?”, and “is this really true?” This pedagogical intentionality ensures students engage critically rather than passively with AI-generated content.

Experimental research employing rigorous methodological designs provides strong evidence for the effectiveness of AI when properly integrated into learning environments. Controlled comparisons between AI-supported and traditional settings demonstrate significant improvements in thinking skills, particularly when AI is integrated with learner-centered methods (Saritepeci & Yildiz Durak, 2024). School-based AI curricula prove more effective than traditional approaches for fostering algorithmic thinking, CT, and problem-solving in K-12 students (Liu et al., 2025).

Domain-specific research further illuminates effective integration strategies. In social studies education, generative AI tools promote evaluative skills by encouraging teachers to critically assess AI-generated lesson plans, thereby modeling analytical processes for students (van den Berg & du Plessis, 2023). Mixed-methods research in the same domain demonstrates that AI chatbots enhance critical inquiry through features such as multiple explanations and non-judgmental practice spaces, which support self-directed learning and a deeper understanding of history (Yetişensoy & Rapoport, 2023). Notably, culturally sensitive design enhances AI's effectiveness by resonating with diverse historical contexts and strengthening students' ability to evaluate multiple perspectives. These domain-specific examples underscore AI's potential for fostering multidimensional CT when integrated with culturally responsive pedagogical approaches.

The synthesis of current research reveals that AI tools, particularly conversational systems like ChatGPT, significantly contribute to CT development by enhancing analysis, synthesis, inquiry, and decision-making skills through personalized learning experiences and exposure to complex problems (Mayasari et al., 2024). However, recent reviews emphasize that realizing this potential requires systematic approaches to implementation (Essien et al., 2024; Khairani Zakaria et al., 2025). Educators must reconsider traditional teaching methods to provide more holistic learning experiences, while institutions should implement comprehensive AI literacy programs to ensure the effective and ethical integration of AI into their teaching processes.

In conclusion, when combined with appropriate pedagogical approaches such as inquiry-based methods, culturally responsive design, and explicit scaffolding for critical evaluation, AI tools can significantly contribute to CT development and offer transformative learning experiences. The technology's potential will be maximized through expanded AI literacy programs, ethical integration frameworks, and continued support for active student participation in AI-mediated learning processes.

The purpose of this study is to examine middle school students' levels of AI and virtual teacher usage in social studies class and the relationship between AI usage and their CT skills.

METHOD

Research Design

This cross-sectional study provides information on middle school students' levels of AI usage and examines the relationship between AI usage and their CT skills.

Participants

Participants included 371 middle school students attending five different middle schools in Amasya Province. Convenience sampling was used to select participants. A series of power analyses were conducted to determine the required sample size. Power analyses indicated that for a medium effect size with a minimum statistical power of .95, the required sample size ranged between 115 and 134 (Faul et al., 2007). Of the students, 235 (63.3%) were female and 136 (36.7%) were male. The students' ages ranged from 11 to 15 years old, with a mean age of 12.64 ($SD = .86$). There were 171 (46.1%) sixth-grade, 104 (28.0%) seventh-grade, and 96 (25.9%) eighth-grade students.

Data Collection Instruments

Personal Information Form

This form was used to collect data on students' grade level, gender, and age. It also gathered information on students' awareness of AI and the frequency of AI tool usage. The form inquired about the most frequently used AI tool and its intended purpose. Students' awareness of the "virtual teacher" concept was also measured. The form collected data on the use of AI tools in social studies classes and the use of AI-powered virtual teachers in those classes. Students were asked about the perceived helpfulness of AI-powered virtual teachers in social studies. The form included questions on the advantages of virtual teachers compared to real teachers. It also examined areas where AI-powered virtual teachers would be most useful in social studies. The form assessed students' willingness to participate in social studies lessons with a virtual teacher. It asked about the skills that AI-powered virtual teachers could help develop. Finally, it collected opinions on the contributions of AI-powered virtual teachers to the delivery of lessons.

Critical Thinking Skills Scale

The Critical Thinking Skills Scale developed by Karabulut et al. (2023) was used to measure middle school students' CT skills. To develop the scale, an item pool was generated utilizing the Critical Thinking Skills Scale, a widely used instrument in the literature. Items appropriate for middle school students were then selected based on expert evaluation. Exploratory factor analysis revealed that the scale consisted of 24 items explaining 41.34% of the total variance. The scale comprises five factors. This five-factor structure was also confirmed via confirmatory factor analysis. Participants indicated their level of agreement with each scale statement by selecting options ranging from "strongly disagree" (1) to "strongly agree" (5). The possible scores that each participant can obtain from the scale range from 24 to 96. Higher scores indicate higher CT disposition. The Cronbach's alpha internal consistency coefficient calculated by Karabulut et al. (2023) was .74. In this study, the Cronbach's alpha coefficient was .72. A sample item from the scale is: "I want to fully understand something I read before making a judgment about it."

Data Collection Process

Data were collected by the researcher between February and May 2025, following the acquisition of necessary ethical permissions from Amasya University. Prior to implementation, students were informed about voluntariness, confidentiality, the right to withdraw, and the purpose of the research. Participation was voluntary among all middle school students, and the instruments were completed in approximately 10 minutes.

Data Analysis

Statistical analyses were conducted using SPSS version 27. Prior to analysis, data accuracy, missing values, outliers, and the assumptions underlying the statistical procedures were assessed (Field, 2024; George & Mallery, 2024; Hair et al., 2018; Tabachnick & Fidell, 2019). Minimum and maximum values, as well as frequency distributions, were reviewed to confirm data accuracy, and all variables fell within the expected range. The dataset contained no missing or outlier values.

Descriptive statistics included frequencies, percentages, means, standard deviations, minimum values, and maximum values. These statistics summarized students' grade level, gender, age, AI awareness, and frequency of AI tool usage. Additionally, they described the most frequently used AI tool, its purpose, and students' awareness of the concept of a virtual teacher. The use of AI tools and AI-powered virtual teachers in social studies classes was also summarized. Finally, students' perceptions regarding the helpfulness and advantages of AI-powered virtual teachers, areas of greatest utility, willingness to participate in lessons with a virtual teacher, perceived skill support, and opinions on contributions to lesson delivery were reported.

Independent samples *t*-tests were conducted to examine differences in CT total scores based on students' AI awareness, awareness of the AI-powered virtual teacher concept, use of AI tools in social studies classes, and use of AI-powered virtual teachers in social studies classes. One-way analysis of variance (ANOVA) was then used to assess differences in CT total scores by AI tool usage frequency, the most frequently used AI tool, and willingness to participate in social studies lessons with a virtual teacher. When ANOVA results were significant, Tukey HSD post-hoc tests were applied.

Effect sizes were reported for all analyses. Cohen's *d* was calculated for independent samples *t*-tests, and eta-squared (η^2) was used for one-way ANOVA. Effect size interpretation followed Cohen's (1992) classification. The significance threshold for all inferential statistics was set at $p < .05$.

FINDINGS

Findings Regarding AI Usage

Table 1 presents descriptive statistics, including the frequency and percentage values, for middle school students' awareness of AI, the frequency of AI tool usage, the most commonly used AI tools, and the purposes of AI use.

Table 1. Descriptive statistics of students' AI usage

Question	*n*	%
Do you know what artificial intelligence (AI) is?		
No	31	8.3
Yes	340	91.7
How often do you use AI tools?		
Never	34	9.2
A few times a month	49	13.2
1-2 times a week	85	22.9
3-4 times a week	89	24.0
Every day	114	30.7
Which AI tool do you use the most?		

continued on following page

Table 1. Continued

Question	*n*	%
ChatGPT	211	56.9
Google Gemini	97	26.1
Other	63	17.0
For what purposes do you use AI tools? (Multiple responses allowed)*		
Doing homework	253	20.7
Asking questions I'm curious about	271	22.2
Entertainment	203	16.6
Generating stories/poems	52	4.3
Playing games	140	11.5
Creating images	94	7.7
Learning foreign languages	92	7.5
Learning programming	40	3.3
Other	28	2.3
Coding	23	1.9
I do not use it	24	2.0

Note. N = 371. * Multiple responses allowed for this question.

As shown in Table 1, 31 students (8.3%) were unfamiliar with AI, while 340 (91.7%) were aware of it. Regarding frequency of AI tool usage: 34 students (9.2%) never used AI tools, 49 (13.2%) used them a few times a month, 85 (22.9%) 1-2 times a week, 89 (24.0%) 3-4 times a week, and 114 (30.7%) used them daily. The most commonly used AI tools were ChatGPT (211 students, 56.9%), Google Gemini (97 students, 26.1%), and other tools (63 students, 17.0%). Purposes for using AI tools included: doing homework (253, 20.7%), asking questions (271, 22.2%), entertainment (203, 16.6%), generating stories/poems (52, 4.3%), playing games (140, 11.5%), creating images (94, 7.7%), learning foreign languages (92, 7.5%), learning programming (40, 3.3%), coding (23, 1.9%), other purposes (28, 2.3%), and 24 students (2.0%) reported not using AI tools for any purpose.

Table 2 presents descriptive statistics on middle school students' awareness and usage of AI-powered virtual teachers.

Table 2. Descriptive statistics of students' awareness of the virtual teacher concept and usage

Question	*n*	%
Do you know the concept of a "virtual teacher"?		
Yes	160	43.1
No	211	56.9
Have you used AI tools (e.g., Grok, ChatGPT) in social studies class?		
Yes	145	39.1
No	226	60.9
Have you used an AI-powered virtual teacher (e.g., an AI that explains lessons or solves problems) in social studies class?		
Yes	135	36.4
No	236	63.6
How helpful would using an AI-powered virtual teacher be for you in social studies class?		
Not helpful	29	7.8
Neutral	139	37.5
Helpful	203	54.7
What advantages do you think a virtual teacher has over a real teacher in social studies class? (Multiple responses allowed)*		
24/7 accessibility	265	28.2
Asking questions without embarrassment	173	18.4
Learning at my own pace	142	15.1
Patience (does not get angry at me)	158	16.8
Ability to re-explain multiple times	201	21.4

Note. $N = 371$. * Multiple responses allowed for this question.

As shown in Table 2, 160 students (43.1%) were familiar with the concept of a virtual teacher, while 211 (56.9%) were not. Regarding the use of AI tools in social studies classes, 145 students (39.1%) utilized them, while 226 (60.9%) did not. For AI-powered virtual teacher usage in social studies class, 135 students (36.4%) used them, while 236 (63.6%) did not. Regarding perceived helpfulness, 29 students (7.8%) stated it would not be helpful, 139 (37.5%) were undecided, and 203 (54.7%) found it helpful. Advantages of virtual teachers over real teachers included: 24/7 accessibility (265, 28.2%), asking questions without embarrassment (173, 18.4%), learning at one's own pace (142, 15.1%), patience (158, 16.8%), and repeated explanations (201, 21.4%).

Table 3 presents descriptive statistics on students' perceptions of the benefits and applications of AI-powered virtual teachers.

Table 3. Descriptive statistics of students' perceptions of virtual teacher benefits and applications

Question	*n*	%
In which areas do you think an AI-powered virtual teacher would be most helpful in social studies class? (Multiple responses allowed)*		
Reviewing misunderstood topics	276	18.3
Getting additional explanations on difficult topics	188	12.5
Better visualizing/understanding historical events and geographic concepts	129	8.6
Preparing for exams	253	16.8
Gaining more information about topics	163	10.8
Assisting with assignments (research, brainstorming)	228	15.1
Increasing general knowledge	97	6.4
Learning to read maps	53	3.5
Choosing project topics	103	6.8
Other	15	1.0
Would you like to have social studies lessons with a virtual teacher?		
No	77	20.8
Neutral	115	31.0
Yes	179	48.2
Which skills do you think an AI-powered virtual teacher could help you develop in social studies? (Multiple responses allowed)*		
Critical thinking	80	6.8
Interpretation and analysis	186	15.8
Problem solving	173	14.7
Presentation skills	132	11.2
Research skills	193	16.4
Assignment assistance (research, brainstorming)	226	19.3
Accessing and evaluating information	164	14.0
Other	20	1.7

Note. N = 371. * Multiple responses allowed for this question.

According to Table 3, students believed an AI-powered virtual teacher would be most helpful in: reviewing misunderstood topics (276, 18.3%), getting additional explanations (188, 12.5%), visualizing historical/geographic concepts (129, 8.6%), exam preparation (253, 16.8%), gaining topic information (163, 10.8%), assignment assistance (228, 15.1%), increasing general knowledge (97, 6.4%), map reading (53, 3.5%), choosing project topics (103, 6.8%), and other areas (15, 1.0%). Regarding willingness to use a virtual teacher for social studies: 77 students (20.8%) opposed it, 115 (31.0%) were neutral, and 179 (48.2%) supported it. For skill development, students identified assignment assistance (226, 19.3%), research skills (193, 16.4%), interpretation/analysis (186, 15.8%), problem solving (173, 14.7%), accessing/evaluating information (164, 14.0%), presentation skills (132, 11.2%), CT (80, 6.8%), and other skills (20, 1.7%).

Table 4 presents descriptive statistics, including frequency and percentage values, regarding middle school students' attitudes and perceptions towards the AI-powered virtual teacher.

Table 4. Descriptive statistics of students' attitudes toward virtual teachers

Statement	*n*	%
AI-powered virtual teachers make learning more enjoyable.		
Strongly disagree	33	8.9
Disagree	73	19.7
Neutral	111	29.9
Agree	105	28.3
Strongly agree	49	13.2
AI-powered virtual teachers offer personalized learning pace.		
Strongly disagree	22	5.9
Disagree	46	12.4
Neutral	96	25.9
Agree	150	40.4
Strongly agree	57	15.4
AI-powered virtual teachers help me understand lessons better.		
Strongly disagree	26	7.0
Disagree	60	16.2
Neutral	120	32.3
Agree	116	33.1
Strongly agree	49	13.2
AI-powered virtual teachers cannot replace my teacher.		
Strongly disagree	50	13.5
Disagree	35	9.4
Neutral	82	22.1
Agree	76	20.5
Strongly agree	128	34.5
I am unsure if AI-powered virtual teachers provide accurate information.		
Strongly disagree	38	10.2

continued on following page

Table 4. Continued

Statement	*n*	%
Disagree	84	22.6
Neutral	140	37.7
Agree	78	21.0
Strongly agree	31	8.4
AI-powered virtual teachers increase my interest in the subject.		
Strongly disagree	47	12.7
Disagree	78	21.0
Neutral	118	31.8
Agree	82	22.1
Strongly agree	46	12.4

Note. $N = 371$.

According to Table 4, middle school students expressed varying attitudes toward AI-powered virtual teachers. For the statement "AI-powered virtual teachers make learning more enjoyable," 33 students (8.9%) strongly disagreed, 73 (19.7%) disagreed, 111 (29.9%) were neutral, 105 (28.3%) agreed, and 49 (13.2%) strongly agreed. Regarding personalized learning pace, 22 students (5.9%) strongly disagreed, 46 (12.4%) disagreed, 96 (25.9%) were neutral, 150 (40.4%) agreed, and 57 (15.4%) strongly agreed. For improved lesson comprehension, 26 students (7.0%) strongly disagreed, 60 (16.2%) disagreed, 120 (32.3%) were neutral, 116 (33.1%) agreed, and 49 (13.2%) strongly agreed. On the statement "AI-powered virtual teachers cannot replace my teacher," 50 students (13.5%) strongly disagreed, 35 (9.4%) disagreed, 82 (22.1%) were neutral, 76 (20.5%) agreed, and 128 (34.5%) strongly agreed. Regarding the accuracy of information, 38 students (10.2%) strongly disagreed, 84 (22.6%) disagreed, 140 (37.7%) were neutral, 78 (21.0%) agreed, and 31 (8.4%) strongly agreed. Finally, for increased interest in the subject, 47 students (12.7%) strongly disagreed, 78 (21.0%) disagreed, 118 (31.8%) were neutral, 82 (22.1%) agreed, and 46 (12.4%) strongly agreed.

Differences in Critical Thinking Scores Based on AI Usage

Table 5 presents the mean and standard deviation values, as well as the results of the independent samples *t*-test, for middle school students' total CT scores based on their level of AI awareness.

Table 5. Independent samples t-test results for middle school students' CT scores based on their AI awareness

Group	*n*	*Mean*	*SD*	*df*	*t*	*p*	*d*
Not aware	31	74.87	7.53	369	-3.36	.001***	-.63
Aware	340	80.26	8.64				

Note. p < .001***.

As shown in Table 5, an independent samples *t*-test revealed a statistically significant difference in CT scores between students aware and unaware of AI ($t(369) = -3.36$, $p < .001$, $d = -.63$). The effect size was moderate. Students aware of AI had significantly higher mean CT scores ($M = 80.26$) compared to those unaware ($M = 74.87$).

Table 6 presents the mean CT scores of middle school students, categorized by their frequency of using AI tools, along with the results of the one-way ANOVA analysis.

Table 6. One-way ANOVA results for middle school students' CT scores based on their frequency of using AI tools

Group	*n*	*Mean*	*SD*	df_1, df_2	*F*	*p*	η^2	**Post Hoc**
1. Never	34	73.56	7.40	4, 366	6.25	.001***	.06	1-2, 1-3, 1-4, 1-5
2. A few times/month	49	81.88	7.77					
3. 1-2 times/week	85	80.21	9.30					
4. 3-4 times/week	89	81.31	8.65					
5. Daily	114	79.32	8.15					

Note. p < .001***.

As shown in Table 6, one-way ANOVA analyses revealed a statistically significant difference in CT mean scores among middle school students based on their frequency of using AI tools ($F(4, 366) = 6.25$, $p < .001$, $\eta^2 = .06$). This difference represents a medium effect size, indicating that frequency of AI tool usage explains 6% of the variance in CT scores. To identify the source of the difference, a post hoc Tukey HSD test was conducted. Results showed that middle school students who used AI tools daily ($M = 79.32$), 3–4 times per week ($M = 81.31$), 1–2 times per week ($M = 80.21$), and several times per month ($M = 81.88$) all had significantly higher CT mean scores than those who never used AI tools ($M = 73.56$).

Table 7 presents the mean CT scores of middle school students, categorized by the AI tools they use most frequently, along with the results of the one-way ANOVA analysis.

Table 7. One-way ANOVA results for middle school students' CT scores based on the most frequently used AI tools

Group	*n*	*Mean*	*SD*	df_1, df_2	*F*	*p*	η^2	Post Hoc
1. ChatGPT	211	81.04	8.53	2, 368	5.02	.007**	.03	1-2, 1-3
2. Google Gemini	97	78.25	8.19					
3. Other	63	78.11	9.32					

Note. $p < .01$**.

As shown in Table 7, the one-way ANOVA revealed a statistically significant difference in CT scores among middle school students based on their most frequently used AI tools ($F(2, 368) = 5.02, p < .01, \eta^2 = .03$). This difference represents a small effect size, indicating that the primary AI tools used account for 3% of the variance in CT scores. To identify the source of the difference, a post hoc Tukey HSD test was conducted. The results showed that middle school students using ChatGPT ($M = 81.04$) had significantly higher CT scores than those using Google Gemini ($M = 78.25$) or other AI tools ($M = 78.11$).

Table 8 presents the total CT scores, mean values, and standard deviation, along with the results of the independent samples *t*-test conducted based on middle school students' awareness of the AI-powered virtual teacher concept.

Table 8. Independent samples t-test results for middle school students' CT scores based on their awareness of the AI-powered virtual teacher concept

Group	*n*	*Mean*	*SD*	*df*	*t*	*p*	*d*
Aware	160	80.91	9.06	369	2.13	.034*	.22
Not aware	211	78.98	8.30				

Note. $p < .05$*.

As shown in Table 8, the independent samples *t*-test revealed a statistically significant difference in the total CT attitude scores of middle school students based on their familiarity with the concept of AI-based virtual teachers ($t(369) = 2.13, p < .05, d = .22$) This difference represents a small effect size, indicating that awareness of AI-powered virtual teachers accounts for 3% of the variance in CT scores. As indicated in Table 8, the mean total CT score of students aware of the concept of AI-based virtual teachers ($M = 80.91$) was significantly higher than that of students unaware of the concept ($M = 78.98$).

Table 9 presents the total CT scores, means, and standard deviation values, as well as the results of the independent samples *t*-test conducted for middle school students based on their usage status of AI tools in the social studies course.

Table 9. Independent samples t-test results for middle school students' CT scores based on their usage status of AI tools in social studies classes

Group	*n*	*Mean*	*SD*	*df*	*t*	*p*	*d*
Aware	145	80.48	8.16	369	1.04	.298	.11
Not aware	226	79.44	8.99				

As shown in Table 9, the independent samples *t*-test results indicated no significant difference in the total mean scores of CT attitudes among middle school students based on their use of AI tools in social studies courses ($t(369) = 1.04$, $p > .05$, $d = .11$).

Table 10 presents the mean and standard deviation values of the total CT scores of middle school students based on their usage of the AI-powered virtual teacher in social studies classes, along with the results of the independent samples t-test conducted.

Table 10. Independent samples t-test results for middle school students' CT scores based on AI-powered virtual teacher usage in social studies classes

Group	*n*	*Mean*	*SD*	*df*	*t*	*p*	*d*
Aware	135	79.90	8.57	369	.14	.890	.01
Not aware	236	79.77	8.75				

As shown in Table 10, the independent samples t-test revealed no significant difference in the total mean scores for CT attitudes among middle school students based on their use of the AI-powered virtual teacher in the social studies course ($t(369) = .14$, $p > .05$, $d = .01$).

Table 11 presents the mean CT scores of middle school students based on their willingness to take classes with a virtual teacher in the social studies course, along with the results of the one-way ANOVA analysis conducted.

Table 11. One-way ANOVA results for middle school students' CT scores based on their willingness to take classes with a virtual teacher in the social studies course

	n	*Mean*	*SD*	df_1, df_2	*F*	*p*	η^2	**Post Hoc**
1. Unwilling	77	76.60	9.86	2, 368	6.95	.001**	.02	1-2, 1-3
2. Neutral	115	80.44	7.75					
3. Willing	179	80.79	8.41					

Note. $p < .01$**.

As presented in Table 11, the one-way ANOVA revealed a statistically significant difference in CT scores among middle school students based on their willingness to learn with virtual teachers in social studies classes ($F(2, 368) = 6.95, p < .01, \eta^2 = 02$). This difference represents a small effect size, indicating that willingness to learn with virtual teachers accounts for 2% of the variance in CT scores. To identify the source of this difference, a post hoc Tukey HSD test was conducted. The results showed that middle school students who were willing to learn with virtual teachers ($M = 80.79$) and those who were neutral toward this approach ($M = 80.44$) exhibited significantly higher CT scores than students unwilling to engage with virtual teachers ($M = 76.60$).

DISCUSSION

This study examined the relationship between AI use and CT skills among middle school students, providing insights into their awareness and utilization of AI and virtual teachers. The findings revealed that nearly all middle school students were aware of AI, and more than half regularly used AI tools. These results align with prior research indicating widespread awareness and utilization of AI tools among middle and high school students (Chiu, 2024; Lee et al., 2021; Martin et al., 2024; Wang et al., 2024). This supports Lampropoulos & Papadakis's (2025) assertion that AI transforms learning experiences by fostering interactive and engaging environments, which is reflected in students' openness to AI-powered tools. AI-powered tools have emerged with the ability to act as intelligent human-like tutors, offering personalized learning experiences that take students' unique characteristics, needs, knowledge, and preferences into account. They have the potential to improve students' learning outcomes, engagement, and motivation, enhance their academic performance, and increase their social skills.

Data from the Turkish Statistical Institute (2024a) Survey on Information and Communication Technology (ICT) Usage in Households and by Individuals confirms the pervasive use of smartphones and social media platforms among youth in Türkiye. Furthermore, recent digitalization initiatives in the Turkish Education System (e.g., the FATİH Project, Education Information Network [EBA]) have increased students' familiarity with technology-based learning tools. The study, titled "Artificial Intelligence and the Future of Teaching and Learning", conducted by the U.S. Department of Education's Office of Educational Technology (2023), also found that students frequently use AI-powered tools.

The study also identified ChatGPT as one of the most commonly preferred AI tools across different age groups. Similarly, the present research found that ChatGPT was the most frequently used AI tool among students. Research by Sidoti et al.

(2025) for the Pew Research Center indicated that 79% of youth are familiar with ChatGPT. Rapid technological adaptation and the integration of technology into education may have facilitated the swift proliferation of AI among Turkish middle school students.

Analysis of middle school students' purposes for using AI reveals that they primarily utilize it to complete homework, ask questions they are curious about, and for entertainment. Sidoti et al. (2025) similarly found that teens who are most familiar with ChatGPT are more likely to frequently use it to ask questions and complete schoolwork. Due to the traditional structure of the Turkish education system, middle school students are subjected to a heavy homework load and are educated within an exam-oriented framework (Eranıl et al., 2024; Martı Emel, 2025). This may prompt students to seek practical solutions, with AI-powered tools acting as intelligent human-like tutors to offer personalized learning experiences (Yim & Su, 2025). Turkish culture traditionally emphasizes respect for elders and hesitancy to question authority figures (Kağıtçıbaşı, 2017). The non-judgmental and consistently accessible nature of AI can readily enable students to satisfy their curiosities. This benefit may be particularly pronounced for students who exhibit shyness and reticence. Finally, the use of AI for entertainment among middle school students may reflect broader habits of social media and technology utilization for leisure in Türkiye (Turkish Statistical Institute, 2024a), which is consistent with research findings that students perceived AI learning as an enjoyable experience (Yim & Su, 2025).

This study found that approximately four out of ten middle school students were familiar with the concept of virtual teachers. International studies indicate that developed countries are more likely to utilize virtual teachers or AI-powered educational tools (Luckin et al., 2016). The 40% awareness rate in Türkiye suggests these technologies are still in the early adoption phase. These findings underscore a pressing need for targeted professional development programs that equip teachers with virtual teaching technologies and empower them to effectively integrate these tools into their pedagogical practices. Policymakers should prioritize investments in teacher training initiatives that address both technical competencies and pedagogical strategies for integrating AI. The Turkish Education System has traditionally been characterized by a teacher-centered structure (Eranıl et al., 2024; Martı Emel, 2025). Consequently, a significant proportion of students expect the physical presence of an instructor throughout the learning process. Additionally, in the context of Turkish educational culture, the high regard for teachers and the personal dimension of the teacher-student relationship may influence the acceptance of the virtual teacher concept. Regarding the use of AI tools in social studies classes, approximately four in ten students reported using these tools in their social studies classes. The interdisciplinary nature of social studies, encompassing historical events, geographical knowledge, and societal processes, makes it suitable for AI integration. While AI tools, such as personalized learning materials and simulations, can enhance learning experiences (Luckin, 2017), the majority of students not yet using them in social studies indicate barriers related to access, awareness, or pedagogical adaptation. This gap underscores the pressing need for curriculum reform and professional development that equip social studies teachers with the knowledge and skills to effectively utilize AI tools in their classrooms.

Although 54.7% of middle school students believed an AI-powered virtual teacher would be helpful in social studies, only 35% reported using one. Research shows global trends of increasing virtual teacher adoption, with AI tools positively impacting knowledge access, problem-solving, and personalized learning (Chen et al., 2020). However, adoption varies based on countries' technological infrastructure, educational policies, and teacher attitudes toward AI. This disparity between perceived value and actual use highlights the importance of policy interventions that address infrastructure gaps, provide equitable access to AI tools, and support teachers in implementing these technologies. Teacher training programs must specifically address concerns about AI replacing human educators while demonstrating how AI can augment, rather than replace, traditional teaching methods. In Türkiye, digital literacy and technology integration are still in development, potentially limiting middle school students' use of advanced tools, such as virtual teachers. Students identified key advantages of virtual teachers over human teachers as 24/7 accessibility, repeated explanations without frustration, and judgment-free questioning. The most critical advantage of the virtual teacher in providing continuous learning support and flexibility in learning time is its 24/7 accessibility (Alam, 2023; Basri, 2024; Rızvı, 2023; Shoukat et al., 2025). After school hours, students have the opportunity to review difficult topics and meet urgent learning demands, such as studying for exams or completing homework. Thus, virtual teachers eliminate physical and temporal constraints of traditional teaching (Alam, 2023; Rızvı, 2023). Another significant advantage of virtual teachers is their ability to explain concepts repeatedly, allowing students to learn at a personalized pace. While it is often impractical for a teacher in a traditional classroom to explain a topic more than two or three times, virtual teachers can patiently repeat the same content as many times as needed (Basri, 2024; Shoukat et al., 2025). This feature may serve as an ideal support mechanism, particularly for students who learn at a slower pace. Furthermore, the ability to ask questions without fear of judgment enables students to overcome the anxiety of asking seemingly simple questions in front of peers or teachers, helping them feel more at ease in the learning process.

Approximately half of the middle school students expressed interest in learning social studies with an AI-powered virtual teacher. They believed that such tools would be most beneficial for reviewing misunderstood topics, exam preparation, receiving additional explanations, and gaining a deeper understanding of the subject.

When examining students' interest in AI-powered virtual teachers within the context of the Turkish Education System, overcrowded classrooms in Türkiye can make it challenging for teachers to provide individualized support to every student (Turkish Statistical Institute, 2024b). This finding has important implications for educational policy and teacher professional development. Given the reality of large class sizes, professional development programs should train teachers to use AI tools as complementary resources that extend their capacity to provide personalized support. Policy initiatives should explore blended learning models that strategically combine human instruction with AI-powered virtual teachers to address the individualization challenges inherent in overcrowded classrooms. Centralized examinations, such as the High School Entrance Exam (LGS), also hold significant importance within the Turkish Education System. Students' perception of AI-powered teachers as a tool for exam preparation appears consistent with this competitive environment. AI's provision of practical solutions and test strategies may also alleviate exam anxiety.

An examination of middle school students' perceptions regarding the capabilities of AI-powered virtual teachers reveals that they most frequently believe these tools could enhance their homework-related skills, including research, idea generation, interpretation and analysis, and problem-solving. Homework is fundamental to learning in Türkiye (Avcı & Özgenel, 2024; Iflazoglu & Hong, 2012), and students often need support for research-intensive social studies homework, such as projects and presentations. Middle school students' belief in the potential of AI-powered teaching to enhance research, source evaluation, problem-solving, and analytical thinking skills highlights the value of virtual teachers in education. By helping students filter reliable sources, suggest relevant keywords, present multiple perspectives, and offer scenario-based simulations for complex social studies topics, AI-powered virtual teachers can support the development of original thinking and critical inquiry skills. These findings suggest that professional development should focus on teaching educators how to design homework assignments that strategically incorporate AI tools to develop students' research and analytical capabilities while maintaining academic integrity. Teachers require training on how to evaluate AI-assisted work and guide students in utilizing these tools ethically and effectively.

Approximately 40% of respondents expressed the belief that virtual teachers would enhance the enjoyment of learning, while 56% highlighted the benefit of personalized pacing. Additionally, 45% anticipated an improved comprehension of the content, and 35% expected a heightened interest in learning. Conversely, 55% of participants asserted that virtual teachers could not serve as substitutes for human educators, and 28% questioned their reliability. The focus on enjoyable and personalized learning, with 40-56% of respondents endorsing these benefits, corroborates research indicating that AI tools facilitate personalized support, brainstorming, research, multimedia analysis, and administrative tasks (Chan & Hu, 2023; Chiu,

2024). Virtual teachers' ability to offer interactive tools such as animations and game-based learning may be more appealing to students than traditional lectures, which they often find monotonous (Lewis, 2014; Mason et al., 2013; Park & Kim, 2015). Virtual teachers can also facilitate student comprehension by helping students better understand the subject matter and by captivating their interest. This is achieved by concretizing abstract subjects, such as historical events and geographical concepts prevalent in social studies, through the provision of visual and auditory support to students (Park & Kim, 2015).

Students' negative perceptions of AI generally stem from their belief that virtual teachers cannot replace human educators. Research by Jose & Jose (2024) revealed that educators' primary concerns about AI stem from feeling professionally threatened and the belief that AI cannot replicate uniquely human teaching skills. This finding highlights the crucial importance of professional development programs that enable teachers to appreciate their indispensable role in education while fostering their confidence in utilizing AI as a pedagogical tool. Teacher training should explicitly address the complementary relationship between human and AI instruction, emphasizing the unique socio-emotional, ethical, and cultural competencies that human teachers bring to the learning environment. This perspective may be influenced by Turkish culture, where teachers are regarded not only as knowledge transmitters but also as role models (Martı Emel, 2025). Furthermore, the limited capacity of virtual teachers to comprehend students' emotional needs could lead to deficiencies in students' social-emotional learning (Graefen & Fazal, 2024).

Students who were aware of AI exhibited significantly higher CT skills than those who were unaware of it. These findings support studies showing AI tools enhance CT across contexts (Boucher et al., 2021; Essien et al., 2024; Khairani Zakaria et al., 2025; Liu & Wang, 2024; Lou, 2018; Wang & Xue, 2024). For instance, studies have identified AI-powered applications as effective tools for developing higher-order skills, particularly in the context of CT (Boucher et al., 2021; Irwanto, 2025; Khairani Zakaria et al., 2025; Liu & Wang, 2024). The significant relationship between AI awareness and CT skills suggests that educational policy should prioritize AI literacy as a core component of curriculum standards. Professional development initiatives must equip teachers with the knowledge and pedagogical approaches necessary to foster students' AI awareness while simultaneously developing their CT capabilities. This potential is especially salient in social studies education. Generative AI tools can foster CT by encouraging students to examine multiple perspectives, support problem-solving through scenario-based simulations, and enhance collaboration via interactive tasks. Such opportunities are directly aligned with the core objectives of social studies, including the cultivation of democratic citizenship, the ability to evaluate diverse viewpoints, and the development of media and information literacy — essential for responsible civic participation in the digital age.

Empirical findings highlight specific mechanisms through which AI tools promote CT skills. Specifically, Khairani Zakaria et al. (2025), through their comprehensive literature review, found that using AI is effective in enhancing students' CT abilities. AI-powered applications offer students opportunities to evaluate events and concepts from diverse perspectives (Sok & Heng, 2023). For instance, in analyzing a historical event, the varied sources and interpretations provided by AI can enable students to move beyond a singular understanding, fostering multi-dimensional thinking. Furthermore, as Boucher et al. (2021) noted, the personalized feedback offered by AI helps students identify deficiencies in their thought processes and make corrections.

The potential of AI to enhance CT, as demonstrated by these studies, is now being seen in concrete implementations within Turkish educational settings. Recent implementations in Turkish educational contexts have shown how AI-facilitated lessons on topics like global citizenship can enhance both CT and cultural empathy. These emerging cases highlight the professional development needs identified in this study, particularly in the context of integrating ethical AI, which ensures cultural responsiveness and equitable access in diverse educational settings, such as Türkiye (Küçükuncular & Ertugan, 2025). Teacher training programs should incorporate modules on culturally responsive AI pedagogy, ethical considerations in AI use, and strategies for ensuring equitable access to AI tools across diverse student populations. Policymakers should establish guidelines and standards for the ethical use of AI in educational contexts that protect student data privacy and ensure transparency in AI-generated content.

This study found a positive correlation between the frequency of AI use and CT skills. Specifically, individuals who never use AI demonstrated significantly higher CT skills compared to those who use it once a month or more. These findings support research indicating a positive relationship between AI use and CT skills. For instance, Mayasari et al. (2024) discovered a moderate positive correlation between students' frequency of AI use and their CT skills. Styve et al. (2024) reported that AI tools such as ChatGPT, GitHub Copilot, and Amazon CodeWhisperer are effective and beneficial for developing students' CT abilities. Fakour & Imani (2025) found ChatGPT to be a useful AI tool for enhancing students' learning and CT skills. However, research by Chan & Tsi (2024) revealed that a significant portion of students believe AI-powered teachers cannot replace human educators. Regular AI use can help students improve their abilities in systematic analysis, data evaluation, and synthesizing alternative perspectives (Chan & Hu, 2023; Kouzov, 2019; Sok & Heng, 2023; Suriano et al., 2025; Wang & Fan, 2025). Concurrently, AI-powered tools can encourage students to think and inquire through interactive scenarios and real-time feedback. Furthermore, AI tools can contribute to the gradual development of students' CT skills by adjusting tasks or questions based on student performance. These findings suggest that professional development should teach educators how to design learning activities that promote frequent and meaningful engagement with AI tools. Teachers need training on how to progressively scaffold AI use, starting with structured activities and gradually moving toward more autonomous student engagement with these technologies.

Differences in CT scores among middle school students, based on the AI program they used, revealed that students utilizing ChatGPT demonstrated higher levels of CT skills compared to those using Google Gemini and other AI tools. Suriano et al. (2025) found that the use of ChatGPT is an effective method for enhancing students' complex thinking skills and that individuals who use and are knowledgeable about ChatGPT tend to have higher CT abilities. Similarly, Wang & Fan (2025) concluded from their meta-analysis that ChatGPT has positive effects on developing students' higher-order thinking skills, improving student performance, and enhancing learning perceptions.

The differentiation in CT skills between students using ChatGPT and those using other AI engines may be attributed to ChatGPT's language processing capabilities and interaction quality, its Socratic questioning approach, distinctions in content presentation, and its performance in the Turkish language (Singh et al., 2023; Suriano et al., 2025; Wang & Fan, 2025; Welsby & Cheung, 2023). For example, ChatGPT's advanced natural language processing algorithms can facilitate more human-like and context-sensitive dialogues with students. Its detailed responses to open-ended questions may help students evaluate topics from multiple perspectives. Furthermore, compared to other AI tools like Google Gemini, ChatGPT provides longer-form and more analytical answers (Singh et al., 2023). This characteristic may contribute to students' enhanced ability to generate diverse scenarios compared to users of other AI tools. Additionally, ChatGPT's performance in Turkish is more advanced than that of other AI tools. These tool-specific differences have important implications for educational policy and teacher training. Policymakers should consider language-specific performance when selecting AI tools for educational contexts and ensure that procurement decisions prioritize tools with strong native language capabilities. Professional development should familiarize teachers with the strengths and limitations of different AI platforms, enabling them to make informed decisions about which tools best serve their pedagogical objectives and students' linguistic needs. Future AI tools should incorporate culturally responsive designs, as suggested by Crowder (2024) and Samuel et al. (2023), to enhance their capacity to comprehend, interpret, and provide culturally relevant examples within local and cultural contexts, thereby better supporting diverse student backgrounds and promoting inclusive CT.

This study found that middle school students who were aware of the concept of AI-powered virtual teachers demonstrated significantly higher levels of CT skills than those who were not. This finding aligns with a systematic literature review on

AI literacy in K-12 education by Casal-Otero et al. (2023), which concluded that students exposed to AI-related learning experiences, such as interacting with virtual tutors or AI-supported tools, developed technical, conceptual, and applied skills that foster CT. Furthermore, another study by Dimitriadou & Lanitis (2023) revealed that students educated in smart classrooms integrating AI technologies, including virtual instructors, enhanced their creative and CT abilities.

There was no significant difference in CT mean scores among middle school students based on their use of AI tools in social studies or their use of AI-powered virtual teachers. However, a significant difference emerged in CT mean scores based on students' willingness to use a virtual teacher for social studies lessons. Specifically, students who were willing to study social studies with a virtual teacher showed significantly higher CT scores than those who were not. These findings suggest that students who are open to novelty, curious, and inclined towards active learning may possess stronger CT skills. The research findings align with previous studies. For example, it has been found that students who are willing to use AI-supported educational tools have a higher CT disposition. Similarly, Dimitriadou & Lanitis (2023) reported that students with high curiosity regarding AI tools tend to have strong CT, problem-solving, and perspective-taking skills. This finding highlights the importance of cultivating positive attitudes toward AI among both students and teachers. Professional development programs should include components that address teachers' attitudes and beliefs about AI, helping them model openness to innovation and technological adoption for their students. Educational policy should support the creation of school environments that encourage experimentation with new technologies and reward innovative pedagogical practices that effectively integrate AI tools.

LIMITATIONS

This study has several limitations. First, it was conducted with a limited number of middle school students in Türkiye's Central Black Sea Region. Consequently, the generalizability of the findings to middle school students in other regions of Turkey, particularly those residing in large metropolitan areas for most of their lives, is constrained. Furthermore, the experiences of Turkish middle school students with AI may differ from those of their counterparts in other parts of the world, thereby limiting the generalizability of these findings globally. Second, this research relied on self-report scales to assess students' CT levels. This approach introduces limitations inherent in self-report measures, such as the tendency for central tendency bias, social desirability bias, and the potential for participants' emotional states to influence their responses. Additionally, the absence of skill-based scales to measure

CT abilities might have led participants to over- or underestimate their CT skills. Third, the study's focus on AI usage patterns specifically within social studies classes may not fully reflect students' frequency of AI use in other subjects. Finally, given that this research employed a cross-sectional design, causal inferences regarding the relationships among the findings cannot be drawn.

PRACTICAL IMPLICATIONS

AI is receiving increasing attention worldwide, but its impact on schools has not been extensively studied. The lack of established frameworks and management protocols for AI adoption in educational settings has led to several unresolved inquiries concerning AI's overall impact on learning environments. The uncertainty regarding AI's impact on the formation of CT, a vital talent that must be nurtured throughout schooling, is particularly concerning. These gaps highlight a pressing need for rigorous research and clear, evidence-based guidelines to inform education policy and practice in the age of AI.

Despite the study's limitations, its findings have significant implications for both practitioners and researchers in education. First, the results indicate a need to develop skills among middle school students that will enable them to use AI tools consciously and critically, including information verification, source evaluation, and ethical use. To this end, AI literacy courses could be integrated into middle school curricula.

AI is attracting heightened global interest; nevertheless, its effects on educational systems are predominantly unexamined. The lack of established frameworks and management protocols for AI adoption in educational settings has led to several unresolved inquiries concerning AI's overall impact on learning environments. The uncertainty regarding AI's impact on the formation of CT, a vital talent that must be nurtured throughout schooling, is particularly concerning. The identified knowledge gaps underscore the necessity for rigorous research and evidence-based guidelines to guide educational policy and practice in the era of AI.

A critical gap in current AI implementation is the challenge of aligning AI tools with national curriculum standards. While this study demonstrates positive correlations between AI use and CT skills, it remains essential that educators carefully evaluate how AI-generated content aligns with established learning objectives and the specific cultural contexts of the social studies curriculum. Notably, the risk of cultural misalignment becomes particularly pronounced when AI systems trained on predominantly Western datasets attempt to address topics central to local history and cultural heritage. To address these challenges, several key conclusions can guide the development of AI literacy initiatives in K-12 education. First, AI literacy should be integrated into existing curricula through an interdisciplinary and competency-based approach, rather than being taught as a separate subject. By integrating AI education with disciplinary content, such as social studies, it can transcend traditional subject boundaries, promoting active, project-based learning that engages students in contextualized activities. Second, AI literacy should enhance learning outcomes in curricular subjects, deepening students' engagement with areas such as historical analysis and civic education. Ultimately, the effectiveness of AI literacy programs hinges on strengthening teachers' competencies through collaborative design processes, which involve educators, curriculum designers, and AI specialists in developing pedagogically sound and contextually relevant strategies for social studies instruction.

The research also suggests that teachers require in-service training to effectively integrate AI tools into social studies instruction. Specifically, such training should focus on how to utilize AI platforms like AI-powered simulations, virtual reality applications, and interactive discussions, while also educating teachers about the limitations and advantages of these tools. Furthermore, to foster students' CT skills, AI tools should be supported with applications such as scenario-based simulations, multi-perspective discussions, and source verification activities. For instance, tools like ChatGPT can facilitate dialogues about historical events, prompting students to evaluate diverse viewpoints.

Virtual teachers should be positioned as complements to, rather than replacements for, human teachers. In this supportive role, educators should leverage virtual teachers for tasks such as preparing lesson materials, providing additional explanations, or addressing students' individual needs. Given the socio-emotional learning limitations of AI tools identified in this research, virtual teachers should be used in a guiding capacity, emphasizing the human aspects of real teachers, such as providing emotional support and serving as role models. In addition, the technological infrastructure of schools in Türkiye should be enhanced to support the widespread adoption of AI-powered educational tools. Integrating AI-powered tools into existing platforms, such as the EBA in Türkiye, would ensure that all students have access to these technologies.

CONCLUSION

This study investigated the use of AI and AI-powered virtual teachers among middle school students in social studies, as well as the relationship between this utilization and CT skills. The findings indicated that most students are aware of AI and engage with it regularly, with ChatGPT identified as the most frequently used AI tool. Students primarily used AI for homework, answering questions, and entertainment purposes. About four in ten students reported using AI tools and virtual teachers in social studies classes. Over half believe that AI-powered virtual teachers could be beneficial. Key advantages include 24-hour accessibility, the ability to ask questions without embarrassment, and personalized learning paces. Students noted that virtual teachers help review difficult topics, prepare for exams, and complete homework.

Students who were aware of and regularly used AI had higher CT skills than those who did not. Similarly, students who understood the concept of AI-powered virtual teachers and wanted to use them in lessons had significantly higher CT skills. Students unfamiliar and unwilling to use them had lower CT skills. However, no link was found between using AI or virtual teachers in social studies and students' CT skills. This suggests that effectiveness in developing CT skills depends on the context, frequency, and level of AI literacy.

The results indicate that AI use is prevalent among students within the Turkish education system, although the adoption of virtual teachers remains limited. Students' positive attitudes toward AI, particularly in relation to personalized learning and accessibility, underscore the educational potential of these technologies. Nevertheless, many students maintain that virtual teachers cannot substitute for human educators, reflecting the esteemed status of teachers in Turkish culture. These concerns further emphasize the necessity of enhancing AI literacy and information verification skills.

The study found a positive correlation between AI awareness and CT skills in middle school students. However, these findings should be considered in conjunction with the ethical and practical challenges of AI in education. Despite the benefits, concerns about data privacy, algorithmic bias, and digital addiction remain. Addressing these issues is essential for responsible and fair AI use in education. Future research should measure academic outcomes and monitor the long-term socio-emotional and ethical impacts of student-AI interactions.

REFERENCES

Alam, A. (2023). Harnessing the power of AI to create intelligent tutoring systems for enhanced classroom experience and improved learning outcomes. In Rajakumar, G., Du, K.-L., & Rocha, Á. (Eds.), *Intelligent communication technologies and virtual mobile networks* (Vol. 171, pp. 571–591). Springer. DOI: 10.1007/978-981-99-1767-9_42

Ali, O., Murray, P. A., Momin, M., Dwivedi, Y. K., & Malik, T. (2024). The effects of artificial intelligence applications in educational settings: Challenges and strategies. *Technological Forecasting and Social Change, 199*, 123076. DOI: 10.1016/j.techfore.2023.123076

Avcı, S., & Özgenel, M. (2024). Adaptation and psychometric evaluation of homework management, teacher and parent involvement scales for middle schoolers in Turkey. *International Journal of Psychology and Educational Studies, 11*(2), 179–200. DOI: 10.52380/ijpes.2024.11.2.1357

Basri, W. S. (2024). Effectiveness of AI-powered tutoring systems in enhancing learning outcomes. *Eurasian Journal of Educational Research (EJER), 110.*

Beck, T. A., & Parker, W. (2021). *Social studies in elementary education* (16th ed.). Pearson.

Boucher, E. M., Harake, N. R., Ward, H. E., Stoeckl, S. E., Vargas, J., Minkel, J., Parks, A. C., & Zilca, R. (2021). Artificially intelligent chatbots in digital mental health interventions: A review. *Expert Review of Medical Devices, 18*(sup1), 37–49. DOI: 10.1080/17434440.2021.2013200

Casal-Otero, L., Catala, A., Fernández-Morante, C., Taboada, M., Cebreiro, B., & Barro, S. (2023). AI literacy in K-12: A systematic literature review. *International Journal of STEM Education, 10*(29), 29. Advance online publication. DOI: 10.1186/s40594-023-00418-7

Chan, C. K. Y., & Hu, W. (2023). Students' voices on generative AI: Perceptions, benefits, and challenges in higher education. *International Journal of Educational Technology in Higher Education, 20*(1), 43. DOI: 10.1186/s41239-023-00411-8

Chan, C. K. Y., & Tsi, L. H. Y. (2024). Will generative AI replace teachers in higher education? A study of teacher and student perceptions. *Studies in Educational Evaluation, 83*, 101395. DOI: 10.1016/j.stueduc.2024.101395

Chen, X., Xie, H., & Hwang, G.-J. (2020). A multi-perspective study on artificial intelligence in education: Grants, conferences, journals, software tools, institutions, and researchers. *Computers and Education: Artificial Intelligence, 1*, 100005. DOI: 10.1016/j.caeai.2020.100005

Chiu, T. K. F. (2024). The impact of Generative AI (GenAI) on practices, policies and research direction in education: A case of ChatGPT and Midjourney. *Interactive Learning Environments, 32*(10), 6187–6203. DOI: 10.1080/10494820.2023.2253861

Clark, C. H., & van Kessel, C. (2025). *AI in social studies education: Tools for thoughtful practice with generative artificial intelligence*. Teachers College Press.

Cohen, J. (1992). A power primer. *Psychological Bulletin, 112*(1), 155–159. https://psycnet.apa.org/doi/10.1037/0033-2909.112.1.155. DOI: 10.1037/0033-2909.112.1.155 PMID: 19565683

Crowder, J. (2024). What happens when a chatbot gives detrimental advice? Who's Responsible? In Crowder, J. (Ed.), *AI chatbots: The good, the bad, and the ugly* (pp. 121–133). Springer Nature Switzerland., DOI: 10.1007/978-3-031-45509-4_13

Darwin, R., Rusdin, D., Mukminatien, N., Suryati, N., Laksmi, E. D., & Marzuki, . (2023). Critical thinking in the AI era: An exploration of EFL students' perceptions, benefits, and limitations. *Cogent Education, 11*(1), 2290342. DOI: 10.1080/2331186X.2023.2290342

Dimitriadou, E., & Lanitis, A. (2023). A critical evaluation, challenges, and future perspectives of using artificial intelligence and emerging technologies in smart classrooms. *Smart Learning Environments, 10*(12), 12. Advance online publication. DOI: 10.1186/s40561-023-00231-3 PMID: 40478141

Eranıl, A. K., Eyice, R., Atan, M., & Alici, T. (2024). Investigations in the Turkish Education System: Structure, process and its reflections. *Denetişim, 30*(30), 1–15. Advance online publication. DOI: 10.58348/denetisim.1383929

Essien, A., Bukoye, O. T., O'Dea, X., & Kremantzis, M. (2024). The influence of AI text generators on critical thinking skills in UK business schools. *Studies in Higher Education, 49*(5), 865–882. DOI: 10.1080/03075079.2024.2316881

Facione, P. A. (1990). *Critical thinking: A statement of expert consensus for purposes of educational assessment and instruction*. The California Academic Press., https://eric.ed.gov/?id=ED315423

Fakour, H., & Imani, M. (2025). Socratic wisdom in the age of AI: A comparative study of ChatGPT and human tutors in enhancing critical thinking skills. *Frontiers in Education, 10*, 1–12. DOI: 10.3389/feduc.2025.1528603

Faul, F., Erdfelder, E., Lang, A.-G., & Buchner, A. (2007). G*Power 3: A flexible statistical power analysis program for the social, behavioral, and biomedical sciences. *Behavior Research Methods*, *39*(2), 2. Advance online publication. DOI: 10.3758/BF03193146 PMID: 17695343

Field, A. P. (2024). *Discovering statistics using IBM SPSS statistics* (6th ed.). SAGE Publications.

George, D., & Mallery, P. (2024). *IBM SPSS Statistics 29 step by step: A simple guide and reference* (18th ed.). Routledge. DOI: 10.4324/9781032622156

Gerlich, M. (2025). AI tools in society: Impacts on cognitive offloading and the future of critical thinking. *Societies (Basel, Switzerland)*, *15*(1), 6. DOI: 10.3390/soc15010006

Gonsalves, C. (2024). Generative AI's impact on critical thinking: Revisiting Bloom's Taxonomy. *Journal of Marketing Education*, 02734753241305980. Advance online publication. DOI: 10.1177/02734753241305980

Graefen, B., & Fazal, N. (2024). From chat bots to virtual tutors: An overview of chat GPT's role in the future of education. *Archives of Pharmacy Practice (Mumbai)*, *15*(2), 43–52. DOI: 10.51847/TOuppjEDSX

Hair, J. F., Black, W. C., Babin, B. J., & Anderson, R. E. (2018). *Multivariate data analysis*. Cengage.

Hanna, M. G., Pantanowitz, L., Jackson, B., Palmer, O., Visweswaran, S., Pantanowitz, J., Deebajah, M., & Rashidi, H. H. (2025). Ethical and bias considerations in artificial intelligence/machine learning. *Modern Pathology*, *38*(3), 100686. DOI: 10.1016/j.modpat.2024.100686 PMID: 39694331

Hartshorne, R., Waring, S. M., & Okraski, H. (2019). Developing well-informed, critically thinking, and active citizens through the connection of modeling & simulation and social studies education. *The Clearing House: A Journal of Educational Strategies, Issues and Ideas*, *92*(1–2), 48–52. DOI: 10.1080/00098655.2019.1571988

Holmes, W., Bialik, M., & Fadel, C. (2019). *Artificial intelligence in education: Promises and implications for teaching & learning* (1st ed.). The Center for Curriculum Redesign.

Iflazoglu, A., & Hong, E. (2012). Homework motivation and preferences of Turkish students. *Research Papers in Education*, *27*(3), 343–363. DOI: 10.1080/02671522.2010.529581

Irwanto, I. (2025). Research trends on artificial intelligence in K-12 education in Asia: A bibliometric analysis using the Scopus database (1996–2025). *Discover Artificial Intelligence*, *5*(1), 155. DOI: 10.1007/s44163-025-00389-4

Jose, J., & Jose, B. J. (2024). Educators' academic insights on artificial intelligence: Challenges and opportunities. *Electronic Journal of e-Learning*, *22*(2), 59–77. DOI: 10.34190/ejel.21.5.3272

Kağıtçıbaşı, Ç. (2017). *Family, Self, and Human Development Across Cultures: Theory and Applications*. Routledge. DOI: 10.4324/9781315205281

Karabulut, H., Gökçe, H., & Kariper, A. (2023). Development of Critical Thinking Skills Scale (Secondary school sample). *Kirikkale University Journal of Social Sciences*, *13*(2), 443–461.

Karakose, T., Tülübaş, T., & Papadakis, S. (2022). Revealing the intellectual structure and evolution of digital addiction research: An integrated bibliometric and science mapping approach. *International Journal of Environmental Research and Public Health*, *19*(22), 14883. DOI: 10.3390/ijerph192214883 PMID: 36429603

Khairani Zakaria, N. Y., Hashim, H., & Jamaludin, K. A. (2025). Exploring the impact of AI on critical thinking development in ESL: A systematic literature review. *Arab World English Journal*, *16*(Special Issue on Artificial Intelligence), 330–347. DOI: 10.24093/awej/AI.19

Kouzov, O. (2019). The new paradigms in education and support of critical thinking with artificial intelligence (AI) tools. *Serdica Journal of Computing*, *13*(1-2), 27–40. DOI: 10.55630/sjc.2019.13.27-40

Küçükuncular, A., & Ertugan, A. (2025). Teaching in the AI era: Sustainable digital education through ethical integration and teacher empowerment. *Sustainability (Basel)*, *17*(16), 7405. DOI: 10.3390/su17167405

Lampropoulos, G., & Papadakis, S. (2025). The educational value of artificial intelligence and social robots. In Lampropoulos, G., & Papadakis, S. (Eds.), *Social Robots in Education: How to Effectively Introduce Social Robots into Classrooms* (Vol. 1194, pp. 3–15). Springer Nature Switzerland. DOI: 10.1007/978-3-031-82915-4_1

Lee, I., Ali, S., Zhang, H., DiPaola, D., & Breazeal, C. (2021). Developing middle school students' AI literacy. *Proceedings of the 52nd ACM Technical Symposium on Computer Science Education*, 191–197. DOI: 10.1145/3408877.3432513

Lewis, D. I. (2014). *The pedagogical benefits and pitfalls of virtual tools for teaching and learning laboratory practices in the biological sciences*. The Higher Education Academy.

Liu, J., Ma, J., & Li, S. (2025). Research on school-based AI curriculum design and practice for cultivating computational thinking in high school students. *Education and Information Technologies, 30*(6), 7949–7993. DOI: 10.1007/s10639-024-13115-x

Liu, W., & Wang, Y. (2024). The effects of using AI tools on critical thinking in English literature classes among EFL learners: An intervention study. *European Journal of Education, 59*(4), e12804. DOI: 10.1111/ejed.12804

Lou, J. (2018). Improvement in university students' critical thinking following a strategic thinking training program. *NeuroQuantology : An Interdisciplinary Journal of Neuroscience and Quantum Physics, 16*(5), 91–96. DOI: 10.14704/nq.2018.16.5.1310

Lubbe, A., Marais, E., & Kruger, D. (2025). Cultivating independent thinkers: The triad of artificial intelligence, Bloom's taxonomy and critical thinking in assessment pedagogy. *Education and Information Technologies, 30*(12), 17589–17622. DOI: 10.1007/s10639-025-13476-x

Luckin, R. (2017). Towards artificial intelligence-based assessment systems. *Nature Human Behaviour, 1*, 0028. https://doi.org/DOI: 10.1038/s41562-017-0028

Luckin, R., Holmes, W., Griffiths, M., & Forcier, L. B. (2016). *Intelligence unleashed. An argument for AI in education*. Pearson.

Martell, C. C. (2018). *Social studies teacher education: Critical issues and current perspectives*. Information Age Publishing, Inc.

Martı Emel, N. (2025). Restructuring attempts in the Turkish Education System from 1980 to the present. *Science. Education and Innovations in the Context of Modern Problems, 8*(5), 207–217. DOI: 10.56334/sei/8.5.22

Martin, F., Zhuang, M., & Schaefer, D. (2024). Systematic review of research on artificial intelligence in K-12 education (2017–2022). *Computers and Education: Artificial Intelligence, 6*, 100195. DOI: 10.1016/j.caeai.2023.100195

Mason, L., Jeon, T., Blair, P., & Glomb, N. (2013). Virtual tutor training: Learning to teach in a multi-user virtual environment. In Ferdig, R. E. (Ed.), *Design* (pp. 51–67). Utilization, and Analysis of Simulations and Game-Based Educational Worlds., DOI: 10.4018/978-1-4666-4018-4.ch004

Mayasari, N., Sastraatmadja, A. H. M., Suparman, T., Mutiara, I. I., & Maqfirah, P. A.-V. (2024). Effectiveness of using artificial intelligence learning tools and customized curriculum on improving students' critical thinking skills in Indonesia. *The Eastasouth Journal of Learning and Educations, 2*(2), 111–118. DOI: 10.58812/esle.v2i02.302

Muthmainnah, I. S., Ibna Seraj, P. M., & Oteir, I. (2022). P. M., & Oteir, I. (2022). Playing with AI to investigate human-computer interaction technology and improving critical thinking skills to pursue 21st century age. *Education Research International, 2022*(6468995), 1–17. Advance online publication. DOI: 10.1155/2022/6468995

Ng, D. T. K., Chan, E. K. C., & Lo, C. K. (2025). Opportunities, challenges and school strategies for integrating generative AI in education. *Computers and Education: Artificial Intelligence, 8*, 100373. DOI: 10.1016/j.caeai.2025.100373

Ng, D. T. K., Leung, J. K. L., Chu, S. K. W., & Qiao, M. S. (2021). Conceptualizing AI literacy: An exploratory review. *Computers and Education: Artificial Intelligence, 2*, 100041. DOI: 10.1016/j.caeai.2021.100041

Ng, D. T. K., Su, J., Leung, J. K. L., & Chu, S. K. W. (2024). Artificial intelligence (AI) literacy education in secondary schools: A review. *Interactive Learning Environments, 32*(10), 6204–6224. DOI: 10.1080/10494820.2023.2255228

Papadakis, S., Lytvynova, S. H., Ivanova, S. M., & Selyshcheva, I. A. (2024b). Advancing lifelong learning with AI-enhanced ICT: A review of 3L-Person 2024. In *CEUR Workshop Proceedings (9th International Workshop on Professional Retraining and Life-Long Learning using ICT: Person-oriented Approach — 3L-Person* 2024, Lviv, Ukraine, September 25, 2023). CEUR-WS.org.

Papadakis, S., Striuk, A. M., Kravtsov, H. M., Shyshkina, M. P., Marienko, M. V., & Danylchuk, H. B. (2024a). Embracing digital innovation and cloud technologies for transformative learning experiences. In *Proceedings of the 11th Workshop on Cloud Technologies in Education (CTE 2023)*, Kryvyi Rih, Ukraine, December 22, 2023. CEUR Workshop Proceedings.

Park, S., & Kim, C. (2015). Boosting learning-by-teaching in virtual tutoring. *Computers & Education, 82*, 129–140. DOI: 10.1016/j.compedu.2014.11.006

Paul, R., & Elder, L. (2014). *Critical thinking: Tools for taking charge of your professional and personal life* (2nd ed.). Pearson Education.

Rızvı, M. (2023). Investigating AI-powered tutoring systems that adapt to individual student needs, providing personalized guidance and assessments. *The Eurasia Proceedings of Educational and Social Sciences, 31*, 67–73. DOI: 10.55549/epess.1381518

Saddhono, K., Suhita, R., Rakhmawati, A., Rohmadi, M., & Sukmono, I. K. (2024). AI and literacy: Developing critical thinking and analytical skills in the digital era. *2024 International Conference on IoT, Communication and Automation Technology (ICICAT)*, 360-365. DOI: 10.1109/ICICAT62666.2024.10922871

Samuel, Y., Brennan-Tonetta, M., Samuel, J., Kashyap, R., Kumar, V., Krishna Kaashyap, S., Chidipothu, N., Anand, I., & Jain, P. (2023). Cultivation of human centered artificial intelligence: Culturally adaptive thinking in education (CATE) for AI. *Frontiers in Artificial Intelligence*, *6*, 1198180. DOI: 10.3389/frai.2023.1198180 PMID: 38106981

Saritepeci, M., & Yildiz Durak, H. (2024). Effectiveness of artificial intelligence integration in design-based learning on design thinking mindset, creative and reflective thinking skills: An experimental study. *Education and Information Technologies*, *29*(18), 25175–25209. DOI: 10.1007/s10639-024-12829-2

Shoukat, W., Rizwan, N., & Khan, M. T. (2025). The role of artificial intelligence (AI) tutors in personalized learning: Benefits and challenges. *Journal of Social Signs Review*, *3*(4), 1–13.

Sidoti, O., Eugenie, P., & Gottfried, J. (2025). *About a quarter of U.S. teens have used ChatGPT for schoolwork – double the share in 2023*. Pew Research Center. https://www.pewresearch.org/short-reads/2025/01/15/about-a-quarter-of-us-teens-have-used-chatgpt-for-schoolwork-double-the-share-in-2023/

Singh, S. K., Kumar, S., & Mehra, P. S. (2023). Chat GPT & Google Bard AI: A Review. *2023 International Conference on IoT, Communication and Automation Technology (ICICAT)*, 1–6. DOI: 10.1109/ICICAT57735.2023.10263706

Sok, S., & Heng, K. (2023). ChatGPT for education and research: A review of benefits and risks. *Cambodian Journal of Educational Research*, *3*(1), 110–121. DOI: 10.62037/cjer.2023.03.01.06

Styve, A., Virkki, O. T., & Naeem, U. (2024). Developing critical thinking practices interwoven with generative AI usage in an introductory programming course. *2024 IEEE Global Engineering Education Conference (EDUCON)*, 1–8. DOI: 10.1109/EDUCON60312.2024.10578746

Su, J., & Yang, W. (2022). Artificial intelligence in early childhood education: A scoping review. *Computers and Education: Artificial Intelligence*, *3*, 100049. DOI: 10.1016/j.caeai.2022.100049

Su, J., & Yang, W. (2023). Unlocking the power of ChatGPT: A framework for applying generative AI in education. *ECNU Review of Education*, *6*(3), 355–366. DOI: 10.1177/20965311231168423

Suriano, R., Plebe, A., Acciai, A., & Fabio, R. A. (2025). Student interaction with ChatGPT can promote complex critical thinking skills. *Learning and Instruction*, *95*, 102011. DOI: 10.1016/j.learninstruc.2024.102011

Tabachnick, B. G., & Fidell, L. S. (2019). *Using multivariate statistics* (6th ed.). Pearson Education.

Tan, Q., & Tang, X. (2025). Unveiling AI literacy in K-12 education: A systematic literature review of empirical research. *Interactive Learning Environments, 33*(9), 1–17. DOI: 10.1080/10494820.2025.2482586

Tülübaş, T., Karakose, T., & Papadakis, S. (2023). A holistic investigation of the relationship between digital addiction and academic achievement among students. *European Journal of Investigation in Health, Psychology and Education, 13*(10), 2006–2034. DOI: 10.3390/ejihpe13100143 PMID: 37887144

Turkish Statistical Institute. (2024a). *Survey on Information and Communication Technology (ICT) Usage in Households and by Individuals.* https://data.tuik.gov.tr/Bulten/Index?p=Hanehalki-Bilisim-Teknolojileri-(BT)-Kullanim-Arastirmasi-2024-53492

Turkish Statistical Institute. (2024b). *National Education Statistics.* https://data.tuik.gov.tr/Bulten/Index?p=Ulusal-Egitim-Istatistikleri-2024-53937

U.S. Department of Education, Office of Educational Technology. (2023). *Artificial Intelligence and the Future of Teaching and Learning: Insights and Recommendations.*

van den Berg, G., & du Plessis, E. (2023). ChatGPT and generative AI: Possibilities for its contribution to lesson planning, critical thinking and openness in teacher education. *Education Sciences, 13*(10), 998. DOI: 10.3390/educsci13100998

Walter, Y. (2024). Embracing the future of Artificial Intelligence in the classroom: The relevance of AI literacy, prompt engineering, and critical thinking in modern education. *International Journal of Educational Technology in Higher Education, 21*(15), 15. Advance online publication. DOI: 10.1186/s41239-024-00448-3

Wang, J., & Fan, W. (2025). The effect of ChatGPT on students' learning performance, learning perception, and higher-order thinking: Insights from a meta-analysis. *Humanities & Social Sciences Communications, 12*(1), 621. DOI: 10.1057/s41599-025-04787-y

Wang, S., Wang, F., Zhu, Z., Wang, J., Tran, T., & Du, Z. (2024). Artificial intelligence in education: A systematic literature review. *Expert Systems with Applications, 252*, 124167. DOI: 10.1016/j.eswa.2024.124167

Wang, Y., & Xue, L. (2024). Using AI-driven chatbots to foster Chinese EFL students' academic engagement: An intervention study. *Computers in Human Behavior, 159*, 108353. DOI: 10.1016/j.chb.2024.108353

Welsby, P., & Cheung, B. M. (2023). ChatGPT. *Postgraduate Medical Journal*, *99*(1176), 1047–1048. DOI: 10.1093/postmj/qgad056 PMID: 37462242

Wu, Y. (2024). Critical thinking pedagogics design in an era of ChatGPT and other AI tools—Shifting from teaching "what" to teaching "why" and "how.". *Journal of Education and Development*, *8*(1), 1–10. DOI: 10.20849/jed.v8i1.1404

Yetişensoy, O., & Rapoport, A. (2023). Artificial intelligence literacy teaching in social studies education. *Journal of Pedagogical Research*, *7*(3), 100–110. DOI: 10.33902/JPR.202320866

Yim, I. H. Y., & Su, J. (2025). Artificial intelligence (AI) learning tools in K-12 education: A scoping review. *Journal of Computers in Education*, *12*, 93–131. DOI: 10.1007/s40692-023-00304-9

KEY TERMS AND DEFINITIONS

Artificial Intelligence (AI): Computational systems designed to perform tasks typically requiring human cognition, such as learning, problem-solving, and decision-making. In education, AI tools analyze data to deliver personalized content, simulations, or feedback.

Critical Thinking (CT) Skills: Cognitive abilities enabling individuals to analyze evidence, question assumptions, synthesize information, and draw reasoned conclusions. These skills include logical reasoning, source evaluation, and multi-perspectival analysis.

Virtual Teacher: An AI system that acts as an instructional guide, providing explanations, answering queries, or facilitating learning activities. Unlike human teachers, it operates digitally and offers 24-hour accessibility.

Personalized Learning: An educational approach where AI tailors content, pace, and resources to individual learners' needs, abilities, and preferences, optimizing engagement and comprehension.

AI Literacy: The competence to understand, ethically use, and critically evaluate AI tools. It encompasses recognizing AI's limitations, verifying outputs, and integrating AI responsibly into the learning process.

Social Studies Education: An educational discipline that draws upon various social sciences to help students understand and interpret the social world, aiming to cultivate democratic values, advanced CT skills, and a global perspective.

Digital Citizenship: The skills and understanding necessary for students to responsibly and effectively navigate the digital world, including the ethical and critical use of technology like AI.

Chapter 9
Designing Culturally Responsive AI Tutors:
Bridging Equity Gaps in Arab K-12 Education

Sani Alkhasawneh
http://orcid.org/0000-0002-4239-463X
Arab Open University, Jordan

ABSTRACT

This chapter discusses why culturally responsive AI tutors are needed in K-12 in underserved Arab communities where learners confront infrastructural, linguistic, and cultural challenges. It points to the existence of the digital divide among refugee/rural learners, the incompatibility between the Arab values and the West-designed AI tools, and the weaknesses of Arabic NLP. Based on the recent case studies of Jordan, Lebanon, Egypt, and the Gulf regions, the chapter offers a culturally adaptive AI framework that focuses on the linguistic diversity of Arabic in AI, attention to ethics, and availability offline. The chapter is closed by providing practical policy advice to policymakers, developers, and teachers so that the AI systems in Arab education remain not only technically beneficial but also socially and culturally significant.

1. INTRODUCTION

Artificial intelligence (AI) technology is rapidly revolutionizing educational models worldwide, offering new opportunities to personalize learning and providing support to diverse students (Lampropoulos & Papadakis, 2025). The recent emergence of generative AI tools, such as ChatGPT, has further prompted discussion about the ability of these tools to democratize education and facilitate sustainable

DOI: 10.4018/979-8-3373-2637-5.ch009

learning processes, even in challenging contexts (Uğraş et al., 2024). However, a significant weakness still exists. As K-12 schools continue to incorporate AI, these applications have been mostly developed within Western systems and cultures. Such a one-size-fits-all approach tends to make them ill-fit the linguistic, cultural, and infrastructural realities of the Arab world (Sahrir et al., 2025).

Standardized AI tutor approaches continue to alienate many Arab learners, as their mechanistic teaching approaches lack pedagogical alignment, Arabic NLP is underrepresented, and there is a severe shortage of culturally customized context (Aljabr et al., 2025; Sahrir et al., 2025). This chapter does diagnose these failures and goes on to put forward a way for equitable and effective AI integration. It claims that in Arab countries, where linguistic complexity, local cultural standards, and special socio-political realities significantly shape education, AI tools cannot simply be copied into the environment; they must be tailored. Based on the empirical case synopsis in Jordan, Saudi Arabia, Egypt, and the refugee education scene, this paper critiques the place of top-down implementation models and, rather, supports the claim of a co-designed, culturally responsive framework on AI. Combining relevance and learning in the region, the chapter comes up with practical guidelines in the pursuit of building AI systems that respect student well-being, encourage true relevance, and have a notable impact on learning across K-12 settings. Finally, the chapter appeals to individuals in policymaking, teaching, and development circles to promote an Arab-focused concept of educational AI that emphasizes proactive strategies for addressing digital divides, empowering learning, and fostering constructive and participatory Arab classrooms.

To conclude, this chapter presents an AI framework that local solutions are reducing the digital divide. The chapter emphasizes a few key areas, including (1) Methodology: Conceptual Synthesis and Framework Development. (2) Comprehensive Literature Review: Culturally Responsive Pedagogy and AI in Education. (3) Contextual Challenges in Arab K-12 Education. (4) Design Principles for a Culturally Responsive AI Tutor. (5) Ethical, Practical, and Implementation Challenges. (6) Recommendations for Policy, Practice, and Future Research. Finally, the chapter provides actionable recommendations for educators, developers, and policymakers to scale these approaches safely and broadly.

2. METHODOLOGY: CONCEPTUAL SYNTHESIS AND FRAMEWORK DEVELOPMENT

This chapter outlines the methodological approach to this inquiry. This study employs conceptual and analytical design rather than relying on empirical data collection. The main goal is to conduct a theoretical inquiry into how the culturally responsive artificial intelligence (AI) tutor can be created to reduce the inequities in the K-12 system among underserved Arab populations. We consider the method suitable for synthesizing various areas of knowledge to create a new conceptual framework, which is in high demand.

2.1. Research Design: Narrative Synthesis and Conceptual Analysis

The study is based on the principles of systematic narrative review and conceptual synthesis that provide its research design. The design does not aim to test hypotheses but to:

· Discuss the insights of disparate but related fields, i.e., educational technology, AI ethics, and culturally responsive pedagogy.

· Criticize, analyze, and interpret the available literature to identify gaps, tensions, and synergies.

· Establish a coherent and practical conceptual model that guides future investigations and applications.

2.2. Data Sources and Search Strategy

To achieve a robust and extensive evidence base, the analysis uses a broad spectrum of scholarly and grey literature.

· Information Sources: Synthesis included peer-reviewed journal articles, authoritative books, policy briefs of international organizations (e.g., UNESCO, World Bank), and conference papers.

· Temporal Scope: The scope of the review is based on literature published between 2020 and 2025, mostly to reflect the latest achievements in AI and the current discussion of educational equity.

· Search Strategy: A systematic search was conducted through electronic databases (Scopus, Web of Science, IEEE Xplore, and ERIC) using a combination of keywords such as (AI tutor or intelligent tutoring system), (culturally responsive or cultural relevance), (digital equity or digital divide), and (Arab world or MENA region).

2.3. Study Selection and Eligibility Criteria

To make literature relevant and grounded, predefined criteria were used in selection to ensure that the literature is relevant.

· **Inclusion Criteria:** Preference was given to sources that: (1) directly discussed AI applications in K-12 education; (2) discussed principles of cultural responsiveness, inclusivity, or pedagogy; (3) discussed issues of digital access or equity; (4) offered case studies or analyses of Arab settings.

· **Exclusion Criteria:** Works were excluded that were technical and not pedagogically reflective, as well as those that only discussed Western situations and had no generalizable implications.

2.4. Analytical Strategy: Thematic Synthesis and Critical Interpretation

The analytical process was conducted using a thematic synthesis method, which was implemented in three stages:

· Familiarization and Coding: The body of literature was systematically analyzed to determine relevant concepts, arguments, and findings.

· Theme Development: The ideas that were frequent were divided into four main analytic themes:

· The infrastructural and socioeconomic dimensions of digital equity and access barriers.

· The technical capabilities and pedagogical implications of AI-powered personalization.

· The theoretical and practical foundations of culturally responsive pedagogy

· Regional case studies and initiatives within the Arab world.

· Synthesis and Model Building: These topics were critically compared, contrasted, and synthesized. Themes were also examined to determine how the relationships between them are interactive, which informs us of the central research problem.

2.5. Conceptual Framework Development

An original conceptual framework was developed at the end of the thematic synthesis. Such a framework is both visual and narrative, as it bridges the fields of AI-driven personalization and the concepts of cultural inclusivity and pedagogical equity. The synthesis is the most important result of this methodological process because it provides a framework for the discussion in the following chapters and for the actionable strategies offered to developers, educators, and policymakers.

The suggested framework has three unique contributions to the field. First, it provides a hybrid architecture that is specifically tailored to Arabic dialects to allow switching between local dialects and Modern Standard Arabic. Second, it integrates a culturally grounded data pipeline with a human-in-the-loop verification process to reduce annotation bias and preserve cultural relevance. Third, it presents new measurement criteria, i.e., dialect sensitivity and cultural appropriateness, which transcend traditional linguistic accuracy. These additions make the framework stand out among the already existing Western academic models and emphasize its ability to influence K-12 schools that are underserved by Arab students.

Figure 1. Three-Layer Educational AI System Architecture

Figure 1 introduces a three-level educational AI system, where an external layer of infrastructure and governance is located, a middle layer is the core technologies, i.e., a hybrid NLP module, a pedagogical reasoning engine, and a data pipeline that are culturally verified, and an inner layer is the educational objectives, e.g., cultural relevance, academic achievement, student engagement, and data safety. The constant improvement of the work process between teachers and communities is possible due to the bidirectional feedback loop. The main contributions of the framework are the support of Arabic dialects with Modern Standard Arabic, a culturally aware human-curated data pipeline to minimize annotation bias, and novel evaluation metrics with sensitivity to dialects and cultural appropriateness, providing a culturally responsive alternative to Western-centric AI paradigms for underserved Arab K–12 schools.

3. COMPREHENSIVE LITERATURE REVIEW: CULTURALLY RESPONSIVE PEDAGOGY AND AI IN EDUCATION

Artificial Intelligence (AI) is drastically altering the fundamentals of Culturally Responsive Pedagogy (CRP), which has long been one of the key pillars of equitable education (Gay, 2010; Ladson-Billings, 1995). Worldwide, AI has been hailed as far more capable of facilitating personalized learning and developing adaptive, interactive programs of education (Xiao et al., 2025; Lampropoulos & Papadakis, 2025). The possibility is also especially intriguing in relation to culturally responsive teaching because AI holds the potential to expand the representation in teaching media and counteract implicit biases (Mariyono & Abror, 2024). Nonetheless, this promise is accompanied by a stark paradox: the technologies that have the potential to promote inclusivity are simultaneously contributing to greater inequity around the world. This process of AI integration reveals both cultural and infrastructural gaps, with tools created and conditioned in and for the Western world being configurationally unsuited to managing the language complexity of Arabic or the subtleties of Arabic social and cultural norms (Elmahdi et al., 2025; Al-Mutawa & Al-Aama, 2024; Lavidas et al., 2022). Issues of algorithm bias, ethical issues related to data privacy, and unequal technological access are not only technical but also highly contextual, and they are particular to the Arab world (Mariyono & Abror, 2024). As a result, researchers desperately propose the need to shift the trend of generic AI products to frameworks built on international collaboration, distinct cultural sensitivity in policymakers, and capacity development on the ground (Elmahdi et al., 2025). This chapter posits the following for the Arab world: It requires an Arab-centered approach to AI adoption, shifting approaches focusing on implementation to enculturation, and making sure ethical frameworks and interdisciplinary partnerships are grounded in the needs and values of Arab learners.

3.1. Theoretical Foundations of Culturally Responsive Pedagogy (CRP)

The culturally relevant pedagogy (CRP) is not defined as a collection of abstract principles; it is a praxis, which mediates the connection between the lived experiences of students and academic learning. The elements on which CRP is founded include the three interwoven tenets, which are academic success, cultural competence, and sociopolitical consciousness (Ladson-Billings, 1995). The concept of academic success is larger than getting high test scores—it is related to having very high expectations of students and building on their cultural knowledge, values, and modes of knowing by tapping those resources to support rigorous achievement (Gay, 2010). Practically, such an approach would mean developing lessons to reaffirm cultural identities and lead the students towards the disciplinary standards that they must master.

Cultural competence asserts that we ought to assist students in valuing and maintaining their cultural identities, and this is in addition to providing them with the capacity to adjust to existing in other cultural environments and to appreciate other cultural contexts. Those who teach using CRP incorporate the language, the traditions, and the stories of students in their classroom (Aronson & Laughter, 2016). Furthermore, cross-culturally fluent teachers provide learners with the ability to survive in multicultural societies. Lastly, sociopolitical awareness dares the students to perceive education as an instrument of change. Through in-depth analysis of matters of inequality and injustice, students acquire the ability to be critical of widely accepted narratives and learn to use their knowledge to the advantage of all (Papadakis et al., 2024a, 2024b).

Putatively, these tenets develop and maintain a positive academic identity by decreasing the amount of dissonance various minority students experience between home and school culture. Instead of viewing difference as lack, CRP authenticates students' cultural capital (Yosso, 2005) that further enhances self-efficacy, sense of belonging, and motivation. It is in this convergence of identities and schooling that culturally relevant pedagogy becomes more than a comprehensive instructional method; it becomes a structure of educational justice as well.

Nonetheless, Artificial Intelligence (AI) in education brings an additional and complicated aspect to this practice. Although AI has the potential to offer personalized learning, the models on which it is trained do not correlate in any way to the cultural contexts and data of Arab learners. This creates a stark contrast. Can a technology that criticizes its culture-blindness and algorithmic biases effectively mediate culturally demanding pedagogy (Buolamwini & Gebru, 2018)? This chapter argues that CRP principles should re-frisk AI to promote equity, not exclusion, in Arab classrooms. AI should be responsive but also culture conscious, which means that a careful synergy of these established pedagogical frameworks and ethically designed technology is needed (Benjamin, 2019).

3.2. The Global AI in Education Discourse: Promises and Hidden Assumptions

Some describe the integration of Artificial Intelligence (AI) into educational systems worldwide as a paradigm shift, given its potential to foster individuality and facilitate accessible learning. Advocates point to the ability of AI to process large amounts of data that can be used to personalize instruction to the speed of students, provide timely feedback, and automate teacher tasks, creating more time to teach students higher-order thinking skills (Lampropoulos & Papadakis, 2025; Uğraş et al., 2024). At a theoretical level, these abilities are consistent with the overall aims of differentiated instruction, which contingently introduces the assumption that AI can become a potent agent of educational diversity. The emergence of generative AI applications, such as ChatGPT, in the recent past has enhanced this potential by finding new applications in content generation, language development, language practice, and the fostering of sustainable educational activities within an under-resourced setting (Uğraş et al., 2024).

Various studies indicate that AI tools, particularly generic ones, are significantly enhancing academic achievements, engagement, and personalized learning among Arab learners. Generative AI tools have already been proven to enhance cognitive performance and learner satisfaction in higher education institutions within the Arab region, and even students have supportive reports on the development of their behavior patterns and learning efficiency after applying the given tools to their studying experiences (Jaboob et al., 2024; Mulyanto et al., 2024; AlAfnan, 2024). AI-driven platforms in learning will allow Arabic language learners to engage in adaptive, interactive, and personalized experiences, where measurable improvements in overall vocabulary, grammar, and conversational abilities will be obtained (Asfar et al., 2024; Garba & Hassan, 2024; Mohideen, 2024; Rohmawaty et al., 2024; Seyidov, 2024). Comparative analysis also indicates that Arab countries have recorded better levels of AI implementation and success in language learning as compared to other regions with better infrastructure and support mechanisms in the form of policy interventions (Septia & Khodr, 2024).

Nevertheless, a set of ongoing issues plagues the region and has the inherent potential to neutralize the benefits mentioned and, without intervention, to deepen existing educational disparities. The communicative complexities of the Arabic language—practiced by deep morphology and the presence of dialects—repeatedly overpower generic AI solutions, and the results are inaccurate and rigid (Borham et al., 2024; Abdo et al., 2024). Moreover, the gaps in the process of integration are amplified by the inability to acquire culturally tailored educational materials, the lack of teacher training, and other widespread digitalization challenges (Rabie, 2023; Alakabawy, 2024). This leads to a significant accessibility gap for students, especially in non-urban regions (Yatri et al., 2023). Most critically, ethical issues related to data privacy and the oversaturation of artificial intelligence, as well as a fundamental absence of culturally sensitive representations within these systems, remain essentially unaddressed (Yatri et al., 2023; AlAfnan, 2024). These issues highlight a significant mismatch between the culturally naive design of mainstream AI and the fundamental principles of culturally responsive teaching, necessitating an innovative solution tailored to the needs of Arabian learners.

Current research shows difficulties in the use of generic AI technologies to teach Arabic. The ambiguity of Arabic and linguistic complexities will be an insurmountable challenge to AI tools such as ChatGPT, which recently demonstrated an inaccurate performance (Al-Ghobesi, 2025; Alakabawy, 2024). Generative AI has the potential to make language learning even more personalized by helping learners acquire knowledge about the Arabic language with the desired level of accuracy, specificity, and cultural relevance; however, its applicability raises concerns about accuracy within context and cultural considerations (Alayba, 2025; Sahrir et al., 2025). To solve these problems, scholars suggest making specific AI models based on Arabic, using the local speech data in a certain region, and collaborating with teachers who teach in Arabic (Sahrir et al., 2025). Moreover, enhancing the skills of educators and students in terms of AI literacy is essential to be able to see the boundaries of the technology, as well as to use it ethically (Alayba, 2025; Yatri et al., 2023). Therefore, while the potential of AI is undeniable, its effective and equitable application in Arab education necessitates a radical departure from generic, one-size-fits-all models. This critical need for a culturally conscious and linguistically specific approach forms the foundation for the design framework proposed in the following section.

3.3. Synthesis: The Imperative for Culturally Conscious AI

The presented analysis indicates a fundamental gap between the principles of Culturally Responsive Pedagogy (CRP) that require incorporating students' cultural identities as essential assets for learning (Ladson-Billings, 1995; Gay, 2010) and the present model of mainstream artificial intelligence systems in education. Where CRP demands accurate affirmation, AI freely provides assimilation; where necessity demands context, AI offers standardization; and where CRP empowers through critical consciousness, AI threatens to entrench bias in the form of algorithmic opacity (Benjamin, 2019; Buolamwini & Gebru, 2018).

This gap does not represent a minor implementation challenge but the actual cause of the brutal mismatch between the world promises of AI and its local failures, especially in cases such as the Arab world (Asfar et al., 2024; Garba & Hassan, 2024; Mohideen, 2024; Rohmawaty et al., 2024; Seyidov, 2024). The potential of personalization, accessibility, and equity becomes meaningless when the tools are designed to be inactive in identifying linguistic complexity, culturally varying content, and differences in ways of knowing (Al-Ghobesi, 2025). As such, the technologies that had come to be depicted as powerful equalizers have posed the danger of becoming tools of a novel digital marginalization and have contributed to the growth of educational inequalities they purport to eliminate (Rabie, 2023; Alakabawy, 2024).

Therefore, it is critically insufficient to merely implement AI; instead, we must fundamentally reinvent it. Such a dire situation requires a significant paradigm shift away from the current methodology of culturally blind AI—which assumes it has no cultural bias—to a new method of culturally conscious AI (Xiao et al., 2025). These systems should be deliberately built from the ground up with the ideals of CRP, which emphasize that ethically creative foresight, community co-design, and a commitment to equity are essential principles rather than additional considerations (Sahrir et al., 2025; Uğraş et al., 2024).

Filling this gap is imperative, which makes this study the focus of my research. In the next section, I will now be examining in more depth how this divide plays out in the Arab K-12 education arena, laying out the practical infrastructural, linguistic, and socio-cultural barriers that an education-sensitive AI must work against.

4. CONTEXTUAL CHALLENGES IN ARAB K-12 EDUCATION

4.1. The Digital Divide: Infrastructure, Access, and Equity

The digital divide among Arab children is very significant due to inadequate infrastructure, including electricity, technology devices, and internet connectivity. Many students from rural and marginalized communities have difficulty accessing online education because they do not have the power or funds for technology (UNESCO, 2021). Due to power issues in Yemen and Iraq, schools are unable to implement digital learning, making it nearly impossible for teachers to utilize digital resources (World Bank, 2022). In the wealthier Gulf states, there are still major differences between city areas and more remote places (GSMA, 2023).

The digital divide in Arab education is primarily evident in the insufficient availability of technology, which hinders the implementation of AI-based learning. Access to reliable electricity, digital tools, and the internet is lacking in many public schools in underserved communities, all of which are required for using educational technology (UNESCO, 2021). Rural communities in Jordan, Egypt, and Yemen face frequent power cuts and lack the resources needed for digital learning centers, making it difficult to integrate AI tutors or digital learning in those areas.

Countries like Lebanon and Jordan face even greater difficulties as home to many refugees. The Syrian conflict and massive refugee flows have severely challenged education systems. Lebanon, where more than 1.5 million Syrian refugees live, does not have enough schools or educational technology (Human Rights Watch, 2022). A lot of the time, Syrian children who are refugees go to classes that are overcrowded and do not have access to computers or the internet (UNHCR, 2023). These children cannot rely on modern technology or education, both of which restrict their learning and contribute to systemic inequalities that AI technology could help address.

Limited infrastructure and displacement underscore the need for technology that is both accessible and culturally appropriate. The first step in implementing AI in Arab education should be to address these fundamental disparities.

4.2. Linguistic Hurdles: Complex Morphology, Dialects, and Data Scarcity

Arabic learners increasingly use AI tutors, but these systems have significant shortcomings because of the lack of linguistic sources, the lack of dialect coverage, and the complexity of Arabic grammar and morphology. Effective learning often requires human judgment and reflective thought. Recent research demonstrates that AI tutors of the new generation enhance different language abilities, among which are grammar, vocabulary, speaking, translation, and text analysis. For example, a virtual tutor was superior to traditional education in terms of cognitive outcomes among more than 120 native learners. Speech tutors that were machine-learned were successful in the detection of pronunciation errors. Adaptive systems that combined visual, auditory, and kinesthetic properties enhanced the learners' performance and satisfaction, even in the case of children with autism spectrum disorders. Nevertheless, other AI tutors were able to make learners more motivated without any tangible learning benefits. All in all, AI tutors offer real-time feedback that is adaptive and personalized and can assist with the difficulties related to Arabic grammar, pronunciation, and vocabulary (Al-Ghobesi, 2025; Hartanto et al., 2023; Abdo et al., 2024).

4.2.1 Key Challenges in Arabic AI Tutors

Discussing the performance limitations of AI tutors, we can identify four major challenges:

4.2.1.1 Data Scarcity and Quality

Most models are based on Modern Standard Arabic (MSA), which is not reflective of other dialects, including Egyptian, Levantine, and Gulf Arabic. Publicly available Arabic corpora are smaller and less diverse than those for English or Chinese, limiting generalization and model robustness (Menashy & Zakharia, 2022). Low-quality data decreases AI accuracy of grammar, morphology, and spelling, which may impede the creation of Arabic AI applications (Al-Ghobesi, 2025).

4.2.1.2 Complex Grammar and Morphology

Arabic is very inflectional, with roots, patterns of derivation, and endings of cases. The issue of morphological ambiguity, including the use of words whose meanings differ based on diacritics, gets in the way of AI accuracy. Even modern models can mix verb conjugation or noun cases (Al-Ghobesi, 2025).

4.2.1.3 Dialectal Variation and Informal Usage

There is variation both at the dialectal level and in the informal form. There is a significant difference in Arabic dialects in terms of grammar and vocabulary. More frequently than not, AI systems that have been trained mostly on MSA are incapable of processing vernacular variations like Moroccan Darija or Egyptian Arabic (Moaiad et al, 2024). There is no way that the AI can differentiate between MSA, and colloquial speech as compared to human instructors who are able to contextualize variations (Al-Ghobesi, 2025).

4.2.1.4 Contextual Understanding

AI does not follow semantic understanding but uses statistical correlations, which tend to misunderstand idioms, metaphors, or expressions that are context-specific (Abdo et al., 2024). When exposed to culturally sensitive phrases, conversational AI models often provide direct or wrong translations (Al-Ghobesi, 2025).

4.2.2 Advances in Arabic Conversational AI (2023–2024)

In the recent past, Arabic conversational AI has been improved significantly, particularly in terms of dialect representation and dataset quality. Specific models with dialects, such as Jais (Gulf Arabic), improve the task performance by an average of 15% in contrast to the common MSA models (Sengupta et al., 2023). Localized text production models like AceGPT (Huang et al., 2024) reduce hallucinations. Detailed assessment systems, including AraBench, consider various NLP tasks that are required to standardize Arabic AI systems (Sajjad et al., 2020). Notwithstanding these accomplishments, difficulties persist insufficient dialect representation, annotation deficiencies, and diminutive dataset sizes relative to high-resource languages. The potential opportunities include improving the dialectal representation (e.g., Maghrebi and Yemeni Arabic). The challenge lies in establishing standard measures for long-context comprehension and multimodal interaction. Enhancing industry-academic partnerships to create high-quality datasets, such as the Meta NLLB project, is another potential opportunity. Xue et al. (2020) propose the use of synthetic data generation, cross-lingual transfer, and crowdsourced annotation to improve the quality of datasets.

Recently, several datasets have been introduced to facilitate Arabic AI development (Table 1). These datasets vary in size, dialect coverage, and quality, which directly impacts model training and evaluation.

Table 1. Key Arabic Conversational AI Datasets (2023–2024)

Dataset	Size / Scale	Primary Task	Key Advancement	Limitation	Source
Jais	13B tokens	Gulf Arabic LLM	+15% improvement in dialect performance	Limited to Gulf Arabic	Sengupta et al., 2023
AceGPT	75B tokens	Text generation	40% fewer hallucinations	Requires fine-tuning	Abdo et al., 2024
AraBench	50K QA pairs	Multi-task evaluation	12 NLP tasks benchmarked	Minimal dialect coverage	Menashy & Zakharia, 2022
MADAR v3	1M sentences	Dialect understanding	32 city-level dialects	Sparse annotations	Alenezi, 2024
ArDialogue-24	120K dialogues	Open-domain conversation	Emotion & sentiment labels	Small scale corpus	Al-Ghobesi, 2025

As Table 1 demonstrates, although large-scale corpora like AceGPT exist, they have a serious limitation in terms of the variety of dialects. This impacts the accuracy of AI tutors, particularly in informal or regional contexts. Table 2 displays the results of experimental studies of AI tutors, which emphasize positive outcomes and ongoing challenges. Virtual teachers strengthen the knowledge of grammar and vocabulary; however, the speech-based systems still face the problem of identifying the correct pronunciation.

Table 2. Reported Performance of AI Tutors in Arabic Language Learning

Study	Learners (N)	AI Method	Focus Area	Main Outcome	Note
Abdo et al., 2024	120	Virtual tutor	Grammar & vocabulary	Outperformed traditional methods	Higher cognitive gains
Alenezi, 2024	80	ML speech tutor	Pronunciation	High error-detection accuracy	Some detection errors remain
Hartanto et al., 2023	60	Adaptive multimodal	Engagement & satisfaction	Increased motivation & participation	Tested with children with ASD

Arabic AI tutors demonstrate a considerable level of language proficiency, though they are constrained by the lack of data, dialect representation, grammar complexities, and contextual understanding. The most recent developments in datasets and models (Jais, AceGPT, AraBench, ArDialogue 2024) show that there is significant improvement. Further work must focus on synthetic data, crowdsourcing annotation, dialect inclusion, and multimodal AIs to improve Arabic AI system performance to match high-resource languages.

4.3. Socio-Cultural Nuances in Learning

The main weakness in Arabic artificial intelligence (AI) programs is their insufficient ability to explore the cultural and contextual nuances that are essential for understanding the diverse speech communities within the Arabic-speaking world. Although AI approaches have displayed remarkable success in dealing with Modern Standard Arabic (MSA), they always suffer when dealing with dialectical variation, culturally coded phrases, and regional specifics of communication norms. By examining the existing AI application to Arabic language teaching and natural language processing (NLP), the research can pinpoint three major areas of problematic practices, specifically (1) failure to identify culturally deterministic communication patterns, (2) insufficient treatment of contextual meanings, and (3) inability to adapt to regional linguistic peculiarities. The existing Arabic-based applications of AI express a major failure in consuming culturally and contextually specific information. Although these systems demonstrate the ability to process formal modern standard Arabic (MSA), they fail to address four main domains of sociolinguistic complexity (Habash, 2023). On the one hand, they generally do not process such elements of cultural framing, such as jokes, proverbs, and indirect language use, that are core properties of Arabic discourse correctly. Second, they have trouble with contextual dependencies, such as words and phrases that have a varied meaning depending on the situation. Third, they often go wrong with the dialectal nuances, such as regional variation in the vocabulary and grammar. Fourth, they usually fail to pick up on fine-grained social coding, including honorifics, politeness strategies, and gendered speaking patterns. These restrictions are based on several structural challenges with the existing AI development paradigms. The training data used is highly biased in that it adheres to formal written rather than natural spoken Arabic, therefore providing a representation bias. Existing Arabic language corpora significantly lack adequate metadata tagging, particularly in relation to cultural context. Instead, most systems remain overly reliant on English-based NLP methods, which are not easily adaptable to the unique characteristics of the Arabic language. Most importantly, there exists an impoverished dialect representation in the training of models, and most materials cater to only MSA and not the variable regional forms used in day-to-day usage.

4.3.1 Culturally Embedded Expressions

AI systems often render culturally sensitive Arabic utterances literally or wrongly interpret them. Proverbs like "   " (which literally means "those who were ashamed died") are often translated word for word, failing to convey their intended cultural meaning related to social rights and reputation. There are cases of religious terms being deprived of culture and religious meaning during the AI processing, especially those that involve commonly used words in the name of God, such as (God willing). Struggling with politeness formulas, the systems are also not able to appreciate very slight yet meaningful variations between such constructions as and (both meaning the same thing but to be used in diverse situations). According to a 2024 study by Al-Mutawa & Al-Aama, 78 percent of the Arabic chatbot answers to culturally loaded questions were rated as inappropriate by the native speakers, which indicates a major deficiency in cultural competence (Al-Mutawa & Al-Aama, 2024).

4.3.2 Context-Dependent Meaning Shifts

The Arabic language has outstanding semantic flexibility, as most words carry vastly different meanings depending on the context of usage, a fact that the current AI frameworks are ill-designed to handle. As an example, the opposite meaning of the word can be an eye in a plain context, whereas it refers to a spy, water source, or pick in other respects. The same applies with , which mainly means "heart" but can also mean "bravery" or "transformation" (such as when you say —"to turn the tables"). The term "hand," (yad), is a term that may mean the physical part of the body, power (baydah al-amr—the thing is in his hands), or generosity (tallit yadik—you have extended your hand/generosity). Such context-sensitive variations in meaning commonly baffle AI systems, which lack the high-fidelity context processing to do model interpretation properly and which regularly yield improper or absurd results when AI systems handle genuine Arabic discourse (Al-Mutawa & Al-Aama, 2024).

4.3.3 Variation of Dialect and Register

There exist many problems of understanding between Modern Standard Arabic (MSA) and the regional dialects owing to the linguistic continuum nature. There is a problem with lexical variations, as examples may include the fact that in MSA, the word "car" is translated by , whereas in Egyptian Arabic, it is translated by , and in Moroccan dialects, it is translated by (Moaiad et al, 2024). Other major differences among dialects include grammatical constructions; for example, the pattern of negation varies, with used in Levantine Arabic and used in Egyptian Arabic (Moaiad et al, 2024). The pragmatic differences exacerbate the issue, as the cultural norms of communication can vary depending on the region people reside in. People tend to reject invitations more subtly in Gulf Arabic than in the Levantine style. These differences present a significant challenge to AI models that have been extensively trained on MSA since they lack practical equipment to cope with the Arabic communication reality (Al-Mutawa & Al-Aama, 2024).

5. DESIGN PRINCIPLES FOR A CULTURALLY RESPONSIVE AI TUTOR

5.1. Frameworks for Culturally Responsive AI: A Global Perspective, Ethical, Practical, and Implementation Challenges

The purpose of the culturally responsive AI design frameworks is to ensure the inclusivity, equity, and relevance of artificial intelligence systems across diverse cultural contexts. These frameworks respond to the demands of AI to respect, reflect, and adapt to the values, knowledge, and lived experiences of various communities as AI becomes more integrated into education, the creative sector, and everyday life.

The most recent research raises the importance of a culturally responsive AI design to suit the needs of a broad range of the population. Research indicates that cultural backgrounds can inform the viewing preferences and expectations of how people are likely to use AI systems (Xiao et al., 2024). A theory of culturally appropriate design of learning spaces inspired by studies of learning sciences and cultural psychology has been advanced (Lee, 2003). To design social robots for multilingual children, it has been noted that the Culturally Localized User Experience (CLUE) Framework was used to emphasize the importance of co-design with the main stakeholders (Kuo et al., 2022). To enhance culturally responsible AI systems, researchers favor AI enculturation and the introduction of regulation (Lukasik & Ozegalska-Lukasik, 2023). These findings underscore the necessity of interdisciplinary research to create AI models that address social and cultural issues while ensuring they remain adaptable to various cultures.

Key Frameworks and Approaches

Culturally localized user experience (CLUE) framework: Deployed in social robot design, it is a participatory design framework that entails co-designing with multicultural learners and stakeholders (students, parents, and teachers) so that robots respond and are accessible in diverse cultural contexts. The second value presented in the framework is the significance of involving cultural informants, who are the users, throughout the design (Kuo et al., 2022).

Adaptive Contextualized Learning (ACL) Framework: In a learner-controlled context, it is used to add the reality of the real world, dynamic scaffolding, and cultural relevance to the learning tools in AI-based education. Customized AI systems, rather than generic ones, greatly enhance learning for local cultures (Elmahdi et al., 2025).

GenAI Culturally Responsive Science Assessment (GenAI-CRSciA) Framework: It is a framework that links generative AI amenities with critical cultural principles (language, knowledge, ethnicity, and religion) to build science assessments that adapt to the cultural combination of the students. It also emphasizes the necessity of elaborate user input to prevent oversimplification of cultural profiles (Faison et al., 2024).

Cultural Intelligence and Adaptive Governance Models These models combine strategies from the West, East, and Africa to inform the ethical development of AI by adopting the concept of flexible governance and cross-cultural cooperation (Kumar et al., 2025).

Mechanisms and Principles

Participatory and Co-Design Methods: The impact can also be achieved with the help of participatory methods that involve the end-users and various stakeholders whose backgrounds are different and thus guarantee that the AI systems are based on actual cultural needs and preferences (Kuo et al., 2022).

Localized and Contextual Content: AI is even more effective to use when it considers local stories, local languages, and local traditions and is used in the sphere of education and the creation of artistic products (Tan et al., 2025; Faison et al., 2024; Elmahdi et al., 2025).

Explainability and Transparency: To create trust and ease of access, frameworks based on explainable AI methods (e.g., SHAP) are used to guide the user as to how cultural principles have been integrated into AI outputs.

Challenges and Limitations

Homogenization of Culture: Other models run the danger of regarding nations or tribes as culturally monolithic and thus ignoring subcultural diversity. Professionals should review and provide extensive background information for precise cultural representation (Faison et al., 2024).

Ethical and Sociocultural Threats: Current issues include ethical threats arising from biased algorithms, insufficient representation of indigenous voices, and concerns regarding privacy. Regulations, feedback loops, and federated learning can address these issues (Elmahdi et al., 2025; Lukasik & Ozegalska-Lukasik, 2023).

Scalability and Access Data: Culturally responsive AI systems may be restricted in terms of scalability, blind spots, and access due to urban-centric samples and uneven internet coverage (Elmahdi et al., 2025).

Futures and Advantages

Increased Efficiency: AI solutions tailored to specific cultures demonstrate improved performance, learning outcomes, and user interaction (Misaki et al., 2024; Elmahdi et al., 2025).

Equity and inclusion: Culturally responsive frameworks assist in reducing bias and cultivating the inclusion of discriminated and indigenous voices (Lukasik & Ozegalska-Lukasik, 2023).

Recommendations: The effort in the future needs to be on rural adjustments, longitudinal studies, and multidisciplinary combinations with a view to having far-reaching, sustainable influences (Elmahdi et al., 2025; Lukasik & Ozegalska-Lukasik, 2023).

In summary, culturally responsive AI development models value the concepts of inclusivity, flexibility, and ethical obligation by integrating the cultural information and collaborative approaches to AI creation. Such frameworks enhance effectiveness, trust, and equity but should be continually based upon diversity, ethical risks, and practical implementation issues to extend the intended benefits of AI to all communities equally.

5.2. Core Pillars for an Arab Context: Linguistic Adaptability, Cultural Representation, and Pedagogical Alignment

An effective culturally applicable tutor to be used by Arab learners must be built upon three main pillars, which are interdependent and far beyond the boundaries of traditional AI. These pillars transform the ideas of Culturally Responsive Pedagogy (CRP) into workable guidelines to present AI creation. Linguistic Adaptability: This principle obliges the AI to go beyond one view of Arabic. Dialectal Flexibility: the system should have the capability to code switch between Modern Standard Arabic (MSA) and the most notable regional dialects (e.g., Levantine, Gulf, and Egyptian). It should be able to understand questions using a local dialect and provide a response that eases the learning of modern standard Arabic without undermining the learner's vernacular (Sahrir et al., 2025). The NLP engine should be carefully designed because of the complexity of the Arabic morphological structure, which contains root-and-pattern recognition and diacritic restoration and accurately weighs lexical and syntax (Habash, 2023). High optimization in low function: Since data may be scarce, optimization criteria are expected to imply efficiency and ability to perform few-shot learning, use low bandwidth, and even work offline (Yatri et al., 2023). Cultural Representation: The AI must be used as a reflection of the reality of the learner herself, rather than an opening to an unknown one. Culturally Relevant Content: The issues, examples, stories, and images must be based on Arab history, social customs, literature, and everyday life (e.g., street markets (souqs) can be used to introduce a mathematical problem, or traditional narratives can be used to understand language (Eppard et al., 2021)). Value-Aware Design: The style of interaction between the system and the user must be in line with the cultural values, which may focus on community learning situations, respect for authority, and the exclusion of information that runs counter to shared social or religious norms (Alenezi, 2024). Betting on Diversity Bias: A thorough exam is necessary to identify and eliminate stereotypes or negative imagery in both written and visual deliverables (Benjamin, 2019). Pedagogical Alignment Technology should support pedagogy, not the reverse. Beyond assessment, the AI should not merely function as an assessment tool; it must also present adaptive scaffolding to break down complex Arabic grammatical situations into manageable segments and provide hints that are bound by both code and cultural context (Gay, 2010). Yielding to the Agenda of Critical Consciousness: In addition to the linguistic mechanics, the tutor shall cover materials that challenge learners to scrutinize social issues relevant to their societies, thereby addressing an aspect of culturally relevant pedagogy related to sociopolitical principles (Ladson-Billings, 1995). Empowerment of Teachers: The design must serve as an assistive copilot for educators, ensuring that it does not attempt to replace them in any of their roles; instead, it should provide practical information regarding student growth and cultural barriers (Almuhanna, 2024).

5.3. Architectural Considerations for Arabic NLP and Content Delivery

Application of the general principles to a practical system requires purposeful design choices that are dissimilar to standard Western-centric AI designs (Al-Ghobesi, 2025; Alenezi, 2024). The aim is to advance beyond systems that fail to convert dialectal input into ones capable of understanding and functioning within the full linguistic and sociolinguistic scope of Arabic.

5.3.1 The Hybrid NLP Architecture: Beyond the Monolithic LLM

A strong tutor cannot rely on a single inexhaustible language model. It requires multi tiered and hybrid architecture (Sengupta et al., 2023)

A dialect recognition module is the first step, as it automatically recognizes the user's dialect (i.e., Gulf, Levantine, or Egyptian) to properly direct inquiries, a necessary precursor to effective code-switching (Sahrir et al., 2025).

A Library of Fine-Tuned, Task-Specific Models: Use smaller and more efficient models fitted with specific tasks over one large model. This approach is more effective for low-resource languages and specific domains (Essa et al., 2025).

A grammar correction model based on Modern Standard Arabic (MSA).

· A machine translation model to translate dialect into MSA that preserves meaning rather than merely interchanging words (Moaiad et al., 2024)

· A model for the retrieval of culturally relevant content, which fetches appropriate instances and problems (Eppard et al., 2021).

The Pedagogical Reasoning Engine serves as the central layer that analyzes the results produced by the specialized models. Its role is to produce a reply that is not only linguistically specific but also pedagogically successful; that way the tutor explains the rule or the cultural background behind his/her correction. This engine applies to the concept of scaffolding (Gay, 2010).

5.3.2 A Curated and Culturally Annotated Data Pipeline

The training data should be selected thoroughly and augmented in far more than text scraping.

Culturally Annotated Corpora: Datasets must be annotated with communicative functionality (e.g., persuasion, apology), cultural context (e.g., religious, tribal, urban), and speech act labeling to educate the AI on the reasoning behind the way words are used (Essa et al., 2025).

Balanced Dialectal Datasets: The compilation of data should proactively ensure coverage of major regional variations, urban/rural differences, and intergenerational language use to avoid bias towards one so-called standard (Essa et al., 2025).

Synthetic Data Generation and Human Verification: Use existing Arabic LLMs (like Jais) to generate practice dialogues and examples, afterwards going through them carefully and correcting them with the help of cultural and linguistic experts. Such a hybrid human-AI loop plays a fundamental role in scaling quality data (Sengupta et al., 2023); Sahrir et al., 2025).

5.3.3 Culturally Informed Measures of Evaluation

Indicators of new evaluation frameworks should be established and implemented to replace those criteria that only determine MSA accuracy.

Enter Level Above Precision: One should test systems on dialectal sensitivity, cultural relevancy, contextual accuracy, and pragmatic competency (e.g., can the AI use honorifics appropriately?). (Al-Mutawa & Al-Aama, 2024).

In the reviewing process, it is essential to enlist Arab linguists and cultural academics to evaluate the AI output, ensuring that it is not only accurate but also respectful and relevant (Eppard et al., 2021).

5.3.4 The Interface (UI/UX) Should be Designed With the User in Mind

Right-to-Left (RTL) orientation: the interface should be natively and flawlessly adapted to RTL scripts, as well as text alignment, navigation bars, and iconography.

Culturally Intuitive Design: The visual design elements (colors, iconography, graphics, and avatars) should appeal to Arab learners, avoiding western-oriented analogy (Nejati et al., 2024).

Accessibility Features: Voice-based input and output is critical to meet oral learning traditions and to provide an alternative to those with lower reading capabilities (Yatri et al., 2023).

6. LESSONS FROM IMPLEMENTATION: EVIDENCE FROM THE ARAB WORLD

The use of artificial intelligence (AI) technologies in educational institutions is gaining more popularity recently in the Arab world. To modernize the educational system in Arab countries, AI has emerged as a potential solution that addresses issues such as overcrowding in classrooms, personalized teaching, and expanding access to high-quality learning opportunities, particularly for underserved communities and inclusive learners. Nonetheless, the process of bringing AI into Arab states and education is challenging, as it depends on cultural, infrastructural, and policy-related issues. This section will review recent empirical research studies on AI technologies in the Arab K-12 environment to better understand their potential effects in the field. These papers illuminate the process of bringing AI into classrooms, the challenges that teachers and learners experience, and the course to a better and fairer implementation. The results are tabulated in the categories listed below: Successes: Beneficial results and positive practices in AI-based education. Failures: Typical problems, shortfalls, and flaws of existing implementations. Recommendations, which consider stakeholders important: Policymakers should receive strategic and regulatory advice to support the implementation of AI in education. Teachers should receive functional advice on how to accommodate classroom needs and effectively engage with students. Designers and developers: Prioritize designs and development to increase cultural and contextual appropriateness. The given thematic framework offers a systematic perspective of assessing and examining the emerging role of AI in Arab education systems, the purpose of which is to eventually guide a more culturally mindful approach.

It presents a set of empirical case studies to illuminate real-world issues and possibilities of introducing educational technology in the context of refugees in the

Arab world. These examples are valuable, as they show on-the-ground evidence to support the theoretical concepts and design principles that have been raised in earlier chapters, emphasizing the non-negotiable elements of culturally responsive AI.

6.1. Recurring Successes: The Documented Potential of AI

The cumulative evidence that is presented by the case studies revealed that there is a strong and consistent pattern of positive results when AI is used well in the Arab education sector. These achievements point to the potential for AI to help resolve long-standing problems.

Improved Learning Outcomes and Test Scores: Various studies have demonstrated a significant improvement in academic performance, and it correlates well with the components of our proposed framework. The impressive gains recorded by Alkhasawneh (2025) in one of the most disadvantaged schools located in Jordan are not only a result of the AI mobile platform but also a policy enabling students to use their own mobile devices. This strategy is in line with the CRP principle of using the cultural assets and environment of students as a medium of learning and hence improving the relevance and effectiveness of learning.

Furthermore, the paradigm assumes that AI will be able to reduce the latent biases and increase representation. The study by Sa'Idah et al. (2024) in Jakarta and Yogyakarta found fluency and grammar improvements can be interpreted as evidence of AI systems providing consistent and unbiased feedback, which can be viewed as a representation of educational justice. The fact that low-achieving students received the best gift of the adaptive system that Alenezi (2024) observed indicates the potential of the AI to become an equalizing force, which is the main goal of CRP. As a result, all of the case studies indicate that AI-enhanced improvements in test scores would be the largest and most consistent in this paradigm when viewed as outcomes of the creation of more inclusive, responsive, and equitable learning environments.

AI facilitated a more personalized learning experience, leading to increased student engagement and motivation. The observed enhancements in engagement and motivation are direct results of this alignment. The ability of the students in the Alenezi (2024) study to make their learning experiences personalized concurs with the CRP concept of considering the diversity in the epistemology and learning style of students, explaining the high rate of engagement by the group (mean=3.42/5). In addition to the enhancement of appeal, AI can help to incorporate culturally relevant aesthetics and examples, thereby increasing relevance and motivation, as was shown in the study conducted by Alkhasawneh (2025) among Jordanian students. This individualization includes not only material but also the communication process and the critical development of skills that are crucial to enabling students to demand their cultural identity and engage with the world. The Almuhanna (2024) study shows that AI-enhanced soft skills, such as creativity and critical thinking, are necessary; from the CRP perspective, these skills serve not only as generic competencies but also as tools for cultural critique and self-expression. In turn, in this strategy, AI-based interaction is not only an indicator of attention but also indicative of a learning process that is adaptive, affirmative, and empowering to students with diverse backgrounds.

Administrative Efficiency: AI tools have significantly reduced administrative tasks for educators, allowing them to focus more on teaching. As argued in a systematic review by Rabie (2023), the use of automated grading and predictive analytics has minimized teacher workload and made it easier to identify at-risk students. Artificial intelligence-based grading systems, predictive analytics, and humanoid robot help desks have reduced the workload on instructors and provided some classroom support (Rabie, 2023; Alzahrani, 2022). With the help of data dashboards, reports generated with AI, and suggestions, teachers planned lessons (Alenezi, 2024; Almuhanna, 2024). Furthermore, the predictive modeling approach supports both short- and long-term risk detection through the incorporation of historical data, offering a scalable and comprehensive solution to the persistent issue of student dropout. Elbouknify et al.'s (2025) predictive AI-driven modeling approach was able to identify students at risk of dropping out of school early with an accuracy of up to 88 percent in Morocco, demonstrating how AI can support school administration. Ultimately, the administrative effectiveness that AI offers includes not only automating grading but also predicting outcomes. To sum up, the administrative efficiency provided by AI, such as automated grading or predictive dropout algorithms, is not just a convenience but a prerequisite to culturally responsive pedagogy. The tools discussed by Rabie (2023), Alenezi (2024), and Elbouknify et al. (2025) address quantitative tasks that pertain to data volumes of education. Thus, in this context, the most significant administrative role of AI tutors is to be more efficient cultural facilitators, mentors, and advocates of their students.

Pandemic and Crisis Response: The role of AI in responding to a pandemic and crisis underscores its basic importance in enhancing the cause of educational equity, which is the central aim of culturally responsive pedagogy. Shutting down physical schools often disrupts the marginalized and rural populations the most. These studies mentioned, such as the review by Alzahrani or the study on M-Learning by Reinprecht et al. (2021), help us understand that AI-driven tools play an essential role in maintaining education continuity. This feat transcends a mere technical accomplishment; it exemplifies cultural receptivity. These technologies will ensure that education does not break down for affected pupils, irrespective of their geographic and socioeconomic background, because they allow remote location access using mobile AI. The framework, as a result, names AI in crisis management as a crucial tool that should be used to uphold the CRP pledge to deliver meaningful learning opportunities to all students regardless of their situations.

6.1.1. Benefits in Refugee Contexts: Access, Inclusion, and Psychosocial Support

When utilized in a considerate manner that takes surrounding circumstances into account, technology and AI have a lot of potential when it comes to assisting refugee education. Improved **Access and Enrollment:** Technology-aided programs and other alternative education pathways have been significant contributors toward Syrian refugee enrollment rates in Jordan returning to their 2013 levels (Krafft et al., 2022). Integration and distance learning platforms can help provide access to education in areas where schooling is interrupted.

Enhanced Engagement and Psychosocial Support: Psychosocial support and culturally relevant digital tools, including Arabic language games and locally relevant stories, greatly increased participation, especially among girls (Tal et al., 2022). These instruments also offered much-needed psychosocial support, reducing feelings of isolation, giving hope, and improving self-esteem through a sense of safety and community. This practical implementation of the main idea of CRP, the scaffold of learning, is based on the cultural knowledge and life experience of students (Ladson-Billings, 1995). The success of the AI tool was not only because of the technological skills but mostly because it extended beyond Arabic language translation. The curriculum directly incorporated well-known stories, folklore, and problem-solving scenarios related to the Levantine setting. For example, math word problems were framed within familiar activities like traditional baking recipes or local market exchanges, while history modules connected broader topics to the rich history of the Levant. Active cultural support alleviates the cognitive strain of learning in an unfamiliar environment, promoting a sense of belonging and validation. It shows that for AI tutors; cultural responsiveness is not a feature that is added but a system design principle that can directly influence engagement and knowledge retention among vulnerable groups of students.

Effective Personalized Learning: AI-based platforms have been employed in personalizing teaching and learning content, linguistic diversity support, and real-time feedback, which elevated learner engagement and learning outcomes (Alkhasawneh, 2025).

Mobile-First Reach: Smartphone penetration among refugees is high (90 percent in one study), presenting an essential channel to deliver education content right into the hands of learners, regardless of the other obstacles to attending schools (Reinprecht et al., 2021). This approach aims to teach more critical soft skills, such as creativity, communication, and critical thinking.

6.2. Systemic Challenges: The Barriers to Fulfilling AI's Promise

Despite its demonstrated capabilities, the integration of AI into Arab education encounters persistent, institutional obstacles that have hindered the realization of its potential in a fair and efficient way.

The Infrastructure Gap: The digital divide poses the greatest challenge, as it contradicts the CRP goal of ensuring that every pupil receives an equivalent educational foundation. The frequent reports of challenges in the technological field (Alenezi, 2024; Rabie, 2023) and the complete lack of AI integration in countries like Libya and Iraq (Alzahrani, 2022) due to poor infrastructure represent more than just operational failures. They represent an institutional failure to act upon and respond to the material conditions of children in rural and underprivileged areas. Lack of reliable internet, hardware, or electricity means that the students cannot contribute dependably to the educational discourse, and this nullifies the purpose of the educational system being culturally relevant. Alasmari (2024) argues that such infrastructural inequity ensures that AI does not reduce disparities but instead worsens them, especially in favor of urban and wealthy pupils and against the disadvantaged. This fact indicates the conclusion of Pehlivan Yilmaz & Gunel (2022) regarding refugee education: until the framework of recognizing and actively addressing the contextual barriers, be they the technological or the pedagogical ones, the task to achieve the objective of student belonging and engagement becomes unavailable.

The Cultural-Linguistic Mismatch: a severe gap between the construction and implementation of AI and the cultural, linguistic, and ethical realities of the Arab classroom. Currently, the solutions that AI offers to create egalitarian learning environments are inherently culturally insensitive, pedagogically disruptive, and ethically ambiguous. The issue of the cultural-linguistic mismatch is not a technical one but a complete violation of the first principle of culturally responsive pedagogy: the affirmation of the cultural and linguistic identities of students. The external system favored by AI technologies designed in the Western context, as seen by Almuhanna (2024) and Rabie (2023), marginalizes the Arabic language and local curricula. The result is effectively communicating to children that the history of their language does not match technological progression, and it is the opposite of a culturally affirming education.

Human Factor: The challenges linked to the human factor, such as the lack of preparation of teachers, cultural resistance, and the lack of digital skills, highlight a severe mistake in the process of AI integration. CRP assigns the educator as a key mediator of culture. However, the studies by Alenezi (2024) and Alzahrani (2023) show that resistance is inevitable without sufficient educational and awareness training, along with a clear narrative that presents AI as an aid rather than a replacement for teachers. The results of Almuhanna (2024) support the idea that advancing AI literacy and developing soft skills are essential for successfully integrating AI, thereby empowering educators as agents of culturally responsive change instead of ostracizing them.

The ethical and governance issues, as well as the lack of inclusiveness for marginalized subgroups, are significant concerns. The ethical and governance issues, as well as the lack of inclusivity of marginalized subgroups, are indicators of serious breaches of trust and equity. Thalji and Alkhasawneh (2025) express data privacy concerns, and Gouseti et al. (2025) highlight the absence of inclusive design, both demonstrating how AI may support the biases and non-representativeness that CRP is supposed to eradicate. The warning that AI will not pay sufficient attention to particular students and the statement by Alasmari (2025) that inclusiveness is often viewed as a secondary concern confirm that, unless specific efforts are undertaken, AI will continue to widen existing inequalities. A major warning is the refugee schooling situation, where technology overshadowed the psychological needs (Zakharia and Menashy, 2020).

Finally, AI needs to develop into a technology that is embraced by culture instead of being an externally imposed technology to achieve its potential in Arab education. This necessitates a fundamental dedication to harmonizing AI development and deployment with the essential principles of culturally responsive pedagogy: honoring linguistic diversity, empowering educators, safeguarding student privacy, and emphasizing equitable inclusion for all learners.

6.3. Synthesis: The Path Forward – Evidence-Based Recommendations

The adoption of the CRP approach implies that there should be a radical transformation from top-down development to joint co-design involvement. The following guidelines can be used to authenticate cultural backgrounds and avoid shallow stereotypes:

An overview of the insights of success and failure could help in giving a conclusive number of evidence-based recommendations, which will be taken into action by key stakeholder groups to ensure that AI and technology can achieve their potential in Arab education, especially the refugee communities.

6.3.1 For Policymakers and Funders

The international funders and policymakers need to establish an enabling environment to support sustainable, equitable, and context-sensitive integration.

- Invest in Infrastructure: Reallocate budgetary funding to ensure sufficient investment in both digital infrastructure (such as internet connectivity and modern hardware) and foundational infrastructure (like stable electricity), particularly targeting rural, underserved, and refugee communities to help reduce the digital divide. We combine the recommendations of Alasmari (2025), Alzahrani (2024), and Alenezi (2024) with the case studies of the refugees. ·
- Create National AI Strategies & Ethical Frameworks: Design national policies concerning the localization of AI tools and consider data privacy, algorithmic bias, and culturally sensitive AI applications. When using cognitive behavioral therapy, combine the suggestions of Almuhanna (2024), Rabie (2023), and Alasmari (2025).
- Fund Long-Term Integration and Teacher Training: Invest in the systematic, continuous professional development of teachers and the process of incorporating effective technology programs into national education systems to make them long-term efforts rather than short-term initiatives in countries (Combine recommendations from Almuhanna (2024), Alzahrani (2024), and Sa'Idah et al. (2024)).
- Mandate Community Co-Design: Require that the funded interventions actively engage the refugees, host population, teachers, and parents in the design and implementation process so that it can be culturally and pedagogically relevant. With this goal in mind, consideration must be given to the scope; that is, the dimensions of the research problem being studied (a key finding in the refugee case studies by Al Tal et al., 2022).

6.3.2 To Developers/NGOs

A Framework of Authentic Co-design of Arab Education for Developers and Non-Governmental Organizations. The effective integration of AI teachers in marginalized Arab groups requires an enormous shift from a top-down, copy-paste model to that of true co-design. Such an approach ensures that tools are not merely translated, but they are culturally sensitive, attentive to the local intellectual resources, and developed in such a way that they are sustainable over the long term. Based on regional evidence, this framework outlines critical action pillars.

1. Emphasize the importance of Arabic natural language processing and the variation among dialects.

Action: Invest in research and development that uncovers the complexity of Arabic that goes beyond Modern Standard Arabic (MSA) to include popular forms of Arabic like Levantine and Egyptian. Develop NLP technologies that are capable of reading and writing content in these dialects to ensure actual accessibility and relevance.

Reason: According to Sa'Idah et al. (2024) and Rabie (2023), the lack of attention to linguistic variety is a basic barrier to its acceptance and effectiveness.

2. Combine Cultural and Linguistic Significance through Cooperation.

Collaborate with local teachers, cultural experts, and community members to co-create content. This will ensure that modules are culturally relevant, Arab-pride-focused, locally integrated, and gender-sensitive in design where necessary.

The key recommendation concerning Almuhanna (2024), Sa'Idah et al. (2024), and case studies of refugees emphasizes the urgent need to implement massive community engagement to move the theory into practice.

3. Accessibility and Infrastructure Accessibility and Infrastructure Engineer.

Task: Build the infrastructure base in the region. Go mobile first, ensure offline functionality, and optimize performance of low-bandwidth (2G) connections. Use easy input features, including voice recognition and uploading images, to minimize typing, and cloud synchronization when it can be connected.

Reason: This is a paramount and constant requirement of Almuhanna (2024) and all the reviewed refugee case studies, which ensure that tools are operational in real-life settings.

6.3.3 For Educators and Implementers

Teachers and frontline implementers are the key protagonists in this integration, and we must empower them to spearhead it

- Demand Training and Become Co-Designers: Pursue professional training proactively and aim to be more than just users. Offer insight to the designers/programmers and contribute to design phases so that they produce the most applicable, pedagogically sound, and ethically developed tools. Almuhanna (2024) endorses Alenezi's (2025) major recommendations.
- Adopt a Blended Formula: Use technology to enhance, not replace, human interaction. Use AI (e.g., to grade) in concert with traditional teacher feedback. A recommendation that can be made based on the voice of refugee case studies and one inferred in the case of teacher attitudes (Al-Waridat, 2024) is to include more games as a means of diversifying the tools that can be used effectively in the classroom.

- Integrate AI literacy and utilize it as a supportive tool. Educate students not only on how to use technology but also on its principles and implications. In addition to that, technology is used not only for the purposes of academic achievement but also to promote psychosocial support, resilience, and social connections through access to game-based learning and virtual communities. One of the main implications derived from the studies of refugees is a direct recommendation from Almuhanna (2024) and Alasmari (2025).
- Community Engagement: Establish a partnership with parents and local organizations and find common ground, developing trust and support in AI utilization (Alenezi, 2024; Rabie, 2023; Reinprecht et al., 2021).).

7. CONCLUSION: STRATEGIC IMPERATIVES OF AI-BASED INTEGRATION OF EDUCATION IN THE ARAB WORLD

This chapter concludes that educational equity in poor Arab classrooms requires cultural intelligence algorithms, not more sophisticated ones. The use of the paradigm of Culturally Responsive Pedagogy (CRP) is not merely the change in technology but rather the moral and pedagogical imperative. The principles of CRP, including identity affirmation, cultural competency, and sociopolitical awareness, provide a basic framework for development beyond AI tools that solely work in Arabic and those that interact with Arab students. The examples and models show that the goal is to make AI tutors that see a student's culture as a learning prerequisite, not a challenge. The direction of future projects should be based on the combination of technological knowledge and deep cultural understanding, which will ensure that the opportunities of AI in education will allow for the improvement, not the saving, of diverse cultural views.

The Arab world finds itself at a pivotal point. The chapter explores an instance of big disparity, highlighting the vast potential that can be displayed and the numerous challenges that are involved in the system. Examples of how AI can promote retention and equity in education include reported successes such as adaptive learning in Saudi Arabia, which increased outcomes by 22 percent, and an AI-based dropout prediction model in the Moroccan education system that successfully identified at-risk students, enabling timely interventions that reduced dropout rates by 88 percent. However, there remain major challenges, such as insufficient infrastructure; thus, 34 percent of the remote schools lack reliable internet connectivity, and the language issue hinders the performance of Arabic NLP.

The further future of Arab tutoring based on AI is exciting and complicated at the same time. Although the contemporary environment is frequently characterized by a lack of equality related to infrastructure, availability of some information, and cultural orientation, it offers numerous opportunities to change everything around dramatically. When used sensitively, AI will lead to educational equality in marginalized and underserved communities, such as refugees, rural students, and students with few trained educators.

It needs to be a multi-layered strategy to turn the vision into reality, i.e., a strategy that combines technological innovation with cultural awareness and educational inclusion. To begin with, investments need to be made in the development of strong local datasets, especially those that are underrepresented speakers of Arabic dialects such as Maghrebi, Gulf Arabic, and Levantine Arabic. Training AI solutions with culturally competent and multilingual information will enhance their ability to understand the real needs of students

Second, it's crucial to address the digital divide to develop offline-enabled, smart, and mobile-friendly artificial intelligence tools. Low-bandwidth settings and low-cost gadgets must enable these solutions to cover a wider range of impoverished areas.

Third, collaborative human-AI environments hold the key to the future of AI learning in the Arab region. Teachers should receive training not only in using AI but also in co-developing and critically evaluating it. Artificial intelligence should be an add-on to the role of a teacher, providing him or her with practical information, adaptive material, and resources in various languages reflecting the life experiences of their students.

Fourth, policymakers should develop systems that will facilitate ethical integration of AI in schools. This may involve creating data privacy laws, ensuring transparency in AI decision-making, and providing incentives to schools that participate in trials of inclusive AI instruments. The government and education ministries should also safeguard the partnerships between the government and any business enterprises to ensure that innovations comply with national curricula and local values.

Finally, community co-design is key to sustainability. A new AI tutor should be created in collaboration with Arab educators, students, and parents rather than serving them. When communities help create the technology they use, they will trust it more and achieve better results.

To sum up, the path towards culturally responsive AI in K-12 education in Arab countries is yet to be written. However, when you and the students have a shared interest in equity, collaboration, and context-sensitive innovation, smart tutoring systems can be built where they do not only provide academic material but also confirm who and what we are through identity, language, and culture. The future lies with those learners who are not only digitally networked but also culturally visible. With every learner gaining the benefit of our full education and care, we are making a more intelligent and equitable future together, one where they can hear themselves, see themselves in the world, and achieve the best out of themselves.

REFERENCES

Abdo, N. I., Alwaely, S. A., Aburezeq, I. M., Alkhazaleh, M. S., Alaqtash, S. K., & El-Zeiny, M. E. (2024). Assessing the extent of AI implementations in Arabic L2 courses. *2024 Fifth International Conference on Intelligent Data Science Technologies and Applications (IDSTA)*, 231–236. https://doi.org/DOI: 10.1109/IDSTA62194.2024.10746992

Al-Ghobesi, A. A. H. (2025). Risks of relying on artificial intelligence in learning Arabic language sciences through the Meta application. *Arts for Linguistic & Literary Studies*, *7*(1), 396–419. DOI: 10.53286/arts.v7i1.2420

Al-Mutawa, R. F., & Al-Aama, A. Y. (2024). Arabic opinion classification of customer service conversations using data augmentation and artificial intelligence. *Big Data and Cognitive Computing*, *8*(12), 196. DOI: 10.3390/bdcc8120196

Al-Tal, R., Sallam, S., & Ali, H. (2022). Syrian crisis impacts on the international refugee education fund in Jordan. *International Journal of Educational Reform*, *34*(2), 320–335. DOI: 10.1177/10567879221124882

Al-Waridat, A. Y. (2024). Attitudes of first through third grade teachers in Al-Rusayfa district toward using artificial intelligence techniques in inclusive education. *Journal of Education, 40*(4.2), 78–110. https://doi.org/DOI: 10.21608/mfes.2024.362288

AlAfnan, M. (2024). Artificial Intelligence and Language: Bridging Arabic and English with Technology. *Journal of Ecohumanism*, *4*(1), 240–256. DOI: 10.62754/joe.v3i8.4961

Alakabawy, B. (2024). Artificial intelligence in the educational stages from kindergarten to university: A systematic review of Arab studies from 2010 to 2023. *E-Learning and Digital Media*, *21*(3), 1–24. DOI: 10.1177/20427530241276140

Alasmari, T. (2025). Artificial intelligence and M-learning in Arabic countries: Innovations, trends, and regional perspectives. [iJIM]. *International Journal of Interactive Mobile Technologies*, *19*(5), 170–194. DOI: 10.3991/ijim.v19i05.52735

Alayba, A. M. (2025). Arabic Natural Language Processing (NLP): A Comprehensive Review of Challenges, Techniques, and Emerging Trends. *Computers*, *14*(11), 497. DOI: 10.3390/computers14110497

Alenezi, A. (2024). Evaluating the effectiveness of AI-powered adaptive learning systems in secondary schools. *International Journal on Studies in Education*, *6*(2), 45–67. DOI: 10.46328/ijonse.264

Aljabr, F., Zakarneh, B., Annamalai, N., & Al Said, N. (2025). Integrating AI: Challenges and opportunities in teaching English writing skills. *World Journal of English Language*, *15*(5), 371. DOI: 10.5430/wjel.v15n5p371

Alkhasawneh, S. (2025). AI-Driven Personalized Mathematics Learning Through Interactive Mobile Platforms: Effects on Achievement and Motivation. [iJIM]. *International Journal of Interactive Mobile Technologies*, *19*(13), 33–54. DOI: 10.3991/ijim.v19i13.54947

Almuhanna, M. A. (2024). Teachers' perspectives of integrating AI-powered technologies in K-12 education for creating customized learning materials and resources. *Education and Information Technologies*, *29*(10), 10343–10371. DOI: 10.1007/s10639-024-13257-y

Alzahrani, A. (2022). A systematic review of artificial intelligence in education in the Arab world. *Amazonia Investiga*, *11*(54), 293–305. DOI: 10.34069/AI/2022.54.06.28

Aronson, B., & Laughter, J. (2016). The theory and practice of culturally relevant education: A synthesis of research across content areas. *Review of Educational Research*, *86*(1), 163–206. DOI: 10.3102/0034654315582066

Asfar, H., Husna, I., Yasmadi, Y., Khairi, A., Suryani, K., Ikhlas, A., & Madona, A. (2024). Innovative Arabic language learning: Redefining language archetypes using artificial intelligence. *Al-Ta'rib. Jurnal Ilmiah Program Studi Pendidikan Bahasa Arab IAIN Palangka Raya*, *12*(2), 293–308. Advance online publication. DOI: 10.23971/altarib.v12i2.8323

Benjamin, R. (2019). *Race after technology: Abolitionist tools for the New Jim Code*. Polity Press.

Borham, S., Ramli, S., & Ghani, M. (2024). AI concepts integration in developing E-Muhadathat kits for non-Arabic speakers. *Ijaz Arabi Journal of Arabic Learning*, *7*(3). Advance online publication. DOI: 10.18860/ijazarabi.v7i3.26568

Buolamwini, J., & Gebru, T. (2018). Gender shades: Intersectional accuracy disparities in commercial gender classification. In *Proceedings of Machine Learning Research* (Vol. 81, pp. 77–91). https://proceedings.mlr.press/v81/buolamwini18a/buolamwini18a.pdf

Elbouknify, I., Berrada, I., Mekouar, L., Iraqi, Y., Bergou, E. H., Belhabib, H., Nail, Y., & Wardi, S. (2025). *AI-based identification and support of at-risk students: A case study of the Moroccan education system* (arXiv:2504.07160) [Preprint]. arXiv. https://doi.org//arXiv.2504.07160DOI: 10.48550

Elmahdi, O. E. H., Balla, A. A. S., Abdelrady, A. H., Othman, E., & Abdelaziz Ahmed, A. (2025). AI-Driven Vocabulary Acquisition in EFL Higher Education: Interdisciplinary Insights into Technological Innovation, Ethical Challenges, and Equitable Access. *Forum for Linguistic Studies*, *7*(4), 477–491. DOI: 10.30564/fls.v7i4.8760

Elsheikh Hago Elmahdi, O., Ahmed Saeed Balla, A., Hussein Abdelrady, A., Othman, E., & Othman Abdelaziz Ahmed, A. (2025). AI-Driven Vocabulary Acquisition in EFL Higher Education: Interdisciplinary Insights into Technological Innovation, Ethical Challenges, and Equitable Access. *Forum for Linguistic Studies*, *7*(4), 477–491. DOI: 10.30564/fls.v7i4.8760

Eppard, J., Kaviani, A., Bowles, M., & Johnson, J. (2021). EdTech culturation: Integrating a culturally relevant pedagogy into educational technology. *Electronic Journal of e-Learning*, *19*(6), 516–530. DOI: 10.34190/ejel.19.6.2065

Essa, N., El-Gayar, M. M., & El-Daydamony, E. M. (2025). Enhanced model for abstractive Arabic text summarization using natural language generation and named entity recognition. *Neural Computing & Applications*, *37*(10), 7279–7301. DOI: 10.1007/s00521-024-10949-x

Faison, M., Nyaaba, M., & Zhai, X. (2024). Generative AI for culturally responsive science assessment: A conceptual framework. *Education Sciences*, *14*(12), 1325. DOI: 10.3390/educsci14121325

Garba, M., & Hassan, A. (2024). Use of AI in learning Arabic language by non-Arabic speakers. *International Journal of Research and Innovation in Social Science*, *8*(8), 2519–2532. Advance online publication. DOI: 10.47772/IJRISS.2024.8080191

Gay, G. (2010). *Culturally responsive teaching: Theory, research, and practice* (2nd ed.). Teachers College Press.

Gouseti, A., James, F., Fallin, L., & Burden, K. (2025). The ethics of using AI in K-12 education: A systematic literature review. *Technology, Pedagogy and Education*, *34*(2), 161–182. DOI: 10.1080/1475939X.2024.2428601

Habash, N. (2023). *Computational modeling of Arabic dialects*. Cambridge University Press.

Hartanto, B., Zaimah, N., Hartanto, E., Zahro, F., Zaimah, R., & Nely, C. (2023). Acceptability and effectiveness analysis of large language model-based artificial intelligence chatbot among Arabic learners. *Mantiqu Tayr: Journal of Arabic Language*, *4*(1), 1–20. Advance online publication. DOI: 10.25217/mantiqutayr.v4i1.3951

Huang, H., Yu, F., Zhu, J., Sun, X., Cheng, H., Song, D., Chen, Z., Alharthi, A., An, B., He, J., Liu, Z., Chen, J., Li, J., Wang, B., Zhang, L., Sun, R., Wan, X., Li, H., & Xu, J. (2024). AceGPT, localizing large language models in Arabic. *Proceedings of the 2024 Conference of the North American Chapter of the Association for Computational Linguistics: Human Language Technologies (*Volume 1*: Long Papers)*, 8139–8163. https://doi.org/DOI: 10.18653/v1/2024.naacl-long.450

Jaboob, M., Hazaimeh, M., & Al-Ansi, A. (2024). Integration of generative AI techniques and applications in student behavior and cognitive achievement in Arab higher education. *International Journal of Human-Computer Interaction*, *41*(1), 353–366. DOI: 10.1080/10447318.2023.2300016

Krafft, C., Assaad, R., & Keo, C. (2022). The Jordan Compact: Impact on education and labor market outcomes of Syrian refugees. *ERF Working Paper Series*.

Kuo, A., Alves-Oliveira, P., Björling, E., & Louie, B. (2022). Designing for culturally responsive social robots: An application of a participatory framework. *Frontiers in Robotics and AI*, *9*, 983408. Advance online publication. DOI: 10.3389/frobt.2022.983408 PMID: 36340576

Ladson-Billings, G. (1995). Toward a theory of culturally relevant pedagogy. *American Educational Research Journal*, *32*(3), 465–491. DOI: 10.3102/00028312032003465

Lampropoulos, G., & Papadakis, S. (2025). The educational value of artificial intelligence and social robots. In *Social Robots in Education* (pp. 3–15). Springer. DOI: 10.1007/978-3-031-82915-4_1

Lavidas, K., Papadakis, S., Manesis, D., Grigoriadou, A. S., & Gialamas, V.Lectures and Lab Classes. (2022). The effects of social desirability on students' self-reports in two social contexts: Lectures vs. lectures and lab classes. *Information (Basel)*, *13*(10), 491. DOI: 10.3390/info13100491

Lavidas, K., Petropoulou, A., Papadakis, S., Apostolou, Z., Komis, V., Jimoyiannis, A., & Gialamas, V. (2022). Factors affecting response rates of the web survey with teachers. *Computers*, *11*(9), 127. DOI: 10.3390/computers11090127

Lee, C. D. (2003). Toward a framework for culturally responsive design in multimedia computer environments: Cultural modeling as a case. *Mind, Culture, and Activity*, *10*(1), 42–61. DOI: 10.1207/S15327884MCA1001_05

Lukasik, S., & Ozegalska-Lukasik, N. (2023). *Culturally responsive artificial intelligence - Problems, challenges and solutions* (arXiv:2312.08467) [Preprint]. arXiv. https://doi.org//arXiv.2312.08467DOI: 10.48550

Mariyono, D., & Abror, M. (2024). AI in enhancing cultural sensitivity. *Jurnal EDUCATIO: Jurnal Pendidikan Indonesia*, *10*(2), 296–310. DOI: 10.29210/1202424847

Menashy, F., & Zakharia, Z. (2022). Crisis upon crisis: Refugee education responses amid COVID-19. *Peabody Journal of Education*, *97*(3), 309–325. DOI: 10.1080/0161956X.2022.2079895

Misaki, D., Ge, X., Xu, C., Markus, H., & Tsai, J. (2024). How culture shapes what people want from AI. *Proceedings of the 2024 CHI Conference on Human Factors in Computing Systems*. https://doi.org/DOI: 10.1145/3613904.3642660

Moaiad, Y., Alobed, M., Alsakhnini, M., & Momani, A. (2024). *Challenges in natural Arabic language processing*. Edelweiss Applied Science and Technology., DOI: 10.55214/25768484.v8i6.3018

Mohideen, H.H. L. M. Mohideen. (2024). Exploring the opportunities of implementing artificial intelligence (AI) technology for teaching Arabic to non-native speakers: A theoretical approach. *Journal of Digital Learning and Distance Education*, *2*(9), 760–767. Advance online publication. DOI: 10.56778/jdlde.v2i9.225

Mulyanto, D., Zaky, M., Ridho, A., & Fata, K. (2024). [Using artificial intelligence to develop Arabic language skills in learning]. *An-Nidzam: Jurnal Manajemen Pendidikan dan Studi Islam, 11*(1), 18–32. https://doi.org/DOI: 10.33507/an-nidzam.v11i1.1940

Nejati, B., Manchi, R., & Schofield, D. (2024). Incorporating cross-cultural design into the user interface. *The International Journal of Multimedia & Its Applications*. https://doi.org/DOI: 10.5121/ijma.2024.16501

Papadakis, S., Lytvynova, S. H., Ivanova, S. M., & Selyshcheva, I. A. (2024). Advancing lifelong learning with AI-enhanced ICT: A review of 3L-Person 2024. *CEUR Workshop Proceedings*, *3679*, 1–11. https://ceur-ws.org/Vol-3679/paper00.pdf

Papadakis, S., Striuk, A. M., Kravtsov, H. M., Shyshkina, M. P., Marienko, M. V., & Danylchuk, H. B. (2024). Embracing digital innovation and cloud technologies for transformative learning experiences. *CEUR Workshop Proceedings*, *3781*, 1–13. https://ceur-ws.org/Vol-3781/paper00.pdf

Pehlivan Yılmaz, A., & Günel, E. (2022). Culturally responsive teaching practices in social studies: Interaction with refugee students in Turkey. *Education in Science*, *47*(212), 121–159. DOI: 10.15390/EB.2022.11338

Rabie, R. M. (2023). The future of education with artificial intelligence and machine learning in the Arab world: A systematic review. *Educational Sciences Journal (Al-Ulum Al-Tarbawiya), 31*(3), 1–35. https://doi.org/DOI: 10.21608/ssj.2023.344574

Reinprecht, C., Suter, R., Parry, B., & Rampelt, F. (2021). No longer a 'lost generation'? Opportunities and obstacles of online and blended learning programmes for Syrian refugees in Jordan and Lebanon. *Journal of Refugee Studies, 34*(3), 3197–3220. DOI: 10.1093/jrs/feab034

Rohmawaty, E., Hilmi, D., Uqba, S., & Saleh, U. (2024). Peran Artificial Intelligence (AI) dalam pembelajaran bahasa Arab mahasiswa pascas jana UIN Maulana Malik Ibrahim Malang. *Khatulistiwa: Jurnal Pendidikan dan Sosial Humaniora, 4*(3). https://doi.org/DOI: 10.55606/khatulistiwa.v4i3.4023

Sa'Idah, M. A., Diantoro, K., Mahmudah, U., Dolan, E., Santoso, N. A., & Junaedi, S. R. P. (2024). Enhancing Arabic language teaching through artificial intelligence: Assessing effectiveness and educational implications. *2024 3rd International Conference on Creative Communication and Innovative Technology (ICCIT)*, 1–8. https://doi.org/DOI: 10.1109/ICCIT62134.2024.10701089

Sahrir, M. S., Albantani, A. M., & Arifin, F. (2025). The use of generative artificial intelligence (AI) in Arabic language education: Insights and implications between Malaysia and Indonesia. [IJRISS]. *International Journal of Research and Innovation in Social Science, 9*(3), 3638–3646. DOI: 10.47772/IJRISS.2025.90300288

Sajjad, H., Abdelali, A., Dalvi, F., Durrani, N., & Vogel, S. (2020). *AraBench: Benchmarking dialectal Arabic–English machine translation.* In Proceedings of the 28th International Conference on Computational Linguistics (COLING 2020) (pp. 5094–5105). International Committee on Computational Linguistics. https://doi.org/DOI: 10.18653/v1/2020.coling-main.447

Sengupta, N., Han, X., Knight, A., Sikka, R., Li, S., Ni, J., . . . Habash, N. (2023). *Jais: A Giant Step for Arabic LLMs* [Preprint]. arXiv. https://doi.org//arXiv.2308.16149DOI: 10.48550

Septia, F., & Khodr, T. S. I. (2024). Unlocking AI's potential in language learning: A comparative study of adoption and effectiveness in Indonesia and Arab countries. *Language, Technology, and Social Media, 2*(1), 60–71. DOI: 10.70211/ltsm.v2i1.78

Seyidov, R. (2024). Arabic language processing: Current status and future prospects of artificial intelligence. *Journal of Namibian Studies: History Politics Culture, 3*(9), 458–471. DOI: 10.59670/jwszy037

Tan, B., Tan, S., & Han, D. (2025). AI-assisted cultural and creative product design framework and case study. *Journal of Communication, Language and Culture.* https://doi.org/DOI: 10.33093/ijomfa.2025.6.1.8

Thalji, N. J., & Alkhasawneh, S. (2025). How can artificial intelligence shape the future of sustainable education? Challenges and opportunities. *Journal of Theoretical and Applied Information Technology*, *103*(9), 3836–3847. https://www.jatit.org/volumes/Vol103No9/20Vol103No9.pdf

Uğraş, H., Uğraş, M., Papadakis, S., & Kalogiannakis, M. (2024). ChatGPT-supported education in primary schools: The potential of ChatGPT for sustainable practices. *Sustainability (Basel)*, *16*(22), 9855. DOI: 10.3390/su16229855

UNHCR. (2023, June 14). *Global trends: Forced displacement in 2022*. United Nations High Commissioner for Refugees. https://www.unhcr.org/global-trends

World Bank. (2022). *Thrive: The role of higher education in refugee students' futures*. https://openknowledge.worldbank.org/handle/10986/37230

Xiao, N., Pei, Y., Yuan, C., Bu, Y., & Cai, Z. (2025). Transforming Education with Artificial Intelligence: A Comprehensive Review of Applications, Challenges, and Future Directions. *International Theory and Practice in Humanities and Social Sciences*, *2*(1), 337–356. DOI: 10.70693/itphss.v2i1.211

Xue, L., Constant, N., Roberts, A., Kale, M., Al-Rfou, R., Siddhant, A., Barua, A., & Raffel, C. (2020). mT5: A massively multilingual pre-trained text-to-text transformer [Preprint]. arXiv. https://arxiv.org/abs/2010.11934

Yatri, D., Anugerahwati, M., & Setyowati, L. (2023). Artificial intelligence (AI) in language learning (English and Arabic class): Students' and teachers' experience and perceptions. *Transformational Language, Literature, and Technology Overview in Learning*, *3*(1), 1–12. DOI: 10.55047/transtool.v3i1.1338

Yosso, T. J. (2005). Whose culture has capital? A critical theory discussion of community cultural wealth. *Race, Ethnicity and Education*, *8*(1), 69–91. DOI: 10.1080/1361332052000341006

Chapter 10
Designing Ethical and Engaging Chatbots for K-12 Education: Voice, Story, and AI

Rama Yusvana
http://orcid.org/0009-0001-6990-2171
Faculty of Engineering Technology, Tun Hussein Onn University of Malaysia, Malaysia

'Aisyah Mohamed Rehan
http://orcid.org/0000-0001-7841-1705
Research Institute for Vocational Education and Training, Tun Hussein Onn University of Malaysia, Malaysia

ABSTRACT

AI integration in K-12 education promises personalised learning but faces engagement, accessibility and ethical challenges. Text-centric tools often fail digital natives. Voice systems and cultural narratives are under-used. This chapter explores how conversational AI chatbot with personas and narrative gamification can bridge these gaps. It evaluates voice-based AI tutors, adaptive storytelling, and inclusive design for equitable, engaging learning. Drawing on narrative-centred learning, universal design for learning, and self-determination theory, it synthesises studies and critiques. Findings show narratives boost engagement via quests, and voice interfaces aid neurodiverse/multilingual learners. Culturally-adaptive personas and low-cost voice systems increase access, yet AI bias and privacy risks require mitigation. The chapter advocates hybrid teacher-AI models. Implications stress

DOI: 10.4018/979-8-3373-2637-5.ch010

ethically grounded, scalable solutions balancing innovation with inclusivity. When designed with narrative elements, AI may support equitable and culturally-relevant classroom practices.

1. INTRODUCTION

The integration of Artificial Intelligence (AI) into K-12 education has emerged as a transformative force, yet student engagement and equitable access remain persistent challenges in modern classrooms (Bougdira & Al Murshidi, 2025). Traditional text-based AI tools, while effective for some learners, often fail to captivate younger students who thrive on interactive and emotionally resonant experiences. Conversational AI chatbot aligns with the intrinsic motivations of digitally-native students but also addresses disparities in accessibility, offering voice-based alternatives to text-reliant tools (Bougdira & Al Murshidi, 2025; Corbeil & Corbeil, 2025). This innovation is urgent because it can reimagine engagement at a time of declining attention spans and diverse learning needs.

Current research underscores the efficacy of gamification and narrative techniques in boosting educational outcomes. Studies demonstrate that storytelling enhances memory retention by embedding information within emotionally charged contexts (Ginting et al., 2024), while gamified learning environments increase motivation through reward systems and progression mechanics (Jaskari & Syrjälä, 2024; Wang et al., 2024). Text-based AI chatbot, such as customised ChatGPT models, have shown promise in personalising instruction (Kumaran et al., 2025), yet their reliance on literacy skills excludes struggling readers and linguistically diverse students. Recent advancements in neural voice synthesis, exemplified by platforms like OpenAI's Voice Engine, now enable expressive, adaptive speech that mimics human mentors (Stragier et al., 2023). However, existing literature predominantly focuses on text interfaces, with limited exploration of voice-driven AI or its capacity to foster emotional connections through character personas (Mehrez et al., 2023).

Despite its promise, the deployment of conversational AI tutors raises unresolved ethical and practical dilemmas. Scholars warn that AI personas risk of perpetuating biases in gender and cultural representation if not thoughtfully designed (O'Connor & Liu, 2024). Additionally, voice data collection poses privacy concerns, particularly for minors, while over-reliance on AI could diminish critical human teacher–student interactions (Shukla & Taneja, 2024). Current studies often sidestep these issues, focusing instead on technical feasibility rather than holistic implementation frameworks. Furthermore, the equity potential of voice-based AI remains underexplored. While it may reduce cognitive load for struggling readers, access to voice-enabled devices in under-resourced schools remains a barrier (Seaborn et al., 2022). These gaps (tabulated in Table 1) underscore the need for a balanced approach that harmonises technological innovation with ethical safeguards and inclusivity.

Recent empirical studies provide strong evidence that AI-driven chatbot can meaningfully support student motivation, engagement, and learning outcomes when grounded in established pedagogical theories. For example, Renfeng et al. (2025) and Li & Chiu (2025) demonstrate how generative AI chatbot enhance learners' autonomy, competence, and relatedness—key dimensions of Self-Determination Theory (SDT)—by providing responsive feedback, stress-free practice, and emotionally engaging dialogue. Wu et al. (2025) further show that satisfaction of these psychological needs mediates stronger behavioural, cognitive, and emotional engagement, reinforcing SDT's relevance. At the same time, research guided by the Community of Inquiry (CoI) framework highlights how chatbots foster social and cognitive presence by simulating supportive peer or instructor dialogue, thereby sustaining collaborative meaning-making (Xie et al., 2024).

Complementing these insights, studies applying Cognitive Load Theory (CLT) in K-12 and higher education contexts (Ngandoh et al., 2025; Olugbade et al., 2024) reveal that well-designed chatbot interfaces can reduce extraneous load and scaffold intrinsic load, enabling learners to focus cognitive resources on conceptual understanding. Together, these findings explain why voice- and narrative-driven chatbots are uniquely poised to enhance K-12 learning: the voice modality strengthens social presence and reduces literacy barriers, while narrative structures contextualise abstract knowledge in emotionally resonant storylines. When integrated, these affordances align with SDT's motivational pathways, CoI's emphasis on social presence, and CLT's cognitive efficiency, offering a robust theoretical rationale for their adoption in classrooms.

Building on these foundations, the chapter later discusses a practical implementation framework (Section 5) that outlines how narrative- and voice-driven chatbots can be deployed in classrooms, while also addressing the ethical safeguards and evolving teacher roles necessary to ensure responsible, pedagogically sound integration. Discussion includes how conversational AI chatbots with voice-driven interactivity can revolutionise K-12 education by fostering engagement, accessibility, and inclusivity. The scope encompasses the integration of narrative gamification, ethical AI design, and culturally adaptive frameworks to address persistent challenges in student motivation, cognitive accessibility, and equitable access. Key objectives include: (1) analysing voice-based AI's role in reducing cognitive load and bridging literacy gaps through multilingual, emotion-aware interfaces; (2) addressing ethical dilemmas in cultural representation, data privacy, and bias mitigation; (3) proposing hybrid teacher-AI collaboration models to balance automation with human mentorship; and (4) advocating for voice-first, low-cost solutions to democratise access in under-resourced regions. These objectives position AI-driven learning as a pedagogically grounded, narrative-supported approach.

2. NARRATIVE AND GAMIFICATION IN K-12 EDUCATION

Recent empirical research underscores that gamification is most effective when it is intentionally grounded in motivational theory and narrative design rather than treated as a superficial layer of points or rewards. Hsia et al. (2025) demonstrated that gamified intelligent tutoring systems aligned with SDT led to measurable gains in skill development and engagement, as learners experienced greater autonomy, competence, and relatedness. Similarly, Alvi (2024) found that gamified experiences which emphasised meaningfulness and personalisation significantly improved students' sense of competence and social presence, thereby enhancing learning outcomes. These studies highlight that when gamified narratives are designed to resonate with learners' intrinsic motivations and framed around purposeful contexts, they not only sustain attention but also foster deeper knowledge retention and transfer.

Engaging and meaningful learning in K-12 requires new techniques that appeal to children's innate motivations and cultural experiences. Section 2 examines how narrative frameworks and gamification tactics create dynamic, immersive classrooms where abstract concepts become quests and academic difficulties match students' aspirations. Using game mechanisms like points, badges, and collaborative challenges with storytelling tactics like heroism, mystery, and discovery, educators can bridge cognitive and emotional learning. Figure 1 illustrates the core principles, theoretical foundations, and ethical considerations of narrative gamification.

2.1. Gamification as a Catalyst for Engagement

Gamification improves engagement when game elements are purposefully aligned with motivational theory rather than added superficially. Studies grounded in SDT show that points, badges and narrative missions enhance autonomy, competence and relatedness, leading to measurable gains in skill development and social presence (Alvi, 2024; Hsia et al., 2025). When these mechanics resonate with learners' intrinsic goals, they not only sustain attention but also foster deeper knowledge retention and transfer. However, poorly designed competition or extrinsic rewards can undermine motivation; balanced gamification therefore emphasises meaningful quests and personalisation over simple leaderboards.

Table 1. Conceptual overview of conversational (voice-based) AI chatbot in K-12 education

Key Themes	Identified Gaps/Challenges	Proposed Solutions / Innovations	Impact/Outcomes
Narrative Engagement	Underutilised emotional/ narrative resonance in AI tutors; passive learning in traditional methods.	Integration of storytelling to contextualise abstract concepts; episodic, mission-based learning.	Increased student motivation, deeper cognitive connections, and contextualised knowledge retention.
Gamification Mechanics	Over-reliance on extrinsic rewards risks undermining intrinsic motivation; inconsistent academic gains.	Balanced gamification (quests, adaptive challenges) aligned with SDT (autonomy, competence).	Sustained engagement, skill mastery, and equitable participation through narrative-driven rewards.
Voice-Based AI Technology	Text-centric tools exclude non-readers, neurodiverse learners, and multilingual students.	Voice interfaces leveraging prosody, multilingual Text-To-Speech (TTS), and real-time emotional modulation.	Enhanced accessibility, reduced cognitive load, and personalised feedback for diverse learners.
Cultural & Ethical Design	Cultural bias in AI personas; gendered/racialised stereotypes in narratives.	Culturally adaptive personas; inclusive voice customisation.	Global inclusivity, trust-building, and validation of diverse identities in educational narratives.
Equity & Accessibility	Digital divide exacerbated by hardware/internet dependency; exclusion of marginalised communities.	Voice-first systems using low-cost devices (basic phones, smart speakers); localised language support.	Democratised access to quality education in low-resource settings (e.g., rural India, sub-Saharan Africa).
Teacher-AI Collaboration	Fear of AI replacing human educators and lack of teacher training for AI integration.	Hybrid models where AI handles repetitive tasks, freeing teachers for mentorship and critical thinking.	Enhanced pedagogical efficiency while preserving the irreplaceable role of human empathy and judgement.

Empirical evidence demonstrates that integrating well-designed gamification into intelligent tutoring systems can significantly enhance both performance and learner experience. Ma et al. (2024) showed that gamified learning environments, structured around activity theory and SDT, produced measurable improvements across multiple dimensions including flow experience, intrinsic motivation, knowledge retention, and transfer performance, with notably large effect sizes. Similarly, Hare et al. (2024) reported that combining an intelligent tutoring system with a serious game not only improved students' performance on pre- and post-tests but also reduced the time and effort required to complete tasks, owing to adaptive scaffolding that supported individual learner needs. Together, these findings highlight that gamified systems, when thoughtfully designed, can stimulate sustained engagement and deepen learning. However, caution is warranted: poorly designed competitive mechanics may undermine intrinsic motivation, leading to fatigue and disengagement. Balancing intrinsic motivators such as autonomy, competence, and relatedness with carefully calibrated extrinsic incentives is therefore critical to maintaining both learner motivation and long-term effectiveness.

Figure 1. Visual illustration of gamification mechanics, narrative frameworks, and their synergistic role in K-12 education, highlighting key theories and ethical considerations.

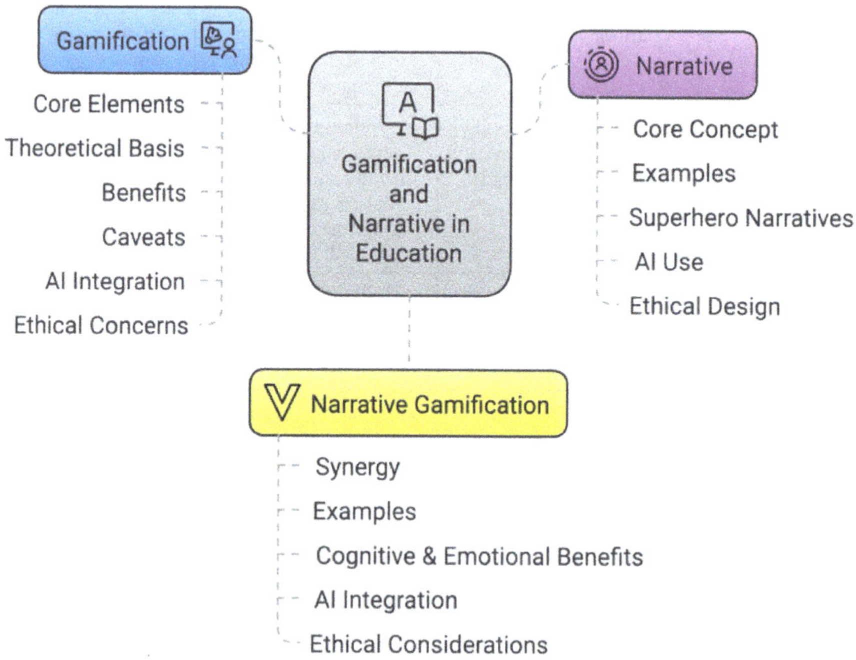

The integration of gamification with theoretical frameworks such as SDT, along with the incorporation of meaningfulness, was emphasised as essential for fostering sustained engagement (Gupta & Goyal, 2022). Concurrently, the importance of balancing utilitarian and hedonic functions to maintain intrinsic motivation was highlighted (Tan et al., 2022). Challenges persist, as an over-reliance on extrinsic rewards has been cautioned against (Gilyazova & Zamoshchanskii, 2020), with alternative strategies prioritising game thinking over superficial mechanics advocated. The potential of gamification to elevate engagement and learning outcomes is affirmed by these studies, provided that its implementation is strategically aligned with pedagogical objectives and learner needs. Taken together, these findings suggest that when gamification is thoughtfully designed in line with SDT and CLT, it not only optimises engagement and performance but also lays the groundwork for the narrative-driven strategies explored in the following section.

2.2. The Power of Narrative and Storytelling

Narrative-centred learning aligns with both CLT and the CoI framework, as well-crafted stories reduce extraneous cognitive load by contextualising abstract concepts while simultaneously fostering social presence through shared characters and plotlines. Narrative-centred learning frameworks have demonstrated significant potential in transforming K-12 education by embedding academic content within immersive story worlds, thereby fostering emotional connections and active engagement. Lee et al. (2023; 2024) highlighted the efficacy of narrative-centred digital games in science education, where fifth-grade students achieved higher learning gains by completing quests and earning in-game rewards, effectively positioning them as protagonists in problem-solving scenarios. Similarly, Vanbecelaere et al. (2023) emphasised adaptive digital games that integrate learning content into compelling narratives, enabling personalised instruction and instant feedback to sustain student involvement. These findings align with Wang et al. (2022), whose Virtual Reality (VR)-based game 'Cellverse' allowed high school students to collaboratively explore cell biology through a diagnostic narrative, turning abstract biological concepts into relatable challenges.

Narrative-centred learning reduces extraneous cognitive load by situating abstract concepts within story worlds, while simultaneously fostering social presence through shared characters and plotlines. Research across subjects—from science to language arts—demonstrates that students achieve higher gains when they become protagonists in problem-solving quests (Lee et al., 2023; Vanbecelaere et al., 2023). Adaptive narratives provide personalised feedback and instant scaffolds, sustaining interest and enabling peer collaboration. To avoid overload, design frameworks such as the "Here Comes the Airplane" model recommend structuring stories into clear episodes with teacher mediation and iterative feedback.

Collaborative narrative experiences, such as those in 'Cellverse' (Wang et al., 2022) illustrated how shared storytelling can deepen understanding through peer interaction and role-based exploration. These approaches resonate with the concept of "impassioned involvement," where students perceive themselves as active contributors to the narrative rather than passive recipients of information. Nevertheless, the success of such interventions depends on iterative design and expert feedback, as demonstrated by the Collaborative Learning Environments in Virtual Reality (CLEVR) team's reliance on user and subject matter input to refine gameplay mechanics and narrative fidelity. Collectively, these studies underscore the transformative role of narratives in K-12 education, particularly when combined with adaptive technologies and collaborative frameworks, offering a pathway to make abstract concepts both accessible and memorable.

2.3. Combining Story and Game: Narrative Gamification

Narrative gamification evokes emotional investment by blending storytelling with game mechanics. Studies highlight that interactivity fosters identity formation and positive attitudes toward subject matter (Buffum, 2015). Yet a balance is required: overly complex stories can obscure learning objectives, and insufficient scaffolding may lead to cognitive overload. Critically evaluating narrative depictions of technology and providing teacher-guided support ensures that gamified stories remain aligned with curricular goals and inclusivity. This synergy sets the stage for integrating voice-based AI, where dynamic narratives and adaptive quests can personalise learning experiences.

3. VOICE-BASED AI INTERACTIONS: EMOTIONAL AND COGNITIVE DIMENSIONS

Voice-based AI technologies are increasingly shaping K-12 education by combining human-like speech with pedagogical design to create conversational environments that feel engaging and cognitively accessible. Within the CoI framework, such vocal interfaces can strengthen social presence, as tone, narrative personalities, and natural dialogue foster a sense of connection between learners and the system. Section 3 examines how these features may reduce cognitive barriers and support inclusivity, while also highlighting the importance of careful attention to accessibility, data privacy, and equity in implementation. Figure 2 illustrates the interplay between emotional resonance, cognitive accessibility, and conversational engagement, underscoring both the potential of voice-based AI to coach and motivate students and the ethical safeguards required to ensure responsible use.

3.1. Emotional Resonance of Voice Interfaces

Engagement in educational settings is enhanced by voice-based interfaces through the leveraging of emotional and personality cues that are absent in text-based systems, fostering a social presence akin to human interaction (Lampropoulos & Papadakis, 2025). The improvement of emotional communication through non-verbal elements, such as animated chat-balloons, was demonstrated (Arn et al., 2024), suggesting that affective exchanges could similarly be enriched by voice interfaces via tone and intonation. Emotional attachment has been identified as a critical factor in sustaining user engagement with conversational AI (Mamun et al., 2025), with the "persona effect" emphasised, where lifelike attributes enhance perceived interactivity. Similarly, anthropomorphism—the attribution of human-like qualities to AI—was found to strengthen trust (Saffarizadeh et al., 2024), particularly when voice-driven interactions mimic empathetic or encouraging tones.

Figure 2. Voice-based AI in K-12 education: Emotional Resonance, Cognitive Accessibility, and Conversational Engagement.

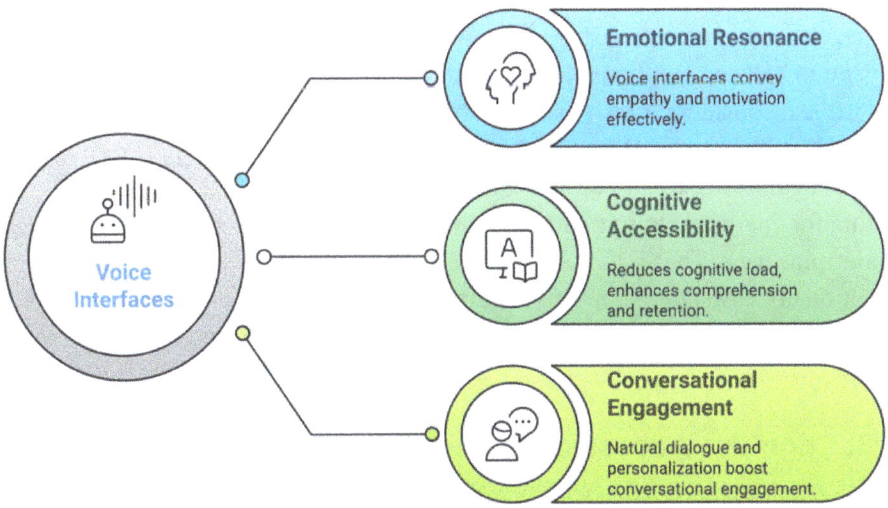

Emerging research on voice-based educational chatbots highlights the critical role of vocal tone, pacing, and prosody in fostering empathy, motivation, and sustained learner engagement. Studies of 'WoeBot', a cognitive-behavioural therapy–based conversational agent, show that users can establish therapeutic bonds at levels comparable to those reported in face-to-face and group counselling, with voice and dialogue patterns perceived as supportive and motivating (Darcy et al., 2021). Qualitative findings further reveal that empathetic pacing and natural prosody encourage reflection, rational thinking, and mindfulness, while reducing the stigma associated with help-seeking (Yeh et al., 2024). Although challenges such as usability barriers and limited emotional nuance persist, participants consistently reported that voice-driven features enhanced the sense of being understood, thereby increasing motivation to persist with tasks and adopt positive behaviours (Yeh et al., 2025). Taken together, these results illustrate that when vocal qualities are carefully designed, educational chatbots can extend beyond information delivery to create emotionally resonant learning companions that scaffold both cognitive and affective dimensions of learning.

The emotional resonance of voice interfaces is further amplified through adaptive feedback mechanisms. Daryanto et al. (2025) highlighted the value of dialogic feedback in interview simulations, where AI's responsive and personalised guidance reduced cognitive burden and fostered deeper reflection. Such dynamics align with Kurian (2025) argument for AI systems capable of recognising unconventional speech patterns, ensuring emotionally attuned responses to children's playful or imaginative communication. However, challenges persist, as Morozova & Nikolaienko (2024) noted that users often resist framing AI as fully human-like, necessitating careful design to balance emotional appeal without over-anthropomorphisation.

Ethical considerations remain paramount. Chubb et al. (2022) stressed the need for ethically grounded designs in conversational AI for children, prioritising safeguards against biases and ensuring transparency. Kurian (2025) echoed this, advocating for guardrails to mitigate risks like erratic emotional responses, which could undermine trust. These studies underscore the potential of voice interfaces to create emotionally resonant, supportive learning environments, provided they integrate ethical frameworks and adaptive emotional intelligence to sustain engagement and confidence in young learners.

3.2. Cognitive Accessibility and Universal Design

Cognitive accessibility is enhanced by voice-based AI systems through the reduction of cognitive load and the provision of multimodal engagement, aligning with UDL principles. The integration of speech interaction in systems such as 'Kid Space' was demonstrated to alleviate parental concerns about screen time while neurodiverse learners were supported through features including captions and adaptive content (Aslan et al., 2024). Similarly, conversational AI was designed for users with motor impairments (Taheri et al., 2023), with the role of voice interfaces in simplifying interactions for individuals with physical challenges being emphasised, thereby broadening accessibility. The alignment of these systems with UDL through auditory alternatives has been highlighted (Matera et al., 2023), with the necessity of voice-driven modalities underscored to ensure equitable access, particularly through inclusive web interfaces for visually impaired users.

Voice interfaces reduce cognitive load by offering multimodal engagement and supporting diverse learners. Grounded in UDL, they provide multiple means of representation and engagement—adaptive pacing, prosody and captions—making content accessible to neurodiverse and multilingual students. Studies show that voice-augmented cues improve comprehension and reduce mental demand, and that combining translation and cultural modelling further scaffolds intrinsic load (Ubur,

2025; Patilima, 2025). Personalisation and emotional engagement amplify these benefits, though challenges remain around latency, contextual awareness and privacy.

Personalisation and emotional engagement further amplify cognitive accessibility. Shilaskar et al. (2024) utilised Natural Language Understanding (NLU) in scholarship counselling chatbots, enabling intuitive interactions that cater to diverse linguistic needs. Zadeh & Sattler (2023) reinforced this by employing conversational AI to generate personalised health narratives, illustrating how voice interfaces can foster engagement through compassionate, context-aware responses. However, challenges persist, such as optimising latency and enhancing contextual awareness, as noted by Aslan et al. (2024), who identified the need for advanced personalisation in AI systems to address varying learner profiles effectively.

The alignment of voice-based AI with UDL principles is evidenced by its capacity to deliver content through multiple modalities. Conversational AI in web browsing has been advocated for to support users with situational or permanent impairments, with auditory channels emphasised as critical for inclusivity (Piro, 2023). This perspective has been echoed through the recognition of chatbots' 24/7 accessibility and accuracy in automating tasks, reducing reliance on text-based interactions (Meshram et al., 2021). Nevertheless, the necessity of ethical safeguards and continuous evaluation has been stressed (Bettayeb et al., 2024) to mitigate biases and ensure responsible implementation. It is affirmed by these studies that voice-first approaches democratise learning, particularly for neuro-diverse learners and individuals with disabilities, through the transformation of abstract concepts into accessible, engaging experiences.

3.3. Conversational Engagement

Natural dialogue and complementary personalities help chatbots foster rapport and sustain attention. Real-time adaptive feedback encourages deeper reflection and supports metacognition (Li et al., 2025; Daryanto et al., 2025). Advances in emotion recognition allow systems to tailor responses, while augmented reality and mixed-modality approaches lower cognitive load for complex tasks. Nevertheless, extended exposure can lead to fatigue or unrealistic expectations. Scheduled novelty, teacher mediation and blended activities help mitigate over-reliance and ensure that AI serves as a supportive tool rather than replacing human educators.

Conversational engagement is further refined through technological advancements in emotional intelligence. A dual framework for emotion recognition and response generation was proposed (Zhang et al., 2024), enabling empathetic tones to be mimicked by AI. Conversational AI was integrated with augmented reality (Monjoree et al., 2024), where cognitive load was reduced through real-time guidance, illustrating how complex tasks can be simplified by voice-driven interactions while immersion is maintained. However, challenges persist, as limitations in AI's ability to interpret children's playful or non-literal language have been noted (Kurian, 2025), necessitating robust training to avoid disengagement.

Figure 3. Conceptual framework illustrating interconnected design dimensions that collectively shape credible, meaningful, and inclusive AI-enhanced learning experiences.

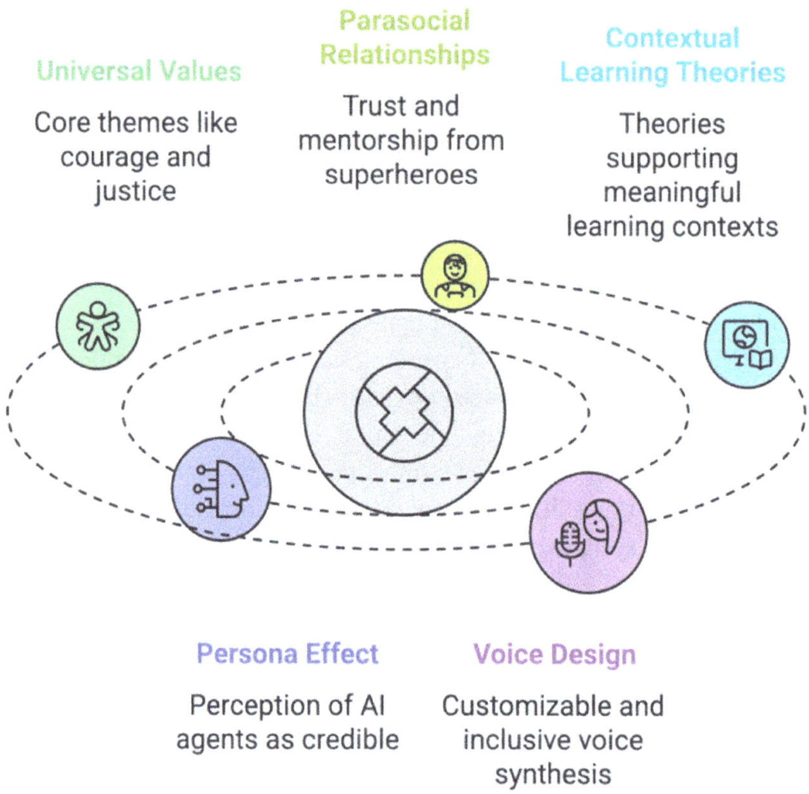

Personalisation and consistency are pivotal for sustaining curiosity. Subitsha et al. (2025) utilised sentiment analysis to tailor instruction, mirroring how a conversational AI might reference past interactions to create continuity. Ye & Li (2020) emphasised persona consistency in chatbots, ensuring the AI's tone and style remain coherent, much like a character maintaining its "mad scientist" or heroic demeanour. Despite these advancements, ethical considerations, such as mitigating biases in training data, Kurian (2025) remain critical to ensure interactions remain inclusive and trustworthy. These studies underscore the potential of voice-based AI to transform learning into an imaginative, socially resonant experience, blending pedagogical efficacy with the allure of storytelling (Figure 3).

While short-term studies (Table 2) highlight that AI chatbots can improve critical thinking skills and boost intrinsic motivation in tasks such as argumentative writing (Zhang et al., 2025), sustaining these benefits over time remains a challenge. Prolonged exposure to conversational agents may lead to student fatigue, particularly if the interactions become repetitive or overly scripted, reducing novelty and engagement. An additional risk lies in over-anthropomorphising AI tutors: when learners begin to attribute human-like authority or emotional understanding to chatbots, they may develop unrealistic expectations or diminish the role of genuine teacher–student relationships. To mitigate these risks, researchers emphasise the importance of scheduled novelty (e.g., rotating prompts, changing personas, or varying interaction modes) to refresh interest, as well as teacher mediation to contextualise and critically frame chatbot responses. Furthermore, mixed-modality approaches—where chatbot interactions are complemented by peer collaboration, teacher feedback, and offline activities—help sustain motivation while preventing cognitive and emotional over-reliance on AI tutors. Together, these strategies ensure that AI chatbots function as supportive tools rather than replacements, balancing technological novelty with pedagogical stability.

Table 2. Summary of representative studies on narrative/gamified voice AI.

Study (Year)	Context/Grade	Modality (Narrative/Voice)	Outcome Metric	Effect/Key Finding	Notes/ limits
Hsia et al. (2025)	University yoga course	Gamified ITS aligned with SDT; narrative quests	Skill gains; autonomy, competence, relatedness	Moderate improvements in engagement and skills when quests resonated with learners' goals	Caution against poorly designed competition; adult sample
Lee et al. (2023); Vanbecelaere et al. (2023)	5th grade science & adaptive games	Narrative-centred digital games	Learning gains; quest completion	Students achieved higher gains and motivation when narratives framed problem-solving; adaptive feedback sustained interest	Requires scaffolding to avoid cognitive overload
Li H et al. (2025); Daryanto et al. (2025)	Secondary language learning; interview practice	Voice chatbots with complementary personalities	Participation rate; self-reflection	Real-time adaptive feedback and voiced personas improved participation and metacognitive reflection	Limited longitudinal data; small samples

continued on following page

Table 2. Continued

Study (Year)	Context/Grade	Modality (Narrative/Voice)	Outcome Metric	Effect/Key Finding	Notes/ limits
Ubur (2025); Patilima (2025)	Neurodiverse and multilingual learners	Voice-augmented interfaces with UDL principles	Comprehensio; cognitive load	Voice cues and captions improved comprehension by 45% and reduced mental demand by 25%; trauma-informed UDL strategies boosted academic and social gains	Requires inclusive design; technology access constraints
Yeh et al. (2024); Yeh et al. (2025)	Therapeutic/ educational chatbot (Woebot)	Voice-enabled conversational agent	Motivation; emotional bond	Users reported strong therapeutic alliance; empathetic pacing encouraged reflection and reduced stigma	Focus on mental health; not exclusively educational

4. PERSONALISED AND ADAPTIVE LEARNING WITH AI TUTORS

AI tutors combine individualised instruction, engaging narrative, and ongoing mentorship to transform K-12 education. Section 4 examines how adaptive algorithms, voice-enabled feedback, and storylines allow AI systems to respond to learner needs, frame setbacks as opportunities for growth, and evolve alongside students. In addition to highlighting these affordances, this section also compares conversational chatbots with other adaptive technologies such as intelligent tutoring systems and personalised learning platforms, identifying both overlaps and distinctions in their pedagogical value. Finally, it introduces an implementation framework that provides practical guidance for integrating chatbots into classroom contexts. Figure 4 illustrates how AI tutors merge computational precision with narrative engagement to democratise high-quality, emotionally resonant instruction.

4.1. Individualised Instruction and Feedback

The integration of AI such as ChatGPT into educational frameworks has demonstrated significant potential in advancing individualised instruction and feedback through real-time personalisation and adaptive learning pathways (Uğraş et al., 2024). Recent studies highlight the efficacy of AI-driven systems in dynamically adjusting content difficulty and pacing based on learner performance. For instance, Huang et al. (2025) proposed a generative AI-enhanced problem-based learning (PT-PBL) model that tailors activities to students' cognitive levels, resulting in improved reading performance and motivation, particularly among highly engaged learners. Similarly, Li T et al. (2025) integrated real-time analytics with generative AI to deliver adaptive scaffolds for self-regulated learning, which fostered metacognitive patterns and enhanced coordination of learning processes. These findings align with Zhou et al. (2025), whose convolutional neural network-based recommendation system dynamically adjusted learning resources by analysing user profiles and performance data, underscoring the scalability of AI in personalising educational experiences.

Adaptive pathways, enabled by AI's diagnostic capabilities, further address learning gaps by tailoring interventions to individual needs. Naseer et al. (2025) demonstrated this through an AI-gamified platform that combined levelling systems and personalised feedback, leading to higher post-test scores and mastery rates compared to non-adaptive systems. Katona & Gyonyoru (2025) reinforced this approach in programming education, where AI-driven adaptive feedback in flipped classrooms improved learning outcomes and student autonomy. However, challenges such as equitable access and accuracy concerns persist, as noted by Sunmboye et al. (2025), who identified demographic disparities in AI tool adoption among medical students.

Assessment in AI-supported classrooms increasingly extends beyond summative tests to include metrics such as knowledge retention, transfer of skills, and ongoing formative analytics. Recent work on AI-driven learning analytics demonstrates that real-time data can identify individual strengths and gaps, enabling feedback that is both adaptive and highly specific (Vashishth et al., 2024). In this context, log files from chatbot conversations—including timestamps, response accuracy, and interaction patterns—offer a rich behavioural dataset for formative assessment. Studies show that transforming raw log data into dashboards and feedback texts provides students with actionable insights, strengthens self-regulated learning, and supports preparation for graded assessments (Hanses et al., 2024). By leveraging such data streams, educators can track engagement, detect misconceptions, and deliver personalised feedback at scale, thus turning conversational interactions into continuous assessment opportunities.

Figure 4. Enhancing education through AI Tutor as personalised, adaptive, and continuous learning companions.

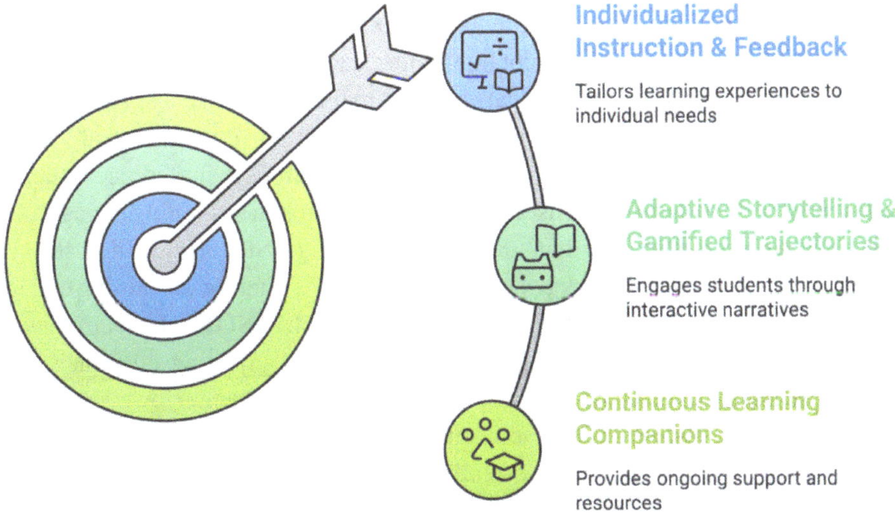

Engagement through interactive and motivational elements, though less explicitly addressed in the literature, is indirectly supported by studies emphasising real-time feedback and gamification. Elevated engagement was reported in language learning through AI-powered chatbots and gamified lessons (Aravind et al., 2025), with vocabulary retention being improved by 25%. The mediating role of digital literacy in optimising engagement with adaptive technologies was highlighted (Yaseen et al., 2025), suggesting that verbal interaction could be enhanced through synergies between voice-driven interfaces and such tools. While heterogeneous student readiness for personalised learning was cautioned against (Sysoyev, 2025), the evidence suggests AI can contribute to more flexible, student-centred learning environments.

4.2. Adaptive Storytelling and Gamified Trajectories.

The enhancement of personalised learning through dynamic narrative adjustments and integrated assessment mechanisms has been driven by the emergence of adaptive storytelling and gamification as pivotal strategies. The effectiveness of AI-driven dynamic branching narratives in tailoring educational experiences has been underscored in recent studies. For instance, GPT-4 was utilised to create interactive city tours (Ferracani et al., 2024), through which adaptive narratives were demonstrated to enhance engagement by aligning content with individual preferences as story paths were influenced by users. Similarly, TinyTeller AI was developed to generate personalised stories for children based on user profiles (Kim et al., 2024), illustrating the potential of AI to adjust narrative complexity in real-time. A genetic algorithm-based Drama Manager was introduced (Utsch et al., 2020), through which non-deterministic plot lines tailored to player models were generated, ensuring content remained within learners' optimal challenge zones. Additionally, personality-based narrative generation was implemented (de Lima et al., 2020), achieving 91.9% accuracy in aligning story events with user preferences, thereby reinforcing the role of individualised narrative adaptation in sustaining engagement.

It is also important to note that adaptive storytelling systems draw their strength from tailoring narratives to students' evolving responses, thereby sustaining engagement through alignment with motivational theories such as SDT, which emphasises autonomy, competence, and relatedness. By dynamically adjusting storylines, these systems can reinforce learners' sense of agency and achievement. However, fairness considerations must also be addressed: without careful oversight, algorithmic biases in narrative generation may inadvertently privilege certain cultural references or learning styles over others. For this reason, teacher mediation remains essential, ensuring that AI-generated narratives are not only motivating but also pedagogically sound and aligned with curricular objectives.

The embedding of continuous feedback within adaptive storytelling frameworks is critically supported by integrated mastery and assessment. The superiority of AI-enhanced adaptive learning paths in improving language proficiency and motivation through real-time adjustments was highlighted, supported by statistical analyses of learner performance (Liu, 2025). An AI Tutor combining customised videos and quizzes with instant feedback was introduced (Shahri et al., 2024), ensuring content dynamically aligns with learner progress. This approach was reinforced through the integration of fuzzy logic into educational games (Jondya et al., 2023), where quiz difficulty and story scenarios are adapted based on user comprehension, resulting in higher mastery rates. The necessity of weaving formative assessments into narrative structures to address evolving learning needs is collectively emphasised.

The preservation of engagement and self-esteem has been shown to be supported by diegetic remediation-where academic challenges are framed as narrative elements. This was demonstrated through an empathic robot that adapts storytelling styles (e.g., pitch, emotion) based on listener feedback (Wang et al., 2022), through which remedial sessions were transformed into immersive "training" experiences. A device-independent storytelling framework was proposed (Khundam & Noël, 2021), allowing varied interaction systems to reframe content delivery as part of a cohesive narrative journey. Further validation of this concept was achieved through personalised hip-hop history narratives based on user input (Olson et al., 2020), with both satisfaction and learning outcomes being enhanced. The integration of remediation into storylines is illustrated by these approaches to maintain motivation while addressing knowledge gaps, thereby aligning with the principles of diegetic learning design.

4.3. AI Tutors as Continuous Learning Companions.

The potential of AI tutors to foster longitudinal personalisation through adaptive mechanisms that evolve with student progress is significantly demonstrated. Fuzzy logic controllers were employed to dynamically adjust learning materials in real-time (Szczepański et al., 2025), addressing diverse learning styles and enabling sustained adaptation over extended periods. Similarly, AI and gamification were integrated to track engagement patterns and performance metrics (Narayanan & Kumaravel, 2024), with rewards allocated based on longitudinal data to maintain motivation. This concept was further advanced through the Knowledge Graph-enhanced framework (KG-RAG), where AI responses were grounded in structured domain knowledge to ensure personalised instruction aligns with students' evolving comprehension (Dong et al., 2025). The capacity of AI tutors to retain and utilise historical data for tailoring lessons is collectively highlighted, thereby supporting long-term academic growth.

The alignment of AI-driven tutoring with curricular goals and assessment systems is critically supported by integrated insights and support. This was demonstrated through an AI Tutor that generates customised quizzes and videos while instant feedback is provided (Shahri et al., 2024), enabling educator monitoring of progress and instructional adjustments. Similarly, AI tutors were embedded in VR environments (Sarshartehrani et al., 2024), where emotional and cognitive states were analysed to deliver personalised programming instruction, aligning with educational psychology principles. Empirical validation of KG-RAG's ability to improve assessment scores by 35% was achieved (Dong et al., 2025), with its role in bridging instructional content with evaluative benchmarks emphasised. The synthesis of learner data by AI tutors to offer actionable insights for students and educators is exemplified, ensuring alignment with academic objectives.

Consistent, equitable access to personalised learning is achievable through AI tutors designed for ubiquitous availability. Sarshartehrani et al. (2024) highlighted immersive VR environments accessible across devices, democratising advanced programming instruction regardless of physical location. Furthermore, Narayanan and Kumaravel (2024) utilised hybrid gamification to sustain engagement among 200 participants, illustrating how AI-driven systems can extend instructional time beyond traditional settings. Therefore, AI tutors have the potential to make personalised tutoring more widely accessible.

Although AI tutors can initially generate strong enthusiasm by offering continuous feedback and narrative-driven interaction, empirical data suggests that engagement may taper over time if experiences become repetitive or overly predictable. To sustain motivation, several strategies are recommended. First, rotating narrative arcs and challenges can refresh novelty and prevent learner fatigue. Second, incorporating periodic human check-ins—for example, brief teacher-led discussions or reflections—anchors the learning experience in authentic social interaction. Finally, adopting hybrid AI–teacher models ensures that chatbots provide adaptive, moment-to-moment scaffolding while teachers maintain oversight, contextualise content, and reinforce long-term goals. Together, these practices balance the efficiency of AI with the irreplaceable pedagogical and relational roles of educators, helping students remain engaged over extended learning periods.

4.4. Implementation Frameworks and Scalability

The implementation of conversational AI in schools must follow a structured, stepwise roadmap (Table 3) to ensure both educational value and long-term sustainability. The first step is a comprehensive needs assessment, in which schools identify specific pedagogical challenges that conversational AI can address. These may include the need for more personalised feedback in language learning, additional practice opportunities for shy or marginalised students, or support for routine administrative tasks such as attendance and timetabling (Khanna, 2025). At this stage, stakeholder engagement is essential: teachers, administrators, parents, and even students should be consulted to clarify expectations and concerns. Ethical and privacy considerations—especially in relation to children's data—must be foregrounded from the beginning, not treated as an afterthought (Anagnostopoulou et al., 2024). Establishing a shared vision at the needs assessment stage creates legitimacy, reduces resistance to adoption, and aligns the technology with existing curricular frameworks.

Following needs assessment, schools must prepare their infrastructure and hardware environment to support conversational AI. At a minimum, this includes reliable internet connectivity, access to servers or cloud storage, and affordable classroom devices such as tablets, laptops, or low-cost smartboards. However, hardware readiness is not simply about availability of equipment. In practice, classrooms are often noisy, students speak with varied accents, and some learners experience speech or hearing disorders. These challenges can undermine AI accuracy if not properly addressed. Thus, schools should incorporate multimodal access options such as keyboard-based input, visual prompts, and noise-cancelling microphones to ensure inclusivity (Mutajwaa & Didas, 2025). Strategic partnerships with telecom providers or device vendors can reduce the financial burden of upgrading infrastructure, particularly in rural or resource-constrained schools. By framing infrastructure not only as a technical requirement but as an equity issue, schools can ensure that no student is disadvantaged by environmental or physical barriers.

Once infrastructure is in place, careful attention must be given to budgeting and cost–benefit analysis, since financial sustainability often determines the success or failure of educational technology initiatives. Budgets should extend beyond the one-time cost of hardware to include recurring expenses such as licensing fees, maintenance, and periodic upgrades. External funding streams—government subsidies, NGO partnerships, or philanthropic contributions—can offset these costs, especially in low-resource contexts (Joshi, 2025). For schools with limited budgets, gradual implementation through pilot projects is more feasible than attempting a full rollout. Lightweight, low-cost solutions such as SMS-based conversational bots or open-source chat frameworks can deliver meaningful functionality while minimising expenditure. Importantly, the cost–benefit calculus should include indirect savings: conversational AI can streamline administrative tasks like timetabling and report summarisation, thereby freeing teachers to devote more time to student engagement (Venkatraman et al., 2024). When viewed through this broader lens, conversational AI is not merely an expense but an investment in institutional efficiency.

Table 3. Implementation framework (roadmap) and scalability for conversational AI in schools.

Stage	Key actions (examples)	Cost–benefit considerations	Accessibility strategies	Key stakeholders
Needs assessment	• Align goals with curriculum and learner needs. • Identify subjects and age groups that could benefit. • Evaluate ethical/privacy requirements.	• Consider whether conversational AI solves a real pedagogical problem. • Weigh expected learning gains against resource requirements.	• Prioritise subjects where conversation adds value (e.g., language practice).	School leaders; curriculum designers; data-protection officers
Infrastructure & hardware	• Ensure reliable internet or select offline-capable models. • Provide devices, headsets/microphones. • Plan for secure data storage.	• Assess cost of licences, devices, bandwidth, and maintenance; explore partnerships for subsidised access.	• Offer multiple input modes (voice/text). • Use noise-cancelling headsets or classroom microphones.	IT departments; telecom providers; vendors
Budgeting & cost-benefit	• Build multi-year budgets covering licences, hardware, training, and upgrades. • Identify funding sources (government grants, NGOs).	• In low-resource contexts, start with pilot projects and scale gradually; voice-only or SMS-based bots reduce device cost.	• Use open-source chatbots where possible to lower costs; partner with local tech hubs.	Finance officers; donors; procurement teams
Teacher training & professional development	• Train teachers to design prompts, monitor interactions, and interpret analytics. • Provide AI ethics and bias-mitigation workshops. • Develop communities of practice for sharing experiences.	• Include teacher time and compensation in budgets; training may reduce long-term support costs by empowering teachers.	• Use blended training (online and in-person) to accommodate teachers' schedules.	Teacher-education centres; professional-development coordinators
Evaluation & feedback	• Define metrics (retention, transfer, engagement, misconceptions). • Use log files and analytics dashboards to track progress. • Conduct periodic surveys and focus groups. • Perform ethical audits.	• Allocate resources for data analysis and ongoing improvements; plan for model retraining.	• Provide accessible feedback reports for students and parents; adapt metrics for diverse populations.	Assessment specialists; data scientists; ethics committees

The long-term scalability of conversational AI hinges on teacher training and professional development. Teachers are not only end-users but also mediators between students and the technology, shaping how AI is used in practice. As such, they require training in prompt engineering, classroom integration strategies, and AI ethics. Training should go beyond basic technical skills to include awareness of algorithmic bias, data privacy, and appropriate scaffolding of AI-mediated interactions. Blended training models—combining online modules with in-person workshops—are particularly effective because they respect teachers' diverse schedules while fostering peer exchange (Caruana et al., 2025). Establishing communities of practice, where educators share experiences and collaboratively refine AI use, strengthens collective capacity. Furthermore, budgeting should explicitly account for teacher time and compensation, as professional development represents not an optional add-on but a core condition for sustainable implementation. Schools that neglect this aspect often face resistance or superficial use of AI tools, undermining scalability.

To ensure ongoing improvement, institutions must implement robust evaluation and feedback mechanisms. Technical performance metrics, such as system accuracy and response times, should be complemented by pedagogical indicators like student engagement, learning outcomes, and equity of access. Data dashboards can provide administrators with insights into patterns of use, while ethical audits and student focus groups add qualitative perspectives that numbers alone cannot capture (Anagnostopoulou et al., 2024). Importantly, evaluation frameworks must be inclusive, recognising that students from diverse linguistic, cultural, and ability backgrounds may interact differently with conversational AI. Feedback loops should therefore extend beyond teachers and administrators to include parents and learners themselves, ensuring that the system adapts to evolving needs and remains accountable to the communities it serves.

Evidence from case studies underscores both the opportunities and challenges of scaling conversational AI in education. In India, pilot projects demonstrated that conversational AI could significantly reduce administrative workload and support language learning, leading to improved efficiency and student engagement (Venkatraman et al., 2024). Conversely, a European deployment faced difficulties when classroom noise and diverse accents undermined system accuracy, frustrating both teachers and students (Caruana et al., 2025). These contrasting experiences reveal that technical sophistication alone is insufficient; contextual adaptation and strong teacher mediation are decisive factors in success. When compared with ITS and adaptive learning platforms, conversational AI distinguishes itself by enabling dialogic, flexible interaction across subjects (Table 4). While ITS excel at structured, domain-specific guidance, they often lack the spontaneity and open-ended dialogue that conversational AI can provide (Mutajwaa & Didas, 2025). A hybrid model—leveraging the structured precision of ITS and the adaptability of conversational

AI—offers a promising pathway for schools seeking to maximise learning outcomes while maintaining scalability.

Table 4. Comparative analysis of AI-powered learning platforms.

	Conversational AI Chatbots	**Intelligent Tutoring Systems (ITS)**	**Adaptive Learning Platforms**
Personalisation Approach	• Conversational, real-time responses based on dialogue history • Provides a general, flexible knowledge base	• Fine-grained, step-by-step guidance on problem-solving paths • Focuses on mastery of specific skills	• Coarse-grained adaptation of curriculum and pacing • Recommends content based on a student model
Learner Agency	• High; students can drive the conversation, explore topics freely • No fixed learning path	• Guided or constrained; system directs the learner through a mastery path	• Varies; system guides the learner's journey by recommending material or next topics
Data Requirements	• Large, general-purpose datasets for training • Fine-tuning on domain-specific corpora	• Domain-specific knowledge models • Student performance data at a granular, step-by-step level	• Curriculum-based knowledge maps • Broader student performance and engagement data
Cost Considerations	• Can be low per-user with open-source models • Usage-based fees for commercial APIs	• Generally high; requires specialised development and licensing • Costs can be prohibitive for many institutions	• Typically a subscription-based licence for a pre-built platform • Cost can vary with scale and features

5. ETHICAL, CULTURAL AND DATA PRIVACY CONSIDERATIONS

Ethics must be central when deploying AI tutors in education, ensuring that issues of bias, cultural relevance, data privacy, and instructor roles are addressed comprehensively. Building on the EU Guidelines for Trustworthy AI, which emphasise principles of transparency, accountability, and human oversight, and the UNESCO AI Competency Framework, which highlights equity, inclusivity, and teacher preparedness, this section examines how AI systems may both perpetuate and reduce social inequalities in classrooms worldwide. The discussion extends to safeguarding children, promoting culturally responsive learning environments, and reinforcing the indispensable role of educators. In this updated structure, Section 5 will also devote attention to teacher roles and bias mitigation, recognising that empowering instructors and addressing systemic bias are prerequisites for trustworthy

AI adoption. Figure 5 illustrates how inclusive design, regulatory compliance, and human oversight interact, underscoring the need to balance AI's potential with fairness, equality, and long-term trust in educational settings.

5.1. Cultural Sensitivity and Localisation

The integration of AI chatbots into K-12 education requires careful attention to cultural sensitivity and localisation to ensure alignment with diverse societal norms. It is emphasised that generative AI systems risk perpetuating cultural biases rooted in dominant training data (Karpouzis, 2024), necessitating technical interventions such as data diversification and culturally aware constraints. Context-aware ethical frameworks are advocated for, particularly in culturally significant domains (Stacchio et al., 2024), to ensure intellectual property and heritage values are respected during AI deployment. Cross-cultural considerations in AI governance are further highlighted as critical (Herrera-Ferrá et al., 2023), with ethical frameworks argued to require balancing universal principles with localised interpretations to address neurocognitive diversity. The need for AI narratives and communication styles to avoid cultural hegemony is collectively underscored, prioritising region-specific humour, deference norms, and correction methods to mitigate misunderstandings.

Figure 5. Promoting inclusive and secure AI in K-12 education by addressing bias, culture, privacy, and human collaboration.

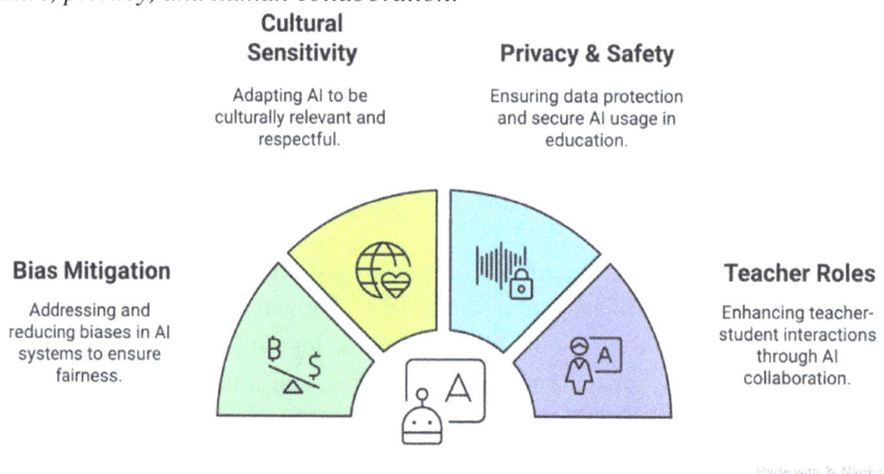

The development of localised personas is necessitated by the leveraging of region-specific archetypes and inclusive design processes. Cultural differences shaping perceptions of AI were demonstrated (Li & Gabriel, 2022), suggesting that personas such as mythic figures or anime mentors could enhance relatability in non-Western contexts. The necessity of macro-level approaches for AI's role in cultural creativity was posited (Morkina, 2021), where collaboration among diverse stakeholders—including educators from underrepresented regions—is required to shape inclusive AI tutoring systems. Transparency and trust were emphasised as critical for culturally aligned AI (Robinson, 2020), exemplified through Nordic policies prioritising democratic values and citizen engagement. The advocacy for AI personas rooted in regional heroism and co-developed with diverse educators is supported, with moderation required to align with local curricula and ethical standards, fostering equitable and context-sensitive learning environments.

Designing conversational AI for education must also account for linguistic diversity (Elwahsh et al., 2025) neurodiversity, and speech disability inclusion to ensure equitable participation. Systems should support multiple languages and dialects, recognising that students may use regional varieties, code-switching, or non-standard grammar in authentic learning contexts. Equally, neurodiverse learners—such as those with autism, ADHD, or dyslexia—benefit from customisable interaction speeds, simplified text, and multimodal prompts such as visual, auditory, or tactile (Zhang et al., 2025). Students with disabilities require features such as screen-reader compatibility, speech-to-text input, and captioning to remove participation barriers. Voice design also carries ethical implications: offering only a single default accent or gender risks reinforcing stereotypes or marginalising learners whose identities differ. Best practice, guided by frameworks such as the EU Guidelines for Trustworthy AI (https://digital-strategy.ec.europa.eu/en/library/ethics-guidelines-trustworthy-ai) and UNESCO's emphasis on equity, is to provide multiple voice options across genders and accents, while transparently explaining how these voices are generated and avoiding caricature or bias. By embedding linguistic and cultural sensitivity alongside neuro- and accessibility-aware design, schools can ensure conversational AI fosters inclusion rather than reproduces existing inequities.

5.2. Data Privacy and Child Safety

The integration of AI chatbots in K-12 education necessitates stringent privacy-by-design frameworks to safeguard children's data and ensure compliance with regulations such as COPPA and GDPR-K. Privacy and security were identified as core ethical concerns (Kamila & Jasrotia, 2025), with transparent data handling and minimised data collection advocated to mitigate risks. Technical measures such as differential privacy and anonymisation during AI training were proposed (Mooradian et al., 2025), aligning with principles of data minimisation and encryption for secure transfers. The urgency of global regulatory alignment was emphasised (Furizal et al., 2024), with localised data processing and anonymous deletion mechanisms highlighted as critical to prevent misuse. Technological solutions to obfuscate identities were reinforced (Bertini, 2023), ensuring data sovereignty while maintaining functionality. The need for parental consent protocols and robust encryption to align AI systems with legal and ethical standards is underscored.

Safeguarding children's data is a central obligation when integrating conversational AI into education (Malaborbor et al., 2024), and this requires a privacy-by-design approach from the outset. Rather than retrofitting security measures after deployment, systems must be built to minimise data collection, restrict storage, and ensure transparency in how information is processed. Data minimisation ensures that only what is strictly necessary—such as anonymised interaction logs—is collected, avoiding sensitive identifiers unless absolutely essential. Consent management is equally critical: students, parents, and guardians must be informed in clear, accessible language about what data is gathered, how it will be used, and for how long it will be stored. Ongoing parental and guardian involvement creates trust, especially in younger age groups, by ensuring that adults can review, approve, or revoke their child's data use. Aligning with frameworks such as the EU General Data Protection Regulation (GDPR) and UNESCO's recommendations, privacy and safety are not optional add-ons but conditions for the ethical use of AI in schools.

Checklist for teachers and administrators evaluating the AI tools for 'Privacy' and 'Safety' aspects may include:

- Does the tool follow privacy-by-design (built-in safeguards, not added later)?
- Is data minimisation applied (only essential data collected, anonymised where possible)?
- Are consent forms provided in plain, age-appropriate language for parents and students?
- Can parents/guardians easily review or withdraw consent at any time?
- Is data storage secure, time-limited, and transparent about where and how it is held?
- Does the provider allow regular audits or external verification of privacy practices?

The prevention of harmful outcomes and maintenance of child-appropriate interactions are critically supported by rigorous safety measures and human oversight. The dual role of AI as both protector and potential intruder was stressed (Lami et al., 2024), necessitating content filtering and strict task constraints to avoid ethical breaches. Ethical concerns—such as workplace fairness and social behaviour—were revealed to directly influence user trust (Sargent et al., 2024), with AI behaviour suggested to adhere to predefined ethical guidelines to sustain reliability. Stakeholder collaboration was advocated (Nguyen et al., 2023), through which frameworks were proposed for educators and policymakers to jointly supervise AI outputs, ensuring alignment with educational and safety goals. The role of interdisciplinary expertise, such as librarian involvement, in enforcing accountability and refining oversight mechanisms was highlighted (Michalak, 2023). The necessity of human-AI collaboration is collectively affirmed, where unpredictable advice is prevented by vetted task limitations and continuous monitoring, fostering a secure and trustworthy learning environment for children.

5.3. Teacher Mediation and Professional Development

The integration of AI chatbots into K-12 education necessitates the redefinition of teacher roles and the addressing of ethical implementation challenges (Lavidas et al., 2022). It has been emphasised that AI tools should augment rather than replace educators, enabling a shift from routine tasks to high-level mentoring and social-emotional support (Sánchez-García et al., 2025; Yang et al., 2024). For instance, the importance of human oversight in AI applications has been highlighted (Sánchez-García et al., 2025), with ethical dilemmas noted to emerge when institutional frameworks fail to align with technological functionalities. Similarly, the necessity of teacher training to clarify rules for AI use has been underscored (Sysoyev, 2024), as students are often found to lack systematic understanding of ethical boundaries during interactions with generative tools. This aligns with findings in which shared responsibility among stakeholders is stressed to govern AI ethics (Park & Milner, 2025), arguing that pedagogical designs must integrate guidelines to mitigate threats to academic integrity while AI's efficiency is harnessed.

Ethical deployment further demands stakeholder transparency and trust-building through inclusive governance. Jeon et al. (2025) advocated for "ethics-in-practice" frameworks that combine community engagement, institutional policies, and democratic deliberations to address societal impacts of AI. Similarly, Wakunuma & Eke, (2024) emphasised the role of AI governance in balancing ethical benefits—such as educational accessibility—with risks like bias and labour exploitation, particularly in underrepresented regions. Gallent Torres et al., (2023) reinforced this by urging institutions to establish clear ethical codes, ensuring transparency in data usage and aligning AI integration with academic integrity policies. However, Quince & Nikolic, (2025) cautions that awareness initiatives must prioritise risk education, as students often overlook ethical challenges while recognising AI's positive potential. Collectively, these studies underscore the need for collaborative efforts among educators, administrators, and policymakers to foster responsible AI adoption while preserving human-centric educational values.

Teachers remain a central role in ensuring that AI tutors are deployed ethically and effectively, and this requires structured investment in AI-literacy certification and ongoing professional development (Choi, 2025). Certification programmes can equip educators with foundational knowledge about how conversational AI systems operate, their limitations, and the ethical risks of bias, privacy breaches, or over-reliance. Professional development frameworks should go beyond one-off workshops to include sustained, modular training that addresses technical skills, prompt design, classroom integration, and ethical oversight. Importantly, teachers should be positioned as co-designers of lessons alongside AI tutors, adapting and contextualising AI outputs to meet the diverse needs of their learners. This co-design process empowers educators to maintain pedagogical authority and ensure that all AI-generated content is aligned with curriculum standards and inclusive teaching practices. Ultimately, teachers remain responsible for safeguarding safe and fair interactions in the classroom, using AI as a supportive tool rather than a substitute for human judgement. By embedding certification, continuous professional learning, and collaborative lesson design, schools can ensure that teachers are not displaced by AI but are instead empowered as ethical stewards of its use.

The modules for AI-Literacy Certification Framework for teachers may include:

- **Module 1**: Foundations of AI in Education – Basic principles of conversational AI, ITS, and adaptive learning tools; understanding strengths and limitations.
- **Module 2**: Ethics and Trustworthiness – Privacy, bias, cultural sensitivity, and alignment with frameworks such as the EU Guidelines for Trustworthy AI and UNESCO's AI Competency Framework.
- **Module 3**: Practical Classroom Integration – Designing prompts, managing AI-student interactions, adapting outputs for different subjects and learner groups.
- **Module 4**: Co-Design and Curriculum Alignment – Collaborating with AI to create lesson plans while ensuring alignment with national curricula, assessment standards, and accessibility requirements.
- **Module 5**: Safeguarding and Oversight – Monitoring safe use, detecting inappropriate or biased outputs, and applying escalation protocols when needed.
- **Module 6**: Continuous Professional Growth – Building communities of practice, sharing best practices, and staying updated on emerging AI tools and regulations.

Completion of such certification could be tied to teacher accreditation or Continuing Professional Development (CPD) credits, reinforcing that ethical AI use is part of professional responsibility. Schools that embed these frameworks ensure that AI tutors remain subordinate to human judgement and pedagogical goals, fostering environments where innovation is balanced by accountability and care.

5.4. Bias Mitigation

The mitigation of biases embedded in algorithmic design and persona representation is necessitated by the integration of AI chatbots in K-12 education, requiring proactive strategies. Fairness-aware learning and transparency are emphasised as critical measures to address skewed training data, which often perpetuate stereotypes in AI outputs (Samala & Rawas, 2025). Similarly, the risks of societal biases (Lavidas et al., 2022) being amplified by generative AI, particularly in synthetic media, are highlighted (Ferrara, 2024), with diverse voice options—varied accents, genders, and local dialects—necessitated to ensure equitable student representation. Bias mitigation across the AI lifecycle is advocated (Aninze & Bhogal, 2024), inclusive persona design such as globally neutral or culturally diverse characters being suggested to counteract gendered or Eurocentric norms. This is aligned with categorisation frameworks proposed to address biases in autonomous systems (Bansal et al., 2023), reinforcing the need for varied archetypes like female STEM mentors to promote inclusivity.

The prioritisation of ethical frameworks and stakeholder collaboration is essential for inclusive development processes. The importance of interdisciplinary efforts to reduce algorithmic biases is underscored (Gray et al., 2024), with strategies such as data diversification recommended to reflect diverse demographics. Checklists for bias reduction during AI development are proposed (Nazer et al., 2023), ensuring personas are co-designed with educators from varied cultural backgrounds. Ethical AI decision-making is noted to demand accountability mechanisms, such as the auditing of voice options for cultural neutrality (Gavrilova, 2023). However, caution is raised that trade-offs between accuracy and fairness may arise even with mitigation techniques like reweighting, necessitating continuous refinement (Ferrara, 2024). The collective advocacy for AI personas rooted in global diversity, combined with technical safeguards like fairness metrics, is emphasised to foster equitable learning environments free from stereotypical influences.

Mitigating algorithmic bias in conversational AI for education requires a combination of technical safeguards and institutional practices (Sowjanya & Srividya, 2024). At the model level, schools and vendors should prioritise fairness-aware model selection, choosing systems that are transparent about training methods and capable of handling diverse linguistic and cultural contexts. Regular dataset diversity audits are essential to ensure that training data includes voices, dialects, and perspectives representative of the student population, thereby reducing the risk of exclusion or stereotyping. In the classroom, real-time monitoring of AI outputs by teachers and administrators acts as a critical safeguard, allowing biased or inappropriate responses to be flagged and corrected before they harm learners. International initiatives such as Linus Foundation's AI Fairness 360 toolkit (https://ai-fairness-360.org/) provide valuable frameworks and open-source tools for testing, measuring, and mitigating bias across different dimensions of equity. While these measures represent important progress, the complexity of bias in educational AI underscores the need for ongoing interdisciplinary research that bridges technical innovation with pedagogy, ethics, and local cultural realities.

The Bias Mitigation Checklist for teachers and administrators may include:

- **Fairness-Aware Model** – Has the vendor provided documentation on fairness or equity testing of the AI model?
- **Dataset Diversity Audit** – Does the tool disclose the diversity of its training data (languages, accents, demographics) or provide evidence of periodic audits?
- **Real-Time Monitoring** – Can teachers or administrators easily flag inappropriate or biased outputs in real-time?
- **Bias Testing Tools** – Has the system been evaluated with established toolkits such as AI Fairness 360 or equivalent frameworks?
- **Transparency and Explainability** – Does the provider explain how decisions are made and allow users to understand why a particular response was generated?
- **Corrective Mechanisms** – Is there a clear process for retraining or updating the AI model when bias is detected?

5.5. Long-Term Risks: Anthropomorphism and Over-Reliance in K-12

Anthropomorphism—students attributing human intentions or authority to an AI Tutor—can inflate perceived accuracy and trust. In K-12, this matters because children are still calibrating epistemic judgement. When a friendly, voice-enabled agent speaks in natural prosody and appears "all-knowing," students may accept answers they do not fully understand, skip verification, or internalise the AI as an academic authority. Over time, this risks shallow understanding (answers without reasoning), reduced self-explanation, and weaker metacognition.

Over-reliance is a related hazard: when the chatbot is always available and instantly helpful, learners may offload planning, retrieval, and evaluation—the very processes that build durable knowledge. In extreme cases, students ask the AI before attempting tasks, teachers become "exception handlers," and classrooms drift toward automation bias: choosing AI-suggested actions even when contradictory evidence exists. These risks are not arguments against AI tutors; they are design and policy problems. Practical mitigations include:

- **De-anthropomorphise the surface**: no human name/avatar, periodic reminders ("I am a tool, not a teacher"), and language that signals uncertainty ("Here are three possibilities…").
- **Force productive struggle**: delay full answers by prompting student reasoning first ("What have you tried? Show one step."), then give graded hints rather than solutions.
- **Transparency** by default: reveal sources or reasoning chains at age-appropriate levels; highlight when the model is guessing or out-of-scope.
- **Human-in-the-loop contracts**: define moments when teacher review is required (e.g., safety-sensitive topics, grading, accommodations).
- **Time** and **scope limits**: cap consecutive AI turns; require periodic reflection prompts ("Why do you think this is correct?").
- **Data minimisation for minors**: default opt-out of data retention; avoid sensitive attributes; log only what is necessary for learning analytics with clear parental/guardian policies.

For voice-driven narrative experiences, add meta-narrative breaks that re-contextualise the agent ("Let's check with your notes/teacher") and dual-channel prompts that make students write or sketch before the agent continues speaking. These small frictions re-centre human agency and preserve the teacher's role as sense-maker and ethicist, not merely an overseer.

6. FUTURE DIRECTIONS AND PROJECTIONS

6.1. Emotionally Intelligent and Empathic AI Tutors

The future development of emotionally intelligent AI tutors is hinged on advancements in understanding and simulating human empathy through interdisciplinary approaches. The ability of Large Language Models (LLMs) to infer users' psychological needs with accuracy comparable to human designers was demonstrated (Zhu et al., 2025), suggesting potential for scalable empathic interactions in educational contexts. Similarly, hardware-level innovations, such as MXene-based memristors, were explored to emulate affective reactions like "empathic blame" (Wang et al., 2024), offering a pathway for emotional responsiveness to be embedded directly into AI systems. These technical strides are aligned with the validation of the Agent Empathic Reactivity Index (AERI) as a robust metric (Lee & Yong Yi, 2024), through which AI's ability to mirror human-like concern and perspective-taking—essential for fostering student engagement—is assessed.

However, Fuchs, (2024) challenged the notion of genuine AI subjectivity, arguing that empathy requires shared "conviviality"—a lived, biological experience—which artificial agents inherently lack. Despite this limitation, Mari et al. (2024) empirically showed that AI voice assistants perceived as empathic significantly enhance user trust and willingness to seek assistance, underscoring the pragmatic value of simulated empathy in educational tools. Drigas et al. (2023) further bridged this gap by proposing metacognitive strategies inspired by emotional intelligence frameworks, advocating for AI tutors to integrate training paradigms that enhance adaptive emotional responses. These studies suggest that while AI may never fully replicate human empathy, combining algorithmic transparency, hardware innovations, and validated metrics like AERI can create functionally empathic tutors capable of supporting K-12 learners' socio-emotional development.

The next frontier in educational technology therefore lies in the integration of affective computing (Geetha & Mala, 2025), where AI tutors are designed to recognise and respond to learners' emotions through cues such as tone of voice, facial expressions, or interaction patterns. By using real-time sentiment analysis, these systems can adapt feedback, pacing, and encouragement to match a student's emotional state, offering motivation when frustration rises or slowing down when confusion is detected. While this capacity holds great promise for more empathic and personalised learning, it also raises significant ethical concerns. Learners must not be subjected to hidden profiling or opaque decision-making, which makes transparent and explainable algorithms essential. Students, teachers, and parents should be able to understand how and why an AI Tutor interprets emotions, and safeguards must be in place to prevent misuse of sensitive emotional data. In this way, emotionally intelligent AI tutors can enhance trust and foster deeper engagement, provided that empathy is balanced by accountability and clarity.

6.2. Immersive and Mixed-Reality Learning Environments

The integration of immersive and mixed-reality technologies into K-12 education has been demonstrated to hold significant potential for enhancing engagement and personalisation. The improvement of student motivation and reduction of injury risks through precise pose estimation in physical education has been highlighted (Shekerbekova et al., 2025), with AI and augmented reality (AR) outperforming traditional methods. Similarly, the Meta-MILE framework, which combines 3D virtual environments and AI-driven personalisation to create adaptive learning pathways, has been proposed (Yeganeh et al., 2025), fostering inclusivity and skill acquisition. Cross-cultural benefits have been further emphasised through the use of

360-degree video and AI translation tools (Shadiev et al., 2024), bridging language barriers and enhancing students' cultural knowledge and attitudes. These findings have been reinforced through the integration of VR with generative AI (GAI) such as ChatGPT (Wang et al., 2025), where personalised feedback is provided, significantly boosting reflective thinking and hands-on abilities in AIoT education.

These immersive technologies are increasingly integrated into conversational AI, offering students interactive simulations and experiential learning opportunities (Lertbumroongchai et al., 2025). To ensure equitable access, however, these environments must be developed with inclusive design for low-resource schools, providing scalable options such as mobile-based AR applications or lightweight VR headsets that reduce hardware costs. Emerging infrastructure, particularly 5G networks and edge computing, enables real-time responsiveness in AR/VR experiences, reducing latency and supporting collaborative, interactive classrooms across geographically dispersed regions. Yet the expansion of immersive environments raises profound ethical considerations around surveillance and data privacy, as these systems often capture biometric, behavioural, and location data. Schools and developers must adopt strict privacy-by-design principles, transparent consent practices, and clear limits on data retention to safeguard learners. Only by balancing innovation with inclusivity and ethical vigilance can immersive and mixed-reality learning environments truly serve as tools for global educational equity.

The persistence of challenges such as ethical concerns, infrastructure costs, and technical limitations has been noted (Uğraş et al., 2025). The Metaverse's infrastructural demands and data security risks were identified as barriers to widespread adoption (Chamola et al., 2025), necessitating strategies for equitable access. Robust cybersecurity measures and inclusive design were advocated for to ensure safe and accessible immersive environments, particularly for learners with diverse needs (Villegas-Ch et al., 2024). Technical hurdles in mixed-reality were addressed through the employment of deep learning models like LSTM-CNN hybrids to predict interaction difficulties (Ogunseiju et al., 2023), though computational costs remain a trade-off. The need for interdisciplinary collaboration, teacher training, and ethical frameworks to harness immersive technologies' full potential while mitigating risks is collectively underscored, paving the way for scalable, future-ready educational models.

While emotionally intelligent tutors and immersive mixed-reality environments offer powerful new opportunities for learning, it is essential to remain cautious about over-reliance on AI. No system can replace the nuanced judgement, empathy, and contextual knowledge that human teachers bring to the classroom. Human oversight must remain central, ensuring that AI serves as a supportive tool rather than an autonomous authority. At the same time, schools must prioritise equitable access, so that advances in AI do not deepen divides between well-resourced and marginalised communities. Finally, because the long-term cognitive, social, and ethical effects of these technologies remain uncertain, there is a pressing need for ongoing interdisciplinary research to track impacts and guide responsible implementation. Only by combining innovation with vigilance can educational AI evolve in ways that genuinely enhance learning while protecting the values of fairness, inclusivity, and trust.

7. CONCLUSION

This chapter has argued that conversational AI chatbots—especially those designed with narrative gamification, voice-based interactivity, and culturally adaptive personas—represent more than just a technological upgrade in K-12 classrooms. They embody a reimagining of education as an experience that resonates emotionally, motivates intrinsically, and adapts equitably to diverse learners. By weaving together evidence from SDT, the CoI, and UDL, we have demonstrated that the central message is clear: when grounded in sound pedagogy and ethical safeguards, AI chatbots are not simply tools for efficiency but story-driven companions that can democratise and humanise learning.

Our contribution lies in synthesising multiple streams of literature—narrative learning, gamification, voice technology, and ethical AI governance—into a single, holistic framework for educational AI. Whereas much of the existing scholarship isolates these strands, this chapter demonstrates their synergistic potential. The framework we propose not only fills a gap in studies that privilege text-based, literate-centric models, but also advances the conversation by positioning culturally adaptive, low-cost voice interfaces as pathways for inclusive access in under-resourced schools. In doing so, we carve out intellectual territory that reframes conversational AI from a technical novelty to a pedagogical paradigm.

At the same time, we acknowledge the limitations and boundaries of this work. Our focus has been on K-12 contexts, leaving unanswered how such frameworks translate into early childhood or higher education. While we emphasise voice and narrative affordances, we have not fully addressed the technical complexities of integrating these systems across varying levels of infrastructure. Nor have we resolved all ethical tensions: questions about long-term emotional dependence on AI tutors, cross-cultural narrative appropriateness, and evolving regulatory landscapes remain open. These limitations do not diminish the argument; rather, they highlight the need for ongoing scrutiny and iterative design.

From these limitations flow several promising directions for future research. Scholars could extend this work by conducting longitudinal studies that measure not only short-term engagement but also sustained academic growth and socio-emotional development. Cross-cultural investigations into persona design and localised storytelling could test how well global frameworks adapt to specific regional contexts. Interdisciplinary collaborations—bringing together computer scientists, educators, ethicists, and cognitive psychologists—are urgently needed to refine bias mitigation techniques, safeguard children's privacy, and design inclusive user interfaces. Finally, datasets capturing multimodal classroom interactions could inform next-generation chatbots that respond not just to words, but to tone, gesture, and emotion.

The implications of this work extend well beyond academic debates about AI pedagogy. For policymakers, our findings underscore that equitable AI integration must be accompanied by investment in teacher training, privacy regulation, and affordable infrastructure. For practitioners, the evidence suggests that chatbots can meaningfully reduce administrative burdens, personalise feedback, and scaffold learning for neurodiverse and multilingual students, provided they are embedded within hybrid teacher-AI models. For society at large, the message is that AI tutors are not the harbingers of teacher obsolescence, but rather exemplars of how technology can be ethically and inclusively harnessed to close educational divides.

This chapter concludes with both a caution and a hope. The caution is that AI will fail if it is treated as a replacement for human teachers, or if it reproduces the inequities and biases it promises to solve. The hope is that, if guided by ethics, inclusivity, and pedagogy, conversational AI chatbots can transform classrooms into vibrant, story-driven communities of learning where every child—regardless of background, language, or ability—feels both capable and seen. The single most important lesson is therefore this: educational AI tool must not be built merely to automate instruction but to amplify humanity.

ACKNOWLEDGEMENT

The authors gratefully acknowledge the support provided by Tun Hussein Onn University of Malaysia (UTHM) and the Malaysian Qualifications Agency (MQA) for the GPPT research grant administered by the UTHM Research Management Center, through Vot No. K-579.

REFERENCES

Alvi, I. (2024). Gamification in Education Management : Fulfilling Students' Intrinsic Needs and Learning Outcomes. *Prabandhan: Indian Journal of Management, 17*(11), 41–60. DOI: 10.17010/pijom/2024/v17i11/174022

Anagnostopoulou, E., Grammatikos, N. A., Apostolou, D., & Mentzas, G. (2024). Trustworthy AI in education: A Roadmap for Ethical and Effective Implementation. *Proceedings of the 13th Hellenic Conference on Artificial Intelligence*, 1–7. https://doi.org/DOI: 10.1145/3688671.3688781

Aninze, A., & Bhogal, J. (2024). Artificial Intelligence Life Cycle: The Detection and Mitigation of Bias. *Proceedings of the 4th International Conference on AI Research, ICAIR 2024*, 40–49. https://www.scopus.com/inward/record.uri?eid=2-s2.0-85215706792&partnerID=40&md5=b6e143bd6aa02cf8eb1411594d249c3f

Aravind, A., Durairaj, M., Chitkara, P., Baker El-Ebiary, Y. A., Muniyandy, E., Ushasree, L., & Ammar, M. B. (2025). Adaptive AI-Based Personalized Learning for Accelerated Vocabulary and Syntax Mastery in Young English Learners. *International Journal of Advanced Computer Science and Applications, 16*(4), 678–687. DOI: 10.14569/IJACSA.2025.0160467

Arn, L., Pak, D., Schwartz, L., Yeh, T., & Huang, E. M. (2024). "Do They Act the Way They Look?": Examining Portrayals of Intelligent Technology in Narrative Media from an Educational Perspective. *ACM International Conference Proceeding Series*. https://doi.org/DOI: 10.1145/3679318.3685337

Aslan, S., Durham, L. M., Alyuz, N., Chierichetti, R., Denman, P. A., Okur, E., Aguirre, D. I. G., Esquivel, J. C. Z., Cordourier Maruri, H. A., Sharma, S., Raffa, G., Mayer, R. E., & Nachman, L. (2024). What is the impact of a multi-modal pedagogical conversational AI system on parents' concerns about technology use by young children? *British Journal of Educational Technology, 55*(4), 1625–1650. DOI: 10.1111/bjet.13399

Bansal, C., Pandey, K. K., Goel, R., Sharma, A., & Jangirala, S. (2023). Artificial intelligence (AI) bias impacts: Classification framework for effective mitigation. *Issues in Information Systems*, *24*(4), 367–389. DOI: 10.48009/4_iis_2023_128

Bertini, F. (2023). Artificial Intelligence and data privacy. *Sistemi Intelligenti*, *35*(2), 477–484. DOI: 10.1422/108143

Bettayeb, A. M., Abu Talib, M., Sobhe Altayasinah, A. Z., & Dakalbab, F. (2024). Exploring the impact of ChatGPT: Conversational AI in education. *Frontiers in Education*, *9*, 1379796. Advance online publication. DOI: 10.3389/feduc.2024.1379796

Bougdira, A., & Al Murshidi, G. (2025). Generative AI as a tool for personalized STEAM K-12 education. In *Prompt Engineering and Generative AI Applications for Teaching and Learning* (pp. 387–409). https://doi.org/DOI: 10.4018/979-8-3693-7332-3.ch023

Buffum, P. S. (2015). Examining the impact narrative interactivity has on fostering identity formation in an educational game. *CHI PLAY 2015 - Proceedings of the 2015 Annual Symposium on Computer-Human Interaction in Play*, 395–398. https://doi.org/DOI: 10.1145/2793107.2810278

Caruana, I., Gilar-Corbí, R., & Palomar, M. (2025). THE AI REVOLUTION IN K-12 EDUCATION: ARE EDUCATORS READY? 6259–6265. https://doi.org/.DOI: 10.21125/inted.2025.1624

Chamola, V., Peelam, M. S., Mittal, U., Hassija, V., Singh, A., Pareek, R., Mangal, P., Sangwan, D., de Albuquerque, V. H. C., Mahmud, M., & Brown, D. J. (2025). Metaverse for Education: Developments, Challenges, and Future Direction. *Computer Applications in Engineering Education*, *33*(3), e70018. Advance online publication. DOI: 10.1002/cae.70018

Choi, E. (2025). AI and Digital Literacy Training Support Strategies for Elementary School Teachers in South Korea: Insights from Needs Analysis and Delphi Survey. *KSII Transactions on Internet and Information Systems*, *19*(2). Advance online publication. DOI: 10.3837/tiis.2025.02.007

Chubb, J., Missaoui, S., Concannon, S., Maloney, L., & Walker, J. A. (2022). Interactive storytelling for children: A case-study of design and development considerations for ethical conversational AI. *International Journal of Child-Computer Interaction*, *32*, 100403. Advance online publication. DOI: 10.1016/j.ijcci.2021.100403

Corbeil, J. R., & Corbeil, M. E. (2025). Teaching and Learning in the Age of Generative AI: Evidence-Based Approaches to Pedagogy, Ethics, and Beyond. In *Teaching and Learning in the Age of Generative AI: Evidence-Based Approaches to Pedagogy, Ethics, and Beyond*. https://doi.org/DOI: 10.4324/9781032688602

Darcy, A., Daniels, J., Salinger, D., Wicks, P., & Robinson, A. (2021). Evidence of human-level bonds established with a digital conversational agent: Cross-sectional, retrospective observational study. Jmir Formative Research, 5(5). *JMIR Formative Research*, *5*(5), e27868. Advance online publication. DOI: 10.2196/27868 PMID: 33973854

Daryanto, T., Ding, X., Wilhelm, L. T., Stil, S., Knutsen, K. M., & Rho, E. H. (2025). Conversate: Supporting Reflective Learning in Interview Practice Through Interactive Simulation and Dialogic Feedback. *Proceedings of the ACM on Human-Computer Interaction*, *9*(1), 1–32. Advance online publication. DOI: 10.1145/3701188

De Lima, E. S., Feijó, B., & Furtado, A. L. (2020). Adaptive storytelling based on personality and preference modeling. *Entertainment Computing*, *34*, 100342. Advance online publication. DOI: 10.1016/j.entcom.2020.100342

Dong, C., Yuan, Y., Chen, K., Cheng, S., & Wen, C. (2025). How to Build an Adaptive AI Tutor for Any Course Using Knowledge Graph-Enhanced Retrieval-Augmented Generation (KG-RAG). *2025 14th International Conference on Educational and Information Technology, ICEIT 2025*, 152–157. https://doi.org/DOI: 10.1109/ICEIT64364.2025.10975937

Drigas, A., Papoutsi, C., & Skianis, C. (2023). Being an Emotionally Intelligent Leader through the Nine-Layer Model of Emotional Intelligence—The Supporting Role of New Technologies. *Sustainability (Basel)*, *15*(10), 8103. Advance online publication. DOI: 10.3390/su15108103

Elwahsh, S., Stern, N., Singh, A., & Ayobi, A. (2025). Linguistic Diversity and Mental Well-Being: Co-Designing Custom AI Chatbots with Multilingual Mothers. Cui 2025 Proceedings of the 2025 ACM Conference on Conversational User Interfaces. Scopus. https://doi.org/DOI: 10.1145/3719160.3736615

Ferracani, A., Bertini, M., Pala, P., Nannotti, G., Principi, F., & Becchi, G. (2024). Personalized Generative Storytelling with AI-Visual Illustrations for the Promotion of Knowledge in Cultural Heritage Tourism. *SUMAC 2024 - Proceedings of the 6th Workshop on the AnalySis, Understanding and ProMotion of HeritAge Contents, Co-Located with: MM 2024*, 28–32. https://doi.org/DOI: 10.1145/3689094.3689465

Ferrara, E. (2024). Fairness and Bias in Artificial Intelligence: A Brief Survey of Sources, Impacts, and Mitigation Strategies. *Sci*, *6*(1), 3. Advance online publication. DOI: 10.3390/sci6010003

Fuchs, T. (2024). Understanding Sophia? On human interaction with artificial agents. *Phenomenology and the Cognitive Sciences*, *23*(1), 21–42. DOI: 10.1007/s11097-022-09848-0

Furizal, R., Ramelan, A., Adriyanto, F., Maghfiroh, H., Ma'arif, A., Kariyamin, K., Masitha, A., & Fawait, A. B. (2024). Concerns of Ethical and Privacy in the Rapid Advancement of Artificial Intelligence: Directions, Challenges, and Solutions. [JRC]. *Journal of Robotics and Control*, *5*(6), 2015–2026. DOI: 10.18196/jrc.v5i6.24090

Gallent Torres, C., Zapata González, A., & Ortego Hernando, J. L. (2023). The impact of Generative Artificial Intelligence in higher education: a focus on ethics and academic integrity. *RELIEVE - Revista Electrónica de Investigación y Evaluación Educativa, 29*(2). https://doi.org/.DOI: 10.30827/relieve.v29i2.29134

Gavrilova, M. L. (2023). Responsible Artificial Intelligence and Bias Mitigation in Deep Learning Systems. *Proceedings of the International Conference on Information Visualisation*, 329–333. https://doi.org/DOI: 10.1109/IV60283.2023.00062

Geetha, A. V., & Mala, T. (2025). Masked Attention-Driven Unified Multitask Representation Learning for Affective Computing. *Scopus.*, 1–8. Advance online publication. DOI: 10.1109/ICDSBS63635.2025.11031501

Gilyazova, O. S., & Zamoshchanskii, I. I. (2020). On motivational tools of gamification in higher education: Theoretical aspect. *Perspektivy Nauki i Obrazovania*, *45*(3), 39–51. DOI: 10.32744/pse.2020.3.3

Ginting, D., Woods, R. M., Barella, Y., Limanta, L. S., Madkur, A., & How, H. E. (2024). The Effects of Digital Storytelling on the Retention and Transferability of Student Knowledge. *SAGE Open*, *14*(3), 21582440241271267. Advance online publication. DOI: 10.1177/21582440241271267

Gray, M., Samala, R., Liu, Q., Skiles, D., Xu, J., Tong, W., & Wu, L. (2024). Measurement and Mitigation of Bias in Artificial Intelligence: A Narrative Literature Review for Regulatory Science. *Clinical Pharmacology and Therapeutics*, *115*(4), 687–697. DOI: 10.1002/cpt.3117 PMID: 38018360

Gupta, P., & Goyal, P. (2022). Is game-based pedagogy just a fad? A self-determination theory approach to gamification in higher education. *International Journal of Educational Management*, *36*(3), 341–356. DOI: 10.1108/IJEM-04-2021-0126

Hanses, M., van Rijn, L., Karolyi, H., & de Witt, C. (2024). Guiding Students Towards Successful Assessments Using Learning Analytics From Behavioral Data to Formative Feedback. In Sahin, M., & Ifenthaler, D. (Eds.), *Assessment Analytics in Education: Designs, Methods and Solutions* (pp. 61–83). Springer International Publishing., DOI: 10.1007/978-3-031-56365-2_4

Hare, R., Tang, Y., & Ferguson, S. (2024). An Intelligent Serious Game for Digital Logic Education to Enhance Student Learning. *IEEE Transactions on Education*, *67*(3), 387–394. DOI: 10.1109/TE.2024.3359001

Herrera-Ferrá, K., Muñoz, J. M., Nicolini, H., Saruwatari Zavala, G., & Martínez Bullé Goyri, V. M. (2023). Contextual and Cultural Perspectives on Neurorights: Reflections Toward an International Consensus. *AJOB Neuroscience*, *14*(4), 360–368. DOI: 10.1080/21507740.2022.2048722 PMID: 35341473

Hsia, L.-H., Lin, Y.-N., Lin, C.-H., & Hwang, G.-J. (2025). Effectiveness of gamified intelligent tutoring in physical education through the lens of self-determination theory. *Computers & Education*, *227*, 105212. Advance online publication. DOI: 10.1016/j.compedu.2024.105212

Huang, C., Zhong, Y., Li, Y., Wang, X., Han, Z., Zhang, D., & Liu, M. (2025). Enhancing student reading performance through a personalized two-tier problem-based learning approach with generative artificial intelligence. *Humanities & Social Sciences Communications*, *12*(1), 645. Advance online publication. DOI: 10.1057/s41599-025-04919-4

Jaskari, M.-M., & Syrjälä, H. (2024). One solution does not fit all: Reward-based and meaningful gamification in higher education. In *Practices and Implementation of Gamification in Higher Education* (pp. 22–49). https://doi.org/DOI: 10.4018/979-8-3693-0716-8.ch002

Jeon, J., Kim, L., & Park, J. (2025). The ethics of generative AI in social science research: A qualitative approach for institutionally grounded AI research ethics. *Technology in Society*, *81*, 102836. Advance online publication. DOI: 10.1016/j.techsoc.2025.102836

Jondya, A. G., & Susanto, K. F., & Cathleen. (2023). Utilizing Simple Fuzzy Logic into An Adaptive Storytelling Mobile Game in Learning Historical Event of Indonesia's Independence Movement. *Proceedings of the 7th 2023 International Conference on New Media Studies, CONMEDIA 2023*, 33–38. https://doi.org/DOI: 10.1109/CONMEDIA60526.2023.10428575

Joshi, S. (2025). Strategic Integration of Artificial Intelligence in U.S. K-12 Education: A Comprehensive Review and Policy Roadmap. *SSRN*. https://doi.org/DOI: 10.5120/ijca2025925428

Kamila, M. K., & Jasrotia, S. S. (2025). Ethical issues in the development of artificial intelligence: Recognizing the risks. *International Journal of Ethics and Systems*, *41*(1), 45–63. DOI: 10.1108/IJOES-05-2023-0107

Karpouzis, K. (2024). Plato's Shadows in the Digital Cave: Controlling Cultural Bias in Generative AI. *Electronics (Basel)*, *13*(8), 1457. Advance online publication. DOI: 10.3390/electronics13081457

Katona, J., & Gyonyoru, K. I. K. (2025). Integrating AI-based adaptive learning into the flipped classroom model to enhance engagement and learning outcomes. *Computers and Education: Artificial Intelligence*, *8*, 100392. Advance online publication. DOI: 10.1016/j.caeai.2025.100392

Khanna, R. (2025). Harnessing AI in Education: Perspectives from Education Leaders. Insights from a National Leadership Roundtable on the Future of Education. SSRN Electronic Journal. https://doi.org/DOI: 10.2139/ssrn.5381208

Khundam, C., & Noël, F. (2021). Storytelling framework with adaptive interaction system for interactive content in virtual museum. *ECTI Transactions on Computer and Information Technology*, *15*(1), 34–49. DOI: 10.37936/ecti-cit.2021151.239948

Kim, M., Kim, T., Nguyen, A., Gomez, E. N., & Jin, J. (2024). TinyTeller AI, an AI-based Adaptive Storytelling Application. *Proceedings - 2024 Artificial Intelligence x Humanities, Education, and Art. AIxHEART*, *2024*, 44–51. DOI: 10.1109/AIxHeart62327.2024.00017

Kumaran, S., Bharathi, B. S., & Pradeepa, R. (2025). A college enquiry text-based AI chatbot using python. *AIP Conference Proceedings*, *3159*(1), 030013. Advance online publication. DOI: 10.1063/5.0247111

Kurian, N. (2025). AI's empathy gap: The risks of conversational Artificial Intelligence for young children's well-being and key ethical considerations for early childhood education and care. *Contemporary Issues in Early Childhood*, *26*(1), 132–139. DOI: 10.1177/14639491231206004

Lami, B., Mohd. Hussein, S., Rajamanickam, R., & Emmanuel, G. K. (2024). The role of artificial intelligence (AI) in shaping data privacy. *International Journal of Law and Management*. https://doi.org/.DOI: 10.1108/IJLMA-07-2024-0242

Lampropoulos, G., & Papadakis, S. (2025). The Educational Value of Artificial Intelligence and Social Robots. In Lampropoulos, G., & Papadakis, S. (Eds.), *Social Robots in Education* (Vol. 1194, pp. 3–15). Springer Nature Switzerland., DOI: 10.1007/978-3-031-82915-4_1

Lavidas, K., Papadakis, S., Manesis, D., Grigoriadou, A. S., & Gialamas, V.Lectures and Lab Classes. (2022). The Effects of Social Desirability on Students' Self-Reports in Two Social Contexts: Lectures vs. Lectures and Lab Classes. *Information (Basel), 13*(10), 491. DOI: 10.3390/info13100491

Lavidas, K., Petropoulou, A., Papadakis, S., Apostolou, Z., Komis, V., Jimoyiannis, A., & Gialamas, V. (2022). Factors Affecting Response Rates of the Web Survey with Teachers. *Computers, 11*(9), 127. DOI: 10.3390/computers11090127

Lee, B., & Yong Yi, M. (2024). Understanding the Empathetic Reactivity of Conversational Agents: Measure Development and Validation. *International Journal of Human-Computer Interaction, 40*(22), 6845–6863. DOI: 10.1080/10447318.2023.2270665

Lee, S., Mott, B., Vandenberg, J., Spires, H. A., & Lester, J. (2023). Examining the Relationship of Gameplay and Learning in a Narrative-Centered Digital Game for Science Education. *IEEE Conference on Computatonal Intelligence and Games, CIG*. https://doi.org/DOI: 10.1109/CoG57401.2023.10333202

Lee, S., Mott, B., Vandenberg, J., Spires, H. A., & Lester, J. (2024). Exploring Gameplay and Learning in a Narrative-Centered Digital Game for Elementary Science Education. *IEEE Transactions on Games, 16*(4), 1–14. DOI: 10.1109/TG.2024.3424689

Lertbumroongchai, K., Janratchakool, W., & Nittayathammakul, V. (2025). Using Virtual Reality and Conversational AI to Enhance High School Students' Intentions to Pursue Computer Science: Insights from the CS RMUTT Virtual Tour. Studies in Media and Communication, 13(3), 87–102. *Scopus*. Advance online publication. DOI: 10.11114/smc.v13i3.7683

Li, H., Xing, W., Li, C., Zhu, W., Lyu, B., Zhang, F., & Liu, Z. (2025). Who Should Be My Tutor? Analyzing the Interactive Effects of Automated Text Personality Styles Between Middle School Students and a Mathematics Chatbot. *15th International Conference on Learning Analytics and Knowledge, LAK 2025*, 910–917. https://doi.org/DOI: 10.1145/3706468.3706537

Li, T., Nath, D., Cheng, Y., Fan, Y., Li, X., Raković, M., Khosravi, H., Swiecki, Z., Tsai, Y.-S., & Gašević, D. (2025). Turning Real-Time Analytics into Adaptive Scaffolds for Self-Regulated Learning Using Generative Artificial Intelligence. *15th International Conference on Learning Analytics and Knowledge, LAK 2025*, 667–679. https://doi.org/DOI: 10.1145/3706468.3706559

Li, Y., & Chiu, T. K. F. (2025). The mediating effects of needs satisfaction on the relationship between teacher support and student engagement with Generative Artificial Intelligence (GenAI) chatbots from a Self-Determination Theory (SDT) perspective. Education and Information Technologies. *Education and Information Technologies*, *30*(14), 20051–20070. Advance online publication. DOI: 10.1007/s10639-025-13574-w

Li, Y., & Gabriel, M. (2022). Diverse Cultures, Universal Capacities: an Interview with Markus Gabriel. *Technology and Language, 3*(1–6), 47–56. https://doi.org/DOI: 10.48417/technolang.2022.01.06

Liu, L. (2025). Impact of AI gamification on EFL learning outcomes and nonlinear dynamic motivation: Comparing adaptive learning paths, conversational agents, and storytelling. *Education and Information Technologies*, *30*(8), 11299–11338. Advance online publication. DOI: 10.1007/s10639-024-13296-5

Malaborbor, R. A. C., Rivera, V. S., Diloy, M. A., De Luna, L. R., Dela Cruz, A. L. Y., & Velasco, A. T. (2024). Enhancing Data Privacy Literacy through Conversational AI: A QandA-Based Approach to Educating Users on the Provisions of the Data Privacy Act of 2012. 271–276. *Scopus.*, 271–276. Advance online publication. DOI: 10.1145/3696230.3696247

Mamun, M. R. A., Ntsweng, O., Baah-Peprah, P., David, A., & Prybutok, V. R. (2025). What Drives User Intention to Continue Using Conversational AI? How Functional and Emotional Values Influence Continuance Intention. *AIS Transactions on Human-Computer Interaction*, *17*(1), 1–34. DOI: 10.17705/1thci.00216

Mari, A., Mandelli, A., & Algesheimer, R. (2024). Empathic voice assistants: Enhancing consumer responses in voice commerce. *Journal of Business Research*, *175*, 114566. Advance online publication. DOI: 10.1016/j.jbusres.2024.114566

Matera, M., Piro, L., Pucci, E., Costabile, M. F., Lanzilotti, R., & Piccinno, A. (2023). Improving Citizen Inclusivity through Conversational AI. The PROTECT Approach. *CEUR Workshop Proceedings*, *3486*, 261–266. https://www.scopus.com/inward/record.uri?eid=2-s2.0-85173828750&partnerID=40&md5=66d2fe8589141c2be62efcdc237cb1ec

Mehrez, A., Adamo, N., Giri, N., & Larson, D. (2023). Fiat Lux! Does the Lighting Design Affect Viewers' Perception of an Animated Character Personality? *Lecture Notes in Computer Science (Including Subseries Lecture Notes in Artificial Intelligence and Lecture Notes in Bioinformatics), 14047 LNCS*, 263–272. https://doi.org/DOI: 10.1007/978-3-031-35979-8_21

Meshram, S., Naik, N., Vr, M., More, T., & Kharche, S. (2021). Conversational AI: Chatbots. *2021 International Conference on Intelligent Technologies, CONIT 2021*. https://doi.org/DOI: 10.1109/CONIT51480.2021.9498508

Michalak, R. (2023). From Ethics to Execution: The Role of Academic Librarians in Artificial Intelligence (AI) Policy-Making at Colleges and Universities. *Journal of Library Administration*, *63*(7), 928–938. DOI: 10.1080/01930826.2023.2262367

Monjoree, U., Aguilar, S. D., Qian, C., Van Huyck, C., Yeh, S.-H., Tranbarger, P., Duane-Tessier, L., Solitare-Renaldo, L., Burte, H., Yasskin, P., Liew, J., Song, D., Quek, F., & Yan, W. (2024). AR-Classroom: Integrating Conversational Artificial Intelligence with Augmented Reality Technology for Learning Spatial Transformations and Their Matrix Representation. *Proceedings - Frontiers in Education Conference, FIE*. https://doi.org/DOI: 10.1109/FIE61694.2024.10893308

Mooradian, N., Franks, P. C., & Srivastav, A. (2025). The impact of artificial intelligence on data privacy: A risk management perspective. *Records Management Journal*, *35*(2), 147–159. Advance online publication. DOI: 10.1108/RMJ-06-2024-0013

Morkina, J. S. (2021). Meaning-constitution Problems in the Digital Culture's Horizon. *Voprosy Filosofii*, *12*(12), 78–89. DOI: 10.21146/0042-8744-2021-12-78-89

Morozova, I., & Nikolaienko, V. (2024). Emotional appeal in ChatGPT prompts: A study of L2 speakers' perceptions | Emotywne prompty i ich percepcja – na przykładzie interakcji nierodzimych użytkowników języka z botem ChatGPT. *Res Rhetorica*, *11*(4), 155–174. DOI: 10.29107/rr2024.4.9

Mutajwaa, S. A., & Didas, M. (2025). Roadmap to Systematic Understanding of Artificial Intelligence Technology Development and Implementation: A Narrative Review of Frameworks, Platforms, Scenarios of Use and Empirical Guide. *Journal of ICT Systems*, *3*(1), 34–62. DOI: 10.56279/jicts.v3i1.126

Narayanan, K. S., & Kumaravel, A. (2024). Hybrid Gamification and AI Tutoring Framework using Machine Learning and Adaptive Neuro-Fuzzy Inference System. *Journal of Advanced Research in Applied Sciences and Engineering Technology*, *42*(2), 221–233. DOI: 10.37934/araset.42.2.221233

Naseer, F., Khan, M. N., Addas, A., Awais, Q., & Ayub, N. (2025). Game Mechanics and Artificial Intelligence Personalization: A Framework for Adaptive Learning Systems. *Education Sciences*, *15*(3), 301. Advance online publication. DOI: 10.3390/educsci15030301

Nazer, L. H., Zatarah, R., Waldrip, S., Ke, J. X. C., Moukheiber, M., Khanna, A. K., Hicklen, R. S., Moukheiber, L., Moukheiber, D., Ma, H., & Mathur, P. (2023). Bias in artificial intelligence algorithms and recommendations for mitigation. *PLOS Digital Health*, *2*(6), e0000278. Advance online publication. DOI: 10.1371/journal.pdig.0000278 PMID: 37347721

Ngandoh, S. T., Riandi, R., Rahmat, A., Muslim, M., Haris, A., Khaeruddin, K., & Friyanto, A. (2025). Enhancing Interactive Media Design Using Cognitive Load Theory Approach: Integrating Artificial Intelligence (Ai) Chatbot. [Scopus.]. *Journal of Engineering Science and Technology*, *20*(2), 71–78.

Nguyen, A., Ngo, H. N., Hong, Y., Dang, B., & Nguyen, B.-P. T. (2023). Ethical principles for artificial intelligence in education. *Education and Information Technologies*, *28*(4), 4221–4241. DOI: 10.1007/s10639-022-11316-w PMID: 36254344

O'Connor, S., & Liu, H. (2024). Gender bias perpetuation and mitigation in AI technologies: Challenges and opportunities. *AI & Society*, *39*(4), 2045–2057. DOI: 10.1007/s00146-023-01675-4

Ogunseiju, O., Akinniyi, A., Gonsalves, N., Khalid, M., & Akanmu, A. (2023). Detecting Learning Stages within a Sensor-Based Mixed Reality Learning Environment Using Deep Learning. *Journal of Computing in Civil Engineering*, *37*(4), 04023011. Advance online publication. DOI: 10.1061/JCCEE5.CPENG-5169

Olson, D. M., Soliman, N., Wang, A., Price, M., Sahu, R., & Harrell, D. F. (2020). Breakbeat narratives: A personalized, conversational interactive storytelling system for museum education. *Conference on Human Factors in Computing Systems - Proceedings*. https://doi.org/DOI: 10.1145/3334480.3382974

Olugbade, D., Edwards, B. I., & Ojo, O. A. (2024). Facilitating Cognitive Load Management and Improved Learning Outcomes and Attitudes in Middle School Technology and Vocational Education Through AI Chatbot. Journal of Technical Education and Training, 16(3), 114–131. *Scopus.* Advance online publication. DOI: 10.30880/jtet.2024.16.03.009

Park, J. J., & Milner, P. (2025). Enhancing Academic Writing Integrity: Ethical Implementation of Generative Artificial Intelligence for Non-Traditional Online Students. *TechTrends*, *69*(1), 176–188. DOI: 10.1007/s11528-024-01024-2

Patilima, H. (2025). Neurodiversity and trauma in early childhood: Implications for inclusive learning. South African Journal of Childhood Education, 15(1). *South African Journal of Childhood Education, 15*(1), a1704. Advance online publication. DOI: 10.4102/sajce.v15i1.1704

Piro, L. (2023). Conversational AI for Web Inclusivity: Technologies, Design Patterns and Development Toolkits. *CEUR Workshop Proceedings, 3481*, 29–35. https://www.scopus.com/inward/record.uri?eid=2-s2.0-85172870199&partnerID=40&md5=503b0ef4f132cdddd5f9817468dd6fd1

Quince, Z., & Nikolic, S. (2025). Student identification of the social, economic and environmental implications of using Generative Artificial Intelligence (GenAI): Identifying student ethical awareness of ChatGPT from a scaffolded multi-stage assessment. *European Journal of Engineering Education*. Advance online publication. DOI: 10.1080/03043797.2025.2482830

Renfeng, J., Gang, Y., & Qi, S. (2025). The Motivational Impact of GenAI Tools in Language Learning: A Quasi-Experiment Study. International Journal of Applied Linguistics United Kingdom, 35(3), 1338–1350. *Scopus*. Advance online publication. DOI: 10.1111/ijal.12701

Robinson, S. C. (2020). Trust, transparency, and openness: How inclusion of cultural values shapes Nordic national public policy strategies for artificial intelligence (AI). *Technology in Society, 63*, 101421. Advance online publication. DOI: 10.1016/j.techsoc.2020.101421

Saffarizadeh, K., Keil, M., Boodraj, M., & Alashoor, T. (2024). "My Name is Alexa. What's Your Name?" The Impact of Reciprocal Self-Disclosure on Post-Interaction Trust in Conversational Agents. *Journal of the Association for Information Systems, 25*(3), 528–568. DOI: 10.17705/1jais.00839

Samala, A. D., & Rawas, S. (2025). Bias in artificial intelligence: Smart solutions for detection, mitigation, and ethical strategies in real-world applications. *IAES International Journal of Artificial Intelligence, 14*(1), 32–43. DOI: 10.11591/ijai.v14.i1.pp32-43

Sánchez-García, P., Diez-Gracia, A., Mayorga, I. R., & Jerónimo, P. (2025). Media Self-Regulation in the Use of AI: Limitation of Multimodal Generative Content and Ethical Commitments to Transparency and Verification. *Journalism and Media, 6*(1), 29. Advance online publication. DOI: 10.3390/journalmedia6010029

Sargent, C. S., Koohang, A., Floyd, K., & Kilburn, R. (2024). Artificial Intelligence: Ethical concerns, trust, and risk. *Issues in Information Systems, 25*(2), 71–83. DOI: 10.48009/2_iis_2024_106

Sarshartehrani, F., Mohammadrezaei, E., Behravan, M., & Gracanin, D. (2024). *Enhancing E-Learning Experience Through Embodied AI Tutors in Immersive Virtual Environments: A Multifaceted Approach for Personalized Educational Adaptation.*, DOI: 10.1007/978-3-031-60609-0_20

Seaborn, K., Miyake, N. P., Pennefather, P., & Otake-Matsuura, M. (2022). Voice in human-agent interaction: A survey. *ACM Computing Surveys*, *54*(4), 1–43. Advance online publication. DOI: 10.1145/3386867

Shadiev, R., Wang, X., Chen, X., Gayevskaya, E., & Borisov, N. (2024). Research on the impact of the learning activity supported by 360-degree video and translation technologies on cross-cultural knowledge and attitudes development. *Education and Information Technologies*, *29*(7), 7759–7791. DOI: 10.1007/s10639-023-12143-3

Shahri, H., Emad, M., Ibrahim, N., Rais, R. N. B., & Al-Fayoumi, Y. (2024). Elevating Education through AI Tutor: Utilizing GPT-4 for Personalized Learning. *Proceedings of the 15th Annual Undergraduate Research Conference on Applied Computing on "AI for a Sustainable Economy." URC 2024*. https://doi.org/DOI: 10.1109/URC62276.2024.10604578

Shekerbekova, S., Kamalova, G., Iskakova, M., Aldabergenova, A., Abdykerimova, E., & Shetiyeva, K. (2025). Exploring the use of Artificial Intelligence and Augmented Reality tools to improve interactivity in Physical Education teaching and training methods | Explorando el uso de herramientas de Inteligencia Artificial y Realidad Aumentada para mejorar la inter. *Retos*, *66*, 1132–1139. DOI: 10.47197/retos.v66.113540

Shilaskar, S., Sheikh, S., Bhatlawande, S., Salve, S., & Shaikh, T. (2024). Empowering Futures: A Dynamic Conversational AI Chatbot System for Facilitating Educational Scholarship Opportunities. *2024 1st International Conference on Trends in Engineering Systems and Technologies, ICTEST 2024*. https://doi.org/DOI: 10.1109/ICTEST60614.2024.10576128

Shukla, R. P., & Taneja, S. (2024). Ethical considerations and data privacy in artificial intelligence. In *Integrating Generative AI in Education to Achieve Sustainable Development Goals* (pp. 86–97). https://doi.org/DOI: 10.4018/979-8-3693-2440-0.ch005

Sowjanya, A. M., & Srividya, K. (2024). NLP-driven chatbots: Applications and implications in conversational AI. In *Conversational Artificial Intelligence* (pp. 713–725). Scopus., DOI: 10.1002/9781394200801.ch39

Stacchio, L., Balloni, E., Gorgoglione, L., Mancini, A., Giovanola, B., Tiribelli, S., & Zingaretti, P. (2024). An ethical framework for trustworthy Neural Rendering applied in cultural heritage and creative industries. *Frontiers of Computer Science, 6*, 1459807. Advance online publication. DOI: 10.3389/fcomp.2024.1459807

Stragier, V., Seddati, O., & Dutoit, T. (2023). Developing an Interactive Agent for Blind and Visually Impaired People. *IMX 2023 - Proceedings of the 2023 ACM International Conference on Interactive Media Experiences*, 248–253. https://doi.org/DOI: 10.1145/3573381.3596471

Subitsha, R. S., Vetrivel, M., Shrimaulik, N., & Saravanan, K. (2025). Natural Language Processing-Driven Learning Platform for Personalized Education. *Proceedings of International Conference on Visual Analytics and Data Visualization, ICVADV 2025*, 174–180. https://doi.org/DOI: 10.1109/ICVADV63329.2025.10961687

Sunmboye, K., Strafford, H., Noorestani, S., & Wilison-Pirie, M. (2025). Exploring the influence of artificial intelligence integration on personalized learning: A cross-sectional study of undergraduate medical students in the United Kingdom. *BMC Medical Education, 25*(1), 570. Advance online publication. DOI: 10.1186/s12909-025-07084-z PMID: 40247306

Sysoyev, P. V. (2024). Ethics and AI-Plagiarism in an Academic Environment: Students' Understanding of Compliance with Author's Ethics and the Problem of Plagiarism in the Process of Interaction with Generative Artificial Intelligence. *Vysshee Obrazovanie v Rossii = Higher Education in Russia, 33*(2), 31–53. .DOI: 10.31992/0869-3617-2024-33-2-31-53

Sysoyev, P. V. (2025). Personalized Learning Based on Artificial Intelligence: How Ready Are Modern Students for New Educational Opportunities. *Vysshee Obrazovanie v Rossii = Higher Education in Russia, 34*(2), 51–71. .DOI: 10.31992/0869-3617-2025-34-2-51-71

Szczepański, M., Gapiński, G., & Marciniak, J. (2025). AI Tutor: Adaptive e-Learning System Using Expert Fuzzy Controllers. *International Conference on Computer Supported Education, CSEDU - Proceedings, 2*, 96–107. https://doi.org/DOI: 10.5220/0013277900003932

Taheri, A., Bhardwaj, P., Caetano, A., Zhong, A., & Sra, M. (2023). Virtual Buddy: Redefining Conversational AI Interactions for Individuals with Hand Motor Disabilities. *UIST 2023 Adjunct - Adjunct Proceedings of the 36th Annual ACM Symposium on User Interface Software and Technology*. https://doi.org/DOI: 10.1145/3586182.3616680

Tan, J. W., Ng, K. B., & Mogali, S. R. (2022). An Exploratory Digital Board Game Approach to the Review and Reinforcement of Complex Medical Subjects Like Anatomical Education: Cross-sectional and Mixed Methods Study. *JMIR Serious Games*, *10*(1), e33282. Advance online publication. DOI: 10.2196/33282 PMID: 35006080

Ubur, S. D. (2025). AI-Driven Interpretation of Nonverbal Communication in AR-Enhanced Real-Time Captions: Effects on Cognitive Load, Comprehension, and User Engagement. 45–51. *Scopus.*, 45–51. Advance online publication. DOI: 10.1145/3698061.3734421

Uğraş, H., Uğraş, M., Papadakis, S., & Kalogiannakis, M. (2024). ChatGPT-Supported Education in Primary Schools: The Potential of ChatGPT for Sustainable Practices. *Sustainability (Basel)*, *16*(22), 9855. DOI: 10.3390/su16229855

Uğraş, H., Uğraş, M., Papadakis, S., & Kalogiannakis, M. (2025). Innovative Early Childhood STEM Education with ChatGPT: Teacher Perspectives. Technology. *Knowledge and Learning*, *30*(2), 809–831. DOI: 10.1007/s10758-024-09804-8

Utsch, M. N. R., Pappa, G. L., Chaimowicz, L., & Prates, R. O. (2020). A new non-deterministic drama manager for adaptive interactive storytelling. *Entertainment Computing*, *34*, 100364. Advance online publication. DOI: 10.1016/j.entcom.2020.100364

Vanbecelaere, S., Demedts, F., Reynvoet, B., & Depaepe, F. (2023). Toward a framework for analyzing adaptive digital games' research effectiveness. *International Journal of Serious Games*, *10*(4), 77–91. DOI: 10.17083/ijsg.v10i4.618

Vashishth, T. K., Sharma, V., Sharma, K. K., Kumar, B., Panwar, R., & Chaudhary, S. (2024). AI-Driven Learning Analytics for Personalized Feedback and Assessment in Higher Education. In Nguyen, T. V. T., & Vo, N. T. M. (Eds.), (pp. 206–230). Advances in Media, Entertainment, and the Arts. IGI Global., DOI: 10.4018/979-8-3693-0639-0.ch009

Venkatraman, S., Brindha, S., Lakshmi, G., Selvi, V. M., & Sandhya, J. (2024). Harnessing the potential of conversational AI: A Roadmap for Academic Applications. *2024 International Conference on Power, Energy, Control and Transmission Systems (ICPECTS)*, 1–5. https://doi.org/DOI: 10.1109/ICPECTS62210.2024.10780187

Villegas-Ch, W., García-Ortiz, J., & Sánchez-Viteri, S. (2024). Educational Advances in the Metaverse: Boosting Learning Through Virtual and Augmented Reality and Artificial Intelligence. *IEEE Access : Practical Innovations, Open Solutions*, *12*, 59093–59112. DOI: 10.1109/ACCESS.2024.3393776

Wakunuma, K., & Eke, D. (2024). Africa, ChatGPT, and Generative AI Systems: Ethical Benefits, Concerns, and the Need for Governance. *Philosophies*, *9*(3), 80. Advance online publication. DOI: 10.3390/philosophies9030080

Wang, A., Thompson, M., Roy, D., Pan, K., Perry, J., Tan, P., Eberhart, R., & Klopfer, E. (2022). Iterative user and expert feedback in the design of an educational virtual reality biology game. *Interactive Learning Environments*, *30*(4), 677–694. DOI: 10.1080/10494820.2019.1678489

Wang, H., Zhang, L., Zheng, C., Gomez, R., Nakamura, K., & Li, G. (2022). *Personalized Storytelling with Social Robot Haru.*, DOI: 10.1007/978-3-031-24670-8_39

Wang, L., Huang, M., & Ismail Kamal, J. (2024). The Application of an Unplugged and Low-Cost Children's Coding Education Tool in a Gamification Context. *Pertanika Journal of Social Science & Humanities*, *32*(2), 387–407. DOI: 10.47836/pjssh.32.2.03

Wang, W.-S., Lin, C.-J., Lee, H.-Y., Huang, Y.-M., & Wu, T.-T. (2025). Integrating feedback mechanisms and ChatGPT for VR-based experiential learning: Impacts on reflective thinking and AIoT physical hands-on tasks. *Interactive Learning Environments*, *33*(2), 1770–1787. DOI: 10.1080/10494820.2024.2375644

Wang, Y., Zhang, Y., Wang, Y., Zhang, H., Wang, X., Xu, R., & Tong, Y. (2024). Realization of Empathy Capability for the Evolution of Artificial Intelligence Using an MXene(Ti3C2)-Based Memristor. *Electronics (Basel)*, *13*(9), 1632. Advance online publication. DOI: 10.3390/electronics13091632

Wu, X., Li, R., & Gwendoline Quek, C. L. (2025). When GenAI chatbots meet self-determination: Unpacking Chinese EFL learners' engagement in chatbot-assisted language learning. Interactive Learning Environments. *Interactive Learning Environments*, 1–21. Advance online publication. DOI: 10.1080/10494820.2025.2538756

Xie, Z., Wu, X., & Xie, Y. (2024). Can interaction with generative artificial intelligence enhance learning autonomy? A longitudinal study from comparative perspectives of virtual companionship and knowledge acquisition preferences. Journal of Computer Assisted Learning, 40(5), 2369–2384. *Scopus*. Advance online publication. DOI: 10.1111/jcal.13032

Yang, Z., Wu, J. G., & Xie, H. (2024). Taming Frankenstein's monster: Ethical considerations relating to generative artificial intelligence in education. *Asia Pacific Journal of Education*. Advance online publication. DOI: 10.1080/02188791.2023.2300137

Yaseen, H., Mohammad, A. S., Ashal, N., Abusaimeh, H., Ali, A., & Sharabati, A.-A. A. (2025). The Impact of Adaptive Learning Technologies, Personalized Feedback, and Interactive AI Tools on Student Engagement: The Moderating Role of Digital Literacy. *Sustainability (Basel)*, *17*(3), 1133. Advance online publication. DOI: 10.3390/su17031133

Ye, W., & Li, Q. (2020). Open Questions for Next Generation Chatbots. *Proceedings - 2020 IEEE/ACM Symposium on Edge Computing, SEC 2020*, 346–351. https://doi.org/DOI: 10.1109/SEC50012.2020.00050

Yeganeh, L. N., Fenty, N. S., Chen, Y., Simpson, A., & Hatami, M. (2025). The Future of Education: A Multi-Layered Metaverse Classroom Model for Immersive and Inclusive Learning. *Future Internet*, *17*(2), 63. Advance online publication. DOI: 10.3390/fi17020063

Yeh, P.-L., Kuo, W.-C., & Tsai, C.-J. (2024). Counseling Students' First Impressions of Using Woebot: A Mental Health Chatbot. Bulletin of Educational Psychology, 56(1), 45–72. *Scopus*. Advance online publication. DOI: 10.6251/BEP.202409_56(1).0003

Yeh, P.-L., Kuo, W.-C., Tseng, B.-L., & Sung, Y.-H. (2025). Does the AI-driven Chatbot Work? Effectiveness of the Woebot app in reducing anxiety and depression in group counseling courses and student acceptance of technological aids. Current Psychology, 44(9), 8133–8145. *Scopus*. Advance online publication. DOI: 10.1007/s12144-025-07359-0

Zadeh, P. M., & Sattler, D. (2023). Improving Accessibility and Readability of Survey Reports in Digital Health Platforms using Conversational AI. *Proceedings - 2023 2023 IEEE International Conference on Bioinformatics and Biomedicine, BIBM 2023*, 4987–4989. https://doi.org/DOI: 10.1109/BIBM58861.2023.10386018

Zhang, Q., Siraj, S. B., & Abdul Razak, R. B. (2025). Effects of AI chatbots on EFL students' critical thinking skills and intrinsic motivation in argumentative writing. Innovation in Language Learning and Teaching. *Innovation in Language Learning and Teaching*, 1–29. Advance online publication. DOI: 10.1080/17501229.2025.2515111

Zhang, S., Hu, H., & Xing, S. (2024). Dual Learning for Conversational Emotion Recognition and Emotional Response Generation. *IEEE Transactions on Affective Computing*, *15*(3), 1241–1252. DOI: 10.1109/TAFFC.2023.3332631

Zhou, X., Liu, M., & Wu, L. (2025). Research on Personalized Learning Resource Recommendation Method for Students Supported by Artificial Intelligence. *Journal of Combinatorial Mathematics and Combinatorial Computing*, *127b*, 1725–1736. DOI: 10.61091/jcmcc127b-096

Zhu, Q., Chong, L., Yang, M., & Luo, J. (2025). Reading Users' Minds With Large Language Models: Mental Inference for Artificial Empathy in Design. *Journal of Mechanical Design*, *147*(6), 061401. Advance online publication. DOI: 10.1115/1.4067527

Chapter 11
Dual Chatbots for K-12 Literature Education:
A Serbian Case Study of AI-Powered Dialogue Systems

Milena Škobo
http://orcid.org/0000-0001-8427-2051
Faculty of Philology, Sinergija University, Bijeljina, Serbia

ABSTRACT

This chapter proposes a dual chatbot model for Serbian K–12 education, combining a subject-general AI assistant with a persona-based chatbot modeled after Danilo Kiš. Grounded in AI-in-education research and aligned with national curricular goals, the model emphasizes teacher agency, pedagogical relevance, and ethical integration. A conceptual roadmap outlines development phases, pilot strategies, and assessment methods while addressing infrastructure gaps and teacher training. The Kiš chatbot shows potential for deepening literary analysis, supporting historical inquiry, and enhancing translation and language learning. Interdisciplinary applications are explored through history, English, and multilingual education, with attention to cross-cultural dialogue and semantic nuance. Ethical considerations—including authenticity, data bias, and pedagogical limits—are examined. The chapter concludes that well-designed AI tools can support inclusive, context-sensitive humanities instruction and offer scalable innovations that enrich student engagement while preserving literary complexity.

DOI: 10.4018/979-8-3373-2637-5.ch011

INTRODUCTION

Artificial intelligence (AI) is no longer a futuristic idea—it is part of the fabric of everyday life. Classrooms, once defined by textbooks and chalkboards, are now increasingly shaped by algorithms, generative models, and conversational agents. Around the world, AI tools are beginning to influence how teachers design lessons, how students engage with knowledge, and how progress is assessed. What makes this moment different from earlier waves of educational technology—computers in labs, smartboards, or learning management systems—is the rise of generative AI and natural language processing. These advances make it possible to deliver instruction that feels personal: chatbots that can explain a concept in multiple ways, offer instant feedback, and adapt to a learner's pace. Especially in language-rich subjects, such as literature, history, or foreign languages, the potential for dialogue-driven support is unprecedented (Cope et al., 2020; Uğraş et al., 2024).

Among these tools, chatbots stand out because they do more than automate tasks—they converse. They can answer questions, model critical reasoning, and create individualized pathways through complex material, often echoing the benefits of one-to-one tutoring (Luckin et al., 2016; Lampropoulos & Papadakis, 2025). International experiments reveal varied designs: some systems assign multiple chatbot "roles" to simulate peer or teacher interaction, while others adopt a Socratic style that forces students to question and justify their reasoning. Yet, for all this momentum, most implementations remain confined to higher education or well-funded pilot programs. Primary and secondary schools—where foundational skills and habits of mind are formed—are only beginning to be touched by this wave.

In Serbia, these global shifts are still at their early stages of development. Chatbots have so far been introduced mainly at the university level, often limited to administrative functions (Vukomanović et al., 2022). The first real cultural-educational pilots—the Branislav Nušić and Nikola Tesla chatbots developed by Škobo and Šović (2025)—mark important steps, but they remain isolated prototypes. Systematic, curriculum-aligned efforts to integrate chatbots into everyday classroom practice are still missing, leaving significant room for experimentation and critical inquiry.

This chapter proposes one such pathway: a dual chatbot model tailored to Serbian K–12 education. It combines a subject-general chatbot, designed to scaffold learning across literature curricula, with a persona-based chatbot that simulates the voice of an author Danilo Kiš. The model is meant not to replace teachers but to enrich their practice—helping students engage in dialogue, sharpen interpretation, and explore literature in ways that conventional methods often cannot sustain.

Although the chapter does not report on empirical findings, it offers a conceptual framework. It asks why a dual chatbot model is worth considering, how it intersects with current international research, and which ethical and pedagogical concerns must be addressed. While anchored in the Serbian language and literature curriculum, the proposed chatbot model raises questions that transcend national borders. Its design —especially the interplay between subject-general and persona-based agents—can be adapted to other languages, literary traditions, and classroom contexts. In this sense, the model becomes a way to examine global tensions in AI integration—particularly in systems marked by infrastructural constraints and rigid curricula. It invites questions such as: How can underfunded systems introduce AI without deepening existing inequalities? What does responsible integration look like when infrastructure, teacher training, and language support are still works in progress?

CHATBOTS IN EDUCATION: FROM ORIGINS TO CONTEMPORARY APPLICATION

The evolution of chatbots in education parallels the broader development of artificial intelligence and its pursuit of simulating human interaction. Although the term chatterbot was coined by Mauldin in 1994 (Molnár & Szűts, 2018), the conceptual roots extend back to systems such as ELIZA and ALICE, which relied on rule-based logic and pattern matching. These early programs were not intended as teaching tools, yet their experiments with natural language interaction laid the groundwork for educational use. Černý (2022) situates this formative stage within psychological inquiry, noting that models like ELIZA and PARRY functioned less as tutors than as probes into human–computer communication. While limited, these projects provided the conceptual basis for later designs that sought to position chatbots as dialogue-based learning partners. The shift from simulation to pedagogy mirrored wider changes in educational technology, moving from behaviorist drills towards more constructivist, interaction-driven environments. Importantly, the artificial identity of a chatbot, when integrated into instructional design, can itself become a pedagogical asset.

Advances in natural language processing reinforced this pedagogical turn. The transition from rule-based programming to neural-network architectures enabled more context-sensitive interaction. Yet, as Černý (2022) emphasizes, the true value of chatbots lies not in technical sophistication alone but in how they are embedded within curricula. Institutional reports echo this view; for example, the Food and Agriculture Organization (2021) describes chatbots as adaptive learning objects capable of scaffolding knowledge, providing feedback, and supporting learners in real time. Still, despite a surge of research since 2017, the field remains criticized for being overly descriptive and lacking systematic frameworks for evaluation.

Systematic reviews highlight this shortcoming. Pérez et al. (2020), synthesizing 80 studies through PRISMA guidelines, distinguish between two main functions:

service assistants providing administrative support and instructional agents engaging directly with learning. These roles often overlap, but they reveal the increasing diversification of applications. Pérez et al. also note that chatbots can, in certain contexts, approximate human tutoring through adaptive feedback. Nonetheless, most studies prioritize technical performance over pedagogy, leaving learning outcomes underexamined. The authors therefore call for frameworks that assess both educational quality and impact, moving beyond fragmented case studies.

Kuhail et al. (2022) mapped 36 educational chatbots across different domains and found that most applications still cluster in computer science, language learning, and general education, with STEM fields remaining underrepresented. Their review highlights design gaps: most chatbots act as teaching agents, while peer or motivational roles remain underdeveloped. Flow-based interaction continues to dominate, leaving little room for the kind of open-ended dialogue essential to language and literature instruction. Personalization is often pursued, but unevenly, and evaluation tends to rely on short-term satisfaction surveys rather than sustained engagement. The absence of user-centered heuristics and personality design stands out as a barrier to long-term effectiveness—underscoring why future models must be developed with learners and teachers in mind rather than as purely technical prototypes.

Different chatbot architectures reveal both strengths and limitations. Rule-based systems are reliable for routine tasks but cannot sustain interpretive dialogue. Retrieval-based systems perform well in structured contexts yet falter when queries are unpredictable or ambiguous (Attigeri et al., 2024). Generative models allow greater flexibility but at the cost of accuracy. Hybrid approaches attempt to balance these trade-offs: combining retrieval with generative layers produces adaptable yet more reliable systems (Day & Shaw, 2021). One empirical demonstration comes from Mikael et al. (2025), where a three-layer hybrid model achieved 97% accuracy and high user satisfaction in educational contexts. These findings illustrate that scalability is best achieved not by privileging one architecture, but by carefully integrating multiple approaches. For K–12 education in particular, this means developing subject- and age-specific systems tailored to local needs. The dual chatbot model proposed in this study situates itself within this trajectory, seeking to align technical development with pedagogy while addressing the realities of classroom integration.

Empirical studies confirm both the opportunities and risks of classroom chatbot use. In Turkish primary schools, Uğraş et al. (2024) reported that ChatGPT supported lesson planning, personalization, and inclusivity in language and mathematics. Yet teachers expressed concern over misinformation, reduced peer interaction, and the erosion of their ethical and emotional role in classrooms. A related study in early childhood STEM contexts found similar benefits for creativity and motivation but also highlighted disparities in digital access and data security (Uğraş et al., 2025). These findings echo broader international evidence: generative AI can increase personalization and motivation (Baidoo-Anu & Owusu Ansah, 2023; Hwang & Chang, 2023; Okonkwo & Ade-Ibijola, 2021), but only when embedded with care and with teachers actively mediating its use. Importantly, evidence from early childhood classrooms remains scarce, as the majority of research still focuses on secondary and higher education (Feser, 2024; Ji et al., 2023). This imbalance points to the need to extend inquiry into K–12 settings, particularly in underexplored contexts such as Serbia.

Methodological issues complicate evaluation further. Lavidas et al. (2022) demonstrate that student self-reports often reflect social desirability bias, especially in performance-intensive contexts such as laboratory-based instruction. This has direct implications for K–12 chatbot studies, where engagement may be overstated. The authors highlight the need for neutral contexts, anonymized participation, and triangulation with observational or qualitative methods. In a related investigation, Lavidas et al. (2022a) also note that teachers' willingness to participate in surveys is shaped by factors such as institutional credibility, questionnaire design, and ethical assurances—all of which are highly relevant to AI research relying on voluntary participation.

Perspectives from adjacent fields reinforce these concerns. Lampropoulos and Papadakis (2025), in their review of social robots in education, emphasize the capacity of such agents to deliver personalized, adaptive learning and foster emotional engagement. Although their focus is on embodied robots, the insights extend directly to chatbots, particularly in relation to inclusivity, affective responsiveness, and teacher acceptance. At the same time, they underline persistent challenges of privacy, standardization, and teacher resistance, underscoring the need for ethical frameworks and professional development prior to wide-scale adoption (Papadakis et al., 2024a, 2024b).

Empirical studies confirm that AI-powered chatbots can support differentiated instruction by clarifying difficult concepts, providing real-time feedback, and assisting with homework (Kasneci et al, 2023; Labadze et al, 2023). Such affordances are particularly valuable in resource-constrained contexts such as Serbia, where heavy teacher workloads limit capacity for individual support. Yet these systems remain less effective for interpretive or open-ended tasks—particularly in literature and the humanities—and overuse may undermine independent critical thinking (Kasneci et al, 2023). Their best role, therefore, is complementary: extending access to knowledge without replacing mentorship, empathy, or pedagogical judgment (Labadze et al, 2023).

Teachers' perceptions are central to AI tools adoption. Chocarro et al. (2021) show that perceived usefulness and performance predict uptake more strongly than digital competence or technical quality. This suggests that context-sensitive design matters more than technological novelty. Similar conclusions appear in studies stressing that alignment with teachers' pedagogical goals outweighs technical sophistication in shaping adoption (Lampropoulos & Papadakis, 2025; Uğraş et al, 2024).

Ethical questions comprising risks of data privacy violations, algorithmic bias, and opacity remain well documented (Dergaa et al, 2023; Williams, 2024; Zhai et al, 2024). A recurring critique is that many tools are developed without teacher input, resulting in weak alignment with classroom practice (Cukurova & Luckin, 2018; Luckin & Cukurova, 2019). As Baidoo-Anu and Owusu Ansah (2023) argue, responsible integration requires institutional safeguards and robust policy frameworks. Other studies point to teachers' limited confidence in pedagogically sound use of AI (Chiu & Chai, 2020; Seufert et al, 2020). Co-design approaches not only ensure curricular alignment but also enhance professional agency and foster higher-order thinking (Dillenbourg, 2016).

International implementations illustrate the possibilities of hybrid and multi-agent approaches. Mikael et al. (2025) highlight how hybrid systems—combining rule-based, retrieval-based, and generative components—can be dynamically routed to serve different classroom needs. In their case, the system proved effective not only in administrative accuracy but also in building trust among users, a reminder that technical design and user perception must advance together. Similarly, Cao et al. (2023) designed a multi-role pedagogical chatbot in computer science education, including Instructor Bot, Peer Bot, Career Advisor Bot, and Emotional Supporter Bot. All these roles enhanced engagement and inquiry. Favero et al. (2024) offer another example with their Socratic chatbot, which improved critical thinking by exposing learners to multiple perspectives. Belda-Medina and Calvo-Ferrer (2022) likewise examined pre-service teachers' interactions with Replika, Kuki, and Wysa, finding generally positive attitudes but moderate intentions for classroom use. Gender differences in satisfaction further suggested that cultural and demographic factors shape reception. More recently, Degen and Asanov (2025) introduced orchestrated multi-agent systems in higher education, reporting that their Socratic AI Tutor significantly improved critical and reflective thinking among pre-service teachers. These experiments illustrate the pedagogical promise of multi-agent or hybrid models, offering a comparative backdrop for the dual chatbot framework developed in this chapter.

Despite such potential, scholars continue to raise reservations about ethical, psychological, and pedagogical risks. Concerns range from plagiarism and compromised academic integrity (Kooli, 2023; Williams, 2024), to reduced creativity and problem-solving when overused (Zhai et al, 2024), to the persistence of the "ELIZA effect," whereby students anthropomorphize chatbots in ways that may foster dependency or distort perceptions of agency. Data protection also remains a pressing issue, with widespread unease about the handling of sensitive information (Belen Saglam et al, 2021). Taking this into account, robust safeguards, regulatory frameworks, and digital literacy training are needed to ensure that chatbots enhance rather than undermine practice. It can be also concluded that it is necessary to adapt global debates on AI integration to the specific institutional, cultural, and technological contexts of each educational system.

These reviews and case studies suggest a clear research agenda: educational chatbots should be developed not as short-lived experiments but as sustainable, context-sensitive systems that address both technical and pedagogical realities. This agenda provides the backdrop for Serbia, where infrastructure, curriculum, and cultural heritage shape how AI can be responsibly integrated.

The Chatbots in the Serbian Educational Context

While educational chatbots are becoming increasingly common in classrooms around the world, Serbia is still at the beginning of this journey—particularly in primary and secondary education. National-level initiatives like the *Strategy for the Development of Artificial Intelligence (2020–2025)* (Government of the RS, 2019, 2020) and the more recent *Ethical Guidelines for the Development and Use of Reliable AI* (2023) (Government of the RS, 2023) reflect growing institutional interest. However, these documents remain advisory, and Serbia has yet to develop a binding framework that would support the meaningful integration of AI tools into school curricula.

Research on how AI is perceived and used in Serbian education is gradually expanding. Several studies have explored teachers' and students' experiences with tools like ChatGPT, though most focus on general attitudes or early-stage use. For example, Tomić and Radovanović (2024) examined how ChatGPT-3.5 could support lesson planning in religious education. Ružičić et al. (2024), in a larger survey of 140 teachers, found that while awareness of AI tools was relatively high, practical use in classrooms remained limited. Common barriers included digital infrastructure gaps, low levels of technical training, and unresolved questions around data privacy.

Building on these earlier accounts, Škobo and Šović (2025a) conducted the first statistical analysis on this topic in Serbia, based on a sample of 135 teachers. Their findings confirmed a pattern seen elsewhere: teachers who felt more familiar with AI tended to view it more positively. At the same time, concerns about ethical and institutional risks significantly shaped teachers' willingness to adopt such tools. Importantly, the data showed no strong link between familiarity and risk perception—suggesting that broader structural issues, not individual hesitations, are the main obstacle.

Similar insights have emerged from student-focused studies. A national survey by Stanković et al. (2024) found high levels of awareness of AI tools among students at all levels, especially at universities. Mandić et al. (2024) focused on final-year education students, who reported limited hands-on experience with ChatGPT but recognized its potential to support lesson planning and reflective practice. In another study, Mekić et al. (2024) found that law students were using AI tools mainly to spark ideas or revise their writing, rather than to complete assignments, and emphasized the importance of critical thinking. Bajčetić et al. (2024) compared first-year medical students' test scores with those of several chatbots (including ChatGPT, Bing, and Bard) on biology questions. While the chatbots performed well on factual knowledge, they showed clear limitations when asked to apply concepts or demonstrate higher-order thinking.

Serbia's first attempts to integrate educational chatbots into learning took shape in 2025 with the Branislav Nušić and Nikola Tesla chatbots (Škobo & Šović, 2025). Designed as cultural-educational tools, these chatbots were initially bilingual (Serbian and English) but evolved over time—Nušić maintaining its bilingual literary orientation, and Tesla expanding into a multilingual assistant—allowing students to interact with iconic national figures while reinforcing Serbian heritage. Though focused on distinct domains—literature and science—both projects shared a broader mission of fostering engagement and cultural identity. However, each followed a single-persona model, operating independently and confined to its respective domain. The dual-model design proposed here builds on these efforts by combining a subject-general tutoring assistant with a literary chatbot (e.g., Danilo Kiš), aiming to blend broad pedagogical support with the motivational and cultural benefits of dialogic encounters with literary figures.

A few other initiatives deserve mention. The ADA chatbot, developed by the Belgrade Business and Arts Academy, helped students register for exams during the COVID-19 pandemic, but was not intended for teaching. Outside Serbia, promising work has been done on BCS (Bosnian/Croatian/Serbian) language-learning chatbots at Arizona State University (Šipka, 2024). These tools offer corrective feedback, work with customized vocabulary, and are aligned with ACTFL standards, demonstrating that pedagogically rich, culturally sensitive chatbots can be successfully built for Slavic languages.

Serbia currently ranks among the top ten global contributors to AI in higher education (Šijan et al., 2025). These innovations have yet to reach most classrooms. There is still no systemic integration of chatbots into Serbia's K–12 curricula, nor formal training for teachers on how to use them. In this context, the dual chatbot model outlined here represents an effort to move from isolated experiments to a more curriculum-aligned solution for Serbian schools.

THE DUAL CHATBOT MODEL

As schools in Serbia begin exploring more creative uses of AI in the classroom, this section introduces a dual chatbot model designed to support literature teaching primarily targeting high schools and philological gymnasiums, combining practical application with curricular alignment. Prior international research studies have shown both the pedagogical potential and the ethical concerns surrounding AI integration—highlighting the need for alignment with teacher agency and national curricula (Uğraş et al., 2024, 2025; Lampropoulos & Papadakis, 2025).

The model includes two components that respond to different classroom needs—from individual revision to interpretive seminars—harmonized with inclusive pedagogies. The first is a subject-general chatbot, envisioned as a curriculum-aligned tutor that offers support across key literary concepts—narrative perspective, genre conventions, stylistic features, and historical contexts. It could support routine tasks—revision, homework, independent study. It would not mimick a personality but provide clear explanations and step-by-step scaffolding tailored to students' different levels of readiness. In this sense, it would require training on digitized Serbian texts, curriculum documents, and annotated corpora. Its design draws on Cognitive Load Theory introduced by John Sweller in 1988, which stresses breaking down complex ideas, as well as on adaptive learning models that adjust content to student understanding (Rincón-Flores et al, 2024; Simon & Zeng, 2024). For example, it might help a fifth grade pupil differentiate between narrator and author in a fable, or support a gymnasium student in analyzing modernist prose. It is designed to reinforce comprehension without displacing the teacher's role.

The second component is a persona-based chatbot, modeled on Danilo Kiš, designed to simulate his literary voice through curated excerpts from his essays and fiction. It would support interpretive tasks, particularly in senior literature classes. This design is informed by the theory of Embodied Conversational Agents and by growing evidence that narrative-driven AI can enhance student motivation in interpretive subjects (Ayedoun et al, 2018). In the Serbian school context, the Kiš chatbot could enrich discussions of themes central to graduation exams. Through simulated dialogue, students might reflect more deeply on literary form and historical context.

The Case of Danilo Kiš: Persona-Based Chatbot in Practice

Danilo Kiš (1935–1989), one of the most influential Serbian writers of the twentieth century, is an especially fitting figure for persona-based chatbot use in literature courses. His major works—*Garden, Ashes* (1965), *Growing Pains* (1970), *A Tomb for Boris Davidovich* (1976), and *The Encyclopedia of the Dead* (1983)—are part of the national curriculum and often appear on graduation exams. With recurring themes of memory, exile, identity, and totalitarian violence, his prose invites ethical reflection and interpretive depth, making it ideal basis for dialogic, AI-supported classroom engagement. His public persona—cosmopolitan, multilingual, and intellectually engaged—is also well documented, providing strong foundations for constructing a pedagogical "digital double."

Kiš's multilingualism—fluent in Serbian, Croatian, Hungarian, French, and Russian—opens additional educational possibilities. As a translator and comparative writer, his voice can support activities ranging from exploring translation choices to modeling cross-cultural literary discourse. The availability of digitized archival materials from the institutions like the Serbian Academy of Sciences and Arts (SASA) further increases the feasibility of developing a well-calibrated, textually grounded chatbot.

The persona-based chatbot would be suited to interpretive seminars, group discussions, or creative exercises. For instance, gymnasium students might explore *Garden, Ashes* through dialog with the Kiš chatbot. This approach aligns with Universal Design for Learning, which promotes multiple access points into material, and with social constructivism, which values knowledge co-construction through dialogue. More recent frameworks also emphasize student agency, AI literacy, and reciprocal human–machine learning (Holmes et al, 2022).

The chatbot would be designed to "speak" in the first person, using rhetorical patterns and themes drawn from Kiš's essays (*Homo Poeticus*, 1990), interviews, and fiction. When students study *A Tomb for Boris Davidovich*, they might ask why Kiš wrote about political repression. The chatbot could synthesize on documentary fiction, trauma, and the writer's moral duty, drawing on sources like *The Anatomy Lesson* (1978) or "Po-etika" (1972). Similarly, when reading *The Encyclopedia of the Dead*, students might explore Kiš's intertextual influences—from Borges and Kafka to Bruno Schulz—developing their interpretive awareness through conversation.

Through simulated exchanges, students could explore Kiš's Jewish-Hungarian heritage, the trauma of the Holocaust, his experience under Yugoslav socialism, and his preoccupation with fragmented identity and silenced histories. In this way, the chatbot would not only transmit knowledge but also foster ethical and emotional engagement, as students connect biography with broader literary and historical questions. This aligns with constructivist approaches that frame learning as co-created through dialogue (Vygotsky, 1978). As Liu and Reinders (2025) suggest, narrative-driven AI chatbots can enhance motivation in literature classrooms—especially among students who may lack initial interest or confidence.

Although Kiš is the focus here, his chatbot provides a model for future expansion. Other literary figures, such as Miloš Crnjanski—with his modernist explorations of migration and alienation—or Borislav Pekić, whose speculative and satirical prose interrogates ethics and power, could offer contrasting perspectives. A multi-persona platform could thus allow students to engage with different authorial "voices," supporting differentiated instruction and varied interpretive approaches, as suggested in the updated UDL 3.0 emphasis on multiple means of engagement (CAST, 2024).

If designed with careful safeguards, the Kiš chatbot could offer significant benefits. Simulated dialogue promotes analytical thinking, low-pressure reflection, and literary empathy by transforming canonical figures into interactive interlocutors. These features must be accompanied by clear disclosures that the bot is a simulation, with responses anchored in textual evidence and expert moderation. Without such transparency, there is a risk of anthropomorphizing or distorting authorial voices—an ethical concern noted in broader AI education debates (Williams, 2024).

The Kiš chatbot offers considerable educational promise. By allowing students to pose questions such as "Do you believe memory can ever be objective?" and receiving context-sensitive responses, it reframes literature not as a fixed body of knowledge but as an ongoing dialogue. This echoes Bakhtin's (1981) idea of the novel as polyphonic, where meaning emerges through the interplay of voices. In practice, the chatbot adds a dialogic layer to the classroom, inviting students to test their interpretations against a simulated literary interlocutor. Paired with a subject-general chatbot, the Kiš model helps maintain both curricular alignment and interpretive inquiry.

The dual chatbot model also aligns with existing research on effective instructional design. Bloom's (1984) "2 Sigma Problem" showed that individualized tutoring greatly enhances student learning. While AI cannot fully replicate a human tutor, chatbots can simulate some adaptive responses to individual needs. For example, Chen et al. (2020) found that conversational interfaces reduce frustration and encourage persistence—particularly useful in literature education, where sustained interpretation is key.

Equally important is the model's potential for differentiated instruction. As Tomlinson (2001) argues, students benefit when learning materials are adapted to varying readiness levels and interests. Within this framework, a general chatbot can guide learners who need extra scaffolding, while the persona-based model, when tailored to advanced learners, can prompt exploration of ethical dilemmas and narrative ambiguity. In classrooms, socially embedded AI tools have also been shown to encourage participation and intellectual risk-taking when used in structured group activities (Holmes et al, 2019).

Design Process of the Dual Chatbot Model

The development of the dual chatbot model requires a structured and transparent design process to ensure both pedagogical alignment and ethical integrity. This process can be understood as a cycle with six interconnected stages, from the initial collection of authentic materials to iterative evaluation in classroom contexts. Each stage involves collaboration between researchers, teachers, students, and domain experts, ensuring that the model remains culturally relevant, curriculum-based, and pedagogically grounded. Table 1 summarizes the main stages of this process.

Table 1. Stages in the Design of the Dual Chatbot Model

Stage	Focus	Key Actions	Participants	Outputs
Data Collection	Build the knowledge base	Gather digitized Serbian texts, national curriculum documents, annotated corpora, essays, interviews, and critical commentary (e.g., Kiš)	Researchers, curriculum experts	Comprehensive and authentic dataset
Model Training	Develop subject-general and persona-based components	Train subject-general chatbot on curricular content, simulate persona chatbot voice using curate texts	A developers, linguists, literary scholars	Prototype dual chatbot
Persona Design	Shape interpretive and dialogic voice	Curate responses for depth (memory, exile, authorship); ensure clear signaling of simulation	Literary experts, teachers	Pedagogically anchored persona
Validation and Co-Design	Classroom alignment	Teacher workshops, pilot sessions, iterative refinement with student feedback	Teachers, students	Classroom-ready tool
Ethical Safeguards	Responsible integration	Address bias, transparency, authorship clarity, age-appropriateness	Researchers, ethics boards	Ethically compliant chatbot
Iteration and Evaluation	Continuous improvement	Longitudinal trials, mixed-methods evaluation, revision cycles	Researchers, teachers, students	Evidence-based refinements

The design process is best understood as a cycle rather than a straight line. It begins with the collection of authentic materials—curriculum documents, annotated literary texts, and expert insights—that form the foundation for training. From there, model training shapes both the subject-general and persona-based components, creating prototypes that can be tested and refined. Persona design requires special care: this means curating Kiš's rhetorical style, worldview, and thematic concerns so that the simulation feels credible yet always framed as a pedagogical construct rather than an authorial substitute.

Once a prototype is established, validation and co-design come into play. Teachers, students, and literary experts engage directly with the tool, ensuring that it reflects classroom realities and curricular demands. At the same time, ethical safeguards must be embedded—making clear to learners that they are interacting with a simulation, preventing anthropomorphism, and protecting data privacy.

The process is not linear but cyclical. Each stage feeds into the next: classroom feedback, testing, and ethical reflection inform new rounds of data collection and retraining, ensuring that the model evolves with practice rather than remaining a static product. What makes the model sustainable is precisely this responsiveness. It is not a fixed product but a living system, continually reshaped by practice, collaboration, and critical review.

IMPLEMENTATION ROADMAP

A phased implementation can be structured around four interrelated domains: prototype development, teacher participation and curricular integration, evaluation and equity, and institutional sustainability.

The roadmap begins with the creation of two prototypes. The subject-general chatbot should offer curricular alignment, conceptual clarity, and differentiated scaffolding based on grade level. Its training corpus would consist of digitized Serbian literary texts, approved schoolbooks, and annotated corpora. To optimize resources, existing open-source models like Falcon, BLOOM, or LLaMA 2 could be fine-tuned using localized data rather than developed from scratch (Touvron et al., 2023; Workshop et al., 2022).

The persona-based chatbot, modeled on Danilo Kiš, requires a more curated approach. It would draw on selected fiction, essays, interviews, and critical interpretations. As Škobo and Petričević (2023) argue, no AI can replicate authorial subjectivity; this chatbot must therefore clearly present itself as a simulated persona, maintaining transparency and appropriateness for pedagogical use.

To test the feasibility of the model, a short pilot could be conducted in two Serbian secondary schools—one general and one philological gymnasium—each with 25–30 students. Over a four-week period, literature classes would incorporate both chatbot types. The subject-general chatbot would support concept reinforcement, while the Kiš chatbot would be used for interpretive dialogue aligned with national curriculum outcomes (e.g., *Bašta, pepeo* or selected works from Serbian modernist prose).

Teachers would co-create lesson prompts such as "What is the role of the narrator here?" or "Danilo, why dcpict your father this way?" Students would alternate between AI interaction and teacher- or peer-led discussions. Data collection would include pre- and post-lesson surveys, teacher logs, anonymized chat transcripts, and small focus groups. The goal is not to generate generalizable findings but to surface practical insights for further refinement.

Teacher involvement is crucial at every stage. Study shows that adoption improves when teachers act as co-designers, not just end-users (Luckin et al., 2016;

Yim & Wegerif, 2024). In Serbia, lesson-study workshops could enable teachers to experiment with chatbot prompts while building AI literacy. Embedding chatbot use within existing curriculum units—e.g., linking *A Tomb for Boris Davidovich* to competencies in postwar prose—would secure relevance and reduce resistance.

Evaluation methods must combine interaction data (e.g., frequency of chatbot queries, time-on-task) with qualitative evidence (e.g., essays, teacher reflections, student interviews). This mixed-methods approach mitigates the limitations of self-report bias (Lavidas et al., 2022). Special attention is needed when discussing sensitive themes like trauma or identity, where shallow engagement could trivialize ethical complexity.

Equity must also be addressed. Urban schools may support real-time AI interactions, but many rural schools in Serbia face limited connectivity and outdated equipment (Škobo & Šović, 2025a). Lightweight or offline-compatible versions of the chatbot will be essential to ensure that all students have access, regardless of geography.

Long-term success depends on formal institutional backing. Endorsement from the Ministry of Education could enable funding pathways and ensure curricular legitimacy. Teacher training should include not only technical competencies but also ethical facilitation skills and critical digital pedagogy (Selwyn, 2019). Eventually, the dual chatbot model could be expanded to other subjects, with persona-based agents for history, philosophy, or civic education, aligned with Serbia's evolving AI strategy and educational priorities.

The roadmap envisions a phased rollout: short-term pilots (1 year) in selected urban schools of 20–30 students per class, with literature teachers as co-design partners; medium-term expansion (2–3 years) to gymnasiums and rural schools through mobile-first adaptations; and long-term integration (5+ years) into national AI and education policy frameworks, in line with Serbia's 2020–2025 AI Strategy. Each stage must follow ethical standards, including informed consent, transparency in data use, and protection of student privacy—conditions vital for both academic credibility and public trust.

Expanding the Model: Interdisciplinary Applications

Although the dual chatbot model is initially designed for Serbian language and literature, its supports interdisciplinary and cross-cultural use. Literature intersects with history, translation studies, and foreign language learning, making it an ideal entry point for broader curricular applications.

In history classes, works such as *A Tomb for Boris Davidovich* and *The Encyclopedia of the Dead* introduce students to themes of repression, ideology, and collective memory. Rather than merely reading about totalitarian trials, students could ask the

Kiš chatbot: *Why did you write about fabricated political confessions*?—and receive a response grounded in his essays, which frame such trials as instruments of erasure and literature as a way to recover silenced voices. These exchanges deepen historical empathy and stimulate ethical reflection (VanSledright, 2004).

In translation and language courses, the chatbot could facilitate critical comparison between student translations, professional versions, and AI-generated outputs. For instance, when ChatGPT mistranslated the French idiom *le compas dans l'œil* as "to have an eagle eye," it overlooked the nuance of proportion and aesthetic judgment (Škobo & Petričević, 2023). Classroom tasks could therefore involve reverse translations, where students produce their own versions and then query the chatbot for justifications of lexical or stylistic choices. Such tasks sharpen linguistic and introduce students to the interpretive nature of literary translation. Bibliometric studies confirm that such dialogic support is among the most impactful uses of chatbots in language learning (Gu & Yu, 2025).

The model also adapts well to comparative literature. Students might explore parallels between Kiš and George Orwell or Milan Kundera by asking the chatbot to simulate an intertextual dialogue: "What would you say to Orwell about writing under dictatorship?" Such activities situate Serbian literature within wider European traditions and foster critical literacy by exposing learners to multiple perspectives.

Beyond the humanities, persona-based agents can enrich different subjects such as Science education, Music, or Civic education. A Mihajlo Pupin chatbot could connect science and history by engaging students in conversations about telecommunications, diplomacy, or immigrant identity, while a Mokranjac chatbot might enrich music education by contextualizing Serbian choral traditions. Such agents could form an integrated digital platform where students converse with multiple cultural-historical figures—not as trivia repositories, but as curated gateways into disciplinary thinking.

The model is also flexible across diverse educational contexts. Well-resourced schools may embed chatbot interactions within multimedia modules, while under-resourced settings could adopt streamlined, mobile-first versions. Regardless of form, the key is maintaining alignment with curricular goals, grounding responses in verified corpora, and clearly signaling the artificial nature of the agent.

Framed as a context-sensitive case study, the Serbian implementation demonstrates how dialogic, culturally grounded AI tools—rooted in national literary and intellectual heritage—can be meaningfully integrated into mainstream curricular practice. The model draws on well-known Serbian cultural figures as entry points for dialogue about literature, science, and national identity. Through these characters, it brings different school subjects into conversation with one another and makes abstract concepts more tangible and personally meaningful for students.

However, this very specificity enables generalization. The framework invites adaptation in other countries by substituting Serbian corpora and historical figures with culturally relevant counterparts—be it Orwell in the UK, Neruda in Chile, or Tagore in India. What makes this transfer viable is not the replication of content, but the design logic: alignment with curricular goals, integration of teacher co-design, transparency about AI's artificiality, and attention to infrastructural inequality. In this sense, the model provides a scalable, ethically conscious pathway for incorporating persona-based chatbots into diverse educational systems—whether as part of digital heritage initiatives, second-language instruction, or interdisciplinary humanities education.

CHALLENGES AND LIMITATIONS

The integration of a dual chatbot model into Serbian K–12 literature classrooms faces obstacles that go well beyond questions of technical design. Its success depends on the broader educational ecosystem—teachers' readiness, the infrastructure available, the financial and institutional frameworks that sustain innovation, and the pedagogical culture in which such tools are embedded. Unless these elements are addressed in tandem, even the most sophisticated chatbot risks adding little real value to classroom practice.

A central challenge is teacher preparedness. Serbian educators have shown growing awareness of AI tools, but recent studies indicate that many remain cautious about classroom use, citing ethical uncertainties, workload pressures, and infrastructural gaps (Škobo & Šović, 2025a). Technical competence alone cannot resolve these concerns. What teachers require is structured professional development that positions them as co-designers of chatbot activities rather than passive implementers. Without this sense of ownership, adoption will be fragmented, uneven, and ultimately fragile.

The physical conditions of schools also weigh heavily. Urban classrooms may have relatively stable internet and up-to-date equipment, but many rural schools still operate with outdated hardware and unreliable connectivity. In such contexts, real-time chatbot use is not only impractical but risks deepening existing educational inequalities. Ensuring equitable participation will therefore require offline-compatible or mobile-first versions of the system, supported by digital literacy initiatives for teachers and students alike.

Sustainability poses a different kind of difficulty. Building a persona-based chatbot modeled on Danilo Kiš demands a carefully curated dataset, editorial oversight, and expert involvement to ensure stylistic fidelity. His works are well digitized, but capturing his literary and philosophical complexity requires a corpus that extends to essays, interviews, and critical commentary. Constructing and maintaining such a resource is labor-intensive and far beyond the reach of generic large language models. From a financial perspective, few Serbian schools could sustain this independently. The more realistic pathway is fine-tuning open-source or commercial platforms with locally relevant corpora. Even so, the effort requires stable funding and institutional backing—whether from the Ministry of Education, EU cultural programs, or cultural foundations—without which the model risks remaining a prototype rather than a durable pedagogical tool.

There are also risks at the level of pedagogy. Chatbots can enhance engagement, but if students begin substituting dialogue with the system for direct engagement with texts, learning may become superficial. The fluency of AI-generated responses can create an illusion of depth, tempting students to treat outputs as authoritative rather than provisional. In a discipline where interpretive plurality and ethical reflection are central, this is a serious danger. To counter it, chatbot use must be embedded in teacher-led activities that require comparison, debate, and close reading—ensuring that the tool stimulates rather than replaces interpretation.

Bias and curricular alignment raise further concerns. Decisions about which texts, commentaries, or perspectives to include in the training data inevitably privilege some interpretations over others. In Serbian literature, where canon formation and identity politics remain contested, such editorial choices can carry particular weight. A chatbot trained on an unbalanced corpus risks narrowing rather than expanding students' exposure to diverse perspectives. Preventing this requires careful curation, regular updates, and sustained teacher oversight to maintain fidelity both to the national curriculum and to plural interpretive traditions.

Finally, credibility depends on systematic evaluation. Student self-reports—while valuable—are notoriously susceptible to social desirability bias (Lavidas et al., 2022). Stronger evidence must come from triangulation: observation of classroom dynamics, teacher feedback, discourse analysis of chatbot–student exchanges, and pre/post measures of interpretive skill. Without such multi-layered evaluation, claims about effectiveness remain speculative, offering little justification for scaling the model beyond pilot programs.

These challenges highlight the conditions under which the dual chatbot model might succeed. Pilot projects in diverse school settings—with teacher input and sustainable funding—are a necessary first step. Only once infrastructural inequalities, sustainability concerns, and evaluation frameworks are addressed can the dual chatbot model progress from a conceptual innovation to a credible supplement to literature instruction.

As an early-stage digital education initiative in a non-English-speaking, post-socialist context, this dual-chatbot framework captures many of the *growing pains* experienced by systems in transition. The specific challenges it addresses—overburdened curricula, teacher shortages, and the absence of culturally grounded digital content—are not exclusive to Serbia. Similar concerns are voiced by teachers and policymakers in other rapidly changing settings. Therefore, this case offers a grounded contribution to wider discussions on how technology-enhanced instruction can remain inclusive, meaningful, and contextually relevant. The model may serve as a transferable, interdisciplinary prototype for education systems undergoing comparable cultural and infrastructural shifts.

ETHICAL CONSIDERATIONS

The structural challenges outlined above—teacher readiness, infrastructure, and sustainability—make it clear that technical design alone cannot determine the success of a dual chatbot model. Equally crucial are the ethical questions that shape how such tools are perceived, trusted, and used in classrooms. These concerns are especially acute in primary and secondary education, where safeguarding responsibilities are highest and students are still developing independent judgment. For this reason, the dual chatbot model proposed here—pairing a subject-general assistant with a persona-based simulation of Danilo Kiš—must embed ethical safeguards from the very start, not as an add-on but as a core design principle.

One of the first concerns is data privacy. Because chatbots inevitably process sensitive personal and learning data, the risk of misuse or unauthorized access is ever present. Williams (2024) observes that while personalization can support learners, minors rarely grasp the permanence of their digital footprints, and deletion is almost impossible once data feeds into training cycles. GDPR provides a legal framework, but enforcement is complicated by opaque algorithmic processes (Hasal et al., 2021). For the dual chatbot model, the safest course is a minimalist approach: avoid collecting identifiers, restrict storage of dialogue histories, and develop offline or low-bandwidth versions where possible. Such design choices not only align with child-specific GDPR protections but also reassure teachers and parents that cultural innovation does not come at the expense of student security.

Bias represents another major risk. Large language models reproduce the patterns and prejudices present in their training data, whether that involves gendered assumptions about professions or distorted representations of culture (Williams, 2024). Reducing these effects requires diverse corpora, regular audits, and clear reminders that chatbot responses are partial, not definitive (Nazer et al., 2023). The danger intensifies with persona-based design. A Kiš chatbot, if trained on unbalanced sources, could flatten the richness of his style or skew interpretations of his work. The result would be cultural distortion rather than enrichment. To avoid this, developers must draw on curated materials, consult literary experts, and ensure that the chatbot itself signals its provisional nature. In practice, this means framing every exchange as interpretation, not authentic voice.

The cognitive risks of over-reliance are equally pressing. Fluent AI-generated outputs can tempt students to substitute machine responses for their own reasoning, gradually eroding curiosity, skepticism, and truth-seeking (Zhai et al., 2024). Literature, however, depends on precisely these dispositions. Unlike factual recall, literary study demands weighing perspectives, interpreting evidence, and reflecting on meaning. If students defer too readily to a general chatbot for summaries or to a persona chatbot for "authorial" interpretations, they risk undermining the very skills literature is meant to cultivate. Research confirms the danger: nearly 70% of students report greater academic passivity and more than a quarter acknowledge weaker decision-making when using dialogue systems (Ahmad et al., 2023; Sabharwal et al., 2023). Neuroscience studies further show diminished activation in pathways associated with planning and reflective judgment (Friedman & Robbins, 2022). To guard against this, the dual model must remain a supplement rather than a replacement, embedded in assignments that press students to critique and compare outputs. A class might, for example, weigh the chatbot's reading of *A Tomb for Boris Davidovich* against scholarly commentary, treating the system as a stimulus for debate rather than a final authority.

Linked to these risks is the question of academic integrity. Because chatbot outputs are polished and convincing, students may be tempted to present them as original work. Detection tools currently catch fewer than 15% of such cases (Khalil & Er, 2023). For literature courses, this problem strikes at the core of the discipline: interpretation must reflect individual judgment, not prefabricated text. Rethinking assessment becomes essential. Oral defenses, comparative exercises, or reflective commentaries can help ensure that students' own voices remain central, while still making room for chatbots as catalysts for dialogue and experimentation.

Closely connected is the issue of hallucinations—outputs that sound plausible but are factually false. Nearly 40% of AI-generated references in one study could not be verified through academic databases (Athaluri et al., 2023). In the dual chatbot framework, this risk takes different forms: the general assistant may produce fabricated citations or misleading explanations, while the persona-based chatbot could go further, misattributing quotations or inventing episodes in Kiš's life. In literature courses, where the distinction between evidence and speculation is foundational, such distortions are particularly harmful. Unless carefully framed, they can harden into misconceptions. Teachers must therefore design activities where verification is routine—for instance, requiring students to test chatbot claims against primary texts or established scholarship—so that the system becomes a partner in critical engagement rather than a source of unquestioned truth.

Students, teachers, and parents must also understand how the chatbot operates, what data it draws on, and where its limits lie. Dergaa et al. (2023) argue that many inaccuracies in AI systems stem from hidden training practices and call for explicit guidelines around honesty and integrity. For persona-based design, this means going further: students must be reminded that they are not conversing with Kiš himself but with an approximation crafted for educational purposes. Without such reminders, stylistic imitation could be mistaken for historical fact. Transparency here is cultural as much as technical: it requires open acknowledgment of the system's artificiality, reinforced by classroom activities that ask students to locate points where the chatbot's interpretations diverge from the text or from scholarly consensus.

Underlying all these safeguards is the role of the teacher. Research consistently shows that educators often lack structured preparation in AI, which leads to uneven or hesitant adoption (Chen et al., 2025; Viberg et al., 2024). Effective professional development must extend beyond technical skills to include ethical awareness, governance, and cultural sensitivity (Daher, 2025; Nyaaba, 2024). For the dual chatbot model, this means equipping teachers to facilitate rather than simply monitor interactions: designing prompts that spark questioning, modeling how to challenge a chatbot's interpretation, and scaffolding debates around conflicting outputs. If no such training is provided, teachers may either rely too heavily on the system or reject it outright, in both cases missing its pedagogical potential.

Finally, ethical deployment depends on sustainability. Too many EdTech projects collapse after short-term pilots for lack of infrastructure or funding (Labadze et al., 2023; Kooli, 2023). Persona-based systems, in particular, require ongoing curation and expert oversight to remain accurate and relevant. Without continuous updates, they risk circulating outdated or distorted interpretations as authoritative. The challenge is not only technical but also distributive: well-funded schools can maintain advanced tools, while under-resourced schools risk being excluded. UNESCO has warned that long-term planning and equitable infrastructure are essential to prevent AI from widening educational divides (Walter, 2024). The implementation of the proposed dual chatbot model requires financial planning that covers corpus updates, localized adaptations, and teacher training refreshers, alongside governance structures that ensure cultural fidelity and ethical oversight.

These considerations highlight the need for a cautious, scaffolded approach. Responsible deployment of the dual chatbot model requires: (1) strict privacy protections aligned with GDPR and child-specific safeguards; (2) proactive monitoring and mitigation of bias; (3) integration strategies that prevent over-reliance and instead foster critical engagement; (4) redesigned assessments to protect academic integrity; (5) transparency about the system's artificial nature; and (6) long-term sustainability, including equitable infrastructure and teacher training. Only when these conditions are met can dual chatbots serve as culturally aligned, pedagogically valuable tools rather than as sources of distortion or dependency.

CONCLUSION

The dual chatbot model proposed in this chapter—pairing a subject-general assistant with a persona-based simulation inspired by Danilo Kiš—shows how artificial intelligence can reframe the possibilities of K–12 literature education. At stake is not simply whether chatbots belong in classrooms, but how they can be mobilized to sustain interpretive depth, critical judgment, and cultural dialogue in a system often constrained by heavy workloads and rigid curricula.

When used deliberately, such tools can do more than lighten the teacher's burden: they can provoke debate, sharpen analysis, and invite students to test the boundaries of interpretation. Oral defenses, reflective commentaries, and comparative tasks become ways to preserve integrity while harnessing AI as a catalyst for inquiry. In this sense, persona-based chatbots challenge students to interrogate authority itself—an intellectual exercise at the heart of literary study.

The practical conditions for this vision are demanding. Teachers must be trained not as passive adopters but as co-designers who guide students through critique and verification. Infrastructure must secure equitable access, ensuring that rural classrooms are not left behind. Governance must guarantee transparency and cultural fidelity so that simulations remain pedagogically trustworthy. Without such scaffolds, the model risks reinforcing dependency or bias rather than expanding horizons.

For research, the path forward is equally clear. We need longitudinal classroom studies that trace how chatbot use affects interpretation, motivation, and critical thinking across diverse contexts. We need comparative trials between urban and rural schools, and between literature and other humanities subjects. We also need exploration of modular, multi-persona platforms—where students can converse not only with Kiš, but with Crnjanski, Pekić, Pupin, or Mokranjac—building a living archive of cultural heritage that speaks directly to learners.

Serbia's case study regarding the application of the dual chatbot model pose a challenge. What happens when literary education meets AI in a system where teachers are overburdened, digital tools are unevenly distributed, and cultural heritage is both contested and underfunded? In asking these questions, the dual chatbot model speaks to conditions that are emerging not just in the Balkans, but across a range of educational settings where ambition outpaces infrastructure. The insights may begin locally, but the dilemmas they expose are anything but provincial.

The real question, then, is not whether AI will find its way into classrooms—it already has—but whether it will be embedded in ways that are equitable, intellectually rigorous, and culturally grounded. If developed with care, dual chatbots can become more than a technical novelty: they can serve as provocations that keep literature alive as dialogue, reminding students that meaning is not given but made.

REFERENCES

Ahmad, S. F., Han, H., Alam, M. M., Rehmat, M., Irshad, M., Arraño-Muñoz, M., & Ariza-Montes, A. (2023). Impact of artificial intelligence on human loss in decision making, laziness and safety in education. *Humanities & Social Sciences Communications*, *10*(1), 1–14. PMID: 37325188

Athaluri, S. A., Manthena, S. V., Kesapragada, V. K. M., Yarlagadda, V., Dave, T., & Duddumpudi, R. T. S. (2023). Exploring the boundaries of reality: Investigating the phenomenon of artificial intelligence hallucination in scientific writing through ChatGPT references. *Cureus*, *15*(4). Advance online publication. DOI: 10.7759/cureus.37432 PMID: 37182055

Attigeri, G., Agrawal, A., & Kolekar, S. V. (2024). Advanced NLP models for technical university information chatbots: Development and comparative analysis. *IEEE Access : Practical Innovations, Open Solutions*, *12*, 29633–29647. DOI: 10.1109/ACCESS.2024.3368382

Ayedoun, E., Hayashi, Y., & Seta, K. (2018). Adding communicative and affective strategies to an embodied conversational agent to enhance second language learners' willingness to communicate. *International Journal of Artificial Intelligence in Education*, *28*(1), 1–23.

Baidoo-Anu, D., & Ansah, L. O. (2023). Education in the era of generative artificial intelligence (AI): Understanding the potential benefits of ChatGPT in promoting teaching and learning. *Journal of AI*, *7*(1), 52–62. DOI: 10.61969/jai.1337500

Bajčetić, A., Mirčić, A., Rakočević, J., Đoković, D., Milutinović, K., & Zaletel, I. (2024). Comparing the performance of artificial intelligence learning models to medical students in solving histology and embryology multiple choice questions. Annals of Anatomy-. *Anatomischer Anzeiger*, *254*, 152261. DOI: 10.1016/j.aanat.2024.152261 PMID: 38521363

Belda-Medina, J., & Calvo-Ferrer, J. R. (2022). Using chatbots as AI conversational partners in language learning. *Applied Sciences (Basel, Switzerland)*, *12*(17), 8427. DOI: 10.3390/app12178427

Belen Saglam, R., Nurse, J. R., & Hodges, D. (2021, July). Privacy concerns in chatbot interactions: When to trust and when to worry. In *International Conference on Human-Computer Interaction* (pp. 391-399). Cham: Springer International Publishing. DOI: 10.1007/978-3-030-78642-7_53

Cao, C. C., Ding, Z., Lin, J., & Hopfgartner, F. (2023). AI Chatbots as multi-role pedagogical agents: Transforming engagement in CS education. arXiv preprint arXiv:2308.03992

CAST. (2024). UDL Guidelines 3.0. Retrieved from https://udlguidelines.cast.org/

Černý, M. (2022). The history of chatbots: The journey from psychological experiment to educational object. *Journal of Applied Technical and Educational Sciences*, *12*(3), 322–322.

Chen, R., Lee, V. R., & Lee, G. (2025). A cross-sectional look at teacher reactions, worries, and professional development needs related to generative AI in an urban school district. *Education and Information Technologies*, *30*(11), 1–38. DOI: 10.1007/s10639-025-13350-w

Chen, X., Xie, H., Zou, D., & Hwang, G. J. (2020). Application and theory gaps during the rise of artificial intelligence in education. *Computers and Education: Artificial Intelligence*, *1*, 100002. DOI: 10.1016/j.caeai.2020.100002

Chiu, T. K., & Chai, C. S. (2020). Sustainable curriculum planning for artificial intelligence education: A self-determination theory perspective. *Sustainability (Basel)*, *12*(14), 5568. DOI: 10.3390/su12145568

Chocarro, R., Cortiñas, M., & Marcos-Matás, G. (2021). Teachers' attitudes towards chatbots in education: A technology acceptance model approach considering the effect of social language, bot proactiveness, and users' characteristics. *Educational Studies*, *49*(2), 295–313. DOI: 10.1080/03055698.2020.1850426

Cope, B., Kalantzis, M., & Searsmith, D. (2020). Artificial intelligence for education: Knowledge and its assessment in AI-enabled learning ecologies. *Educational Philosophy and Theory*, •••, 1–17.

Cukurova, M., & Luckin, R. (2018). *Measuring the impact of emerging technologies in education: A pragmatic approach*. Springer.

Daher, R. (2025). Integrating AI literacy into teacher education: A critical perspective paper. *Discover Artificial Intelligence*, *5*(1), 217. DOI: 10.1007/s44163-025-00475-7

Day, M. Y., & Shaw, S. R. (2021, August). AI customer service system with pre-trained language and response ranking models for university admissions. In 2021 IEEE 22nd International Conference on Information Reuse and Integration for Data Science (IRI) (pp. 395-401). IEEE. DOI: 10.1109/IRI51335.2021.00062

Degen, P. B., & Asanov, I. (2025). Beyond Automation: Socratic AI, Epistemic Agency, and the Implications of the Emergence of Orchestrated Multi-Agent Learning Architectures. arXiv preprint arXiv:2508.05116.

Dergaa, I., Chamari, K., Zmijewski, P., & Saad, H. B. (2023). From human writing to artificial intelligence generated text: Examining the prospects and potential threats of ChatGPT in academic writing. *Biology of Sport*, *40*(2), 615–622. DOI: 10.5114/biolsport.2023.125623 PMID: 37077800

Dillenbourg, P. (2016). The evolution of research on digital education. *International Journal of Artificial Intelligence in Education*, *26*(2), 544–560. DOI: 10.1007/s40593-016-0106-z

Favero, L., Pérez-Ortiz, J. A., Käser, T., & Oliver, N. (2024, October). Enhancing critical thinking in education by means of a Socratic chatbot. In International Workshop on AI in Education and Educational Research (pp. 17-32). Cham: Springer Nature Switzerland.

Feser, M. S. (2024). PARENTS' VIEWS ON THE USE OF AI-BASED CHATBOTS SUCH AS ChatGPT IN HIGH SCHOOL (STEM) EDUCATION. *Journal of Baltic Science Education*, *23*(1), 4–8. DOI: 10.33225/jbse/24.23.04

Friedman, N. P., & Robbins, T. W. (2022). The role of prefrontal cortex in cognitive control and executive function. *Neuropsychopharmacology : Official Publication of the American College of Neuropsychopharmacology*, *47*(1), 72–89. DOI: 10.1038/s41386-021-01132-0 PMID: 34408280

Government of the RS (2019). Strategy for the development of artificial intelligence in the Republic of Serbia for the period 2020–2025. Službeni glasnik RS, 96/2019. [In Serbian]

Government of the RS (2020). Action plan for the period 2020–2022 for the implementation of the Artificial Intelligence Development Strategy in the Republic of Serbia for the period 2020–2025. Službeni glasnik RS, 81/2020. [In Serbian]

Government of the RS (2023). Conclusion on the adoption of the Ethical Guidelines for the development, application and use of reliable and responsible artificial intelligence. Službeni glasnik RS, 23/2023. [In Serbian]

Gu, W., & Yu, Z. (2025). A bibliometric analysis of the application of AI chatbots in language learning contexts. *Quality & Quantity*, *59*(1), 639–661. DOI: 10.1007/s11135-024-01946-2

Hasal, M., Nowaková, J., Ahmed Saghair, K., Abdulla, H., Snášel, V., & Ogiela, L. (2021). Chatbots: Security, privacy, data protection, and social aspects. *Concurrency and Computation, 33*(19), e6426. DOI: 10.1002/cpe.6426

Holmes, W., Bialik, M., & Fadel, C. (2019). *Artificial intelligence in education promises and implications for teaching and learning*. Center for Curriculum Redesign.

Holmes, W., Porayska-Pomsta, K., Holstein, K., Sutherland, E., Baker, T., Shum, S. B., Santos, O. C., Rodrigo, M. T., Cukurova, M., Bittencourt, I. I., & Koedinger, K. R. (2022). Ethics of AI in education: Towards a community-wide framework. *International Journal of Artificial Intelligence in Education, 34*(3), 504–526. DOI: 10.1007/s40593-021-00239-1

Hwang, G. J., & Chang, C. Y. (2023). A review of opportunities and challenges of chatbots in education. *Interactive Learning Environments, 31*(7), 4099–4112. DOI: 10.1080/10494820.2021.1952615

Ji, Y., Zou, X., Li, T., & Zhan, Z. (2023, November). The effectiveness of ChatGPT on pre-service teachers' STEM teaching literacy, learning performance, and cognitive load in a teacher training course. In *Proceedings of the 2023 6th international conference on educational technology management* (pp. 16-22). DOI: 10.1145/3637907.3637948

Kasneci, E., Seßler, K., Küchemann, S., Bannert, M., Dementieva, D., Fischer, F., Gasser, U., Groh, G., Günnemann, S., Hüllermeier, E., Krusche, S., Kutyniok, G., Michaeli, T., Nerdel, C., Pfeffer, J., Poquet, O., Sailer, M., Schmidt, A., Seidel, T., & Kasneci, G. (2023). ChatGPT for good? On opportunities and challenges of large language models for education. *Learning and Individual Differences, 103*, 102274. DOI: 10.1016/j.lindif.2023.102274

Khalil, M., & Er, E. (2023). Will chatgpt get you caught? Rethinking of Plagiarism Detection. *Computer Science*.

Kooli, C. (2023). Chatbots in education and research: A critical examination of ethical implications and solutions. *Sustainability (Basel), 15*(7), 5614. DOI: 10.3390/su15075614

Kuhail, M. A., Alturki, N., Alramlawi, S., & Alhejori, K. (2022). Interacting with educational chatbots: A systematic review. *Education and Information Technologies*, •••, 1–46.

Labadze, L., Grigolia, M., & Machaidze, L. (2023). Role of AI chatbots in education: Systematic literature review. *International Journal of Educational Technology in Higher Education, 20*(1), 56. DOI: 10.1186/s41239-023-00426-1

Lampropoulos, G., & Papadakis, S. (2025). The educational value of artificial intelligence and social robots. In *Social robots in education* (pp. 3–15). Springer. DOI: 10.1007/978-3-031-82915-4_1

Lavidas, K., Papadakis, S., Manesis, D., Grigoriadou, A. S., & Gialamas, V.Lectures and Lab Classes. (2022). The effects of social desirability on students' self-reports in two social contexts: Lectures vs. lectures and lab classes. *Information (Basel), 13*(10), 491. DOI: 10.3390/info13100491

Lavidas, K., Petropoulou, A., Papadakis, S., Apostolou, Z., Komis, V., Jimoyiannis, A., & Gialamas, V. (2022a). Factors affecting response rates of the web survey with teachers. *Computers, 11*(9), 127. DOI: 10.3390/computers11090127

Liu, M., & Reinders, H. (2025). Do AI chatbots impact motivation? Insights from a preliminary longitudinal study. *System, 128*, 103544. DOI: 10.1016/j.system.2024.103544

Luckin, R., & Cukurova, M. (2019). Designing educational technologies in the age of AI: A learning sciences-driven approach. *British Journal of Educational Technology, 50*(6), 2824–2838. DOI: 10.1111/bjet.12861

Luckin, R., Holmes, W., Griffiths, M., & Forcier, L. B. (2016). *Intelligence unleashed: An argument for AI in education*. Pearson Education.

Mandić, D. P., Miščević, G. M., & Bujišić, L. G. (2024). Evaluating the quality of responses generated by ChatGPT. Metodička teorija i praksa, 27(1), 5-19

Mekić, E. S., Jovanović, M. N., Kuk, K. V., Prlinčević, B. P., & Savić, A. M. (2024). Enhancing educational efficiency: Generative AI chatbots and DevOps in Education 4.0. *Computer Applications in Engineering Education, 32*(6), e22804. DOI: 10.1002/cae.22804

Mikael, K., Cemil, Ö. Z., Rashid, T. A., & Nariman, G. S. (2025). A Hybrid Chatbot Model for Enhancing Administrative Support in Education: Comparative Analysis, Integration, and Optimization. IEEE Access.

Molnár, G., & Szüts, Z. (2018, September). The role of chatbots in formal education. In 2018 IEEE 16th international symposium on intelligent systems and informatics (SISY) (pp.197-202). IEEE. Subotica, Serbia. DOI: 10.1109/SISY.2018.8524609

Nazer, L. H., Zatarah, R., Waldrip, S., Ke, J. X. C., Moukheiber, M., Khanna, A. K., Hicklen, R. S., Moukheiber, L., Moukheiber, D., Ma, H., & Mathur, P. (2023). Bias in artificial intelligence algorithms and recommendations for mitigation. *PLOS Digital Health, 2*(6), e0000278. DOI: 10.1371/journal.pdig.0000278 PMID: 37347721

Nyaaba, M. (2024). Transforming teacher education in developing countries: The role of generative AI in bridging theory and practice. arXiv preprint arXiv:2411.10718.

Okonkwo, C. W., & Ade-Ibijola, A. (2021). Chatbots applications in education: A systematic review. *Computers and Education: Artificial Intelligence*, *2*, 100033. DOI: 10.1016/j.caeai.2021.100033

Papadakis, S., Lytvynova, S. H., Ivanova, S. M., & Selyshcheva, I. A. (2024b). *Advancing lifelong learning with AI-enhanced ICT: A review of 3L-Person 2024.* In *CEUR Workshop Proceedings (9th International Workshop on Professional Retraining and Life-Long Learning using ICT: Person-oriented Approach — 3L-Person 2024, Lviv, Ukraine, September 25, 2023).* CEUR-WS.org.

Papadakis, S., Striuk, A. M., Kravtsov, H. M., Shyshkina, M. P., Marienko, M. V., & Danylchuk, H. B. (2024a). *Embracing digital innovation and cloud technologies for transformative learning experiences.* In *Proceedings of the 11th Workshop on Cloud Technologies in Education (CTE 2023), Kryvyi Rih, Ukraine, December 22, 2023.* CEUR Workshop Proceedings.

Pérez, J. Q., Daradoumis, T., & Puig, J. M. M. (2020). Rediscovering the use of chatbots in education: A systematic literature review. *Computer Applications in Engineering Education*, *28*(6), 1549–1565. DOI: 10.1002/cae.22326

Rincón-Flores, E. G., Castano, L., Guerrero Solis, S. L., Olmos Lopez, O., Rodríguez Hernández, C. F., Castillo Lara, L. A., & Aldape Valdés, L. P. (2024). Improving the learning-teaching process through adaptive learning strategy. *Smart Learning Environments*, *11*(1), 27. DOI: 10.1186/s40561-024-00314-9

Ružičić, V., Simeunović, M., & Gojgic, N. (2024). Prerequisites for Higher Quality Education: Teachers' Attitudes on the Application of Artificial Intelligence Tools in Teaching. In 10th International Scientific Conference Technics, Informatics and Education-TIE 2024. Faculty of Technical Sciences Čačak, University of Kragujevac.

Sabharwal, D., Kabha, R., & Srivastava, K. (2023). Artificial intelligence (ai)-powered virtual assistants and their effect on human productivity and laziness: Study on students of delhi-ncr (india) & fujairah (uae). Journal of Content. *Community and Communication*, *17*(9), 162–174. DOI: 10.31620/JCCC.06.23/12

Selwyn, N. (2019). *Should Robots Replace Teachers? AI and the Future of Education*. Polity Press.

Seufert, S., Guggemos, J., & Sailer, M. (2020). Technology-related knowledge, skills, and attitudes of pre-and in-service teachers: The current situation and emerging trends. *Computers in Human Behavior, 115*, 106552. DOI: 10.1016/j.chb.2020.106552 PMID: 32921901

Šijan, A., Ilić, L., Predić, B., Viduka, D., & Renčić, D. (2025). Bibliometric analysis of artificial intelligence applications in higher education using web of science database. Facta Universitatis, Series: Teaching, Learning and Teacher Education, 119-130.

Simon, P. D., & Zeng, L. M. (2024). Behind the scenes of adaptive learning: A scoping review of teachers' perspectives on the use of adaptive learning technologies. *Education Sciences, 14*(12), 1413. DOI: 10.3390/educsci14121413

Šipka, D. (2024). Developing Bosnian/Croatian/Serbian Conversational Chatbots Using MYAI Builder. *Russian Language Journal, 74*(1), 12. DOI: 10.70163/0036-0252.1402

Škobo, M., & Petričević, V. (2023). Navigating the challenges and opportunities of literary translation in the age of AI: Striking a balance between human expertise and machine power. Društvene i humanističke studije, 8(2 (23)), 317-336.

Škobo, M., & Šović, M. (2025). The Digital Doppelgängers of Nikola Tesla and Branislav Nušić: A New Approach to Interactive Learning And Cultural Heritage. Paper presented at Sinteza 2025 - International Scientific Conference on Information Technology, Computer Science, and Data Science

Škobo, M., & Šović, M. (2025a). Teachers' perspectives on Chatbots and AI agents in primary and secondary education. *International Journal on Studies in Education, 7*(2), 410–442. DOI: 10.46328/ijonse.352

Stanković, N., Stankovic, I., Marković, G., & Blagojević, M. (2024). The Role of AI Tools in Education: Opportunities and Challenges. In 10th International Scientific Conference Technics, Informatics and Education-TIE 2024. Faculty of Technical Sciences Čačak, University of Kragujevac.

Tomić, B. M., & Radovanović, N. D. (2024). The application of artificial intelligence in the context of the educational system in Serbia, with a special focus on religious education. *Socioloski Pregled, 58*(2), 435–459. DOI: 10.5937/socpreg58-48911

Tomlinson, C. A. (2001). How to differentiate instruction in mixed-ability classrooms. Association for supervision and curriculum development.

Touvron, H., Lavril, T., Izacard, G., Martinet, X., Lachaux, M. A., Lacroix, T., . . . Lample, G. (2023). Llama: Open and efficient foundation language models. arXiv preprint arXiv:2302.13971.

Uğraş, H., Uğraş, M., Papadakis, S., & Kalogiannakis, M. (2024). ChatGPT-supported education in primary schools: The potential of ChatGPT for sustainable practices. *Sustainability (Basel)*, *16*(22), 9855. DOI: 10.3390/su16229855

Uğraş, H., Uğraş, M., Papadakis, S., & Kalogiannakis, M. (2025). Innovative Early Childhood STEM Education with ChatGPT: Teacher Perspectives. Technology. *Knowledge and Learning*, *30*(2), 809–831. DOI: 10.1007/s10758-024-09804-8

VanSledright, B. A. (2004). What does it mean to think historically… and how do you teach it. *Social Education*, *68*(3), 230–233.

Viberg, O., Cukurova, M., Feldman-Maggor, Y., Alexandron, G., Shirai, S., Kanemune, S., & Kizilcec, R. F. (2024). What explains teachers' trust in AI in education across six countries? *International Journal of Artificial Intelligence in Education*, •••, 1–29.

Vukomanović, A., Deretić, N., Kabiljo, M., & Matić, R. (2022). An example of chatbot in the field of education in the Republic of Serbia. Journal of process management and new technologies, 10(1-2), 125-139.

Vygotsky, L. S. (1978). *Mind in society: The development of higher psychological processes* (Vol. 86). Harvard University Press.

Walter, Y. (2024). Embracing the future of Artificial Intelligence in the classroom: The relevance of AI literacy, prompt engineering, and critical thinking in modern education. *International Journal of Educational Technology in Higher Education*, *21*(1), 15. DOI: 10.1186/s41239-024-00448-3

Williams, R. T. (2024, January). The ethical implications of using generative chatbots in higher education. [). Frontiers Media SA.]. *Frontiers in Education*, *8*, 1331607. DOI: 10.3389/feduc.2023.1331607

Workshop, B., Scao, T. L., Fan, A., Akiki, C., Pavlick, E., Ilić, S., . . . Bari, M. S. (2022). Bloom: A 176b-parameter open-access multilingual language model. arXiv preprint arXiv:2211.05100.

Yim, I. H. Y., & Wegerif, R. (2024). Teachers' perceptions, attitudes, and acceptance of artificial intelligence (AI) educational learning tools: An exploratory study on AI literacy for young students. *Future in Educational Research*, *2*(4), 318–345. DOI: 10.1002/fer3.65

Zhai, C., Wibowo, S., & Li, L. D. (2024). The effects of over-reliance on AI dialogue systems on students' cognitive abilities: A systematic review. *Smart Learning Environments*, *11*(1), 28. DOI: 10.1186/s40561-024-00316-7

Chapter 12
Adaptive Gamification and Learning Analytics for Computational Thinking Development in Early and Primary Teacher Education

Alkinoos Ioannis Zourmpakis
http://orcid.org/0000-0002-4390-6799
University of Thessaly, Greece

ABSTRACT

Computational Thinking (CT) has emerged as a critical skill across preschool and primary education, yet the lack of teachers with expertise in CT and the ability to use adaptive learning applications poses a significant barrier. This article proposes an innovative professional development program to equip pre-service teachers in preschool and primary education with essential CT competencies. The program is based on the Technological Pedagogical and Content Knowledge (TPACK) framework while utilizing an adaptive gamification environment with the use of learning analytics. The methodology guides participants through unplugged activities and hands-on coding, using a custom application that personalizes the learning path while providing instructors with real-time data. The main objective of it isn't only to build core CT skills but also to enable them to use them across subjects and to model the teacher's modern role as a facilitator that can use educational data to make strategic pedagogical decisions and effectively enhance learning in technology-rich environments.

DOI: 10.4018/979-8-3373-2637-5.ch012

1. INTRODUCTION

Computational Thinking (CT) originates from computer science and is a modern skill set that is vital for students in the 21st century, as it allows them to analyze and solve problems across disciplines like mathematics, natural sciences, and computing (Ogegbo & Ramnarain, 2022; Wing, 2006). As such, in recent years there have been many calls to equip students with CT skills from an early age throughout Europe (Vuorikari et al., 2022), leading to efforts to integrate it into K-12 curricula (Zhang & Nouri, 2019). However, these efforts face significant obstacles, such as the lack of specialized teachers who can teach CT effectively (Liu, 2023; Menekse, 2015). The process of integrating CT into education is not an easy task. It is a complex matter that requires both the dedication and involvement of teachers, as well as the systematic reform of the educational framework and structure (Liu et al., 2024).

Alongside CT, another significant and emerging learning method that has shown steady growth in recent years is adaptive learning, which refers to the use of technologies that monitor and analyze student progress to modify teaching approaches based on data and other sources of information (Pelletier et al., 2021). This type of learning dynamically adjusts the level and type of content presented to students according to their skills and abilities, often using both automated systems and teacher intervention to improve learning outcomes (Werbach & Hunter, 2012). A notable development associated with adaptive learning is adaptive gamification, which personalizes learning by incorporating game elements tailored to the user's characteristics, without, however, using excessive elements that lead to cognitive overload (Codish & Ravid, 2014; Monterrat et al., 2015). Although promising, adaptive gamification is still in an early stage of development (Zourmpakis et al., 2023a).

In recent years, due to new challenges and demands, education is undergoing a process of restructuring and redefinition, especially after the coronavirus period (Shehaj, 2022; Zancajo et al., 2022). The role of the teacher is a key element of the learning process. Over time, the duties and responsibilities of teachers have undergone significant changes. One of these is providing strategic support to students to promote self-directed learning, according to UNESCO (2008). More specifically, there is a need to redefine the professional skills of teachers (Torrance & Forde, 2017) and to enhance their training to enable the development of key skills, such as collaboration, critical thinking, problem-solving, and scientific and digital literacy in today's world (Dede, 2010; Haryani et al., 2021; Liu et al., 2024). Moreover, concerning digital educational environments, teachers play a crucial role in promoting engagement, either by guiding or by creating socio-cognitive conflict situations so that students can discuss and solve problems, thereby promoting active learning. Consequently, the teacher is called upon to assume the role of a guide/facilitator, guiding and supporting discussions (Thorman & Fidalgo, 2014). For effective learning management, teachers are encouraged to analyze, manage, and utilize learning analytics (LA) to more accurately assess when and how to intervene in discussions and to keep communication focused and meaningful (Hew, 2016; Rienties et al., 2017). Through the analysis of this data, teachers can enhance their role as guides and partners in the learning process, applying proactive strategies to improve learning outcomes (Herodotou et al., 2019; Ouyang & Scharber, 2017; Wong et al., 2019). This requires the development of new teaching competencies and skills, such as the ability to understand, utilize, and in some cases, even design, if possible, activities that motivate students through carefully designed and implemented pedagogical practices (Ma et al., 2015; Mah & Ifenthaler, 2019; Zourmpakis et al., 2022).

2. LITERATURE REVIEW

2.1 Computational Thinking and Science Education

Even though the integration of CT in the past was taking place after primary education (Haseski & Ilic, 2019), there is a growing consensus that its implementation should begin earlier (Vuorikari et al., 2022). Early and primary education can provide a great opportunity for introducing CT, since children's transition from concrete to abstract reasoning (Flannery & Bers, 2013; Piaget, 1973) tends to make them more responsive to CT practices, such as abstraction, decomposition, algorithmic thinking, etc. (Bers, 2018; Kalogiannakis & Papadakis, 2020). What is more, during the last decade, CT has been increasingly gaining ground as more of a foundational skill, such as literacy and numeracy (Santosa & Sukmawati, 2024; Tariq et al., 2025). CT development is not only confined to the aspect of programming, as it can equip students with a set of interconnected practices related to problem-solving and inquiry, which can be transferred and applied across subjects (Barr & Stephenson, 2011; National Research Council, 2012; NGSS Lead States, 2013). Consequently, CT can be viewed as a universal skill that aims at building and improving vital skills and capacities such as problem-solving, creativity, collaboration, and persistence (Strawhacker et al., 2018; Stamatios, 2024).

CT development can greatly benefit other subjects in early and primary education, such as STEM education. The Next Generation Science Standards (NGSS) have long highlighted the powerful synergy between scientific inquiry and computational thinking, as it can offer powerful methods for exploring, modeling, and understanding scientific phenomena (NGSS Lead States, 2013). To be more precise, CT concepts, such as abstraction, pattern recognition, process iteration, and model improvement, can help students to understand how scientific process and reasoning, like making hypotheses, designing experiments, analyzing data, and improving explanations, work (Basu et al., 2016; Tariq et al., 2025).

Nevertheless, in order to effectively teach CT in primary and early education, age-appropriate methods and tools are a must, especially in early education. The pedagogical goal is much more than to develop technical skills but to foster a new form of literacy, where coding is used to express ideas and create meaningful projects (Bers, 2018; Vee, 2017). While "unplugged" activities like physical games are common, digital environments tend to provide more authentic coding experiences (Sullivan & Bers, 2019). It is vital to utilize applications that provide an accessible environment for students to test their ideas hands-on and engage with foundational computer science concepts without causing cognitive overload, like ScratchJr in early education and Scratch in primary education (Kalogiannakis & Papadakis, 2022; Bers, 2018), while at the same time incorporating pedagogical learning strategies that will be able to leverage the already playful nature of these tools to encourage experimentation and collaboration (Bers, 2012), such as integrating game-based learning and gamification practices.

Despite the clear benefits of early CT integration in education, there are several issues in this research field. CT skills assessment methods tend to focus exclusively on computational concepts rather than encompassing the broader practices and perspectives that CT entails (Cutumisu et al., 2019; Lockwood & Mooney, 2017). Moreover, research in early education as well as validating CT development in young children is still limited (Haseski & Ilic, 2019; Cutumisu et al., 2019; Cakir et al., 2021; Katchapakirin et al., 2022). However, the most urgent and crucial issue lies with teachers, as the lack of training in pedagogical frameworks and assessment tools makes them unwilling to integrate CT effectively into their teaching.

2.2 Computational Thinking and Teacher Education

In recent years, Computational Thinking (CT) has become a focus of international educational reform, with regions such as the USA, EU, China, and Australia heavily focusing on policies to incorporate CT into primary and secondary curricula (Grover & Pea, 2013; Wang et al., 2019; Caeli & Bundsgaard, 2020). Research on CT education has examined a variety of different approaches, including the development of programming tools and the creation of CT-integrated curricula (Grover & Pea, 2013). Nevertheless, three significant challenges continue to hinder the pedagogical development of CT in education: a) teachers often lack a deep understanding of information/computational systems and the pedagogical strategies required for differentiated instruction, b) students may not have the necessary knowledge or motivation to engage in the problem-solving process, and c) there are resource limitations, such as a lack of technological/digital tools in schools (Sentance &

Csizmadia, 2017). Additionally, another significant issue concerning research on CT education is that the majority of studies have focused on students, with limited focus on the CT competencies of teachers, especially pre-service teachers. They frequently encounter challenges to apply CT in programming due to a lack of academic background in computer science training or related fields, low self-efficacy, or lack of support (Menekse, 2015; Mouza et al., 2018; Sentance & Csizmadia, 2017; Yadav et al., 2016).

Research indicates that training pre-service teachers on teaching CT appears to have positive effects on their attitudes and perceptions towards computer science, thereby increasing the likelihood of integrating CT into their teaching practices (Yadav et al., 2017). Nevertheless, much of the existing research centers on short-term professional development for in-service teachers, while studies focusing on pre-service teacher preparation are even more limited (Bower et al., 2017; Hestness et al., 2018; Haines et al., 2019). Addressing the challenges of integrating CT into primary and secondary education requires a comprehensive approach that empowers teachers with both the knowledge and practical skills to deliver CT effectively. Teacher development programs, especially those that promote sustained engagement, are vital for building the capacity for effective CT education. Therefore, it is important to integrate CT into the education of pre-service teachers, allowing them to develop the necessary competencies necessary for effective instruction (Yadav et al., 2017; Esteve-Mon et al., 2020).

2.3 Adaptive Learning and Adaptive Gamification

Traditional pedagogical strategies often assume that all students have the same characteristics and needs, resulting in the implementation of "one-size-fits-all" teaching approaches where all students follow the same learning path, regardless of their individual differences (O'Bannon & Thomas, 2015). However, students seem to differ significantly in their habits, needs, learning pace, and abilities. Personalized learning environments, which adapt to these differences, can offer significant benefits, as they enable teaching to be tailored to each student's unique learning needs (Hassan et al., 2021; Koivisto & Hamari, 2019). Adaptive learning is a personalized educational approach that uses technology to tailor learning experiences to meet the individual needs, preferences, and progress of students (Codish & Ravid, 2014). Using algorithms based on learning data and/or its processing by artificial intelligence systems, adaptive learning systems adjust content, delivery, and pace of instruction based on student performance, activity, and engagement (Gligorea et al., 2023). This real-time adaptation contributes to improved learning by increasing student participation and active engagement, while also improving overall learning outcomes (Gligorea et al., 2023).

Adaptive gamification refers to the adaptation and integration of various game mechanisms and features, depending on the actions, preferences, and characteristics of individual users or students (Codish & Ravid, 2014). This approach draws on elements from the methodologies of adaptive learning and gamification. Although there are references in the literature to certain adaptive gamification methodologies, most are general and do not cover the specifics of cognitive subjects, such as learning strategies (Kalogiannakis et al., 2021; Zourmpakis et al., 2023b). Furthermore, there is limited information on how to adapt game elements and which models or criteria are most appropriate for adaptive gamification environments (Koivisto & Hamari, 2019; Klock et al., 2020). Effective design and a sound pedagogical approach to environments are crucial to ensure that adaptive gamification enhances student engagement and effectiveness over time (Böckle et al., 2017; Zourmpakis et al., 2023a; Zourmpakis et al., 2024).

2.4 Learning Analytics

Active learning, which is facilitated through collaborative activities, communication, and discussions, plays a central role in the engagement and success of students in online learning environments (Garrison et al., 2000). However, simply providing opportunities for interaction does not automatically lead to collaboration or active engagement (Tseng et al., 2016). The strategic use of educational data from digital tools offers opportunities to transform teaching by helping educators determine when and how to intervene effectively in learning activities (Hew, 2016; Rienties et al., 2017).

More specifically, Learning Management Systems (LMS), such as Moodle, offer teachers the ability to access and analyze student behavior data through Learning Analytics features. These systems can also link to external analytics platforms, allowing teachers to visualize and group student behaviors for deeper analysis (Tlili et al., 2023). Furthermore, participation and interaction in online learning environments have a direct impact on learning (Ellis et al., 2017). However, challenges still exist regarding teachers' ability to interpret and effectively use learning analytics data to promote student interaction and engagement (Altun & Kokoc, 2019; Van Leeuwen, 2019) as well as classroom management. By the term "classroom management," we mean all the actions a teacher takes to support the cognitive and socio-emotional development of students. Its main purpose is the development and maintenance of a suitable learning environment, taking into account the planned academic curriculum as well as the social and emotional skills and competencies of the students. In this regard, five types of actions are recognized that teachers should undertake to improve their classroom management (Hickey & Schafer 2006; Moltudal et al., 2022): a) Engagement in relation to learning, b) The goals of teaching and learning strategies, c) Student relationships with each other and with the teacher, d) Managing changes in behavior and knowledge over time, and e) The prevention and handling of behavioral problems. This requires the development of new teaching skills by teachers, including the ability to understand, utilize, and, if possible, design activities that consider the dynamics/characteristics of students, promote student engagement and participation, and also make it possible to manage and/or prevent potential problems.

3. PROPOSED PROFESSIONAL DEVELOPMENT PROGRAM FOR CT DEVELOPMENT FOR PRESCHOOL AND PRIMARY EDUCATION

The roles of the teachers have changed over the years as they are increasingly turned away from the traditional role as providers of knowledge and more as strategically supporting students as facilitators and promoting self-directed learning (UNESCO, 2008). However, this role change must also be initiated in their training and education, not just their teaching in class. The purpose of this research is to pioneer a professional development program designed to equip preschool and primary education pre-service teachers with CT skills through the use of adaptive gamification environments and Learning Analytics. The primary objective is not only building teachers' CT skills but also linking CT to other subjects and promoting and understanding the role of the teacher as a strategic facilitator that utilizes educational data in a self-directed adaptive learning process.

Specifically, upon completion, participating teachers will be proficient in the four core concepts of computational thinking, i.e. decomposition, abstraction, pattern recognition, and algorithm design and how to potentially apply CT in other subjects. Also, the program aims at empowering them to become teacher trainers themselves, enabling a scalable and sustainable model for professional development program that can be used within the educational community.

3.1 The Adaptive Gamification Environment and Learning Analytics

The professional development program will center on a custom-built adaptive gamification application that can provide the instructor with educational data. The environment will be developed using the Unity3D game engine, making it accessible for desktop and potentially mobile devices. The design that will be followed will be based on the established frameworks of Zourmpakis et al. (2023b) with the addition of some guidelines from Ng et al. (2021). It will combine adaptive criteria, learning strategies, game elements, and content in all stages of gameplay, initially, throughout it, and in the end of activities and sections (Böckle et al., 2017; Zourmpakis et al., 2023b). Meaning the application will dynamically adjust game mechanics and content based on the user's real-time performance and actions (Zourmpakis et al., 2023b; Ng et al., 2021).

Following the Zourmpakis framework, the adaptive gamification environment will adapt to the "player type" of the learner, providing game elements and adjusting them if necessary, during gameplay. Regarding the activities, some will follow a predetermined format with divergent prepared answers and corresponding feedback to assist the learner. In these tasks, the utilization of learning analytics will be critical. However, other tasks will utilize AI-driven personalization. To be more specific, some activities will incorporate an AI-based Intelligent NPC (Non-Player Character) (Campitiello et al., 2024) to provide realism and allow learners to freely test their ideas and problem-solving skills. Moreover, it could also adjust the difficulty of specific tasks based on the learner's performance, thus maintaining player challenge and engagement (Bontchev et al., 2024). The Intelligent NPC will be adjusted to the story behind each specific learning scenario and programmed to act accordingly in its role. Learning analytics will also be vital in this case.

Each CT concept will initially be taught in individual learning scenarios by interactive unplugged tasks. After the completion of all learning lessons, the teachers will be guided to a block-based environment similar to Scratch, where they will attempt to utilize what they learn, experiment, and solve some additional challenges.

During gameplay, the instructor will have access to a dashboard on another device displaying educational analytics both during and after teaching sessions. This feedback will help them monitor progress, identify difficulties, refine their instructional strategies, and intervene when they deem it necessary. Consequently, as the application will export data on a private server where the instructor will have access, internet connection will be mandatory.

3.2 Theoretical Framework and structure of the Professional Development Program

To effectively integrate technology into teaching, this professional development program follows the theoretical framework of Technological Pedagogical and Content Knowledge (TPACK), as proposed by Mishra and Koehler (2006). TPACK provides a holistic approach to teacher training by focusing on the dynamic interplay between three core knowledge domains: technology, pedagogy, and content. It tries to equip teachers with the cognitive skills and knowledge to seamlessly integrate technology into the classroom, rather than prescribing a standardized approach for all teachers in different teaching scenarios. This involves merging a teacher's knowledge of content, students, pedagogy, and technology. Rather than advocating a single teaching approach using technology, TPACK emphasizes the importance of context and student characteristics in the process of integrating technology. Consequently, TPACK is always applied within the unique context of a teaching/learning situation, and its effectiveness depends on teachers' ability to adapt pedagogically to the context (Kelly, 2008).

The training program is structured as a sequential, multi-step process based on the work of Kong & Lai (2022), Ng et al. (2021), and Zourmpakis et al. (2022). It combines unplugged activities with hands-on coding while incorporating gamification aspects (Ng et al., 2021; Zourmpakis et al., 2022) and the ‘to play, to think, to code, to reflect’ pedagogy (Kong & Lai, 2022). This pedagogical model encourages gamefulness and thoughtful planning before programming and iteration. The steps that follows are:

1. **Pedagogical and Content Introduction (PCK):** Teachers are introduced to the four basic principles of the curriculum unit (CK), including its concepts, practices, such as problem solving, and perspectives, to ensure they understand the targeted learning outcomes. The ‘to play, to think, to code, to reflect’ pedagogy (PK) is also introduced even though it will be applied later.
2. **Introduction to the Adaptive Gamification Environment (TPK):** Teachers are familiarized with the adaptive gamification environment, its features, and the specific tools it incorporates.
3. **Unplugged CT Concepts (TCK):** Each of the four computational thinking (CT) principles is taught individually through “unplugged” activities. Each lesson follows the problem-based approach, which is incorporated entirely within the application. During gameplay, the instructor utilized the educational data from the application to provide targeted feedback.
4. **Introduction to the Tools (TCK):** Teachers are introduced to the features of the incorporated block-based programming environment which is similar to Scratch, and its specific tools.
5. **Hands-On Programming (TPACK):** Teachers apply their knowledge in the block-based programming environment, completing tasks through cycles of testing and debugging. The “to play, to think, to code, to reflect” model is utilized in this step, except for “to reflect,” which will be applied later. Firstly, teachers explore a finished program to understand its functionality (to play). They then engage in guided discussions to decompose the application’s logic and design a plan for its construction (to think). Next, they use the block-based environment to transform their plan into a working program (to code). Similarly

to the previous stage, the instructor monitors progress both in class and via the analytics dashboard and provides support.

6. **Consolidation and Creativity (TPACK):** Teachers conduct group discussion, brainstorming new ideas and reinforcing their understanding of the tools and concepts, fostering a creative and forward-thinking perspective (to reflect). They are encouraged to think beyond coding and explore application in other subjects, such as STEM or even everyday life.
7. **Content Knowledge Reflection (CK):** Teachers summarize the key CT concepts and practices they have learned to reinforce retention.
8. **Pedagogical Reflection (PCK):** In the final step, teachers assess the pedagogies used and consider how the entire process can be optimized for student learning.

Regarding the program's effectiveness, a mixed-method approach could be most beneficial. The development of teachers' CT skills will be measured using the Algorithmic Thinking Test for Adults (ATTA) (Lafuente Martínez et al., 2022), both at the start and the end of the program. Additionally, regarding teachers TPACK knowledge perceptions, self-efficacy, attitudes toward the use of technological tools, and intentions to use the application in the future a questionnaire will be used, in the same format (before and after) as the ATTA questionnaire. The questionnaire is based on literature and on the works of Papadakis et al., 2024 (Teo, 2009; Wong et al., 2013; Pusparini et al., 2017; Sharma & Srivastava, 2020; Tzafilkou et al., 2021). Moreover, if the teachers apply their knowledge and train other with the same application, then an observation checklist, based on the literature (Kafyulilo et al., 2015; Schmidt-Crawford et al., 2016; Hong et al., 2020) and on the MEIS TPACK Observation Checklist (Michigan Information Education System, n.d.), can also be utilized. Furthermore, individual semi-structured interviews will be conducted after the program to gather qualitative insights into the teachers' experiences, challenges, and perspectives on using adaptive gamification and learning analytics for CT development.

4. CONCLUSION

The effective integration of CT into primary and preschool education depends largely on how well teachers are prepared. In order to address this, we proposed an innovative professional development program designed to meet this critical need by preparing pre-service teachers with essential CT skills through a novel approach integrating adaptive gamification and learning analytics. Although the program can be effectively used with in-service teachers, this proposal prioritized pre-service teachers because they are often more open to new teaching methods and pedagogies.

Furthermore, they might be more willing to train their peers after the program and later apply this collaborative model with their colleagues at school.

The theoretical foundation that we based the professional development program on is the TPACK framework. As opposed to treating technology, pedagogy, and content as separate domains, TPACK emphasizes the dynamic interplay between them, which is essential for meaningful technology integration (Mishra & Koehler, 2006). The program is structured to develop this synthesized knowledge by having teachers engage with CT concepts by utilizing different approaches and methodologies, like the problem-based approach, gamification and "to play, to think, to code, to reflect pedagogy (Kong & Lai, 2022; Zourmpakis et al., 2023b). The use of the TPACK framework in developing teachers' CT skills has been shown to yield significant positive results (Kong et al., 2023). What is more, the use of a TPACK-based professional development program regarding the preparation and development of teachers' TPACK and implementation of an adaptive gamification environment in education has shown that it can improve teachers' TPACK knowledge, skills, motivation and self-efficacy (Papadakis et al., 2024; Zourmpakis et al., 2023c). Furthermore, adaptive learning environments have shown that they can support teachers' TPACK knowledge development (Elmaadaway & Abouelenein, 2023). Consequently, the integration of adaptive gamification is particularly promising, as it offers a personalized learning pathway that adjusts to each teacher's progress, moving beyond the limitations of "one-size-fits-all" instruction and potentially leading to greater engagement and efficacy (Papadakis et al., 2024; Zourmpakis et al., 2023b).

An innovating and promising feature of this proposal is the strategic use of educational data, or learning analytics (Yang et al., 2025). It equips instructors with real-time insights, allowing for timely interventions and a data-informed learning process (Kennedy et al., 2025). However, at the same time, it demonstrates how teachers need to focus on learning to analyze and utilize student data to guide learning and manage the classroom effectively as facilitators in today's technology-rich learning environments (Johler et al., 2022; Wiley et al., 2024).

Conclusively, this proposed program aims not only to develop teachers' CT as a technical skill but also as a transferable problem-solving approach applicable to other disciplines as well, especially towards STEM education. In order to do so, it is imperative to develop programs that boost teachers' competence and confidence as well, enabling them to integrate CT meaningfully in the lessons regardless of content. Examining participants' learning experiences, their interaction with the application, and the program's overall impact will offer valuable information and insights into the competencies needed and necessary changes to maximize adaptive learning technologies. However, it should be noted that a teacher's role is still particularly vital in today's context of data-driven decision-making (Baker, 2016). He is still at the core of the educational process by learning to use emerging technologies while balancing technological, pedagogical, and content-related dimensions and making strategic interventions (UNICEF, 2018). Further research should focus on validating the program's effectiveness with large participant groups and assessing the long-term effects on both teaching practices and student outcomes.

REFERENCES

Altun, A., & Kokoc, M. (2019). Following the learners' traces: Profiling learners and visualizing the learning process for building better learning experiences. In Khine, M. S. (Ed.), *Emerging Trends in Learning Analytics: Leveraging the Power of Education Data* (pp. 100–121). Brill., DOI: 10.1163/9789004399273_007

Baker, R. S. (2016). Stupid tutoring systems, intelligent humans. *International Journal of Artificial Intelligence in Education, 26*(2), 600–614. DOI: 10.1007/s40593-016-0105-0

Barr, V., & Stephenson, C. (2011). Bringing computational thinking to K-12: What is involved and what is the role of the computer science education community? *ACM Inroads, 2*(1), 48–54. DOI: 10.1145/1929887.1929905

Basu, S., Biswas, G., Sengupta, P., Dickes, A., Kinnebrew, J. S., & Clark, D. (2016). Identifying middle school students' challenges in computational thinking-based science learning. *Research and Practice in Technology Enhanced Learning, 11*(1), 13. DOI: 10.1186/s41039-016-0036-2 PMID: 30613246

Bers, M. U. (2012). *Designing digital experiences for positive youth development: From playpen to playground.* Oxford University Press. DOI: 10.1093/acprof:oso/9780199757022.001.0001

Bers, M. U. (2018). Coding and computational thinking in early childhood: The impact of ScratchJr in Europe. *European Journal of STEM Education, 3*(3), 8. DOI: 10.20897/ejsteme/3868

Böckle, M., Novak, J., & Bick, M. (2017). Towards Adaptive Gamification: A Synthesis of Current Developments. In *Proceedings of the 25th European Conference on Information Systems (ECIS), (pp.* 158–174*).* Guimarães, Portugal.

Bontchev, B., Naydenov, I., & Adamov, I. (2024). Intelligent adaptation of difficulty and npc behavior in serious video games for learning. *IFAC-PapersOnLine, 58*(3), 187–192. DOI: 10.1016/j.ifacol.2024.07.148

Bower, M., Wood, L. N., Lai, J. W., Highfield, K., Veal, J., Howe, C., Lister, R., & Mason, R. (2017). Improving the computational thinking pedagogical capabilities of school teachers. *Australian Journal of Teacher Education (Online), 42*(3), 53–72. DOI: 10.14221/ajte.2017v42n3.4

Caeli, E. N., & Bundsgaard, J. (2020). Computational thinking in compulsory education: A survey study on initiatives and conceptions. *Educational Technology Research and Development, 68*(1), 551–573. DOI: 10.1007/s11423-019-09694-z

Campitiello, L., Beatini, V., & Di Tore, S. (2024, January). Non-player character smart in virtual learning environment: Empowering education through artificial intelligence. In *Workshop on Artificial Intelligence with and for Learning Sciences: Past, Present, and Future Horizons* (pp. 131-137). Cham: Springer Nature Switzerland. https://doi.org/DOI: 10.1007/978-3-031-57402-3_14

Codish, D., & Ravid, G. (2014). Personality based gamification-Educational gamification for extroverts and introverts. In *Proceedings of the 9th CHAIS Conference for the Study of Innovation and Learning Technologies: Learning in the Technological Era* (pp. 36-44). Ra'anana: The Open University of Israel.

Cutumisu, M., Adams, C., & Lu, C. (2019). A scoping review of empirical research on recent computational thinking assessments. *Journal of Science Education and Technology*, *28*(6), 651–676. DOI: 10.1007/s10956-019-09799-3

Dede, C. (2010). Comparing frameworks for 21st century skills. *21st century skills: Rethinking how students learn, 20*(2010), 51-76.

Ellis, R. A., Han, F., & Pardo, A. (2017). Improving learning analytics–Combining observational and self-report data on student learning. *Journal of Educational Technology & Society, 20*(3), 158-169. https://www.jstor.org/stable/ 26196127.

Elmaadaway, M. A. N., & Abouelenein, Y. A. M. (2023). In-service teachers' TPACK development through an adaptive e-learning environment (ALE). *Education and Information Technologies*, *28*(7), 8273–8298. DOI: 10.1007/s10639-022-11477-8 PMID: 36571083

Esteve-Mon, F., Llopis, M., & Adell-Segura, J. (2020). Digital competence and computational think ing of student teachers. [iJET]. *International Journal of Emerging Technologies in Learning*, *15*(2), 29–41. DOI: 10.3991/ijet.v15i02.11588

Flannery, L. P., & Bers, M. U. (2013). Let's dance the "robot hokey-pokey!" children's programming approaches and achievement throughout early cognitive development. *Journal of Research on Technology in Education*, *46*(1), 81–101. DOI: 10.1080/15391523.2013.10782614

Garrison, D. R., Anderson, T., & Archer, W. (2000). Critical inquiry in a text-based environment: Computer conferencing in higher education. *The Internet and Higher Education*, *2*(2), 16–22. DOI: 10.1016/S1096-7516(00)00016-6

Gligorea, I., Cioca, M., Oancea, R., Gorski, A. T., Gorski, H., & Tudorache, P. (2023). Adaptive learning using artificial intelligence in e-learning: A literature review. *Education Sciences*, *13*(12), 1216. DOI: 10.3390/educsci13121216

Grover, S., & Pea, R. (2013). Computational thinking in K–12: A review of the state of the field. *Educational Researcher, 42*(1), 38–43. DOI: 10.3102/0013189X12463051

Haines, S., Krach, M., Pustaka, A., Li, Q., & Richman, L. (2019). The effects of computational thinking professional development on STEM teachers' perceptions and pedagogical practices. *Athens Journal of Sciences, 6*(2), 97–122. DOI: 10.30958/ajs.6-2-2

Haryani, E., Coben, W. W., Pleasants, B. A., & Fetters, M. K. (2021). Analysis of teachers' resources for integrating the skills of creativity and innovation, critical thinking and problem solving, collaboration, and communication in science classrooms. *Jurnal Pendidikan IPA Indonesia, 10*(1), 92–102. DOI: 10.15294/jpii.v10i1.27084

Haseski, H. I., & Ilic, U. (2019). An investigation of the data collection instruments developed to measure computational thinking. *Informatics in Education, 18*(2), 297–319. DOI: 10.15388/infedu.2019.14

Hassan, M. A., Habiba, U., Majeed, F., & Shoaib, M. (2021). Adaptive gamification in e-learning based on students' learning styles. *Interactive Learning Environments, 29*(4), 545–565. DOI: 10.1080/10494820.2019.1588745

Herodotou, C., Rienties, B., Verdin, B., & Boroowa, A. (2019). Predictive Learning Analytics "At Scale": Towards Guidelines to Successful Implementation in Higher Education Based on the Case of the Open University UK. *Journal of Learning Analytics, 6*(1), 85–95. DOI: 10.18608/jla.2019.61.5

Hestness, E., Ketelhut, D. J., McGinnis, J. R., & Plane, J. (2018). Professional knowledge building within an elementary teacher professional development experience on computational thinking in science education. *Journal of Technology and Teacher Education, 26*(3), 411–435.

Hew, K. F. (2016). Promoting engagement in online courses: What strategies can we learn from three highly rated MOOCS. *British Journal of Educational Technology, 47*(2), 320–341. DOI: 10.1111/bjet.12235

Hickey, D. T., & Schafer, N. J. (2006). Design-based, participation-centered approaches to classroom management. In C. M. Evertson, & C. S. Weinstein, C. S. (Eds.), Handbook of classroom management: research, practice, and contemporary issues. (pp. 281–308). Routledge.

Hong, J. C., Ye, J. H., Chen, P. H., & Yu, Y. Y. (2020). A checklist development for meaningful learning in classroom observation. *International Journal of Information and Education Technology (IJIET), 10*(10), 728–735. DOI: 10.18178/ijiet.2020.10.10.1450

Johler, M., Krumsvik, R. J., Bugge, H. E., & Helgevold, N. (2022, April). Teachers' perceptions of their role and classroom management practices in a technology rich primary school classroom. In *Frontiers in Education* (Vol. 7, p. 841385). Frontiers Media SA. https://doi.org/DOI: 10.3389/feduc.2022.841385

Kafyulilo, A., Fisser, P., Pieters, J., & Voogt, J. (2015). ICT use in science and mathematics teacher education in Tanzania: Developing technological pedagogical content knowledge. *Australasian Journal of Educational Technology*, *31*(4), 381–399. DOI: 10.14742/ajet.1240

Kalogiannakis, M., & Papadakis, S. (Eds.). (2020). *Handbook of research on tools for teaching computational thinking in P-12 education*. IGI Global. DOI: 10.4018/978-1-7998-4576-8

Kalogiannakis, M., Papadakis, S., & Zourmpakis, A.-I. (2021). Gamification in Science Education. A Systematic Review of the Literature. *Education Sciences*, *11*(1), 22. DOI: 10.3390/educsci11010022

Katchapakirin, K., Anutariya, C., & Supnithi, T. (2022). ScratchThAI: A conversation-based learning support framework for computational thinking development. *Education and Information Technologies*, *27*(6), 8533–8560. DOI: 10.1007/s10639-021-10870-z

Kelly, M. (2008). Incorporating Context Into TPCK-Based Instructional Design. In K. McFerrin, R. Weber, R. Carlsen & D. Willis (Eds.), *Proceedings of SITE 2008--Society for Information Technology & Teacher Education International Conference* (pp. 5257-5262). Las Vegas, Nevada, USA: Association for the Advancement of Computing in Education (AACE).

Kennedy, J., Gabriel, F., Korolkiewicz, M., Rets, I., & Rienties, B. (2025, February). Actionable learning analytics in education: an opportunity to close the learning loop. In *Frontiers in Education* (Vol. 10, p. 1571177). Frontiers Media SA. https://doi.org/DOI: 10.3389/feduc.2025.1571177

Klock, A. C. T., Gasparini, I., Pimenta, M. S., & Hamari, J. (2020). Tailored gamification: A review of literature. *International Journal of Human-Computer Studies*, *144*, 102495. DOI: 10.1016/j.ijhcs.2020.102495

Koivisto, J., & Hamari, J. (2019). The rise of motivational information systems: A review of gamification research. *International Journal of Information Management*, *45*, 191–210. DOI: 10.1016/j.ijinfomgt.2018.10.013

Kong, S. C., & Lai, M. (2022). A proposed computational thinking teacher development framework for K-12 guided by the TPACK model. *Journal of Computers in Education*, *9*(3), 379–402. DOI: 10.1007/s40692-021-00207-7

Kong, S. C., Lai, M., & Li, Y. (2023). Scaling up a teacher development programme for sustainable computational thinking education: TPACK surveys, concept tests and primary school visits. *Computers & Education, 194*, 104707. DOI: 10.1016/j.compedu.2022.104707

Lafuente Martínez, M., Lévêque, O., Benítez, I., Hardebolle, C., & Zufferey, J. D. (2022). Assessing computational thinking: Development and validation of the algorithmic thinking test for adults. *Journal of Educational Computing Research, 60*(6), 1436–1463. DOI: 10.1177/07356331211057819

Liu, Z. (2023). Integrating computational thinking into k-12 education: Bridging the gap between theories and practices: Bridging the gap between theories and practices. *STEM Education Review, 1*. Advance online publication. DOI: 10.54844/stemer.2023.0467

Liu, Z., Gearty, Z., Richard, E., Orrill, C. H., Kayumova, S., & Balasubramanian, R. (2024). Bringing computational thinking into classrooms: A systematic review on supporting teachers in integrating computational thinking into K-12 classrooms. *International Journal of STEM Education, 11*(1), 51. DOI: 10.1186/s40594-024-00510-6

Lockwood, J., & Mooney, A. (2017). A pilot study investigating the introduction of a computer-science course at second level focusing on computational thinking. *The Irish Journal of Education/Iris Eireannach an Oideachais, 42*, 108-127. https://www.jstor.org/stable/26607242

Ma, J., Han, X., Yang, J., & Cheng, J. (2015). Examining the necessary condition for engagement in an online learning environment based on learning analytics approach: The role of the instructor. *The Internet and Higher Education, 24*, 26–34. DOI: 10.1016/j.iheduc.2014.09.005

Mah, D.-K., & Ifenthaler, D. (2019). What do first-year students need? Digital badges for academic support to enhance student retention. *Journal of Applied Research in Higher Education, 12*(1), 86–96. DOI: 10.1108/JARHE-12-2018-0258

Menekse, M. (2015). Computer science teacher professional development in the United States: A review of studies published between 2004 and 2014. *Computer Science Education, 25*(4), 325–350. DOI: 10.1080/08993408.2015.1111645

Michigan Information Education System. (n.d.). Retrieved September 1, 2022 from https://studylib.net/doc/6828389/section-1--tpack-observation-checklist---meis

Mishra, P., & Koehler, M. J. (2006). Technological pedagogical content knowledge: A framework for teacher knowledge. *Teachers College Record, 108*(6), 1017–1054. DOI: 10.1111/j.1467-9620.2006.00684.x

Moltudal, S. H., Krumsvik, R. J., & Høydal, K. L. (2022). Adaptive learning technology in primary education: Implications for professional teacher knowledge and classroom management. *Frontiers in Education, 7*, 830536. DOI: 10.3389/feduc.2022.830536

Monterrat, B., Desmarais, M., Lavoué, E., & George, S. (2015). A player model for adaptive gamification in learning environments. In *Artificial Intelligence in Education: 17th International Conference, AIED 2015, Madrid, Spain, June 22-26, 2015.* [Springer International Publishing.]. *Proceedings, 17*, 297–306.

Mouza, C., Yadav, A., & Ottenbreit-Leftwich, A. (2018). Developing computationally literate teachers: Current perspectives and future directions for teacher preparation in computing education. *Journal of Technology and Teacher Education, 26*(3), 333–352. https://www.learntechlib.org/primary/p/184602/

National Research Council, Division of Behavioral, Board on Science Education, & Committee on a Conceptual Framework for New K-12 Science Education Standards. (2012). *A framework for K-12 science education: Practices, crosscutting concepts, and core ideas*. national academies press.

Ng, A. K., Atmosukarto, I., Cheow, W. S., Avnit, K., & Yong, M. H. (2021). Development and implementation of an online adaptive gamification platform for learning computational thinking. In *2021 IEEE Frontiers in Education Conference (FIE)* (pp. 1-6). IEEE. https://doi.org/DOI: 10.1109/FIE49875.2021.9637467

NGSS Lead States. (2013). *Next generation science standards: For states, by states*. National Academies Press.

Ogegbo, A. A., & Ramnarain, U. (2022). A systematic review of computational thinking in science classrooms. *Studies in Science Education, 58*(2), 203–230. DOI: 10.1080/03057267.2021.1963580

Ouyang, F., & Scharber, C. (2017). The influences of an experienced instructor's discussion design and facilitation on an online learning community development: A social network analysis study. *The Internet and Higher Education, 35*, 34–47. DOI: 10.1016/j.iheduc.2017.07.002

Papadakis, S. (2020). Apps to promote computational thinking concepts and coding skills in children of preschool and pre-primary school age. In *Mobile learning applications in early childhood education* (pp. 101–121). IGI Global Scientific Publishing. DOI: 10.4018/978-1-7998-1486-3.ch006

Papadakis, S. (2022). Apps to promote computational thinking and coding skills to young age children: A pedagogical challenge for the 21st century learners. [EDUPIJ]. *Educational Process: International Journal, 11*(1), 7–13. DOI: 10.22521/edupij.2022.111.1

Papadakis, St., Zourmpakis, A., Kasotaki, S., & Kalogiannakis, M. (2024). Teachers' Perspectives on Integrating Adaptive Gamification Applications into Science Teaching. *Journal of Electrical Systems, 20*(11s), 2593–2600. DOI: 10.52783/jes.7917

Pelletier, K. K., Brown, M., Brooks, D. C., McCormack, M., Reeves, J., Arbino, N., Bozkurt, A., Crawford, S., Czerniewicz, L., Gibson, R., Linder, K., Mason, J., & Mondelli, V. (2021). Australian Higher Education. In *2021 EDUCAUSE Horizon Report: Teaching and Learning Edition* (pp. 37-38). EDUCAUSE Publications.

Piaget, J. (1973). *The Child and Reality: Problems of Genetic Psychology* (Rosin, A., Trans.). Grossman.

Pusparini, F., Riandi, R., & Sriyati, S. (2017, September). Developing technological pedagogical content knowledge (TPACK) in animal physiology. In *Journal of Physics: Conference Series* (Vol. 895, No. 1, p. 012059). IOP Publishing. https://doi.org/DOI: 10.1088/1742-6596/895/1/012059

Rienties, B., Cross, S., & Zdrahal, Z. (2017). Implementing a learning analytics intervention and evaluation framework: What works?. *Big data and learning analytics in higher education: Current theory and practice*, 147-166. https://doi.org/DOI: 10.1007/978-3-319-06520-5_10

Santosa, E. B., & Sukmawati, F. (2024). Level of computational thinking and technological literacy skills to improve pre-service teacher learning innovation. *Jurnal Kependidikan: Jurnal Hasil Penelitian Dan Kajian Kepustakaan Di Bidang Pendidikan. Pengajaran Dan Pembelajaran, 10*(1), 338–352. DOI: 10.33394/jk.v10i1.10872

Schmidt-Crawford, D. A., Tai, S. J. D., Wang, W., & Jin, Y. (2016). Understanding teachers' TPACK through observation. In *Handbook of technological pedagogical content knowledge (TPACK) for educators* (pp. 107-118). Routledge.

Sentance, S., & Csizmadia, A. (2017). Computing in the curriculum: Challenges and strategies from a teacher's perspective. *Education and Information Technologies*, *22*(2), 469–495. DOI: 10.1007/s10639-016-9482-0

Sharma, L., & Srivastava, M. (2020). Teachers' motivation to adopt technology in higher education. *Journal of Applied Research in Higher Education*, *12*(4), 673–692. DOI: 10.1108/JARHE-07-2018-0156

Shehaj, A. (2022). Revolutionized learning: Education policy and digital reform in the eurozone. *European Policy Analysis*, *8*(3), 312–326. DOI: 10.1002/epa2.1158

Stamatios, P. (2024). Can preschoolers learn computational thinking and coding skills with ScratchJr? A systematic literature review. *International Journal of Educational Reform*, *33*(1), 28–61. DOI: 10.1177/10567879221076077

Strawhacker, A., Lee, M., & Bers, M. U. (2018). Teaching tools, teachers' rules: Exploring the impact of teaching styles on young children's programming knowledge in ScratchJr. *International Journal of Technology and Design Education*, *28*(2), 347–376. DOI: 10.1007/s10798-017-9400-9

Sullivan, A., & Bers, M. U. (2019). Computer science education in early childhood: The case of ScratchJr. *Journal of Information Technology Education. In Practice*, *18*, 113–138. DOI: 10.28945/4437

Tariq, R., Aponte Babines, B. M., Ramirez, J., Alvarez-Icaza, I., & Naseer, F. (2025). Computational thinking in STEM education: Current state-of-the-art and future research directions. *Frontiers of Computer Science*, *6*, 1480404. DOI: 10.3389/fcomp.2024.1480404

Teo, T. (2009). The impact of subjective norm and facilitating conditions on pre-service teachers' attitude toward computer use: A structural equation modeling of an extended technology acceptance model. *Journal of Educational Computing Research*, *40*(1), 89–109. DOI: 10.2190/EC.40.1.d

Thorman, J., & Fidalgo, P. (2014). Guidelines for online course moderation and community building from a student's perspective. *Journal of Online Learning and Teaching*, *10*(3), 374–388.

Tlili, A., Denden, M., Essalmi, F., Jemni, M., Chang, M., & Chen, N.-S. (2023). Automatic model ing learner's personality using learning analytics approach in an intelligent Moodle learning platform. *Interactive Learning Environments*, **•••**, 1–15. DOI: 10.1080/10494820.2019.1636084

Torrance, D., & Forde, C. (2017). Redefining what it means to be a teacher through professional standards: Implications for continuing teacher education. *European Journal of Teacher Education*, *40*(1), 110–126. DOI: 10.1080/02619768.2016.1246527

Tseng, S., Tsao, Y.-W., Yu, L.-C., Chan, C.-L., & Lai, K. R. (2016). Who will pass? Analyzing learner behaviors in MOOCs. *Research and Practice in Technology Enhanced Learning*, *11*(8), 8. Advance online publication. DOI: 10.1186/s41039-016-0033-5 PMID: 30613241

Tzafilkou, K., Perifanou, M. A., & Economides, A. A. (2021). Teachers' trainers' intention and motivation to transfer ICT training: The role of ICT individual factors, gender, and ICT self-efficacy. *Education and Information Technologies*, *26*(5), 5563–5589. DOI: 10.1007/s10639-021-10541-z

UNESCO. (2008). *UNESCO's ICT Competency Standards for Teachers.* https://unesdoc.unesco.org/ark:/48223/pf0000156207

UNICEF. (2018). *Raising Learning Outcomes: the opportunities and challenges of ICT for learning*. Retrieved from https://www.unicef.org/esa/media/2636/file/UNICEF-AKF-IU-2018-ICT-Education-WCAR-ESAR.pdf

Van Leeuwen, A. (2019). Teachers' perceptions of the usability of learning analytics reports in a flipped university course: When and how does information become actionable knowledge? *Educational Technology Research and Development*, *67*(5), 1043–1064. DOI: 10.1007/s11423-018-09639-y

Vee, A. (2017). *Coding literacy: How computer programming is changing writing*. Mit Press. DOI: 10.7551/mitpress/10655.001.0001

Vuorikari, R., Kluzer, S., & Punie, Y. (2022). *DigComp 2.2, The Digital Competence framework for citizens—With new examples of knowledge, skills and attitudes*. Publications Office of the European Union., DOI: 10.2760/115376

Wang, S., Wu, H., Kim, J. H., & Andersen, E. (2019). Adaptive learning material recommendation in online language education. In *Artificial Intelligence in Education: 20th International Conference, AIED 2019, Chicago, IL, USA, June 25-29, 2019* [Springer International Publishing.]. *Proceedings*, *20*(Part II), 298–302.

Werbach, K., & Hunter, D. (2012). *For the win* (Vol. 51). Philadelphia: Wharton digital press.

Wiley, K., Dimitriadis, Y., & Linn, M. (2024). A human-centred learning analytics approach for developing contextually scalable K-12 teacher dashboards. *British Journal of Educational Technology*, *55*(3), 845–885. DOI: 10.1111/bjet.13383

Wing, J. M. (2006). Computational thinking. *Communications of the ACM, 49*(3), 33–35. DOI: 10.1145/1118178.1118215

Wong, J., Baars, M., de Koning, B. B., van der Zee, T., Davis, D., Khalil, M., Houben, G. J., & Paas, F. (2019). Educational theories and learning analytics: From data to knowledge: The whole is greater than the sum of its parts. *Utilizing learning analytics to support study success*, 3-25. DOI: 10.1007/978-3-319-64792-0_1

Wong, K.-T., Osman, R., Goh, P. S. C., & Rahmat, M. K. (2013). Understanding Student Teachers' Behavioural Intention to Use Technology: Technology Acceptance Model (TAM) Validation and Testing. *International Journal of Instruction, 6*(1), 89–104.

Yadav, A., Gretter, S., Hambrusch, S., & Sands, P. (2016). Expanding computer science education in schools: Understanding teacher experiences and challenges. *Computer Science Education, 26*(4), 235–254. DOI: 10.1080/08993408.2016.1257418

Yadav, A., Stephenson, C., & Hong, H. (2017). Computational thinking for teacher education. *Communications of the ACM, 60*(4), 55–62. DOI: 10.1145/2994591

Yang, C. C., Wu, J. Y., & Ogata, H. (2025). Learning analytics dashboard-based self-regulated learning approach for enhancing students'e-book-based blended learning. *Education and Information Technologies, 30*(1), 35–56. DOI: 10.1007/s10639-024-12913-7

Zancajo, A., Verger, A., & Bolea, P. (2022). Digitalization and beyond: The effects of Covid-19 on post-pandemic educational policy and delivery in Europe. *Policy and Society, 41*(1), 111–128. DOI: 10.1093/polsoc/puab016

Zhang, L., & Nouri, J. (2019). A systematic review of learning computational thinking through Scratch in K-9. *Computers & Education, 141*, 103607. DOI: 10.1016/j.compedu.2019.103607

Zourmpakis, A. I., Kalogiannakis, M., & Papadakis, S. (2023a). Adaptive gamification in science education: An analysis of the impact of implementation and adapted game elements on students' motivation. *Computers, 12*(7), 143. DOI: 10.3390/computers12070143

Zourmpakis, A. I., Kalogiannakis, M., & Papadakis, S. (2024). The effects of adaptive gamification in science learning: A comparison between traditional inquiry-based learning and gender differences. *Computers, 13*(12), 324. DOI: 10.3390/computers13120324

Zourmpakis, A.-I., Kalogiannakis, M., & Papadakis, S. (2024). Education of Elementary Teachers on The Use of Adaptive Gamification Environment in Science Education. In Sardag, M., Kaya, G., & Sogut, M. (Eds.) *Proceedings Book Series-I of the ESERA 2023 Conference. Connecting Science Education with Cultural Heritage, Strand 4 - Digital Resources for Science Teaching and Learning* (co-ed. Napal, M., & Romano-Garcia, L.), 224-237, Cappadocia, Türkiye. Nobel Bilimsel Eserler.

Zourmpakis, A. I., Papadakis, S., & Kalogiannakis, M. (2022). Education of preschool and elementary teachers on the use of adaptive gamification in science education. *International Journal of Technology Enhanced Learning, 14*(1), 1–16. DOI: 10.1504/IJTEL.2022.120556

Zourmpakis, I.-A., Kalogiannakis, M., & Papadakis, St. (2023b). A Review of the Literature for Designing and Developing a Framework for Adaptive Gamification in Physics Education. In Taşar, M.-F., & Heron, P.-R.-L. (Eds.), *The International Handbook of Physics Education Research: Teaching Physics* (pp. 5.1–5.26). AIP Publishing., DOI: 10.1063/9780735425712_005

Chapter 13
AI-Powered Learning in the Global South:
Lessons From ChatGPT Use in Tanzanian Universities

Neema Mduma
http://orcid.org/0000-0002-4364-3124
Nelson Mandela African Institution of Science and Technology, Tanzania

ABSTRACT

This chapter explores how ChatGPT, a popular Artificial Intelligence (AI) tool, is being used in Tanzanian universities to support teaching and learning. It presents findings from a study conducted at the University of Dar es Salaam, University of Dodoma and Nelson Mandela African Institution of Science and Technology. The chapter discusses how students and lecturers are using ChatGPT, the benefits they experience and the challenges they face such as poor internet access, lack of training and missing university policies. While the study focuses on higher education, the findings also inform K–12 education by showing how AI can serve as virtual tutors, support personalized learning and expose policy or infrastructure gaps in schools. The chapter offers recommendations, policy suggestions and areas for future research. It fills an important gap, since few studies examine AI use in Tanzanian higher education. The insights shared can help universities and policymakers make better decisions about using AI tools in a responsible way.

INTRODUCTION: ARTIFICIAL INTELLIGENCE IN EDUCATION

Artificial Intelligence (AI) is rapidly reshaping education worldwide by transforming how students learn and lecturers teach (Vieriu & Petrea, 2025; Ruano-

DOI: 10.4018/979-8-3373-2637-5.ch013

Borbalan, 2025). Beyond its growing presence in classrooms, AI tools have been used to personalize learning, automate grading and improve student support services (Luckin et al., 2016; Walter, 2024). One of the most significant advancements in this area is the development of Large Language Models (LLM) like ChatGPT, which are capable of generating human-like text and providing instant feedback to users (Dwivedi et al., 2023; Meyer et al., 2023).

Research has also highlighted the broader educational value of AI, including its use in social robots to support interactive learning (Lampropoulos & Papadakis, 2025). Studies further show that ChatGPT can assist teaching in primary and early childhood education, particularly in Science, Technology, Engineering and Mathematics (STEM) activities (Uğraş, Uğraş, Papadakis, & Kalogiannakis, 2024a, 2024b). These examples show that the application of ChatGPT and similar AI tools is expanding across multiple educational contexts globally, not just in higher education. Notably, recent studies have shown its use in K–12 education, including early childhood and primary levels, particularly for STEM learning, language support and interactive classroom tasks (Uğraş et al., 2024a; 2024b; Lampropoulos & Papadakis, 2025). This suggests that insights from higher education may inform AI integration strategies in earlier stages of schooling (Lavidas, Papadakis et al., 2022).

In Tanzania, universities are gradually adopting these AI tools to support both students and lecturers in higher education (Matto, 2024; Sarakikya & Kitula, 2024; Ngulugulu & Mgina, 2024). ChatGPT, developed by OpenAI is a smart chatbot that can answer questions, explain difficult topics and assist with writing tasks (Ray, 2023; Dwivedi et al., 2023). It works by processing text input and producing relevant responses which makes it useful for academic purposes such as summarizing information, improving grammar, generating ideas and supporting research (Chukwuere, 2024; Dwivedi et al., 2023). Similar to findings in global studies, students in Tanzania are exploring ChatGPT informally to supplement their learning, often without institutional frameworks to guide responsible use.

To understand the use of AI in Tanzanian higher education, it is important to consider how the system itself is structured. Higher education in Tanzania is overseen by the Ministry of Education, Science and Technology (MoEST) and regulated by the Tanzania Commission for Universities (TCU), which is responsible for accreditation and quality assurance. The system is made up of both public and private universities where, public universities are mainly funded through government allocations, tuition fees and research grants. Private universities, on the other hand, are often sponsored by faith-based organizations, non-governmental organizations or private investors. Funding challenges are common in both types of institutions, but they are more visible in public universities where large student populations stretch available resources (Mgaiwa & Ishengoma, 2023; Mgaiwa, 2018).

The Higher Education Students' Loans Board (HESLB) also plays an important role by providing loans to students to cover tuition and living expenses. However, limited resources mean that not all applicants are supported. These funding constraints, together with an increased number of student enrollments, have led to large class sizes, staff shortages and limited access to modern teaching facilities. This environment makes digital innovations like ChatGPT most valuable (Mubofu & Kainkwa, 2023).

As class sizes grow and academic resources remain limited, students often struggle to receive individual attention from lecturers (Matto, 2024; Mubofu & Kainkwa, 2023). ChatGPT can help bridge this gap by acting as a virtual tutor, offering round-the-clock academic support (Al Shloul et al., 2024; Shabbir et al., 2024). For lecturers, it can save time by helping prepare lecture notes, create tests and draft assignments (Kondoro, 2025; Atlas, 2023). These benefits are most valuable in resource-constrained environments where both staff and students face competing demands (Simatupang et al., 2025; Shabbir et al., 2024).

While these benefits are promising, the successful use of ChatGPT also depends on broader policy frameworks. National strategies such as the Tanzania Development Vision 2050 (United Republic of Tanzania, 2025) and the Education Sector Development Programme (ESDP) highlight the importance of ICT integration and digital skills for national development (United Republic of Tanzania, 2025; MoEST, 2025a). However, while these strategies provide direction at the national level, universities continue to face everyday challenges that affect how such policies are put into practice. Comparative global studies show that policy design and institutional culture significantly affect technology acceptance in education (Lavidas et al., 2022). These insights help to frame Tanzania's case within wider debates about how educational institutions can adapt to fast-changing AI tools.

At the same time, the integration of ChatGPT in higher education also presents several challenges (García-López et al., 2025; Baig & Yadegaridehkordi, 2024; Naznin et al., 2025). For instance, it's estimated that 86% of rural people in Tanzania are not connected to the internet, compared to 44.6% in urban areas, highlighting a serious digital divide that affects students in rural areas (Internet Society, 2019). Also, only 17% of women have mobile internet access, compared to 35% of men, further worsening inequity (UNESCO, 2023). Combined with limited access to digital devices, these figures show that many students, particularly in rural or underserved areas, are at a disadvantage (Amoah et al., 2025; Indrawati et al., 2025). Concerns also remain about misuse, with some students copying answers without understanding the material (Bin-Nashwan et al., 2023; Li et al., 2024). Moreover, the lack of clear institutional policies adds to uncertainty about how AI should be used responsibly in academic settings (Matto & Ponera, 2025; Funa & Gabay, 2025).

Despite these challenges, the potential of ChatGPT in Tanzanian universities remains promising. With proper training, guidelines and improved access to digital infrastructure, this AI tool could play a major role in shaping the future of education in the country. This chapter explores how ChatGPT is currently used in Tanzanian universities. It also examines its impact on teaching and learning, the barriers to its effective use and recommendations for moving forward.

While the primary focus is on higher education, the insights gained are not limited to universities. Many of the lessons also apply directly to K-12 settings where virtual tutors can support homework, reading practice and basic skills reinforcement. Prior work shows that AI can assist primary and early childhood learning and classroom interaction, including formative feedback and language support (Uğraş et al., 2024a; Uğraş et al., 2024b; Lampropoulos & Papadakis, 2025). In Tanzania, national priorities emphasize digital inclusion and AI literacy across both higher and basic education (MoEST, 2025a; MoEST, 2025). This means that the chapter also provides insights that can guide K-12 schools in considering safe and effective ways to adopt AI-powered virtual tutors.

LITERATURE REVIEW: CHATGPT IN HIGHER EDUCATION

The use of ChatGPT is becoming more common in Tanzanian universities as both students and lecturers explore new ways to improve learning and teaching (Mbwambo & Kaaya, 2024; Komba, 2024). Unlike traditional learning tools, ChatGPT offers a two-way interaction where users can ask questions and get instant, human-like answers. This makes it more engaging than static textbooks or recorded lectures (Njiku et al., 2024; Komba, 2024).

While these trends are visible in Tanzania, they also reflect broader developments across Africa and globally. Studies in South Africa and Botswana, for example, have shown that students are experimenting with ChatGPT to support academic writing, problem-solving and exam preparation (Chukwuere, 2024; Indrawati et al., 2025). Similar findings have been reported in Asia and Europe, where ChatGPT is increasingly used for personalized tutoring, language support and critical thinking development (Naznin et al., 2025; Baig & Yadegaridehkordi, 2024). This suggests that Tanzanian universities are part of a wider global shift in higher education, even though challenges such as infrastructure gaps and digital inequality are more pronounced in the local context (Internet Society, 2019; UNESCO, 2023).

The integration of ChatGPT can also be better understood through established theoretical frameworks. The Technology Acceptance Model (TAM) has been widely used to explain how students and lecturers adopt digital tools, emphasizing the role of perceived usefulness and ease of use (Davis, 1989; Venkatesh & Davis,

2000). Similarly, Diffusion of Innovations (DOI) theory (Rogers, 2003) highlights how early adopters can influence wider acceptance within academic communities. These frameworks help situate the Tanzanian case in a broader scholarly context, showing that depends on access to technology as well as cultural, institutional and social factors.

Furthermore, several meta-analyses have highlighted the potential of AI tools like ChatGPT to transform higher education worldwide. Dwivedi et al. (2023) and García-López et al. (2025) argue that while benefits such as efficiency, creativity and accessibility are clear, unresolved concerns about academic integrity, plagiarism and over-reliance remain. These global insights resonate with local findings in Tanzania, where lecturers acknowledge both the opportunities and risks of using ChatGPT (Kondoro, 2025; Matto, 2024).

In the Tanzanian context, ChatGPT is helping students manage the pressures of large classes and limited lecturer availability. Many students describe it as a "study companion" that can explain difficult topics in areas like law, computer science and economics, often by simplifying complex concepts into everyday language. This kind of support is more useful for first-year students who are still adjusting to university life and academic expectations (Matto, 2024; Mubofu & Kainkwa, 2023). Students also report using ChatGPT to review course material, practice exam questions and brainstorm ideas for projects.

Another important use is in academic writing where students often struggle with grammar, clarity and organization, especially when English is not their first language. ChatGPT offers immediate feedback that helps them polish their writing and gain confidence in structuring assignments. As Kondoro (2025) notes, many students feel that AI support improves their ability to communicate ideas more effectively, even if they still rely on lecturers for final review and feedback.

Lecturers are also beginning to use ChatGPT, though often more cautiously. Some report that it helps them prepare lecture notes, generate questions for classroom discussions and summarize complex research for teaching purposes. Others see it as a way to save time on routine tasks so they can focus more on mentoring and direct interaction with students (Papadakis et al., 2024a, 2024b). However, most lecturers treat ChatGPT as a supplementary tool rather than a replacement for their expertise. Furthermore, some prefer not to disclose their use of it, fearing it might be viewed as unprofessional (Kondoro, 2025).

Despite its growing use, there are differences from one institution to another. Larger urban universities with better internet access and infrastructure report more frequent and diverse uses of ChatGPT, while students in other settings face barriers such as weak connectivity, limited devices and lack of awareness (Matto & Ponera, 2025). These gaps highlight the importance of investment in infrastructure and training if all students are to benefit equally.

Overall, student perceptions are mostly positive, with many seeing ChatGPT as a way to work more independently and explore new ideas (Komba, 2024; Mbwambo & Kaaya, 2024). At the same time, concerns remain about academic honesty, as some students admit to copying AI-generated responses without fully understanding the material. This shows the importance of universities providing training and guidelines so that ChatGPT is used responsibly, in ways that support learning rather than replace it.

While most studies in this chapter examine higher education, related evidence from K-12 shows similar patterns for AI-supported tutoring and classroom use. Studies in primary and early childhood contexts report that ChatGPT-supported activities can encourage learning and prompt critical thinking, provided teachers guide use and teach AI literacy (Uğraş et al., 2024a; Uğraş et al., 2024b; Walter, 2024). Work on social robots in education also highlights how AI mediation can support engagement and differentiation for younger learners (Lampropoulos & Papadakis, 2025). Taken together, this literature suggests that the benefits and risks described for university students such as feedback, personalization, language support, over-reliance and integrity also appear in K-12 settings. In schools, however there is an even stronger need for teacher guidance and age-appropriate safeguards.

CASE STUDIES FROM TANZANIAN UNIVERSITIES

To understand how ChatGPT is being adopted and experienced in Tanzanian universities, this section presents case studies from different types of institutions; the University of Dar es Salaam (UDSM), the University of Dodoma (UDOM) and the Nelson Mandela African Institution of Science and Technology (NM-AIST). The goal is to provide evidence from the ground to support the wider discussions in this chapter about AI adoption, opportunities and challenges in higher education.

Study Objectives

The main objectives of this study were to:

i) To investigate the level of awareness and use of ChatGPT among university students and lecturers.
ii) To understand how ChatGPT is used in academic work and teaching support.
iii) To identify barriers and enablers of ChatGPT adoption in Tanzanian universities.
iv) To compare the use of ChatGPT across different institutional settings.

Study Design

The study followed a qualitative approach involving three higher learning institutions in Tanzania which are UDSM, UDOM and NM-AIST. These universities were selected to represent a range of academic environments in terms of size, focus areas, student backgrounds and levels of digital development. The aim was to gather a balanced view of how ChatGPT is being used in different university settings in the country.

UDSM is one of Tanzania's oldest and most established universities with a large and diverse student population, along with a relatively advanced digital infrastructure. Many students at UDSM have access to computer labs, personal laptops and campus Wi-Fi, especially within faculties like Engineering, Social Sciences and Education.

UDOM is one of the largest universities in Tanzania in terms of student enrollment. It has several colleges and attracts students from different regions, including many from rural backgrounds. Although UDOM has made investments in digital infrastructure, not all students have consistent access to internet or personal devices.

NM-AIST is a research-based institution with a strong emphasis on science, engineering, Information and Communication Technology (ICT) and innovation. All students are postgraduates pursuing Master's or PhD programs, and they come from both within Tanzania and other countries across the region. Many students have personal laptops and are more tech-savvy than their counterparts at other public universities.

Ethical Considerations

This study followed ethical guidelines to make sure all participants were treated with respect and fairness. Participation was voluntary and no one was forced or pressured to take part in the research. Before data collection, each participant was informed about the purpose of the study and how the information would be used.

Participants were also assured that their responses would remain confidential. Their names, identities or any personal information were not recorded or included in the study report. The focus was only on collecting general views and experiences related to the use of ChatGPT in university settings. During the interviews and discussions, participants were free to skip any question they did not want to answer or stop at any point without giving a reason. The research team made sure that all conversations and notes were handled carefully and stored in a secure manner. After the data was collected and analyzed, all identifying details were removed to protect participants' privacy.

Data Collection Methods

Semi-structured interviews, focus group discussions and short questionnaires were used as the main tools to collect information on how ChatGPT is being used in Tanzanian universities. These tools were chosen to allow participants to share their thoughts freely while also giving the researcher a way to collect useful data.

Semi-structured interviews were conducted with lecturers and ICT support staff at each university. These interviews followed a flexible guide that included key questions and allowed for open discussion. This helped the researcher explore individual experiences and opinions in more depth. Lecturers were asked about their awareness of ChatGPT, whether they use it in teaching or academic work and what challenges or benefits they have observed. ICT staff were asked about digital access, internet infrastructure and any university-level efforts related to AI or digital learning tools.

Focus Group Discussions (FGDs) were held with groups of students at each university. Each group had between six and eight participants from different academic programs. The FGDs allowed students to share how they learned about ChatGPT, how they use it, what they find helpful or difficult and whether they received any guidance or training. These discussions also helped to understand peer-to-peer learning, where students share tools and tricks with each other informally.

Short questionnaires were also used to gather basic information about how often students and lecturers use ChatGPT, what they use it for and what devices or internet access they rely on. These questionnaires provided quick insights that supported the more detailed conversations in interviews and group discussions. The questions were kept simple and short to encourage honest and easy responses, especially for participants with limited time.

Data collection was done over a three-week period from February to March 2025. During this time, the research team visited all three universities to collect information from students, lecturers and ICT staff. The team worked closely with coordinators at each institution to help identify suitable participants and arrange times for interviews, focus group discussions and questionnaire sessions. This coordination made it easier to reach a wide range of participants and ensure that the data collection activities fit well into the academic schedules of each university.

Participants

A total of 48 participants were involved in this study. These participants were selected to reflect different roles, experiences and academic backgrounds within each of the three universities. The group included students, lecturers and administrative or ICT support staff.

Among them, 24 students took part in focus group discussions. Each university contributed 8 students, selected from various academic levels and programs. The selection included both undergraduate and postgraduate students, depending on the type of institution. For example, at NM-AIST, all students were postgraduates, while UDSM and UDOM included a mix of first year to final-year undergraduate students. The students represented different fields such as Education, Social Sciences, Engineering and ICT. This mix helped to ensure that the study captured a broad view of how ChatGPT is used across academic disciplines.

In addition, 15 lecturers were interviewed through one-on-one conversations, with 5 lecturers chosen from each university. The lecturers came from a range of departments, including those that are traditionally more theory-based like Humanities and Education, as well as those in technical areas like Engineering and ICT. Some of the lecturers had used ChatGPT personally, while others had only heard about it through students or colleagues. Their views provided important insight into how staff perceive the use of AI tools in teaching and academic work.

To understand the institutional context, the study also included 9 administrative and ICT support staff, with 3 participants from each university. These staff members were responsible for digital services, e-learning systems or academic coordination. Their input helped explain the availability of digital infrastructure, current efforts to support AI use and the level of institutional readiness to adopt new technologies like ChatGPT.

Data Analysis

After data collection was completed, the research team reviewed and organized the information gathered from interviews, focus group discussions and questionnaires. Because this was a qualitative study, the focus was not on numbers alone but also on understanding the experiences, views and patterns shared by participants across the three universities.

The audio recordings from interviews and focus group discussions were transcribed into written text. These transcripts were then read several times to identify common themes, ideas and concerns raised by students, lecturers and ICT staff. Key points were grouped into categories such as “ways students use ChatGPT,” “challenges with access,” “attitudes of lecturers” and “institutional efforts.”

For the questionnaire data, basic statistics were used to summarize responses. These included the number of students who had used ChatGPT, how often they used it and what they used it for. Bar charts were created to help visualize these findings.

The graphs made it easier to compare results across the three institutions and to spot similarities and differences in how ChatGPT is being used.

To ensure fairness, the analysis looked at each university separately before making cross-university comparisons. This allowed the research team to see how digital access, student background and university type influenced the use of ChatGPT. The combination of open-ended discussions and simple numerical data gave a rich picture of how ChatGPT is currently used in Tanzanian universities. This approach helped to understand what is happening and why certain patterns exist.

RESULTS

University of Dar es Salaam (UDSM)

At the University of Dar es Salaam, student awareness and use of ChatGPT were found to be relatively high. Most students who took part in the study had already used ChatGPT, especially those studying in the faculties of Humanities, Education and Information and Communication Technology (ICT). Out of the eight students selected from UDSM, six said they had used ChatGPT at least once. They mainly used it for writing assignments, correcting grammar and preparing for exams.

Figure 1. ChatGPT Usage Among Students at UDSM

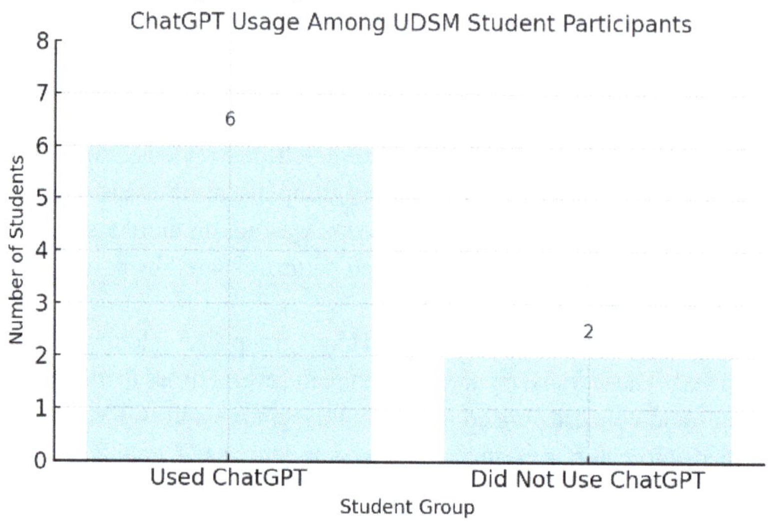

The Figure 1 above shows the number of students who used ChatGPT compared to those who had not. As seen in the graph, only two students had never used it, while the rest were familiar with the platform and had tried it at least once.

Students shared that they usually accessed ChatGPT through their mobile phones using campus Wi-Fi or personal data bundles. Most of them were using the free version, which sometimes limited their experience due to slow responses or restricted access during busy hours. Still, they found it helpful, especially when working on individual tasks outside of class.

Lecturers at UDSM also noticed that students were starting to use AI tools more often. Some lecturers had used ChatGPT themselves to prepare teaching materials or draft sample texts. However, many said they were not comfortable talking about it publicly, as there was no official policy or training on how to use AI in academic settings. This lack of clear guidance made some lecturers cautious, even though they saw the benefits of the tool.

One ICT support officer who was interviewed said something that stood out:

"Students are already using ChatGPT. It's happening. What we lack is guidance on how to use it in a good way."

This quote highlights a key issue at UDSM where, the technology is already being used, but both students and staff need proper direction on how to use it responsibly. The university has the infrastructure such as computer labs and Wi-Fi but more efforts are needed to provide training, set rules and raise awareness about ethical and productive use of ChatGPT in academic work.

University of Dodoma (UDOM)

At the University of Dodoma, the use of ChatGPT among students was lower compared to other universities in this study. Out of the eight student participants from UDOM, only four said they had used ChatGPT before. The Figure 2 below shows an equal split between students who had used the tool and those who had not.

Figure 2. ChatGPT Usage Among Students at UDOM

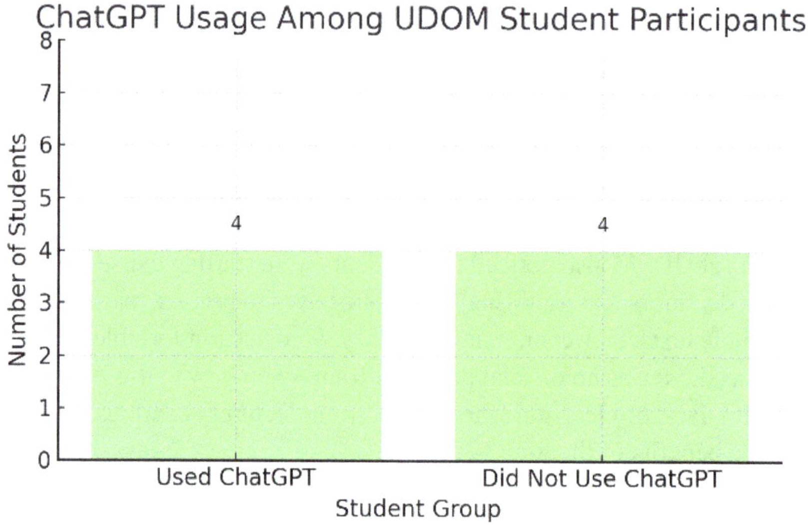

Students who had used ChatGPT said they mostly accessed it through their mobile phones. They used it occasionally, often for small tasks like checking grammar, summarizing lecture notes or getting help with difficult words in assignments. Their use was not frequent and they mentioned that the experience sometimes felt slow or limited because they were using the free version with unstable internet.

A key reason for the low usage at UDOM was poor internet access. Several students said they faced difficulties connecting to reliable Wi-Fi, especially in hostels or outside lecture hours. Many of them relied on mobile data, which they described as expensive and not always fast enough to support AI tools. One student shared,

> *"Sometimes I want to use ChatGPT to check my work, but the connection is too weak or I don't have enough data."*

Despite these challenges, UDOM stood out in one area; institutional efforts to raise awareness about AI. One department in the College of Informatics and Virtual Education organized a seminar on AI and digital tools in early 2025, which was attended by over 200 students. The seminar introduced tools like ChatGPT and encouraged students to explore how they could support learning.

Lecturers at UDOM had mixed views about ChatGPT. Some showed interest in how the tool could help with lesson planning, generating test questions or giving quick feedback on assignments. However, others were concerned that students might misuse it to complete work without proper understanding. One lecturer explained,

> *"We don't want students to stop thinking for themselves. We need to guide them on how to use AI wisely."*

Overall, the case of UDOM shows that even in universities where digital access is limited, there is growing interest in AI tools. The efforts by some departments to promote awareness are a positive sign, but students still face several barriers like data costs and poor connectivity. With better infrastructure and more structured training, tools like ChatGPT could play a bigger role in improving learning at UDOM.

Nelson Mandela African Institution of Science and Technology (NM-AIST)

Among the three universities studied, NM-AIST showed the highest level of ChatGPT use. All eight student participants from NM-AIST had used the tool before, and several of them said they used it regularly, even on a daily basis. The Figure 3 below shows that every student involved in the study had tried ChatGPT, with none reporting that they had never used it.

Figure 3. ChatGPT Usage Among Students at NM-AIST

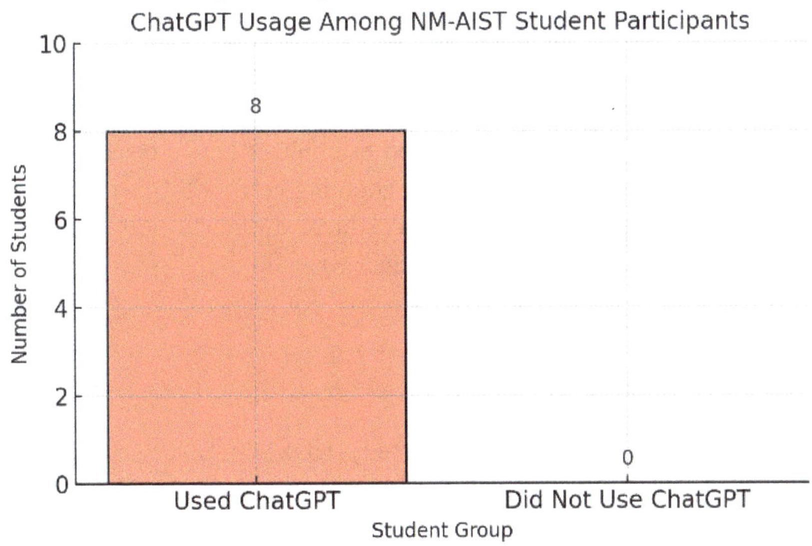

Students explained that they found ChatGPT very helpful, especially for academic tasks that require writing and organization. They used it to write project reports, rephrase technical content to make it easier to understand and prepare for presentations. Some mentioned that ChatGPT helped them express scientific ideas, especially when writing in English, which is not their first language.

Students at NM-AIST are mostly postgraduates, and many of them have a strong background in technology and research. They have access to personal laptops and the university offers reliable internet access across most parts of the campus. This makes it easier for them to explore and use AI tools like ChatGPT in their day-to-day academic work.

Lecturers at NM-AIST also showed a more open and positive attitude towards ChatGPT compared to lecturers at UDSM and UDOM. Three out of five lecturers interviewed were already using ChatGPT in their work. Some used it to prepare lecture materials, while others used it to support student research. One lecturer in the school of Life Sciences and Bioengineering (LiSBE) shared that he helped students draft abstracts for their research papers using ChatGPT. After drafting, they would hold review sessions to discuss and improve the writing together. He said this approach saved time and helped students learn how to write well.

An ICT officer from NM-AIST made a statement that captured the university's forward-thinking attitude:

"At NM-AIST, the mindset is different. We see ChatGPT as a tool to support innovation, not something to fear."

This mindset reflects the university's focus on science, innovation and problem-solving. The institution encourages its staff and students to explore new technologies and use them to improve learning, teaching and research. While there are still no official policies in place to guide the use of AI tools, the university environment is already creating space for experimentation and growth.

Therefore, NM-AIST represents a good example of how a research-based and tech-savvy institution can lead the way in adopting new tools like ChatGPT. With the right infrastructure, skilled users and a positive attitude towards innovation, AI can become a powerful support tool in higher education.

CROSS-CASE ANALYSIS

The three universities involved in this study; UDSM, UDOM and NM-AIST offered different experiences and levels of engagement with ChatGPT. By comparing their cases, we can see how factors like digital access, academic focus, institutional culture and support affect how AI tools are used in higher education (Table 1).

Table 1. Summary of ChatGPT Usage, Access and Institutional Support Across the Three Universities

Theme	UDSM	UDOM	NM-AIST
Student Awareness	High	Moderate	Very High
Access to Devices	Good	Mixed	Good
Internet Reliability	Moderate	Low	High
Formal AI Training	None	Some awareness efforts	Emerging in curriculum
Lecturer Use	Informal and cautious	Limited	Active and exploratory
Institutional Policy	Not yet developed	Not yet developed	In early stages

Student Awareness and Usage

Student awareness of ChatGPT varied across the three universities. At UDSM, awareness was high and most students had tried using ChatGPT, mainly for assignments and exam preparation. At UDOM, awareness was moderate, with only half of the students in the study having used the tool. Usage at UDOM was also more basic; students mostly used ChatGPT for grammar checking and brief summaries. In contrast, all students from NM-AIST had used ChatGPT, often for advanced academic tasks such as report writing and rephrasing technical research content. This shows that institutions with stronger digital skills and a focus on innovation are more likely to see regular and effective AI use.

Digital Access and Infrastructure

Access to devices like laptops and smartphones was fairly consistent across all three institutions. However, UDOM had a more mixed situation, with some students depending completely on shared facilities. The big difference was in internet quality as UDSM and NM-AIST had more reliable Wi-Fi, especially in learning areas, while students at UDOM often struggled with slow or unreliable connections. Poor internet access was a major reason why students at UDOM did not use ChatGPT more often, even if they were interested.

AI Training and Guidance

None of the universities had formal training programs for using AI tools, but some early steps had been taken. At UDOM, a department had organized an awareness seminar that introduced ChatGPT and other AI tools to students. NM-AIST had gone a step further by beginning to include AI-related topics in coursework and encouraging hands-on exploration. UDSM had not yet taken any formal action, even though both students and staff were using the tool informally. This suggests that AI use is growing from the bottom up driven by users rather than institutions.

Lecturer Engagement

Lecturers' views and use of ChatGPT differed across all institutions, with most at UDSM and UDOM being cautious. Some used ChatGPT privately but were hesitant to talk about it openly, mainly due to concerns about academic integrity or lack of clear guidance. At NM-AIST, lecturers were more open and some were even using ChatGPT as part of teaching strategies. They used it in tasks such as helping students write abstracts or simplify complex topics. However, they also acknowledged some disadvantages including the risk of hallucinations. In such cases, the tool may generate inaccurate or misleading information. This makes it necessary for users to have prior knowledge of the topic and to double-check outputs before use. Lecturer support is very important, as it shapes how students use AI and whether it is seen as a learning tool or a shortcut.

Institutional Readiness and Policy

None of the three universities had clear internal policies about AI use at the time of the study however, there was a difference in attitude. At UDOM and UDSM, the lack of policy created uncertainty, and many users felt they were "on their own" when using ChatGPT. NM-AIST, while also lacking formal policy, had a more open environment that encouraged discussion and exploration of new tools. It is important to note that all institutions were aware of the National Guidelines for Artificial Intelligence in Education, but had not yet adapted them into university-level rules or strategies.

Key Patterns and Lessons

One of the most important lessons from this study is that students need reliable access to the internet and digital devices to make full use of AI tools. In places where students have strong Wi-Fi and access to personal laptops or university computer labs such as NM-AIST and parts of UDSM; ChatGPT is used more often and in more useful ways. Students in these environments were able to explore the tool not just for grammar checking or simple answers, but also for writing reports, preparing presentations and improving their academic writing. On the other hand, students at UDOM, who struggled with internet access and data costs, used ChatGPT less frequently and mostly for basic tasks. This shows that improving digital infrastructure is key to helping more students benefit from AI in education.

Another pattern is that the culture and focus of the university affects how people view and use AI. At NM-AIST, where the focus is on research, science and innovation, both students and lecturers were more open to using ChatGPT. They saw it as a tool to support learning, make research easier and improve communication. The university encourages students to try new technology, which creates a supportive environment for using AI. In contrast, some lecturers at UDOM and UDSM were hesitant or uncertain about using ChatGPT because there was no clear direction from their institutions. This shows that when a university promotes innovation and digital learning, it becomes easier for AI tools to be accepted and used in helpful ways.

Across all three universities, students and staff showed interest in using ChatGPT, but many of them said they had never received any training. Some students were using the tool only for quick answers, without knowing how to check if the information was correct. Others were not aware of all the features that could help with academic writing or research. Lecturers also said they were not sure how to include ChatGPT in their teaching. These findings show that training is very important to guide the proper use of AI tools in ways that supports learning and uphold academic standards. Training can also help prevent misuse and promote responsible use of technology.

Furthermore, the study showed that policies are missing in most universities. Even though students and staff are already using ChatGPT, many are not sure what is allowed and what is not. Some lecturers are using the tool privately, but they avoid talking about it because they fear it may be seen as unprofessional. Without rules and guidelines, people are left to guess what is acceptable. This creates confusion and can lead to problems, such as students using AI to complete assignments without understanding the content. Having university-level policies would help set clear expectations, support ethical use and give students and lecturers the confidence to use AI tools in a responsible manner. These findings, though based on university settings, also offer valuable insights for AI use in K–12 education.

CHALLENGES AND OPPORTUNITIES OF CHATGPT IN TANZANIAN UNIVERSITIES

While ChatGPT is beginning to find its place in Tanzanian universities, its use is shaped by both serious challenges and promising opportunities. Barriers such as poor internet connectivity, high costs, lack of awareness and unclear policies limit how effectively the tool can be used. On the other hand, ChatGPT also presents new possibilities for improving teaching, learning, administration and innovation if these challenges are addressed.

The effective use of ChatGPT in Tanzanian universities is constrained by persistent digital and policy gaps. Internet connectivity remains inconsistent, especially outside major campuses, creating inequities in access (Internet Society, 2019; UNESCO, 2023). Furthermore, the absence of clear institutional policies leads to uncertainty about acceptable use, limiting the integration of AI into teaching and learning (Matto & Ponera, 2025; Funa & Gabay, 2025). These structural challenges recur throughout this study and shape the unequal adoption of ChatGPT across institutions.

Another important factor influencing the use of ChatGPT in Tanzanian universities is awareness and digital literacy. This factor determines whether students and lecturers are able to use the tool effectively for learning and teaching. Although many students have heard of the tool, some use it only for quick answers without checking the accuracy or learning how to apply it in their studies. Lecturers also show mixed feelings, with some using ChatGPT to prepare materials while others remain hesitant due to limited training or institutional support (Kondoro, 2025). As Matto and Ponera (2025) explain, knowing how to use AI responsibly through critical questioning, verification of responses and avoiding over-reliance is just as important as access. Without training, both students and staff risk misusing ChatGPT or failing to benefit from its full potential.

Furthermore, cost of accessing advanced features forces most students to rely on the free version of the tool. Most students use the free version of ChatGPT, which is often slow, limited in quality and unreliable when many users are online. Matto (2024) observes that this creates frustration among students who want to use the tool for assignments or exam preparation. Since the premium version is expensive, access to advanced features remains out of reach for many. Universities could play an important role by negotiating institutional licenses or providing alternatives through affordable or open-source platforms.

In addition to that, concerns about academic integrity have also emerged. Some students rely on ChatGPT to complete assignments without understanding the content, which raises questions about plagiarism and the quality of learning. Lecturers worry that this reliance may reduce students' ability to think critically and write independently (Komba, 2024). Addressing this requires guidance and training so that students use ChatGPT as a support tool rather than a shortcut.

Despite the many challenges identified, the use of ChatGPT also presents opportunities for enhancing teaching, learning and student support in Tanzanian universities. It can improve access to information and assist students outside the classroom by acting as a tutor available at any time. Universities could also integrate ChatGPT into their websites and student portals to provide quick responses to questions about registration, timetables or library services so as to reduce the administrative pressure. For learning, ChatGPT can help students strengthen their research, writing and problem-solving skills, as well as prepare them for future careers through support with job applications and interview practice.

There is also potential for fostering innovation where, students and research groups can use ChatGPT to explore ideas, structure projects and develop local solutions to real-world problems. Universities could encourage such innovation through training hubs and partnerships with the private sector. This would support entrepreneurship and prepare graduates for the growing role of AI in the job market.

Another opportunity is making education more inclusive particularly by supporting students who learn better in Swahili or other local languages. As ChatGPT and similar tools develop, they can be adapted to work better with Swahili and other local languages. This would support students who learn best in their mother tongue and improve access for those from rural or underserved backgrounds. At the same time, AI tools can help universities collect and analyze learning data to track student progress and provide early support where needed.

Furthermore, ChatGPT opens doors for collaboration where, Tanzanian universities can learn from international experiences and share their own lessons with global partners. By building partnerships with universities abroad and engaging with AI experts, institutions can strengthen their capacity. Involving the private sector can also help them position themselves as active contributors to the global conversation on AI in education.

IMPLICATIONS FOR K-12 AND VIRTUAL TUTORS IN TANZANIA

Although the evidence of this chapter comes from universities, the findings also have implications for basic education. The same access constraints that limit university use such as unreliable connectivity and device gaps are often more severe in primary and secondary schools. Any plan for introducing virtual tutors in K-12 must therefore combine pedagogy with improvements in connectivity and access to devices (UNESCO, 2023; MoEST, 2025a).

Beyond infrastructure, teacher capacity is another essential factor. Just as lecturers require support, schoolteachers also need practical AI literacy. This includes learning how to design effective prompts, check the accuracy of AI outputs, guide students to think for themselves and use AI mainly as a tool for feedback rather than ready-made answers (Walter, 2024). Strengthening local language support, particularly in Swahili, would further ensure that virtual tutors are inclusive and equitable for younger learners across diverse regions.

Equally important are safeguards to ensure responsible use of AI tools. Introducing age-appropriate safeguards, privacy protections and classroom rules can help prevent over-reliance on AI and protect student data. To support this, small pilot programs could be developed within existing structures such as after-school tuitions or remedial classes that many schools already run to help struggling learners. In addition, targeted support could be introduced in early secondary (Pre-Form I) to strengthen the transition from primary to secondary education, which is often a difficult stage for many students. These pilots could be co-designed with teachers and aligned with national curriculum priorities to ensure that virtual tutor initiatives are relevant, practical and supportive of Tanzania's broader education goals (MoEST, 2025; MoEST, 2025a).

COMPARATIVE PERSPECTIVES ON TANZANIA AND OTHER RESOURCE-CONSTRAINED CONTEXTS

This chapter focuses on Tanzanian universities, but it is also important to compare their experiences with those of other countries in sub-Saharan Africa and beyond. Such comparisons help reveal whether the challenges and opportunities in Tanzania are unique or part of broader trends in resource-constrained education systems.

In Kenya, universities face similar barriers related to internet costs, limited infrastructure and unequal access to digital devices. Mtebe and Raisamo (2014) found that although many Kenyan and Tanzanian lecturers recognize the potential of digital technologies, poor internet and limited institutional support slow down adoption. Recent studies confirm that while Kenyan students are eager to use AI tools, they often rely on mobile data due to connectivity constraints, similar to Tanzanian students (Woldegiorgis, 2025).

In Nigeria, ChatGPT has quickly gained popularity among students, especially for assignment support, summarization and grammar checking. However, Saidu (2024) reported that many lecturers worry about plagiarism and student over-reliance on AI. These concerns strongly reflect Tanzanian lecturers' hesitations. At the same time, universities in Nigeria, like in Tanzania, often lack formal policies to guide ethical AI use, which leads to inconsistent practices.

South Africa presents a slightly different case where, some universities have begun formal experiments with AI in the classroom, supported by stronger digital infrastructure compared to Tanzania. Yet, Tarisayi (2024) notes that challenges of academic integrity, data privacy and lecturer skepticism remain strong. This shows that even in better-resourced institutions, ethical and pedagogical questions are central to AI adoption.

Beyond Africa, similar trends appear in Indonesia and India. In Indonesian universities, students show strong enthusiasm for ChatGPT but limited institutional guidance and inadequate lecturer training restrict its responsible use (Simatupang et al. 2025). In India, students use ChatGPT mostly for academic writing and coding, but concerns about accuracy, bias and misuse remain (Dwivedi et al., 2023).

What makes Tanzania's case stand out is the recent development of the National Guidelines for Artificial Intelligence in Education (MoEST, 2025). While many countries in the region are still in early stages of policy discussion, Tanzania has already taken steps to outline national strategies for safe and effective AI use. This positions Tanzania as a leader in framing policy, even though practical challenges like internet access, affordability and digital skills remain.

DISCUSSION

The findings from this study show that the use of ChatGPT is growing in Tanzanian universities, even though there are still many challenges. Students and lecturers are already using the tool in different ways, but most of them are doing so without proper guidance, training or support from their institutions. This indicates that AI tools are entering higher education faster than university policies and systems can adapt, creating both opportunities and risks.

One of the main issues that appeared across all three universities is the lack of internet access. Even students who are interested in using ChatGPT are often blocked by slow or unreliable internet and high data costs. For instance, students at UDOM reported that they could not rely on ChatGPT regularly because "data costs and poor Wi-Fi" made access difficult, while students at NM-AIST noted that stable internet allowed them to integrate it into daily academic routines. This confirms what other studies have found, technology cannot help students if they cannot access it (Matto, 2024; Komba, 2024).

Institutional culture also plays a significant role in how AI is accepted. At NM-AIST, the culture encourages innovation, which has made it easier for both students and lecturers to explore new technologies. At UDSM and UDOM, some lecturers are still not sure or even afraid to use AI, mostly because there are no clear rules. This observation aligns with findings of Matto and Ponera (2025), who show that institutional leadership significantly impacts AI adoption.

The study also shows that while many students are using ChatGPT, they often do not fully understand how to use it well. Without digital skills training, some students use ChatGPT only for basic tasks like grammar checks or quick answers. Others copy AI-generated content without learning. This supports the argument that access alone is not enough; teacher training and digital literacy programs are equally important if AI is to be used responsibly and effectively (Matto & Ponera, 2025). The need for capacity building goes beyond students; many lecturers admitted they lacked confidence in using ChatGPT and wanted structured institutional training before incorporating it into teaching.

Lecturers also expressed mixed attitudes toward ChatGPT. Some see it as a useful tool to prepare lessons or support students with writing. Others however, are worried about academic honesty and fear that students will use it to cheat. This fear combined with the lack of institutional policy, led some lecturers to use ChatGPT privately without disclosing it to colleagues. This underscores the importance of AI governance frameworks at the university level including policies, institutional guidelines and academic integrity safeguards (Hasanein & Sobaih, 2023).

Beyond the problem of plagiarism, the use of ChatGPT in universities also brings up broader ethical issues that need serious consideration. AI tools like ChatGPT raise concerns about privacy, data protection and bias. Students often provide personal or sensitive academic information to the platform, yet most universities in Tanzania have no frameworks to safeguard how such data is managed. This gap reflects global debates about responsible AI use, where questions of transparency, fairness and accountability remain fundamental (Dwivedi et al., 2023; García-López et al., 2025). Addressing these issues requires both institutional policies and alignment with national strategies.

Furthermore, the findings from this chapter demonstrate how adoption patterns in Tanzania both confirm and extend TAM and DOI. Consistent with TAM, usefulness and ease of access were decisive factors in students' willingness to adopt ChatGPT. However, institutional culture and policy gaps also shaped attitudes, pointing to the need to extend the model to include governance factors in low-resource settings. Similarly, DOI's focus on innovators and early adopters is evident in NM-AIST's openness, yet the slow diffusion in UDOM shows how infrastructural barriers can hinder even motivated adopters. These insights suggest that while global theories help explain adoption, local constraints significantly modify their applicability.

POLICY IMPLICATIONS AND RECOMMENDATIONS

The findings of this study show that universities in Tanzania need both strong policies and practical actions to make the use of ChatGPT and other AI tools safe, fair, and effective. One of the most urgent short-term steps is for universities to develop institutional guidelines. These should explain how AI can be used in teaching, learning and research, while also protecting academic integrity and preventing misuse. Simple and practical rules will help both students and staff know what is acceptable.

For immediate action, universities and teacher-training colleges can partner with MoEST to create school-ready models of AI use that include age-appropriate prompts. Pilot programs should include teacher professional development, parental communication and child-safeguarding and privacy protocols, in line with national guidance. This higher-ed to K-12 pipeline would help ensure that virtual tutors are introduced in ways that are pedagogically sound, culturally appropriate and safe for younger learners.

Many students and lecturers struggle because of poor or unreliable internet. In the short term, universities with support from government and private partners, should expand Wi-Fi on campuses, improve computer labs and work with service providers to make internet more affordable. Without reliable access, AI tools will only benefit a few students instead of everyone.

Students and lecturers also need immediate training on responsible ChatGPT use. Such training should cover how to ask good questions, check accuracy, avoiding over-reliance and thinking critically about the responses. Training can be added to student orientation and staff development programs so that responsible AI use becomes part of everyday academic life.

Because most students use the free version of ChatGPT, which has limitations, universities should provide short-term guidance on how to make the best use of it. Where resources allow, institutions can also explore offering limited access to premium features for academic purposes. This could be done through institutional subscriptions, pilot programs or partnerships to ensure that students have equal opportunities to benefit from advanced features regardless of their financial background.

In the longer term, universities should also encourage local research and innovation by supporting AI in education projects and developing tools adapted to Tanzanian needs and languages. This will help institutions create solutions that are more inclusive and relevant. Such efforts would strengthen the capacity of universities to use AI responsibly and build local expertise that reduces dependence on external technologies.

At the strategic level, universities must align their efforts with the national frameworks including Tanzania Development Vision 2050, National Guidelines for Artificial Intelligence in Education and the Education Sector Development Programme. These guidelines provide a shared framework, but each university must adapt them into strategies and action plans. Alignment will help ensure that AI is introduced in a way that supports national education goals while also protecting students and lecturers.

Furthermore, the government and education stakeholders should establish long-term grants, partnerships with technology companies and research initiatives to support innovation and capacity building. This mechanism will allow universities to strengthen infrastructure and adapt to new developments in AI and digital education.

CONTRIBUTION OF THE STUDY

This study helps to fill a knowledge gap about how ChatGPT is being used in higher learning institutions in Tanzania. So far, very few studies have been done in this area and there is limited information about how students and lecturers are engaging with AI tools like ChatGPT.

By focusing on three different universities, the study provides a well-defined picture of what is really happening on the ground. It shows that many students are already using ChatGPT, but often without proper training or support. It also highlights the challenges that come with poor internet access, lack of policies and limited digital skills. These are real issues that universities and education stakeholders need to understand and address.

Most of the research on AI in education comes from countries with stronger digital systems. This study is different because it looks at the Tanzanian context, where students may not have the same level of access to technology. It shows how limited conditions affect the way AI tools are used and why support must be adapted to fit those conditions.

The study also brings in the voices of students, lecturers and ICT staff. This makes the findings more practical and useful for anyone working in the education sector. Policymakers, university leaders and education stakeholders can use this information to make better decisions about how to support the responsible use of AI in universities.

CONCLUSION

This study has explored how ChatGPT is being used in higher education institutions in Tanzania, focusing on three universities; UDSM, UDOM and NM-AIST. The findings show that while the use of AI tools like ChatGPT is still new, it is growing fast especially among students who are eager to find new ways to support their learning. Many students are already using ChatGPT for assignments, grammar checking and exam preparation, often without formal training or guidance. Lecturers are also beginning to explore its use, although some are cautious because there are no university policies.

The study highlighted several challenges including limited internet access, lack of training and the absence of official guidelines. These barriers make it difficult for both students and lecturers to fully benefit from AI tools. However, the study also shows that there is strong interest in using AI, especially in institutions that promote research and innovation like NM-AIST. This interest is a good sign and shows that the education sector is ready to embrace new tools, if the right support is provided.

Beyond technical and institutional barriers, the study also raises important ethical considerations. Academic integrity remains a concern, as some students may be tempted to use ChatGPT to complete assignments without fully understanding the content. Issues of privacy and data protection are also critical, since users often share personal or academic information with the platform without knowing how this data is stored or used. Moreover, ChatGPT and similar AI systems are developed based on data from other contexts, so they may carry cultural or language biases that do not fit Tanzanian realities. These risks highlight the importance of responsible AI use that prioritizes fairness, accountability and transparency.

This study also points to several directions for future research. There is a need to examine the long-term effects of regular AI use on students' academic performance, critical thinking and writing skills. More research is required on ethical concerns, particularly around plagiarism and how universities adapt their assessment methods. Studies should also compare public and private universities to understand different adoption levels and challenges. In addition, exploring how AI can support non-academic functions such as administration, student support services and career guidance would give a more complete view of its potential impact on higher education.

Although the focus here is on universities, the findings also offer guidance for K-12 education. Building reliable access, training teachers in AI literacy, prioritizing Swahili-ready tools and putting strong safeguards in place are key starting points. With careful piloting under the ESDP and MoEST's AI guidelines, Tanzania has the opportunity to extend the benefits of AI from campuses to classrooms in a safe and equitable way.

AUTHOR DISCLOSURE STATEMENT

This chapter received limited assistance from digital writing tools, which were used for language editing and formatting. All research design, data collection, analysis, interpretation and substantive content are entirely the work of the author. The use of these tools did not influence the originality, integrity or validity of the findings presented in this chapter.

ACKNOWLEDGMENT

The author would like to thank BakiShule organization for funding this study.

REFERENCES

Al Shloul, T., Mazhar, T., Abbas, Q., Iqbal, M., Ghadi, Y. Y., Shahzad, T., Mallek, F., & Hamam, H. (2024). Role of activity-based learning and ChatGPT on students' performance in education. *Computers and Education: Artificial Intelligence*, *6*, 100219. DOI: 10.1016/j.caeai.2024.100219

Amoah, A., Asiama, R. K., & Kwablah, E. (2025). ChatGPT early usage among students: A global evidence of determinants. *Development and Sustainability in Economics and Finance*, *7*, 100065. DOI: 10.1016/j.dsef.2025.100065

Atlas, S. (2023). ChatGPT for higher education and professional development: A guide to conversational AI. The University of Rhode Island. https://digitalcommons.uri.edu/cba_facpubs/548

Baig, M. I., & Yadegaridehkordi, E. (2024). ChatGPT in higher education: A systematic literature review and research challenges. *International Journal of Educational Research*, *127*, 102411. DOI: 10.1016/j.ijer.2024.102411

Bin-Nashwan, S. A., Sadallah, M., & Bouteraa, M. (2023). Use of ChatGPT in academia: Academic integrity hangs in the balance. *Technology in Society*, *75*, 102370. DOI: 10.1016/j.techsoc.2023.102370

Chukwuere, J. (2024). Today's academic research: The role of ChatGPT writing. *Journal of Information Systems and Informatics*, *6*(1), 30–46. Advance online publication. DOI: 10.51519/journalisi.v6i1.639

Davis, F. D. (1989). Perceived usefulness, perceived ease of use, and user acceptance of information technology. *Management Information Systems Quarterly*, *13*(3), 319–340. DOI: 10.2307/249008

Dwivedi, Y. K., Kshetri, N., Hughes, L., Slade, E. L., Jeyaraj, A., Kar, A. K., Baabdullah, A. M., Koohang, A., Raghavan, V., Ahuja, M., Albanna, H., Albashrawi, M. A., Al-Busaidi, A. S., Balakrishnan, J., Barlette, Y., Basu, S., Bose, I., Brooks, L., Buhalis, D., & Wright, R. (2023). Opinion Paper: "So what if ChatGPT wrote it?" Multidisciplinary perspectives on opportunities, challenges and implications of generative conversational AI for research, practice and policy. *International Journal of Information Management, 71*, 102642. Advance online publication. DOI: 10.1016/j.ijinfomgt.2023.102642

Funa, A. A., & Gabay, R. A. E. (2025). Policy guidelines and recommendations on AI use in teaching and learning: A meta-synthesis study. *Social Sciences & Humanities Open, 11*, 101221. DOI: 10.1016/j.ssaho.2024.101221

Garcia-López, I. M., González González, C. S., Ramírez-Montoya, M.-S., & Molina-Espinosa, J.-M. (2025). Challenges of implementing ChatGPT in education: Systematic literature review. *International Journal of Educational Research Open, 8*, 100401. DOI: 10.1016/j.ijedro.2024.100401

Hasanein, A. M., & Sobaih, A. E. E. (2023). Drivers and consequences of ChatGPT use in higher education: Key stakeholder perspectives. *European Journal of Investigation in Health, Psychology and Education, 13*(11), 2599–2614. DOI: 10.3390/ejihpe13110181 PMID: 37998071

Indrawati, I., Letjani, K. P., Kurniawan, K., & Muthaiyah, S. (2025). Adoption of ChatGPT in educational institutions in Botswana: A customer perspective. *Asia Pacific Management Review, 30*(1), 100346. DOI: 10.1016/j.apmrv.2024.100346

Internet Society. (2019, January 7). Community networks in Tanzania: Helping to close the connectivity gap. Internet Society. https://www.internetsociety.org/blog/2019/01/community-networks-in-tanzania-helping-to-close-connectivity-gap/

Komba, M. M. (2024). The influence of ChatGPT on digital learning: Experience among university students. *Global Knowledge, Memory and Communication*. Advance online publication. DOI: 10.1108/GKMC-10-2023-0390

Kondoro, A. M. (2025). AI writing assistants in Tanzanian universities: Adoption trends, challenges, and opportunities. In *Proceedings of the Fourth Workshop on Intelligent and Interactive Writing Assistants* (pp. 37–46). ACL Anthology., https://aclanthology.org/2025.in2writing-1.4.pdf DOI: 10.18653/v1/2025.in2writing-1.4

Lampropoulos, G., & Papadakis, S. (2025). The Educational Value of Artificial Intelligence and Social Robots. In *Social Robots in Education* (pp. 3–15). Springer., https://link.springer.com/chapter/10.1007/978-3-031-82915-4_1 DOI: 10.1007/978-3-031-82915-4_1

Lavidas, K., Papadakis, S., Manesis, D., Grigoriadou, A. S., & Gialamas, V.Lectures and Lab Classes. (2022). The effects of social desirability on students' self-reports in two social contexts: Lectures vs. lectures and lab classes. *Information (Basel), 13*(10), 491. DOI: 10.3390/info13100491

Lavidas, K., Petropoulou, A., Papadakis, S., Apostolou, Z., Komis, V., Jimoyiannis, A., & Gialamas, V. (2022). Factors affecting response rates of the web survey with teachers. *Computers, 11*(9), 127. DOI: 10.3390/computers11090127

Li, B., Jiang, J., Ma, L., Huang, Y., & Wu, X. (2024). Mitigating University Students' Reliance on Chatgpt. Proceedings of the 2024 8th International Seminar on Education, Management and Social Sciences (ISEMSS 2024), Advances in Social Science, Education and Humanities Research, 867. https://doi.org/DOI: 10.2991/978-2-38476-297-2_31

Luckin, R., Holmes, W., Griffiths, M., & Forcier, L. B. (2016). Intelligence unleashed: An argument for AI in education. Pearson Education. https://static.googleusercontent.com/media/edu.google.com/en//pdfs/Intelligence-Unleashed-Publication.pdf

Matto, G. (2024). Is ChatGPT building or destroying education? Perception of university students in Tanzania. *Journal of Education and Learning Technology, 5*(4), 38–51. DOI: 10.38159/jelt.2024541

Matto, G., & Ponera, J. M. (2025). Artificial intelligence in higher education institutions in Tanzania: Analysis of policy perspectives. *Interdisciplinary Journal of Education Research, 7*(1), a13. DOI: 10.38140/ijer-2025.vol7.1.13

Mbwambo, N. M., & Kaaya, P. B. (2024). ChatGPT in education: Applications, concerns and recommendations. *Journal of ICT Systems, 2*(1), 107–124. DOI: 10.56279/jicts.v2i1.87

Meyer, J. G., Urbanowicz, R. J., Martin, P. C. N., O'Connor, K., Li, R., Peng, P.-C., Bright, T. J., Tatonetti, N., Won, K. J., Gonzalez-Hernandez, G., & Moore, J. H. (2023). ChatGPT and large language models in academia: Opportunities and challenges. *BioData Mining, 16*(1), 20. DOI: 10.1186/s13040-023-00339-9 PMID: 37443040

Mgaiwa, S. J. (2018). The paradox of financing public higher education in Tanzania and the fate of quality education: The experience of selected universities. *SAGE Open, 8*(2), 2158244018771729. Advance online publication. DOI: 10.1177/2158244018771729

Mgaiwa, S. J., & Ishengoma, J. M. (2023). Financing higher education in Tanzania through students' loans scheme and its impact on equitable access. *Heliyon, 9*(3), e13943. DOI: 10.1016/j.heliyon.2023.e13943 PMID: 36895382

Ministry of Education. Science and Technology (MoEST). (2025). National guidelines for artificial intelligence in education. https://www.moe.go.tz/sites/default/files/NATIONAL%20GUIDELINES%20FOR%20ARTIFICIAL%20INTELIGENCE%20N%20EDUCATION.pdf

Ministry of Education. Science and Technology (MoEST). (2025). Education sector development plan, 2025/26–2029/30. United Republic of Tanzania. https://www.moe.go.tz/sites/default/files/ESDP%202025-26%20hadi%202029-30%20Final-%2026%20February%202025.pdf

Mtebe, J. S., & Raisamo, R. (2014). Challenges and instructors' intention to adopt and use open educational resources in higher education in Tanzania and Kenya. *International Review of Research in Open and Distance Learning*, *15*(1), 249–271. DOI: 10.19173/irrodl.v15i1.1687

Mubofu, C., & Kainkwa, E. (2023). University lecturers' feelings, awareness and attitudes towards Open Education Resources: Experience from two higher learning institutions in Tanzania. *Open Praxis*, *15*(4), 328–341. DOI: 10.55982/openpraxis.15.4.555

Naznin, K., Al Mahmud, A., Nguyen, M. T., & Chua, C. (2025). ChatGPT integration in higher education for personalized learning, academic writing, and coding tasks: A systematic review. *Computers*, *14*(2), 53. DOI: 10.3390/computers14020053

Ngulugulu, M. M., & Mgina, H. J. (2024). Utilization of educational artificial intelligence tools in higher learning institutions in Tanzania: A literature review. *International Journal of Novel Research and Development*, *9*(4). https://www.ijnrd.org/papers/IJNRD2404376.pdf

Njiku, J., Ismail, M. J., Yunus, S., & Abdulla, A. A. (2024). Exploring ChatGPT's potential to enhance learning outcomes: A study of university students' beliefs and practices. International Conference on Global Innovation for a Sustainable Future. https://www.researchgate.net/publication/389920573_Exploring_ChatGPT%27s_Potential_to_Enhance_Learning_Outcomes_A_Study_of_University_Students%27_Beliefs_and_Practices

Papadakis, S., Lytvynova, S. H., Ivanova, S. M., & Selyshcheva, I. A. (2024b). *Advancing lifelong learning with AI-enhanced ICT: A review of 3L-Person 2024.* In *CEUR Workshop Proceedings (9th International Workshop on Professional Retraining and Life-Long Learning using ICT: Person-oriented Approach — 3L-Person 2024, Lviv, Ukraine, September 25, 2023).* CEUR-WS.org.

Papadakis, S., Striuk, A. M., Kravtsov, H. M., Shyshkina, M. P., Marienko, M. V., & Danylchuk, H. B. (2024a). *Embracing digital innovation and cloud technologies for transformative learning experiences.* In *Proceedings of the 11th Workshop on Cloud Technologies in Education (CTE 2023), Kryvyi Rih, Ukraine, December 22, 2023.* CEUR Workshop Proceedings.

Ray, P. P. (2023). ChatGPT: A comprehensive review on background, applications, key challenges, bias, ethics, limitations and future scope. *Internet of Things and Cyber-Physical Systems*, *3*, 121–154. DOI: 10.1016/j.iotcps.2023.04.003

Rogers, E. M. (2003). *Diffusion of innovations* (5th ed.). Free Press., https://books.google.co.tz/books/about/Diffusion_of_Innovations_5th_Edition.html?id=9U1K5LjUOwEC&redir_esc=y

Ruano-Borbalán, J. (2025). *The transformative impact of artificial intelligence on higher education: A critical reflection on current trends and future directions.* International Journal of Chinese Education., DOI: 10.1177/2212585X251319364

Saidu, A. M. (2024). ChatGPT usage and plagiarism in academic writing: The mediating role of academic integrity among Nigerian universities' students. In P. A. Okebukola (Ed.), AI and ethics, academic integrity and the future of quality assurance in higher education (pp. 86–97). Nigeria: Global University Network for Innovation (GUNi). https://www.researchgate.net/publication/386245533

Sarakikya, G. M., & Kitula, P. R. (2024). Application of artificial intelligence platforms and its influence on education of students in higher learning institutions in Arusha City, Tanzania. *Journal of Research Innovation and Implications in Education*, *8*(4). Advance online publication. DOI: 10.59765/nvthtd5

Shabbir, A., Rizvi, S., Alam, M. M., & Su'ud, M. M. (2024). Beyond boundaries: Navigating the positive potential of ChatGPT, empowering education in underdeveloped corners of the world. *Heliyon*, *10*(16), e35845. DOI: 10.1016/j.heliyon.2024.e35845 PMID: 39224307

Simatupang, E. C., Ismail, I., Waluyo, B., & Panmei, B. (2025). ChatGPT in education: The influence of institutional support and peer dynamics in Indonesian higher education. *Internet Reference Services Quarterly*, *29*(2), 225–244. DOI: 10.1080/10875301.2025.2461476

Tarisayi, K. S. (2024). Artificial intelligence in South African universities: Ethical concerns and pedagogical implications. *Journal of Education Studies in South Africa*, *38*(2), 55–72. DOI: 10.10520/ejc-jedsaf_v38_n2_a5

Uğraş, H., Uğraş, M., Papadakis, S., & Kalogiannakis, M. (2024a). ChatGPT-supported education in primary schools: The potential of ChatGPT for sustainable practices. *Sustainability (Basel), 16*(22), 9855. DOI: 10.3390/su16229855

Uğraş, H., Uğraş, M., Papadakis, S., & Kalogiannakis, M. (2024b). Innovative Early Childhood STEM Education with ChatGPT: Teacher Perspectives. Technology, Knowledge and Learning, 1-23. https://link.springer.com/article/10.1007/s10758-024-09804-8

UNESCO. (2023, September 6). In Tanzania, adolescent girls and young women expand digital literacy and skills. UNESCO. https://www.unesco.org/en/articles/adolescent-girls-and-young-women-tanzania-expand-digital-literacy-and-skills

United Republic of Tanzania. (2025). Tanzania Development Vision 2050 (Dira 2050). President's Office, Planning and Investment. https://www.planning.go.tz/uploads/documents/sw-1752762713-DIRA%20YA%20TAIFA%20YA%20MAENDELEO%202050.pdf

Venkatesh, V., & Davis, F. D. (2000). A theoretical extension of the technology acceptance model: Four longitudinal field studies. *Management Science, 46*(2), 186–204. DOI: 10.1287/mnsc.46.2.186.11926

Vieriu, A. M., & Petrea, G. (2025). The impact of artificial intelligence (AI) on students' academic development. *Education Sciences, 15*(3), 343. DOI: 10.3390/educsci15030343

Walter, Y. (2024). Embracing the future of artificial intelligence in the classroom: The relevance of AI literacy, prompt engineering, and critical thinking in modern education. *International Journal of Educational Technology in Higher Education, 21*(1), 15. DOI: 10.1186/s41239-024-00448-3

Woldegiorgis, E. T. (2025). Challenges of integrating technology in East African higher education systems in the post-pandemic era: Emerging academic cultures. *Technology, Pedagogy and Education, 56*(2), e13533. DOI: 10.1080/1475939X.2025.2520589

Compilation of References

Abdelsalam Mohamed Mostafa, M. (2025). Bridging the digital divide: AI, VR, and AR for equitable K-12 education. *SSRN*. http://dx.doi.org/DOI: 10.2139/ssrn.5124551

Abdo, N. I., Alwaely, S. A., Aburezeq, I. M., Alkhazaleh, M. S., Alaqtash, S. K., & El-Zeiny, M. E. (2024). Assessing the extent of AI implementations in Arabic L2 courses. *2024 Fifth International Conference on Intelligent Data Science Technologies and Applications (IDSTA)*, 231–236. https://doi.org/DOI: 10.1109/IDSTA62194.2024.10746992

Abendroth, D., & colleauges. (2025). *Generative ai outlook report: Exploring the intersection between technology, society and policy* (tech. rep. No. JRC142598). European Commission Joint Research Centre (JRC). https://publications.jrc.ec.europa.eu/repository/bitstream/ JRC142598/JRC142598 01.pdf

Abubakari, M. S., Shafik, W., & Hidayatullah, A. F. (2024). Evaluating the Potential of Artificial Intelligence in Islamic Religious Education: A SWOT Analysis Overview. In *AI-Enhanced Teaching Methods* (pp. 216–239). IGI Global. DOI: 10.4018/979-8-3693-2728-9.ch010

Access, A. O. (2024). *Ai and collaboration: Practical tips for teachers* [Details how teachers can use AI for designing group experiences, forming equitable teams, and creating rubrics and reflection surveys]. https://avidopenaccess.com/ai-collaboration/

Addo, S. A. (2023). Are You Ready to Teach AI in Schools? Teachers' Perspectives of Teaching AI in K-12 Settings. *ACM International Conference Proceeding Series*. DOI: 10.1145/3610969.3610973

Addo, S. A., & Sentance, S. (2023). Teachers' Motivation for Teaching AI in K-12 settings. *ACM International Conference Proceeding Series*. DOI: 10.1145/3633083.3633192

Adzima, R., Rochsantiningsih, D., & Suparno, S. (2023). Perspectives and preferences towards teaching culture in efl classroom: senior high school context in indonesia. International Journal of Multicultural and Multireligious Understanding, 10(6), 274. https://doi.org/DOI: 10.18415/ijmmu.v10i6.4728

Ahmad, S. F., Han, H., Alam, M. M., Rehmat, M. K., Irshad, M., Arraño-Muñoz, M., & Ariza-Montes, A. (2023). Impact of artificial intelligence on human loss in decision making, laziness and safety in education. *Humanities & Social Sciences Communications*, *10*(1), 311. DOI: 10.1057/s41599-023-01787-8 PMID: 37325188

Ahmad, S., Rahmat, M., Mubarik, M., Alam, M., & Hyder, S. (2021). Artificial intelligence and its role in education. *Sustainability (Basel)*, *13*(22), 12902. DOI: 10.3390/su132212902

AI, S. (2024). *Competency-based learning: Definition, benefits, and implementation* [Explains principles of competency-based education including equity, measurable competencies, transparency, personalised support, and growth-based assessment]. https://www.saima. ai/competency-based-learning

Ain, Q., & Imtiaz, R. (2025). The role of technology in speech-language therapy: Perceptions, effectiveness, and challenges in a resource-limited setting. *Journal of Health and Rehabilitation Research*, *5*(1), 1–8.

Aithal, P. S., & Aithal, S. (2023). How to increase emotional infrastructure of higher education institutions. [IJMTS]. *International Journal of Management, Technology, and Social Sciences*, *8*(3), 356–394. DOI: 10.47992/IJMTS.2581.6012.0307

Ajuwon, O., Animashaun, E., & Chiekezie, N.Olanike Abiola AjuwonEnitan Shukurat AnimashaunNjideka Rita Chiekezie. (2024). Advancing human resources management practices in educational institutions: Enhancing teacher retention and student outcomes using ai. *International Journal of Management & Entrepreneurship Research*, *6*(8), 2488–2506. DOI: 10.51594/ijmer.v6i8.1367

Akavova, A., Temirkhanova, Z., & Lorsanova, Z. (2025). Adaptive learning and artificial intelligence in the educational space. *E3S Web of Conferences, 451*. https://doi.org/DOI: 10.1051/e3sconf/202345106011

Akbarani, R. (2024). Use of artificial intelligence in english language teaching. *International Journal of English Learning and Applied Linguistics (Ijelal)*, *4*(1), 14–23. DOI: 10.21111/ijelal.v4i1.10756

Akgun, S., & Greenhow, C. (2022). Artificial Intelligence (AI) in Education: Addressing Societal and Ethical Challenges in K-12 Settings. *Proceedings of International Conference of the Learning Sciences, ICLS*. DOI: 10.1007/s43681-021-00096-7

Akram, Z., Sethi, A., Mehreen, A., & Sohail, M. (2021). The assessment of emotional intelligence in medical faculty working at poonch medical college (pmc), ajk. *Journal of University Medical & Dental College*, *12*(1), 1–8. DOI: 10.37723/jumdc.v12i1.499

Al Shloul, T., Mazhar, T., Abbas, Q., Iqbal, M., Ghadi, Y. Y., Shahzad, T., Mallek, F., & Hamam, H. (2024). Role of activity-based learning and ChatGPT on students' performance in education. *Computers and Education: Artificial Intelligence*, *6*, 100219. DOI: 10.1016/j.caeai.2024.100219

AlAfnan, M. (2024). Artificial Intelligence and Language: Bridging Arabic and English with Technology. *Journal of Ecohumanism*, *4*(1), 240–256. DOI: 10.62754/joe.v3i8.4961

Alakabawy, B. (2024). Artificial intelligence in the educational stages from kindergarten to university: A systematic review of Arab studies from 2010 to 2023. *E-Learning and Digital Media*, *21*(3), 1–24. DOI: 10.1177/20427530241276140

Alam, A. (2023). Harnessing the power of AI to create intelligent tutoring systems for enhanced classroom experience and improved learning outcomes. In Rajakumar, G., Du, K.-L., & Rocha, Á. (Eds.), *Intelligent communication technologies and virtual mobile networks* (Vol. 171, pp. 571–591). Springer. DOI: 10.1007/978-981-99-1767-9_42

Alasmari, T. (2025). Artificial intelligence and M-learning in Arabic countries: Innovations, trends, and regional perspectives. [iJIM]. *International Journal of Interactive Mobile Technologies*, *19*(5), 170–194. DOI: 10.3991/ijim.v19i05.52735

Alawneh, Y. J. J., Sleema, H., Salman, F. N., Alshammat, M. F., & Oteer, R. S., & ALrashidi, N. K. N. (2024). Adaptive learning systems: Revolutionizing higher education through ai-driven curricula. *2024 International Conference on Knowledge Engineering and Communication Systems (ICKECS)*, *1*, 1–5. DOI: 10.1109/ICKECS61492.2024.10616675

Alayba, A. M. (2025). Arabic Natural Language Processing (NLP): A Comprehensive Review of Challenges, Techniques, and Emerging Trends. *Computers*, *14*(11), 497. DOI: 10.3390/computers14110497

Albahli, S. (2025). Advancing Sustainable Educational Practices Through AI-Driven Prediction of Academic Outcomes. *Sustainability (Basel)*, *17*(3), 1087. DOI: 10.3390/su17031087

Alenezi, A. (2024). Evaluating the effectiveness of AI-powered adaptive learning systems in secondary schools. *International Journal on Studies in Education*, *6*(2), 45–67. DOI: 10.46328/ijonse.264

Aleven, V., McLaghlin, E. A., Glenn, R. A., & Koedinger, K. R. (2016). Instruction based on adaptive learning technologies. In Mayer, R. E., & Alexander, P. A. (Eds.), *Handbook of research on learning and instruction* (pp. 522–560). Routledge., DOI: 10.4324/9781315736419

Aleven, V., Rowe, J., Huang, Y., & Mitrovic, A. (2023). Domain modeling for AIED systems with connections to modeling student knowledge: A review. In du Boulay, B., Mitrovic, A., & Yacef, K. (Eds.), *Handbook of artificial intelligence in education* (pp. 127–169). Edward Elgar Publishing. DOI: 10.4337/9781800375413.00017

Al-Ghobesi, A. A. H. (2025). Risks of relying on artificial intelligence in learning Arabic language sciences through the Meta application. *Arts for Linguistic & Literary Studies*, *7*(1), 396–419. DOI: 10.53286/arts.v7i1.2420

Ali, O., Murray, P. A., Momin, M., Dwivedi, Y. K., & Malik, T. (2024). The effects of artificial intelligence applications in educational settings: Challenges and strategies. *Technological Forecasting and Social Change*, *199*, 123076. DOI: 10.1016/j.techfore.2023.123076

Aljabr, F., Zakarneh, B., Annamalai, N., & Al Said, N. (2025). Integrating AI: Challenges and opportunities in teaching English writing skills. *World Journal of English Language*, *15*(5), 371. DOI: 10.5430/wjel.v15n5p371

Alkhasawneh, S. (2025). AI-Driven Personalized Mathematics Learning Through Interactive Mobile Platforms: Effects on Achievement and Motivation. [iJIM]. *International Journal of Interactive Mobile Technologies*, *19*(13), 33–54. DOI: 10.3991/ijim.v19i13.54947

Al-Mughairi, H. and Bhaskar, P. (2024). Exploring the factors affecting the adoption ai techniques in higher education: insights from teachers' perspectives on chatgpt. Journal of Research in Innovative Teaching & Learning. https://doi.org/DOI: 10.1108/JRIT-09-2023-0129

Almuhanna, M. A. (2024). Teachers' perspectives of integrating AI-powered technologies in K-12 education for creating customized learning materials and resources. *Education and Information Technologies*, *29*(10), 10343–10371. DOI: 10.1007/s10639-024-13257-y

Al-Mutawa, R. F., & Al-Aama, A. Y. (2024). Arabic opinion classification of customer service conversations using data augmentation and artificial intelligence. *Big Data and Cognitive Computing*, *8*(12), 196. DOI: 10.3390/bdcc8120196

Alrashedi, N. T., Alsulami, S. M. H., Flatah, A. I., Najmi, A. H., & Alhalafawy, W. S. (2024). The effects of gamified platforms on enhancing learners' ambition. *Journal of Ecohumanism*, *3*(8), 3393–3403. DOI: 10.62754/joe.v3i8.5004

Alrawashdeh, G. S. (2023). *Personalized and adaptive learning technology for early grade reading: Evidence from MENA* [Doctoral dissertation, University of Illinois at Urbana-Champaign]. https://hdl.handle.net/2142/121495

Alrawashdeh, G. S., & Castillo, N. M. (2025a). Responsible AI in Personalized Adaptive Learning: A Global Review of 40 Products. In Papadakis, S. (Ed.), *AI Roles and Responsibilities in Education* (pp. 171–198). Springer Nature Switzerland., DOI: 10.1007/978-3-031-96855-6_8

Alrawashdeh, G. S., & Castillo, N. M. (2025b). Student agency in personalized and adaptive learning technologies: From conceptualization to application. *Education and Information Technologies*, *30*(18), 26125–26149. Advance online publication. DOI: 10.1007/s10639-025-13772-6

Alrayes, A., Henari, T., & Ahmed, D. (2024). Chatgpt in education – understanding the bahraini academics perspective. *Electronic Journal of e-Learning*, *22*(2), 112–134. DOI: 10.34190/ejel.22.2.3250

Alshehri, B. (2023). Pedagogical paradigms in the ai era: Insights from saudi educators on the long-term implications of ai integration in classroom teaching. *IJESA*, *2*(8), 159–180. DOI: 10.59992/IJESA.2023.v2n8p7

Al-Tal, R., Sallam, S., & Ali, H. (2022). Syrian crisis impacts on the international refugee education fund in Jordan. *International Journal of Educational Reform*, *34*(2), 320–335. DOI: 10.1177/10567879221124882

Altun, A., & Kokoc, M. (2019). Following the learners' traces: Profiling learners and visualizing the learning process for building better learning experiences. In Khine, M. S. (Ed.), *Emerging Trends in Learning Analytics: Leveraging the Power of Education Data* (pp. 100–121). Brill., DOI: 10.1163/9789004399273_007

Alvi, I. (2024). Gamification in Education Management : Fulfilling Students' Intrinsic Needs and Learning Outcomes. *Prabandhan: Indian Journal of Management*, *17*(11), 41–60. DOI: 10.17010/pijom/2024/v17i11/174022

Al-Waridat, A. Y. (2024). Attitudes of first through third grade teachers in Al-Rusayfa district toward using artificial intelligence techniques in inclusive education. *Journal of Education, 40*(4.2), 78–110. https://doi.org/DOI: 10.21608/mfes.2024.362288

Alzahrani, A. (2022). A systematic review of artificial intelligence in education in the Arab world. *Amazonia Investiga, 11*(54), 293–305. DOI: 10.34069/AI/2022.54.06.28

Al-Zahrani, A. M. (2024). Unveiling the shadows: Beyond the hype of AI in education. *Heliyon, 10*(9), e30696. DOI: 10.1016/j.heliyon.2024.e30696 PMID: 38737255

American Federation of Teachers & Common Sense Education. (2024, June). *Guardrails for AI in education: Practical guidance for districts and schools* [Includes guidance on educator autonomy, bargaining, PD, privacy; accessed 2025-10-11]. https://www.aft.org/sites/ default/files/media/documents/2024/Commonsense Guardrails AI 0604.pdf

Amer, S. (2022). The importance of teaching culture in the foreign language classroom. *JOFOA*, (46). Advance online publication. DOI: 10.37376/jofoa.vi46.2653

Amgott, N., & Renfroe, D. (2025). Implementing AI Chatbots in L2 University Courses: Building Pragmatic Competence and Critical Digital Literacy. In Rethinking Language Education in the Age of Generative AI (pp. 185-205). Routledge.

Amoah, A., Asiama, R. K., & Kwablah, E. (2025). ChatGPT early usage among students: A global evidence of determinants. *Development and Sustainability in Economics and Finance*, *7*, 100065. DOI: 10.1016/j.dsef.2025.100065

Anagnostopoulou, E., Grammatikos, N. A., Apostolou, D., & Mentzas, G. (2024). Trustworthy AI in education: A Roadmap for Ethical and Effective Implementation. *Proceedings of the 13th Hellenic Conference on Artificial Intelligence*, 1–7. https://doi.org/DOI: 10.1145/3688671.3688781

Andreadakis, Z. E. (2025 in press). Teaching with AI personas: Designing for Co-CreAItivity in ECE. In Papadakis, S. (Ed.), *AI applications in preschool and primary education: Teaching with artificial intelligence* (pp. xx–xx). Springer.

Angelelli, C. V., de Campos Ribeiro, G. M., Severino, M. R., Johnstone, E., Borzenkova, G., & da Silva, D. C. O. (2023). Developing critical thinking skills through gamification. *Thinking Skills and Creativity*, *49*, 101354. DOI: 10.1016/j.tsc.2023.101354 PMID: 37360225

Aninze, A., & Bhogal, J. (2024). Artificial Intelligence Life Cycle: The Detection and Mitigation of Bias. *Proceedings of the 4th International Conference on AI Research, ICAIR 2024*, 40–49. https://www.scopus.com/inward/record.uri?eid=2-s2.0-85215706792&partnerID=40&md5=b6e143bd6aa02cf8eb1411594d249c3f

Antonopoulou, H., Halkiopoulos, C., Gkintoni, E., & Katsimpelis, A. (2022). Application of gamification tools for identification of neurocognitive and social function in distance learning education. *International Journal of Learning. Teaching and Educational Research, 21*(5), 367–400.

Aravind, A., Durairaj, M., Chitkara, P., Baker El-Ebiary, Y. A., Muniyandy, E., Ushasree, L., & Ammar, M. B. (2025). Adaptive AI-Based Personalized Learning for Accelerated Vocabulary and Syntax Mastery in Young English Learners. *International Journal of Advanced Computer Science and Applications, 16*(4), 678–687. DOI: 10.14569/IJACSA.2025.0160467

Arn, L., Pak, D., Schwartz, L., Ych, T., & Huang, E. M. (2024). "Do They Act the Way They Look?": Examining Portrayals of Intelligent Technology in Narrative Media from an Educational Perspective. *ACM International Conference Proceeding Series*. https://doi.org/DOI: 10.1145/3679318.3685337

Aronson, B., & Laughter, J. (2016). The theory and practice of culturally relevant education: A synthesis of research across content areas. *Review of Educational Research, 86*(1), 163–206. DOI: 10.3102/0034654315582066

Asfar, H., Husna, I., Yasmadi, Y., Khairi, A., Suryani, K., Ikhlas, A., & Madona, A. (2024). Innovative Arabic language learning: Redefining language archetypes using artificial intelligence. *Al-Ta'rib. Jurnal Ilmiah Program Studi Pendidikan Bahasa Arab IAIN Palangka Raya, 12*(2), 293–308. Advance online publication. DOI: 10.23971/altarib.v12i2.8323

Aslan, S., Durham, L. M., Alyuz, N., Chierichetti, R., Denman, P. A., Okur, E., Aguirre, D. I. G., Esquivel, J. C. Z., Cordourier Maruri, H. A., Sharma, S., Raffa, G., Mayer, R. E., & Nachman, L. (2024). What is the impact of a multi-modal pedagogical conversational AI system on parents' concerns about technology use by young children? *British Journal of Educational Technology, 55*(4), 1625–1650. DOI: 10.1111/bjet.13399

Athaluri, S. A., Manthena, S. V., Kesapragada, V. K. M., Yarlagadda, V., Dave, T., & Duddumpudi, R. T. S. (2023). Exploring the boundaries of reality: Investigating the phenomenon of artificial intelligence hallucination in scientific writing through ChatGPT references. *Cureus, 15*(4). Advance online publication. DOI: 10.7759/cureus.37432 PMID: 37182055

Atlas, S. (2023). ChatGPT for higher education and professional development: A guide to conversational AI. The University of Rhode Island. https://digitalcommons.uri.edu/cba_facpubs/548

Attigeri, G., Agrawal, A., & Kolekar, S. V. (2024). Advanced NLP models for technical university information chatbots: Development and comparative analysis. *IEEE Access : Practical Innovations, Open Solutions, 12*, 29633–29647. DOI: 10.1109/ACCESS.2024.3368382

Augenstein, S. (2024, May 7). *The stumbling blocks for artificial intelligence in K–12 education. EdTech Magazine*. https://edtechmagazine.com/k12/article/2024/05/stumbling-blocks-artificial-intelligence-k-12-education

Avcı, S., & Özgenel, M. (2024). Adaptation and psychometric evaluation of homework management, teacher and parent involvement scales for middle schoolers in Turkey. *International Journal of Psychology and Educational Studies, 11*(2), 179–200. DOI: 10.52380/ijpes.2024.11.2.1357

Ayedoun, E., Hayashi, Y., & Seta, K. (2018). Adding communicative and affective strategies to an embodied conversational agent to enhance second language learners' willingness to communicate. *International Journal of Artificial Intelligence in Education, 28*(1), 1–23.

Ayeni, O., Hamad, N., Chisom, O., Osawaru, B., & Adewusi, O. (2024). Ai in education: A review of personalized learning and educational technology. *GSC Advanced Research and Reviews, 18*(2), 261–271. DOI: 10.30574/gscarr.2024.18.2.0062

Baidoo-Anu, D., Rasooli, A., DeLuca, C., & Cheng, L. (2023). Conceptions of classroom assessment and approaches to grading: teachers' and students' perspectives. *Education Inquiry*, 1–29. DOI: 10.1080/20004508.2023.2244136

Baidoo-Anu, D., & Ansah, L. O. (2023). Education in the era of generative artificial intelligence (AI): Understanding the potential benefits of ChatGPT in promoting teaching and learning. *Journal of AI, 7*(1), 52–62. DOI: 10.61969/jai.1337500

Baig, M. I., & Yadegaridehkordi, E. (2024). ChatGPT in higher education: A systematic literature review and research challenges. *International Journal of Educational Research, 127*, 102411. DOI: 10.1016/j.ijer.2024.102411

Baillifard, A., Gabella, M., Lavenex, P. B., & Martarelli, C. S. (2025). Effective learning with a personal AI tutor: A case study. *Education and Information Technologies, 30*(1), 297–312. DOI: 10.1007/s10639-024-12888-5

Bains, A., Spaulding, C., Ricketts, J., & Krishnan, S. (2023). Providing choice enhances reading enjoyment and motivation.

Bajčetić, A., Mirčić, A., Rakočević, J., Đoković, D., Milutinović, K., & Zaletel, I. (2024). Comparing the performance of artificial intelligence learning models to medical students in solving histology and embryology multiple choice questions. Annals of Anatomy-. *Anatomischer Anzeiger, 254*, 152261. DOI: 10.1016/j.aanat.2024.152261 PMID: 38521363

Baker, B. A., Davis, S., Wilkins-Yel, K. G., Mukherjee, A., & Paneto, A. (2023). "It's the Teacher's Responsibility:" Examining Pre-service and In-service Teachers' Responses to Racial Discrimination. *Journal of Educational & Psychological Consultation, 33*(2), 201–229. Advance online publication. DOI: 10.1080/10474412.2022.2104300

Baker, R. S. (2016). Stupid tutoring systems, intelligent humans. *International Journal of Artificial Intelligence in Education, 26*(2), 600–614. DOI: 10.1007/s40593-016-0105-0

Bang, H. J., Olander, K., & Lenihan, E. (2020). Testing a research-based digital learning tool. *CALICO Journal, 37*(3), 277–308. DOI: 10.1558/cj.40544

Bansal, C., Pandey, K. K., Goel, R., Sharma, A., & Jangirala, S. (2023). Artificial intelligence (AI) bias impacts: Classification framework for effective mitigation. *Issues in Information Systems, 24*(4), 367–389. DOI: 10.48009/4_iis_2023_128

Barnes, E., & Hutson, J. (2024). Natural language processing and neurosymbolic ai: The role of neural networks with knowledge-guided symbolic approaches. *Journal of Artificial Intelligence and Robotics, 2*(1).

Barr, V., & Stephenson, C. (2011). Bringing computational thinking to K-12: What is involved and what is the role of the computer science education community? *ACM Inroads, 2*(1), 48–54. DOI: 10.1145/1929887.1929905

Barua, P., Vicnesh, J., Gururajan, R., Oh, S., Palmer, E., Azizan, M., Kadri, N. A., & Acharya, U. (2022). Artificial intelligence enabled personalised assistive tools to enhance education of children with neurodevelopmental disorders—A review. *International Journal of Environmental Research and Public Health, 19*(3), 1192. DOI: 10.3390/ijerph19031192 PMID: 35162220

Barzani, S., Aslam, M., & Aslam, T. (2021). The role of technology in ell classes in turkish republic of northern cyprus. *International Journal of Language Education, 5*(2), 30. DOI: 10.26858/ijole.v5i2.14109

Baskara, F. (2023). Ai-driven dynamics: Chatgpt transforming elt teacher-student interactions. *Lensa Kajian Kebahasaan Kesusastraan Dan Budaya, 13*(2), 261. DOI: 10.26714/lensa.13.2.2023.261-275

Basri, W. S. (2024). Effectiveness of AI-powered tutoring systems in enhancing learning outcomes. *Eurasian Journal of Educational Research (EJER), 110.*

Bastani, H., Bastani, O., Sungu, A., & Ge, H., Kabakci, O¨., & Mariman, R. (2025). Generative ai without guardrails can harm learning: Evidence from high school mathematics. *Proceedings of the National Academy of Sciences.* . 2422633122DOI: 10.1073/pnas.2422633122

Bastani, H., Bastani, O., Sungu, A., Ge, H., Kabakcı, O., & Mariman, R. (2024). Generative ai can harm learning. *SSRN, 4895486,* •••. https://papers.ssrn.com/sol3/papers.cfm?abstract_id=4895486

Basu, S., Biswas, G., Sengupta, P., Dickes, A., Kinnebrew, J. S., & Clark, D. (2016). Identifying middle school students' challenges in computational thinking-based science learning. *Research and Practice in Technology Enhanced Learning, 11*(1), 13. DOI: 10.1186/s41039-016-0036-2 PMID: 30613246

Beck, T. A., & Parker, W. (2021). *Social studies in elementary education* (16th ed.). Pearson.

Belda-Medina, J., & Calvo-Ferrer, J. R. (2022). Using chatbots as AI conversational partners in language learning. *Applied Sciences (Basel, Switzerland), 12*(17), 8427. DOI: 10.3390/app12178427

Belen Saglam, R., Nurse, J. R., & Hodges, D. (2021, July). Privacy concerns in chatbot interactions: When to trust and when to worry. In *International Conference on Human-Computer Interaction* (pp. 391-399). Cham: Springer International Publishing. DOI: 10.1007/978-3-030-78642-7_53

Benita, F., Virupaksha, D., Wilhelm, E., & Tunçer, B. (2021). A smart learning ecosystem design for delivering Data-driven Thinking in STEM education. *Smart Learning Environments, 8*(1), 1–20. DOI: 10.1186/s40561-021-00153-y PMID: 40477256

Benjamin, R. (2019). *Race after technology: Abolitionist tools for the New Jim Code*. Polity Press.

Bernacki, M. L., Greene, M. J., & Lobczowski, N. G. (2021). A systematic review of research on personalized learning: Personalized by whom, to what, how, and for what purpose(s)? *Educational Psychology Review, 33*(4), 1675–1715. DOI: 10.1007/s10648-021-09615-8

Bers, M. U. (2012). *Designing digital experiences for positive youth development: From playpen to playground*. Oxford University Press. DOI: 10.1093/acprof:oso/9780199757022.001.0001

Bers, M. U. (2018). Coding and computational thinking in early childhood: The impact of ScratchJr in Europe. *European Journal of STEM Education*, *3*(3), 8. DOI: 10.20897/ejsteme/3868

Bertini, F. (2023). Artificial Intelligence and data privacy. *Sistemi Intelligenti*, *35*(2), 477–484. DOI: 10.1422/108143

Bettayeb, A. M., Abu Talib, M., Sobhe Altayasinah, A. Z., & Dakalbab, F. (2024). Exploring the impact of ChatGPT: Conversational AI in education. *Frontiers in Education*, *9*, 1379796. Advance online publication. DOI: 10.3389/feduc.2024.1379796

Betts, A., Thai, K. P., & Gunderia, S. (2021). Personalized mastery learning ecosystems: Using Bloom's four objects of change to drive learning in adaptive instructional systems. In Sottilare, R. A., & Schwarz, J. (Eds.), *Adaptive instructional systems. Design and evaluation* (Vol. 12792, pp. 29–52). Springer., DOI: 10.1007/978-3-030-77857-6_3

Bhardwaj, A., Sharma, M., Kumar, S., Sharma, S., & Sharma, P. C. (2024). Transforming pediatric speech and language disorder diagnosis and therapy: The evolving role of artificial intelligence. *Health Sciences Review (Oxford, England)*, *12*, 100188. DOI: 10.1016/j.hsr.2024.100188

Bhowmik, D., & Kim, M. (2022). Ethical governance of AI in education: Challenges and frameworks for equitable access. *Journal of Educational Technology Research*, *45*(2), 175–192. DOI: 10.5281/zenodo.15667060

Bhowmik, S. (2023). K-12 ESL Writing Instruction: Learning to Write or Writing to Learn Language? *TESL Canada Journal*, *39*(2). Advance online publication. DOI: 10.18806/tesl.v39i2/1376

Bhowmik, S., & Kim, M. (2022). ESL Writing Instruction in K-12 Settings: Pedagogical Approaches and Classroom Techniques. *Language and Literature*, *24*(2), 174–197. Advance online publication. DOI: 10.20360/langandlit29612

Bhuyan, B. P., Ramdane-Cherif, A., Tomar, R., & Singh, T. (2024). Neuro-symbolic artificial intelligence: A survey. *Neural Computing & Applications*, *36*(21), 12809–12844. DOI: 10.1007/s00521-024-09960-z

Bin-Nashwan, S. A., Sadallah, M., & Bouteraa, M. (2023). Use of ChatGPT in academia: Academic integrity hangs in the balance. *Technology in Society*, *75*, 102370. DOI: 10.1016/j.techsoc.2023.102370

Blasco, A., & Charisi, V. (2024). AI chatbots in K-12 education: An experimental study of Socratic vs. non-Socratic approaches and the role of step-by-step reasoning. *SSRN*. https://dx.doi.org/DOI: 10.2139/ssrn.5040921

Bloom, B. S. (1968). Learning for mastery. *Evaluation Comment*, *1*(2), 1–12.

Böckle, M., Novak, J., & Bick, M. (2017). Towards Adaptive Gamification: A Synthesis of Current Developments. In *Proceedings of the 25th European Conference on Information Systems (ECIS), (pp.* 158–174*)*. Guimarães, Portugal.

Bontchev, B., Naydenov, I., & Adamov, I. (2024). Intelligent adaptation of difficulty and npc behavior in serious video games for learning. *IFAC-PapersOnLine*, *58*(3), 187–192. DOI: 10.1016/j.ifacol.2024.07.148

Borham, S., Ramli, S., & Ghani, M. (2024). AI concepts integration in developing E-Muhadathat kits for non-Arabic speakers. *Ijaz Arabi Journal of Arabic Learning*, *7*(3). Advance online publication. DOI: 10.18860/ijazarabi.v7i3.26568

Boucher, E. M., Harake, N. R., Ward, H. E., Stoeckl, S. E., Vargas, J., Minkel, J., Parks, A. C., & Zilca, R. (2021). Artificially intelligent chatbots in digital mental health interventions: A review. *Expert Review of Medical Devices, 18*(sup1), 37–49. DOI: 10.1080/17434440.2021.2013200

Bougdira, A., & Al Murshidi, G. (2025). Generative AI as a tool for personalized STEAM K-12 education. In *Prompt Engineering and Generative AI Applications for Teaching and Learning* (pp. 387–409). https://doi.org/DOI: 10.4018/979-8-3693-7332-3.ch023

Bouneffouf, D., & Aggarwal, C. C. (2022). Survey on applications of neurosymbolic artificial intelligence. *arXiv preprint arXiv:2209.12618.*

Bower, M., Wood, L. N., Lai, J. W., Highfield, K., Veal, J., Howe, C., Lister, R., & Mason, R. (2017). Improving the computational thinking pedagogical capabilities of school teachers. *Australian Journal of Teacher Education (Online)*, *42*(3), 53–72. DOI: 10.14221/ajte.2017v42n3.4

Bown, Oliver, Grace, K., Ocampo Blanco, R., & Ibarrola, F. (2025). "coffee so good, you'll want to slap your barista": Evaluating AI co-creation through dialogic actions. *Creativity Research Journal*, 1–17. https://doi.org/DOI: 10.1080/10400419.2025.2501735

Bradex, M. A. (2016). *Blended learning: A case study using ALEKS and small group instruction to increase math literacy of English learners* [Doctoral Dissertation, California State University]. ScholarWorks. http://hdl.handle.net/10211.3/190298

Brown, J. C. (2017). A metasynthesis of the complementarity of culturally responsive and inquiry-based science education in K-12 settings: Implications for advancing equitable science teaching and learning. *Journal of Research in Science Teaching*, *54*(9), 1143–1173. Advance online publication. DOI: 10.1002/tea.21401

Brown, M. R. (2023). Educators' accounts of White racial advantage in K-12 settings: Mitigating disadvantages for non-White students. *Multicultural Education Review, 15*(3), 185–203. Advance online publication. DOI: 10.1080/2005615X.2023.2287697

Brusilovsky, P. (1996). Methods and techniques of adaptive hypermedia. *User Modeling and User-Adapted Interaction, 6*(2–3), 87–129. DOI: 10.1007/BF00143964

Brynjolfsson, E., Li, D., & Raymond, L. R. (2023, November). *Generative AI at work* (NBER Working Paper No. 31161). National Bureau of Economic Research. https://doi.org/DOI: 10.3386/w31161

Bubeck, S., Chandrasekaran, V., Eldan, R., Gehrke, J., Horvitz, E., Kamar, E., Lee, P., Lee, Y. T., Li, Y., Lundberg, S., Nori, H., Palagni, H., Ribeiro, M., & Yi, Z. (2023). *Sparks of artificial general intelligence: Early experiments with gpt- 4. Procedia - Social and Behavioral Sciences Elsevier BV*. Elsevier BV.

Buffum, P. S. (2015). Examining the impact narrative interactivity has on fostering identity formation in an educational game. *CHI PLAY 2015 - Proceedings of the 2015 Annual Symposium on Computer-Human Interaction in Play*, 395–398. https://doi.org/DOI: 10.1145/2793107.2810278

Bulut, O., Beiting-Parrish, M., Casabianca, J. M., Slater, S. C., Jiao, H., Song, D., Ormerod, C., Fabiyi, D. G., Ivan, R., Walsh, C., Rios, O., Wilson, J., Yildirim-Erbasli, S. N., Wongvorachan, T., Liu, J. X., Tan, B., & Morilova, P. (2025). The rise of artificial intelligence in educational measurement: Opportunities and ethical challenges. *Chinese/English Journal of Educational Measurement and Evaluation, 5*(3). Advance online publication. DOI: 10.59863/MIQL7785

Buolamwini, J., & Gebru, T. (2018). Gender shades: Intersectional accuracy disparities in commercial gender classification. In *Proceedings of Machine Learning Research* (Vol. 81, pp. 77–91). https://proceedings.mlr.press/v81/buolamwini18a/buolamwini18a.pdf

Burden, P. R. (2025). *Classroom management: Creating a successful K-12 learning community*. John Wiley & Sons.

Caeli, E. N., & Bundsgaard, J. (2020). Computational thinking in compulsory education: A survey study on initiatives and conceptions. *Educational Technology Research and Development, 68*(1), 551–573. DOI: 10.1007/s11423-019-09694-z

Cai, C. J., Winter, S., Steiner, D., Wilcox, L., & Terry, M. (2019). "hello AI": Uncovering the onboarding needs of medical practitioners for human-AI collaborative decision-making. *Proceedings of the ACM on Human-Computer Interaction, 3*(CSCW), 1–24. https://doi.org/DOI: 10.1145/3359206

Campaña, K. V., & Solomon, B. G. (2025). Classification accuracy of i-Ready and prior year state exams on year-end outcomes. *Assessment for Effective Intervention, 50*(3), 153–162. DOI: 10.1177/15345084251338860

Campitiello, L., Beatini, V., & Di Tore, S. (2024, January). Non-player character smart in virtual learning environment: Empowering education through artificial intelligence. In *Workshop on Artificial Intelligence with and for Learning Sciences: Past, Present, and Future Horizons* (pp. 131-137). Cham: Springer Nature Switzerland. https://doi.org/DOI: 10.1007/978-3-031-57402-3_14

Cao, C. C., Ding, Z., Lin, J., & Hopfgartner, F. (2023). AI Chatbots as multi-role pedagogical agents: Transforming engagement in CS education. arXiv preprint arXiv:2308.03992

Cao, B., & Tutor, A. (2023). Solution for china disadvantaged and underresourced children. *Lect. Notes Educ. Psychol. Public Media, 32*(1), 133–141. DOI: 10.54254/2753-7048/32/20230834

Capps, R. (2025, June 17). 22 New Jobs A.I. Could Give You. *The New York Times*. https://www.nytimes.com/2025/06/17/magazine/ai-new-jobs.html

Carroll, J. J. (2024). Effects of Lexia Reading Core5 on non-ELL upper elementary students' reading comprehension [Doctoral dissertation, Walden University].

Caruana, I., Gilar-Corbí, R., & Palomar, M. (2025). THE AI REVOLUTION IN K-12 EDUCATION: ARE EDUCATORS READY? 6259–6265. https://doi.org/.DOI: 10.21125/inted.2025.1624

Casal-Otero, L., Catala, A., Fernández-Morante, C., Taboada, M., Cebreiro, B., & Barro, S. (2023). AI literacy in K-12: A systematic literature review. *International Journal of STEM Education, 10*(29), 29. Advance online publication. DOI: 10.1186/s40594-023-00418-7

CAST. (2024). UDL Guidelines 3.0. Retrieved from https://udlguidelines.cast.org/

CAST. (2024). Universal design for learning guidelines version 3.0 [Graphic organizer and guidance]. https://udlguidelines.cast.org/more/downloads/

CEDEFOP. (2024). *AI competency framework for teachers (summary of UNESCO framework)* [Summarises UNESCO's AI Competency Framework for Teachers; accessed 2025-10-11]. https://www.cedefop.europa.eu/en/news/ai-competency-framework-teachers

Černý, M. (2022). The history of chatbots: The journey from psychological experiment to educational object. *Journal of Applied Technical and Educational Sciences, 12*(3), 322–322.

Chae, H., Kim, M., Kim, C., Jeong, W., Kim, H., Lee, J., & Yeo, J. (2023). Tutoring: Instruction-grounded conversational agent for language learners. *Proceedings of the AAAI Conference on Artificial Intelligence, 37*(13), 16413–16415. DOI: 10.1609/aaai.v37i13.27063

Chaer, H., Jafar, S., Intiana, S. R. J., & Setiawan, I. (2024). Pengajaran bahasa berdasarkan teori aktivitas budaya engeström: Integrasi konteks budaya dalam pembelajaran bahasa. *Jurnal Humanitas Katalisator Perubahan Dan Inovator Pendidikan, 10*(2), 235–254. DOI: 10.29408/jhm.v10i2.25562

Chamola, V., Peelam, M. S., Mittal, U., Hassija, V., Singh, A., Pareek, R., Mangal, P., Sangwan, D., de Albuquerque, V. H. C., Mahmud, M., & Brown, D. J. (2025). Metaverse for Education: Developments, Challenges, and Future Direction. *Computer Applications in Engineering Education, 33*(3), e70018. Advance online publication. DOI: 10.1002/cae.70018

Chan, C. K. Y., & Hu, W. (2023). Students' voices on generative AI: Perceptions, benefits, and challenges in higher education. *International Journal of Educational Technology in Higher Education, 20*(1), 43. DOI: 10.1186/s41239-023-00411-8

Chan, C. K. Y., & Tsi, L. H. Y. (2024). Will generative AI replace teachers in higher education? A study of teacher and student perceptions. *Studies in Educational Evaluation, 83*, 101395. DOI: 10.1016/j.stueduc.2024.101395

Chan, W., An, A., & Davoudi, H. (2023). A Case Study on ChatGPT Question Generation. *2023 IEEE International Conference on Big Data (BigData)*, 1647–1656. DOI: 10.1109/BigData59044.2023.10386520

Chen, W. J. (2023). Improving the e-learning experience: A primarily gamification-based approach to conceptualizing and designing a user-friendly and visually appealing solution for primary students and teachers [Doctoral dissertation, Technische Hochschule Ingolstadt].

Chen, J., Shi, B., Chen, Q., & Qiu, J. (2023). Comparisons of convergent thinking: A perspective informed by culture and neural mechanisms. *Thinking Skills and Creativity, 49*(101343), 101343. DOI: 10.1016/j.tsc.2023.101343

Chen, M. (2025). The impact of AI-assisted personalized learning on student academic achievement. *US-China Education Review A, 15*(6), 441–450. DOI: 10.17265/2161-623X/2025.06.008

Chen, R., Lee, V. R., & Lee, G. (2025). A cross-sectional look at teacher reactions, worries, and professional development needs related to generative AI in an urban school district. *Education and Information Technologies*, *30*(11), 1–38. DOI: 10.1007/s10639-025-13350-w

Chen, S., Fang, Y., Shi, G., Sabatini, J., Greenberg, D., Frijters, J., & Graesser, A. C. (2021). Automated disengagement tracking within an intelligent tutoring system. *Frontiers in Artificial Intelligence*, *3*, 595627. Advance online publication. DOI: 10.3389/frai.2020.595627 PMID: 33748746

Chen, X., Xie, H., & Hwang, G.-J. (2020). A multi-perspective study on artificial intelligence in education: Grants, conferences, journals, software tools, institutions, and researchers. *Computers and Education: Artificial Intelligence*, *1*, 100005. DOI: 10.1016/j.caeai.2020.100005

Chen, X., Xie, H., Zou, D., & Hwang, G. J. (2020). Application and theory gaps during the rise of artificial intelligence in education. *Computers and Education: Artificial Intelligence*, *1*, 100002. DOI: 10.1016/j.caeai.2020.100002

Chen, Y., Chu, H., & Chueh, C. (2025). Effect of teachers' emotional intelligence on emotional blackmail at work with emotional labor as the mediating variable and burnout as the moderating variable. *Psychology in the Schools*, *62*(5), 1583–1597. DOI: 10.1002/pits.23412

Chiu, T. K. F. (2021). A holistic approach to the design of artificial intelligence (AI) education for K-12 schools. *TechTrends*, *65*(6), 796–807. DOI: 10.1007/s11528-021-00637-1

Chiu, T. K. F. (2024). The impact of Generative AI (GenAI) on practices, policies and research direction in education: A case of ChatGPT and Midjourney. *Interactive Learning Environments*, *32*(10), 6187–6203. DOI: 10.1080/10494820.2023.2253861

Chiu, T. K., & Chai, C. S. (2020). Sustainable curriculum planning for artificial intelligence education: A self-determination theory perspective. *Sustainability (Basel)*, *12*(14), 5568. DOI: 10.3390/su12145568

Chocarro, R., Cortiñas, M., & Marcos-Matás, G. (2021). Teachers' attitudes towards chatbots in education: A technology acceptance model approach considering the effect of social language, bot proactiveness, and users' characteristics. *Educational Studies*, *49*(2), 295–313. DOI: 10.1080/03055698.2020.1850426

Choi, E. (2025). AI and Digital Literacy Training Support Strategies for Elementary School Teachers in South Korea: Insights from Needs Analysis and Delphi Survey. *KSII Transactions on Internet and Information Systems, 19*(2). Advance online publication. DOI: 10.3837/tiis.2025.02.007

Chubb, J., Missaoui, S., Concannon, S., Maloney, L., & Walker, J. A. (2022). Interactive storytelling for children: A case-study of design and development considerations for ethical conversational AI. *International Journal of Child-Computer Interaction, 32*, 100403. Advance online publication. DOI: 10.1016/j.ijcci.2021.100403

Chukwuere, J. (2024). Today's academic research: The role of ChatGPT writing. *Journal of Information Systems and Informatics, 6*(1), 30–46. Advance online publication. DOI: 10.51519/journalisi.v6i1.639

Cipriano, C., & McCarthy, M. F. (2023). Towards an inclusive social and emotional learning. *Social and Emotional Learning: Research, Practice, and Policy, 2*, 100008. Advance online publication. DOI: 10.1016/j.sel.2023.100008

Clark, C. T., Chrisman, A., & Lewis, S. G. (2022). (Un)standardizing emotions: An ethical critique of social and Emotional Learning Standards. *Teachers College Record (1970), 124*(7), 131–149. DOI: 10.1177/01614681221111432

Clark, C. H., & van Kessel, C. (2025). *AI in social studies education: Tools for thoughtful practice with generative artificial intelligence*. Teachers College Press.

Clayback, K. A., Williford, A. P., & Vitiello, V. E. (2023). Identifying Teacher Beliefs and Experiences Associated with Curriculum Implementation Fidelity in Early Childhood Education. *Prevention Science, 24*(1), 27–38. Advance online publication. DOI: 10.1007/s11121-022-01414-z PMID: 35921059

Coates, H., James, R., & Baldwin, G. (2005). A critical examination of the effects of learning management systems on university teaching and learning. *Tertiary Education and Management, 11*(1), 19–36. DOI: 10.1080/13583883.2005.9967137

Codish, D., & Ravid, G. (2014). Personality based gamification-Educational gamification for extroverts and introverts. In *Proceedings of the 9th CHAIS Conference for the Study of Innovation and Learning Technologies: Learning in the Technological Era* (pp. 36-44). Ra'anana: The Open University of Israel.

Coenen, A., Davis, L., Ippolito, D., Reif, E., & Yuan, A. (2021). Wordcraft: A human-AI collaborative editor for story writing. In *arXiv [cs.CL]*. arXiv. https://arxiv.org/abs/2107.07430

Cohen, J. (1992). A power primer. *Psychological Bulletin, 112*(1), 155–159. https://psycnet.apa.org/doi/10.1037/0033-2909.112.1.155. DOI: 10.1037/0033-2909.112.1.155 PMID: 19565683

Colelough, B. C., & Regli, W. (2025). Neuro-symbolic ai in 2024: A systematic review. *arXiv preprint arXiv:2501.05435*.

Colton, S., & Wiggins, G. A. (2012). Computational creativity: The final frontier? In *Proceedings of the 20th European conference on artificial intelligence* (pp. 21–26). IOS Press.

Common Sense Education. (2025). *AI professional learning for educators (self-paced courses and certification)* [Includes AI Basics, Safe & Responsible Use, AI Literacy Certification; accessed 2025-10-11]. https://www.commonsense.org/education/training/ai

Cope, B., Kalantzis, M., & Searsmith, D. (2020). Artificial intelligence for education: Knowledge and its assessment in AI-enabled learning ecologies. *Educational Philosophy and Theory*, •••, 1–17.

Corbeil, J. R., & Corbeil, M. E. (2025). Teaching and Learning in the Age of Generative AI: Evidence-Based Approaches to Pedagogy, Ethics, and Beyond. In *Teaching and Learning in the Age of Generative AI: Evidence-Based Approaches to Pedagogy, Ethics, and Beyond*. https://doi.org/DOI: 10.4324/9781032688602

Cosyn, E., Uzun, H., Doble, C., & Matayoshi, J. (2021). A practical perspective on knowledge space theory: ALEKS and its data. *Journal of Mathematical Psychology, 101*, 102512. Advance online publication. DOI: 10.1016/j.jmp.2021.102512

Couch, J. D. (2023). *Rewiring education: How technology can unlock every student's potential*. BenBella Books.

Craig, S. D., Hu, X., Graesser, A. C., Bargagliotti, A. E., Sterbinsky, A., Cheney, K. R., & Okwumabua, T. (2013). The impact of a technology-based mathematics after-school program using ALEKS on student's knowledge and behaviors. *Computers & Education, 68*, 495–504. DOI: 10.1016/j.compedu.2013.06.010

Crawford, K., & Huling, H. (2023). Building Classroom Community in Elementary Literacy Methods Courses. *Georgia Journal of Literacy, 45*(1). Advance online publication. DOI: 10.56887/galiteracy.69

Crowder, J. (2024). What happens when a chatbot gives detrimental advice? Who's Responsible? In Crowder, J. (Ed.), *AI chatbots: The good, the bad, and the ugly* (pp. 121–133). Springer Nature Switzerland., DOI: 10.1007/978-3-031-45509-4_13

Crowder, N. A. (1959). Automatic tutoring by means of intrinsic programming. In Galanter, E. (Ed.), *Automatic teaching: The state of the art* (pp. 109–116). Wiley.

Cukurova, M., & Luckin, R. (2018). *Measuring the impact of emerging technologies in education: A pragmatic approach*. Springer.

Curriculum Associates. (n.d.). *Literacy tours*. Curriculum Associates. https://www.curriculumassociates.com/programs/tours

Cutumisu, M., Adams, C., & Lu, C. (2019). A scoping review of empirical research on recent computational thinking assessments. *Journal of Science Education and Technology*, *28*(6), 651–676. DOI: 10.1007/s10956-019-09799-3

D'Mello, S. K., Biddy, Q., Breideband, T., Bush, J., Chang, M., Cortez, A., Flanigan, J., Foltz, P. W., Gorman, J. C., Hirshfield, L., Monica Ko, M.-L., Krishnaswamy, N., Lieber, R., Martin, J., Palmer, M., Penuel, W. R., Philip, T., Puntambekar, S., Pustejovsky, J., & Whitehill, J. (2024). From learning optimization to learner flourishing: Reimagining AI in Education at the Institute for Student-AI Teaming (iSAT). *AI Magazine*, *45*(1), 61–68. DOI: 10.1002/aaai.12158

Daher, R. (2025). Integrating AI literacy into teacher education: A critical perspective paper. *Discover Artificial Intelligence*, *5*(1), 217. DOI: 10.1007/s44163-025-00475-7

Darcy, A., Daniels, J., Salinger, D., Wicks, P., & Robinson, A. (2021). Evidence of human-level bonds established with a digital conversational agent: Cross-sectional, retrospective observational study. Jmir Formative Research, 5(5). *JMIR Formative Research*, *5*(5), e27868. Advance online publication. DOI: 10.2196/27868 PMID: 33973854

Darwin, R., Rusdin, D., Mukminatien, N., Suryati, N., Laksmi, E. D., & Marzuki, . (2023). Critical thinking in the AI era: An exploration of EFL students' perceptions, benefits, and limitations. *Cogent Education*, *11*(1), 2290342. DOI: 10.1080/2331186X.2023.2290342

Daryanto, T., Ding, X., Wilhelm, L. T., Stil, S., Knutsen, K. M., & Rho, E. H. (2025). Conversate: Supporting Reflective Learning in Interview Practice Through Interactive Simulation and Dialogic Feedback. *Proceedings of the ACM on Human-Computer Interaction*, *9*(1), 1–32. Advance online publication. DOI: 10.1145/3701188

Davis, F. D. (1989). Perceived usefulness, perceived ease of use, and user acceptance of information technology. *Management Information Systems Quarterly*, *13*(3), 319–340. DOI: 10.2307/249008

Dawat, E. (2023). Advancing education through data analytics and artificial intelligence: A comprehensive literature review. *International Journal of Research Publications, 137*(1). Advance online publication. DOI: 10.47119/IJRP1001371120235686

Day, M. Y., & Shaw, S. R. (2021, August). AI customer service system with pre-trained language and response ranking models for university admissions. In 2021 IEEE 22nd International Conference on Information Reuse and Integration for Data Science (IRI) (pp. 395-401). IEEE. DOI: 10.1109/IRI51335.2021.00062

De Lima, E. S., Feijó, B., & Furtado, A. L. (2020). Adaptive storytelling based on personality and preference modeling. *Entertainment Computing, 34*, 100342. Advance online publication. DOI: 10.1016/j.entcom.2020.100342

De Smet, L., Venturato, G., De Raedt, L., & Marra, G. (2025). Relational neurosymbolic markov models. *Proceedings of the AAAI Conference on Artificial Intelligence, 39*(15), 16181–16189. DOI: 10.1609/aaai.v39i15.33777

De Souza, A. S., & Kochhann, A. (2023). Extensionist training in the landscape of opportunities and challenges for reframing teacher education in K-12 settings: A systematic literature review. *REVISTA FOCO, 16*(10), e3297. Advance online publication. DOI: 10.54751/revistafoco.v16n10-065

Dean, S. N., & Gilbert, A. (2024). 'Watching what they can do on their own is beautiful': A navigation of shared agency in school-based outdoor environmental education. *Journal of Adventure Education and Outdoor Learning*. Advance online publication. DOI: 10.1080/14729679.2024.2314605

Dear, B. (2017). *The friendly orange glow: The untold story of the plato system and the dawn of cyberculture*. Pantheon.

DeBiasMe: De-biasing Human-AI Interactions with Metacognitive AIED (AI in Education) Interventions. (n.d.). Retrieved June 16, 2025, from https://arxiv.org/html/2504.16770v1

Dede, C. (2010). Comparing frameworks for 21st century skills. *21st century skills: Rethinking how students learn, 20*(2010), 51-76.

Deep, S., Athimoolam, K., & Enoch, T. (2024). Optimizing administrative efficiency and student engagement in education: The impact of ai. *International Journal of Current Science Research and Review, 07*(10). Advance online publication. DOI: 10.47191/ijcsrr/V7-i10-34

Degen, P. B., & Asanov, I. (2025). Beyond Automation: Socratic AI, Epistemic Agency, and the Implications of the Emergence of Orchestrated Multi-Agent Learning Architectures. arXiv preprint arXiv:2508.05116.

Dehghanzadeh, H., Farrokhnia, M., Dehghanzadeh, H., Taghipour, K., & Noroozi, O. (2024). Using gamification to support learning in K-12 education: A systematic literature review. *British Journal of Educational Technology*, *55*(1), 34–70. DOI: 10.1111/bjet.13335

Dembe, A. (2024). Advancing personalized learning through educational artificial intelligence: Challenges, opportunities, and future directions. *Res Invent J Eng Phys Sci*, *3*(1), 89–101.

Denny, P., McDonald, F., Empson, R., Kelly, P., & Petersen, A. (2018, April). Empirical support for a causal relationship between gamification and learning outcomes. In *Proceedings of the 2018 CHI Conference on Human Factors in Computing Systems* (pp. 1–13). DOI: 10.1145/3173574.3173885

Dergaa, I., Chamari, K., Zmijewski, P., & Ben Saad, H. (2023). From human writing to artificial intelligence generated text: Examining the prospects and potential threats of ChatGPT in academic writing. *Biology of Sport*, *40*(2), 615–622. DOI: 10.5114/biolsport.2023.125623 PMID: 37077800

Deveci Topal, A., Dilek Eren, C., & Kolburan Geçer, A. (2021). Chatbot application in a 5th grade science course. *Education and Information Technologies*, *26*(5), 6241–6265. DOI: 10.1007/s10639-021-10627-8 PMID: 34177344

Dieker, L., Hines, R., Wilkins, I., Hughes, C., Scott, K., Smith, S., & Shah, S. (2024). Using an artificial intelligence (ai) agent to support teacher instruction and student learning. *Journal of Special Education Preparation*, *4*(2), 78–88. DOI: 10.33043/d8xb94q7

Diliberti, M. K., Lake, R. J., & Weiner, S. R. (2025). *More districts are training teachers on artificial intelligence: Findings from the American School District Panel.* RAND Corporation. https://www.rand.org/pubs/research_reports/RRA956-31.html

Diliberti, M. K., Schwartz, H. L., Doan, S., Shapiro, A., Rainey, L. R., & Lake, R. J. (2024). *Using artificial intelligence tools in K–12 classrooms* (Research Report No. RRA956-21). RAND Corporation. https://www.rand.org/pubs/research_reports/RRA956-21.html

Dillenbourg, P. (2016). The evolution of research on digital education. *International Journal of Artificial Intelligence in Education*, *26*(2), 544–560. DOI: 10.1007/s40593-016-0106-z

Dimitriadou, E., & Lanitis, A. (2023). A critical evaluation, challenges, and future perspectives of using artificial intelligence and emerging technologies in smart classrooms. *Smart Learning Environments*, *10*(12), 12. Advance online publication. DOI: 10.1186/s40561-023-00231-3 PMID: 40478141

Dinu, M.-C. (2024). Parameter choice and neuro-symbolic approaches for deep domain-invariant learning. *arXiv preprint arXiv:2410.06235*.

Divanji, R. A., Bindman, S., Tung, A., Chen, K., Castaneda, L., & Scanlon, M. (2023). A one stop shop? Perspectives on the value of adaptive learning technologies in K-12 education. *Computers and Education Open*, *5*, 100157. Advance online publication. DOI: 10.1016/j.caeo.2023.100157

Doignon, J. P., & Falmagne, J. C. (1985). Spaces for the assessment of knowledge. *International Journal of Man-Machine Studies*, *23*(2), 175–196. DOI: 10.1016/S0020-7373(85)80031-6

Doignon, J., & Falmagne, J. (1999). *Knowledge spaces*. Springer., DOI: 10.1007/978-3-642-58625-5

Doignon, J., & Falmagne, J. (2011). *Learning spaces*. Springer., DOI: 10.1007/978-3-642-01039-2

Dollinger, M., Liu, D., Arthars, N., & Lodge, J. (2019). Working Together in Learning Analytics Towards the Co-Creation of Value. *Journal of Learning Analytics*, *6*(2), 10–26. DOI: 10.18608/jla.2019.62.2

Dong, C., Yuan, Y., Chen, K., Cheng, S., & Wen, C. (2025). How to Build an Adaptive AI Tutor for Any Course Using Knowledge Graph-Enhanced Retrieval-Augmented Generation (KG-RAG). *2025 14th International Conference on Educational and Information Technology, ICEIT 2025*, 152–157. https://doi.org/DOI: 10.1109/ICEIT64364.2025.10975937

Doshi, A. R., & Hauser, O. P. (2024). Generative AI enhances individual creativity but reduces the collective diversity of novel content. *Science Advances*, *10*(28), eadn5290. Advance online publication. DOI: 10.1126/sciadv.adn5290 PMID: 38996021

Drigas, A., Papoutsi, C., & Skianis, C. (2023). Being an Emotionally Intelligent Leader through the Nine-Layer Model of Emotional Intelligence—The Supporting Role of New Technologies. *Sustainability (Basel)*, *15*(10), 8103. Advance online publication. DOI: 10.3390/su15108103 du Plooy, E., Casteleijn, D., & Franzsen, D. (2024). Personalized adaptive learning in higher education: A scoping review of key characteristics and impact on academic performance and engagement. *Heliyon, 10*(21), e39630. DOI: 10.1016/j.heliyon.2024.e39630 PMID: 39524879

Dumbuya, E. (2023). Personalized learning through artificial intelligence: Revolutionizing education. *Available at SSRN* 5023248.

Dumont, H., & Ready, D. D. (2023). On the promise of personalized learning for educational equity. *NPJ Science of Learning*, *8*(26), 26. Advance online publication. DOI: 10.1038/s41539-023-00174-x PMID: 37542046

Dusseault, B. (2024). *AI and education policy 101: The evolving landscape and examples from early adopters*. Center on Reinventing Public Education. https://crpe.org/ai-and-education-policy-101-the-evolving-landscape-and-examples-from-early-adopters/

Dutta, S., Ranjan, S., Mishra, S., Sharma, V., Hewage, P., & Iwendi, C. (2024, February). Enhancing educational adaptability: A review and analysis of AI-driven adaptive learning platforms. *2024 4th International Conference on Innovative Practices in Technology and Management (ICIPTM)*. https://doi.org/DOI: 10.1109/ICIPTM59628.2024.10563448

Dwivedi, Y. K., Kshetri, N., Hughes, L., Slade, E. L., Jeyaraj, A., Kar, A. K., Baabdullah, A. M., Koohang, A., Raghavan, V., Ahuja, M., Albanna, H., Albashrawi, M. A., Al-Busaidi, A. S., Balakrishnan, J., Barlette, Y., Basu, S., Bose, I., Brooks, L., Buhalis, D., & Wright, R. (2023). Opinion Paper: "So what if ChatGPT wrote it?" Multidisciplinary perspectives on opportunities, challenges and implications of generative conversational AI for research, practice and policy. *International Journal of Information Management*, *71*, 102642. Advance online publication. DOI: 10.1016/j.ijinfomgt.2023.102642

Eden, C., Chisom, O., & Adeniyi, I. (2024). Integrating ai in education: opportunities, challenges, and ethical considerations. Magna Scientia Advanced Research and Reviews, 10(2), 006-013. https://doi.org/DOI: 10.30574/msarr.2024.10.2.0039

Elbouknify, I., Berrada, I., Mekouar, L., Iraqi, Y., Bergou, E. H., Belhabib, H., Nail, Y., & Wardi, S. (2025). *AI-based identification and support of at-risk students: A case study of the Moroccan education system* (arXiv:2504.07160) [Preprint]. arXiv. https://doi.org//arXiv.2504.07160DOI: 10.48550

Ellikkal, A., & Rajamohan, S. (2025). AI-enabled personalized learning: Empowering management students for improving engagement and academic performance. *Vilakshan - XIMB. Journal of Management*, *22*(1), 28–44. DOI: 10.1108/XJM-02-2024-0023

Elliott, D. (2024). This ai tutor could make humans "10 times smarter", its creator says [Squirrel Ai adaptive learning system helping address teaching gaps in China; cites UNESCO estimate of 44 million additional teachers needed by 2030 to reach SDG 4:contentReference[oaicite:1]index=1]. *World Economic Forum (Forum Stories)*. https: //www.weforum.org/stories/2024/07/ai-tutor-china-teaching-gaps/

Ellis, R. A., Han, F., & Pardo, A. (2017). Improving learning analytics–Combining observational and self-report data on student learning. *Journal of Educational Technology & Society, 20*(3), 158-169. https://www.jstor.org/stable/ 26196127.

Elmaadaway, M. A. N., & Abouelenein, Y. A. M. (2023). In-service teachers' TPACK development through an adaptive e-learning environment (ALE). *Education and Information Technologies*, *28*(7), 8273–8298. DOI: 10.1007/s10639-022-11477-8 PMID: 36571083

Elmahdi, O. E. H., Balla, A. A. S., Abdelrady, A. H., Othman, E., & Abdelaziz Ahmed, A. (2025). AI-Driven Vocabulary Acquisition in EFL Higher Education: Interdisciplinary Insights into Technological Innovation, Ethical Challenges, and Equitable Access. *Forum for Linguistic Studies*, *7*(4), 477–491. DOI: 10.30564/fls.v7i4.8760

Elwahsh, S., Stern, N., Singh, A., & Ayobi, A. (2025). Linguistic Diversity and Mental Well-Being: Co-Designing Custom AI Chatbots with Multilingual Mothers. Cui 2025 Proceedings of the 2025 ACM Conference on Conversational User Interfaces. Scopus. https://doi.org/DOI: 10.1145/3719160.3736615

Eppard, J., Kaviani, A., Bowles, M., & Johnson, J. (2021). EdTech culturation: Integrating a culturally relevant pedagogy into educational technology. *Electronic Journal of e-Learning*, *19*(6), 516–530. DOI: 10.34190/ejel.19.6.2065

Eranıl, A. K., Eyice, R., Atan, M., & Alici, T. (2024). Investigations in the Turkish Education System: Structure, process and its reflections. *Denetişim*, *30*(30), 1–15. Advance online publication. DOI: 10.58348/denetisim.1383929

Essa, N., El-Gayar, M. M., & El-Daydamony, E. M. (2025). Enhanced model for abstractive Arabic text summarization using natural language generation and named entity recognition. *Neural Computing & Applications*, *37*(10), 7279–7301. DOI: 10.1007/s00521-024-10949-x

Essien, A., Bukoye, O. T., O'Dea, X., & Kremantzis, M. (2024). The influence of AI text generators on critical thinking skills in UK business schools. *Studies in Higher Education, 49*(5), 865–882. DOI: 10.1080/03075079.2024.2316881

Esteve-Mon, F., Llopis, M., & Adell-Segura, J. (2020). Digital competence and computational think ing of student teachers. [iJET]. *International Journal of Emerging Technologies in Learning, 15*(2), 29–41. DOI: 10.3991/ijet.v15i02.11588

Evans, J. E. (2024). *The effectiveness of ALEKS to address Grade 8 students' math deficiencies* [Doctoral dissertation, Walden University]. Walden Dissertations and Doctoral Studies. https://scholarworks.waldenu.edu/dissertations/16447/

Evans, R., & Sinha, N. (2024). Bridging the gap: Diversity initiatives in ai education. *AAAI-SS, 3*(1), 474–477. DOI: 10.1609/aaaiss.v3i1.31260

Ezzaim, A., Dahbi, A., Aqqal, A., & Haidine, A. (2024). AI-based learning style detection in adaptive learning systems: A systematic literature review. *Journal of Computers in Education.* Advance online publication. DOI: 10.1007/s40692-024-00328-9

Facione, P. A. (1990). *Critical thinking: A statement of expert consensus for purposes of educational assessment and instruction.* The California Academic Press., https://eric.ed.gov/?id=ED315423

Fakour, H., & Imani, M. (2025). Socratic wisdom in the age of AI: A comparative study of ChatGPT and human tutors in enhancing critical thinking skills. *Frontiers in Education, 10*, 1–12. DOI: 10.3389/feduc.2025.1528603

Falco, G., Shneiderman, B., Badger, J., Carrier, R., Dahbura, A., Danks, D., Eling, M., Goodloe, A., Gupta, J., Hart, C., Jirotka, M., Johnson, H., LaPointe, C., Llorens, A. J., Mackworth, A. K., Maple, C., Pálsson, S. E., Pasquale, F., Winfield, A., & Yeong, Z. K. (2021). Governing AI safety through independent audits. *Nature Machine Intelligence, 3*(7), 566–571. DOI: 10.1038/s42256-021-00370-7

Familoni, B., & Onyebuchi, N.Babajide Tolulope FamiloniNneamaka Chisom Onyebuchi. (2024). Advancements and challenges in ai integration for technical literacy: A systematic review. *Engineering Science & Technology Journal, 5*(4), 1415–1430. DOI: 10.51594/estj.v5i4.1042

Fariani, R. I., Junus, K., & Santoso, H. B. (2023). A systematic literature review on personalised learning in the higher education context. *Technology. Knowledge and Learning, 28*(2), 449–476. DOI: 10.1007/s10758-022-09628-4

Faul, F., Erdfelder, E., Lang, A.-G., & Buchner, A. (2007). G*Power 3: A flexible statistical power analysis program for the social, behavioral, and biomedical sciences. *Behavior Research Methods*, *39*(2), 2. Advance online publication. DOI: 10.3758/BF03193146 PMID: 17695343

Favero, L., Pérez-Ortiz, J. A., Käser, T., & Oliver, N. (2024, October). Enhancing critical thinking in education by means of a Socratic chatbot. In International Workshop on AI in Education and Educational Research (pp. 17-32). Cham: Springer Nature Switzerland.

Federation of American Scientists (Day One Project). (2024, June). *Establish a teacher AI literacy development program* [Policy memo proposing national K-12 teacher AI literacy PD; accessed 2025-10-11]. https://fas.org/publication/teacher-ai-literacy-development/

Feldstein, J., Dilkas, P., Belle, V., & Tsamoura, E. (2024). Mapping the neuro-symbolic ai landscape by architectures: A handbook on augmenting deep learning through symbolic reasoning. *arXiv preprint arXiv:2410.22077.*

Feng, M., Brezack, N., & Heffernan, N. (2025, July 21–23). *Scaling what works cost-consciously: A cost analysis of an AI-enhanced tool for middle school math learning. Proceedings of the Twelfth ACM Conference on Learning @ Scale (L@S '25)*, pp. 315–319. https://doi.org/DOI: 10.1145/3698205.3733947

Fernsel, L., & coauthors. (2025). An auditability framework for ai-based learning analytics systems. *Proceedings of the 17th International Conference on Computer Supported Education (CSEDU 2025).* https://www.scitepress.org/Papers/2025/132543/132543.pdf

Ferracani, A., Bertini, M., Pala, P., Nannotti, G., Principi, F., & Becchi, G. (2024). Personalized Generative Storytelling with AI-Visual Illustrations for the Promotion of Knowledge in Cultural Heritage Tourism. *SUMAC 2024 - Proceedings of the 6th Workshop on the AnalySis, Understanding and ProMotion of HeritAge Contents, Co-Located with: MM 2024*, 28–32. https://doi.org/DOI: 10.1145/3689094.3689465

Ferrara, E. (2024). Fairness and Bias in Artificial Intelligence: A Brief Survey of Sources, Impacts, and Mitigation Strategies. *Sci*, *6*(1), 3. Advance online publication. DOI: 10.3390/sci6010003

Ferster, B. (2014). *Teaching machines: Learning from the intersection of education and technology*. Johns Hopkins University Press. DOI: 10.1353/book.36140

Feser, M. S. (2024). PARENTS' VIEWS ON THE USE OF AI-BASED CHATBOTS SUCH AS ChatGPT IN HIGH SCHOOL (STEM) EDUCATION. *Journal of Baltic Science Education*, *23*(1), 4–8. DOI: 10.33225/jbse/24.23.04

Field, A. P. (2024). *Discovering statistics using IBM SPSS statistics* (6th ed.). SAGE Publications.

Fitas, R. (2025a). Inclusive education with ai: Supporting special needs and tackling language barriers. *arXiv preprint arXiv:2504.14120.*

Fitas, R., Ghosh, K., & Maity, S. (2025). Leveraging ai in education: Benefits, responsibilities, and trends. *Education: Benefits, Responsibilities, and Trends (February 01, 2025).* for California Community Colleges, A. S. (2023). Ai-powered education: Authentic assessments and learning [Describes authentic assessments evaluating creativity and collaboration and how AI can support project-based learning and multimodal assignments]. *ASCCC Open Education Resources.* https://asccc-oer-oedtresources.org/ai-powered-education

Fitas, R. (2025b). Neuro-symbolic ai for advanced signal and image processing: A review of recent trends and future directions. *IEEE Access : Practical Innovations, Open Solutions*, *13*, 143360–143376. DOI: 10.1109/ACCESS.2025.3598909

Fitria, T. (2021). Grammarly as ai-powered english writing assistant: Students' alternative for writing english. *Metathesis Journal of English Language Literature and Teaching*, *5*(1), 65. DOI: 10.31002/metathesis.v5i1.3519

Flannery, R. (2025, February 18). *Derek Li and Squirrel AI aim to lead the future of AI-driven education.* Forbes. https://www.forbes.com/sites/forbeschina/2025/02/18/derek-li-and-squirrel-ai-aim-to-lead-the-future-of-ai-driven-education/

Flannery, L. P., & Bers, M. U. (2013). Let's dance the "robot hokey-pokey!" children's programming approaches and achievement throughout early cognitive development. *Journal of Research on Technology in Education*, *46*(1), 81–101. DOI: 10.1080/15391523.2013.10782614

for Lifelong Learning. U. I. (2024). Lifelong learning in the age of ai: How can we bridge the digital divide? [Discusses human-centred lifelong learning, bridging the digital divide, open resources, Universal Design for Learning, and participatory governance]. *UNESCO Institute for Lifelong Learning Blog*. https://uil.unesco.org/en/news/lifelong-learning- age-ai-how-can-we-bridge-digital-divide

Forbes, S. A., Ross, M. E., & Chesser, S. S. (2011). Single-subject designs and action research in the K-12 setting. *Educational Research and Evaluation*, *17*(3), 161–173. Advance online publication. DOI: 10.1080/13803611.2011.599555

Foundation, W. F. (2024). *New survey reveals teachers believe ai can boost creativity and classroom learning* [Reports that nearly half of teachers use AI weekly, only 25% have PD, 56% want training, and describes pilot tools for literacy and personalised hints]. https://www.waltonfamilyfoundation.org/about/newsroom/new-survey-reveals- teachers-believe-ai-can-boost-creativity-and-classroom-learning

Friedman, N. P., & Robbins, T. W. (2022). The role of prefrontal cortex in cognitive control and executive function. *Neuropsychopharmacology : Official Publication of the American College of Neuropsychopharmacology*, *47*(1), 72–89. DOI: 10.1038/s41386-021-01132-0 PMID: 34408280

Fuchs, T. (2024). Understanding Sophia? On human interaction with artificial agents. *Phenomenology and the Cognitive Sciences*, *23*(1), 21–42. DOI: 10.1007/s11097-022-09848-0

Funa, A. A., & Gabay, R. A. E. (2025). Policy guidelines and recommendations on AI use in teaching and learning: A meta-synthesis study. *Social Sciences & Humanities Open*, *11*, 101221. DOI: 10.1016/j.ssaho.2024.101221

Furizal, R., Ramelan, A., Adriyanto, F., Maghfiroh, H., Ma'arif, A., Kariyamin, K., Masitha, A., & Fawait, A. B. (2024). Concerns of Ethical and Privacy in the Rapid Advancement of Artificial Intelligence: Directions, Challenges, and Solutions. [JRC]. *Journal of Robotics and Control*, *5*(6), 2015–2026. DOI: 10.18196/jrc.v5i6.24090

Fu, Y., & Weng, Z. (2024). Navigating the ethical terrain of ai in education: A systematic review on framing responsible human-centered ai practices. *Computers and Education: Artificial Intelligence*, *7*, 100306. DOI: 10.1016/j.caeai.2024.100306

Gada, T., & Chudasama, S. (2024). Impact of artificial intelligence on student attitudes, engagement, and learning. *International Research Journal of Modernization in Engineering Technology and Science*. Advance online publication. DOI: 10.56726/IRJMETS56247

Gadde, H. (2023). Leveraging AI for Scalable Query Processing in Big Data Environments. *International Journal of Advanced Engineering Technologies and Innovations*, *1*(02), 435–465.

Gaeta, A., Orciuoli, F., Pascuzzo, A., & Peduto, A. (2024). Evaluating the ability of large language models to generate motivational feedback. In Sifaleras, A., & Lin, F. (Eds.), *Generative intelligence and intelligent tutoring systems, ITS 2024*. Springer., DOI: 10.1007/978-3-031-63028-6_15

Gallent Torres, C., Zapata González, A., & Ortego Hernando, J. L. (2023). The impact of Generative Artificial Intelligence in higher education: a focus on ethics and academic integrity. *RELIEVE - Revista Electrónica de Investigación y Evaluación Educativa, 29*(2). https://doi.org/.DOI: 10.30827/relieve.v29i2.29134

Gao, Q., & An, H. (2024). Technology-neutral Illusion: The Ethical and Social Challenges in the Age of Artificial Intelligence. Sociology. *Philosophical Psychology*, *1*(2), 33–40.

Garba, M., & Hassan, A. (2024). Use of AI in learning Arabic language by non-Arabic speakers. *International Journal of Research and Innovation in Social Science*, *8*(8), 2519–2532. Advance online publication. DOI: 10.47772/IJRISS.2024.8080191

Garcia-López, I. M., González González, C. S., Ramírez-Montoya, M.-S., & Molina-Espinosa, J.-M. (2025). Challenges of implementing ChatGPT in education: Systematic literature review. *International Journal of Educational Research Open*, *8*, 100401. DOI: 10.1016/j.ijedro.2024.100401

Garcia, M. B. (2024). The paradox of artificial creativity: Challenges and opportunities of generative AI artistry. *Creativity Research Journal*, ●●●, 1–14. DOI: 10.1080/10400419.2024.2354622

Garrison, D. R., Anderson, T., & Archer, W. (2000). Critical inquiry in a text-based environment: Computer conferencing in higher education. *The Internet and Higher Education*, *2*(2), 16–22. DOI: 10.1016/S1096-7516(00)00016-6

Gates, A. (2024). *Teachers' perceptions of the impact of iReady on student reading achievement for students in response to intervention* [Doctoral dissertation, Kennesaw State University]. DigitalCommons @ Kennesaw State University. https://digitalcommons.kennesaw.edu/dissertations/26

Gaur, M., & Sheth, A. (2024). Building trustworthy neurosymbolic ai systems: Consistency, reliability, explainability, and safety. *AI Magazine*, *45*(1), 139–155. DOI: 10.1002/aaai.12149

Gavrilova, M. L. (2023). Responsible Artificial Intelligence and Bias Mitigation in Deep Learning Systems. *Proceedings of the International Conference on Information Visualisation*, 329–333. https://doi.org/DOI: 10.1109/IV60283.2023.00062

Gay, G. (2010). *Culturally responsive teaching: Theory, research, and practice* (2nd ed.). Teachers College Press.

Geetha, A. V., & Mala, T. (2025). Masked Attention-Driven Unified Multitask Representation Learning for Affective Computing. *Scopus.*, 1–8. Advance online publication. DOI: 10.1109/ICDSBS63635.2025.11031501

Geng, F., Zhou, N., & Yu, S. (2024). Exploring the effect of l2 writing teachers' emotional intelligence on their professional well-being: The mediating role of emotional labour strategies. *European Journal of Education, 60*(1), e12850. Advance online publication. DOI: 10.1111/ejed.12850

Gentile, M., Città, G., Perna, S., & Allegra, M. (2023). Do we still need teachers? Navigating the paradigm shift of the teacher's role in the AI era. *Frontiers in Education, 8*, 1161777. Advance online publication. DOI: 10.3389/feduc.2023.1161777

George, A. S. (2024). Technology Tension in Schools: Addressing the Complex Impacts of Digital Advances on Teaching, Learning, and Wellbeing. *Partners Universal Multidisciplinary Research Journal, 1*(3), 49–65.

George, B., & Wooden, O. (2023). Managing the strategic transformation of higher education through artificial intelligence. *Administrative Sciences, 13*(9), 196. DOI: 10.3390/admsci13090196

George, D., & Mallery, P. (2024). *IBM SPSS Statistics 29 step by step: A simple guide and reference* (18th ed.). Routledge. DOI: 10.4324/9781032622156

Gerlich, M. (2025). AI tools in society: Impacts on cognitive offloading and the future of critical thinking. *Societies (Basel, Switzerland), 15*(1), 6. DOI: 10.3390/soc15010006

Getman, Y., Phan, N., Al-Ghezi, R., Voskoboinik, E., Singh, M., Grosz, T., Kurimo, M., Salvi, G., Svendsen, T., Strömbergsson, S., Smolander, A., & Ylinen, S. (2023). Developing an AI-assisted low-resource spoken language learning app for children. *IEEE Access : Practical Innovations, Open Solutions, 11*, 86025–86037. DOI: 10.1109/ACCESS.2023.3304274

Giantini, G. (2023). The sophistry of the neutral tool. Weaponizing artificial intelligence and big data into threats toward social exclusion. *AI and Ethics, 3*(4), 1049–1061. DOI: 10.1007/s43681-023-00311-7

Gilyazova, O. S., & Zamoshchanskii, I. I. (2020). On motivational tools of gamification in higher education: Theoretical aspect. *Perspektivy Nauki i Obrazovania, 45*(3), 39–51. DOI: 10.32744/pse.2020.3.3

Ginting, D., Woods, R. M., Barella, Y., Limanta, L. S., Madkur, A., & How, H. E. (2024). The Effects of Digital Storytelling on the Retention and Transferability of Student Knowledge. *SAGE Open, 14*(3), 21582440241271267. Advance online publication. DOI: 10.1177/21582440241271267

Gligorea, I., Cioca, M., Oancea, R., Gorski, A. T., Gorski, H., & Tudorache, P. (2023). Adaptive learning using artificial intelligence in e-learning: A literature review. *Education Sciences, 13*(12), 1216. DOI: 10.3390/educsci13121216

Global Learning Council. (2022). *Kli: A theoretical framework for improving student learning* [Summarises the Knowledge–Learning–Instruction framework and its role in linking knowledge types, learning processes, and instructional methods]. https: / / www. globallearningcouncil . org / posts / kli - a - theoretical - framework- for-improving-student-learning

Gonsalves, C. (2024). Generative AI's impact on critical thinking: Revisiting Bloom's Taxonomy. *Journal of Marketing Education*, 02734753241305980. Advance online publication. DOI: 10.1177/02734753241305980

Goodwin, M. E. (2017). *Using a math tutorial program to decrease the number of failed grades the first semester helping the college achieve a 91% first-year retention rate* [Conference presentation]. 2017 FYEE Conference, Florida, United States.

Gorgun, G., & Bulut, O. (2022). Identifying aberrant responses in intelligent tutoring systems: An application of anomaly detection methods. *Psychological Test and Assessment Modeling, 64*(4), 359–384.

Gouseti, A., James, F., Fallin, L., & Burden, K. (2025). The ethics of using AI in K-12 education: A systematic literature review. *Technology, Pedagogy and Education, 34*(2), 161–182. DOI: 10.1080/1475939X.2024.2428601

Government of the RS (2019). Strategy for the development of artificial intelligence in the Republic of Serbia for the period 2020–2025. Službeni glasnik RS, 96/2019. [In Serbian]

Government of the RS (2020). Action plan for the period 2020–2022 for the implementation of the Artificial Intelligence Development Strategy in the Republic of Serbia for the period 2020–2025. Službeni glasnik RS, 81/2020. [In Serbian]

Government of the RS (2023). Conclusion on the adoption of the Ethical Guidelines for the development, application and use of reliable and responsible artificial intelligence. Službeni glasnik RS, 23/2023. [In Serbian]

GovTech Singapore. (2025, January 21). *AI in education: Transforming Singapore's education system with student learning space.* https://www.tech.gov.sg/technews/ai-in-education-transforming-singapore-education-system-with-student-learning-space

Grace, K., Maher, M. L., Davis, N., & Eltayeby, O. (2018). Surprise walks: Encouraging users towards novel concepts with sequential suggestions. In *Proceedings of the 9th International Conference on Computational Creativity (ICCC 2018). Association of Com- putational Creativity.*

Graefen, B., & Fazal, N. (2024). From chat bots to virtual tutors: An overview of chat GPT's role in the future of education. *Archives of Pharmacy Practice (Mumbai), 15*(2), 43–52. DOI: 10.51847/TOuppjEDSX

Graesser, A. C., Hu, X., Nye, B. D., VanLehn, K., Kumar, R., Heffernan, C., Heffernan, N., Woolf, B., Olney, A. M., Rus, V., Andrasik, F., Pavlik, P., Cai, Z., Wetzel, J., Morgan, B., Hampton, A. J., Lippert, A. M., Wang, L., Cheng, Q., & Baer, W. (2018). Electronixtutor: An intelligent tutoring system with multiple learning resources for electronics [Describes topic and knowledge component mapping, course calendars, and mastery tracking in an ITS]. *International Journal of STEM Education, 5*(1), 15. DOI: 10.1186/s40594-018-0110-y PMID: 30631705

Graesser, A. C., Hu, X., & Sottilare, R. (2018). Intelligent tutoring systems. In Fischer, F., Hmelo-Silver, C. E., Goldman, S. R., & Reimann, P. (Eds.), *International handbook of the learning sciences* (pp. 246–255). Routledge. DOI: 10.4324/9781315617572-24

Grant, A. A., Cook, M. A., & Ross, S. M. (2023). *The impacts of i-Ready personalized instruction on student reading achievement.* Johns Hopkins University. https://files.eric.ed.gov/fulltext/ED644594.pdf

Grassini, S. (2023). Shaping the Future of Education: Exploring the Potential and Consequences of AI and ChatGPT in Educational Settings. *Education Sciences, 13*(7), 692. DOI: 10.3390/educsci13070692

Gray, M., Samala, R., Liu, Q., Skiles, D., Xu, J., Tong, W., & Wu, L. (2024). Measurement and Mitigation of Bias in Artificial Intelligence: A Narrative Literature Review for Regulatory Science. *Clinical Pharmacology and Therapeutics, 115*(4), 687–697. DOI: 10.1002/cpt.3117 PMID: 38018360

Grilli, L., & Pedota, M. (2024). Creativity and artificial intelligence: A multilevel perspective. *Creativity and Innovation Management, 33*(2), 234–247. DOI: 10.1111/caim.12580

Grover, S., & Pea, R. (2013). Computational thinking in K–12: A review of the state of the field. *Educational Researcher, 42*(1), 38–43. DOI: 10.3102/0013189X12463051

Gupta, P., & Goyal, P. (2022). Is game-based pedagogy just a fad? A self-determination theory approach to gamification in higher education. *International Journal of Educational Management, 36*(3), 341–356. DOI: 10.1108/IJEM-04-2021-0126

Guskey, T. R. (1997). *Implementing mastery learning*. Wadsworth.

Gu, W., & Yu, Z. (2025). A bibliometric analysis of the application of AI chatbots in language learning contexts. *Quality & Quantity*, *59*(1), 639–661. DOI: 10.1007/s11135-024-01946-2

Gyawali, Y., & Mehandroo, M. (2022). Artificial intelligence in english language teaching: Navigating the future with emerging perspectives. *Journal of Language and Linguistics in Society*, (26), 21–27. DOI: 10.55529/jlls.26.21.27

Habash, N. (2023). *Computational modeling of Arabic dialects*. Cambridge University Press.

Ha, D., & Nguyen, A. (2024). Artificial intelligence-based assessment in elt exam creation: A case study of van lang university lecturers. *Saudi Journal of Language Studies*, *5*(1), 34–49. DOI: 10.1108/SJLS-06-2024-0030

Haines, S., Krach, M., Pustaka, A., Li, Q., & Richman, L. (2019). The effects of computational thinking professional development on STEM teachers' perceptions and pedagogical practices. *Athens Journal of Sciences*, *6*(2), 97–122. DOI: 10.30958/ajs.6-2-2

Hair, J. F., Black, W. C., Babin, B. J., & Anderson, R. E. (2018). *Multivariate data analysis*. Cengage.

Halverson, L. R., Spring, K. J., Huyett, S., Henrie, C. R., & Graham, C. R. (2023). Blended Learning Research in Higher Education and K-12 Settings. In *Learning, Design, and Technology*. DOI: 10.1007/978-3-319-17727-4_31-2

Hamid, R., & Barzenji, Z. (2024). Evaluating the effectiveness of gamification in online education: Strategies for promoting active learning and student retention. *International Journal of Post Axial: Futuristic Teaching and Learning*, 97–110.

Hanna, M. G., Pantanowitz, L., Jackson, B., Palmer, O., Visweswaran, S., Pantanowitz, J., Deebajah, M., & Rashidi, H. H. (2025). Ethical and bias considerations in artificial intelligence/machine learning. *Modern Pathology*, *38*(3), 100686. Advance online publication. DOI: 10.1016/j.modpat.2024.100686 PMID: 39694331

Hanses, M., van Rijn, L., Karolyi, H., & de Witt, C. (2024). Guiding Students Towards Successful Assessments Using Learning Analytics From Behavioral Data to Formative Feedback. In Sahin, M., & Ifenthaler, D. (Eds.), *Assessment Analytics in Education: Designs, Methods and Solutions* (pp. 61–83). Springer International Publishing., DOI: 10.1007/978-3-031-56365-2_4

Harati, H., Sujo-Montes, L., Tu, C.-H., Armfield, S., & Yen, C.-J. (2021). Assessment and learning in knowledge spaces (ALEKS) adaptive system impact on students' perception and self-regulated learning skills. *Education Sciences*, *11*(10), 603. Advance online publication. DOI: 10.3390/educsci11100603

Hare, R., Tang, Y., & Ferguson, S. (2024). An Intelligent Serious Game for Digital Logic Education to Enhance Student Learning. *IEEE Transactions on Education*, *67*(3), 387–394. DOI: 10.1109/TE.2024.3359001

Harms, M. B., & Garrett-Ruffin, S. D. (2023). Disrupting links between poverty, chronic stress, and educational inequality. npj Science of Learning, 8(1), 50.

Hart, J. (2025, June 11). *AI tutoring in schools: How personalized learning technology is changing K-12 education in 2025*. The Hunt Institute. https://hunt-institute.org/resources/2025/06/ai-tutoring-alpha-school-personalized-learning-technology-k-12-education/

Hartanto, B., Zaimah, N., Hartanto, E., Zahro, F., Zaimah, R., & Nely, C. (2023). Acceptability and effectiveness analysis of large language model-based artificial intelligence chatbot among Arabic learners. *Mantiqu Tayr: Journal of Arabic Language*, *4*(1), 1–20. Advance online publication. DOI: 10.25217/mantiqutayr.v4i1.3951

Hartley, J. R., & Sleeman, D. H. (1973). Towards more intelligent teaching systems. *International Journal of Man-Machine Studies*, *5*(2), 215–236. DOI: 10.1016/S0020-7373(73)80033-1

Hartshorne, R., Waring, S. M., & Okraski, H. (2019). Developing well-informed, critically thinking, and active citizens through the connection of modeling & simulation and social studies education. *The Clearing House: A Journal of Educational Strategies, Issues and Ideas*, *92*(1–2), 48–52. DOI: 10.1080/00098655.2019.1571988

Haryani, E., Coben, W. W., Pleasants, B. A., & Fetters, M. K. (2021). Analysis of teachers' resources for integrating the skills of creativity and innovation, critical thinking and problem solving, collaboration, and communication in science classrooms. *Jurnal Pendidikan IPA Indonesia*, *10*(1), 92–102. DOI: 10.15294/jpii.v10i1.27084

Hasal, M., Nowaková, J., Ahmed Saghair, K., Abdulla, H., Snášel, V., & Ogiela, L. (2021). Chatbots: Security, privacy, data protection, and social aspects. *Concurrency and Computation*, *33*(19), e6426. DOI: 10.1002/cpe.6426

Hasanein, A. M., & Sobaih, A. E. E. (2023). Drivers and consequences of ChatGPT use in higher education: Key stakeholder perspectives. *European Journal of Investigation in Health, Psychology and Education*, *13*(11), 2599–2614. DOI: 10.3390/ejihpe13110181 PMID: 37998071

Haseski, H. I., & Ilic, U. (2019). An investigation of the data collection instruments developed to measure computational thinking. *Informatics in Education, 18*(2), 297–319. DOI: 10.15388/infedu.2019.14

Hassan, M. A., Habiba, U., Majeed, F., & Shoaib, M. (2021). Adaptive gamification in e-learning based on students' learning styles. *Interactive Learning Environments, 29*(4), 545–565. DOI: 10.1080/10494820.2019.1588745

Hawkins, R., & Kern, L. (2024). *Higher Expectations: How to Survive Academia, Make It Better for Others, and Transform the University*. Between the Lines.

Heffernan, N. T., & Heffernan, C. L. (2014). The assistments ecosystem: Building a platform that brings scientists and teachers together for minimally invasive research on human learning and teaching. *International Journal of Artificial Intelligence in Education, 24*(4), 470–497. DOI: 10.1007/s40593-014-0024-x

Henkel, O., Horne-Robinson, H., Kozhakhmetova, N., & Lee, A. (2024). Effective and scalable math support: Evidence on the impact of an ai-tutor on math achievement in ghana. *arXiv preprint*. https://arxiv.org/abs/2402.09809 DOI: 10.1007/978-3-031-64315-6_34

Herawati, R. (2025). Integrating artificial intelligence (ai) into sustainable tourism management in indonesia and the impact on customer experience: a literature review., 36. https://doi.org/DOI: 10.1117/12.3058730

Herawati, A., Yusuf, S., Ilfiandra, I., Taufik, A., & Habibi, A. (2024). Exploring the role of artificial intelligence in education, students preferences and perceptions. *Al-Ishlah Jurnal Pendidikan, 16*(2), 1029–1040. DOI: 10.35445/alishlah.v16i2.4784

Herodotou, C., Rienties, B., Verdin, B., & Boroowa, A. (2019). Predictive Learning Analytics "At Scale": Towards Guidelines to Successful Implementation in Higher Education Based on the Case of the Open University UK. *Journal of Learning Analytics, 6*(1), 85–95. DOI: 10.18608/jla.2019.61.5

Herrera-Ferrá, K., Muñoz, J. M., Nicolini, H., Saruwatari Zavala, G., & Martínez Bullé Goyri, V. M. (2023). Contextual and Cultural Perspectives on Neurorights: Reflections Toward an International Consensus. *AJOB Neuroscience, 14*(4), 360–368. DOI: 10.1080/21507740.2022.2048722 PMID: 35341473

Hess, F. M. (2023). *The great school rethink*. Harvard Education Press.

Hestness, E., Ketelhut, D. J., McGinnis, J. R., & Plane, J. (2018). Professional knowledge building within an elementary teacher professional development experience on computational thinking in science education. *Journal of Technology and Teacher Education, 26*(3), 411–435.

Hew, K. F. (2016). Promoting engagement in online courses: What strategies can we learn from three highly rated MOOCS. *British Journal of Educational Technology*, *47*(2), 320–341. DOI: 10.1111/bjet.12235

Hickey, D. T., & Schafer, N. J. (2006). Design-based, participation-centered approaches to classroom management. In C. M. Evertson, & C. S. Weinstein, C. S. (Eds.), Handbook of classroom management: research, practice, and contemporary issues. (pp. 281–308). Routledge.

Hidayatullah, A. F., Kalinaki, K., Aslam, M. M., Zakari, R. Y., & Shafik, W. (2023). Fine-Tuning BERT-Based Models for Negative Content Identification on Indonesian Tweets. *ICITDA 2023 - Proceedings of the 2023 8th International Conference on Information Technology and Digital Applications*. DOI: 10.1109/ICITDA60835.2023.10427046

Hill, K. (2025, May 14). The Professors Are Using ChatGPT, and Some Students Aren't Happy About It. *The New York Times*. https://www.nytimes.com/2025/05/14/technology/chatgpt-college-professors.html

Hollands, F., Bowden, A. B., Belfield, C., Levin, H. M., Cheng, H., Shand, R., Pan, Y., & Hanisch-Cerda, B. (2014). Cost-effectiveness analysis in practice: Interventions to improve high school completion. *Educational Evaluation and Policy Analysis*, *36*(3), 307–326. DOI: 10.3102/0162373713511850

Holman, K., Marino, M., Vasquez, E., Taub, M., Hunt, J., & Tazi, Y. (2024). Navigating ai-powered personalized learning in special education: A guide for preservice teacher faculty. *Journal of Special Education Preparation*, *4*(2), 90–95. DOI: 10.33043/5b2xqcb3

Holmes, W. (2019). *Artificial intelligence in education: Promises and implications for teaching and learning*. Independently Published., https://discovery.ucl.ac.uk/id/eprint/10139722/

Holmes, W., Bialik, M., & Fadel, C. (2019). *Artificial intelligence in education promises and implications for teaching and learning*. Center for Curriculum Redesign.

Holmes, W., Bialik, M., & Fadel, C. (2019). *Artificial intelligence in education: Promises and implications for teaching & learning* (1st ed.). The Center for Curriculum Redesign.

Holmes, W., Porayska-Pomsta, K., Holstein, K., Sutherland, E., Baker, T., Shum, S. B., Santos, O. C., Rodrigo, M. T., Cukurova, M., Bittencourt, I. I., & Koedinger, K. R. (2022). Ethics of AI in education: Towards a community-wide framework. *International Journal of Artificial Intelligence in Education*, *34*(3), 504–526. DOI: 10.1007/s40593-021-00239-1

Hong, J. C., Ye, J. H., Chen, P. H., & Yu, Y. Y. (2020). A checklist development for meaningful learning in classroom observation. *International Journal of Information and Education Technology (IJIET)*, *10*(10), 728–735. DOI: 10.18178/ijiet.2020.10.10.1450

Hooshyar, D., Azevedo, R., & Yang, Y. (2024). Augmenting deep neural networks with symbolic educational knowledge: Towards trustworthy and interpretable ai for education. *Machine Learning and Knowledge Extraction*, *6*(1), 593–618. DOI: 10.3390/make6010028

Hou, R., Fu¨tterer, T., Bu¨hler, B., Bozkir, E., Gerjets, P., Trautwein, U., & Kasneci, E. (2024). Automated assessment of encouragement and warmth in classrooms leveraging multimodal emotional features and chatgpt. *International conference on artificial intelligence in education*, 60–74. DOI: 10.1007/978-3-031-64302-6_5

Hsia, L.-H., Lin, Y.-N., Lin, C.-H., & Hwang, G.-J. (2025). Effectiveness of gamified intelligent tutoring in physical education through the lens of self-determination theory. *Computers & Education*, *227*, 105212. Advance online publication. DOI: 10.1016/j.compedu.2024.105212

Huang, J., Li, Z., Naik, M., & Lim, S.-N. (2023). Laser: A neuro-symbolic framework for learning spatial-temporal scene graphs with weak supervision. *arXiv preprint arXiv:2304.07647*.

Huang, C., Zhong, Y., Li, Y., Wang, X., Han, Z., Zhang, D., & Liu, M. (2025). Enhancing student reading performance through a personalized two-tier problem-based learning approach with generative artificial intelligence. *Humanities & Social Sciences Communications*, *12*(1), 645. Advance online publication. DOI: 10.1057/s41599-025-04919-4

Huang, D., Nan, Z., Hu, X., Jin, P., Peng, S., Wen, Y., Zhang, R., Du, Z., Guo, Q., & Pu, Y.. (2023). Anpl: Towards natural programming with interactive decomposition. *Advances in Neural Information Processing Systems*, *36*, 69404–69440.

Huang, H., Yu, F., Zhu, J., Sun, X., Cheng, H., Song, D., Chen, Z., Alharthi, A., An, B., He, J., Liu, Z., Chen, J., Li, J., Wang, B., Zhang, L., Sun, R., Wan, X., Li, H., & Xu, J. (2024). AceGPT, localizing large language models in Arabic. *Proceedings of the 2024 Conference of the North American Chapter of the Association for Computational Linguistics: Human Language Technologies (*Volume 1*: Long Papers)*, 8139–8163. https://doi.org/DOI: 10.18653/v1/2024.naacl-long.450

Huang, J., Lee, Y., & Kwon, O. (2023). Direct: Toward dialogue-based reading comprehension tutoring. *IEEE Access : Practical Innovations, Open Solutions, 11*, 8978–8987. DOI: 10.1109/ACCESS.2022.3233224

Huang, R., Ritzhaupt, A. D., Sommer, M., Zhu, J., Stephen, A., Valle, N., Hampton, J., & Li, J. (2020). The impact of gamification in educational settings on student learning outcomes: A meta-analysis. *Educational Technology Research and Development*, *68*(4), 1875–1901. DOI: 10.1007/s11423-020-09807-z

Humburg, M., Dragnić-Cindrić, D., Hmelo-Silver, C. E., Glazewski, K., Lester, J. C., & Danish, J. A. (2024). Integrating youth perspectives into the design of AI-supported collaborative learning environments. *Education Sciences*, *14*(11), 1197. DOI: 10.3390/educsci14111197

Hunt, M., Yan, Y., Meyer, B., & Liu, H. (2025). Managing literacy interventions through professional learning communities: A case study on organizational change in education systems. *Humanities & Social Sciences Communications*, *12*(1), 402. Advance online publication. DOI: 10.1057/s41599-025-04744-9

Hwang, G.-J., & Chang, C.-Y. (2023). A review of opportunities and challenges of chatbots in education. *Interactive Learning Environments*, *31*(7), 4099–4112. DOI: 10.1080/10494820.2021.1952615

Никитина, И., & Ishchenko, T. (2024). The impact of ai on teachers: Support or replacement? *SJPU*, *65*(4), 93–99. DOI: 10.23856/6511

Ibrahim, A. (2024). Assessing the knowledge and perception of artificial intelligence for teaching and research among lecturers in the faculties of arts in nigeria. *Journal of Global Research in Education and Social Science*, *18*(2), 25–33. DOI: 10.56557/jogress/2024/v18i28671

Idham, A., Rauf, W., & Rajab, A. (2024). Navigating the transformative impact of artificial intelligence on english language teaching: Exploring challenges and opportunities. *JES*, *4*(1), 8–14. DOI: 10.56185/jes.v4i1.620

Iflazoglu, A., & Hong, E. (2012). Homework motivation and preferences of Turkish students. *Research Papers in Education*, *27*(3), 343–363. DOI: 10.1080/02671522.2010.529581

Iman, M. Z., Asis, A. A., & Rahma, A. U. Z. (2024). Enhancing personalized learning: The impact of artificial intelligence in education. *Edu Spectrum: Journal of Multidimensional Education*, *1*(2), 101–112. DOI: 10.70063/eduspectrum.v1i2.55

Indrawati, I., Letjani, K. P., Kurniawan, K., & Muthaiyah, S. (2025). Adoption of ChatGPT in educational institutions in Botswana: A customer perspective. *Asia Pacific Management Review*, *30*(1), 100346. DOI: 10.1016/j.apmrv.2024.100346

Ingkavara, T., Panjaburee, P., Srisawasdi, N., & Sajjapanroj, S. (2022). The use of a personalized learning approach to implementing self-regulated online learning. *Computers and Education: Artificial Intelligence*, *3*, 100086. Advance online publication. DOI: 10.1016/j.caeai.2022.100086

Internet Society. (2019, January 7). Community networks in Tanzania: Helping to close the connectivity gap. Internet Society. https://www.internetsociety.org/blog/2019/01/community-networks-in-tanzania-helping-to-close-connectivity-gap/

Irwanto, I. (2025). Research trends on artificial intelligence in K-12 education in Asia: A bibliometric analysis using the Scopus database (1996–2025). *Discover Artificial Intelligence*, *5*(1), 155. DOI: 10.1007/s44163-025-00389-4

Isaeva, R., Karasartova, N., Dznunusnalieva, K., Mirzoeva, K., & Mokliuk, M. (2024). Enhancing learning effectiveness through adaptive learning platforms and emerging computer technologies in education. *Jurnal Ilmiah Ilmu Terapan Universitas Jambi*, *9*(1), 144–160. DOI: 10.22437/jiituj.v9i1.37967

ISTE. (2017). *Iste standards for educators* [Seven role-based standards (Learner, Leader, Citizen, Collaborator, Designer, Facilitator, Analyst); accessed 2025-10-11]. https://iste.org/standards/iste-standards-for-educators

Jaboob, M., Hazaimeh, M., & Al-Ansi, A. (2024). Integration of generative AI techniques and applications in student behavior and cognitive achievement in Arab higher education. *International Journal of Human-Computer Interaction*, *41*(1), 353–366. DOI: 10.1080/10447318.2023.2300016

Jain, N. (2025). Ai as a catalyst for educational equity: Addressing global teacher shortages and learning disparities. *International Journal of Scientific Research in Computer Science, Engineering and Information Technology, 11*(1).

Jain, R., Saha, T., & Saha, S. (2023). T-vaks: a tutoring-based multimodal dialog system via knowledge selection.. https://doi.org/DOI: 10.3233/FAIA230388

Jaskari, M.-M., & Syrjälä, H. (2024). One solution does not fit all: Reward-based and meaningful gamification in higher education. In *Practices and Implementation of Gamification in Higher Education* (pp. 22–49). https://doi.org/DOI: 10.4018/979-8-3693-0716-8.ch002

Jayavardhini, P. (2024). Ai study partner: Development of an llm and gen ai-enhanced study assistant tool. *Interantional Journal of Scientific Research in Engineering and Management*, *08*(03), 1–5. DOI: 10.55041/IJSREM29626

Jeon, J., Kim, L., & Park, J. (2025). The ethics of generative AI in social science research: A qualitative approach for institutionally grounded AI research ethics. *Technology in Society*, *81*, 102836. Advance online publication. DOI: 10.1016/j.techsoc.2025.102836

Jia, F., Fu, Y., Zheng, J., & Li, F. (2025). Embodied AI agent for co-creation ecosystem: Elevating human-AI co-creation through emotion recognition and dynamic personality adaptation. In *Preprints*. DOI: 10.20944/preprints202501.0946.v1

Jian, M. (2023). Personalized learning through ai. *AEI*, *5*(1), 16–19. DOI: 10.54254/2977-3903/5/2023039

Ji, Y., Zou, X., Li, T., & Zhan, Z. (2023, November). The effectiveness of ChatGPT on pre-service teachers' STEM teaching literacy, learning performance, and cognitive load in a teacher training course. In *Proceedings of the 2023 6th international conference on educational technology management* (pp. 16-22). DOI: 10.1145/3637907.3637948

Ji, Z., Lee, N., Frieske, R., Yu, T., Su, D., Xu, Y., Ishii, E., Bang, Y., Madotto, A., & Fung, P. (2023). Survey of hallucination in natural Language Generation. *ACM Computing Surveys*. Advance online publication. DOI: 10.1145/3571730

Johler, M., Krumsvik, R. J., Bugge, H. E., & Helgevold, N. (2022, April). Teachers' perceptions of their role and classroom management practices in a technology rich primary school classroom. In *Frontiers in Education* (Vol. 7, p. 841385). Frontiers Media SA. https://doi.org/DOI: 10.3389/feduc.2022.841385

Jöhnk, J., Weißert, M., & Wyrtki, K. (2021). Ready or not, AI comes—An interview study of organizational AI readiness factors. *Business & Information Systems Engineering*, *63*(1), 5–20. DOI: 10.1007/s12599-020-00676-7

Jondya, A. G., & Susanto, K. F., & Cathleen. (2023). Utilizing Simple Fuzzy Logic into An Adaptive Storytelling Mobile Game in Learning Historical Event of Indonesia's Independence Movement. *Proceedings of the 7th 2023 International Conference on New Media Studies, CONMEDIA 2023*, 33–38. https://doi.org/DOI: 10.1109/CONMEDIA60526.2023.10428575

Jordanous, A. (2017). Co-creativity and perceptions of computational agents in co-creativity. *International Conference on Innovative Computing and Cloud Computing*, 159–166. http://www.telegraph.co.uk/theatre/what-to-see/

Jose, J., & Jose, B. J. (2024). Educators' academic insights on artificial intelligence: Challenges and opportunities. *Electronic Journal of e-Learning*, *22*(2), 59–77. DOI: 10.34190/ejel.21.5.3272

Joshi, S. (2025). Strategic Integration of Artificial Intelligence in U.S. K-12 Education: A Comprehensive Review and Policy Roadmap. *SSRN*. https://doi.org/DOI: 10.5120/ijca2025925428

Judijanto, L. (2025a). A bibliometric analysis of adaptive learning in K-12 education. *The Eastasouth Journal of Learning and Education*, *3*(1), 75–86. DOI: 10.58812/esle.v3i01.496

Judijanto, L. (2025b). The role of data supervisors in the implementation of privacy policies: A literature review. *Jurnal Komunikasi*, *3*(3), 139–146.

Kafyulilo, A., Fisser, P., Pieters, J., & Voogt, J. (2015). ICT use in science and mathematics teacher education in Tanzania: Developing technological pedagogical content knowledge. *Australasian Journal of Educational Technology*, *31*(4), 381–399. DOI: 10.14742/ajet.1240

Kağıtçıbaşı, Ç. (2017). *Family, Self, and Human Development Across Cultures: Theory and Applications*. Routledge. DOI: 10.4324/9781315205281

Kalogiannakis, M., & Papadakis, S. (Eds.). (2020). *Handbook of research on tools for teaching computational thinking in P-12 education*. IGI Global. DOI: 10.4018/978-1-7998-4576-8

Kalogiannakis, M., Papadakis, S., & Zourmpakis, A.-I. (2021). Gamification in Science Education. A Systematic Review of the Literature. *Education Sciences*, *11*(1), 22. DOI: 10.3390/educsci11010022

Kamila, M. K., & Jasrotia, S. S. (2025). Ethical issues in the development of artificial intelligence: Recognizing the risks. *International Journal of Ethics and Systems*, *41*(1), 45–63. DOI: 10.1108/IJOES-05-2023-0107

Karabulut, H., Gökçe, H., & Kariper, A. (2023). Development of Critical Thinking Skills Scale (Secondary school sample). *Kirikkale University Journal of Social Sciences*, *13*(2), 443–461.

Karakose, T., Tülübaş, T., & Papadakis, S. (2022). Revealing the intellectual structure and evolution of digital addiction research: An integrated bibliometric and science mapping approach. *International Journal of Environmental Research and Public Health*, *19*(22), 14883. DOI: 10.3390/ijerph192214883 PMID: 36429603

Karamuk, E. (2025). The automation trap: Unpacking the consequences of over-reliance on AI in education and its hidden costs. In Garcia, M. B., Rosak-Szyrocka, J., & Bozkurt, A. (Eds.), *Pitfalls of AI integration in education: Skill obsolescence, misuse, and bias* (pp. 151–174). IGI Global Scientific Publishing. DOI: 10.4018/979-8-3373-0122-8.ch007

Karki, B., & Karki, T. (2025). Integrating ai in english language teaching: Challenges and opportunities. *Dristikon a Multidisciplinary Journal*, *15*(1), 13–28. DOI: 10.3126/dristikon.v15i1.77118

Karpouzis, K. (2024). Plato's Shadows in the Digital Cave: Controlling Cultural Bias in Generative AI. *Electronics (Basel)*, *13*(8), 1457. Advance online publication. DOI: 10.3390/electronics13081457

Kasneci, E., Seßler, K., Küchemann, S., Bannert, M., Dementieva, D., Fischer, F., Gasser, U., Groh, G., Günnemann, S., Hüllermeier, E., Krusche, S., Kutyniok, G., Michaeli, T., Nerdel, C., Pfeffer, J., Poquet, O., Sailer, M., Schmidt, A., Seidel, T., & Kasneci, G. (2023). ChatGPT for good? On opportunities and challenges of large language models for education. *Learning and Individual Differences*, *103*, 102274. DOI: 10.1016/j.lindif.2023.102274

Kaswan, K. S., Dhatterwal, J. S., & Ojha, R. P. (2024). Ai in personalized learning. In *Advances in technological innovations in higher education* (pp. 103–117). CRC Press. DOI: 10.1201/9781003376699-9

Katchapakirin, K., Anutariya, C., & Supnithi, T. (2022). ScratchThAI: A conversation-based learning support framework for computational thinking development. *Education and Information Technologies*, *27*(6), 8533–8560. DOI: 10.1007/s10639-021-10870-z

Katiyar, N., Awasthi, M. V. K., Pratap, R., Mishra, M. K., Shukla, M. N., Tiwari, M., & Singh, R. (2024). Ai-driven personalized learning systems: Enhancing educational effectiveness. *Educational Administration: Theory and Practice*, *30*(5), 11514–11524.

Katiyar, N., Awasthi, V. K., Pratap, R., Mishra, K., Shukla, N., Singh, R., & Tiwari, M. (2024). AI-driven personalized learning systems: Enhancing educational effectiveness. *Educational Administration: Theory and Practice*, *30*(5), 11514–11524. DOI: 10.53555/kuey.v30i5.4961

Katona, J., & Gyonyoru, K. I. K. (2025). Integrating AI-based adaptive learning into the flipped classroom model to enhance engagement and learning outcomes. *Computers and Education: Artificial Intelligence*, *8*, 100392. Advance online publication. DOI: 10.1016/j.caeai.2025.100392

Kaufman, J. H., ... (2025). *Uneven adoption of artificial intelligence tools among u.s. teachers and principals* (RRA134-25). RAND Corporation. https://www.rand .org/pubs/ research reports/RRA134-25.html

Kautz, H. (2022). The third ai summer: Aaai robert s. engelmore memorial lecture. *AI Magazine*, *43*(1), 105–125. DOI: 10.1002/aaai.12036

Kavitha, K., & Joshith, V. P. (2024). Pedagogical incorporation of artificial intelligence in K-12 science education: A decadal bibliometric mapping and systematic literature review (2013–2023). *Journal of Pedagogical Research*, *8*(4), 437–465. DOI: 10.33902/JPR.202429218

Kayyali, M. (2024). Immersive Technologies: Virtual and Augmented Reality in Higher Education. In Reshaping learning with next generation educational technologies (pp. 99-114). IGI Global.

Kayyali, M. (2025). E-Learning Platforms and Their Influence on Lifelong Learning. In Impact of Digitalization on Education and Social Sustainability (pp. 155-176). IGI Global.

Kayyali, M. (2026). AI in Higher Education: The Risk of Excluding Vulnerable Learners. In AI and New Forms of Exclusion (pp. 57-82). IGI Global Scientific Publishing.

Kebritchi, M., Hirumi, A., Kappers, W., & Henry, R. (2009). Analysis of the supporting websites for the use of instructional games in K-12 settings. *British Journal of Educational Technology*, *40*(4), 733–754. Advance online publication. DOI: 10.1111/j.1467-8535.2008.00854.x

Keller, F. S., & Sherman, J. G. (1974). *The Keller plan handbook; essays on a personalized system of instruction*. W. A. Benjamin.

Kelly, M. (2008). Incorporating Context Into TPCK-Based Instructional Design. In K. McFerrin, R. Weber, R. Carlsen & D. Willis (Eds.), *Proceedings of SITE 2008--Society for Information Technology & Teacher Education International Conference* (pp. 5257-5262). Las Vegas, Nevada, USA: Association for the Advancement of Computing in Education (AACE).

Kennedy, J., Gabriel, F., Korolkiewicz, M., Rets, I., & Rienties, B. (2025, February). Actionable learning analytics in education: an opportunity to close the learning loop. In *Frontiers in Education* (Vol. 10, p. 1571177). Frontiers Media SA. https://doi.org/DOI: 10.3389/feduc.2025.1571177

Khairani Zakaria, N. Y., Hashim, H., & Jamaludin, K. A. (2025). Exploring the impact of AI on critical thinking development in ESL: A systematic literature review. *Arab World English Journal, 16*(Special Issue on Artificial Intelligence), 330–347. DOI: 10.24093/awej/AI.19

Khalil, M., & Er, E. (2023). Will chatgpt get you caught? Rethinking of Plagiarism Detection. *Computer Science*.

Khanna, R. (2025). Harnessing AI in Education: Perspectives from Education Leaders. Insights from a National Leadership Roundtable on the Future of Education. SSRN Electronic Journal. https://doi.org/DOI: 10.2139/ssrn.5381208

Khan, S. (2024). *Brave New Words: How AI Will Revolutionize Education (and why That's a Good Thing)*. Penguin.

Khazanchi, R., Di Mitri, D., & Drachsler, H. (2023). Measuring efficacy of ALEKS as a supportive instructional tool in K-12 math classroom with underachieving students. *Journal of Computers in Mathematics and Science Teaching, 42*(2), 155–176. DOI: 10.70725/204333qjmwhs

Khizar, A. (2024). Artificial intelligence and neurosurgery: A revolution in the field. *Pakistan Journal of Neurological Sciences, 18*(04). Advance online publication. DOI: 10.56310/pjns.v18i04.244

Khosravi, H., Shum, S. B., Chen, G., Conati, C., Tsai, Y.-S., Kay, J., Knight, S., Martinez-Maldonado, R., Sadiq, S., & Gašević, D. (2022). Explainable artificial intelligence in education. *Computers and Education: Artificial Intelligence, 3*(100074), 100074. DOI: 10.1016/j.caeai.2022.100074

Khundam, C., & Noël, F. (2021). Storytelling framework with adaptive interaction system for interactive content in virtual museum. *ECTI Transactions on Computer and Information Technology, 15*(1), 34–49. DOI: 10.37936/ecti-cit.2021151.239948

Kim, M. S., & Yu, F. (2023). 'Teacher data literacies practice' meets 'pedagogical documentation': A scoping review. In *Review of Education* (Vol. 11, Issue 2). DOI: 10.1002/rev3.3414

Kim, K., Kwon, K., Ottenbreit-Leftwich, A., Bae, H., & Glazewski, K. (2023). Exploring middle school students' common naive conceptions of Artificial Intelligence concepts, and the evolution of these ideas. *Education and Information Technologies, 28*(8), 9827–9854. Advance online publication. DOI: 10.1007/s10639-023-11600-3

Kim, M., Kim, T., Nguyen, A., Gomez, E. N., & Jin, J. (2024). TinyTeller AI, an AI-based Adaptive Storytelling Application. *Proceedings - 2024 Artificial Intelligence x Humanities, Education, and Art. AIxHEART, 2024*, 44–51. DOI: 10.1109/AIxHeart62327.2024.00017

Kinyaduka, B. D. (2024). Multiplicity theory and its implications in education. *Global Journal of Social Sciences Studies, 10*(1), 13–29. DOI: 10.55284/gjss.v10i1.1018

Klock, A. C. T., Gasparini, I., Pimenta, M. S., & Hamari, J. (2020). Tailored gamification: A review of literature. *International Journal of Human-Computer Studies, 144*, 102495. DOI: 10.1016/j.ijhcs.2020.102495

Koedinger, K. R., Anderson, J. R., Hadley, W. H., & Mark, M. A. (1997). Intelligent tutoring goes to school in the big city. *International Journal of Artificial Intelligence in Education, 8*, 30–43. https://kilthub.cmu.edu/articles/journal contribution/Intelligent Tutoring Goes To School in the Big City/6470153

Koivisto, J., & Hamari, J. (2019). The rise of motivational information systems: A review of gamification research. *International Journal of Information Management, 45*, 191–210. DOI: 10.1016/j.ijinfomgt.2018.10.013

Komba, M. M. (2024). The influence of ChatGPT on digital learning: Experience among university students. *Global Knowledge, Memory and Communication.* Advance online publication. DOI: 10.1108/GKMC-10-2023-0390

Kondoro, A. M. (2025). AI writing assistants in Tanzanian universities: Adoption trends, challenges, and opportunities. In *Proceedings of the Fourth Workshop on Intelligent and Interactive Writing Assistants* (pp. 37–46). ACL Anthology., https://aclanthology.org/2025.in2writing-1.4.pdf DOI: 10.18653/v1/2025.in2writing-1.4

Kong, S. C., & Lai, M. (2022). A proposed computational thinking teacher development framework for K-12 guided by the TPACK model. *Journal of Computers in Education, 9*(3), 379–402. DOI: 10.1007/s40692-021-00207-7

Kong, S. C., Lai, M., & Li, Y. (2023). Scaling up a teacher development programme for sustainable computational thinking education: TPACK surveys, concept tests and primary school visits. *Computers & Education, 194*, 104707. DOI: 10.1016/j.compedu.2022.104707

Kooli, C. (2023). Chatbots in education and research: A critical examination of ethical implications and solutions. *Sustainability (Basel), 15*(7), 5614. DOI: 10.3390/su15075614

Kopp, W. (2025, January). *Nurturing a thriving teaching profession in an AI-enhanced world* [OECD Education and Skills Today blog; accessed 2025-10-11]. https://oecdedutoday. com/nurturing-a-thriving-teaching-profession-in-an-ai-enhanced-world/

Kordzadeh, N., & Ghasemaghaei, M. (2022). Algorithmic bias: Review, synthesis, and future research directions. *European Journal of Information Systems, 31*(3), 388–409. DOI: 10.1080/0960085X.2021.1927212

Kouzov, O. (2019). The new paradigms in education and support of critical thinking with artificial intelligence (AI) tools. *Serdica Journal of Computing, 13*(1-2), 27–40. DOI: 10.55630/sjc.2019.13.27-40

Krafft, C., Assaad, R., & Keo, C. (2022). The Jordan Compact: Impact on education and labor market outcomes of Syrian refugees. *ERF Working Paper Series*.

Krisnawati, K., Irwan, I., Yusnan, M., & Acoci, . (2024). Exploring the relationship between academic achievement and emotional intelligence in upper primary school students. *International Journal of Learning Reformation in Elementary Education, 3*(01), 42–50. DOI: 10.56741/ijlree.v3i01.487

Küçükuncular, A., & Ertugan, A. (2025). Teaching in the AI era: Sustainable digital education through ethical integration and teacher empowerment. *Sustainability (Basel), 17*(16), 7405. DOI: 10.3390/su17167405

Kuhail, M. A., Alturki, N., Alramlawi, S., & Alhejori, K. (2022). Interacting with educational chatbots: A systematic review. *Education and Information Technologies*, •••, 1–46.

Kulik, C.-L. C., Kulik, J. A., & Bangert-Drowns, R. L. (1990). Effectiveness of mastery learning programs: A meta-analysis. *Review of Educational Research, 60*(2), 265–299. DOI: 10.3102/00346543060002265

Kumaran, S., Bharathi, B. S., & Pradeepa, R. (2025). A college enquiry text-based AI chatbot using python. *AIP Conference Proceedings, 3159*(1), 030013. Advance online publication. DOI: 10.1063/5.0247111

Kumor, T., Uribe-Flórez, L., Trespalacios, J., & Yang, D. (2024). ALEKS in high school mathematics classrooms: Exploring teachers' perceptions and use of this tool. *TechTrends*, *68*(3), 506–519. DOI: 10.1007/s11528-024-00955-0

Kuo, A., Alves-Oliveira, P., Björling, E., & Louie, B. (2022). Designing for culturally responsive social robots: An application of a participatory framework. *Frontiers in Robotics and AI*, *9*, 983408. Advance online publication. DOI: 10.3389/frobt.2022.983408 PMID: 36340576

Kurian, N. (2025). AI's empathy gap: The risks of conversational Artificial Intelligence for young children's well-being and key ethical considerations for early childhood education and care. *Contemporary Issues in Early Childhood*, *26*(1), 132–139. DOI: 10.1177/14639491231206004

Labadze, L., Grigolia, M., & Machaidze, L. (2023). Role of AI chatbots in education: Systematic literature review. *International Journal of Educational Technology in Higher Education*, *20*(1), 56. Advance online publication. DOI: 10.1186/s41239-023-00426-1

Ladson-Billings, G. (1995). Toward a theory of culturally relevant pedagogy. *American Educational Research Journal*, *32*(3), 465–491. DOI: 10.3102/00028312032003465

Lafuente Martínez, M., Lévêque, O., Benítez, I., Hardebolle, C., & Zufferey, J. D. (2022). Assessing computational thinking: Development and validation of the algorithmic thinking test for adults. *Journal of Educational Computing Research*, *60*(6), 1436–1463. DOI: 10.1177/07356331211057819

Lami, B., Mohd. Hussein, S., Rajamanickam, R., & Emmanuel, G. K. (2024). The role of artificial intelligence (AI) in shaping data privacy. *International Journal of Law and Management*. https://doi.org/.DOI: 10.1108/IJLMA-07-2024-0242

Lampropoulos, G., & Papadakis, S. (2025). The educational value of artificial intelligence and social robots. In Lampropoulos, G., & Papadakis, S. (Eds.), *Social robots in education: How to effectively introduce social robots into classrooms* (Vol. 1194, pp. 3–15). Springer., DOI: 10.1007/978-3-031-82915-4_1

Lamrani, R., & Abdelwahed, E. H. (2020). Game-based learning and gamification to improve skills in early years education. *Computer Science and Information Systems*, *17*(1), 339–356. DOI: 10.2298/CSIS190511043L

Larkin, I. M., Brantley-Dias, L., & Lokey-Vega, A. (2016). Job satisfaction, organizational commitment, and turnover intention of online teachers in the K-12 setting. *Online Learning : the Official Journal of the Online Learning Consortium*, *20*(3). Advance online publication. DOI: 10.24059/olj.v20i3.986

Latif, G., Alghazo, R., Pilotti, M. A., & Brahim, G. B. (2022). Identifying "at-risk" students: An AI-based prediction approach. *International Journal of Computing and Digital Systems, 11*(1), 1051–1059. DOI: 10.12785/ijcds/110184

Lavidas, K., Papadakis, S., Manesis, D., Grigoriadou, A. S., & Gialamas, V.Lectures and Lab Classes. (2022a). The effects of social desirability on students' self-reports in two social contexts: Lectures vs. lectures and lab classes. *Information (Basel), 13*(10), 491. DOI: 10.3390/info13100491

Lavidas, K., Petropoulou, A., Papadakis, S., Apostolou, Z., Komis, V., Jimoyiannis, A., & Gialamas, V. (2022b). Factors affecting response rates of the web survey with teachers. *Computers, 11*(9), 127. DOI: 10.3390/computers11090127

Lawrence, L., Echeverría, V., Yang, K., Aleven, V., & Rummel, N. (2023). How teachers conceptualise shared control with an ai co-orchestration tool: A multiyear teacher-centred design process. *British Journal of Educational Technology, 55*(3), 823–844. DOI: 10.1111/bjet.13372

Lechuga, C. G., Matayoshi, J., & Doroudi, S. (2025). Looking beyond a single score: Examining student mathematical strengths using aleks data. *Educational Assessment, 30*(3), 219–247. DOI: 10.1080/10627197.2025.2485928

Lee, B., & Yong Yi, M. (2024). Understanding the Empathetic Reactivity of Conversational Agents: Measure Development and Validation. *International Journal of Human-Computer Interaction, 40*(22), 6845–6863. DOI: 10.1080/10447318.2023.2270665

Lee, C. D. (2003). Toward a framework for culturally responsive design in multimedia computer environments: Cultural modeling as a case. *Mind, Culture, and Activity, 10*(1), 42–61. DOI: 10.1207/S15327884MCA1001_05

Lee, I., Ali, S., Zhang, H., DiPaola, D., & Breazeal, C. (2021). Developing middle school students' AI literacy. *Proceedings of the 52nd ACM Technical Symposium on Computer Science Education*, 191–197. DOI: 10.1145/3408877.3432513

Lee, J. H., Sioutis, M., Ahrens, K., Alirezaie, M., Kerzel, M., & Wermter, S. (2023). Neuro-symbolic spatio-temporal reasoning. In *Compendium of neurosymbolic artificial intelligence* (pp. 410–429). IOS Press. DOI: 10.3233/FAIA230151

Lee, S., Mott, B., Vandenberg, J., Spires, H. A., & Lester, J. (2023). Examining the Relationship of Gameplay and Learning in a Narrative-Centered Digital Game for Science Education. *IEEE Conference on Computatonal Intelligence and Games, CIG*. https://doi.org/DOI: 10.1109/CoG57401.2023.10333202

Lee, S., Mott, B., Vandenberg, J., Spires, H. A., & Lester, J. (2024). Exploring Gameplay and Learning in a Narrative-Centered Digital Game for Elementary Science Education. *IEEE Transactions on Games*, *16*(4), 1–14. DOI: 10.1109/TG.2024.3424689

Lertbumroongchai, K., Janratchakool, W., & Nittayathammakul, V. (2025). Using Virtual Reality and Conversational AI to Enhance High School Students' Intentions to Pursue Computer Science: Insights from the CS RMUTT Virtual Tour. Studies in Media and Communication, 13(3), 87–102. *Scopus*. Advance online publication. DOI: 10.11114/smc.v13i3.7683

Létourneau, A., Deslandes Martineau, M., Charland, P., Karran, J. A., Boasen, J., & Léger, P. M. (2025). A systematic review of AI-driven intelligent tutoring systems (ITS) in K-12 education. *NPJ Science of Learning*, *10*(1), 29. DOI: 10.1038/s41539-025-00320-7 PMID: 40368938

Levin, H. M., & McEwan, P. J. (2001). *Cost-effectiveness analysis: Methods and applications* (2nd ed.). Sage.

Lewis, D. I. (2014). *The pedagogical benefits and pitfalls of virtual tools for teaching and learning laboratory practices in the biological sciences*. The Higher Education Academy.

Li, B., Jiang, J., Ma, L., Huang, Y., & Wu, X. (2024). Mitigating University Students' Reliance on Chatgpt. Proceedings of the 2024 8th International Seminar on Education, Management and Social Sciences (ISEMSS 2024), Advances in Social Science, Education and Humanities Research, 867. https://doi.org/DOI: 10.2991/978-2-38476-297-2_31

Li, H., Xing, W., Li, C., Zhu, W., Lyu, B., Zhang, F., & Liu, Z. (2025). Who Should Be My Tutor? Analyzing the Interactive Effects of Automated Text Personality Styles Between Middle School Students and a Mathematics Chatbot. *15th International Conference on Learning Analytics and Knowledge, LAK 2025*, 910–917. https://doi.org/DOI: 10.1145/3706468.3706537

Li, S., & Wang, W. (2022). Effect of blended learning on student performance in K-12 settings: A meta-analysis. In *Journal of Computer Assisted Learning* (Vol. 38, Issue 5). DOI: 10.1111/jcal.12696

Lim, C. (2025). DeBiasMe: De-biasing human-AI interactions with metacognitive AIED (AI in Education) interventions. In *arXiv [cs.HC]*. arXiv. https://arxiv.org/abs/2504.16770

Li, T., Nath, D., Cheng, Y., Fan, Y., Li, X., Raković, M., Khosravi, H., Swiecki, Z., Tsai, Y.-S., & Gašević, D. (2025). Turning Real-Time Analytics into Adaptive Scaffolds for Self-Regulated Learning Using Generative Artificial Intelligence. *15th International Conference on Learning Analytics and Knowledge, LAK 2025*, 667–679. https://doi.org/DOI: 10.1145/3706468.3706559

Liu, M. (2023). Exploring the application of artificial intelligence in foreign language teaching: challenges and future development. SHS Web of Conferences, 168, 03025. https://doi.org/DOI: 10.1051/shsconf/202316803025

Liu, J., Ma, J., & Li, S. (2025). Research on school-based AI curriculum design and practice for cultivating computational thinking in high school students. *Education and Information Technologies*, *30*(6), 7949–7993. DOI: 10.1007/s10639-024-13115-x

Liu, L. (2025). Impact of AI gamification on EFL learning outcomes and nonlinear dynamic motivation: Comparing adaptive learning paths, conversational agents, and storytelling. *Education and Information Technologies*, *30*(8), 11299–11338. Advance online publication. DOI: 10.1007/s10639-024-13296-5

Liu, M., & Reinders, H. (2025). Do AI chatbots impact motivation? Insights from a preliminary longitudinal study. *System*, *128*, 103544. DOI: 10.1016/j.system.2024.103544

Liu, T. C. (2022). A case study of the adaptive learning platform in a Taiwanese elementary school: Precision education from teachers' perspectives. *Education and Information Technologies*, *27*(5), 6295–6316. DOI: 10.1007/s10639-021-10851-2 PMID: 35013667

Liu, W., & Wang, Y. (2024). The effects of using AI tools on critical thinking in English literature classes among EFL learners: An intervention study. *European Journal of Education*, *59*(4), e12804. DOI: 10.1111/ejed.12804

Liu, Z. (2023). Integrating computational thinking into k-12 education: Bridging the gap between theories and practices: Bridging the gap between theories and practices. *STEM Education Review*, *1*. Advance online publication. DOI: 10.54844/stemer.2023.0467

Liu, Z., Gearty, Z., Richard, E., Orrill, C. H., Kayumova, S., & Balasubramanian, R. (2024). Bringing computational thinking into classrooms: A systematic review on supporting teachers in integrating computational thinking into K-12 classrooms. *International Journal of STEM Education*, *11*(1), 51. DOI: 10.1186/s40594-024-00510-6

Li, Y., & Chiu, T. K. F. (2025). The mediating effects of needs satisfaction on the relationship between teacher support and student engagement with Generative Artificial Intelligence (GenAI) chatbots from a Self-Determination Theory (SDT) perspective. Education and Information Technologies. *Education and Information Technologies, 30*(14), 20051–20070. Advance online publication. DOI: 10.1007/s10639-025-13574-w

Li, Y., & Gabriel, M. (2022). Diverse Cultures, Universal Capacities: an Interview with Markus Gabriel. *Technology and Language, 3*(1–6), 47–56. https://doi.org/DOI: 10.48417/technolang.2022.01.06

Lockwood, J., & Mooney, A. (2017). A pilot study investigating the introduction of a computer-science course at second level focusing on computational thinking. *The Irish Journal of Education/Iris Eireannach an Oideachais, 42*, 108-127. https://www.jstor.org/stable/26607242

Lonn, S., & Teasley, S. D. (2009). Saving time or innovating practice? investigating perceptions and uses of learning management systems. *Computers & Education, 53*(3), 686–694. DOI: 10.1016/j.compedu.2009.04.008

Looi, C.-K., & Jia, F. (2025). Personalization capabilities of current technology chatbots in a learning environment: An analysis of student-tutor bot interactions. *Education and Information Technologies, 30*(10), 14165–14195. DOI: 10.1007/s10639-025-13369-z

Louis, M., & ElAzab, M. (2023). Will AI replace Teacher? *International Journal of Internet Education, 22*(2), 9–21. DOI: 10.21608/ijie.2023.312491

Lou, J. (2018). Improvement in university students' critical thinking following a strategic thinking training program. *NeuroQuantology : An Interdisciplinary Journal of Neuroscience and Quantum Physics, 16*(5), 91–96. DOI: 10.14704/nq.2018.16.5.1310

Lubbe, A., Marais, E., & Kruger, D. (2025). Cultivating independent thinkers: The triad of artificial intelligence, Bloom's taxonomy and critical thinking in assessment pedagogy. *Education and Information Technologies, 30*(12), 17589–17622. DOI: 10.1007/s10639-025-13476-x

Luckin, R. (2017). Towards artificial intelligence-based assessment systems. *Nature Human Behaviour, 1*, 0028. https://doi.org/DOI: 10.1038/s41562-017-0028

Luckin, R., Holmes, W., Griffiths, M., & Forcier, L. B. (2016). Intelligence unleashed: An argument for AI in education. Pearson Education. https://static.googleusercontent.com/media/edu.google.com/en//pdfs/Intelligence-Unleashed-Publication.pdf

Luckin, R., & Cukurova, M. (2019). Designing educational technologies in the age of AI: A learning sciences-driven approach. *British Journal of Educational Technology*, *50*(6), 2824–2838. DOI: 10.1111/bjet.12861

Luckin, R., Holmes, W., Griffiths, M., & Forcier, L. B. (2016). *Intelligence unleashed. An argument for AI in education.* Pearson.

Luckin, R., Holmes, W., Griffiths, M., & Forcier, L. B. (2016). *Intelligence unleashed: An argument for AI in education.* Pearson Education.

Madden, V. J. (2024). Vocal Awareness and K-12 Education: A Qualitative Research Study. *Voice & Speech Review*, *18*(1), 18–33. Advance online publication. DOI: 10.1080/23268263.2022.2062851

Madhu, N., Latha, P., & Savitha, N. (2024). Revolutionizing education: Harnessing ai for personalized learning pathways and student success. *International Journal for Multidisciplinary Research*, *6*(5).

Maghsudi, S., Lan, A., Xu, J., & Van Der Schaar, M. (2021). Personalized education in the artificial intelligence era: What to expect next. *IEEE Signal Processing Magazine*, *38*(3), 37–50. DOI: 10.1109/MSP.2021.3055032

Mah, D.-K., & Ifenthaler, D. (2019). What do first-year students need? Digital badges for academic support to enhance student retention. *Journal of Applied Research in Higher Education*, *12*(1), 86–96. DOI: 10.1108/JARHE-12-2018-0258

Ma, J., Han, X., Yang, J., & Cheng, J. (2015). Examining the necessary condition for engagement in an online learning environment based on learning analytics approach: The role of the instructor. *The Internet and Higher Education*, *24*, 26–34. DOI: 10.1016/j.iheduc.2014.09.005

Major, L., Francis, G. A., & Tsapali, M. (2021). The effectiveness of technology-supported personalised learning in low- and middle-income countries: A meta analysis. *British Journal of Educational Technology*, *52*(5), 1935–1964. DOI: 10.1111/bjet.13116

Malaborbor, R. A. C., Rivera, V. S., Diloy, M. A., De Luna, L. R., Dela Cruz, A. L. Y., & Velasco, A. T. (2024). Enhancing Data Privacy Literacy through Conversational AI: A QandA-Based Approach to Educating Users on the Provisions of the Data Privacy Act of 2012. 271–276. *Scopus.*, 271–276. Advance online publication. DOI: 10.1145/3696230.3696247

Mamun, M. R. A., Ntsweng, O., Baah-Peprah, P., David, A., & Prybutok, V. R. (2025). What Drives User Intention to Continue Using Conversational AI? How Functional and Emotional Values Influence Continuance Intention. *AIS Transactions on Human-Computer Interaction, 17*(1), 1–34. DOI: 10.17705/1thci.00216

Mandić, D. P., Miščević, G. M., & Bujišić, L. G. (2024). Evaluating the quality of responses generated by ChatGPT. Metodička teorija i praksa, 27(1), 5-19

Maqsood, M., Zahid, A., Asghar, T., Farooqi, S., & Shahbaz, M. (2024). Issues in teaching english in a cultural context. *Migration Letters : An International Journal of Migration Studies, 21*(S4), 1020–1027. DOI: 10.59670/ml.v21iS4.7411

Mari, A., Mandelli, A., & Algesheimer, R. (2024). Empathic voice assistants: Enhancing consumer responses in voice commerce. *Journal of Business Research, 175*, 114566. Advance online publication. DOI: 10.1016/j.jbusres.2024.114566

Mariyono, D., & Abror, M. (2024). AI in enhancing cultural sensitivity. *Jurnal EDUCATIO: Jurnal Pendidikan Indonesia, 10*(2), 296–310. DOI: 10.29210/1202424847

Marpaung, S. F., Sembiring, A. W., Azzahra, N., & Hallawa, S. (2023). Educational ethics in developing character learners. edumaspul. *Jurnal Pendidikan, 7*(2), 5721–5729.

Marple, S., Jaquet, K., Laudone, A., Sewell, J., & Liepmann, K. (2019). *i-Ready in 7th grade math classes: A mixed methods case study.* WestEd. https://www.wested.org/resource/iready-in-7th-grade-math/

Martell, C. C. (2018). *Social studies teacher education: Critical issues and current perspectives.* Information Age Publishing, Inc.

Martı Emel, N. (2025). Restructuring attempts in the Turkish Education System from 1980 to the present. *Science. Education and Innovations in the Context of Modern Problems, 8*(5), 207–217. DOI: 10.56334/sei/8.5.22

Martin, F., Chen, Y., Moore, R. L., & Westine, C. D. (2020). Systematic review of adaptive learning research designs, context, strategies, and technologies from 2009 to 2018. *Educational Technology Research and Development, 68*(4), 1903–1929. DOI: 10.1007/s11423-020-09793-2 PMID: 32837122

Martin, F., Zhuang, M., & Schaefer, D. (2024). Systematic review of research on artificial intelligence in K-12 education (2017–2022). In *Computers and Education* (Vol. 6). Artificial Intelligence., DOI: 10.1016/j.caeai.2023.100195

Mason, L., Jeon, T., Blair, P., & Glomb, N. (2013). Virtual tutor training: Learning to teach in a multi-user virtual environment. In Ferdig, R. E. (Ed.), *Design* (pp. 51–67). Utilization, and Analysis of Simulations and Game-Based Educational Worlds., DOI: 10.4018/978-1-4666-4018-4.ch004

Matayoshi, J., Uzun, H., & Cosyn, E. (2023). Analyzing response times and answer feedback tags in an adaptive assessment. In Wang, N., Rebolledo-Mendez, G., Dimitrova, V., Matsuda, N., & Santos, O. C. (Eds.), *Artificial intelligence in education. Posters and late breaking results, workshops and tutorials, industry and innovation tracks, practitioners, doctoral consortium and blue sky. AIED 2023*. Springer., DOI: 10.1007/978-3-031-36336-8_46

Matera, M., Piro, L., Pucci, E., Costabile, M. F., Lanzilotti, R., & Piccinno, A. (2023). Improving Citizen Inclusivity through Conversational AI. The PROTECT Approach. *CEUR Workshop Proceedings*, *3486*, 261–266. https://www.scopus.com/inward/record.uri?eid=2-s2.0-85173828750&partnerID=40&md5=66d2fe8589141c2be62efcdc237cb1ec

Mat, N. C., & Jamaludin, K. A. (2024). Effectiveness of practices and applications of student-centered teaching and learning in primary schools: A systematic literature review. *International Journal of Academic Research in Progressive Education and Development*, *13*(3), 1025–1044.

Matto, G. (2024). Is ChatGPT building or destroying education? Perception of university students in Tanzania. *Journal of Education and Learning Technology*, *5*(4), 38–51. DOI: 10.38159/jelt.2024541

Matto, G., & Ponera, J. M. (2025). Artificial intelligence in higher education institutions in Tanzania: Analysis of policy perspectives. *Interdisciplinary Journal of Education Research*, *7*(1), a13. DOI: 10.38140/ijer-2025.vol7.1.13

Mayasari, N., Sastraatmadja, A. H. M., Suparman, T., Mutiara, I. I., & Maqfirah, P. A.-V. (2024). Effectiveness of using artificial intelligence learning tools and customized curriculum on improving students' critical thinking skills in Indonesia. *The Eastasouth Journal of Learning and Educations*, *2*(2), 111–118. DOI: 10.58812/esle.v2i02.302

Mbwambo, N. M., & Kaaya, P. B. (2024). ChatGPT in education: Applications, concerns and recommendations. *Journal of ICT Systems*, *2*(1), 107–124. DOI: 10.56279/jicts.v2i1.87

McGehee, N. (2024). *Breaking barriers: A meta-analysis of educator acceptance of AI technology in education.* Michigan Virtual. https://michiganvirtual.org/research/publications/breaking-barriers-a-meta-analysis-of-educator-acceptance-of-ai-technology-in-education/

McGraw Hill. (n.d.-a). *All about knowledge checks.* Retrieved August 26, 2025, from https://www.aleks.com/resources/ALEKS_Knowledge_Checks_Overview_for_Students.pdf

McGraw Hill. (n.d.-b). *ALEKS in Canada – Adaptive learning & assessment for math, chemistry, statistics & more.* Retrieved August 26, 2025, from https://ca.aleks.com/

McGraw Hill. (n.d.-c). *ALEKS program overview.* Retrieved August 26, 2025, from https://info.mheducation.com/rs/128-SJW-347/images/ALEKS-Overview-Brochure.pdf

McLaren, B. M., Herckis, L., Teffera, L., Branstetter, L., & Rose, C. P.. (2024). Community college information technology education: Curriculum mapping, a learning science framework, and AI learning technologies [Describes curriculum mapping with KLI to align knowledge components with intelligent tutors and collaborative learning]. *Proceedings of the 2024 Annual Meeting of the American Educational Research* DOI: 10.3102/2111565

Means, B., Roschelle, J., Penuel, W., Sabelli, N., & Haertel, G. (2003). Chapter 5: Technology's contribution to teaching and policy: Efficiency, standardization, or transformation? *Review of Research in Education*, *27*(1), 159–181. DOI: 10.3102/0091732X027001159

Meecha, C. (2023). Professional Development within the K-12 Setting. In *Career Pathways in Adult Education.* Perspectives and Opportunities., DOI: 10.4324/9781003259602-23

Mehrez, A., Adamo, N., Giri, N., & Larson, D. (2023). Fiat Lux! Does the Lighting Design Affect Viewers' Perception of an Animated Character Personality? *Lecture Notes in Computer Science (Including Subseries Lecture Notes in Artificial Intelligence and Lecture Notes in Bioinformatics), 14047 LNCS*, 263–272. https://doi.org/DOI: 10.1007/978-3-031-35979-8_21

Mejeh, M., & Rehm, M. (2024). Taking adaptive learning in educational settings to the next level: Leveraging natural language processing for improved personalization. *Educational Technology Research and Development*, *72*(3), 1597–1621. DOI: 10.1007/s11423-024-10345-1

Mekić, E. S., Jovanović, M. N., Kuk, K. V., Prlinčević, B. P., & Savić, A. M. (2024). Enhancing educational efficiency: Generative AI chatbots and DevOps in Education 4.0. *Computer Applications in Engineering Education*, *32*(6), e22804. DOI: 10.1002/cae.22804

Menashy, F., & Zakharia, Z. (2022). Crisis upon crisis: Refugee education responses amid COVID-19. *Peabody Journal of Education*, *97*(3), 309–325. DOI: 10.1080/0161956X.2022.2079895

Menekse, M. (2015). Computer science teacher professional development in the United States: A review of studies published between 2004 and 2014. *Computer Science Education*, *25*(4), 325–350. DOI: 10.1080/08993408.2015.1111645

Meng, X., & Yang, Y. (2025). Self-evolving generative AI tutors: Reinforcement learning-augmented ITS for personalized, proactive, and context-aware student engagement. *Research Square*. https://doi.org/DOI: 10.21203/rs.3.rs-6107039/v1

Meshram, S., Naik, N., Vr, M., More, T., & Kharche, S. (2021). Conversational AI: Chatbots. *2021 International Conference on Intelligent Technologies, CONIT 2021*. https://doi.org/DOI: 10.1109/CONIT51480.2021.9498508

Meyer, J. G., Urbanowicz, R. J., Martin, P. C. N., O'Connor, K., Li, R., Peng, P.-C., Bright, T. J., Tatonetti, N., Won, K. J., Gonzalez-Hernandez, G., & Moore, J. H. (2023). ChatGPT and large language models in academia: Opportunities and challenges. *BioData Mining*, *16*(1), 20. DOI: 10.1186/s13040-023-00339-9 PMID: 37443040

Mgaiwa, S. J. (2018). The paradox of financing public higher education in Tanzania and the fate of quality education: The experience of selected universities. *SAGE Open*, *8*(2), 2158244018771729. Advance online publication. DOI: 10.1177/2158244018771729

Mgaiwa, S. J., & Ishengoma, J. M. (2023). Financing higher education in Tanzania through students' loans scheme and its impact on equitable access. *Heliyon*, *9*(3), e13943. DOI: 10.1016/j.heliyon.2023.e13943 PMID: 36895382

Miao, F., Holmes, W., Huang, R., & Zhang, H. (2021). *Artificial intelligence and education. Guidance for policy-makers*. United Nations Educational, Scientific and Cultural Organization (UNESCO). https://doi.org/DOI: 10.54675/PCSP7350

Michalak, R. (2023). From Ethics to Execution: The Role of Academic Librarians in Artificial Intelligence (AI) Policy-Making at Colleges and Universities. *Journal of Library Administration*, *63*(7), 928–938. DOI: 10.1080/01930826.2023.2262367

Michigan Information Education System. (n.d.). Retrieved September 1, 2022 from https://studylib.net/doc/6828389/section-1--tpack-observation-checklist---meis

Mikael, K., Cemil, Ö. Z., Rashid, T. A., & Nariman, G. S. (2025). A Hybrid Chatbot Model for Enhancing Administrative Support in Education: Comparative Analysis, Integration, and Optimization. IEEE Access.

Miller, P., & DiCerbo, K. (2024). LLM Based Math Tutoring: Challenges and Dataset. *EdArXiv*. https://doi.org/DOI: 10.35542/osf.io/5zwv3

Mills, N. J. D. (2021). ALEKS constructs as predictors of high school mathematics achievement for struggling students. *Heliyon*, *7*(6), e07345. Advance online publication. DOI: 10.1016/j.heliyon.2021.e07345 PMID: 34195443

Ministry of Education. Science and Technology (MoEST). (2025). Education sector development plan, 2025/26–2029/30. United Republic of Tanzania. https://www.moe.go.tz/sites/default/files/ESDP%202025-26%20hadi%202029-30%20Final-%2026%20February%202025.pdf

Ministry of Education. Science and Technology (MoEST). (2025). National guidelines for artificial intelligence in education. https://www.moe.go.tz/sites/default/files/NATIONAL%20GUIDELINES%20FOR%20ARTIFICIAL%20INTELIGENCE%20N%20EDUCATION.pdf

Mintz, J., Holmes, W., Liu, L., & Perez-Ortiz, M. (2023). Artificial intelligence and K-12 education: Possibilities, pedagogies and risks. *Computers in the Schools*, *40*(4), 325–333. DOI: 10.1080/07380569.2023.2279870

Miri, M., & Pishghadam, R. (2021). Toward an emotioncy based education: A systematic review of the literature. *Frontiers in Psychology*, *12*, 727186. Advance online publication. DOI: 10.3389/fpsyg.2021.727186 PMID: 34421775

Misaki, D., Ge, X., Xu, C., Markus, H., & Tsai, J. (2024). How culture shapes what people want from AI. *Proceedings of the 2024 CHI Conference on Human Factors in Computing Systems*. https://doi.org/DOI: 10.1145/3613904.3642660

Mishra, P., & Koehler, M. J. (2006). Technological pedagogical content knowledge: A framework for teacher knowledge. *Teachers College Record*, *108*(6), 1017–1054. DOI: 10.1111/j.1467-9620.2006.00684.x

Moaiad, Y., Alobed, M., Alsakhnini, M., & Momani, A. (2021). *Challenges in natural Arabic language processing*. Edelweiss Applied Science and Technology., DOI: 10.55214/25768484.v8i6.3018

Mohideen, H.H. L. M. Mohideen. (2024). Exploring the opportunities of implementing artificial intelligence (AI) technology for teaching Arabic to non-native speakers: A theoretical approach. *Journal of Digital Learning and Distance Education*, *2*(9), 760–767. Advance online publication. DOI: 10.56778/jdlde.v2i9.225

Molnár, G., & Szüts, Z. (2018, September). The role of chatbots in formal education. In 2018 IEEE 16th international symposium on intelligent systems and informatics (SISY) (pp.197-202). IEEE. Subotica, Serbia. DOI: 10.1109/SISY.2018.8524609

Moltudal, S. H., Krumsvik, R. J., & Høydal, K. L. (2022). Adaptive learning technology in primary education: Implications for professional teacher knowledge and classroom management. *Frontiers in Education*, *7*, 830536. DOI: 10.3389/feduc.2022.830536

Monjoree, U., Aguilar, S. D., Qian, C., Van Huyck, C., Yeh, S.-H., Tranbarger, P., Duane-Tessier, L., Solitare-Renaldo, L., Burte, H., Yasskin, P., Liew, J., Song, D., Quek, F., & Yan, W. (2024). AR-Classroom: Integrating Conversational Artificial Intelligence with Augmented Reality Technology for Learning Spatial Transformations and Their Matrix Representation. *Proceedings - Frontiers in Education Conference, FIE*. https://doi.org/DOI: 10.1109/FIE61694.2024.10893308

Monterrat, B., Desmarais, M., Lavoué, E., & George, S. (2015). A player model for adaptive gamification in learning environments. In *Artificial Intelligence in Education: 17th International Conference, AIED 2015, Madrid, Spain, June 22-26, 2015.* [Springer International Publishing.]. *Proceedings*, *17*, 297–306.

Mooradian, N., Franks, P. C., & Srivastav, A. (2025). The impact of artificial intelligence on data privacy: A risk management perspective. *Records Management Journal*, *35*(2), 147–159. Advance online publication. DOI: 10.1108/RMJ-06-2024-0013

Morandín-Ahuerma, F. (2023). *Ten UNESCO recommendations on the ethics of artificial intelligence*. https://doi.org/DOI: 10.31219/osf.io/csyux

Morkina, J. S. (2021). Meaning-constitution Problems in the Digital Culture's Horizon. *Voprosy Filosofii*, *12*(12), 78–89. DOI: 10.21146/0042-8744-2021-12-78-89

Morozova, I., & Nikolaienko, V. (2024). Emotional appeal in ChatGPT prompts: A study of L2 speakers' perceptions | Emotywne prompty i ich percepcja – na przykładzie interakcji nierodzimych użytkowników języka z botem ChatGPT. *Res Rhetorica*, *11*(4), 155–174. DOI: 10.29107/rr2024.4.9

Morrison, G. (2023). Literature Review: The Impact of Invisibility on Diasporic Indigenous Students in K-12 Settings. In *Journal of Latinos and Education*. DOI: 10.1080/15348431.2023.2291682

Moruzzi, C., & Margarido, S. (2024, May 11). A user-centered framework for human-AI co-creativity. *Extended Abstracts of the CHI Conference on Human Factors in Computing Systems*. CHI '24: CHI Conference on Human Factors in Computing Systems, Honolulu HI USA. DOI: 10.1145/3613905.3650929

Mousavinasab, E., Zarifsanaiey, N., Niakan Kalhori, S. R., Rakhshan, M., Keikha, L., & Saeedi, M. G. (2021). Intelligent tutoring systems: A systematic review of characteristics, applications, and evaluation methods. *Interactive Learning Environments*, *29*(1), 142–163. DOI: 10.1080/10494820.2018.1558257

Mouza, C., Yadav, A., & Ottenbreit-Leftwich, A. (2018). Developing computationally literate teachers: Current perspectives and future directions for teacher preparation in computing education. *Journal of Technology and Teacher Education*, *26*(3), 333–352. https://www.learntechlib.org/primary/p/184602/

Mtebe, J. S., & Raisamo, R. (2014). Challenges and instructors' intention to adopt and use open educational resources in higher education in Tanzania and Kenya. *International Review of Research in Open and Distance Learning*, *15*(1), 249–271. DOI: 10.19173/irrodl.v15i1.1687

Mubofu, C., & Kainkwa, E. (2023). University lecturers' feelings, awareness and attitudes towards Open Education Resources: Experience from two higher learning institutions in Tanzania. *Open Praxis*, *15*(4), 328–341. DOI: 10.55982/openpraxis.15.4.555

Mudawy, A. (2024). Investigating efl faculty members' perceptions of integrating artificial intelligence applications to improve the research writing process: a case study at majmaah university. https://doi.org/DOI: 10.31235/osf.io/k4ub8

Muller, M., & Strohmayer, A. (2022, April). Forgetting practices in the data sciences. In *Proceedings of the 2022 CHI Conference on Human Factors in Computing Systems* (pp. 1-19).

Mulyanto, D., Zaky, M., Ridho, A., & Fata, K. (2024). [Using artificial intelligence to develop Arabic language skills in learning]. *An-Nidzam: Jurnal Manajemen Pendidikan dan Studi Islam, 11*(1), 18–32. https://doi.org/DOI: 10.33507/an-nidzam.v11i1.1940

Mutajwaa, S. A., & Didas, M. (2025). Roadmap to Systematic Understanding of Artificial Intelligence Technology Development and Implementation: A Narrative Review of Frameworks, Platforms, Scenarios of Use and Empirical Guide. *Journal of ICT Systems*, *3*(1), 34–62. DOI: 10.56279/jicts.v3i1.126

Muthmainnah, I. S., Ibna Seraj, P. M., & Oteir, I. (2022). P. M., & Oteir, I. (2022). Playing with AI to investigate human-computer interaction technology and improving critical thinking skills to pursue 21st century age. *Education Research International*, *2022*(6468995), 1–17. Advance online publication. DOI: 10.1155/2022/6468995

Nagy, E., Sik, D., Biczo, Z., Zimányi, K., Pörzse, G., & Molnár, G. (2024). Advanced digital and artificial intelligence-based solutions for interactive, collaborative learning support. *2024 IEEE 7th International Conference and Workshop Óbuda on Electrical and Power Engineering (CANDO-EPE)*, 103–108. https://doi.org/DOI: 10.1109/CANDO-EPE65072.2024.10772869

Namjoo, F., Liaghat, E., Shabaziasl, S., Modabernejad, Z., & Morshedi, H. (2023). Students experience on self-study through ai. aitechbesosci, 1(3), 35-42. https://doi.org/DOI: 10.61838/kman.aitech.1.3.6

Nanney, B. (2020). Student-centered learning. *The SAGE Encyclopedia of Higher Education*. https://api.semanticscholar.org/CorpusID:64196280

Narayanan, K. S., & Kumaravel, A. (2024). Hybrid Gamification and AI Tutoring Framework using Machine Learning and Adaptive Neuro-Fuzzy Inference System. *Journal of Advanced Research in Applied Sciences and Engineering Technology*, *42*(2), 221–233. DOI: 10.37934/araset.42.2.221233

Naseer, F., Khan, M. N., Addas, A., Awais, Q., & Ayub, N. (2025). Game Mechanics and Artificial Intelligence Personalization: A Framework for Adaptive Learning Systems. *Education Sciences*, *15*(3), 301. Advance online publication. DOI: 10.3390/educsci15030301

National Research Council, Division of Behavioral, Board on Science Education, & Committee on a Conceptual Framework for New K-12 Science Education Standards. (2012). *A framework for K-12 science education: Practices, crosscutting concepts, and core ideas*. national academies press.

Nazaretsky, T., Ariely, M., Cukurova, M., & Alexandron, G. (2022). Teachers' trust in ai-powered educational technology and a professional development program to improve it. *British Journal of Educational Technology*, *53*(4), 914–931. DOI: 10.1111/bjet.13232

Nazer, L. H., Zatarah, R., Waldrip, S., Ke, J. X. C., Moukheiber, M., Khanna, A. K., Hicklen, R. S., Moukheiber, L., Moukheiber, D., Ma, H., & Mathur, P. (2023). Bias in artificial intelligence algorithms and recommendations for mitigation. *PLOS Digital Health*, *2*(6), e0000278. Advance online publication. DOI: 10.1371/journal.pdig.0000278 PMID: 37347721

Naznin, K., Al Mahmud, A., Nguyen, M. T., & Chua, C. (2025). ChatGPT integration in higher education for personalized learning, academic writing, and coding tasks: A systematic review. *Computers*, *14*(2), 53. DOI: 10.3390/computers14020053

Nehring, J., Moyer-Packenham, P., & North, M. (2023). Assessing the effectiveness of an artificial intelligence tutoring system for improving college-level mathematics preparedness in high school students. *Issues in Information Systems*, *24*(1), 128–141. DOI: 10.48009/1_iis_2023_111

Nejati, B., Manchi, R., & Schofield, D. (2024). Incorporating cross-cultural design into the user interface. *The International Journal of Multimedia & Its Applications*. https://doi.org/DOI: 10.5121/ijma.2024.16501

Ng, A. K., Atmosukarto, I., Cheow, W. S., Avnit, K., & Yong, M. H. (2021). Development and implementation of an online adaptive gamification platform for learning computational thinking. In *2021 IEEE Frontiers in Education Conference (FIE)* (pp. 1-6). IEEE. https://doi.org/DOI: 10.1109/FIE49875.2021.9637467

Ngandoh, S. T., Riandi, R., Rahmat, A., Muslim, M., Haris, A., Khaeruddin, K., & Friyanto, A. (2025). Enhancing Interactive Media Design Using Cognitive Load Theory Approach: Integrating Artificial Intelligence (Ai) Chatbot. [Scopus.]. *Journal of Engineering Science and Technology*, *20*(2), 71–78.

Ng, D. T. K., Chan, E. K. C., & Lo, C. K. (2025). Opportunities, challenges and school strategies for integrating generative AI in education. *Computers and Education: Artificial Intelligence*, *8*, 100373. DOI: 10.1016/j.caeai.2025.100373

Ng, D. T. K., Leung, J. K. L., Chu, S. K. W., & Qiao, M. S. (2021). Conceptualizing AI literacy: An exploratory review. *Computers and Education: Artificial Intelligence*, *2*, 100041. DOI: 10.1016/j.caeai.2021.100041

Ng, D. T. K., Su, J., Leung, J. K. L., & Chu, S. K. W. (2024). Artificial intelligence (AI) literacy education in secondary schools: A review. *Interactive Learning Environments*, *32*(10), 6204–6224. DOI: 10.1080/10494820.2023.2255228

NGSS Lead States. (2013). *Next generation science standards: For states, by states*. National Academies Press.

Ngulugulu, M. M., & Mgina, H. J. (2024). Utilization of educational artificial intelligence tools in higher learning institutions in Tanzania: A literature review. *International Journal of Novel Research and Development*, *9*(4). https://www.ijnrd.org/papers/IJNRD2404376.pdf

Nguyen, A., Ngo, H. N., Hong, Y., Dang, B., & Nguyen, B.-P. T. (2023). Ethical principles for artificial intelligence in education. *Education and Information Technologies*, *28*(4), 4221–4241. DOI: 10.1007/s10639-022-11316-w PMID: 36254344

Nichols, T. P., & Dixon-Román, E. (2024). Platform governance and education policy: Power and politics in emerging edtech ecologies. *Educational Evaluation and Policy Analysis*, *46*(2), 309–328. DOI: 10.3102/01623737231202469

Nie, A., Chandak, Y., Suzara, M., Ali, M., Woodrow, J., Peng, M., Sahami, M., Brunskill, E., & Piech, C. (2024). The GPT surprise: Offering large language model chat in a massive coding class reduced engagement but increased adopters exam performances. In *arXiv [cs.CY]*. arXiv. https://doi.org/DOI: 10.31219/osf.io/qy8zd

Niloy, A. C., Akter, S., Sultana, N., Sultana, J., & Rahman, S. I. U. (2024). Is Chatgpt a menace for creative writing ability? An experiment. *Journal of Computer Assisted Learning*, *40*(2), 919–930. https://onlinelibrary.wiley.com/doi/10.1111/jcal.12929. DOI: 10.1111/jcal.12929

Nitkin, D., Ready, D. D., & Bowers, A. J. (2022). Using technology to personalize middle school math instruction: Evidence from a blended learning program in five public schools. *Frontiers in Education*, *7*, 646471. Advance online publication. DOI: 10.3389/feduc.2022.646471

Njiku, J., Ismail, M. J., Yunus, S., & Abdulla, A. A. (2024). Exploring ChatGPT's potential to enhance learning outcomes: A study of university students' beliefs and practices. International Conference on Global Innovation for a Sustainable Future. https://www.researchgate.net/publication/389920573_Exploring_ChatGPT%27s_Potential_to_Enhance_Learning_Outcomes_A_Study_of_University_Students%27_Beliefs_and_Practices

Noy, S., & Zhang, W. (2023). Experimental evidence on the productivity effects of generative artificial intelligence. *Science*, *381*(6654), 187–192. DOI: 10.1126/science.adh2586 PMID: 37440646

Nu'n˜ez-Molina, C., Mesejo, P., & Ferna'ndez-Olivares, J. (2024). A review of symbolic, subsymbolic and hybrid methods for sequential decision making. *ACM Computing Surveys*, *56*(11), 1–36. DOI: 10.1145/3663366

Nur, N., Goh, S. J., Patel, J., & Mizrahi, M. (2024). Navigating the ethical landscape of ai integration in educational settings. In *INTED2024 Proceedings* (pp. 7654-7663). IATED. DOI: 10.21125/inted.2024.2040

Nwana, H. S. (1990). Intelligent tutoring systems: An overview. *Artificial Intelligence Review*, *4*(4), 251–277. DOI: 10.1007/BF00168958

Nyaaba, M. (2024). Transforming teacher education in developing countries: The role of generative AI in bridging theory and practice. arXiv preprint arXiv:2411.10718.

Nyaaba, M., Zhai, X., & Faison, M. Z. (2024). Generative AI for culturally responsive science assessment: A conceptual framework. *Education Sciences*, *14*(12), 1325. DOI: 10.3390/educsci14121325

O'Connor, S., & Liu, H. (2024). Gender bias perpetuation and mitigation in AI technologies: Challenges and opportunities. *AI & Society*, *39*(4), 2045–2057. DOI: 10.1007/s00146-023-01675-4

OECD. (2023). *Oecd digital education outlook 2023: Towards an effective digital education ecosystem*. DOI: 10.1787/c74f03de-en

Ogegbo, A. A., & Ramnarain, U. (2022). A systematic review of computational thinking in science classrooms. *Studies in Science Education*, *58*(2), 203–230. DOI: 10.1080/03057267.2021.1963580

Ogunseiju, O., Akinniyi, A., Gonsalves, N., Khalid, M., & Akanmu, A. (2023). Detecting Learning Stages within a Sensor-Based Mixed Reality Learning Environment Using Deep Learning. *Journal of Computing in Civil Engineering*, *37*(4), 04023011. Advance online publication. DOI: 10.1061/JCCEE5.CPENG-5169

Ogunsina, M., Efunniyi, C. P., Osundare, O. S., Folorunsho, S. O., & Akwawa, L. A. (2024). Neuro-symbolic integration in autonomous robotics: A framework for enhanced decision-making. *Engineering Science & Technology Journal*, *5*(9). Advance online publication. DOI: 10.51594/estj.v5i9.1546

Okonkwo, C. W., & Ade-Ibijola, A. (2021). Chatbots applications in education: A systematic review. *Computers and Education: Artificial Intelligence*, *2*, 100033. DOI: 10.1016/j.caeai.2021.100033

Okunade, A. (2024). The role of artificial intelligence in teaching of science education in secondary schools in nigeria. *European Journal of Computer Science and Information Technology*, *12*(1), 57–67. DOI: 10.37745/ejcsit2013/vol12n15767

Olson, D. M., Soliman, N., Wang, A., Price, M., Sahu, R., & Harrell, D. F. (2020). Breakbeat narratives: A personalized, conversational interactive storytelling system for museum education. *Conference on Human Factors in Computing Systems - Proceedings*. https://doi.org/DOI: 10.1145/3334480.3382974

Olugbade, D., Edwards, B. I., & Ojo, O. A. (2024). Facilitating Cognitive Load Management and Improved Learning Outcomes and Attitudes in Middle School Technology and Vocational Education Through AI Chatbot. Journal of Technical Education and Training, 16(3), 114–131. *Scopus*. Advance online publication. DOI: 10.30880/jtet.2024.16.03.009

Onesi-Ozigagun, O., Ololade, Y., Eyo-Udo, N., & Ogundipe, D. (2024). Revolutionizing education through ai: A comprehensive review of enhancing learning experiences. *International Journal of Applied Research in Social Sciences*, *6*(4), 589–607. DOI: 10.51594/ijarss.v6i4.1011

Open, A. I., Achiam, J., Adler, S., Agarwal, S., Ahmad, L., Akkaya, I., Aleman, F. L., Almeida, D., Altenschmidt, J., Altman, S., Anadkat, S., Avila, R., Babuschkin, I., Balaji, S., Balcom, V., Baltescu, P., Bao, H., Bavarian, M., Belgum, J., & Zoph, B. (2023a). GPT-4 Technical Report. In *arXiv [cs.CL]*. arXiv. https://arxiv.org/abs/2303.08774

Organisation for Economic Co-operation and Development (OECD). (2022). AI and the future of skills: Challenges for education and assessment. OECD Publishing. https://oecd.ai/en/

Orhani, S. (2024). Deep Learning in Math Education. *International Journal of Research and Innovation in Social Science*, *8*(4), 270–278. DOI: 10.47772/IJRISS.2024.804022

Orlikowski, W. J. (1992). The duality of technology: Rethinking the concept of technology in organizations. *Organization Science*, *3*(3), 398–427. DOI: 10.1287/orsc.3.3.398

Osadchaia, V., Ivanova, O., & Getman, E. (2020). Cross-cultural communication issues of educating bicultural students.. https://doi.org/DOI: 10.31483/r-75019

Ouyang, F., & Scharber, C. (2017). The influences of an experienced instructor's discussion design and facilitation on an online learning community development: A social network analysis study. *The Internet and Higher Education*, *35*, 34–47. DOI: 10.1016/j.iheduc.2017.07.002

Ouyang, F., Wu, M., Zheng, L., Zhang, L., & Jiao, P. (2023). Integration of artificial intelligence performance prediction and learning analytics to improve student learning in online engineering course. *International Journal of Educational Technology in Higher Education*, *20*(1), 4. Advance online publication. DOI: 10.1186/s41239-022-00372-4 PMID: 36683653

Overby, K. (2011). Student-centered learning. *Essai*, *9*(1), 32.

Özgür, T. (2023). Active learning improves academic achievement and learning retention in K-12 settings: A meta-analysis. *I-Manager's Journal on School Educational Technology*, *18*(3), jsch.18.3.19288. Advance online publication. DOI: 10.26634/jsch.18.3.19288

Pachman, M., Arguel, A., Lockyer, L., Kennedy, G., & Lodge, J. M. (2016). Eye tracking and early detection of confusion in digital learning environments: Proof of concept. *Australasian Journal of Educational Technology*, *32*(6), 58–71. DOI: 10.14742/ajet.3060

Padmanaban, H. (2024). Machine learning algorithms scaling on large-scale data infrastructure. *Journal of Artificial Intelligence General science (JAIGS) ISSN: 3006-4023, 3*(1), 171–196.

Pahuja, R. (2024). Ethical Dimensions of Informed Consent: Principles, Processes, and Case Studies. Ethical Frameworks in Special Education: A Guide for Researchers (Volume 2nd), 116.

Pan, Y., Ke, F., & Xu, X. (2022). A systematic review of the role of learning games in fostering mathematics education in K-12 settings. In *Educational Research Review* (Vol. 36). DOI: 10.1016/j.edurev.2022.100448

Pane, J. F., Steiner, E. D., Baird, M. D., Hamilton, L. S., ... (2015). *Continued progress: Promising evidence on personalized learning* (tech. rep.). RAND Corporation. Santa Monica, CA. https://www.rand.org/pubs/research reports/RR1365.html

Papadakis, S., Lytvynova, S. H., Ivanova, S. M., & Selyshcheva, I. A. (2024b). *Advancing lifelong learning with AI-enhanced ICT: A review of 3L-Person 2024.* In *CEUR Workshop Proceedings (9th International Workshop on Professional Retraining and Life-Long Learning using ICT: Person-oriented Approach — 3L-Person 2024, Lviv, Ukraine, September 25, 2023).* CEUR-WS.org.

Papadakis, S., Striuk, A. M., Kravtsov, H. M., Shyshkina, M. P., Marienko, M. V., & Danylchuk, H. B. (2024a). *Embracing digital innovation and cloud technologies for transformative learning experiences.* In *Proceedings of the 11th Workshop on Cloud Technologies in Education (CTE 2023), Kryvyi Rih, Ukraine, December 22, 2023.* CEUR Workshop Proceedings.

Papadakis, S. (2020). Apps to promote computational thinking concepts and coding skills in children of preschool and pre-primary school age. In *Mobile learning applications in early childhood education* (pp. 101–121). IGI Global Scientific Publishing. DOI: 10.4018/978-1-7998-1486-3.ch006

Papadakis, S. (2022). Apps to promote computational thinking and coding skills to young age children: A pedagogical challenge for the 21st century learners. [EDUP-IJ]. *Educational Process: International Journal, 11*(1), 7–13. DOI: 10.22521/edupij.2022.111.1

Papadakis, S., Lytvynova, S. H., Ivanova, S. M., & Selyshcheva, I. A. (2024). Advancing lifelong learning with AI-enhanced ICT: A review of 3L-Person 2024. *CEUR Workshop Proceedings, 3679*, 1–11. https://ceur-ws.org/Vol-3679/paper00.pdf

Papadakis, S., Striuk, A. M., Kravtsov, H. M., Shyshkina, M. P., Marienko, M. V., & Danylchuk, H. B. (2024). Embracing digital innovation and cloud technologies for transformative learning experiences. *CEUR Workshop Proceedings, 3781*, 1–13. https://ceur-ws.org/Vol-3781/paper00.pdf

Papadakis, St., Zourmpakis, A., Kasotaki, S., & Kalogiannakis, M. (2024). Teachers' Perspectives on Integrating Adaptive Gamification Applications into Science Teaching. *Journal of Electrical Systems, 20*(11s), 2593–2600. DOI: 10.52783/jes.7917

Park, J. J., & Milner, P. (2025). Enhancing Academic Writing Integrity: Ethical Implementation of Generative Artificial Intelligence for Non-Traditional Online Students. *TechTrends, 69*(1), 176–188. DOI: 10.1007/s11528-024-01024-2

Park, S., & Kim, C. (2015). Boosting learning-by-teaching in virtual tutoring. *Computers & Education, 82*, 129–140. DOI: 10.1016/j.compedu.2014.11.006

Park, W., & Kwon, H. (2023). Implementing artificial intelligence education for middle school technology education in republic of korea. *International Journal of Technology and Design Education, 34*(1), 109–135. DOI: 10.1007/s10798-023-09812-2 PMID: 36844448

Partelow, L. (2024, September 19). *Using learning science to analyze the risks and benefits of AI in K-12 education*. Center for American Progress. https://www.americanprogress.org/article/using-learning-science-to-analyze-the-risks-and-benefits-of-ai-in-k-12-education/

Patilima, H. (2025). Neurodiversity and trauma in early childhood: Implications for inclusive learning. South African Journal of Childhood Education, 15(1). *South African Journal of Childhood Education, 15*(1), a1704. Advance online publication. DOI: 10.4102/sajce.v15i1.1704

Paul, R., & Elder, L. (2014). *Critical thinking: Tools for taking charge of your professional and personal life* (2nd ed.). Pearson Education.

Pehlivan Yılmaz, A., & Günel, E. (2022). Culturally responsive teaching practices in social studies: Interaction with refugee students in Turkey. *Education in Science, 47*(212), 121–159. DOI: 10.15390/EB.2022.11338

Pelletier, K. K., Brown, M., Brooks, D. C., McCormack, M., Reeves, J., Arbino, N., Bozkurt, A., Crawford, S., Czerniewicz, L., Gibson, R., Linder, K., Mason, J., & Mondelli, V. (2021). Australian Higher Education. In *2021 EDUCAUSE Horizon Report: Teaching and Learning Edition* (pp. 37-38). EDUCAUSE Publications.

Pendy, B. (2023). Artificial intelligence: The future of education. *Jurnal Indonesia Sosial Sains*, *2*(11). Advance online publication. DOI: 10.59141/jiss.v2i11.801

Pérez, J. Q., Daradoumis, T., & Puig, J. M. M. (2020). Rediscovering the use of chatbots in education: A systematic literature review. *Computer Applications in Engineering Education*, *28*(6), 1549–1565. DOI: 10.1002/cae.22326

Piaget, J. (1973). *The Child and Reality: Problems of Genetic Psychology* (Rosin, A., Trans.). Grossman.

Piro, L. (2023). Conversational AI for Web Inclusivity: Technologies, Design Patterns and Development Toolkits. *CEUR Workshop Proceedings*, *3481*, 29–35. https://www.scopus.com/inward/record.uri?eid=2-s2.0-85172870199&partnerID=40&md5=503b0ef4f132cdddd5f9817468dd6fd1

Pusparini, F., Riandi, R., & Sriyati, S. (2017, September). Developing technological pedagogical content knowledge (TPACK) in animal physiology. In *Journal of Physics: Conference Series* (Vol. 895, No. 1, p. 012059). IOP Publishing. https://doi.org/DOI: 10.1088/1742-6596/895/1/012059

Qin, Q., & Ao, L. (2023). *A new world of open space - reflections and perspectives of chinese scholars on the digital transformation of education and future education research*. MCET., DOI: 10.1007/978-3-031-33023-0_27

Qiu, B., Zhu, Y., Du, L., & Feng, C. (2024). Analysis and reflection on the teaching application of artificial intelligence technology in the context of big data. *Curriculum and Teaching Methodology*, *7*(4). Advance online publication. DOI: 10.23977/curtm.2024.070404

Quince, Z., & Nikolic, S. (2025). Student identification of the social, economic and environmental implications of using Generative Artificial Intelligence (GenAI): Identifying student ethical awareness of ChatGPT from a scaffolded multi-stage assessment. *European Journal of Engineering Education*. Advance online publication. DOI: 10.1080/03043797.2025.2482830

Rabie, R. M. (2023). The future of education with artificial intelligence and machine learning in the Arab world: A systematic review. *Educational Sciences Journal (Al-Ulum Al-Tarbawiya), 31*(3), 1–35. https://doi.org/DOI: 10.21608/ssj.2023.344574

Rafner, J., Beaty, R. E., Kaufman, J. C., Lubart, T., & Sherson, J. (2023). Creativity in the age of generative AI. *Nature Human Behaviour*, *7*(11), 1836–1838. DOI: 10.1038/s41562-023-01751-1 PMID: 37985916

Ragone, G., Ali, S. A., Esposito, A., Good, J., Howland, K., & Presicce, C. (2024). Child-centered AI for empowering creative and inclusive learning experiences. *Proceedings of the 23rd Annual ACM Interaction Design and Children Conference*, 1035–1037. DOI: 10.1145/3628516.3661157

Rahayu, N. W., Ferdiana, R., & Kusumawardani, S. S. (2023). A systematic review of learning path recommender systems. *Education and Information Technologies*, *28*(6), 7437–7460. DOI: 10.1007/s10639-022-11460-3

Rane, N., Choudhary, S., & Rane, J. (2023). Education 4.0 and 5.0: Integrating artificial intelligence (AI) for personalized and adaptive learning.

Rathore, A., Sultana, N., Zareen, S., & Ahmed, A. (2023). Artificial intelligence and curriculum prospects for elementary school. *Pakistan Journal of Humanities and Social Sciences*, *11*(4). Advance online publication. DOI: 10.52131/pjhss.2023.v11i4.1909

Ray, P. P. (2023). ChatGPT: A comprehensive review on background, applications, key challenges, bias, ethics, limitations and future scope. *Internet of Things and Cyber-Physical Systems*, *3*, 121–154. DOI: 10.1016/j.iotcps.2023.04.003

Regan, K., & King-Sears, M. (2023). A Scaffolded Model for Preparing Doctoral Students to Teach in Higher Education. *Journal of Special Education Preparation*, *3*(3), 38–47. Advance online publication. DOI: 10.33043/JOSEP.3.3.38-47

Reinprecht, C., Suter, R., Parry, B., & Rampelt, F. (2021). No longer a 'lost generation'? Opportunities and obstacles of online and blended learning programmes for Syrian refugees in Jordan and Lebanon. *Journal of Refugee Studies*, *34*(3), 3197–3220. DOI: 10.1093/jrs/feab034

Reiß, M. (2021). The use of ai in education: Practicalities and ethical considerations. *London Review of Education*, *19*(1). Advance online publication. DOI: 10.14324/LRE.19.1.05

Renaissance. (2023). Trends in student outcome measures: The role of individualized practice with Freckle for math and Freckle for ELA. Renaissance Learning, Inc.

Renaissance. (2024). Trends in student outcome measures: The role of individualized practice with Freckle for math and Freckle for ELA. Renaissance Learning, Inc.

Renfeng, J., Gang, Y., & Qi, S. (2025). The Motivational Impact of GenAI Tools in Language Learning: A Quasi-Experiment Study. International Journal of Applied Linguistics United Kingdom, 35(3), 1338–1350. *Scopus*. Advance online publication. DOI: 10.1111/ijal.12701

Rice, M. F., Cantergiani, K., & Macias, D. (2023). A research-based conceptual framework for inclusive K-12 online, distance, and digital education. *Journal of Research on Technology in Education*. Advance online publication. DOI: 10.1080/15391523.2023.2264982

Rienties, B., Cross, S., & Zdrahal, Z. (2017). Implementing a learning analytics intervention and evaluation framework: What works?. *Big data and learning analytics in higher education: Current theory and practice*, 147-166. https://doi.org/ DOI: 10.1007/978-3-319-06520-5_10

Rincón-Flores, E. G., Castano, L., Guerrero Solis, S. L., Olmos Lopez, O., Rodríguez Hernández, C. F., Castillo Lara, L. A., & Aldape Valdés, L. P. (2024). Improving the learning-teaching process through adaptive learning strategy. *Smart Learning Environments*, *11*(1), 27. DOI: 10.1186/s40561-024-00314-9

Ritter, S., Anderson, J. R., Koedinger, K. R., & Corbett, A. (2007). Cognitive tutor: Applied research in mathematics education. *Psychonomic Bulletin & Review*, *14*(2), 249–255. DOI: 10.3758/BF03194060 PMID: 17694909

Rızvı, M. (2023). Investigating AI-powered tutoring systems that adapt to individual student needs, providing personalized guidance and assessments. *The Eurasia Proceedings of Educational and Social Sciences*, *31*, 67–73. DOI: 10.55549/epess.1381518

Rizvi, S., Waite, J., & Sentance, S. (2023). Artificial Intelligence teaching and learning in K-12 from 2019 to 2022: A systematic literature review. *Computers and Education: Artificial Intelligence*, *4*, 100145. Advance online publication. DOI: 10.1016/j.caeai.2023.100145

Robinson, S. C. (2020). Trust, transparency, and openness: How inclusion of cultural values shapes Nordic national public policy strategies for artificial intelligence (AI). *Technology in Society*, *63*, 101421. Advance online publication. DOI: 10.1016/j.techsoc.2020.101421

Rogers, F. H., & Sabarwal, S. (2020). The covid-19 pandemic: Shocks to education and policy responses.

Rogers, E. M. (2003). *Diffusion of innovations* (5th ed.). Free Press.

Rohmawaty, E., Hilmi, D., Uqba, S., & Saleh, U. (2024). Peran Artificial Intelligence (AI) dalam pembelajaran bahasa Arab mahasiswa pascas jana UIN Maulana Malik Ibrahim Malang. *Khatulistiwa: Jurnal Pendidikan dan Sosial Humaniora, 4*(3). https://doi.org/DOI: 10.55606/khatulistiwa.v4i3.4023

Röhrs, S., Rohn, S., & Pfeifer, Y. (2024). Risk Classification of Food Incidents Using a Risk Evaluation Matrix for Use in Artificial Intelligence-Supported Risk Identification. *Foods, 13*(22), 3675. DOI: 10.3390/foods13223675 PMID: 39594090

Ruano-Borbalán, J. (2025). *The transformative impact of artificial intelligence on higher education: A critical reflection on current trends and future directions.* International Journal of Chinese Education., DOI: 10.1177/2212585X251319364

Ružičić, V., Simeunović, M., & Gojgic, N. (2024). Prerequisites for Higher Quality Education: Teachers' Attitudes on the Application of Artificial Intelligence Tools in Teaching. In 10th International Scientific Conference Technics, Informatics and Education-TIE 2024. Faculty of Technical Sciences Čačak, University of Kragujevac.

Ryan, R. M., & Deci, E. L. (2000). Self-determination theory and the facilitation of intrinsic motivation, social development, and well-being. *American Psychologist,* 55(1), 68–78. DOI: 10.1037/0003-066X.55.1.68

Sa'Idah, M. A., Diantoro, K., Mahmudah, U., Dolan, E., Santoso, N. A., & Junaedi, S. R. P. (2024). Enhancing Arabic language teaching through artificial intelligence: Assessing effectiveness and educational implications. *2024 3rd International Conference on Creative Communication and Innovative Technology (ICCIT)*, 1–8. https://doi.org/DOI: 10.1109/ICCIT62134.2024.10701089

Sabbagh, C. (2009). Ethics and teaching. In *International handbook of research on teachers and teaching* (pp. 683–693). Springer. DOI: 10.1007/978-0-387-73317-3_42

Sabharwal, D., Kabha, R., & Srivastava, K. (2023). Artificial intelligence (ai)-powered virtual assistants and their effect on human productivity and laziness: Study on students of delhi-ncr (india) & fujairah (uae). Journal of Content. *Community and Communication, 17*(9), 162–174. DOI: 10.31620/JCCC.06.23/12

Saddhono, K., Suhita, R., Rakhmawati, A., Rohmadi, M., & Sukmono, I. K. (2024). AI and literacy: Developing critical thinking and analytical skills in the digital era. *2024 International Conference on IoT, Communication and Automation Technology (ICICAT)*, 360-365. DOI: 10.1109/ICICAT62666.2024.10922871

Saffarizadeh, K., Keil, M., Boodraj, M., & Alashoor, T. (2024). "My Name is Alexa. What's Your Name?" The Impact of Reciprocal Self-Disclosure on Post-Interaction Trust in Conversational Agents. *Journal of the Association for Information Systems*, *25*(3), 528–568. DOI: 10.17705/1jais.00839

Sahlman, W. A., Ciechanover, A. M., & Grandjean, E. (2024, November). *Khanmigo: Revolutionizing learning with GenAI.* Harvard Business School Case 824-059. https://www.hbs.edu/faculty/Pages/item.aspx?num=64929

Sahrir, M. S., Albantani, A. M., & Arifin, F. (2025). The use of generative artificial intelligence (AI) in Arabic language education: Insights and implications between Malaysia and Indonesia. [IJRISS]. *International Journal of Research and Innovation in Social Science*, *9*(3), 3638–3646. DOI: 10.47772/IJRISS.2025.90300288

Saidu, A. M. (2024). ChatGPT usage and plagiarism in academic writing: The mediating role of academic integrity among Nigerian universities' students. In P. A. Okebukola (Ed.), AI and ethics, academic integrity and the future of quality assurance in higher education (pp. 86–97). Nigeria: Global University Network for Innovation (GUNi). https://www.researchgate.net/publication/386245533

Sajjad, H., Abdelali, A., Dalvi, F., Durrani, N., & Vogel, S. (2020). *AraBench: Benchmarking dialectal Arabic–English machine translation.* In Proceedings of the 28th International Conference on Computational Linguistics (COLING 2020) (pp. 5094–5105). International Committee on Computational Linguistics. https://doi.org/DOI: 10.18653/v1/2020.coling-main.447

Sallas, A. J. (2024). The Logic of Possibility: On the Concept of Deus Ex Machina (Doctoral dissertation, The University of Western Ontario).

Salman, J. (2023, March 20). *How ed tech can worsen racial inequality. The Hechinger Report.* https://hechingerreport.org/how-edtech-can-worsen-racial-inequality/

Samala, A. D., & Rawas, S. (2025). Bias in artificial intelligence: Smart solutions for detection, mitigation, and ethical strategies in real-world applications. *IAES International Journal of Artificial Intelligence*, *14*(1), 32–43. DOI: 10.11591/ijai.v14.i1.pp32-43

Samsonova, O. (2023). Use of i-Ready in tiered instruction for ESL students: A quantitative case study. *The International Journal of Childbirth Education*, *4*(2), 85–105. DOI: 10.33422/ijce.v4i2.503

Samuel, Y., Brennan-Tonetta, M., Samuel, J., Kashyap, R., Kumar, V., Krishna Kaashyap, S., Chidipothu, N., Anand, I., & Jain, P. (2023). Cultivation of human centered artificial intelligence: Culturally adaptive thinking in education (CATE) for AI. *Frontiers in Artificial Intelligence*, *6*, 1198180. DOI: 10.3389/frai.2023.1198180 PMID: 38106981

Sánchez-García, P., Diez-Gracia, A., Mayorga, I. R., & Jerónimo, P. (2025). Media Self-Regulation in the Use of AI: Limitation of Multimodal Generative Content and Ethical Commitments to Transparency and Verification. *Journalism and Media*, *6*(1), 29. Advance online publication. DOI: 10.3390/journalmedia6010029

Sanchez-Gonzalez, M., & Terrell, M. (2023). Flipped classroom with artificial intelligence: Educational effectiveness of combining voice-over presentations and ai. *Cureus*. Advance online publication. DOI: 10.7759/cureus.48354 PMID: 37937181

Santosa, E. B., & Sukmawati, F. (2024). Level of computational thinking and technological literacy skills to improve pre-service teacher learning innovation. *Jurnal Kependidikan: Jurnal Hasil Penelitian Dan Kajian Kepustakaan Di Bidang Pendidikan. Pengajaran Dan Pembelajaran*, *10*(1), 338–352. DOI: 10.33394/jk.v10i1.10872

Sanusi, I. T., Olaleye, S. A., Oyelere, S. S., & Dixon, R. A. (2022). Investigating learners' competencies for artificial intelligence education in an African K-12 setting. *Computers and Education Open*, *3*, 100083. Advance online publication. DOI: 10.1016/j.caeo.2022.100083

Sarakikya, G. M., & Kitula, P. R. (2024). Application of artificial intelligence platforms and its influence on education of students in higher learning institutions in Arusha City, Tanzania. *Journal of Research Innovation and Implications in Education*, *8*(4). Advance online publication. DOI: 10.59765/nvthtd5

Sargent, C. S., Koohang, A., Floyd, K., & Kilburn, R. (2024). Artificial Intelligence: Ethical concerns, trust, and risk. *Issues in Information Systems*, *25*(2), 71–83. DOI: 10.48009/2_iis_2024_106

Sari, F. W., & Wati, T. L. (n.d.). Influence of problem based learning model on elementary school student critical thinking abilities: Pengaruh model pembelajaran problem based learning terhadap kemampuan berpikir kritis siswa sekolah dasar.

Sari, H. E., Tumanggor, B., & Efron, D. (2024). Improving educational outcomes through adaptive learning systems using ai. *International Transactions on Artificial Intelligence*, *3*(1), 21–31. DOI: 10.33050/italic.v3i1.647

Saritepeci, M., & Yildiz Durak, H. (2024). Effectiveness of artificial intelligence integration in design-based learning on design thinking mindset, creative and reflective thinking skills: An experimental study. *Education and Information Technologies, 29*(18), 25175–25209. DOI: 10.1007/s10639-024-12829-2

Sarshartehrani, F., Mohammadrezaei, E., Behravan, M., & Gracanin, D. (2024). *Enhancing E-Learning Experience Through Embodied AI Tutors in Immersive Virtual Environments: A Multifaceted Approach for Personalized Educational Adaptation.*, DOI: 10.1007/978-3-031-60609-0_20

Sat, M., & Kadirhan, Z. (2024). Unveiling competence in the classroom: A multidimensional assessment of computer science teachers' self-efficacy in coding education. *Education and Information Technologies*. Advance online publication. DOI: 10.1007/s10639-024-12503-7

Saxe, R. S. (2021). *The effects of using an online reading program to improve learning for special education students* [Doctoral dissertation, Liberty University]. Liberty University Digital Commons. https://digitalcommons.liberty.edu/doctoral/2998

Saxena, S., Singh, H., Prashar, M., & Mishra, M. (2025). Cost-benefit analysis of AI-driven learning systems: Long-term financial and educational impacts. *2025 4th OPJU International Technology Conference (OTCON) on Smart Computing for Innovation and Advancement in Industry 5.0.* https://doi.org/DOI: 10.1109/OTCON65728.2025.11070340

Schilling, M. R., & Grohs, J. (2023). Developing a Tool for the Assessment of Systems Thinking in K-12 Settings. *Proceedings - Frontiers in Education Conference, FIE*. DOI: 10.1109/FIE58773.2023.10343175

Schmidt-Crawford, D. A., Tai, S. J. D., Wang, W., & Jin, Y. (2016). Understanding teachers' TPACK through observation. In *Handbook of technological pedagogical content knowledge (TPACK) for educators* (pp. 107-118). Routledge.

Schwartz, B. (2005). *The paradox of choice: Why more is less*. HarperPerennial. https://www.amazon.com/Paradox-Choice-Why-More-Less/dp/0060005696

Seaborn, K., Miyake, N. P., Pennefather, P., & Otake-Matsuura, M. (2022). Voice in human-agent interaction: A survey. *ACM Computing Surveys, 54*(4), 1–43. Advance online publication. DOI: 10.1145/3386867

Selwyn, N. (2019). *Should robots replace teachers?: AI and the future of education*. https://books.google.com/books?hl=en&lr=&id=wcm1DwAAQBAJ&oi=fnd&pg=PT6&ots=KJyzbuX8eY&sig=ZiVlmN9ec5lz-xDILXpwRDl-Nyc

Selwyn, N. (2011). Education and technology: Key issues and debates. *Continuum*.

Selwyn, N. (2019). *Should Robots Replace Teachers? AI and the Future of Education*. Polity Press.

Selwyn, N. (2022). The future of ai and education: Some cautionary notes. *European Journal of Education*, *57*(4), 620–631. DOI: 10.1111/ejed.12532

Sentance, S., & Csizmadia, A. (2017). Computing in the curriculum: Challenges and strategies from a teacher's perspective. *Education and Information Technologies*, *22*(2), 469–495. DOI: 10.1007/s10639-016-9482-0

Seo, K., Yoo, M., Dodson, S., & Jin, S.-H. (2024). Augmented teachers: K–12 teachers' needs for artificial intelligence's complementary role in personalized learning. *Journal of Research on Technology in Education*, *57*(4), 876–893. DOI: 10.1080/15391523.2024.2330525

Septia, F., & Khodr, T. S. I. (2024). Unlocking AI's potential in language learning: A comparative study of adoption and effectiveness in Indonesia and Arab countries. *Language, Technology, and Social Media*, *2*(1), 60–71. DOI: 10.70211/ltsm.v2i1.78

Seufert, S., Guggemos, J., & Sailer, M. (2020). Technology-related knowledge, skills, and attitudes of pre-and in-service teachers: The current situation and emerging trends. *Computers in Human Behavior*, *115*, 106552. DOI: 10.1016/j.chb.2020.106552 PMID: 32921901

Seyidov, R. (2024). Arabic language processing: Current status and future prospects of artificial intelligence. *Journal of Namibian Studies: History Politics Culture*, *3*(9), 458–471. DOI: 10.59670/jwszy037

Shabbir, A., Rizvi, S., Alam, M. M., & Su'ud, M. M. (2024). Beyond boundaries: Navigating the positive potential of ChatGPT, empowering education in underdeveloped corners of the world. *Heliyon*, *10*(16), e35845. DOI: 10.1016/j.heliyon.2024.e35845 PMID: 39224307

Shadiev, R., Wang, X., Chen, X., Gayevskaya, E., & Borisov, N. (2024). Research on the impact of the learning activity supported by 360-degree video and translation technologies on cross-cultural knowledge and attitudes development. *Education and Information Technologies*, *29*(7), 7759–7791. DOI: 10.1007/s10639-023-12143-3

Shafik, W. (2024b). Enhancing AI-Enabled Education Through Mobile Learning and Bring Your Own Device (BYOD) Integration. In *Exploring Youth Studies in the Age of AI* (pp. 140–173). IGI Global. DOI: 10.4018/979-8-3693-3350-1.ch008

Shafik, W. (2024d). Mobile Learning and Bring Your Own Device (BYOD): Enhancing Education in the Digital Age. In *Integrating Cutting-Edge Technology Into the Classroom* (pp. 240–267). IGI Global. DOI: 10.4018/979-8-3693-3124-8.ch012

Shafik, W. (2024e). Towards Trustworthy and Explainable AI Educational Systems. In *Explainable AI for Education: Recent Trends and Challenges* (pp. 17–41). Springer. DOI: 10.1007/978-3-031-72410-7_2

Shafik, W. (2025). Human-Computer Interaction (HCI) Technologies in Socially-Enabled Artificial Intelligence. In *Future of Digital Technology and AI in Social Sectors* (pp. 121–150). IGI Global. DOI: 10.4018/979-8-3693-5533-6.ch005

Shafik, W. (2024a). Deep Learning Impacts in the Field of Artificial Intelligence. In *Deep Learning Concepts in Operations Research* (pp. 9–26). Auerbach Publications., DOI: 10.1201/9781003433309-2

Shafik, W. (2024c). Generative AI for Social Good and Sustainable Development. In Raza, K., Ahmad, N., & Singh, D. (Eds.), *Generative AI: Current Trends and Applications. Studies in Computational Intelligence* (Vol. 1177). Springer., DOI: 10.1007/978-981-97-8460-8_10

Shah, P. (2023). *AI and the future of education: Teaching in the age of artificial intelligence*. Sybex. https://www.amazon.com/AI-Future-Education-Artificial-Intelligence/dp/1394219245/ref=bmx_dp_1lrbfu8o_d_sccl_3_2/147-0051106-7973500?pd_rd_w=NeXZ0&content-id=amzn1.sym.628e3119-8afd-4af2-be6b-18415b51e649&pf_rd_p=628e3119-8afd-4af2-be6b-18415b51e649&pf_rd_r=0TG6690Q2BV2DN2A5FEZ&pd_rd_wg=faMQc&pd_rd_r=c06ba4e0-ff1a-4844-8330-a376feaf4fc4&pd_rd_i=1394219245&psc=1

Shahri, H., Emad, M., Ibrahim, N., Rais, R. N. B., & Al-Fayoumi, Y. (2024). Elevating Education through AI Tutor: Utilizing GPT-4 for Personalized Learning. *Proceedings of the 15th Annual Undergraduate Research Conference on Applied Computing on "AI for a Sustainable Economy." URC 2024*. https://doi.org/DOI: 10.1109/URC62276.2024.10604578

Sharma, L., & Srivastava, M. (2020). Teachers' motivation to adopt technology in higher education. *Journal of Applied Research in Higher Education*, *12*(4), 673–692. DOI: 10.1108/JARHE-07-2018-0156

Shazly, R. (2021). Effects of artificial intelligence on english speaking anxiety and speaking performance: A case study. *Expert Systems: International Journal of Knowledge Engineering and Neural Networks*, *38*(3), e12667. Advance online publication. DOI: 10.1111/exsy.12667

Shehaj, A. (2022). Revolutionized learning: Education policy and digital reform in the eurozone. *European Policy Analysis*, *8*(3), 312–326. DOI: 10.1002/epa2.1158

Shekerbekova, S., Kamalova, G., Iskakova, M., Aldabergenova, A., Abdykerimova, E., & Shetiyeva, K. (2025). Exploring the use of Artificial Intelligence and Augmented Reality tools to improve interactivity in Physical Education teaching and training methods | Explorando el uso de herramientas de Inteligencia Artificial y Realidad Aumentada para mejorar la inter. *Retos*, *66*, 1132–1139. DOI: 10.47197/retos.v66.113540

Shelton, J. (2023). *The education myth: How human capital trumped social democracy*. Cornell University Press.

Shen, Z., Piao, Y., Tan, C., Lin, R., Zhao, X., & Wan, X. (2022). Project co-art: Improving children's imagination through AI-based human-computer co-creation. *2022 IEEE Smartworld, Ubiquitous Intelligence & Computing, Scalable Computing & Communications, Digital Twin, Privacy Computing, Metaverse, Autonomous & Trusted Vehicles (SmartWorld/UIC/ScalCom/DigitalTwin/PriComp/Meta)*, 1597–1602. DOI: 10.1109/SmartWorld-UIC-ATC-ScalCom-DigitalTwin-PriComp-Metaverse56740.2022.00231

Shilaskar, S., Sheikh, S., Bhatlawande, S., Salve, S., & Shaikh, T. (2024). Empowering Futures: A Dynamic Conversational AI Chatbot System for Facilitating Educational Scholarship Opportunities. *2024 1st International Conference on Trends in Engineering Systems and Technologies, ICTEST 2024*. https://doi.org/DOI: 10.1109/ICTEST60614.2024.10576128

Shivarkar, A. (2025, May 16). *AI in Education Market Size to Hit USD 112.30 Bn by 2034*. Precedence Research. https://www.precedenceresearch.com/ai-in-education-market

Shoukat, W., Rizwan, N., & Khan, M. T. (2025). The role of artificial intelligence (AI) tutors in personalized learning: Benefits and challenges. *Journal of Social Signs Review*, *3*(4), 1–13.

Shukla, R. P., & Taneja, S. (2024). Ethical considerations and data privacy in artificial intelligence. In *Integrating Generative AI in Education to Achieve Sustainable Development Goals* (pp. 86–97). https://doi.org/DOI: 10.4018/979-8-3693-2440-0.ch005

Sidoti, O., Eugenie, P., & Gottfried, J. (2025). *About a quarter of U.S. teens have used ChatGPT for schoolwork – double the share in 2023*. Pew Research Center. https://www.pewresearch.org/short-reads/2025/01/15/about-a-quarter-of-us-teens-have-used-chatgpt-for-schoolwork-double-the-share-in-2023/

Šijan, A., Ilić, L., Predić, B., Viduka, D., & Rančić, D. (2025). Bibliometric analysis of artificial intelligence applications in higher education using web of science database. Facta Universitatis, Series: Teaching, Learning and Teacher Education, 119-130.

Silva, T. B. (2016). *The effects of the i-Ready computer assisted instruction program on the reading and fluency achievement of first graders* [Doctoral dissertation, California State University]. ScholarWorks. http://hdl.handle.net/10211.3/200863

Simatupang, E. C., Ismail, I., Waluyo, B., & Panmei, B. (2025). ChatGPT in education: The influence of institutional support and peer dynamics in Indonesian higher education. *Internet Reference Services Quarterly*, *29*(2), 225–244. DOI: 10.1080/10875301.2025.2461476

Simon, P. D., & Zeng, L. M. (2024). Behind the scenes of adaptive learning: A scoping review of teachers' perspectives on the use of adaptive learning technologies. *Education Sciences*, *14*(12), 1413. DOI: 10.3390/educsci14121413

Simons, M., & Masschelein, J. (2021). Looking after school: A critical analysis of personalization in education.

Sinatra, A. M., Graesser, A. C., Hu, X., Goodwin, G., & Rus, V. (Eds.). (2023). *Design recommendations for intelligent tutoring systems: Vol. 10. SWOT analysis of ITS*. U.S. Army Research Laboratory. https://www.gifttutoring.org/documents/163

Singer, N. (2023, June 26). In Classrooms, Teachers Put A.I. Tutoring Bots to the Test. *The New York Times*. https://www.nytimes.com/2023/06/26/technology/newark-schools-khan-tutoring-ai.html

Singh, N. (2011). Student-centered learning (scl) in classrooms—A comprehensive overview. *Educational Quest-An International Journal of Education and Applied Social Sciences*, 2(2), 275–282.

Singh, S. K., Kumar, S., & Mehra, P. S. (2023). Chat GPT & Google Bard AI: A Review. *2023 International Conference on IoT, Communication and Automation Technology (ICICAT)*, 1–6. DOI: 10.1109/ICICAT57735.2023.10263706

Šipka, D. (2024). Developing Bosnian/Croatian/Serbian Conversational Chatbots Using MYAI Builder. *Russian Language Journal*, *74*(1), 12. DOI: 10.70163/0036-0252.1402

Škobo, M., & Petričević, V. (2023). Navigating the challenges and opportunities of literary translation in the age of AI: Striking a balance between human expertise and machine power. Društvene i humanističke studije, 8(2 (23)), 317-336.

Škobo, M., & Šović, M. (2025). The Digital Doppelgängers of Nikola Tesla and Branislav Nušić: A New Approach to Interactive Learning And Cultural Heritage. Paper presented at Sinteza 2025 - International Scientific Conference on Information Technology, Computer Science, and Data Science

Škobo, M., & Šović, M. (2025a). Teachers' perspectives on Chatbots and AI agents in primary and secondary education. *International Journal on Studies in Education, 7*(2), 410–442. DOI: 10.46328/ijonse.352

Sleeman, D., & Brown, J. S. (Eds.). (1982). *Intelligent tutoring systems*. Academic Press.

Smirani, L., & Yamani, H. (2024). Analysing the Impact of Gamification Techniques on Enhancing Learner Engagement, Motivation, and Knowledge Retention: A Structural Equation Modelling Approach. *Electronic Journal of e-Learning, 22*(9), 111–124. DOI: 10.34190/ejel.22.9.3563

Sok, S., & Heng, K. (2023). ChatGPT for education and research: A review of benefits and risks. *Cambodian Journal of Educational Research, 3*(1), 110–121. DOI: 10.62037/cjer.2023.03.01.06

Solé-Beteta, X., Navarro, J., Gajšek, B., Guadagni, A., & Zaballos, A. (2022). A data-driven approach to quantify and measure students' engagement in synchronous virtual learning environments. *Sensors (Basel), 22*(9), 3294. DOI: 10.3390/s22093294 PMID: 35590984

Sottilare, R., Graesser, A., Hu, X., & Goldberg, B. (Eds.). (2014). *Design recommendations for intelligent tutoring systems: Vol 2. Instructional management*. U.S. Army Research Laboratory. https://www.gifttutoring.org/documents/44

Sottilare, R., Graesser, A., Hu, X., & Holden, H. (Eds.). (2013). *Design recommendations for intelligent tutoring systems: Vol. 1. Learner modeling*. U.S. Army Research Laboratory. https://www.gifttutoring.org/documents/42

Sowjanya, A. M., & Srividya, K. (2024). NLP-driven chatbots: Applications and implications in conversational AI. In *Conversational Artificial Intelligence* (pp. 713–725). Scopus., DOI: 10.1002/9781394200801.ch39

Spencer, J. A., Ullucci, K., & Howard, T. C. (2022). *Anti-Blackness at school: Creating affirming educational spaces for African American students*. Teachers College Press.

Stacchio, L., Balloni, E., Gorgoglione, L., Mancini, A., Giovanola, B., Tiribelli, S., & Zingaretti, P. (2024). An ethical framework for trustworthy Neural Rendering applied in cultural heritage and creative industries. *Frontiers of Computer Science, 6*, 1459807. Advance online publication. DOI: 10.3389/fcomp.2024.1459807

Stamatios, P. (2024). Can preschoolers learn computational thinking and coding skills with ScratchJr? A systematic literature review. *International Journal of Educational Reform, 33*(1), 28–61. DOI: 10.1177/10567879221076077

Stamper, J., Xiao, R., & Hou, X. (2024). Enhancing LLM-based feedback: Insights from intelligent tutoring systems and the learning sciences. In Olney, A. M., Chounta, I.-A., Liu, Z., Santos, O. C., & Bittencourt, I. I. (Eds.), *Artificial intelligence in education, AIED 2024*. Springer., DOI: 10.1007/978-3-031-64315-6_3

Stanković, N., Stankovic, I., Marković, G., & Blagojević, M. (2024). The Role of AI Tools in Education: Opportunities and Challenges. In 10th International Scientific Conference Technics, Informatics and Education-TIE 2024. Faculty of Technical Sciences Čačak, University of Kragujevac.

Stanley, K. O., & Lehman, J. (2015). *Why greatness cannot be planned: The myth of the objective*. Springer. DOI: 10.1007/978-3-319-15524-1

Stasser, T. (2023). Elt in the digitale age: We have come a long way. *Arbeiten Aus Anglistik Und Amerikanistik*, *48*(1), 121–136. DOI: 10.24053/AAA-2023-0006

Stewart, T. (2023). "Nobody Asked Me!" Unleashing the Collective Voice of Special Education Teacher-Activists to Understand the Impact of Caseload Policies on Teacher Burnout, Attrition, and Student Learning Outcomes. American University.

Stragier, V., Seddati, O., & Dutoit, T. (2023). Developing an Interactive Agent for Blind and Visually Impaired People. *IMX 2023 - Proceedings of the 2023 ACM International Conference on Interactive Media Experiences*, 248–253. https://doi.org/DOI: 10.1145/3573381.3596471

Strawhacker, A., Lee, M., & Bers, M. U. (2018). Teaching tools, teachers' rules: Exploring the impact of teaching styles on young children's programming knowledge in ScratchJr. *International Journal of Technology and Design Education*, *28*(2), 347–376. DOI: 10.1007/s10798-017-9400-9

Strielkowski, W., Grebennikova, V., Lisovskiy, A., Rakhimova, G., & Vasileva, T. (2025). AI-driven adaptive learning for sustainable educational transformation. *Sustainable Development (Bradford)*, *33*(2), 1921–1947. DOI: 10.1002/sd.3221

Styve, A., Virkki, O. T., & Naeem, U. (2024). Developing critical thinking practices interwoven with generative AI usage in an introductory programming course. *2024 IEEE Global Engineering Education Conference (EDUCON)*, 1–8. DOI: 10.1109/EDUCON60312.2024.10578746

Subitsha, R. S., Vetrivel, M., Shrimaulik, N., & Saravanan, K. (2025). Natural Language Processing-Driven Learning Platform for Personalized Education. *Proceedings of International Conference on Visual Analytics and Data Visualization, ICVADV 2025*, 174–180. https://doi.org/DOI: 10.1109/ICVADV63329.2025.10961687

Su, J., & Yang, W. (2022). Artificial intelligence in early childhood education: A scoping review. *Computers and Education: Artificial Intelligence*, *3*, 100049. DOI: 10.1016/j.caeai.2022.100049

Su, J., & Yang, W. (2023). Unlocking the power of ChatGPT: A framework for applying generative AI in education. *ECNU Review of Education*, *6*(3), 355–366. DOI: 10.1177/20965311231168423

Sullivan, A., & Bers, M. U. (2019). Computer science education in early childhood: The case of ScratchJr. *Journal of Information Technology Education. In Practice*, *18*, 113–138. DOI: 10.28945/4437

Sungur Gul, K., Saylan Kirmizigul, A., Ates, H., & Garzon, J. (2023). Advantages and Challenges of STEM Education in K-12: Systematic Review and Research Synthesis. *International Journal of Research in Education and Science*, *9*(2), 283–307. Advance online publication. DOI: 10.46328/ijres.3127

Sunmboye, K., Strafford, H., Noorestani, S., & Wilison-Pirie, M. (2025). Exploring the influence of artificial intelligence integration on personalized learning: A cross-sectional study of undergraduate medical students in the United Kingdom. *BMC Medical Education*, *25*(1), 570. Advance online publication. DOI: 10.1186/s12909-025-07084-z PMID: 40247306

Sun, S., Else-Quest, N. M., Hodges, L. C., French, A. M., & Dowling, R. (2021). The effects of ALEKS on mathematics learning in K-12 and higher education: A meta-analysis. *Investigations in Mathematics Learning*, *13*(3), 182–196. DOI: 10.1080/19477503.2021.1926194

Sun, W. (2023). The impact of automatic speech recognition technology on second language pronunciation and speaking skills of EFL learners: A mixed methods investigation. *Frontiers in Psychology*, *14*, 1210187. DOI: 10.3389/fpsyg.2023.1210187 PMID: 37663357

Suppes, P., & Morningstar, M. (1969). Computer-assisted instruction: Two computer-assisted instruction programs are evaluated. *Science*, *166*(3903), 343–350. DOI: 10.1126/science.166.3903.343 PMID: 5812034

Suriano, R., Plebe, A., Acciai, A., & Fabio, R. A. (2025). Student interaction with ChatGPT can promote complex critical thinking skills. *Learning and Instruction*, *95*, 102011. DOI: 10.1016/j.learninstruc.2024.102011

Suweni, D., Ruswanto, R., Prasmoro, B., & Hawanti, S. (2024). The importance of culture recognition in teaching english. *Khazanah Pendidikan*, *18*(2), 458. DOI: 10.30595/jkp.v18i2.25709

Swain, M., Randel, B., & Dvorak, R. N. (2020). *Impact evaluation of reading i-Ready instruction for elementary grades using 2018–2019 data* (Report No. 107). HumRRO. https://eric.ed.gov/?id=ED604746

Swargiary, K. (2024). The impact of AI-driven personalized learning and intelligent tutoring systems on student engagement and academic achievement: Ethical implications and the digital divide. *SSRN.* https://ssrn.com/abstract=4897241 DOI: 10.2139/ssrn.4897241

Sysoyev, P. V. (2024). Ethics and AI-Plagiarism in an Academic Environment: Students' Understanding of Compliance with Author's Ethics and the Problem of Plagiarism in the Process of Interaction with Generative Artificial Intelligence. *Vysshee Obrazovanie v Rossii = Higher Education in Russia, 33*(2), 31–53. .DOI: 10.31992/0869-3617-2024-33-2-31-53

Sysoyev, P. V. (2025). Personalized Learning Based on Artificial Intelligence: How Ready Are Modern Students for New Educational Opportunities. *Vysshee Obrazovanie v Rossii = Higher Education in Russia, 34*(2), 51–71. .DOI: 10.31992/0869-3617-2025-34-2-51-71

Syuhra, M., Chandra, N. E., & Rosalina, E. (2025). Artificial intelligence in english language teaching: A systematic literature review of tools, impact, and challenges. *Veles Voice of English Language Education Society*, *9*(1), 193–205. DOI: 10.29408/veles.v9i1.29745

Szabó, F., & Szoke, J. (2024). How does generative ai promote autonomy and inclusivity in language teaching? *ELT Journal*, *78*(4), 478–488. DOI: 10.1093/elt/ccae052

Szczepański, M., Gapiński, G., & Marciniak, J. (2025). AI Tutor: Adaptive e-Learning System Using Expert Fuzzy Controllers. *International Conference on Computer Supported Education, CSEDU - Proceedings, 2*, 96–107. https://doi.org/ DOI: 10.5220/0013277900003932

Tabachnick, B. G., & Fidell, L. S. (2019). *Using multivariate statistics* (6th ed.). Pearson Education.

Taha, T. B., & Abdulrahman, M. S. (2023). The impact of technology on students' psychological and educational performance. [Jurnal Informatika dan Sains]. *JISA*, *6*(1), 91–95. DOI: 10.31326/jisa.v6i1.1661

Taheri, A., Bhardwaj, P., Caetano, A., Zhong, A., & Sra, M. (2023). Virtual Buddy: Redefining Conversational AI Interactions for Individuals with Hand Motor Disabilities. *UIST 2023 Adjunct - Adjunct Proceedings of the 36th Annual ACM Symposium on User Interface Software and Technology*. https://doi.org/DOI: 10.1145/3586182.3616680

Tammets, K., & Ley, T. (2023). Integrating ai tools in teacher professional learning: A conceptual model and illustrative case. *Frontiers in Artificial Intelligence*, *6*, 1255089. Advance online publication. DOI: 10.3389/frai.2023.1255089 PMID: 38130325

Tan, B., Tan, S., & Han, D. (2025). AI-assisted cultural and creative product design framework and case study. *Journal of Communication, Language and Culture*. https://doi.org/DOI: 10.33093/ijomfa.2025.6.1.8

Tang, J. (2024). The role of artificial intelligence in improving the efficiency of piano online learning. *Journal of Computational Methods in Sciences and Engineering*, *25*(2), 1504–1518. DOI: 10.1177/14727978241300381

Tang, Z. (2025). Using artificial intelligence in english language teaching: Benefits and challenges. *Journal of Education and Educational Research*, *12*(2), 1–4. DOI: 10.54097/e8f9jw03

Tan, J. W., Ng, K. B., & Mogali, S. R. (2022). An Exploratory Digital Board Game Approach to the Review and Reinforcement of Complex Medical Subjects Like Anatomical Education: Cross-sectional and Mixed Methods Study. *JMIR Serious Games*, *10*(1), e33282. Advance online publication. DOI: 10.2196/33282 PMID: 35006080

Tanksley, T. C. (2024). "We're changing the system with this one": Black students using critical race algorithmic literacies to subvert and survive AI-mediated racism in school. *English Teaching*, *23*(1), 36–56. DOI: 10.1108/ETPC-08-2023-0102

Tan, L. Y., Hu, S., Yeo, D. J., & Cheong, K. H. (2025). Artificial intelligence-enabled adaptive learning platforms: A review. *Computers and Education: Artificial Intelligence*, *9*, 100429. Advance online publication. DOI: 10.1016/j.caeai.2025.100429

Tan, Q., & Tang, X. (2025). Unveiling AI literacy in K-12 education: A systematic literature review of empirical research. *Interactive Learning Environments*, *33*(9), 1–17. DOI: 10.1080/10494820.2025.2482586

Tariq, R., Aponte Babines, B. M., Ramirez, J., Alvarez-Icaza, I., & Naseer, F. (2025). Computational thinking in STEM education: Current state-of-the-art and future research directions. *Frontiers of Computer Science*, *6*, 1480404. DOI: 10.3389/fcomp.2024.1480404

Tarisayi, K. S. (2024). Artificial intelligence in South African universities: Ethical concerns and pedagogical implications. *Journal of Education Studies in South Africa*, *38*(2), 55–72. DOI: 10.10520/ejc-jedsaf_v38_n2_a5

Taylor, D. L., Yeung, M., & Bashet, A. Z. (2021). Personalized and adaptive learning. In Ryoo, J., & Winkelmann, K. (Eds.), *Innovative learning environments in STEM higher education* (pp. 17–34). Springer., DOI: 10.1007/978-3-030-58948-6_2

Teo, T. (2009). The impact of subjective norm and facilitating conditions on pre-service teachers' attitude toward computer use: A structural equation modeling of an extended technology acceptance model. *Journal of Educational Computing Research*, *40*(1), 89–109. DOI: 10.2190/EC.40.1.d

Thakur, M., Reddy, C., Kishor, B., Murthy, B., Nag, A., & Doss, S. (2024). AI and education: Bridging the gap to personalized, efficient, and accessible learning. In *Handbook of Research on AI Applications in Education* (pp. 131–160). IGI Global., DOI: 10.4018/979-8-3693-8151-9.ch005

Thalji, N. J., & Alkhasawneh, S. (2025). How can artificial intelligence shape the future of sustainable education? Challenges and opportunities. *Journal of Theoretical and Applied Information Technology*, *103*(9), 3836–3847. https://www.jatit.org/volumes/Vol103No9/20Vol103No9.pdf

Thamarasseri, I. (2025). Gamification in education: Improving learning outcomes and student motivation. *International Journal of Educational Psychology*, *1*(1), 19–26.

The AI Education Project (aiEDU). (2025). *Professional learning for educators* [PD offerings and AI readiness resources for educators; accessed 2025-10-11]. https://aiedu.org/professional- learning

The Diary Of A CEO [@TheDiaryOfACEO]. (2025, June 16). *Godfather of AI: I Tried to Warn Them, But We've Already Lost Control! Geoffrey Hinton*. Youtube. https://www.youtube.com/watch?v=giT0ytynSqg&t=311s

Thorman, J., & Fidalgo, P. (2014). Guidelines for online course moderation and community building from a student's perspective. *Journal of Online Learning and Teaching*, *10*(3), 374–388.

Tlili, A., Adarkwah, M. A., Lo, C. K., Bozkurt, A., Burgos, D., Bonk, C. J., Costello, E., Mishra, S., Stracke, C. M., & Huang, R. (2024). Taming the Monster: How can Open Education Promote the Effective and Safe use of Generative AI in Education? *Journal of Learning for Development, 11*(3), 398–413. DOI: 10.56059/jl4d.v11i3.1657

Tlili, A., Denden, M., Essalmi, F., Jemni, M., Chang, M., & Chen, N.-S. (2023). Automatic model ing learner's personality using learning analytics approach in an intelligent Moodle learning platform. *Interactive Learning Environments,* •••, 1–15. DOI: 10.1080/10494820.2019.1636084

Tomić, B. M., & Radovanović, N. D. (2024). The application of artificial intelligence in the context of the educational system in Serbia, with a special focus on religious education. *Socioloski Pregled, 58*(2), 435–459. DOI: 10.5937/socpreg58-48911

Tomlinson, C. A. (2001). How to differentiate instruction in mixed-ability classrooms. Association for supervision and curriculum development.

Torrance, D., & Forde, C. (2017). Redefining what it means to be a teacher through professional standards: Implications for continuing teacher education. *European Journal of Teacher Education, 40*(1), 110–126. DOI: 10.1080/02619768.2016.1246527

Touvron, H., Lavril, T., Izacard, G., Martinet, X., Lachaux, M. A., Lacroix, T., . . . Lample, G. (2023). Llama: Open and efficient foundation language models. arXiv preprint arXiv:2302.13971.

Tracey, L., Cockerill, M., Elliott, L., Fairhurst, C., Mandefield, L., Fountain, I., & O'Keeffe, J. (2024). The benefits of computer-assisted learning for struggling readers in elementary schools in England. *Journal of Applied Developmental Psychology.*

Tripathi, T., Sharma, S. R., Singh, V., Bhargava, P., & Raj, C. (2025). Teaching and learning with ai: A qualitative study on k-12 teachers' use and engagement with artificial intelligence. *Frontiers in Education, 10,* 1651217. Advance online publication. DOI: 10.3389/feduc.2025.1651217

Tseng, S., Tsao, Y.-W., Yu, L.-C., Chan, C.-L., & Lai, K. R. (2016). Who will pass? Analyzing learner behaviors in MOOCs. *Research and Practice in Technology Enhanced Learning, 11*(8), 8. Advance online publication. DOI: 10.1186/s41039-016-0033-5 PMID: 30613241

Tülübaş, T., Karakose, T., & Papadakis, S. (2023). A holistic investigation of the relationship between digital addiction and academic achievement among students. *European Journal of Investigation in Health, Psychology and Education, 13*(10), 2006–2034. DOI: 10.3390/ejihpe13100143 PMID: 37887144

Turkish Statistical Institute. (2024a). *Survey on Information and Communication Technology (ICT) Usage in Households and by Individuals.* https://data.tuik.gov.tr/Bulten/Index?p=Hanehalki-Bilisim-Teknolojileri-(BT)-Kullanim-Arastirmasi-2024-53492

Turkish Statistical Institute. (2024b). *National Education Statistics.* https://data.tuik.gov.tr/Bulten/Index?p=Ulusal-Egitim-Istatistikleri-2024-53937

Tzafilkou, K., Perifanou, M. A., & Economides, A. A. (2021). Teachers' trainers' intention and motivation to transfer ICT training: The role of ICT individual factors, gender, and ICT self-efficacy. *Education and Information Technologies*, *26*(5), 5563–5589. DOI: 10.1007/s10639-021-10541-z

Tzirides, A., Galla, M., Cope, B., & Kalantzis, M. (2025). Thinking Through AI: Advancing cognitive and collaborative research for AI in education. In *EdArXiv*. https://doi.org/DOI: 10.35542/osf.io/s8hqe_v1

U.S. Department of Education, Office of Educational Technology. (2023). *Artificial Intelligence and the Future of Teaching and Learning: Insights and Recommendations.*

U.S. Department of Education, Office of Educational Technology. (2023a, May). *Artificial intelligence and the future of teaching and learning: Insights and recommendations* (tech. rep.). U.S. Department of Education. Washington, DC. https://www.ed.gov/sites/ ed/files/documents/ai-report/ai-report.pdf

U.S. Department of Education, Office of Educational Technology. (2023b). Artificial intelligence and the future of teaching and learning: Insights and recommendations.

U.S. Department of Education, Office of Educational Technology. (2023c). *Artificial intelligence and the future of teaching and learning: Insights and recommendations* (tech. rep.) (Highlights formative-assessment applications, help-seeking detection, fairness concerns, and the need for human feedback loops). U.S. Department of Education. https://www.ed. gov/sites/ed/files/documents/ai-report/ai-report.pdf

U.S. Department of Education. (2023). *Artificial intelligence and future of teaching and learning: Insights and recommendations.* Office of Educational Technology. https://www.ed.gov/sites/ed/files/documents/ai-report/ai-report.pdf

Ubur, S. D. (2025). AI-Driven Interpretation of Nonverbal Communication in AR-Enhanced Real-Time Captions: Effects on Cognitive Load, Comprehension, and User Engagement. 45–51. *Scopus.*, 45–51. Advance online publication. DOI: 10.1145/3698061.3734421

Ugˇras¸, H., Ugˇras¸, M., Papadakis, S., & Kalogiannakis, M. (2024). Chatgpt-supported education in primary schools: The potential of chatgpt for sustainable practices [Article number 9855]. *Sustainability (Basel)*, *16*(22), 9855. DOI: 10.3390/su16229855

Ugˇras¸, H., Ugˇras¸, M., Papadakis, S., & Kalogiannakis, M. (2025). Innovative early childhood stem education with chatgpt: Teacher perspectives [First online 2024]. *Technology. Knowledge and Learning*, *30*(2), 809–831. DOI: 10.1007/s10758-024-09804-8

Uğraş, H., Uğraş, M., Papadakis, S., & Kalogiannakis, M. (2024b). Innovative Early Childhood STEM Education with ChatGPT: Teacher Perspectives. Technology, Knowledge and Learning, 1-23. https://link.springer.com/article/10.1007/s10758-024-09804-8

Ulfa, K. (2023). The transformative power of artificial intelligence (ai) to elevate english language learning. *Majalah Ilmiah Methoda*, *13*(3), 307–313. DOI: 10.46880/methoda.Vol13No3.pp307-313

UNESCO & International Task Force on Teachers for Education 2030. (2025, April). Global report on teachers: What you need to know [Article summarizing the Global Report on Teachers (released 26 February 2024)]. https://www.unesco.org/en/articles/global- report-teachers-what-you-need-know

UNESCO Global Education Monitoring Report Team. (2023). *Global education monitoring report 2023: Technology in education: A tool on whose terms?* (Open Access under CC-BY-SA 3.0 IGO). UNESCO. Paris. https: / / unesdoc . unesco . org / ark: /48223 / pf0000385723

UNESCO Inclusive Policy Lab. (2024, May). Ai education and esg/sdgs: Towards student-centered learning [Latest update 20 January 2025]. https:// en. unesco. org/ inclusivepolicylab/ e- teams/ ai- education- and- esgsdgs- towards- student-centered- learning

UNESCO. (2008). *UNESCO's ICT Competency Standards for Teachers*. https://unesdoc.unesco.org/ark:/48223/pf0000156207

UNESCO. (2021). Recommendation on the ethics of artificial intelligence. United Nations Educational, Scientific and Cultural Organization. https://www.unesco.org/en/articles/recommendation-ethics-artificial-intelligence

UNESCO. (2022)K-12 AI curricula: a mapping of government-endorsed AI curricula. (2022). UNESCO. DOI: 10.54675/ELYF6010

UNESCO. (2023, September 6). In Tanzania, adolescent girls and young women expand digital literacy and skills. UNESCO. https://www.unesco.org/en/articles/adolescent-girls-and-young-women-tanzania-expand-digital-literacy-and-skills

UNESCO. (2023a). AI competency framework for students and teachers. United Nations Educational, Scientific and Cultural Organization. https://www.unesco.org/en/articles/ai-competency-framework-teachers

UNESCO. (2023b). Guidelines for AI literacy in education systems. United Nations Educational, Scientific and Cultural Organization. https://unesdoc.unesco.org/ark:/48223/pf0000386693

UNESCO. (2025a, April). Meeting every learner where they are [Article updated 9 May 2025]. https://www.unesco.org/en/articles/meeting-every-learner-where-they-are

UNESCO. (2025b). What you need to know about inclusion in education [Accessed: 2025-08-06]. https://www.unesco.org/en/inclusion-education/need-know

UNHCR. (2023, June 14). *Global trends: Forced displacement in 2022*. United Nations High Commissioner for Refugees. https://www.unhcr.org/global-trends

UNICEF. (2018). *Raising Learning Outcomes: the opportunities and challenges of ICT for learning*. Retrieved from https://www.unicef.org/esa/media/2636/file/UNICEF-AKF-IU-2018-ICT-Education-WCAR-ESAR.pdf

UNICEF. (2020). *Policy guidance on artificial intelligence for children*. United Nations Children's Fund., DOI: 10.1111/chso.12915

United Republic of Tanzania. (2025). Tanzania Development Vision 2050 (Dira 2050). President's Office, Planning and Investment. https://www.planning.go.tz/uploads/documents/sw-1752762713-DIRA%20YA%20TAIFA%20YA%20MAENDELEO%202050.pdf

Usher, M., Hershkovitz, A., & Forkosh-Baruch, A. (2021). From data to actions: Instructors' decision making based on learners' data in online emergency remote teaching. *British Journal of Educational Technology*, *52*(4), 1338–1356. DOI: 10.1111/bjet.13108

Utsch, M. N. R., Pappa, G. L., Chaimowicz, L., & Prates, R. O. (2020). A new non-deterministic drama manager for adaptive interactive storytelling. *Entertainment Computing*, *34*, 100364. Advance online publication. DOI: 10.1016/j.entcom.2020.100364

Valente, S., Veiga-Branco, A., Rebelo, H., Lourenço, A., & Cristóvão, A. (2020). The relationship between emotional intelligence ability and teacher efficacy. *Universal Journal of Educational Research*, *8*(3), 916–923. DOI: 10.13189/ujer.2020.080324

van den Berg, G., & du Plessis, E. (2023). ChatGPT and generative AI: Possibilities for its contribution to lesson planning, critical thinking and openness in teacher education. *Education Sciences*, *13*(10), 998. DOI: 10.3390/educsci13100998

van Leeuwen, A., Strauß, A., & Rummel, N. (2023). Participatory design of teacher dashboards: Navigating the tension between teacher input and theories on teacher professional vision. *Frontiers in Artificial Intelligence, 6*, 1039739. VanLehn, K. (2011). The relative effectiveness of human tutoring, intelligent tutoring systems, and other tutoring systems. *Educational Psychologist, 46*(4), 197–221. https://doi .org/DOI: 10.3389/frai.2023.1039739

Van Leeuwen, A. (2019). Teachers' perceptions of the usability of learning analytics reports in a flipped university course: When and how does information become actionable knowledge? *Educational Technology Research and Development*, *67*(5), 1043–1064. DOI: 10.1007/s11423-018-09639-y

Vanbecelaere, S., Demedts, F., Reynvoet, B., & Depaepe, F. (2023). Toward a framework for analyzing adaptive digital games' research effectiveness. *International Journal of Serious Games*, *10*(4), 77–91. DOI: 10.17083/ijsg.v10i4.618

VanLehn, K. (2011). The relative effectiveness of human tutoring, intelligent tutoring systems, and other tutoring systems. *Educational Psychologist*, *46*(4), 197–221. DOI: 10.1080/00461520.2011.611369

VanSledright, B. A. (2004). What does it mean to think historically… and how do you teach it. *Social Education*, *68*(3), 230–233.

Varsik, S., & Vosberg, L. (2024). *"The potential impact of Artificial Intelligence on equity and inclusion in education", OECD Artificial Intelligence Papers, No. 23*. OECD Publishing., DOI: 10.1787/15df715b-

Vartanian, A. M. (2024). Fostering Environmental Responsibility in U.S. K-12 Education: A Comparative Study of Strategies Integrating STEM. *Journal of Advanced Research in Education*, *3*(1), 31–42. Advance online publication. DOI: 10.56397/JARE.2024.01.05

Vartiainen, H., Kahila, J., Tedre, M., López-Pernas, S., & Pope, N. (2024). Enhancing children's understanding of algorithmic biases in and with text-to-image generative AI. *New Media & Society*. Advance online publication. DOI: 10.1177/14614448241252820

Vashishth, T. K., Sharma, V., Sharma, K. K., Kumar, B., Panwar, R., & Chaudhary, S. (2024). AI-Driven Learning Analytics for Personalized Feedback and Assessment in Higher Education. In Nguyen, T. V. T., & Vo, N. T. M. (Eds.), (pp. 206–230). Advances in Media, Entertainment, and the Arts. IGI Global., DOI: 10.4018/979-8-3693-0639-0.ch009

Vasilev, I. (2024). Motivating unmotivated students and strategies for success in vet: A guide for vet educators. *E-Magazine. Pedagogical Forum*, (4), 70–82. DOI: 10.15547/PF.2024.025

Vee, A. (2017). *Coding literacy: How computer programming is changing writing*. Mit Press. DOI: 10.7551/mitpress/10655.001.0001

Venkatesh, V., & Davis, F. D. (2000). A theoretical extension of the technology acceptance model: Four longitudinal field studies. *Management Science*, *46*(2), 186–204. DOI: 10.1287/mnsc.46.2.186.11926

Venkatraman, S., Brindha, S., Lakshmi, G., Selvi, V. M., & Sandhya, J. (2024). Harnessing the potential of conversational AI: A Roadmap for Academic Applications. *2024 International Conference on Power, Energy, Control and Transmission Systems (ICPECTS)*, 1–5. https://doi.org/DOI: 10.1109/ICPECTS62210.2024.10780187

Viberg, O., Cukurova, M., Feldman-Maggor, Y., Alexandron, G., Shirai, S., Kanemune, S., & Kizilcec, R. F. (2024). What explains teachers' trust in AI in education across six countries? *International Journal of Artificial Intelligence in Education*, •••, 1–29.

Vieriu, A. M., & Petrea, G. (2025). The impact of artificial intelligence (AI) on students' academic development. *Education Sciences*, *15*(3), 343. DOI: 10.3390/educsci15030343

Villegas-Ch, W., García-Ortiz, J., & Sánchez-Viteri, S. (2024). Educational Advances in the Metaverse: Boosting Learning Through Virtual and Augmented Reality and Artificial Intelligence. *IEEE Access : Practical Innovations, Open Solutions*, *12*, 59093–59112. DOI: 10.1109/ACCESS.2024.3393776

Villegas-Ch, W., García-Ortiz, J., & Sánchez-Viteri, S. (2024). Personalization of learning: Machine learning models for adapting educational content to individual learning styles. *IEEE Access : Practical Innovations, Open Solutions*, *12*, 121114–121130. DOI: 10.1109/ACCESS.2024.3452592

Vinchon, F., Lubart, T., Bartolotta, S., Gironnay, V., Botella, M., Bourgeois-Bougrine, S., Burkhardt, J.-M., Bonnardel, N., Corazza, G. E., Glăveanu, V., Hanchett Hanson, M., Ivcevic, Z., Karwowski, M., Kaufman, J. C., Okada, T., Reiter-Palmon, R., & Gaggioli, A. (2023). Artificial intelligence & creativity: A manifesto for collaboration. *The Journal of Creative Behavior*, *57*(4), 472–484. DOI: 10.1002/jocb.597

Vlachopoulos, D., & Makri, A. (2021). Quality teaching in online higher education: The perspectives of 250 online tutors on technology and pedagogy. [iJET]. *International Journal of Emerging Technologies in Learning*, *16*(6), 40–56. DOI: 10.3991/ijet.v16i06.20173

Vukomanović, A., Deretić, N., Kabiljo, M., & Matić, R. (2022). An example of chatbot in the field of education in the Republic of Serbia. Journal of process management and new technologies, 10(1-2), 125-139.

Vuorikari, R., Kluzer, S., & Punie, Y. (2022). *DigComp 2.2, The Digital Competence framework for citizens—With new examples of knowledge, skills and attitudes*. Publications Office of the European Union., DOI: 10.2760/115376

Vygotsky, L. S. (1978). *Mind in society: The development of higher psychological processes* (Rev. ed.). Harvard University Press.

Wahed, S., & Pitterson, N. (2024). Empowering Diverse Learners: Embracing Culturally Relevant Pedagogy (CRP) in Engineering, Higher Education, and K-12 Settings. *Lecture Notes in Networks and Systems, 901 LNNS*. DOI: 10.1007/978-3-031-53022-7_20

Wahed, A., & Pitterson, N. (2024). Artificial intelligence and robotics in K–12 instruction: Emerging policies and practices. *Computers & Education Advances*, *38*(4), 241–268. DOI: 10.1016/j.ssaho.2025.101533

Wakunuma, K., & Eke, D. (2024). Africa, ChatGPT, and Generative AI Systems: Ethical Benefits, Concerns, and the Need for Governance. *Philosophies*, *9*(3), 80. Advance online publication. DOI: 10.3390/philosophies9030080

Walkington, C., & Bernacki, M. L. (2020). Appraising research on personalized learning: Definitions, theoretical alignment, advancements, and future directions. *Journal of Research on Technology in Education*, *52*(3), 235–252. DOI: 10.1080/15391523.2020.1747757

Walter, Y. (2024). Embracing the future of Artificial Intelligence in the classroom: The relevance of AI literacy, prompt engineering, and critical thinking in modern education. *International Journal of Educational Technology in Higher Education*, *21*(15), 15. Advance online publication. DOI: 10.1186/s41239-024-00448-3

Wang, R. E., Ribeiro, A. T., Robinson, C. D., Loeb, S., & Demszky, D. (2024b). *Tutor copilot: A human-ai approach for scaling real-time expertise (preregistered rct report)* (tech. rep.). National Student Support Accelerator (Stanford University). https://nssa.stanford.edu/ sites/default/files/Tutor%20CoPilot.pdf

Wang, R., & Demszky, D. (2024). Edu-ConvoKit: An Open-Source Library for Education Conversation Data. In K.-W. Chang, A. Lee, & N. Rajani (Eds.), *Proceedings of the 2024 Conference of the North American Chapter of the Association for Computational Linguistics: Human Language Technologies (*Volume 3*: System Demonstrations)* (pp. 61–69). Association for Computational Linguistics. DOI: 10.18653/v1/2024.naacl-demo.6

Wang, R., Zhang, Q., Robinson, C., Loeb, S., & Demszky, D. (2024a). Bridging the novice-expert gap via models of decision-making: A case study on remediating math mistakes. *Proceedings of the 2024 Conference of the North American Chapter of the Association for Computational Linguistics: Human Language Technologies (*Volume 1*: Long Papers)*. Proceedings of the 2024 Conference of the North American Chapter of the Association for Computational Linguistics: Human Language Technologies (Volume 1: Long Papers), Mexico City, Mexico. DOI: 10.18653/v1/2024.naacl-long.120

Wang, X., Wrede, S., van Rijn, L., & Wo¨hrle, J. (2023). Ai-based quiz system for personalised learning. *ICERI2023 Proceedings*, 5025–5034.

Wang, A., Thompson, M., Roy, D., Pan, K., Perry, J., Tan, P., Eberhart, R., & Klopfer, E. (2022). Iterative user and expert feedback in the design of an educational virtual reality biology game. *Interactive Learning Environments*, *30*(4), 677–694. DOI: 10.1080/10494820.2019.1678489

Wang, H., Zhang, L., Zheng, C., Gomez, R., Nakamura, K., & Li, G. (2022). *Personalized Storytelling with Social Robot Haru.*, DOI: 10.1007/978-3-031-24670-8_39

Wang, J., & Fan, W. (2025). The effect of ChatGPT on students' learning performance, learning perception, and higher-order thinking: Insights from a meta-analysis. *Humanities & Social Sciences Communications*, *12*(1), 621. DOI: 10.1057/s41599-025-04787-y

Wang, L., Huang, M., & Ismail Kamal, J. (2024). The Application of an Unplugged and Low-Cost Children's Coding Education Tool in a Gamification Context. *Pertanika Journal of Social Science & Humanities*, *32*(2), 387–407. DOI: 10.47836/pjssh.32.2.03

Wang, P., Wang, F., & Li, Z. (2023). Exploring the ecosystem of K-12 online learning: An empirical study of impact mechanisms in the post-pandemic era. *Frontiers in Psychology*, *14*, 1241477. Advance online publication. DOI: 10.3389/fpsyg.2023.1241477 PMID: 37829067

Wang, R. E., Ribeiro, A. T., Robinson, C. D., Loeb, S., & Demszky, D. (2024a). Tutor copilot: A human-ai approach for scaling real-time expertise. https://arxiv.org/abs/2410.03017 DOI: 10.21203/rs.3.rs-5363154/v1

Wang, S., Wang, F., Zhu, Z., Wang, J., Tran, T., & Du, Z. (2024). Artificial intelligence in education: A systematic literature review. *Expert Systems with Applications*, *252*, 124167. DOI: 10.1016/j.eswa.2024.124167

Wang, S., Wu, H., Kim, J. H., & Andersen, E. (2019). Adaptive learning material recommendation in online language education. In *Artificial Intelligence in Education: 20th International Conference, AIED 2019, Chicago, IL, USA, June 25-29, 2019* [Springer International Publishing.]. *Proceedings*, *20*(Part II), 298–302.

Wang, W.-S., Lin, C.-J., Lee, H.-Y., Huang, Y.-M., & Wu, T.-T. (2025). Integrating feedback mechanisms and ChatGPT for VR-based experiential learning: Impacts on reflective thinking and AIoT physical hands-on tasks. *Interactive Learning Environments*, *33*(2), 1770–1787. DOI: 10.1080/10494820.2024.2375644

Wang, Y., & Xue, L. (2024). Using AI-driven chatbots to foster Chinese EFL students' academic engagement: An intervention study. *Computers in Human Behavior*, *159*, 108353. DOI: 10.1016/j.chb.2024.108353

Wang, Y., Zhang, Y., Wang, Y., Zhang, H., Wang, X., Xu, R., & Tong, Y. (2024). Realization of Empathy Capability for the Evolution of Artificial Intelligence Using an MXene(Ti3C2)-Based Memristor. *Electronics (Basel)*, *13*(9), 1632. Advance online publication. DOI: 10.3390/electronics13091632

Wan, Z., Liu, C.-K., Yang, H., Raj, R., Li, C., You, H., Fu, Y., Wan, C., Li, S., & Kim, Y.. (2024). *Towards efficient neuro-symbolic ai: From workload characterization to hardware architecture*. IEEE Transactions on Circuits and Systems for Artificial Intelligence.

Watters, A. (2021). *Teaching machines: The history of personalized learning*. MIT Press. https://mitpress.mit.edu/9780262363754/teaching-machines/

Webb, S. (2024). A Design Thinking Mixed Methods Study on Learned Empathy Through Multicultural Education.

Wegerif, R. (2011). Towards a dialogic theory of how children learn to think. *Thinking Skills and Creativity*, *6*(3), 179–190. DOI: 10.1016/j.tsc.2011.08.002

Weiss, D. J., & Şahin, A. (2024). *Computerized adaptive testing: From concept to implementation*. The Guilford Press.

Welsby, P., & Cheung, B. M. (2023). ChatGPT. *Postgraduate Medical Journal, 99*(1176), 1047–1048. DOI: 10.1093/postmj/qgad056 PMID: 37462242

Werbach, K., & Hunter, D. (2012). *For the win* (Vol. 51). Philadelphia: Wharton digital press.

What Works Clearinghouse. (2013). *Dreambox learning: Intervention report* (tech. rep.). Institute of Education Sciences, U.S. Department of Education. https://ies.ed .gov/ncee/wwc/ Docs/InterventionReports/wwc dreambox 121013.pdf

White, C. J. (2025). *The Complete Childhood Mental Health Workbook: A Comprehensive Guide for Navigating ADHD, Anxiety, Autism and More*. Casey Joe White.

White, S. V., Childs, J., Koshy, S., & Scott, A. (2024). Policy implementation in the era of responsible artificial intelligence (ai) use in k-12 education. *Proceedings of the 2024 on RESPECT Annual Conference*, 81–85. DOI: 10.1145/3653666.3656097

Wiley, K., Dimitriadis, Y., & Linn, M. (2024). A human-centred learning analytics approach for developing contextually scalable K-12 teacher dashboards. *British Journal of Educational Technology, 55*(3), 845–885. DOI: 10.1111/bjet.13383

William, M. (2024). *Creative patterns in the age of ai: Securing america's education edge* [Argues for investing in teacher training, AI infrastructure, and curricular reform to cultivate creative and interdisciplinary learning]. https://www.brookings .edu/articles/creative- patterns-in-the-age-of-ai-securing-americas-education-edge/

Williams, R. T. (2024, January). The ethical implications of using generative chatbots in higher education. []. Frontiers Media SA.]. *Frontiers in Education, 8*, 1331607. DOI: 10.3389/feduc.2023.1331607

Wing, J. M. (2006). Computational thinking. *Communications of the ACM, 49*(3), 33–35. DOI: 10.1145/1118178.1118215

Winkler, R., & Söllner, M. (2018). *Unleashing the potential of chatbots in education: A state-of-the-art analysis. Academy of Management Proceedings, 2018*(1). https:// doi.org/DOI: 10.5465/AMBPP.2018.15903abstract

Woldegiorgis, E. T. (2025). Challenges of integrating technology in East African higher education systems in the post-pandemic era: Emerging academic cultures. *Technology, Pedagogy and Education, 56*(2), e13533. DOI: 10.1080/1475939X.2025.2520589

Wolfenden, F. (2022). *TPD@Scale: Designing teacher professional development with ICTs to support system-wide improvement in teaching* (tech. rep.) (Working paper; accessed 2025-10-11). TPD@Scale Coalition for the Global South / Foundation for Information Technology Education and Development (FIT-ED). https:// oro.open. ac.uk/ 86337/ 1 / Working % 20Paper % 20 - %20Designing % 20TPD % 20with % 20ICTs % 20to % 20Support%20System-Wide%20Improvement%20 in%20Teaching.pdf

Wolfenden, F. (2024). A framework for strengthening teacher professional development systems with ICT [Extended framework building on TPD@Scale; accessed 2025-10-11]. //oro.open.ac.uk/96423/1/A-Framework-for-Strengthening-Teacher -Professional-Development-Systems-with-ICT2024%20(1).pdf">https://oro.open.ac .uk/96423/1/A-Framework-for-Strengthening-Teacher-Professional-Development-Systems-with-ICT 2024%20(1).pdf

Wolff, R., & Ludvik, M. J. B. (2023). Outcomes-based program review: Closing achievement gaps in-and outside the classroom with alignment to predictive analytics and performance metrics.

Wong, J., Baars, M., de Koning, B. B., van der Zee, T., Davis, D., Khalil, M., Houben, G. J., & Paas, F. (2019). Educational theories and learning analytics: From data to knowledge: The whole is greater than the sum of its parts. *Utilizing learning analytics to support study success*, 3-25. DOI: 10.1007/978-3-319-64792-0_1

Wong, K.-T., Osman, R., Goh, P. S. C., & Rahmat, M. K. (2013). Understanding Student Teachers' Behavioural Intention to Use Technology: Technology Acceptance Model (TAM) Validation and Testing. *International Journal of Instruction*, *6*(1), 89–104.

Workshop, B., Scao, T. L., Fan, A., Akiki, C., Pavlick, E., Ilić, S., . . . Bari, M. S. (2022). Bloom: A 176b-parameter open-access multilingual language model. arXiv preprint arXiv:2211.05100.

World Bank. (2022). *Thrive: The role of higher education in refugee students' futures*. https://openknowledge.worldbank.org/handle/10986/37230

Wulantari, N. P., Rachman, A., Sari, M. N., Uktolseja, L. J., & Rofi'i, A. (2023). The role of gamification in English language teaching: A literature review. *Journal of Education*, *6*(1), 2847–2856.

Wu, X., Li, R., & Gwendoline Quek, C. L. (2025). When GenAI chatbots meet self-determination: Unpacking Chinese EFL learners' engagement in chatbot-assisted language learning. Interactive Learning Environments. *Interactive Learning Environments*, 1–21. Advance online publication. DOI: 10.1080/10494820.2025.2538756

Wu, Y. (2024). Critical thinking pedagogics design in an era of ChatGPT and other AI tools—Shifting from teaching "what" to teaching "why" and "how.". *Journal of Education and Development*, *8*(1), 1–10. DOI: 10.20849/jed.v8i1.1404

Xiao, J., Bozkurt, A., Nichols, M., Pazurek, A., Stracke, C. M., Bai, J. Y. H., Farrow, R., Mulligan, D., Nerantzi, C., Sharma, R. C., Singh, L., Frumin, I., Swindell, A., Honeychurch, S., Bond, M., Dron, J., Moore, S., Leng, J., van Tryon, P. J. S., & Themeli, C. (2025). Venturing into the Unknown: Critical Insights into Grey Areas and Pioneering Future Directions in Educational Generative AI Research. *TechTrends*, *69*(3), 582–597. DOI: 10.1007/s11528-025-01060-6

Xiao, N., Pei, Y., Yuan, C., Bu, Y., & Cai, Z. (2025). Transforming Education with Artificial Intelligence: A Comprehensive Review of Applications, Challenges, and Future Directions. *International Theory and Practice in Humanities and Social Sciences*, *2*(1), 337–356. DOI: 10.70693/itphss.v2i1.211

Xie, Z., Wu, X., & Xie, Y. (2024). Can interaction with generative artificial intelligence enhance learning autonomy? A longitudinal study from comparative perspectives of virtual companionship and knowledge acquisition preferences. Journal of Computer Assisted Learning, 40(5), 2369–2384. *Scopus.* Advance online publication. DOI: 10.1111/jcal.13032

Xi, L. (2024). Research on the english writing teaching model in the ai era. *MMSE*, *6*(3), 111. DOI: 10.22158/mmse.v6n3p111

Xue, L., Constant, N., Roberts, A., Kale, M., Al-Rfou, R., Siddhant, A., Barua, A., & Raffel, C. (2020). mT5: A massively multilingual pre-trained text-to-text transformer [Preprint]. arXiv. https://arxiv.org/abs/2010.11934

Xu, T., Wang, J., Zhang, G., Zhang, L., & Zhou, Y. (2023). Confused or not: Decoding brain activity and recognizing confusion in reasoning learning using EEG. *Journal of Neural Engineering*, *20*(2), 026018. DOI: 10.1088/1741-2552/acbfe0 PMID: 36854180

Xu, Z., Wijekumar, K., Ramirez, G., Hu, X., & Irey, R. (2019). The effectiveness of intelligent tutoring systems on K-12 students' reading comprehension: A meta-analysis. *British Journal of Educational Technology*, *50*(6), 3119–3137. DOI: 10.1111/bjet.12758

Yadav, A., Gretter, S., Hambrusch, S., & Sands, P. (2016). Expanding computer science education in schools: Understanding teacher experiences and challenges. *Computer Science Education*, *26*(4), 235–254. DOI: 10.1080/08993408.2016.1257418

Yadav, A., Stephenson, C., & Hong, H. (2017). Computational thinking for teacher education. *Communications of the ACM*, *60*(4), 55–62. DOI: 10.1145/2994591

Yang, C. C., Wu, J. Y., & Ogata, H. (2025). Learning analytics dashboard-based self-regulated learning approach for enhancing students'e-book-based blended learning. *Education and Information Technologies*, *30*(1), 35–56. DOI: 10.1007/s10639-024-12913-7

Yang, H., & Kyun, S. (2022). The current research trend of artificial intelligence in language learning: A systematic empirical literature review from an activity theory perspective. *Australasian Journal of Educational Technology*, •••, 180–210. DOI: 10.14742/ajet.7492

Yang, Z., Wu, J. G., & Xie, H. (2024). Taming Frankenstein's monster: Ethical considerations relating to generative artificial intelligence in education. *Asia Pacific Journal of Education*. Advance online publication. DOI: 10.1080/02188791.2023.2300137

Yannakakis, G. N., Liapis, A., & Alexopoulos, C. (2014). *Mixed-Initiative Co-Creativity*. https://antoniosliapis.com/papers/mixed_initiative_co-creativity.pdf

Yaseen, H., Mohammad, A. S., Ashal, N., Abusaimeh, H., Ali, A., & Sharabati, A.-A. A. (2025). The Impact of Adaptive Learning Technologies, Personalized Feedback, and Interactive AI Tools on Student Engagement: The Moderating Role of Digital Literacy. *Sustainability (Basel)*, *17*(3), 1133. Advance online publication. DOI: 10.3390/su17031133

Yatri, D., Anugerahwati, M., & Setyowati, L. (2023). Artificial intelligence (AI) in language learning (English and Arabic class): Students' and teachers' experience and perceptions. *Transformational Language, Literature, and Technology Overview in Learning*, *3*(1), 1–12. DOI: 10.55047/transtool.v3i1.1338

Yau, K. W., Chai, C. S., Chiu, T. K. F., Meng, H., King, I., & Yam, Y. (2023). A phenomenographic approach on teacher conceptions of teaching Artificial Intelligence (AI) in K-12 schools. *Education and Information Technologies*, *28*(1), 1041–1064. Advance online publication. DOI: 10.1007/s10639-022-11161-x

Ydo, Y. (2020). Inclusive education: Global priority, collective responsibility. *Prospects*, *49*(3), 97–101. DOI: 10.1007/s11125-020-09520-y PMID: 33235396

Ye, W., & Li, Q. (2020). Open Questions for Next Generation Chatbots. *Proceedings - 2020 IEEE/ACM Symposium on Edge Computing, SEC 2020*, 346–351. https://doi.org/DOI: 10.1109/SEC50012.2020.00050

Yeganeh, L. N., Fenty, N. S., Chen, Y., Simpson, A., & Hatami, M. (2025). The Future of Education: A Multi-Layered Metaverse Classroom Model for Immersive and Inclusive Learning. *Future Internet, 17*(2), 63. Advance online publication. DOI: 10.3390/fi17020063

Yeh, P.-L., Kuo, W.-C., & Tsai, C.-J. (2024). Counseling Students' First Impressions of Using Woebot: A Mental Health Chatbot. Bulletin of Educational Psychology, 56(1), 45–72. *Scopus.* Advance online publication. DOI: 10.6251/BEP.202409_56(1).0003

Yeh, P.-L., Kuo, W.-C., Tseng, B.-L., & Sung, Y.-H. (2025). Does the AI-driven Chatbot Work? Effectiveness of the Woebot app in reducing anxiety and depression in group counseling courses and student acceptance of technological aids. Current Psychology, 44(9), 8133–8145. *Scopus.* Advance online publication. DOI: 10.1007/s12144-025-07359-0

Yetişensoy, O., & Rapoport, A. (2023). Artificial intelligence literacy teaching in social studies education. *Journal of Pedagogical Research, 7*(3), 100–110. DOI: 10.33902/JPR.202320866

Yeung, W. L., & Ng, O. L. (2023). Characterizing touchscreen actions in technology-enhanced embodied learning for mathematics instruction in K-12 setting – A systematic review (2010–2023). *Computers & Education, 205*, 104881. Advance online publication. DOI: 10.1016/j.compedu.2023.104881

Yeung, W. L., & Ng, O. L. (2024). Using empathy maps to support design-thinking enhanced transdisciplinary STEM innovation in K-12 setting. *International Journal of Technology and Design Education, 34*(4), 1325–1350. Advance online publication. DOI: 10.1007/s10798-023-09861-7

Yildirim-Erbasli, S. N., & Bulut, O. (2021). Conversation-based assessments: Real-time assessment and feedback. *eLearn Magazine, 2021*(12). https://doi.org/DOI: 10.1145/3508017.3495533

Yildirim-Erbasli, S. N., Bulut, O., Demmans Epp, C., & Cui, Y. (2025). Advancing students' assessment experiences with conversational agents. *Educational Technology Research and Development, 73*(3), 1811–1834. DOI: 10.1007/s11423-025-10472-3

Yildirim-Erbasli, S. N., Gorgun, G., & Bulut, O. (2024). Enhancing self-regulated learning with artificial intelligence-powered learning analytics. In Ulutaş, N. K., & Höl, D. (Eds.), *Emergent practices of learning analytics in K-12 classrooms* (pp. 57–83). IGI Global., DOI: 10.4018/979-8-3693-0066-4.ch004

Yilmaz, B. (2017). *Effects of adaptive learning technologies on math achievement: A quantitative study of ALEKS math software* [Doctoral dissertation, University of Missouri-Kansas City]. MOspace. https://hdl.handle.net/10355/60519

Yim, I. H. Y., & Su, J. (2025). Artificial intelligence (AI) learning tools in K-12 education: A scoping review. *Journal of Computers in Education*, *12*, 93–131. DOI: 10.1007/s40692-023-00304-9

Yim, I. H. Y., & Wegerif, R. (2024). Teachers' perceptions, attitudes, and acceptance of artificial intelligence (AI) educational learning tools: An exploratory study on AI literacy for young students. *Future in Educational Research*, *2*(4), 318–345. DOI: 10.1002/fer3.65

Yosso, T. J. (2005). Whose culture has capital? A critical theory discussion of community cultural wealth. *Race, Ethnicity and Education*, *8*(1), 69–91. DOI: 10.1080/1361332052000341006

Youvan, D. C. (2024). Illuminating Intelligence: Bridging Humanity and Artificial Consciousness.

Yu, C., & Yao, G.. (2024). Enhancing student engagement with ai-driven personalized learning systems. [ITEE]. *International Transactions on Education Technology*, *3*(1), 1–8.

Yulianti, K. (2023). Students' experience with online personalized learning in character building-civics course at a private university in indonesia. *Proceedings of the 2023 7th International Conference on Education and E-Learning*, 85–89. DOI: 10.1145/3637989.3637999

Yu, Y., Han, L., Du, X., & Yu, J. (2022). An oral english evaluation model using artificial intelligence method. *Mobile Information Systems*, *2022*, 1–8. DOI: 10.1155/2022/3998886

Zadeh, P. M., & Sattler, D. (2023). Improving Accessibility and Readability of Survey Reports in Digital Health Platforms using Conversational AI. *Proceedings - 2023 2023 IEEE International Conference on Bioinformatics and Biomedicine, BIBM 2023*, 4987–4989. https://doi.org/DOI: 10.1109/BIBM58861.2023.10386018

Zafari, M., Bazargani, J. S., Sadeghi-Niaraki, A., & Choi, S.-M. (2022a). Artificial intelligence applications in K-12 education: A systematic literature review. *IEEE Access : Practical Innovations, Open Solutions*, *10*, 61905–61921. DOI: 10.1109/ACCESS.2022.3179356

Zancajo, A., Verger, A., & Bolea, P. (2022). Digitalization and beyond: The effects of Covid-19 on post-pandemic educational policy and delivery in Europe. *Policy and Society*, *41*(1), 111–128. DOI: 10.1093/polsoc/puab016

Zhai, C., Wibowo, S., & Li, L. D. (2024). The effects of over-reliance on AI dialogue systems on students' cognitive abilities: A systematic review. *Smart Learning Environments*, *11*(1), 1–37. DOI: 10.1186/s40561-024-00316-7

Zhai, X., Chu, X., Chai, C. S., Jong, M. S. Y., Istenic, A., Spector, M., Liu, J.-B., Yuan, J., & Li, Y. (2021a). A review of artificial intelligence (AI) in education from 2010 to 2020. *Complexity*, *2021*(1), 1–18. DOI: 10.1155/2021/8812542

Zhang, L., & Nouri, J. (2019). A systematic review of learning computational thinking through Scratch in K-9. *Computers & Education*, *141*, 103607. DOI: 10.1016/j.compedu.2019.103607

Zhang, P., & Tur, G. (2024). A systematic review of ChatGPT use in K-12 education. *European Journal of Education*, *59*(2), e12599. Advance online publication. DOI: 10.1111/ejed.12599

Zhang, Q., Siraj, S. B., & Abdul Razak, R. B. (2025). Effects of AI chatbots on EFL students' critical thinking skills and intrinsic motivation in argumentative writing. Innovation in Language Learning and Teaching. *Innovation in Language Learning and Teaching*, 1–29. Advance online publication. DOI: 10.1080/17501229.2025.2515111

Zhang, S. (2024). Research on english language and literature teaching strategies based on situational teaching method. *Journal of Contemporary Educational Research*, *8*(10), 44–47. DOI: 10.26689/jcer.v8i10.8571

Zhang, S., Hu, H., & Xing, S. (2024). Dual Learning for Conversational Emotion Recognition and Emotional Response Generation. *IEEE Transactions on Affective Computing*, *15*(3), 1241–1252. DOI: 10.1109/TAFFC.2023.3332631

Zhang, Y., Shi, Y., & Bi, F. (2023). Personalizing students' learning needs by a teaching decision optimization method. *International Journal of Emerging Technologies in Learning*, *18*(16), 222–236. DOI: 10.3991/ijet.v18i16.42707

Zhao, T. (2023). Ai in educational technology. DOI: 10.20944/preprints202311.0106.v1

Zhou, E., & Lee, D. (2024). Generative artificial intelligence, human creativity, and art. *PNAS Nexus*, *3*(3), gae052. Advance online publication. DOI: 10.1093/pnasnexus/pgae052 PMID: 38444602

Zhou, X., Liu, M., & Wu, L. (2025). Research on Personalized Learning Resource Recommendation Method for Students Supported by Artificial Intelligence. *Journal of Combinatorial Mathematics and Combinatorial Computing*, *127b*, 1725–1736. DOI: 10.61091/jcmcc127b-096

Zhu, Q., Chong, L., Yang, M., & Luo, J. (2025). Reading Users' Minds With Large Language Models: Mental Inference for Artificial Empathy in Design. *Journal of Mechanical Design*, *147*(6), 061401. Advance online publication. DOI: 10.1115/1.4067527

Zhu, Y. (2024). Research on digital virtual humans in the metaverse for smart teaching. *Lecture Notes in Education Psychology and Public Media*, *54*(1), 127–135. DOI: 10.54254/2753-7048/54/20241542

Zourmpakis, A.-I., Kalogiannakis, M., & Papadakis, S. (2024). Education of Elementary Teachers on The Use of Adaptive Gamification Environment in Science Education. In Sardag, M., Kaya, G., & Sogut, M. (Eds.) *Proceedings Book Series-I of the ESERA 2023 Conference. Connecting Science Education with Cultural Heritage, Strand 4 - Digital Resources for Science Teaching and Learning* (co-ed. Napal, M., & Romano-Garcia, L.), 224-237, Cappadocia, Türkiye. Nobel Bilimsel Eserler.

Zourmpakis, A. I., Kalogiannakis, M., & Papadakis, S. (2023a). Adaptive gamification in science education: An analysis of the impact of implementation and adapted game elements on students' motivation. *Computers*, *12*(7), 143. DOI: 10.3390/computers12070143

Zourmpakis, A. I., Kalogiannakis, M., & Papadakis, S. (2024). The effects of adaptive gamification in science learning: A comparison between traditional inquiry-based learning and gender differences. *Computers*, *13*(12), 324. DOI: 10.3390/computers13120324

Zourmpakis, A. I., Papadakis, S., & Kalogiannakis, M. (2022). Education of preschool and elementary teachers on the use of adaptive gamification in science education. *International Journal of Technology Enhanced Learning*, *14*(1), 1–16. DOI: 10.1504/IJTEL.2022.120556

Zourmpakis, I.-A., Kalogiannakis, M., & Papadakis, St. (2023b). A Review of the Literature for Designing and Developing a Framework for Adaptive Gamification in Physics Education. In Taşar, M.-F., & Heron, P.-R.-L. (Eds.), *The International Handbook of Physics Education Research: Teaching Physics* (pp. 5.1–5.26). AIP Publishing., DOI: 10.1063/9780735425712_005

Беганцова, И., Акутина, С., & Щелина, Т. (2020). The question of students' preparedness for studying in the digital educational environment.. https://doi.org/
DOI: 10.3897/ap.2.e0207

About the Contributors

Stamatios Papadakis is an Assistant Professor in Educational Technology at the Department of Preschool Education at the University of Crete, Greece. His scientific and research interests focus on integrating EdTech apps in preschool and primary education, novice programming environments, mobile learning, and the application of generative AI in education. His work aims to enhance early childhood learning experiences through innovative technologies. Dr. Papadakis has been a prolific researcher and editor, contributing to numerous books and journals in educational technology.

***

Alpay Aksin is an associate professor in the Social Studies Education Department at Amasya University's Faculty of Education. His primary research interests are cultural heritage and education, teacher education and competencies, technology integration in social studies, and the role of new media tools in education.

Danielle Alexander is a Ph.D. candidate in the Literacy, Culture, and Language program at Oakland University. Her research centers on secondary writing instruction, with a particular focus on writing teacher identity and its influence on how writing is taught and learned.

Sani Alkhasawneh is an Assistant Professor of Educational Technology in the Educational Studies Programme at the Faculty of Education, Arab Open University, Amman, Jordan. Her research interests focus on the integration of artificial intelligence in education, personalized learning environments, instructional design, and the use of emerging technologies to enhance teaching and learning. Dr. Alkhasawneh has published several studies in the fields of educational technology and e-learning. (E-mail: s_khasawneh@aou.edu.jo)

Ghaida Alrawashdeh is an Assistant Professor of Digital Learning and Literacies at Oakland University. Her work explores how educational technology can support teaching and learning in resource-constrained environments. She specializes in AI, personalized learning, and literacy development.

Okan Bulut is a Professor of Measurement, Evaluation, and Cognition and a member of the Centre for Research in Applied Measurement and Evaluation (CRAME) in the Faculty of Education at the University of Alberta, Canada. His current research interests lie at the intersection of artificial intelligence (AI), educational data mining, and learning analytics. Through the use of AI-driven algorithms and natural language processing, he aims to develop intelligent systems that can dynamically adapt to learners' preferences, cognitive styles, and performance trajectories.

Mustafa Kayyali is an ardent advocate for excellence in higher education, driven by a relentless pursuit of quality, recognition, and innovation. Their journey in academia started with a Master's in Quality Management and Evaluation in Higher Education from Universitat Oberta de Catalunya, followed by a Ph.D. in Quality Management from Azteca University. These academic pursuits have laid a strong foundation for their expertise in Accreditation, Quality Assurance, and Higher Education Rankings. As an entrepreneur, researcher, translator, and publisher, they are deeply involved in various facets of the academic world. Their diverse interests encompass Management, Translation, Interpretation, and Academic consulting, contributing to a well-rounded understanding of the industry. Throughout their career, they have made significant contributions to academic literature, with more than 40 published papers and 30 book chapters to my name. Additionally, they take pride in having translated 6 books, bridging language gaps, and promoting knowledge exchange on a global scale. They are committed to fostering positive change in higher education and contributing to its continuous improvement.

Joyce Xinle Liu is a doctoral student at the University of Alberta. Her research interests focus on applications of computational psychometrics in low-stakes and high-stakes educational assessments, to enhance assessment design and gain deeper insight into students' learning and competencies.

Xiaoxiao Liu is a doctoral student in the Measurement, Evaluation, and Data Science program at the University of Alberta. Her research focuses on AI-enhanced conversation-based assessments, critical thinking, and the use of process data analytics in large-scale educational assessments such as PISA and TIMSS. Her work has been published in peer-reviewed journals, including Computers & Education and the Journal of Computer Assisted Learning. She has also presented her research at major international conferences, such as the International Meeting of the Psychometric Society (IMPS) and the National Council on Measurement in Education (NCME).

Neema Mduma is a computer scientist and senior lecturer at the Nelson Mandela African Institution of Science and Technology (NM-AIST) specializing in Artificial Intelligence (AI) and Machine Learning (ML). She is the founder of an initiative called BakiShule which promotes Science, Technology, Engineering, and Mathematics (STEM) to girls in secondary school in Tanzania. Dr. Mduma also serves as a Principal Investigator in various projects that use AI and ML to address challenges in agriculture, health, education, and other sectors. Additionally, she reviews for scientific journals and conferences and most recently she was appointed by the Minister of State, President's Office Planning and Investment, as a member of the technical team for drafting the Tanzania Development Vision 2050.

'Aisyah Binti Mohamed Rehan is a Senior Lecturer in the Department of Chemical Engineering Technology at the Faculty of Engineering Technology, Universiti Tun Hussein Onn Malaysia (UTHM). She also serves as Head of Department for Global Cooperation and Data Analysis at the Malaysian Research Institute for Vocational Education and Training (MyRIVET). She received her PhD in Biological Sciences from The University of Auckland, New Zealand, and MSc in Human Molecular Genetics from Imperial College London. Her research interests encompass biotechnology, structural biology, protein bioinformatics, and the development of sustainable bioproducts. She has contributed to numerous national and international research projects focusing on marine bioproducts, recombinant enzymes, and the bioengineering of natural resources. A Professional Technologist registered with the Malaysia Board of Technologists (MBOT), Dr. 'Aisyah Rehan actively promotes Digital TVET and innovative STEM education within the 5th Industrial Revolution context through research, curriculum leadership, and industry collaboration.

Vivit Rosmayanti, S.Pd.I., M.Pd was born in Botta on June 26, 1987. She has over 10 years of experience teaching at the University. She obtained a bachelor's degree in English Education from Alauddin State Islamic University. She completed her master's and doctoral degrees in English Education from Makassar State University. She is currently a lecturer in the Post Graduate Program, Department of English Education at Makassar State University, South Sulawesi, Indonesia. She is also actively writing research articles to be published in nationally and internationally accredited journals. She has written in some chapter books, monographs, and reference books. She is interested in teaching methods for teaching English. Her research interests include language teaching methodology, ICT instruction, and ESP teaching.

Wasswa Shafik (Member, IEEE) received a Bachelor of Science degree in information technology from Ndejje University, Uganda, a Master of Engineering degree in Information Technology (Computer and Communication Networks) from Yazd University, Iran, and a PhD in Computer Science with the School of Digital Science, Universiti Brunei Darussalam, Brunei Darussalam. He is also the Founder and Research Director of the Dig Connectivity Research Laboratory (DCRLab) after serving as a Research Associate at the Network Interconnectivity Research Laboratory at Yazd University. Prior to this, he worked as a Community Data Analyst at Population Services International (PSI-Uganda), a Community Data Officer at the Programme for Accessible Health Communication (PACE-Uganda), a Research Assistant at the Socio-Economic Data Centre (SEDC-Uganda), Uganda, an Assistant Data Officer at TechnoServe, Kampala, Uganda, and Asmaah Charity Organization as Cheif Executive Officer. He has hundreds of publications with renowned publishers. His research interests include Artificial Intelligence, Neural Networks, Computer Vision, Smart Agriculture, Digital Health, and Green Computing.

Rebecca Vornberger is a doctoral candidate in Literacy, Culture, and Language at Oakland University with a dissertation focused on Large Language Model Literacy. She is a Special Lecturer in the Writing and Rhetoric department at Oakland University.

Rama Yusvana, CBiol, MRSB, is a Technologist (Ts) and Senior Lecturer at the Faculty of Engineering Technology, Tun Hussein Onn University of Malaysia (UTHM). He specialises in Digital TVET, Agentive Artificial Intelligence (AI) in Education, and Biotechnology / Bioengineering. His research and teaching focus on advancing biological sciences as well as AI-assisted learning ecosystems, and engineering-technology education through the integration of ethical and inclusive AI practices. He currently leads several research initiatives funded by the Malaysian Qualifications Agency (MQA) and UTHM's research grant, including projects exploring student readiness for Digital TVET and the potential role of Agentive AI in higher education, sustainable products (such as plant-based bioplastic, etc). Dr. Yusvana is also actively involved in curriculum innovation and development, applied research, and capacity building for the 5th Industrial Revolution. He is a Chartered Biologist (CBiol) and Member of the Royal Society of Biology (MRSB), UK.

Alkinoos-Ioannis Zourbakis is a postdoctoral researcher at the University of Thessaly, Department of Special Education, Greece. He graduated from the Department of Primary Education, Rethymno, University of Crete in 2015.

He also completed his M.Ed. in Education - Education with the Use of New Technologies at the University of the Aegean, Rhodes, Greece in the School of Humanities, Department of Primary Education in 2019. In addition, he completed his PhD at the University of Crete, Department of Early Childhood Education in 2024, entitled: "Teacher Training in the use of Adaptive Gamification in Science Teaching". His research interests are science education, teacher professional development, educational technologies, ICT, educational robotics, learning analytics, computational thinking development, adaptive technologies, AI in research and education, and STEM learning. He has worked as a project member of Erasmus+ KA2 projects on international mobility and teaching, and on the design and development of blended and distance learning environments for teaching advanced STEM subjects to science teacher candidates and the creation of a master syllabus aimed at building capacities for the transition to a circular economy. Education 2024-now University of Thessaly: Postdoctoral researcher in the Department of Special Education 2020-2024 University of Crete: PhD in the Department of Early Childhood Education. 2017-2019 University of the Aegean: Master's degree in Education Sciences - Education with the Use of New Technologies. 2011-2015 University of Crete: Bachelor's Degree in Primary Education.

Index

A

C

D

E

G

H

I